Commerce and

Russell Smith

Alpha Editions

This edition published in 2019

ISBN : 9789353807832

Design and Setting By
Alpha Editions
email - alphaedis@gmail.com

COMMERCE AND INDUSTRY

BY

J. RUSSELL SMITH

PROFESSOR OF ECONOMIC GEOGRAPHY, COLUMBIA UNIVERSITY, NEW YORK CITY

REVISED EDITION

NEW YORK
HENRY HOLT AND COMPANY

PREFACE TO SECOND EDITION

We stand on the threshold of a new time. We face a new world. Men's minds have changed. The map is changed. The world of industry is changed by financial disturbance, by the dislocations of war, and by a flock of new inventions no thousand years before 1850 ever witnessed. All these things react on each other and give a new and changed usefulness to our old earth. Never before did we have so many good reasons for needing to know about this world which is our home.

This book is an attempt to explain how the earth becomes the home of man especially those men who are pleased to call themselves civilized.

How does climate affect man? How does the soil feed him and furnish him materials for shelter, tools, heat, power and industry? How do the form, location, and surface features of the land affect his efforts at trade? These questions, whose answers form so large a part of economic and commercial geography are of great importance in education and especially in vocational courses. In giving these explanations of the earth, I have always tried to answer the natural question "Why?" Therefore I have had to tell fewer facts in order to leave space for the explanations. This makes less to remember and more to understand. The book aims, therefore, not to be a mere catalog of facts and statistics. The more important facts are there, but the important thing is that the meaning and causes of the facts are set forth as vividly as possible. The physiographic influence in industry is not given in a separate formal statement at the beginning of the discussion of each country, but is treated in connection with the industrial fact which is being explained. Thus, in showing how wheat happens to be grown in a given region, we are explaining both wheat and the region—bringing cause and effect together.

More than half of the book is devoted to the United States. Of foreign countries, Latin America and the Orient receive more than usual attention because of our coming trade expansion with those countries. In the part of the book dealing with the United States,

v

I have described industries rather than regions or states. The wheat industry, for example, arises from certain environmental conditions that exist in many states and many countries. Therefore I have not hesitated to refer, by way of comparison, to the great wheat-producing regions in other countries. Thus the industries of the United States are treated in their world aspects, permitting a briefer and more local treatment of the same industries in the part of the book devoted to foreign countries. Wherever possible, comparisons have been made between countries and regions. As a result of this, the chapter on a given country does not contain all the information about that country in the book. Those who wish to collect all the information the book contains about any topic are referred to the alphabetical index, which is unusually full. A statistical appendix is also included for purposes of reference.

Some one will ask why we publish statistics of 1913 in the edition of 1920. The answer is plain. This is a text book and for a text book the figures of the war period are of little value. We want to study a normal world. Not a world sick of a fever. Every user of this book should, however, have a copy of the latest issue of the U. S. Department of Agriculture which can be secured gratis from Senators and Representatives in Congress. It contains invaluable statistics of agricultural production throughout the world. The U. S. Geological Survey Annual on the Mineral Resources of the U. S. and the Statistical Abstract from the Department of Commerce complete a very useful desk collection of first aids to fine illustrations of geographic and economic principles.

The third part of the book deals with world trade routes and the laws of trade—and contains certain generalizations that can be appreciated only in the light of such facts as are set forth in the preceding sections of the book. In this section also I have forecast some possible future developments such as the great increase of our trade with the tropics; the utilization of the hills of New England and the semi-deserts of Arizona through tree crops; the improvement of farming in the South through diversification; the extraction of nitrogen from the air; the utilization, as coal and oil fail, of water, wind, tide, and even the sunshine itself as sources of power.

COLUMBIA UNIVERSITY,
  NEW YORK CITY,
  November 27, 1919.

CONTENTS

vii

viii CONTENTS

PART III

WORLD COMMERCE

COMMERCE AND INDUSTRY

COMMERCE AND INDUSTRY

INTRODUCTION

OUR CHANGING ENVIRONMENT

1. The Size of and Kinds of Our Environment

Man's small share of the universe.—A certain tribe of microbes is said to live only in the tiny crack of space that lies between the surface of our teeth and the film of moisture that clings to them. Outside of this space the microbe is like a man travelling through a fiery desert or an icy waste. This film home sounds like a very small place in which hosts of beings must be born, grow and produce their young, but when we look at ourselves, we can see that man is very much like this little enemy that sends him to the dentist. It is a very tiny part of the universe that must serve as the home of man.

Look at the limitless space that astronomers call the universe. Thousands, perhaps millions of suns float through it, some of them larger than our own sun. One speck of this vast realm is our little solar system, our vast sun with eight planets swinging round it and warmed by it.

So far as we know this planet is the only place where men could live in all this vast universe of worlds, even if we could freely visit every part. Further, we certainly know that there is a very small part of this, our own world, on which we can live. No man has been 300 feet beneath the surface of the sea and lived. The greatest height man has been able to climb is not five miles above the level of the sea. Our new-found ability to fly costs enough effort, cash and danger to show us that after all we must spend most of our time crawling about the surface of this our world. We cannot go much below or much above that surface.

Few parts of the earth are good.—Yet further than this, examination of the earth's surface shows that within this little narrow surface belt which may, indeed be likened to the microbe's home in the film of a tooth, most of the land for one reason or another does not seem to be a very good place for us to make our homes. Some of it is too hot, some of it is too cold, some of it is too wet, some of it is too dry, some of it is too high. Thus we find that because of the

varied goodness of the earth as home for man there are few places
where men are many and many places where men are few.

19th Century discoveries.—The 19th Century was one of large explorations and conquests of the earth.   Men established trade on all
seas, in all continents.   Tremendous new inventions gave us powers
over material things such as men had only thought of before as
material for fairy tales.   This new science, the new industry, the
new machines, the new railroads, steamships, this world trade,
helped the 19th Century to increase the people of the world from
1,000,000,000 to 1,600,000,000.

Social order or chaos.—Six thousand years before Christ the
Assyrians had big cities on the banks of the Euphrates and Tigris
rivers in the rich plain of Mesopotamia.   They had schools, libra-
ries, banks, transacting business much as our banks do.   Then
came anarchy and marauding bands, but hundreds of years later
the Persians restored order.   Their roads, mail carriers, commerce,
peace and prosperity reached from the Aegean Sea far in the highlands of Persia.   Their empire also fell to be followed later by similar periods of prosperity, commerce, culture, art and civilization,
under the Greeks, the Carthaginians, the Romans and the Venetians.

The biggest facts of history are (1) that in periods of order we
may have civilization, (2) that in periods of anarchy we cannot
have civilization and (3) civilization and anarchy have succeeded
each other for thousands of years, giving social environment that
ranged from good to very bad.

Our new-found ability to have world trade gives us a new interest
in world order or world peace.   World trade means that each
people needs access to all the earth.   With world trade Belgium
became populous.   With a blockade that shut her off from the
world she would have starved but for the Belgian relief.   Russian
Armenia, a little 20,000 square miles of territory, south of the Caucasus Mountains, east of the Black Sea, had bought its agricultural
machinery from Germany before the war.   Five years of the blockade and war reduced Armenian food supply to the point where
140,000 people starved within a year after the armistice because
they could not resume trade and in December, 1919, hundreds of
thousands faced starvation unless they could succeed in getting a
loan from the United States whereby they might get food to carry
them to the next harvest and plows and seed and plant a crop and
resume their life as farmers.

World environment and world citizenship.—Let us assume that
men will have intelligence enough and fairness enough to organize

shortly some kind of a World Government that will give world order and reasonable justice among men. Prosperity will then come to Belgium and Armenia and China and every other country where people are willing to work. Increased trade will make every country more and more dependent on many others. The age of national independence is gone, and the age of national interdependence is coming, we are becoming citizens of the world, in spite of ourselves. The only way we can escape it is to live the life of hermits clothed in bark and the skin of wild beasts.

If we are to have a new world—environment through a new and enlarging world trade it becomes all the more important to know the physical environment, the basis of this trade, as it shows itself in the fitness of the different parts of the earth as the home of man.

The value of lands to man.—The earth becomes the home of man by furnishing him food, clothes, house or shelter, fuel, luxuries, and tools and materials of industry which enable him to produce and transport goods. So nearly universal are these wants that virtually all men have all six classes of goods. Even savages have luxuries in the form of toys, ornaments, and musical instruments. Each particular method by which a man gets some useful commodity leads to an industry often of world-wide distribution.

All these materials for a living come directly or indirectly out of the crust of the earth. Most of our goods come indirectly through the intermediate stages of plant and animal life, the earth itself supplying directly but a small part of our wants. The plants grow from the earth. We cut them into pieces, shape them into tools, and build our houses and barns. We eat them or clothe ourselves with their fibers, we extract their juices and dig their roots for drugs and medicines. We burn them for fuel, turn them into articles of luxury, and thus make them help in the supply of some of the wants for each of the six classes of goods. The animals in turn eat the plants and each other, and furnish us their meat and milk as nourishment; their wool and furs become our clothing, their skins make our shoe leather, the tents of the nomad, the belts of the engine wheel, the bindings of our choicest books.

2. The Influence of Climate

Climate and civilization.—To understand how the earth supplies our needs, we must first consider climate. Climate decides the way in which a land produces, and whether men shall be lazy or vigorous, many or few. The land and the climate make the physical environment, and the environment permits the products and makes the man and the race. If the climate is too cold, there can be little growth or population, as in Greenland, and if it is too warm, there is much growth of plants but little progress in man, as in Borneo, New Guinea, or the Amazon Valley. Civilization is a product of adversity. The great civilizations of all time seem to have arisen where nature made production possible only a part of the year, and thus made it necessary for man to work and save up for the time when he could not produce.

Effect of tropic abundance.—Accordingly, there have been no great civilizations in the warm, moist parts of the torrid zone (Fig. 2), where nature does the most to make easy the support of life. The climate is continually warm, and the rainfall is sufficiently regular over vast areas to keep vegetation always green and growing. A few banana plants by the hut, and a little patch of sweet potatoes will live and yield for years, for there is no frost to kill the plants. The forest is full of nuts, wild fruit, and game; the streams are alive with fish. Wood in abundance supplies the little fuel man needs for cooking, and if he would make himself a drum or any simple tool, the raw materials of the forest lie at his hand in great abundance. A little shelter of palm leaves keeps off the rain (Fig. 1); the warm climate removes the need of further shelter or many clothes. Accordingly, the native of these regions may sit and doze most of the time, as, for untold generations, his ancestors have done before him —enervated by plenty. He does not get the work habit or become ambitious. For this reason lands of perennial plenty have never been lands of power. Most of them are still in "the forest primeval," and ruled by the energetic sons of frosty climates. Thus nearly all of Africa and that part of Asia within the tropics have been taken as colonies by the peoples of Europe. The only absolutely independent territory in all Africa is Abyssinia, where the cool climate of a high plateau stimulates the people into a vigor and activity that has enabled them, with the aid of a powerful leader, to protect themselves from annexation.

Intermittent climate.—After our summer (the growing season), our winter's frost and snow bring death or hibernation to the whole vegetable kingdom, and drive man to the protection of house and warm clothing. In such climates we must either starve, eat wild animals, or eat what we have saved by our work during the summer. Therefore we have worked. A similar but less severe climatic goad to man's activity is furnished by climates that are alternately productive and non-productive through variations in the rainfall. The first great nations in the world's history had their empires in the valleys of the Euphrates and the Nile, where a fertile soil and a good moisture supply made great crops followed by blistering drought, a kind of warm winter so far as food production was con-

FIG. 1.—The Jamaica negro finds life in the tropics to be easy. (Hamburg American S. S. Co.)

cerned. Thus Babylon and Nineveh were rich and cultured cities at a time when all Europe lay in barbarism, and the pyramids were built before the drought-driven Joseph went down to Egypt. These valleys got their early start because their advantages as the home of man were almost unrivalled. They had a warm climate, fertile soil, and a protected location. Each year the rivers overflowed, fertilizing the soil with the muddy waters and promoting the growth of a crop by irrigation. The necessity of food to last through the dry season naturally produced the habit of working and saving, and

resulted in a sufficient surplus of goods to support life while attention
was given to learning and the things we call civilization.

FIG. 2.—World rainfall, annual.   (After Mark S. W. Jefferson.)

█████ Very heavy—an annual rainfall, including melted snow, of over 80 inches.
▧▧▧▧ Heavy—an annual fall of from 40 to 80 inches.
▨▨▨▨ Light—an annual fall of from 20 to 40 inches.
▭▭▭▭ Scant—Less than 20 inches in the year.

Note the rainfall and heat in regions of high development of civilization.
Compare this with **Fig.** 3.

The influence of an unfavorable environment.—To an extent we
rarely notice, the environment makes the race.   It is a common mis-
take of the historian to say that peoples have certain qualities in-

herently. It is much more correct to say that primitive or savage peoples are primitive or savage because of the stinginess or peculiari-

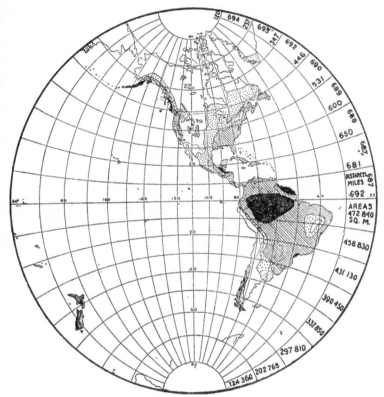

Fig. 2.—(Continued.)

ties of nature's gifts to the land in which they happen to live, and not because of bad qualities which they may inherently possess. The environment, in making the race, has given the qualities. The Eskimo upon the bleak, windy, treeless, bitter-cold shore of the Arctic Sea, in a climate where he constantly faces the danger of freezing and starving and where he, therefore, needs much protection from the cold in the form of fuel, clothes, house, or food, has almost nothing with which to build houses, make clothes, or prepare food. Accordingly, the population is exceedingly sparse and

can support itself only along the seacoast where the few advantages
of the land may be combined with the more numerous advantages

FIG. 3.—World distribution of population.   (After Mark S. W. Jefferson.)

Grade of peopling.   People to 1 square mile.

Very dense		250 or more
Dense		125 to 520
Moderate		26 to 125
Thin		2½ to 26
Scanty		less than 2½

Note the close relation of heavy population and intermittent climate.

of the sea with its fish and seals. Shall the Eskimo be dismissed
as a barbarian or praised as a master of a ferocious environment?
In winning a living from such meager and almost exclusively animal

sources the Eskimo has shown great ingenuity. Even the kyak or
canoe, the most complex of his implements of industry, is made of

FIG. 3.—(Continued.)

bones and tough skins bound together with sinews and rawhide
thongs, unless perchance the ocean currents bring a little drift wood
from afar. For fuel, with which they cook their food but do not
heat their houses, they use the fat of seal, walrus or whale blubber.
Yet the Eskimo himself is not a bad, weak, or stupid fellow. His
many fine qualities are highly praised by explorers. Upon being
put to school he has shown that he can learn with the rest of us. The
severity and poverty of his environment have made economic progress impossible.

Peoples dependent on one resource.—Other peoples have succeeded in living in countries with almost as few natural aids as are possessed by the Eskimo, but culture has been held in check. The South Sea Islander has lived on coral islands a few feet above the waves, where his resources were limited to the cocoanut-palm upon the strand and fish that came from the sea. Yet with these limited resources he has managed to keep strong and healthy and fill in some manner all his needs. When he wanted a saw, he got it by fastening shark's teeth into a piece of wood. His other equipment was made by equally ingenious devices.

Upon the plains of central Asia people have for ages lived in a land where the one resource was grass. Flocks of sheep, cows, horses, goats and camels fed upon the grass. The herdsmen upon their horses followed the flocks as they roamed the flat plains in search of grass. These people were nomads because they had to go wherever they could find grass. Their diet was milk, cheese, and meat, and grain obtained by barter at some oasis; their clothing, wool and skins; their shelter, a felt or leather tent stretched over a few precious poles which they had carried with them for hundreds of miles from the banks of some mountain stream. Burning cow dung made the fire. A little metal was bought from trading caravans.

3. INFLUENCE OF NATURAL PROTECTION AND BEASTS OF BURDEN

Two other things have been necessary to enable man to become civilized. One is beasts of burden to do his work; the other is sheltered localities where he could be free from robbers and danger of conquest. Athens and Sparta were in sheltered nooks. Rome started on a hill crest easy to defend. The cliff-dwelling Indian of New Mexico, secure in his nest, was more civilized than the Indians of the open and unprotected Mississippi Valley who were in almost constant warfare. Both suffered from the lack of domestic animals.

4. THE NECESSITY FOR COMMERCE

Importance of transportation.—It requires a variety of natural resources and of industries to supply the wants of man. This variety may exist in a small locality or products of widely separated districts may be brought to one place by commerce. Since many regions have little variety of resource, commerce is usually necessary to get together the variety of things necessary to support us. Commerce is first of all dependent upon transportation. Men can trade without money, and by signs they can trade with a people whose speech they do not understand. The important thing in all commerce is the fact that the goods *can be moved*.

Commerce without the railroad.—Without the boat or railroad, commerce is a minor thing. The horse-drawn wagon enters into modern commerce only for short hauls, as in taking goods to and from the railway or boat. Where commerce depends entirely upon muscle, as the caravan of wagon or pack animals, we have the commercial conditions which made the Middle Ages.

The first great commercial enterprises of which we know were carried on by means of caravans, such as set out from Egypt in the days of Pharaoh, and from Babylon in the days of Nebuchadnezzar. Only the most costly goods are worth caravan freight rates. In lands dependent on caravan trading nearly everything that man uses must be produced in his immediate locality. The high cost of transportation, where commerce still depends on muscle, drives man back almost entirely upon his own resources. In vast areas of Alaska, northern British America, northeastern Europe, northern and central Asia, Africa, and South America progress is greatly hindered by lack of modern transportation facilities.

Civilization depends upon commerce.—Thus the man in a land of few resources, before modern commerce comes, must develop great ingenuity and great power to do without. Such has been the life of the Eskimo, of the Indian, of the nomad (Kirghiz) plainsmen of Central Asia, of the American frontiersman as he went westward and settled in the wilderness. The Eskimo's house is made of snow, the Indian wigwam of skins, the nomad herdsman makes a tent of felt, the frontiersman's house is of logs or turf (Fig. 4). None of these men can get material for any other kind of a house.

Under these conditions man needs commerce badly. Without a great deal of commerce no large community can rise. Thus, in the days before steam, civilization could rise only in a few spots with great variety of resource or locations easy of access to ships. The interiors of continents remained practically empty. Empty also were most lands of only one resource.

5. The World Market

A new world.—Within the last hundred years the use of coal, iron, and steam, has given us a new world. For ages the fight with the cold environment was slow. In recent times it has been most swift. The railroad with its accompanying car of coal has emancipated man from dependence upon the local fuel supply furnished by forests, or annual crops as in China; and has permitted a great rush of civilized humanity into cold interior regions such as the Mississippi

Fig. 4.—Sod house of the new settler on the treeless prairie of North Dakota, built of the resources at hand. Commerce has made the minimum contribution to it. No wooden house is so warm.

Valley and the plains of Canada, Russia, and Siberia. Instead of the local market, we have the world market. Instead of the local environment, we are coming to have a world environment. The railway and the steamboat make it possible for a backwoods district having but one product in abundance, to supply its inhabitants with all the varieties of goods in the metropolis, because it can sell its one product and buy in return the many different things that the people need. When crops are good, the farmers of Saskatchewan or Argentina who sell only wheat, buy goods from a thousand distant factories. They can do this only when a railroad, the most controlling of all factors of commerce by land, comes near enough to make possible the marketing of the grain and the bringing in of manufactures. Such has been the history of the settlement of all that vast farm-land plain lying beyond the Mississippi River and reaching from the Gulf of Mexico northward beyond Winnipeg. The heart of Russia and Siberia is now being pierced by new lines of railway, making possible the emigration of the Russian peasants into untilled Asia, as the Americans and Canadians are going westward into empty Canada.

The railway, the profound changer of man's environment, is now spreading into new territories more rapidly than ever before. The environment of mankind is undergoing the greatest and most sudden revolution that it has ever experienced. It is the change from the local environment in which the people lived on local supplies, to the world environment to which one abundant export commodity admits us, and which by its uniformity tends to make us all alike. This world environment creates a world commerce and a world market which we must understand before we can grasp man's relation to any community.

6. World Commerce and the World Market

The staple commodities of the world trade.—A world market exists for any commodity that is either produced or consumed over a large part of the world, and is sufficiently portable and durable to permit people in widely separated regions to be interested in buying and selling the same consignments of it. In the days of the sailing vessel, the world market was unimportant, because, with the unsatisfactory, slow, and costly means of communication, only a few valuable and non-perishable commodities could be transported long distances. The staple commodities of the world trade and the world market of that day were spices, silks, tea, coffee, furs, and curios made by the peoples of the different races.

The staple articles of a century ago are no longer the staples of the great world market. True, they are handled in greater quantities than ever, but cheap and bulky goods have now become the staples since all continents have their railroads and all oceans their steamships. Thus spices, for which India was once so important, are now tenth in her list of exports. A century ago, tea, coffee, and spices were the chief foods on the world market. Today the important food staples are wheat, corn, oats, rice, sugar, beef, pork, mutton, butter, potatoes, apples, oranges, and bananas. These are the chief foods of the white race, and, in part, of the other races also.

World trade prevents famine.—The fact that staple foods can be produced in the heart of one continent one year and sold cheaply in the heart of another continent the next year means to most of us a comfort and security usually unrecognized, because we have nothing with which to contrast it. We know nothing of famine in America or western Europe in our day, yet two centuries ago it was a nightmare that haunted all peoples. If a season happened to be too dry or too wet, or some sudden blight or disease made a local crop a failure, the people of the locality had to go hungry because there was no means of carrying bulky foods any great distance. Now, with the swift steamship and the railroad we can prevent famine by bringing in food from across the ocean (Fig. 5). Thus in times of shortage we import wheat from Canada, rice from Asia, and even such bulky goods as meat from Argentina, potatoes from Europe, and oranges from Japan, provided, of course, that we have the money or credit with which to buy. Millions of people have recently starved in India near to good transportation facilities because they lacked means with which to buy.

Changes in world trade during the last century.—The world market staples of clothing a hundred years ago were silk and furs— luxuries for the rich. Today they are cotton, wool, hides, skins, cotton-cloth, shoes, and hats—the clothes of the masses. In almost every school-room in the United States is clothing of wool, cotton, or leather from two or three continents. A century ago world commerce brought for the equipment of man in his activities little but lumber, trinkets, and curios. Today there is a world market for iron (Fig. 6), steel, cement, coal, ores, locomotives, machinery, jute, Manila hemp, and other fibers, so that the school building and the dwelling-house usually have in them materials that have been carried thousands of miles (Fig. 7).

The ability to buy and sell in the world market has quadrupled the population of the western world. It has revolutionized our daily life and our industries. It enables us to take full advantage of natural resources and to produce on a large scale for the people of distant states or foreign lands.

7. WORLD COMMERCE AND AGRICULTURE

Farming in the domestic epoch.—Farming, like manufacture,

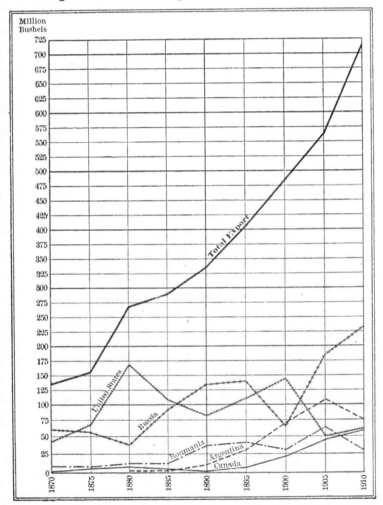

FIG. 5.—World export of wheat and flour has increased over fivefold in forty years.

has been revolutionized by world commerce. In 1786 a Massachusetts farmer wrote a book telling just how he supported his family.[1] With the wheat and corn and buckwheat that grew in his fields he furnished the family bread. The chickens, pigs, sheep, and an occasional beef animal that he slaughtered furnished the meat. His garden furnished all the vegetables and his orchard all the fruits, many of which were dried for winter use. The farm produced the family food. For clothing, his wife spun and wove the wool which he sheared from the sheep; and the flax that grew in the corner of a field was made into linen. The skin of the meat animals was tanned and made into the family's shoes. Thus were they clothed. The trees from the wood lot furnished the boards to

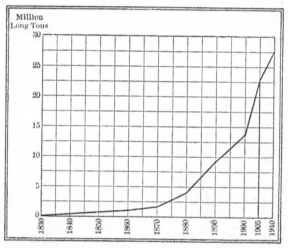

FIG. 6.—United States production of pig iron, 1830–1910.
(Iron production is considered an index of trade activity.)

build the house, the logs for the fire, and the rails for such fences as were not of stone. Like most farmers of that time, he was a fairly good worker in wood, and had a little blacksmith shop, so that he made practically all of his own tools on rainy days and in snowy winter weather. As everything was done at home, we call this the domestic epoch. Only a few things were needed from the outside world, such as salt, pepper, and iron for the little forge. These outside products cost him $10 a year, permitting him to save $150 out of the $160 received for the wheat and cattle that he sold. This

[1] See MacMaster, J. B., History of the People of the United States, Vol. I.

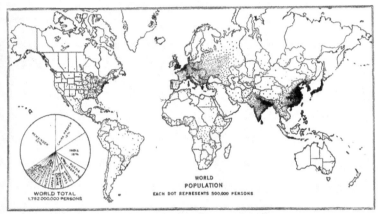

(Finch and Baker.)

Compare the location of the world's people and the world's wheat fields and you can see three things: (1) the development of the world's market; (2) the strength of the German plan of world conquest; (3) the strength of a League of Nations, if it can be carried out as planned by people who are willing to treat all orderly nations fairly.

1. The wheat map and the population map show that most of the wheat must be carried hundreds of miles to the people who eat it. Therefore, without transportation, there can be no bread for millions.

2. The German military plan was, first, to make a lightning rush at Paris and the channel ports, which almost succeeded. When this failed, the next plan was to cut off the British bread supply by the submarine, and starve the British into submission. Few people realize how desperately near this came to succeeding.

The conquest of the United States, according to German military plan, was to be effected by capturing a part of the east coast, holding a line made by the natural defenses of Lake Champlain, the Hudson river, the Susquehanna river, the Potomac river. This left a short land line easily held in the mountains. It would cut our eastern city populations off from their bread supply more surely than the submarine would have cut off the British supply.

3. The League of Nations can control any nation without fighting it by the simple process of stopping trade in bread and other things.

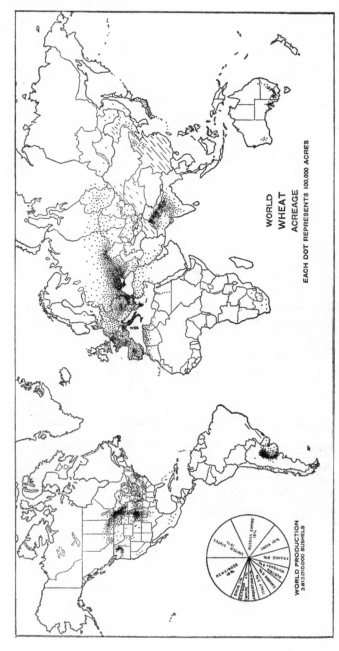

WORLD
WHEAT
ACREAGE

EACH DOT REPRESENTS 100,000 ACRES

WORLD PRODUCTION
3,813,010,000 BUSHELS

If we look at the place where wheat is grown and the places where it is not grown, we can easily see that, after all, a large part of the human race has easily got along without it. Its importance to us is a matter of habit, but habits in diet, once they are formed, are hard to change. (Finch and Baker.)

completeness of support was obtained by an amount of hard work
and discomfort that would not be tolerated in this age of commerce
and division of labor.

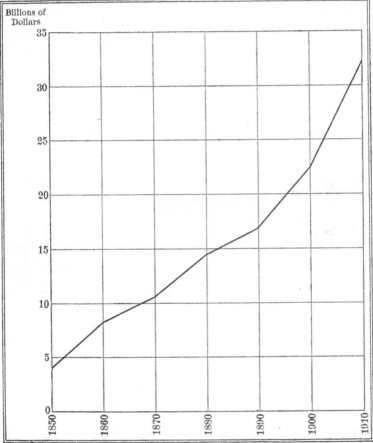

FIG. 7.—The growth of world commerce, 1850–1910. Combined imports
and exports of foreign commerce of leading countries. A sevenfold increase
in sixty years.

Farming in the commercial epoch.—Since the coming of the epoch
of coal, steam, and machinery, the farmer, especially the American
farmer, sells more and buys more, and his family usually does less

work. His shoes and clothes are factory-made, the lumber for his barn often comes from afar, as does the coal for his stove and the stove itself, as well as the tools, the wagon, and often the horse that draws the wagon. A much greater farm product is required to support a family by the commercial than by the domestic system. The increased product goes to pay for things not done on the farm. In the matter of clothing, a flock of fifteen sheep yielding 75 pounds of fleece would abundantly clothe a family with homespun. If the same 75 pounds of unwashed wool were sold at thirty cents a pound, the resulting $22.50 would scarcely buy one-fifth as much ready-made woolen clothing. Many farms that supported large families in the domestic epoch will not do so by the same kind of

Fig. 8.—The frame house, barn, outbuildings, silos, water tank, fences, and machinery of a modern American dairy farm require much wood and iron, often brought long distances. Compare with Fig. 4. (U. S. Dept. Agr.)

agriculture in the commercial epoch, and hence have been abandoned.

Money crops and supply crops.—In the commercial system, the most important consideration in connection with farming is the money crop. Every farm or every farming community has one or more crops which are usually sold and converted into cash, and hence usually called money crops. Among the world's great money crops are grain, sugar, animals, fruits and vegetables, cotton, wool, coffee, tea, and tobacco. The money crops do not occupy half the land in American farms, for most of the land is devoted to what may be called supply crops, that is, crops which are used entirely upon the farm and are sold, if at all, in some indirect form. For example, nearly half of the American farm lands are in grass. Some of it the animals eat in summer, the rest is made into hay for winter forage, so that, while important, the pasture and hay are not sold directly, but supply the means for producing something else. On many farms there may be fields of corn, oats, hay, grass, and rye, yet these are all supply crops contributing to the one money crop of milk, butter, lambs, cattle, swine or horses.

The complete self-support and the well-nigh money-free life of which the Massachusetts farmer wrote 125 years ago, is gone; but a strong trace of it remains in the fact that many things on the farm are still grown for home use. Thus a dollar for the farmer is often as valuable as two dollars to the city man, because he buys many things cheaply where they are grown, in addition to producing many things for home use.

8. The Understanding of Lands

Industrial factors.—In studying lands as the home of man, it is necessary to give close attention to climate, and to give much

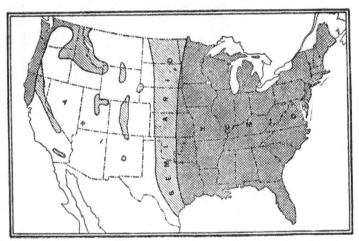

Fig. 9.—Map showing arid, semi-arid and humid regions of the United States. (After Newell.) (From Modern Geography by Salisbury, Barrows, and Tower.)

more attention to agriculture than to manufacturing. Agriculture is carried on almost everywhere. A nation may not have manufactures, but nearly every nation has agriculture, which furnishes

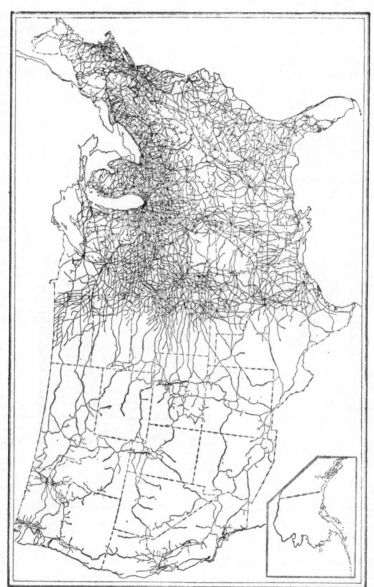

FIG. 10.—The railroads of the United States in 1911. Note the relation between rainfall and railroads, which are a close index of human activity. As an example of the influence of one climatic factor, compare the population of the states marked arid, with that of some large Eastern city or state.

raw materials for the local or foreign factory, and food for man and beast.

Manufacturing is comparatively simple in that it goes on in buildings under man-made conditions. Agriculture is carried on in the open, exposed to all the whims of wind, rain, sun, and frost. There are many animals and many plants and many kinds of soil, so that agriculture is very complex, very scientific. In explaining it there is much that must be told. In agriculture, the soil is of great importance, for it furnishes fertility, but climate furnishes the heat, light, and moisture, which are also essential to plant growth. Climate thus becomes one of the great keys enabling us to understand countries (Figs. 9 and 10). Other important factors in commerce and industry are minerals, topography (surface), and accessibility. Furthermore it is often necessary to go beyond these natural factors and to know the history and government of the inhabitants.

The United States a world in itself.—In this study of man making a living, we will first study the United States, taking up one after the other the great industries by which our people are supported. The United States is a world in itself. It has a great abundance and variety of natural resources, and a very favorable climate. These things have made it the richest nation in the world and have enabled it to have varied industries. Its lands range from the subtropic orange groves of Florida and California to the cold temperate shores of lakes Superior and Champlain. Its rainfall varies from the deserts of the Great Basin to the heavy soakings of West Washington and Louisiana. Its fields and forests are vast and its rich mines yield all the important minerals except tin and potash, and we have recently found a new way to secure potash from the sea.

Owing to the great importance of bread and breadstuffs, we should begin our study of commercial goods with the cereals.

PART I

THE UNITED STATES

CHAPTER I

THE CEREALS

Importance of cereals.—Some cereal food is used by practically all peoples who can get it, for it is nearly a complete ration.[1] The grain-producing plants such as wheat, corn, and rice, store starch, gluten, oils, and other elements of nutrition in their seeds, thereby providing for the nourishment of the young plant before it can get its roots well into the earth. This food is furnished to the men of many lands by a much larger number of plants than we, as a wheat-eating nation, commonly realize.

The peoples of China, India, and Africa make great use of members of the sorghum and millet families, plants that grow quickly and resist summer drought well. The people of the United States having come from climates that suit wheat, corn, oats, rye, barley, rice, and buckwheat, have continued to grow these crops in this country even in localities better suited to some other crop. Finally we shall find out what each locality will produce best. This process of fitting our crops to our land will be somewhat interfered with by the fact that we esteem and will pay more for some grains than for others. Here, as in most other lands, wheat is the cereal most desired for bread.

I. WHEAT

The plant and its climatic requirements.—Like all other cereals, wheat is a grass, and in the first part of its growth the plant consists of a tuft of green blades. Later it sends up stalks of straw that support the grain-bearing heads. The number of stalks and heads

---

[1] Proteid, the tissue or muscle-maker, is contained to some extent in all the grains from wheat, the richest in proteid, to rice the poorest. Starch, the great carbo-hydrate food or energy maker, is also present in all of them, so that the grains, by containing both the great food elements, are almost perfect food.

26

depends on the size and vigor of the plant, and these are greatly dependent upon the duration of cool, moist weather. If this cool, moist season of formative growth is long, the grass-like development is good and the heads many. A shorter damp period shortens the grain yield. The formative period is therefore important. In milder climates like the region south of Dakota, this period of formative growth includes the winter; hence the term "winter wheat"

FIG. 11.—Average dates of the beginning of winter wheat harvest. (After U. S. Crop Reporter.)

(see Fig. 11). Where the winters are too severe, as in North Dakota and West Canada, the formative period falls wholly in the spring and summer, hence the name "spring wheat."

After the moist weather of the formative period, there should be warm, bright, dry weather to ripen and harden the grain. Abundance of summer rain is fatal to extensive wheat growth, for fungus diseases attack the plant, and the grain often moulds or decays.

This double requirement of a cool, moist formative period and a

warm, sunny ripening period, explains the importance of wheat
in regions of rainy winter and dry summer, like our Pacific slope.
These facts explain also its absence from lands of heavy summer

FIG. 12.—Rainfall, June, July, and August. (After Mark S. W. Jefferson.)

Heavy—more than 10 inches of rain and melted snow in the three
months.
Light—from 6 to 10 inches in the three months.
Scant—less than 6 inches in the three months.

All the great wheat regions are in or along the margins of the regions of scant
summer rain.

rainfall, like the coasts of the Gulf of Mexico (see Fig. 12). On
the rainy Gulf slope so favorable for cotton, wheat becomes less and
less possible as one goes south, and the little that is grown in the

northern margins of the east Gulf States and in Carolina has the lowest yield per acre found anywhere among English speaking peoples. Large amounts of wheat are grown in the regions producing corn, but the same region cannot be equally well adapted for both wheat and corn, because the latter, like cotton, requires a considerable summer rain. This is fatal to best wheat growing.

Parts of the corn belt of the United States have, in addition, another difficulty for wheat growing in the alternate freezing and thawing of the late winter and early spring. This is much worse than solid and continuous freezing. The expansion and resultant lifting of the top soil by freezing, and the contraction of the thaw, gradually pull the wheat plant out of the ground. As a result, wheat is much less important in many corn-belt localities, especially Illinois and southern Iowa, than it was 25 or 30 years ago, because the people finally learned that this land is better adapted for corn and oats. The wheat regions have been shifted southwestward into Kansas, Oklahoma, and Texas, into a less frosty climate for winter wheat, and also northward into the colder Red River Valley of the North and to the plains of Canada, where the rigors of the winter climate have no direct effect upon the wheat because it is spring-sown (Fig. 12).

In this region there is a very neat adjustment of crop to climate. The rather scanty rain has its maximum in early summer, so here, as in California with its wet winter, wheat is sown at the beginning of the rains and harvested at the end of the rains.

Wheat thrives with much less moisture than corn. It is a crop that approaches the desert's edge. It is important on the eastern, western, and northern margins of our arid belt, which centers in the Great Basin between the Rocky Mountains and the Sierras. To the west of the Great Basin, across the Sierras in California, is the great valley of that state, since 1860 one of the important wheat regions of the country. It's essentially Mediterranean conditions of winter rain and summer drought give it the best wheat climate in America.

It is unfortunate that there is not more land in California with an arable surface and a wheat rainfall. As it is, orchards, alfalfa, and the drought-resisting barley have already caused a sharp decline in the California wheat crop.

A second wheat belt is found as we go north and northwest from the deserts of the Great Basin, into an area of increased rainfall,

This rainfall makes possible the wheat areas of eastern Oregon and Washington (Fig. 13). Here some wheat is grown in localities with less than 12 inches of rainfall per year.

The most important wheat belt in America closely follows the line of 20 inches of rainfall and reaches from Texas north through Oklahoma, Kansas, Nebraska, the Dakotas, and Minnesota into Canada, where it expands into a vast area of great promise for the future (Fig. 12).

For several reasons, we do not yet know how large this wheat area is. We do not know where its northeastern edge is because it is a temperature line set by the number of days between spring frost and autumn frost. If we have a quick growing variety of wheat, it can grow farther north where the season is shorter.

In similar fashion, the western and southwestern limit of this central North American wheat field, if eventually it is found to stop short of the Rocky Mountains, is again a climatic line, the line of light rain.

Both of these climatic lines are strangely unfixed. It seems like a jest, but the location of these climate lines depends in part upon mechanical invention.

A little figuring makes this plain. Anything that makes cultivation easier, so that one man may cultivate more acres of ground, makes it possible to cultivate with profit land which before could not be cultivated. If the wheat growers of Canada and the United States had to depend upon the wooden plows used by our colonial ancestors in Massachusetts and Pennsylvania, and cut the crop with sickles, small indeed would be the wheat region of Canada or of Dakota. This brings us to the whole question of the relation of machinery to wheat, in which we have had astonishing changes in the past; and the end is not yet, for the farm tractor, which seems to be in its infancy, is perhaps the most revolutionary farm machine ever invented.

Effect of machinery on wheat production.—The production of wheat has been made much cheaper and easier by mechanical inventions. Eighteenth century wheat was cut in the Scriptural way by sickle. The laborer with one hand grasped a few stalks of the grain and cut them off with a sweep of the sickle held in the other hand (Fig. 15). The next implement in general use was the cradle, invented in New England in 1806. It was a kind of scythe provided with fingers to catch and throw into an even row the straw it cut. In 1851 Cyrus McCormick, of Virginia, made a reaper which cut and dropped the grain in bundles to be bound by hand. Then came the self-binders, or reapers that also tie the

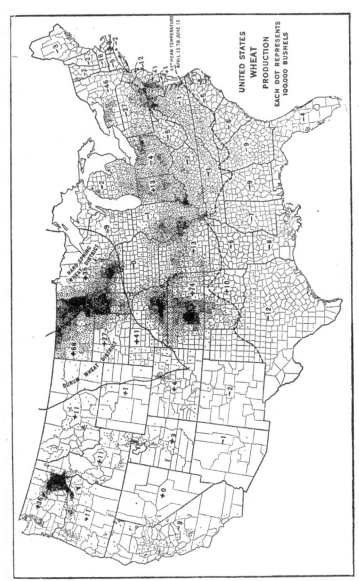

UNITED STATES
WHEAT
PRODUCTION

EACH DOT REPRESENTS
100,000 BUSHELS

The plus and minus figures on this map show the amount of wheat which the state had to import per year on the average before the Great War. It is surprising how many of our states are like England in being dependent on imported bread stuff.

Compare with the cotton map and we see how cotton's climate is wheat's enemy. (Adapted from Finch and Baker.)

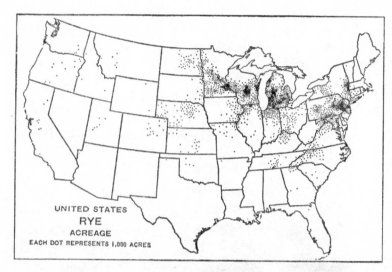

UNITED STATES
RYE
ACREAGE
EACH DOT REPRESENTS 1,000 ACRES

FIG. 14.—The rye maps of the United States and Europe show an enormous difference in the importance of this grain in the two regions. Among other things, they show the difference between the wealth of the people in the two continents. In America, we have not yet been forced near to the limits of our grain growing region. We have been able to extend the wheat region and therefore have neglected the less desirable barley and rye.

Our wheat belt merges off in three directions to the zones where three other grains are more at home. Toward the south, with its moist summer, is the land of corn. Toward the west, with drought, is the land of barley. Toward the north, with frost, is the land of rye. When America has as many people as Europe, our rye area will be much larger than it is now. We will be growing rye on many sandy stretches and now unused, or little used, upland fields between Carolina and the plateaus north of the St. Lawrence, between Canada and Nova Scotia.

Europe is ahead of America in rye growing partly because she has such a large area of cold, sandy plain to the north of her wheat belt. We may some day have a large rye belt to the north of the American wheat belt, but it will not be as large as that of Europe because of the large area of rough country north and east of the Great Lakes. (Finch and Baker.)

bundles, and finally the binders that carry the bundles and drop them in piles where the shocks are to be made (Fig. 16). A driver with three horses operating one of these machines has no difficulty in performing as much work as was done 50 years ago by from five to seven men working arduously with cradles and rakes. The work is occasionally done by women, as the physical effort has been reduced until one now merely drives horses and regulates the cutting by adjusting easily operated levers on the reaper.

FIG. 15.—Arabs in Tunis harvesting wheat by primitive methods preparatory to threshing it under the feet of camels. The Bedouin is little influenced by our machine industry.

Similar improvements have been made in threshing, which is equally a part of wheat production. Men are still living in the United States who in their youth helped thresh by driving horses around and around upon the sheaves that their feet might shatter out the grains upon the threshing floor. A method similar to this, in which the horses drag a rolling stone around the threshing floor is still in use in Russia, Turkey, and other countries adjacent to the Black and Mediterranean Seas. In more progressive regions, under the influence of high wages, the steam thresher (Fig. 17) does nearly all the work. In the United States, it is common for one of these machines to thresh a thousand bushels of wheat per day and be taken at evening to the next farm by its own traction engine. These revolutionary improvements in wheat production have cheapened its labor cost from 133 minutes of human labor per bushel in 1830 to 10 minutes in 1904.

Similar improvements have been made in machinery to prepare the soil and plant the seed.

The machinery for planting, harvesting, and threshing wheat has also been adapted, with minor changes, to do the same work for the

Fig. 16.—Harvesting by machinery in the United States. The machine cuts, binds, and carries the sheaves of small grain. (International Harvester Co.)

other small grains—rye, oats, barley, and buckwheat, and even rice. The cheapening that results from the easier production permits wheat to become more universally used as food. It is now eaten by many people in the southern United States who previously made a larger use of corn; by others in Germany and Austria, who had been living on rye bread; and even by the Chinese and Japanese, who are increasing their use of it as a luxury to replace partially their cheaper foods of barley, rye, millet, and the more expensive rice.

Where wheat is grown on hundreds of acres, still more specialized machines are used, the most complicated of which is the combined

FIG. 17.—American thresher at work.   (International Harvester Co.)

harvester and thresher. This machine can be used only when very dry summers, such as occur in the Columbia River basin and the great valley of California, permit the grain to dry out on the stalk so that shocking it up to cure it is not necessary. Here the combined harvester and thresher, driven by steam or drawn by twenty-five or thirty horses, sweeps over the great fields and daily puts into sacks the thoroughly dry grain of thirty acres of waving wheat fields. These machines were invented shortly after the railroad had given us commercial access to extensive level, treeless, fertile plains

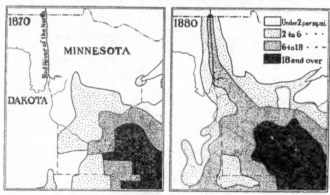

FIG. 18.—(a) Map showing distribution of population in region of Red River of the North in 1870. (b) Population map of region of Red River of the North in 1880. The level, treeless, fertile plain of the Red River Valley was settled almost entirely by wheat growers, and the population of Dakota increased from 14,000 to 135,000 between 1870 and 1880.

and prairies in the center of the continent, and settlement and wheat growing went forward with great speed. The population in this granary of our country is not large because one man can cultivate so great an acreage that a single family can easily take care of several hundred acres. It is populated by machines rather than by men.

Another mechanical invention has increased wheat growing and influenced the speed of settlement in the region north of Minneapolis (Fig. 18). The wheat that grows there is so hard and brittle that the husk broke up when ground by the old-fashioned mill stones, and the flour was dark and not desired. The gradual reduction by repeated pressing between steel rollers makes fine white flour and suddenly gave spring wheat flour the leadership of the market.

The one-crop system of the agricultural frontier.—Wheat, which is valuable, salable, and easily transported, is often the best money crop that can be produced in newly settled regions, hence it is grown year after year for 10 to 20 years after settlement. This gradually exhausts the soil, and the declining yield then makes it necessary to rotate the crops, to grow clover and to keep animals in order to build up the soil again. This is the cycle of the agricultural frontier. It has been witnessed in Illinois, Iowa, Minnesota, Dakota, and is now going on in Washington, Canada, Argentina, Siberia, and other regions, where the early farmers wasted their soil resources by the one-crop system.

The Red River Valley of the North, comprising the major part of the wheat districts of Minnesota, North Dakota, and Manitoba, like the black-earth districts of southern Russia, now experiences decline in yield and approaches the end of its continuous wheat production. With the possible exception of the Russian black-earth belt, there never was in the whole world an easier place than the Red River country for the growth of wheat. This fertile plain, the bed of a glacial lake, often for miles literally as flat as a floor, without a stone or tree, lends itself perfectly to the use of the most modern machinery and large scale production. Year after year wheat has been grown until the declining yield has made the farmers turn to other crops— the raising of horses, the keeping of cattle, the making of butter. The total yield from these districts does not decline because of the steadily increased percentage of the land that goes into wheat in the one-crop period and the improved yields that follow the introduction of crop rotation and live stock.

At the present time in western Canada, where new railroads are being built across open, empty, treeless plains, the new settlers are again beginning with continuous wheat growing which will be kept up one, two, or three decades before they too must take to other crops and to keeping cattle. In the meantime these wheat crops on the virgin prairie soil of the harvest frontier are larger than those of the Red River Valley. It is possible that the Canadian region suitable for the extension of wheat growing reaches 60° north, and extends from Lake Winnipeg to the Rockies. If experience proves this to be true, the wheat-growing possibilities are enormous, and the continuous cropping method will have land to support it for several decades.

The Italian farmers, who are now going to the Argentine Republic

at the rate of 100,000 per year, are having an identical experience
upon the magnificent black-soil plains that lie along the western
banks of the Parana River.   The Russian peasant also exploits in
the same way when he emigrates to central Siberia and settles on
those endless plains called steppes where now the trans-Siberian
railroad has made possible the export of grain.   After a time these
Siberians also must rotate crops, keep cattle, and export butter and

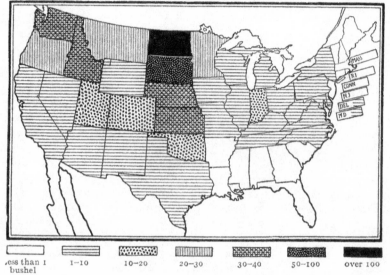

| less than 1 bushel | 1–10 | 10–20 | 20–30 | 30–40 | 50–100 | over 100 |

FIG. 19.—United States production of wheat per capita, by states.   Wheat
figures, three-year average, 1909–11.   Pop., 1910.   Compare with rainfall map
(Fig. 9).   Note emphasis of belt of low rainfall from Texas to Dakota, also in
Washington and Idaho.

eggs to London, as do their brethren in the older and more developed
lands of Russia and West Siberia.
    Despite the leadership of the central wheat districts of the United
States, their yield is less per acre than that of the North Atlantic
States, and far less than it is in northwest Europe.   But on these
cheap, carelessly tilled lands of the frontier, the yield *per man* is
much greater (Fig. 19) than on the more laboriously tilled fields of
Europe.   The distribution of the world's wheat crop is a fine
illustration of the fact that products are often grown in places that
are not best suited to them.   This does not prevent the crop from

being the best thing to grow in that particular place. Thus, western Kansas is not the best place in the world to grow wheat, but owing to a combination of many reasons wheat is the most profitable

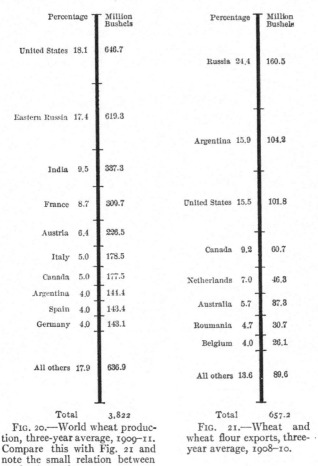

Percentage		Million Bushels
United States	18.1	646.7
Eastern Russia	17.4	619.3
India	9.5	387.3
France	8.7	309.7
Austria	6.4	226.5
Italy	5.0	178.5
Canada	5.0	177.5
Argentina	4.0	141.4
Spain	4.0	143.4
Germany	4.0	143.1
All others	17.9	636.9
Total		3,822

Fig. 20.—World wheat production, three-year average, 1909–11. Compare this with Fig. 21 and note the small relation between production and export.

Percentage		Million Bushels
Russia	24.4	160.5
Argentina	15.9	104.2
United States	15.5	101.8
Canada	9.2	60.7
Netherlands	7.0	46.3
Australia	5.7	37.3
Roumania	4.7	30.7
Belgium	4.0	26.1
All others	13.6	89.6
Total		657.2

Fig. 21.—Wheat and wheat flour exports, three-year average, 1908–10.

crop that can be grown there. (See table of crop comparisons in Appendix.)

Situation of wheat exporting regions compared.—The wheat exporters of southern Europe, on the Black Sea, share with the exporters of the Argentine Republic the advantage of cheap ocean transportation. The wheat exporters of the United States and Canada grow their surplus for export in the heart of a continent a thousand miles or more from seaports. That this last region nevertheless takes its place among export regions is due solely to the excellence of the transportation conditions which have made possible the bringing of wheat to ocean harbors where it could be exported. In 1825 the Erie Canal connected the Hudson River with the Great Lakes and made possible boat transportation from the shores of the Great Lakes to New York at a fraction of the previous cost. This made possible the extensive growing of wheat in western New York, northern Ohio, Michigan and other lake shore districts. Ohio ranked first among the wheat-growing states in 1839. Twenty-five years after the canal opened the lake shores to the world market railroads began to reach out from these inland waterways across the plains and from that time to this wheat has gone eastward to the sea in millions of bushels, being gathered together in the great markets, first at Chicago, and later at St. Louis, Kansas City, Milwaukee, Duluth, Port Arthur, and Winnipeg. It is probable that within a few years new railroads will be built from the Canadian wheat country to Hudson Bay, where for a short time after wheat harvest steamers can get out with the Canadian wheat crop before the ice closes this great and at present unused arm of the sea. At the present time, however, the whole movement of wheat east of the Rocky Mountains is to the Atlantic and Gulf ports, most of it passing down the basin of the Great Lakes, whence, as a result of railroad agreements, it scatters to reach the sea at all ports between Montreal and Norfolk. From Kansas and southward, the Gulf is nearer than the Atlantic and much wheat reaches the ocean steamer at New Orleans and Galveston.

The wheat of the Columbia River basin is exported from Portland and the Puget Sound ports. Some of the Pacific Coast export goes to the Orient but most of it still goes to Europe by cheap water transportation, which has always been less expensive than an over-land journey to an eastern port.

The Siberian wheat plains, drained to the frozen Arctic and shut off by mountains from the southern sea, have the worst situation of all wheat exporters with regard to the sea. The Siberian crop must make the long rail journey to the Baltic or White Seas unaided by any such gift of nature as the American Great Lakes or the

Danube River. For this reason the Siberian plain has been the last of the world's great plains to be settled. The recent railroads have enabled it to become a wheat exporter but its crop combined with that of the adjacent provinces of Central Asia amounted to but 93 million bushels in 1912, while that of Minnesota was 67 million (94 in 1910), North Dakota 99 million (90 in 1910) and Kansas 68 million (87 in 1910). But Siberia has the resources of great area, fertile soil, and the population of Russia promises plenty of immigrants.

Manufacture and commerce in wheat.—Minneapolis is the greatest flour milling city in America. It is situated at the gateway to the spring wheat plains that reach more than a thousand miles to the northwest. Power for its mills is furnished by the Falls of St. Anthony on the upper Mississippi. Other flour manufacturing centers are Niagara Falls, Buffalo, and Rochester, three cities of New York state having water power and also located on the grain route to the East. Breakfast foods are also made entirely or in part from wheat, and are manufactured in most of the larger cities where rail or water routes make it easy to bring in the grain and where the dense population affords a ready market for the finished product. Bran, the outer covering of the grain, and middlings, the germ, which are important cattle foods, are produced at all the great milling centers.

Wheat was an important export of New Amsterdam (New York) as early as 1656, and has been important ever since. In colonial times it went chiefly to the West Indies where wheat does not grow. During most of the nineteenth century the trade has been chiefly with Europe and wheat has been the leading agricultural export of the North. The future, however, promises to see our export of wheat decline in importance and in quantity. It first declined in favor of flour exports. But there is now in progress a conspicuous decline in the export of both wheat and flour, because our increasing population leaves a smaller and smaller surplus for other lands. The phenomenal crop of 1914 promises to be but a temporary exception. California furnishes an interesting example of this change. That state, once a great wheat exporter, reached her maximum wheat acreage in 1893. Since that time alfalfa fields and fruit orchards have cut in on the wheat area until it does not now supply even the needs of the state. The California bean crop is more valuable than the wheat crop. Canada, Argentina, and Siberia possess the new lands for the one-crop farmer to cultivate and rob, and thus supply the world market.

Our future wheat supply.—We can greatly increase our wheat production by the introduction of better varieties from other lands, by breeding better varieties of the grain, and by improved cultivation and fertilization of our fields. The recent introduction to the United States and Canada of a drought-resisting variety of wheat known as Durum, from the arid lands of eastern Europe, has resulted in the extension of the wheat area into the drier lands of our desert edge, which before were practically useless. This variety of wheat contains much gluten and is thus very valuable for the manufacture of macaroni. More than 50 million bushels per year are now grown in the United States.

The introduction of new varieties gives new *materials* for the plant breeders to use (Fig. 22). Plant explorers are now scouring all possible corners of the world in search of plants especially adapted to particular purposes and conditions. These plants, specialized in one quality to the point of perfection, can be used as parent plants by the plant breeders. In 1910 wild wheat (a plant supposed to be extinct) was found growing on the arid slopes of Mount Hermon in Palestine. This is a plant of such promise for scores of millions of hopelessly arid western acres that the United States Department of Agriculture at once sent an expert to study it in its native habitat.

2. Rye

Botanically, rye is closely allied to wheat, which it resembles in physical appearance. It will grow where wheat grows, but the grain is smaller, less nutritious, and hence less valuable. That rye is grown, nevertheless, is due to the fact that a crop will mature in poorer and sandier soil, in a colder climate, and with less care than will wheat. For these reasons rye was relatively more important in the United States before the settlement of the fertile, level west, than it now is. At the present time we produce in this country only about one-twenty-fifth as much rye as wheat. It is grown chiefly in the mountain districts or on poorer and more hilly lands, but almost never on land which will yield a good crop of wheat. The chief centers of production are the Appalachian region from the Potomac and the Ohio northward to Lake Champlain, and the glacial districts between Minneapolis and Lake Michigan. As the conditions of east Canada resemble those of the eastern United States, rye is grown to a similar extent there. It is of very great

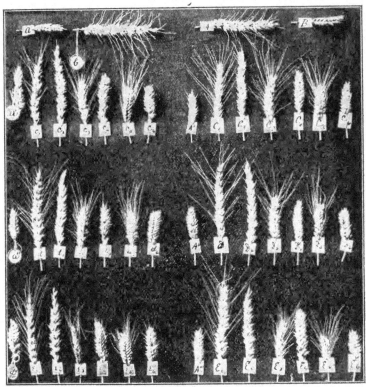

FIG. 22.—An experiment in plant breeding,cross-bred wheat showing great variation in offspring of hybrids.

ab, = parents.
a′a″a‴ = offspring of abCross.

$\left.\begin{array}{l}c_1c_2 \\ d_1d_2 \\ e_1e_2\end{array}\right\}$ etc. = offspring of a′a″a‴.

A.B. = parents same variety as ab but crossed the other way.
A′A″A″ = hybrid offspring of AB-cross.

$\left.\begin{array}{l}C_1C_2 \\ D_1D_2 \\ E_1E_2\end{array}\right\}$ etc = offspring of hybrids A′ A″A‴.

The hybrid offspring show every possible combination of the visible qualities of the parent stocks. By this means new varieties of great value in Washington and Minnesota have been produced.

importance in northern Europe, especially Russia and Germany where there is much sandy soil in a cool climate.

3. Oats

Soil requirements and distribution.—The soil requirements of the oat plant are not unlike those for wheat. In its climatic requirements it can stand nearly as much heat, but it requires more rain and will also grow in a colder climate. Its moisture requirement bars it from the regions of Mediterranean climate, like California, with their hot dry summers. It is commonly spring sown in localities where the other small grains are fall sown, and the grain is chiefly used as forage, especially for horses. For these reasons it is grown to some extent in nearly all the important northern wheat regions and also in rye and northern barley regions. In the southern part of the winter wheat belt, winter sown oats are grown and have the advantage of ripening earlier in the season.

Oats grown on same farm as Indian corn.—The fact that oats may be sown early in spring and will stand the hot summer, makes it a very important grain in the corn belt of the United States. In much of this territory the moisture of summer and the alternate freezing and thawing of the open winter are alike unfavorable for wheat. Oats, standing more moisture and not being hurt by a little frost, fit nicely into these climatic and agricultural conditions by being sown very early in the spring before corn can be planted. The crop requires no attention until harvest time, which does not occur until after the corn has been both planted and cultivated. Then while the corn is maturing, after the hay harvest or possibly before it, the oats are harvested. The excellent way in which these crops dovetail together makes the field of oats as well as the field of corn and the field of hay parts of the great corn belt farm system. In this way is grown the greater part of the United States oat crop, which amounts to nearly a billion bushels, giving us first place among oat producers.

4. Barley

Barley closely resembles wheat in appearance, is the hardiest of the important cereals, and has a much wider climatic range than wheat.

The wheat limit in Russia is near Petrograd, but barley goes on to the Arctic. It is neighbor alike to the sledge-drawing reindeer and the desert-crossing camel. It is important in northern Norway and Sweden, and in the adjacent Lapland, growing beneath the midnight sun, and ripening 150 miles beyond the Arctic Circle

in 70° north latitude. It is regularly grown in Finland and north
Russia to the shores of the Arctic Ocean, and its ability to resist
droughts and heat causes it to be grown as
far south as the Nile Valley, Abyssinia, and
the east point of Africa near the equator.

The grain lacks gluten, and for that reason
it will not make the sticky dough necessary
to good light bread. But because barley
yields nearly twice as much per acre as does
wheat, it is a great forage crop where corn
cannot be grown, as on the Pacific slope of
the United States, and beyond the corn belt
in the plains from Texas to Dakota (Fig. 23).
It will thrive with less rain than wheat
and is consequently replacing wheat in California, which now produces a quarter of our
barley crop. Barley is also used for making
beer, and half of the American crop is
grown in a district reaching from Dakota to
Milwaukee, a great brewing center.

5. Buckwheat

Buckwheat, an unimportant cereal, is
among grains as the goat is among animals
—conspicuous for its ability to nourish
itself where the supply of nourishment is
meager. It grows so quickly that it can
be sown in midsummer after other crops
have failed, or have been harvested, and
yet ripen before frost. Its qualities combine to make it a crop for farms of rough
and mountainous localities, such as the
Appalachian Plateau in New York and
Pennsylvania, and parts of New England

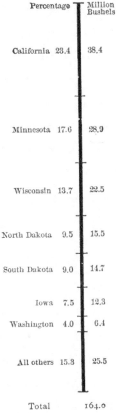

	Percentage	Million Bushels
California	23.4	38.4
Minnesota	17.6	28.9
Wisconsin	13.7	22.5
North Dakota	9.5	15.5
South Dakota	9.0	14.7
Iowa	7.5	12.3
Washington	4.0	6.4
All others	15.8	25.5
Total		164.0

Fig. 23.—United States barley production, three-year average, 1909–11.

and Canada. Its chief use is for making griddle cakes in regions
where maple syrup is easy to obtain.

6. Rice

Rice characteristics and rice climate.—Without rice the human
race would be greatly handicapped for locally grown cereal food in

the torrid zone and in some parts of the warm temperate zone where there is a heavy summer rain, as along the Gulf coast in the United States. In such a climate all the European grains—wheat, barley, rye, oats, and buckwheat—fail miserably, and corn (maize) is not at its best, owing to the bad effects of the moisture which prevents the grains from hardening. Commerce would find difficulty in filling the gap because it is so difficult to keep these northern grains from spoiling in a hot moist climate. Trouble is often experienced in shipping corn down the Mississippi River and through the Gulf of Mexico to Europe, because the humidity causes the grain to heat and mould. It is indeed fortunate that countries with these climatic conditions can grow rice, Asia's great gift to the world, a grain which thrives under wet summer conditions and which, owing to the dryness of the kernels and to a protecting husk, can be kept without deterioration—a tremendous advantage. This grain is to the regions with wet summers what wheat is to the regions with dry summers. The two plants do not thrive in the same region unless, as is the case in a few districts of China and Japan, a **crop** of winter wheat can be harvested before the beginning of summer rains which furnish the proper conditions for rice.

Distribution of rice.—Unfortunately, rice, like barley, has little gluten and will not make light bread, but its great keeping qualities make it a food prized in nearly all lands engaged in commerce. It has been grown in the Orient for ages and was early imported as food by the American colonists. After the surprising success of the governor of South Carolina in raising a patch of rice in his garden in 1694, rice growing became an important industry in that colony and in Georgia. Swamps along the seacoast and rivers could readily be dyked off, irrigated, and cultivated by negro slaves in the Oriental way. These two states have grown rice of excellent quality down to the present day, but they are now suffering from the competition of the newest and most interesting of all the world's rice fields, that upon plains near the Gulf coast not far from the boundary between Louisiana and Texas. In this level, well-watered, marshy and little-used district, the machinery and methods of wheat growing have been adapted to rice growing.

The conquest of this primeval Oriental hand-labor garden crop by American farm machinery has enabled one man to take care of 80 acres of rice in a year. Although he is paid twenty times as much as the Chinese laborer, he produces rice more cheaply because

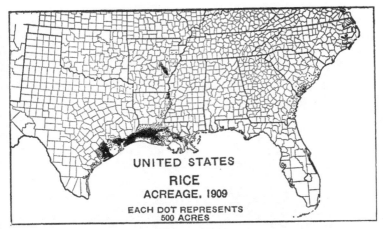

UNITED STATES
RICE
ACREAGE. 1909
EACH DOT REPRESENTS
500 ACRES

(Finch and Baker.)

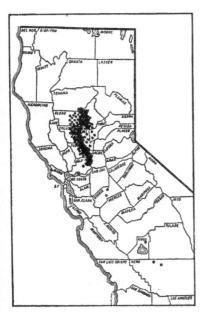

A rapidly increasing rice industry is one of the most recent steps in California's surprising capture of old world crops. The level, new-made soil of the Sacramento Valley furnishes a fine site, and the melting shows from the forest-clad mountains give plenty of water for irrigation. This is much like the rice industry of the Po valley in Italy, where an arm of the sea has been similarly filled with water-born soil, now irrigated by the meltings of mountain snow fields. This successful growth of rice in the cool temperate zone of the United States shows that we might have a very large rice industry scattered through many states if we chose to flood all available lowlands.

(Finch and Baker.)

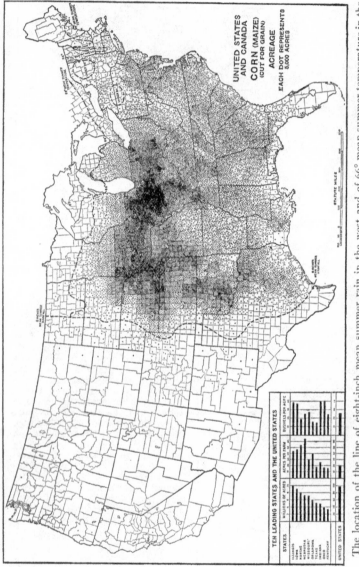

UNITED STATES
AND CANADA
CORN (MAIZE)
(CUT FOR GRAIN)
ACREAGE
EACH DOT REPRESENTS
5,000 ACRES

The location of the line of eight-inch mean summer rain in the west and of 66° mean summer temperature in the north and on Appalachian highlands shows how definitely the corn region is fenced in by climatic factors. The locations of the hilly and rough Ozark and Appalachian plateaus are very clearly shown, also the swamp and sandy lands of the coastal plain. (Finch and Baker.)

the Chinaman cares for only 1 or 2 acres by his arduous hand labor.

This new rice region produces many times as much rice as does the more expensively managed swamp district along the South Atlantic Coast. It is possible that before long the United States will become a rice exporter rather than, as now, an importer. But it will take a good many years for the American rice growers to get acquainted with their new industry and to become acclimated (if possible) in the necessarily damp climate which accompanies the irrigation of land upon the warm and moist shores of the Gulf of Mexico. The attempts at "upland rice culture" in Arkansas and the Sacramento Valley have not as yet been a commercial success—so great is the dependence of this aquatic plant upon a saturated soil.

Since large areas in China, Japan, India, Indo-China, and the East Indian islands have both the humid air and wet soil, rice is the chief crop and chief grain food of several hundred million people.

7. CORN OR MAIZE

Uses of corn.—Corn is properly called the king of American forage plants. It differs from wheat in having a stalk an inch in diameter, and 6 to 15 feet high. The ear is sometimes a foot long. Corn is commonly planted in rows and the ground between them is cultivated to prevent the growth of weeds and to keep the soil loose and moist. Its large size and the cultivation permit it to be grown on rough and recently cleared ground where small grains would not thrive. For these reasons it was of especial service to the early colonists. It could be grown in small clearings in the forest too rough and too shady for other grains. It yielded twice as much as the small grains, was easily kept, and could be served as food in many forms—as parched corn, made by heating the whole grain in a frying pan or over an open fire; as hominy, which is the cracked corn thoroughly boiled; as mush or samp, made by boiling the meal; or, finally, as cornbread. The husk that protected the grain served in the mattress for the colonist's bed; the stalks and leaves fed the horses and cows through the winter, even after they had served for months as a thatch for the temporary shed that shielded the animals from storm. Because of its ability to grow on rough ground it is of great service to the people of such localities as the Appalachian district from Georgia to New York. This locality with its inferior corn crop furnishes a good example of the influence of environment on history. About the only way in which corn can be exported from these plateaus is by converting it into whisky or live stock. Owing to the fact that the United

FIG. 24.—Scene in the Piedmont section of North Carolina. Hill ruined by erosion while in corn—a land-destroying crop on rolling or hilly land because the cultivation greatly aids the washing away of the surface soil. Girdled trees, wasteful rail fences. (U. S. Dept. Agr.)

States Government taxes whisky a dollar a gallon there has been a century-long struggle between the collector of revenue and the illicit distiller, the "moonshiner" as he is called, of the Appalachian Mountains. The mountaineer feels that it is a tyranny for the Government to tax the only thing he can sell. This feeling took its strongest form in Washington's administration, when the people of western Pennsylvania, objecting to the tax, arose in insurrection against the new Republic in the so-called "Whisky Rebellion."

Climatic requirements.—Corn cannot stand frost, but will mature if there is a 5-months growing season, and a hot midsummer with sufficient rainfall (Fig. 25) to keep up the growth of the plant. Accordingly, regions with a cool summer, all North Europe, most of New England north of latitude 44°, and Canada, excepting a part of Ontario, cannot well produce a crop of ripened corn. Selection and breeding are producing quick maturing strains, some of which will ripen in 100 days of growth. By this means the corn belt may be extended farther north. The heat requirement of the maize plant includes warm nights as well as warm days, so that many arid regions having very hot days and cool nights, such as Nevada and the Pacific Slope are not suited to the profitable production of corn despite an apparently satisfactory average temperature. For this reason it is not yet an important crop in the irrigated west but interesting variety adjustments are being tried out.

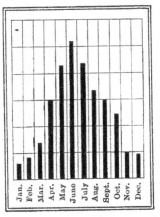

Fig. 25.—Rainfall in inches per month at Omaha. The heaviest rainfall comes just when the growing corn needs it most. Each horizontal line marks an inch.

Although a lover of heat, corn does not do its best in the continuous heat of the tropics, the greatest yield of grain being in the central temperate zone. The cultivation of corn in a small way is, however, widely scattered throughout the warmer parts of the world between 45° north latitude and 40° south latitude.

Corn Belts.—The United States produces twice as much corn as all the rest of the world (Fig. 26). It is grown from the Gulf of Mexico to the Great Lakes, and from the Atlantic Ocean to western Kansas, and in scattered areas beyond, but the region of greatest production, the so-called American corn belt, reaches from central Ohio to central Kansas, and from Kentucky to Wisconsin. It in-

cludes all the state of Iowa, nearly all of the states of Missouri,
Illinois and Indiana, Ohio, and about half of Kansas and Nebraska
(Fig. 27). This region is one of the finest agricultural sections in
the entire world. For hundreds of miles the almost level prairies

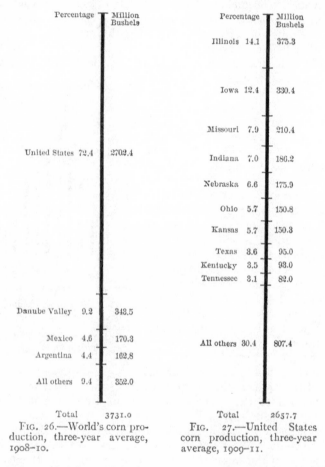

Percentage		Million Bushels		Percentage		Million Bushels
				Illinois	14.1	375.3
				Iowa	12.4	330.4
				Missouri	7.9	210.4
United States	72.4	2702.4		Indiana	7.0	186.2
				Nebraska	6.6	175.9
				Ohio	5.7	150.8
				Kansas	5.7	150.3
				Texas	3.6	95.0
				Kentucky	3.5	93.0
				Tennessee	3.1	82.0
Danube Valley	9.2	343.5				
Mexico	4.6	170.3		All others	30.4	807.4
Argentina	4.4	162.8				
All others	9.4	352.0				
Total		3731.0		Total		2657.7

FIG. 26.—World's corn production, three-year average,
1908–10.

FIG. 27.—United States
corn production, three-year
average, 1909–11.

are rarely varied by undulations steep enough to interfere with the
laying out of roads on meridians and parallels at regular intervals
of 1 mile. This soil that lies so beautifully for tillage is naturally
fertile, and so free from stones that the worker can ride the culti-

vator with which he tends the corn. Some of these cultivators till both sides of one row of corn, and some of them even take two rows at once. Thus, an unaided farmer with his team can cultivate a large area of corn, sometimes more than 40 acres, and produce the grain that was so wonderfully cheap for many years (Fig. 28). Serious droughts are infrequent in the corn belt. The abundant rainfall of summer comes in short showers which do not seriously interfere with agricultural operations, and the heat is sufficient to

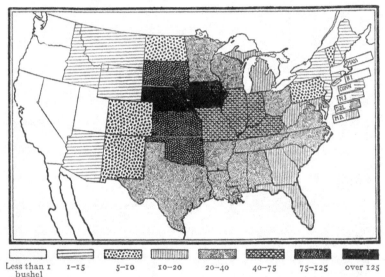

Less than 1   1–15   5–10   10–20   20–40   40–75   75–125   over 125
bushel

FIG. 28.—United States corn production per capita by states, three-year average, 1909–11. Pop. 1910.

make a most excellent growth of corn. The percentage of sunshine, an important factor, is high.

Relation of corn to other products of corn belt.—Corn is not the only crop in the corn belt. On a single farm there may be, in addition to corn, fields of oats and hay which require the farmer's labor at different seasons from the corn; also there will often be a field of grass upon which cattle can graze.

A surprisingly small portion of the corn-belt grain goes directly to the market. Most of it is sold in the more condensed forms of beef, pork, mutton, horses, and mules (Fig. 29).

An interesting adjustment of production to transportation factors is shown by the way distance decides whether the corn-belt farmer ships meat or grain. In 1910, 48 per cent of the corn of Illinois, near St. Louis and Chicago, was shipped out of the county where it was produced. In Kansas the corresponding figure was 22 per cent, in Texas, yet farther from the markets, it was only 7 per cent.

Corn in the South and East.—Corn is the second crop in importance in the cotton lands of the South. Although these lands are

Fig. 29.—Iowa corn field and corn condensers, 140 hogs fed on corn and molasses feed, gained 1⅔ lb. each per day for 100 days. (Champion Feed Milling Co., Lyons, Ia.)

well adapted to corn growing, cotton is so overwhelmingly the main crop that the corn crop is often insufficient for local use, and import from the corn belt is necessary. Corn, but little used as human food in the northern half of the United States, is in common use in the southern states. Two shortcomings of corn suffice to explain its small use as breadstuff where wheat is available; first, it has no gluten and so will not make a dough, or light bread; second, the bread loses much of its palatability upon getting cold.

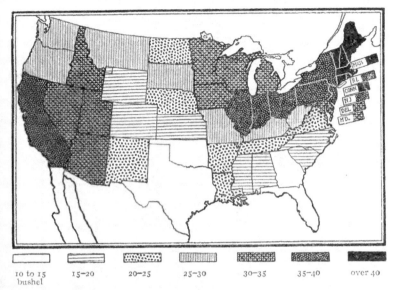

10 to 15 bushel	15–20	20–25	25–30	30–35	35–40	over 40

United States corn production in bushels per acre by states, three-year average, 1909–11. The states that grow but little make the largest yield per acre.

In the case of failure of her wheat crop, there would be famine in Italy without the import of grain. In America we have the great reservoir resource of corn, not fully understood by many during the Great War. We grow three to four times as much of it per year as we do of wheat, sometimes more than that. Nearly all of the corn is fed to our animals (see Fig. 29). In case of a great shortage of wheat, all we need to do is to eat a fifth or a fourth of our corn and reduce temporarily our animal industries to that extent. This would of course mean a reduction in the meat supply, but it would still leave us more meat than the people of any nation on the continent of Europe ate even before the War.

We made a tiny start in that direction during the War, by making a slight reduction of meat during our meatless days and mixing a little corn meal with our wheat flour. We did not like the new bread, for people rarely like to make changes in their diet. Even the hungry people of Europe often resented the eating of corn, which has nevertheless been the food for millions of people for thousands of years.

Corn is also an important crop in the Middle Atlantic States and its growth is extending to the northward. This extension is aided by the use of the silo, a barrel-like structure, 10 to 20 feet in diameter and 30 to 50 feet high, made of wood or concrete (see Fig. 8). By means of the silo the entire corn plant, stalk, leaf, ear and husk, when chopped into bits, may be kept moist, warm, and edible for cattle for 1 or 2 years. In this form, called silage, corn yields

FIG. 32.—Average dates of the beginning of planting corn. (U. S. Crop Report, U. S. Dept. Agr.)

its greatest possible food value for live stock, and is much used in the feeding of dairy and beef cattle. Since it can be put away some weeks before it is fully matured, it can be grown much farther north than can the ripened grain. After the "roasting ears" or "green corn" have gone to the market or the cannery, the stalks are sometimes used in the silo for dairy cows.

The improvement and extension of corn growing.—Great improvement in corn growing takes place from year to year as the scientific agriculturists teach the needs of the plant, breed new and better varieties, and select the seed to take advantage of the known laws of heredity. Boys' corn clubs are doing much to increase the yield of corn. In a recent corn test[1] in Illinois one large field yielded 48 bushels to the acre while a similar adjacent field yielded 77 bushels to the acre, the only element of difference being the superior well-selected seed that produced the larger crop. The breeding of earlier ripening kinds will doubtless make possible a greater growth of corn in parts of the northern United States and Canada where it is not now a dependable crop.

New kinds of corn.—Kaffir corn and Chinese sorghum are two of the new kinds of corn (so-called) that have recently been introduced to the United States with great benefit and greater promise. Both are members of the sorghum family. Like Durum wheat, they can stand much drought. Kaffir corn comes from arid South Africa. Others have recently come from the drier parts of China and they are already being grown by the millions of acres in Kansas and Oklahoma, where they have of late proved themselves more valuable per acre than the water-loving Indian corn. The grains are small and round like little peas. The appearance of the plants is like that of broom corn, but they are satisfactory stock food and are bringing about some westward extension of the corn area.

QUESTIONS

1. Why is the moist open winter of Washington state and England so good for wheat?

2. How does wheat thrive in the climate of the cotton belt? In that of the Great Valley of California?

3. How does the changeable winter weather of Illinois suit wheat?

4. How does the plant explorer increase our possible wheat production? The plant breeder?

5. Why was rye more important in Colonial America than it is now? Why was corn the agricultural mainstay of the American colonist?

6. How does a labor adjustment promote the growth of oats in the corn belt?

7. Why is corn the worst of all grains as a soil destroyer?

8. What quality of the barley plant promises to make it very important in the western half of the United States?

9. What has been the great American achievement in rice growing?

10. How does corn get to market?

11. How may the silo extend the zone of corn culture?

12. How have Kaffir corn and sorghum influenced the corn area?

[1] J. R. Steward: Proceedings American Breeders Association, Omaha meeting, 1909.

CHAPTER II

THE ANIMAL INDUSTRIES

1. MEAT AND THE MEAT SUPPLY

Meat a luxury.—Among most peoples of the world, meat is something of a luxury and is becoming more so. That it is not a necessity is shown by the fact that millions of people, as the Chinese and Japa-

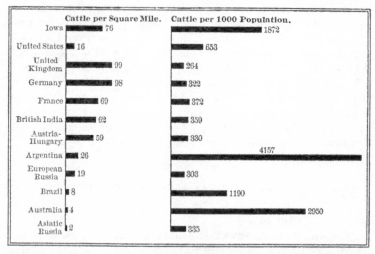

FIG. 33.—The chart of ratios of cattle to land and to population shows how the frontier, as Argentina, leads the old lands like England and Germany in cattle per capita. The per capita consumption of meat in Australia and Argentina is about 250 lb. per year. In United States it is about 160; United Kingdom, 120; France, 80; Italy, 45.

nese, eat it but rarely and many not at all. Some, as the Hindoos, are even forbidden by their religion to eat flesh. An examination of the table of food values (see appendix) shows the sufficiency of vegetable foods, and this sufficiency is a fortunate fact, for many millions of the human race in Asia and Europe can rarely afford to eat meat because of their poverty. It is a luxury possessed chiefly by the people of lands of sparse population, where for that reason meat is cheap (Fig. 33). Man always has the choice of eating plant products directly or, if land is cheap and plant products abundant, he can feed them to animals and then eat the animals. The latter is much the more expensive form, for the making of a pound of meat requires the grass from much land, or it requires from 5 to 10 pounds of grain, the equivalent of eight to fifteen 1-pound loaves of bread. In densely peopled regions where there is not food enough for both man and beast, man eats the vegetable food and does without the beasts.

Japan probably presents the most extreme example of a people

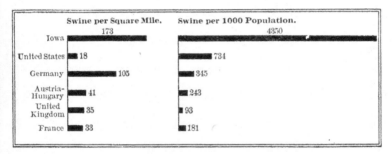

FIG. 34.—Germany is surprisingly close to Iowa in hogs per square mile, but her dense population makes meat relatively scarce. Meat export is a product of sparse populations.

who maintain a high civilization with few animals. With the exception of the cold northern Island of Hokkaido, the whole country has a population of from 400 to 500 people per square mile. With nearly 50 millions of people, the Empire has of horses and cattle combined but 5½ per cent as many, while the number of sheep and hogs is but ⅛ of 1 per cent of the number of people. Both of these figures are utterly insignificant in comparison to those for the United States (113 and 130 per cent, respectively), or even to those of Europe (Fig. 34).

The rising price of meat.—As long as the American people could keep on spreading into fresh new lands, animals were abundant and meat was cheap. By the beginning of the twentieth century we had come to the end of our new lands, and since that time we have been exhausting the land we had and increasing our population so that animals are becoming relatively scarce.[1] That makes the price of meat rise and the relative scarcity seems likely to continue and even to increase because of these geographic reasons.

2. SWINE

Swine are the meat animals of grain-growing lands as sheep are of grass-growing lands. Thus pastoral New Mexico has but one hog to fifty sheep, and Iowa, a great corn state, has eight hogs to one sheep. The hog was originally an animal of forest countries, living upon acorns, nuts, roots, grubs, and other highly nutritious foods. Consequently, in domestication he must have somewhat similar foods, since his small stomach is not adapted to a complete diet of bulky grasses. In his original forest home he converted the abundance of autumn nuts into a layer of fat which covered his body and carried him through the hungry time of winter. Therefore, the rich grains of the farm suit him exactly. He is still fond of the nuts and acorns of his original forest home, but is able to eat anything from a piece of meat or garbage to the weeds which his owner pulls from the garden. Tame, harmless, hardy, and prolific[2] the hog is an admirable dooryard scavenger and meat producer for the cottagers of many lands, and has attained an almost world-wide distribution, being of great local importance as a food supply in many countries where he is of no commercial value. Where an abundance of food and good care are possible the hog easily becomes a commercial product because of its rapid multiplication.

Relation of the hog industry to grain growing.—Since the hog must have some kind of concentrated food such as acorns, nuts or grain, he is a natural product of the regions producing cheap grains. The chief regions producing hogs for export, therefore, are those in which

[1] The United States Department of Agriculture estimate for 1914 shows that in the very short time since 1910 the ratio of domestic animals to population in the United States has declined, as follows: horses 3.5 per cent; mules 9.8 per cent; milch cows, 4.4 per cent; beef cattle 19.2 per cent; swine 5.2 per cent; sheep 11.6 per cent. These are figures of profound significance. Our per capita consumption of meat is estimated to have declined 10 pounds in 5 years since 1909. The very high prices of 1914–15 have produced a slight increase in numbers of meat animals.

[2] It is a rare flock of sheep that increases 100 per cent per year, while ten- to fifteen-fold increase of swine is common. Their production in the United States and other countries is greatly hampered by the outbreak of the swine plague or hog cholera, a disease which the recently discovered process of inoculation seems able to hold in check.

corn or barley abound. [Compare Figs. 28, 30 and 36, showing distribution of swine and corn in the United States.] Since corn has long been the cheapest and is also the most fattening of the grains, and

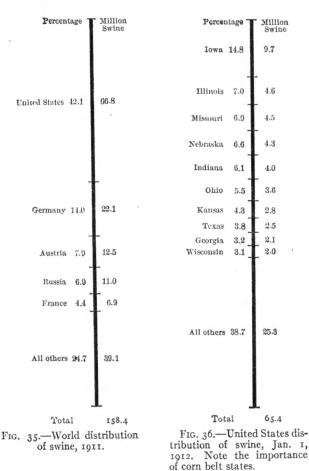

Percentage	Million Swine
United States 42.1	66.8
Germany 14.0	22.1
Austria 7.9	12.5
Russia 6.9	11.0
France 4.4	6.9
All others 24.7	39.1
Total	158.4

FIG. 35.—World distribution of swine, 1911.

Percentage	Million Swine
Iowa 14.8	9.7
Illinois 7.0	4.6
Missouri 6.9	4.5
Nebraska 6.6	4.3
Indiana 6.1	4.0
Ohio 5.5	3.6
Kansas 4.3	2.8
Texas 3.8	2.5
Georgia 3.2	2.1
Wisconsin 3.1	2.0
All others 38.7	25.3
Total	65.4

FIG. 36.—United States distribution of swine, Jan. 1, 1912. Note the importance of corn belt states.

since corn is much more important than barley for hog feed, the corn belt of the United States is the leading hog-exporting region of the whole world. It might as well be called the hog belt as the corn belt. Chiefly because of this corn belt, twice as many hogs are found in the United States as in any two foreign countries (Fig. 35). The farmer in Iowa, Kansas or Nebraska nearly always grows one or two fields of corn, and often keeps from 20 to 100 hogs, which he feeds almost entirely upon the corn. Fully one-third of the American corn crop goes to the market in the form of pork. Hogs are reared to some extent in practically all parts of the United States, but chiefly where corn is grown (Fig. 36). On the Pacific slope barley is used to some extent as a substitute for corn. Several hundred thousand hogs live on mast in the national forests and the mountaineers in parts of the Ozarks and Appalachians derive most of their meat supply from "razor back" hogs that shift for themselves and live entirely upon roots, nuts, acorns and other forest pickings.

3. CATTLE

Distribution of cattle.—Wherever there are wide spaces of untilled grass lands we are likely to find cattle. They were the animal pioneers during the nineteenth century upon the vast plains that the white man won from the wild animals and native peoples in North America, South America, Australia, and central Asia. On account of their size, strength, and speed, they can combat dangers, or, if necessary, flee from them. Their ability to withstand heat and moisture has enabled them to go into lower latitudes than sheep. With the exception of the humid plains of the mid-tropics, they are to be found from the Straits of Magellan to Hudson Bay.

In the first stage of the occupation of new plains, before transportation has been well developed, the only export products furnished by cattle are the non-perishable hides and tallow. Later the bones are gathered up to make into fertilizers to restore phosphorus to worn-out lands. However, the ability of cattle to walk long distances enables them to be raised far from the railroad. Thus we had a vast area in the West which was for a time devoted to cattle under the care of the picturesque but passing cowboys.

The great open plain west of the one hundredth meridian and reaching from west Texas far into Canada was too dry for good farming; therefore the pioneer farmers could not take it for homesteads, as they had taken up all Iowa and the eastern parts of Kansas and Nebraska. Hence, people branded their cattle, and turned them out upon the plain in great numbers to pick up their living as the buffalo had done. At an annual round-up all the cattle

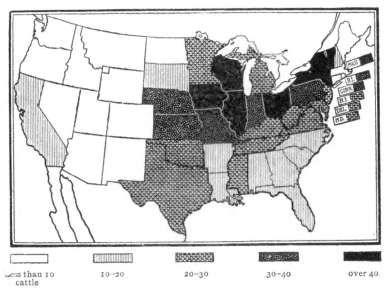

Less than 10 cattle   10–20   20–30   30–40   over 40

FIG. 37.—Cattle in United States per square mile, by states, Jan. 1, 1912.

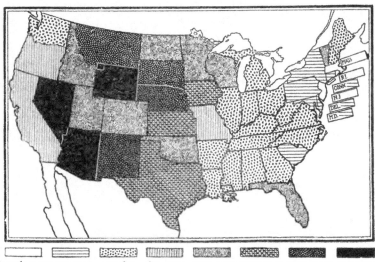

Less than 100 cattle   100–300   300–600   600–1000   1000–1500   1500–2000   2000–3000   over 3000

FIG. 38.—Cattle in United States per 1000 inhabitants, by states, Jan. 1, 1912.
(U. S. Dept. Agr.) Pop. 1910.

in a large area were brought together, each man took the cattle that had his brand and sold them. The freedom of the range naturally led to an overstocking. The grass, especially in periods of drought, was eaten so close that it could not produce seed, and in many places it died out and was replaced by inedible weeds. The

FIG. 39.—Erosion of California pasture land after too close pasturing, Marin County. Great resource destruction follows abuse of pastures. (Photo G. K. Gilbert.)

disappearance of the grass exposed the soil to erosion by both wind and water (Fig. 39) as that the plains cannot now support so many cattle as they once did.

The migration of beef cattle.—The range cattle spend 1 or 2 years upon these western plains living on grass, and are then shipped lean and hungry into the corn belt where the farmers keep them for a few months, fattening them on corn before sending them off to the great markets for slaughter. Some of these cattle are fattened on the farms as far east as Pennsylvania and other Atlantic states. In the hilly country of southwestern Virginia, northeastern Tennessee and West Virginia, there is a section of good grass country where young cattle are raised and sent to the farm lands of the great valley and the Piedmont sections of Virginia and Maryland for fattening.

This migration of the animals in their production and in their going to market provides easy means for the rapid spread of diseases. Within recent years there have been bad outbreaks of the foot and mouth disease, a terrible disease usually fatal to all cattle. It has swept the cattle away by hundreds of thousands in South America and Africa, and occasionally the germs come with hides to this country. An infection from stockyards of Chicago and Buffalo has been spread over many districts by the scattering of cattle to be fattened on eastern farms. We have thus been compelled to establish rigorous and efficient quarantine regulations.

Importance of cattle on arid lands with some irrigation.—Irrigation in the West is important to the cattle industry (Figs. 41 and 42). Indeed, beef is the chief commodity shipped from most of the irrigated districts of the United States. Alfalfa leads all other irrigated crops in the area under cultivation. This plant is the richest of all the clovers. It sends its roots to great depths in the ground and when the moisture supply is abundant it yields heavy crops of hay, in from three to six cuttings a year, according to climate. Fortunately, the irrigable valleys are widely scattered throughout the cattle range from Canada to Mexico, and from western Kansas to western Oregon, so that these favorable alfalfa fields are really scattered oases in the scanty and semi-arid pas-

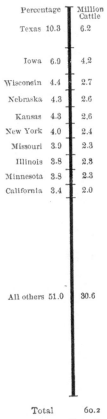

	Percentage	Million Cattle
Texas	10.3	6.2
Iowa	6.9	4.2
Wisconsin	4.4	2.7
Nebraska	4.3	2.6
Kansas	4.3	2.6
New York	4.0	2.4
Missouri	3.9	2.3
Illinois	3.8	2.3
Minnesota	3.8	2.3
California	3.4	2.0
All others	51.0	30.6
Total		60.2

FIG. 40.—Cattle, including milch cows, in United States, Jan. 1, 1912.

tures. During winter and the seasons of drought, alfalfa hay
supplies the cattle from the ranges with abundant food and sometimes fattens them for market.

4. Possible Extension of Meat Production

Cattle in southern states.—The southern states have great but

Fig. 41.—Map showing the irrigable lands of the United States and their admirable distribution over the arid region. (United States Reclamation Service.)

unappreciated cattle-producing possibilities. The northern farmer
must build large barns to protect his animals and their food from
the cold and storms of winter. He must feed his animals full half
the year from the results of his summer's toil. In Alabama or
Florida there is so little winter that a barn is scarcely necessary,
and the growing season is so much longer that more forage can be
produced on a given piece of land than in the northern states. The

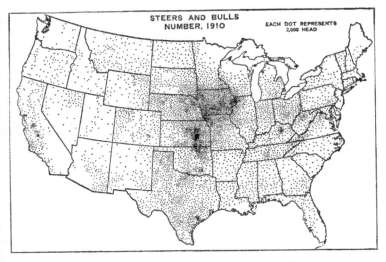

Cattle from western ranges stop in western corn belt to get fat.
United States Swine. (Finch and Baker.)

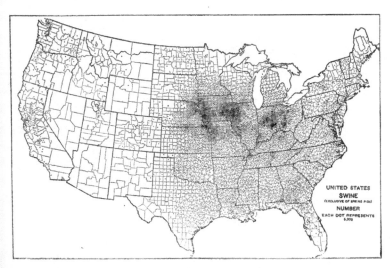

Compare this with the corn map. Corn and swine go together.
Alfalfa Acreage. (Finch and Baker.).

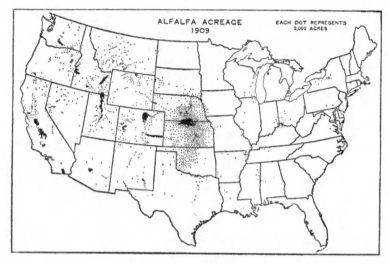

ALFALFA ACREAGE
1909

EACH DOT REPRESENTS
2,000 ACRES

(Finch and Baker.)

The map of alfalfa distribution shows well the location of our irrigated lands. It is easy to pick out the course of the upper Arkansas river, the North and South Platte, the Yellowstone, the Rio Grande, and the string of oases at the foot of the Wasatch Mountains which makes up agricultural Utah.

The value of our irrigated lands is greatly enhanced because they are scattered over a vast region of small rainfall, where cattle live in scanty pastures for a season, and pass their winters, or periods of drought, feasting on the hay stacks in the irrigated alfalfa meadows beside the irrigation ditches. Many alfalfa growers make a business of raising hay and selling it to a man who drives his cattle into the stack yard and feeds the alfalfa on the spot.

The alfalfa crop in the very large region in central Kansas and Nebraska is not irrigated. Here the soils are porous and deep, so that the alfalfa, with roots ten, twenty, thirty, even fifty or sixty feet long, can go to great depths and get enough water in land of moderate rainfall to prosper amazingly. If better varieties or better methods can give an alfalfa crop that will thrive in the east and south as it does in Kansas, it will be a great gain to our people, because of the excellence of alfalfa in the making of milk, a food whose value we are just beginning to appreciate for children who would be strong, and adults who would live long.

cattle can also pasture nearly all the year. Thus the industry requires less capital and labor than in the North. One serious disadvantage to the cattle raiser in the South has been the tick, a parasite which abounds in the timbered districts and which is often carried to other distant areas by shipped cattle. These ticks, which cling to the skin of the animal in great numbers, not only keep the animals thin by sucking their blood, but often transmit the germ

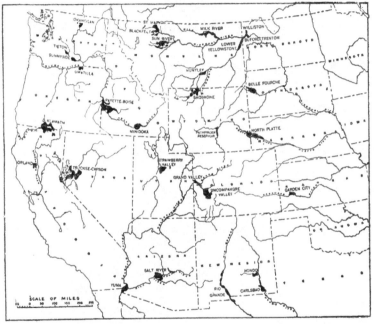

FIG. 42.—Principal irrigation projects undertaken by U. S. Government. (U. S. Reclamation Service.)

of "Texas fever," an often fatal cattle disease. But successful methods of tick eradication are steadily doing away with this danger (Fig. 43) even in the worst infested districts. Hence the South should rapidly take its place as the leading cattle producing region of America.

The South has even greater advantages for hog production than for cattle production. In the Gulf and South Atlantic States it is possible to grow at nearly all seasons of the year a great variety, and

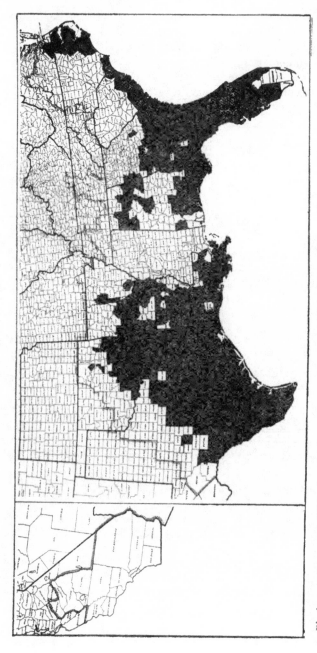

Black area shows tick infected and quarantined area of 1918. Shaded line to north of it shows original limits of quarantine. Millions of cattle have been soused, head, ears, and all, clear under the surface of ill-smelling disinfecting liquids in especially prepared vats, so that now big, fat cattle can replace little, weazened, fever victims in the fields of the South. (U. S. Dept. Agr.)

complete succession of forage plants which the hogs can eat in the field without the trouble of harvesting by human effort. Some of these crops are alfalfa, red clover, crimson clover, cow peas, soy beans, wheat, winter barley (for pasture) and vetches. The last three are not injured by frost and will grow four-fifths of the time in the open winters of the Gulf slope (Fig. 44).

FIG. 44.—Two-story farming. Georgia porkers rooting up the remnants of a sweet potato crop in a young pecan orchard. The pecan is a coming substitute for meat.

5. THE EFECT OF IMPROVED METHODS OF SHIPPING AND PRESERVING MEAT

The invention of artificial refrigeration (Fig. 45) has done much to make possible the slaughtering of animals nearer the place where they were raised. Previous to the development of refrigeration the meat of beef animals in some sections was thrown away, and only the hides, horns and tallow saved. About 1875 the invention of the refrigerator car made it possible to send dressed beef from Chicago to Boston more cheaply than the live animals could be sent. In 1879 came a sure method of hermetically sealing meat in cans so

Fig. 45.—Quarters of beef on trolleys in cold storage rooms where they will keep good for weeks. (Joseph Campbell Co., Camden, N. J.)

that it would keep for a long period, thus giving another force to locate the slaughtering industry at the great cattle markets rather than at the centers of consumption. Consequently, packing plants are located in the great cities nearest to the places where the cattle are fattened. Cincinnati and Chicago were the first packing-house centers, but Omaha, Kansas City, and, to a lesser extent, St. Paul, have now become great centers. Plants are being established also at Fort Worth and Waco in northern Texas still nearer to the cattle-raising districts, but Chicago is yet, as it has long been, the greatest meat-packing center in the world, partly because of its favorable location at the junction of many transportation lines both by rail and water, and partly because it had an early start in the business and so has developed a class of men specially trained in the skillful management of what has come to be a many-sided industry.

The modern meat-packing plant handles cattle, hogs or sheep, according to the demands of the market, and is one of the most wonderful examples existing of speed, mechanical perfection, and the use of by-products. So perfect is the utilization of the refuse that absolutely nothing is wasted. The meat product of the packing house goes out as fresh, salt, smoked, canned, or pickled meat. Grease not fit for culinary use is made into soap. All other parts not otherwise used, are made into fertilizer. The total number of inedible products is over 100. Owing to the development of cold storage and refrigerator cars, an ever-increasing proportion of fresh meat is now distributed from the great packing centers to cities and small towns, chiefly in the northeastern part of the United States. It is also put into the chilled chambers of the ocean steamers at the Atlantic ports, and sent to Liverpool, London, Antwerp, and Hamburg to feed the dense populations of Europe. There is a considerable export of pork to the West Indian Islands and other tropical countries. For this trade salt pork has the advantage of being cheap and of keeping well. Our export of meat products has declined sharply in recent years, and 1913 witnessed some imports of fresh meat from Argentina. This will not stop the rising price. It is a world market price.

The future supply and price of meat.—The nineteenth century was a period of industrial discovery and commercial expansion by means of farm and factory machinery, railways, steamboats and refrigeration. This permitted the western world to have for a few decades the cheapest meat supply we are ever likely to have. There are no more great plains to discover in America or elsewhere, and the population is increasing much faster than the number of meat animals. As a result meat is today rising in price in practically all parts of the world. For this there is no remedy in sight, and it may not be an entirely fanciful prediction that fifty years hence a juicy beef steak will be the center piece at the banquet table.

6. HAY

Relation of hay to the animal industries.—Grass is the natural food of most of our domesticated quadrupeds. Pastures or grass fields where animals can feed in summer are the commonest feature of American farms. Hay, the dry grass or pasture product, kept over in barns or stacks for winter use, is almost equally common. In the harvesting of this crop we see one of the direct results of intermittent climate which stops growth. It is not necessary to make hay in lands where grass will grow the year round, as it does in many parts of the torrid zone. Hay is usually a supply crop, to be eaten by the animals of the farm and becomes salable in the form of live animals, meat, butter, cheese, milk, wool, and hides. Every time one eats any of these foods he uses a commodity that could not have been produced in usable quantities but for hay, and when there is a shortage in hay, dairy products and meat are high in price.

Distribution of hay production.—In the semi-arid regions, like the Great Plains of the central part of America, nature herself makes good hay. Here the rain comes in the early summer making the grass grow rapidly. With the increasing dryness of late summer, the grass dries and stands for months rich and nutritious.

The cultivated hay crop is general in the north temperate zone and also in parts of the south temperate zone, except on the natural hay plains; and it is rapidly increasing in irrigated sections. In the United States, Canada, and Europe it is a very important crop. It even exceeds the wheat crop in value in the United States, and about equals it in area.

In the United States the corn belt is the great hay center also, a fact which shows very clearly that zones producing one farm crop only are not common. The corn-belt farms are often divided into four fields of about 40 acres each, and it is not uncommon for one field to be in corn, one to be in oats, wheat or barley, one to be in pasture for the cattle in summer, and one to be in hay for the cattle in winter.

Methods of making hay.—Methods of making hay have greatly improved through the recent invention of machinery. So great is the saving of labor (Fig. 46) that, in some of the alfalfa fields of the West, it is said that hay can be made at a labor cost of $1 per ton, making it the cheapest of animal foods, and enabling the productive alfalfa lands to bring a very high price for American farm lands.

Hay in irrigated sections.—The most productive of all hay plants is the alfalfa, a clover which lives for many years, which can slumber through months of drought, and spring into rapid growth the very day that water is applied, and can produce five or six tons of hay per

FIG. 46.—By the use of these devices alfalfa hay is cut, gathered and thrown upon the rick without wagon or pitchfork, or the force of human muscle. (U. S. Reclamation Service.)

season in three or four cuttings on rich irrigated land. To crown its virtues, alfalfa hay is richer in protein than is wheat flour. Hay, therefore, reaches great importance on the irrigated districts (Fig. 47) interspersed among the arid and semi-arid lands of the West, where in some places alfalfa alone makes satisfactory stock raising possible.

Hay in commerce.—The bulkiness of hay in proportion to value makes it comparatively unknown in foreign commerce. Our domestic hay movement is much larger than is the foreign. Hay is regularly sent from the corn belt to the cotton belt, where in a region that might produce forage for its own animals and a surplus for export, the people are devoting themselves so exclusively to cotton growing that they frequently buy food for their work animals. Hay is also of considerable importance in local commerce in various parts of America where horses work in cities, in mountainous regions or forest regions, as at lumbering and mining. The many cities of New England and the northeastern states make this region the

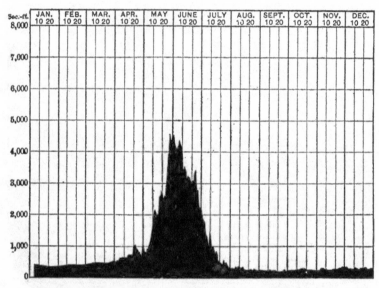

FIG. 47.—Discharge of water in 1900 from the Arkansas River, a stream fed by Rocky Mountain snows, near Canyon, Colo. (U. S. Geol. Surv.). The maximum of water in the growing season is very valuable in raising alfalfa and other irrigated crops which are so important in supporting our animal industry.

greatest American hay market and therefore the farmers of New York and New England find the selling of hay more important to them than do the farmers of other states. In many districts of New England it is almost the only crop grown and sold from many half-abandoned farms where no fields are being plowed. The rapidly increasing use of the automobile in city traffic may be expected to decrease materially the city demand for hay. This will be an advantage to the nation, since the hay can be used in feeding the more profitable meat or dairy animals.

7. DAIRY PRODUCTS

The dairy products and their uses.—Milk, intended only for the offspring of the particular species producing it, has been taken by man at various times and places from many animals. As a result of long selection and improvement, the goat and the cow have become especially adapted for this service. The breeds of cattle are of two classes—the beef animals that tend to get fat if well fed, and the dairy or milk breeds that tend to give much milk if well fed. The dairy products are first raw milk and then a number of manufactures of milk, chiefly cheese, butter, and condensed milk. Cheese, a condensed form of milk, is a substitute for meat (see table of food analyses, appendix); and butter is a fat, supplying well the deficiency of the albuminous and starchy foods. For this reason it is so well liked with bread.

That part of the fat of milk which separates as cream can be condensed into lumps of butter by mere stirring at proper temperature, and kept for weeks, or in cold storage for months; the milk can be converted into white fleecy curds and the curds into cheese which keeps for months; and, by the driving off of water by the processes called condensation and evaporation, milk can be reduced in bulk and canned like fruit so that it will keep for years. Thus, many parts of the world hitherto unaccustomed to dairy products have, since the development of world commerce, adopted their use.

Characteristics and location of the dairy industry.—Dairying as an important industry depends entirely upon cow's milk. It has arisen in lands of moderate coolness where the rainfall is sufficient to make the succulent grass and other forage required by cows giving profitable quantities of milk. Owing to the bulk, weight, and perishable nature of milk, it must be produced near to the market if it is to be consumed while fresh. Thus New York, our empire state, leads all other states in its number of milch cows; and Pennsylvania, second in population, ranks high in milch cows.

Within a few decades great improvements have been made in the processes of manufacture of dairy products, and like cloth making, it has passed from the home to the factory.

Dairying marks an important stage in the intensification of agriculture, which means increasing the income from a given piece of land. There are two ways by which a farmer may get more product: one is to take more land; the other to put more care and labor on the land he has. Upon the Great Plains with their scanty population there are millions of cows, but the available butter, milk, and cheese are inadequate for the use of the people, because the cow, with little care from her owner, is allowed to run upon the great range with the calf which drinks all of her milk. In this instance the farmer makes his profit by selling beef. In New York and other eastern states, on the other hand, the land is hilly, the farms

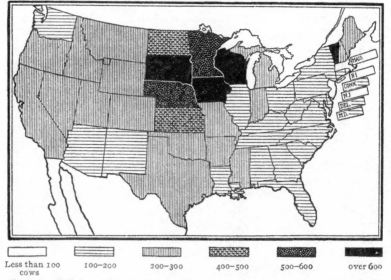

Less than 100 cows   100–200   200–300   400–500   500–600   over 600

FIG. 48.—Milch cows in United States per 1000 inhabitants, by states, Jan. 1, 1912. (U. S. Dept. Agr.) Pop., 1910.

are small, and the farmer cannot raise enough cattle to support him if he uses the method of the beef producer of the Plains.

But a few cows eating his pasture grass, his hay, his corn fodder, or silage and much of his grain will, day by day produce enough milk to make him a comfortable income. Therefore, it comes about that New York State besides furnishing vast quantities of market milk, also ranks high in the manufacture of butter and condensed milk. These latter products, concentrated and easy to transport, tend to come from locations somewhat remote from the large cities, and their production is moving westward into the corn belt, gradually replacing the less intensive meat industry (see Table of Cattle in Appendix). (Fig. 48.)

Wisconsin, next to New York, is the leading dairy state, while

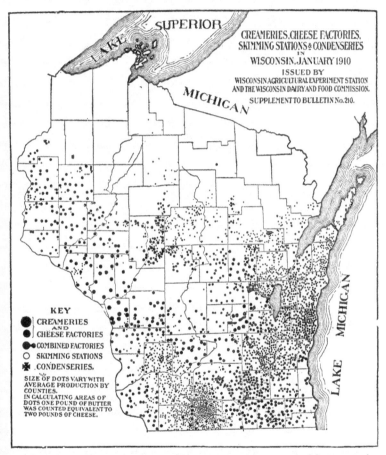

CREAMERIES, CHEESE FACTORIES, SKIMMING STATIONS & CONDENSERIES
IN
WISCONSIN. JANUARY 1910
ISSUED BY
WISCONSIN AGRICULTURAL EXPERIMENT STATION
AND THE WISCONSIN DAIRY AND FOOD COMMISSION.
SUPPLEMENT TO BULLETIN No. 210.

KEY
● CREAMERIES
AND
◖ CHEESE FACTORIES
●◖ COMBINED FACTORIES
○ SKIMMING STATIONS
✸ CONDENSERIES.
SIZE OF DOTS VARY WITH
AVERAGE PRODUCTION BY
COUNTIES.
IN CALCULATING AREAS OF
DOTS ONE POUND OF BUTTER
WAS COUNTED EQUIVALENT TO
TWO POUNDS OF CHEESE.

FIG. 49.—The distribution of an industry in Wisconsin, a state with great variation of geographical conditions.

Illinois, Iowa, and Dakota are steadily growing. Wisconsin and the lower peninsula of Michigan developed a dependence upon dairy products earlier and to a greater degree than the states of the corn belt proper because their land is not quite so well situated for corn, and therefore the people have been compelled to turn earlier from grain growing and make their land profitable by other means, such as potato growing and dairying. In Wisconsin, the State University has, through its school of agriculture, given a conspicuous aid to the dairy industry by inventions, investigations, and teaching throughout the state. In 1909 there were 2,969 creameries and cheese factories in this one state (Fig. 49).

It is a surprising fact that the United States with all its land and agricultural wealth has not become an important exporter of dairy products (see Appendix). We have the land, but we have so much of it that we have not yet been compelled to use it so intensively as the dairy industry compels. Dairy exports are a sign of meager agricultural opportunity per man, as in Holland, Denmark, and Switzerland.

The large amount of labor involved in making butter is causing a rapid development of substitutes. The best known is oleomargarine, made largely from beef fat (margarine) by a cleaner process than butter making. Olive oil, cotton seed oil, peanut oil, and other vegetable oils are also used as butter substitutes in the pure form or in various combinations with butter and margarine.

8. Sheep

Origin and importance of the sheep.—It is generally thought that our ancestors found the sheep upon the mountains of central Asia, a mottled animal of black, white, and brown, whose pelt has made us the best of all protections against the cold and aided our advance into the land of frost and snow. History contains no record of the origin of cloth making, so remote was its beginning. For many ages before the coming of cheap cotton (about 1800) (see chapter on textiles), woolen cloth was the chief clothing material in the temperate zone, and sheep were much more universally kept than they now are.

Factors affecting the distribution of sheep industry.—Before the beginning of the railway epoch, sheep were distributed upon the farms of Europe and America, and most countries were nearly self-supporting with regard to supplies of wool and mutton. But the period of world settlement and world commerce following the railway and steamship about 1850 led to an entire revolution in the sheep

and wool situation of the world. A sheep industry on the largest
scale that has ever been or is ever likely to be seen, resulted from
the throwing open of large areas of land in North and South America,
Africa, Australia, and central Asia which could be best used as sheep
ranges.

Probably because of mountain ancestry, the sheep is a good
climber for rough pastures, and a good traveller. He can go far for
his food and water, or to market. He is well fitted for the utilization

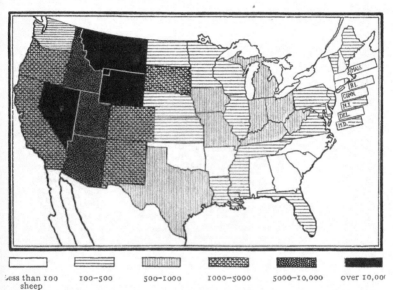

₋ess than 100 sheep	100–500	500–1000	1000–5000	5000–10,000	over 10,00⟨

FIG. 50.—Sheep in United States per 1000 population, by states, Jan. 1, 1912.
Pop., 1910.

of land not fit for the plow, and regions with greatest dependence
upon sheep are those parts of the earth's surface which for some
reason are not available for cultivation. It may be that the land is
too rough and too wet, as in the Scotch Highlands with their heavy
rains. Semi-aridity, however, is the greatest reason why land is
devoted to pasturage of sheep rather than to cultivation of grain
and other crops.

Value of sheep to regions remote from markets.—A third reason
why land may be devoted only to sheep is its inaccessibility for the

marketing of the heavy and less valuable products of agriculture in which transportation costs must be relatively high. Grain requires a railroad close at hand. Cattle, unless their meat can be marketed, have nothing to yield but the hide and tallow which is relatively of less value than the fleeces, skins, and tallow of sheep. Consequently, sheep flocks give the people of remote plains the greatest possible cash income, and the opening of new lands between 1850 and 1890

Fig. 51.—By artificial selection for one quality some strains of Merino sheep have become racks for wrinkly skins, and every wrinkle covered with fine wool until the sheep is almost blinded by it.

caused an enormous increase in the number of sheep throughout the whole world.

Sheep have for several decades competed with cattle for the grass of the plains and mountains of the United States beyond the one hundredth meridian. Upon these western plains as upon other great sheep-growing plains, there is a special method of caring for the sheep. Owing to the defenseless character of these stupid animals they require constant care and may not be allowed to shift for themselves as do cattle. The herder with a couple of dogs takes a flock of two or three thousand sheep and follows them for days and weeks, being met at appointed places by supply wagons sent out by his employer. The sheep dogs, with the inherited qualities of many generations, are much more skillful helpers in driving them than men could be, and the herder's rifle protects from wolves, foxes, and dogs, while the flocks are commonly put into corrals or fenced enclosures at night. It is common for the lambs from the range flocks of our western states to be shipped eastward like the range cattle to the corn belt in the autumn for fattening.

Sheep upon the farms of eastern United States.—The older sheep regions, namely, the farms of eastern United States and Europe, which were the sole dependence for sheep before 1850, still support sheep, but only in small flocks grazing in fenced fields. Because they receive the personal care of their owners such small flocks fare much better and produce a larger proportion of lambs than can be raised in the large flocks upon the range, where less attention is given them. Many of the eastern sheep owners make a specialty of rearing their lambs in the winter season and sending them to market early in the year when they command a very high price.

There is a tendency for the sheep of the distant West to be of the best wool-producing breeds (Fig. 51) and for those of the eastern farms to be of the best mutton breeds. Why?

New England, with its rocky and little-used farms, offers one of the best places in the United States for the extension of sheep growing. The rocky lands produce grass, and there might be worked out a combination of hill pasture and valley-grown winter forage such as exists in the arid West with its irrigated valleys.

Were it not for the ravages of sheep-killing dogs, the United States would have many million more sheep than it now has, for we have much suitable land not fully used.

9. THE AMERICAN HORSE INDUSTRY

Horses of the European breeds early made their escape from the Spanish settlements in Mexico and ran wild on the western plains and mountains for three centuries. These half wild horses usually called Indian ponies or cayuses have, like the Texas longhorn cattle of Spanish origin, now almost disappeared through admixture with the European breeds brought from the eastern states.

Distribution of the horse industry.—One of the best-known centers of American horse production is the blue-grass region of central Kentucky, with the city of Lexington as its center. This plain of eight or ten thousand square miles is underlaid by a bed of limestone which upon exposure to the air breaks up into a soil of great fertility and one in which blue grass grows to perfection. This is one of the best of pasture grasses, especially for horses, which may be called one of the chief money crops of this region. The small area of the Kentucky blue-grass region causes it to be of far less total importance in horse production than is the corn belt.

Throughout the whole extent of the corn belt alongside the farms where some men are fattening pigs and others fattening cattle, still others have droves of colts usually of the heavy draft breeds originally brought from France, Scotland, or Belgium. When 5 or 6 years old, these horses are sent by carloads to the eastern cities and to many agricultural districts in the East where the farmers find it more profitable to raise crops suited to nearby markets, and where they buy their horses because they can so easily come from afar.

There are occasional horse ranches on the Great Plains of the United States from Canada to Mexico, whence horses are sent to the mining and timber camps of the mountains.

The raising of a few colts as a supply crop and occasionally as a money crop is carried on in almost all parts of the United States. It is of greater importance in the Piedmont section of northern Virginia than in any other district east of the Appalachians. Excellent cavalry horses are produced here and the United States Government maintains a remount station at Fort Royal.

The distribution of the mule.—The ability of the mule to resist a more humid climate than the horse gives him prominence over the horse in the tropics and in the southern part of the United States. In Illinois, Iowa, and Kansas (in 1912) the mules comprised only one-twentieth of the 4¼ millions of equine draft animals but more than half of the 1⅜ millions in Alabama, Mississippi, and Louisiana were mules.

The American mule industry.—The finest mules in the United States are grown in the horse belt of Kentucky and adjacent districts of Tennessee. Missouri is probably the greatest mule-producing region of the United States and under a single roof in St. Louis 5,000 mules are sometimes for sale. From this market, and from Kentucky and Tennessee, they are distributed over a very wide area in the United States and in foreign countries. They are particularly desired in army transportation.

10. Poultry

The value of poultry.—The poultry industry seems to attract far less attention than its importance merits. The annual production of eggs and poultry, according to the Yearbook of the United States Department of Agriculture for 1911, was worth $750,000,000. Hence the output of the poultry yard is more valuable than all the gold and iron produced in the United States. It is even greater than the whole world's production of gold, silver, and diamonds.

The wide distribution of poultry.—That the importance of the lowly hen is so little realized may be partly explained by the fact that poultry raising is a widely distributed industry, usually conducted on a small scale. We also fail to realize its importance because of the difficulty of securing statistics, the absence of large financial or speculative operations in connection with poultry and eggs, the small influence of legislation upon them, and the small part they play in international trade. Poultry keeping is none the less important and is undoubtedly the most universal form of animal industry in the United States and also in Europe, east Asia, and other foreign countries. The names of breeds attest their world-wide distribution—Peking and Muscovy ducks; Cochin, Brama, Leghorn, Hamburg, Minorca, Indian Game, Wyandotte and Plymouth Rock chickens; Brabant geese.

"The very large majority of the fowls in this country are found in comparatively small numbers (42 per farm in 1900) on a very large number of farms, where they gather their own subsistence, and receive practically no care. The consequence is that the eggs are produced at little cost. The development of this industry to an extent incredibly larger than it is at the present time is among the easy possibilities."[1]

There has been a marked increase in the number of specialized poultry farms since 1900. One of the causes of this change is the work done by the mechanical incubator. It hatches the chicks on a very large scale, and is almost as successful as the small scale operations of the hen, which is thereby left free to devote her whole time to the production of eggs.

[1] Distribution and Magnitude of the Poultry and Egg Industry. United States Department of Agriculture, Yearbook, 1902.

Poultry is equally well fitted to be a by-product in extensive agriculture or a main product in intensive agriculture, with a strong tendency to be important where intensive agriculture prevails. Parts of the corn belt have unusual opportunities to fatten poultry. In Maine and New Hampshire the eggs are about double the value of the poultry.

Poultry raising and especially egg production are easily increased with a little care and skillful handling. The application of the laws of animal breeding and feeding causes large increase in the average egg output. The average egg production from our 300,-000,000 hens is about 80 per hen per year. Test pens of fowls given special care have averaged 240. If the average could be brought to only half that figure it would be an increase of 150 to 200 million dollars per year.

Owing to the high value of output in proportion to food, it should be emphasized that the distribution of the poultry industry depends more on man and less on the environment than any other of the animal industries thus far discussed.

QUESTIONS

1. What is the geographic explanation of the meat situation in Japan and the United States?

2. What is usually the first use that civilized man makes of an open plain?

3. Why does an American beef animal commonly live in two places?

4. Why would our irrigated land be of less value if it were all in one place?

5. Which has greater possibility of increased meat production, that part of the United States west of 100° longitude or south of 36° latitude? Give some reasons for your answer.

6. What was the effect of the refrigerator car upon the location of slaughtering industry? Explain.

7. Why is dairying more intensive than meat production?

8. What are the characteristics of a region that is devoted largely to sheep production?

9. Compare the value of the poultry, and gold mining industries?

NOTE.—Fishing industries have not yet been discussed.

CHAPTER III

THE VEGETABLE INDUSTRIES

Food value of vegetables.—The cereals give us bread, the animals give us meat, but the foods we call vegetables give us substitutes for both. The chief food element of the potato and the cereals is starch, one of the two most universal food elements of all mankind. It is classed as a carbo-hydrate—energy food. It helps to make fat and heat to keep the body warm, and gives energy for work. Starch is the surplus nutrition stored within the plants for their own future needs or for their offspring. Sometimes it is packed in the seeds, as in the grains; or in the roots, as in sweet potatoes; or in underground stems, as in the white potatoes; or even in the trunks of some of the trees, as in the sago palm. The other great food element, proteid, the tissue or muscle maker (see table of food values, appendix) is furnished by milk, meat, cheese, eggs, most of the nuts, and the leguminous plants, of which peas and beans are the best and commonest examples.

Location of vegetable industries.—Vegetables form an important supply crop in every section of the United States, but only in certain localities are they a money crop. These localities are determined partly by conditions of soil and climate, but largely by proximity to markets. On account of their bulk and their perishable nature, vegetables are largely consumed near the place of production. The desire for fresh vegetables is a strong impetus to commerce in them, and with the improvement of transportation there is a rapidly increasing commerce in fresh vegetables. For example, Britain alone imports 60 to 70 million dollars worth per year and has in addition a lively local trade between her own warmer southwest and the interior cities.

1. THE POTATO

Origin and use.—The potato, second only to breadstuffs as a starch food, is probably exceeded only by bread in the number of times per year it is eaten by the average European or American. The plant is a native of America, growing wild on Mexican and Andean plateaus, whence it was taken to Europe. Introduced into Ireland in 1586 by Sir Walter Raleigh, it soon became important, and it has long since established itself as the great starch food in cool climates. It is probably the plant most commonly grown in the vegetable gardens of Europe and America; but its growth as a money crop is quite restricted, offering in this respect a marked contrast to wheat. The potato and rice are rivals in supplying starch other than bread for the tables of Europe and America, but owing to differing climatic requirements the two plants are rarely rival claimants for the farmer's attention. The recently discovered art of making potato flour has given the otherwise perishable tuber a new means of competing with rice, but this flour has not had time to gain very wide use outside of Germany where it was first manufactured, and proved of great use during the food scarcity of 1914–15 brought on by the war.

Climatic requirements of the potato.—The potato is a crop of wide climatic range, because it can stand a cool climate and mature in a short season. A few hundred bushels are annually grown at Dawson City in the Klondike on the Upper Yukon, and it is cultivated as far south as the sub-tropics in Florida and Egypt. It also tolerates a variety of soils. It grows well on medium heavy land suitable also for wheat or corn, but tends to become important as a main starch food for people, and a money crop for farmers, in regions where it is too cool for corn to grow to the best advantage, or where the soil is too sandy and light for large yields of small grains. It does not do well on heavy clay. The regions that best meet the potato conditions are northern and northeastern United States, Canada, and north Europe. It does not thrive without irrigation in the dry summer of the Mediterranean type of climate.

The yield of potatoes.—The bulky tuber yields six times as many bushels per acre as does wheat, and does it in less time. Therefore it is of great value in enabling land to support dense populations, although a bushel of potatoes is not so nutritious as a bushel of grain (see table of food values, appendix). A 10-year average yield per acre in the United States is for wheat, 14.3 bushels; corn, 26 bushels; potatoes, 92 bushels. Owing to the laborious method of preparing the seed, the expensive fertilizers necessary, the continuous cultivation, and protection from insects and blights, the potato crop requires more labor than any of the grains. Hence potato fields are smaller than grain fields, and the crop is well fitted

FIG. 52.—The corn was planted after a 200 bushels to the acre crop of pota toes. Cow-peas were sown among the corn—three crops in one year. Eastern North Carolina. Possible over large areas. This has been called intensive-extensive agriculture. The *yields* are intensive. The *method* is extensive in that it uses horses and machines, and can be carried on over large areas.

to intensive agriculture where a small area must, by much labor, be made to yield a large product, such as is necessary in countries of dense populations (Fig. 52). Thus the average potato yield in Germany is more than double the yield in America, but many sections of the United States make as good an average as does Germany. The potato harvest, toward the end of summer, leaves the ground in excellent condition for a fine crop of winter grain which usually follows it.

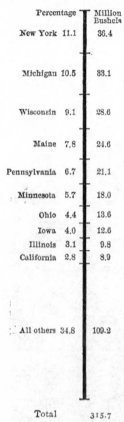

Distribution of the potato industry.—Owing to the average American's ability to raise corn or to buy higher priced foods, the potato is less sought as food in America than it is in Europe. The chief centers of its growth lie north and east of the corn belt (Fig. 53). It is grown to a great extent as a money crop in certain sandy areas in Wisconsin, Minnesota, Michigan, and also in parts of Pennsylvania, New York, and New England, especially Maine. In the adjacent and similar parts of Canada it is of even greater relative importance.

Our 5,700 squares miles in potato fields are but a tiny patch in comparison to our area. A large crop gluts the market, and actual overproduction or the fear of overproduction and the consequent low price is the limiting factor in potato production.

Possibilities of extension of the potato industry.—The price to the grower fluctuates between ten cents and a dollar and a half a bushel, between absolute loss and large profits. The existing farms and men and equipment of America could, if assured a price of a cent a pound, easily double the potato crop without producing any corresponding lessening of other crops, and there is abundant room to grow ten or twenty times as many potatoes without interfering with other crops. If we had the facilities for making a surplus of 40 million or 400 million bushels of potatoes into flour, cow feed, starch and alcohol, as is the case in Germany, it would be a boon to American agriculture. Agricultural overproduction is a

Percentage | Million Bushels
New York 11.1 | 36.4
Michigan 10.5 | 33.1
Wisconsin 9.1 | 28.6
Maine 7.8 | 24.6
Pennsylvania 6.7 | 21.1
Minnesota 5.7 | 18.0
Ohio 4.4 | 13.6
Iowa 4.0 | 12.6
Illinois 3.1 | 9.8
California 2.8 | 8.9
All others 34.8 | 109.2
Total 315.7

FIG. 53.—United States potato production, two-year average, 1910–11.

fact of unappreciated importance in checking the production of perishable commodities of which the potato is an example.

The potato in commerce.—The supply of early potatoes for northern markets from southern lands gives rise to an important commerce in many parts of the world, which is really a part of the trade in vegetables. Thus, Algeria derives a large income from potatoes which reach Paris in thirty-five to forty hours. Egypt sends the first potatoes of the season across the Mediterranean to northwest Europe.

On account of the great bulk and weight of potatoes in proportion to value, and because of their perishable nature, they are much less important in foreign trade than in domestic production. As a whole, they have a tendency to become a national supply crop, with commerce limited to emergencies and early supplies. When, as occasionally happens, we have a shortage in this country, they come to us by millions of bushels from Canada, Ireland, Scotland, Germany, and Egypt. We have a small export of potatoes to Caribbean lands where the warm climate makes their growth unsatisfactory.

The sweet potato supplies the same need in human diet, and differs from the white potato only in the greater amount of sugar and nourishment that it contains (see table of food values, appendix). The sweet potato is a perennial where there is no frost, yet it will grow a crop in the warm summer as far north as Iowa or New York, and is a crop of considerable importance in American agriculture. Fortunately the sweet potato requires even lighter and sandier soil than the white potato and is, therefore, much grown on the sandy lands of the coastal plain in New Jersey, Maryland, and Virginia, where it is largely produced for shipment to the northern states. Similar sandy spots in Iowa and other north-central states render similar service for the interior of the United States and western Canada. This crop is also very widely grown throughout the southern states as a local food supply, where the people have the alternative of rice or sweet potatoes as their chief starch food in addition to corn or wheat bread.

2. OTHER VEGETABLE INDUSTRIES

Garden vegetables.—Nearly every farm has a vegetable garden. Owing to the large yield of a small plot of ground under intensive care, such gardens are very common in villages and small towns of both Europe and America. Aided by the food and income from this source, the retired farmer of America is able to live comfortably in country towns on surprisingly small cash income from other sources.

In the European and American gardens are to be found a large variety of plants that represent in their origin every continent and almost every country in the world. In many cases they have been cultivated until they bear little resemblance to their original form, and in our list of vegetables is found in edible form every part of a plant—roots, stems, leaf stalks, leaves, blossoms, pods, seeds.

The nitrogen-producing legumes or pulse.—The most important of all the plants commonly called vegetables is the group of legumes called pulse in the Old World, comprising the many kinds of peas and beans. These differ from all other vegetables in the large amount of proteids or nitrogenous food, meat substitutes, which they contain (see table of food analysis, appendix). Nitrogen, as food for man, beast, or plant, is expensive to buy in spite of the fact that three-fourths of the air is nitrogen. Owing to its chemical inertness, nitrogen is hard to obtain in available forms. The legumes have upon their roots nodules (Fig. 54) which are colonies of the microscopic plants called bacteria. These organisms catch nitrogen freely from the air and make it available for plant food and thus the legumes by means of the bacteria on their roots render mankind a service of incalculable value by giving nitrogenous food for man, beast, or plant. By the aid of these bacteria, the legumes can grow in poor soil and leave it the richer in nitrogen because of the nodules on the roots that remain in the ground (Fig. 55). This fact recently discovered is one of the greatest agencies for the future enrichment of the race through the restoration of worn-out soils.

The pulse plants, represented chiefly by peas in northern climates and beans in southern climates, are less widely used in the United States than in any other populous country. This is because our people can afford the expensive nitrogenous foods, meat, cheese, and milk, of which we use more per person than any other large group of civilized people.

The trade in vegetables.—Fifty years ago each town and city depended upon its immediate locality for vegetables, and there is at the present time a large area near almost every city where farmers grow fields of peas, beans, cabbages and other garden crops, of which the family garden has but a short row or two. The vegetables from these market gardens are usually consumed in the nearby market in the season of ripening, but months before the local supply is ready similar products are sold in the city market. The best are

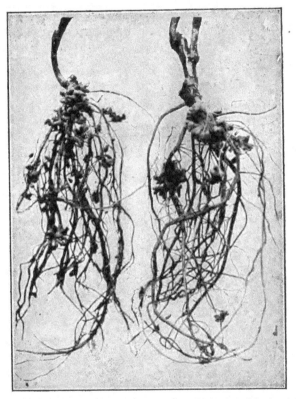

FIG. 54.—The roots of the sweet pea, one of the legumes, with the nodules made by the nitrogen-gathering bacteria.

produced in nearby hothouses, but the great bulk is brought by the refrigerator car, fast freight, and the coasting steamer. This trade is of very recent origin and is increasing rapidly. It could not come until rapid transportation and refrigeration made possible the handling of perishable commodities. In emancipating the city from dependence on local fields these improved transportation facilities

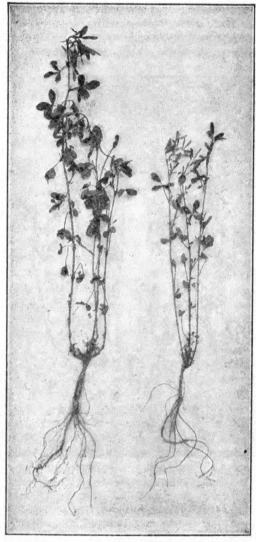

FIG. 55.—Two alfalfa plants treated alike in every respect except that the larger one had nodules on its roots to supply it with nitrogen while the smaller had none.

have caused the development of an enormous trucking industry in rather concentrated areas throughout the entire length of the Atlantic Plain from the east end of Long Island to the tip of Florida.

Vegetable production on the Atlantic Plain.—The Atlantic Plain is a nearly level area lying between the Atlantic Ocean and the first stratum of hard rock that limits the sands and clays of the plain and causes, in the rivers crossing it, a series of waterfalls extending in a nearly straight line from New York southwestward through the cities of Trenton, Philadelphia, Baltimore, Washington, Richmond, Raleigh, N. C., and Columbia, S. C. The sandy soil of this plain suffices for the growth of excellent peas, melons, cabbages, strawberries, etc., which are composed almost entirely of water. The Atlantic Plain has an advantage even over the Piedmont and Appalachian districts lying to the west, with their fertile but heavy clays, because the sandy soil being drier can be cultivated earlier in the spring.

From this plain there comes throughout the cooler part of the year a procession of vegetable products that follows the advance of the seasons (Fig. 56). When October turns the fields of New Jersey and Long Island brown, the huckster and the groceryman of the northern cities are just beginning to sell beans, lettuce, eggplants, and cucumbers from south Florida. As the spring advances northward, so does the location of the truck harvest, which includes potatoes and all kinds of vegetables. Next after the supplies of Florida come those from the district about Savannah, Ga., then the Charleston, S. C., district, including the nearby islands, has its turn, followed by New Berne and Wilmington in eastern North Carolina. Next comes Norfolk, Va., one of the greatest trucking centers in the United States, with steamboats running to Washington, Baltimore, Philadelphia, New York, and Boston. This port ships enormous quantities of early potatoes and strawberries to the northern cities, to be followed in its turn by the peninsula known as the "Eastern Shore" between the Chesapeake Bay and the sea.

The bulky nature of products of this class gives a great advantage to the producer who can haul the crop to market in his own wagon. Hence there is a great concentration of production near the larger cities, especially within a 30-mile radius of Philadelphia, where good truck land is within easy reach of city market.

The vegetable industry of the Mississippi Valley.—The bulk of the vegetable products of the Mississippi Valley is consumed locally and thus does not enter largely into inter-state commerce. Chicago and other cities in the central states draw their off-season supplies partly from certain sandy districts in Tennessee, Mississippi, northeastern Texas, and in southern Texas on the Gulf plain, near the mouth of the Rio Grande.

The California vegetable industry.—The open winter of California gives that state an important vegetable industry which probably reaches its highest development on the reclaimed delta lands ("tules") at the mouths of the San Joaquin and Sacramento Rivers.

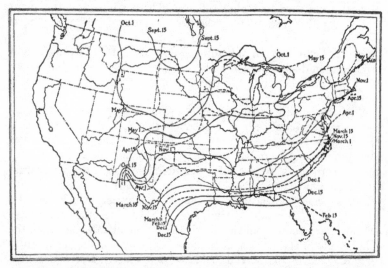

FIG. 56.—Map of United States showing average dates of last killing frost in spring (broken lines) and first killing frost in autumn (solid lines). Note the length of the growing season at some particular places. (After U. S. Weather Bureau. From Modern Geography by Salisbury, Barrows, and Tower.)

These deltas are especially fine for the production of asparagus, which is grown in vast fields. Some of it is shipped to the Atlantic states while fresh, but most of it is canned.[1] The great drawback of the California trucker is the long distance and high freight rates to the eastern markets to which 12,000 carloads of vegetables went in 1914. Transportation is less of a deterrent on the dried beans, con-

[1] For the influence of canning on the vegetable industry, see latter art of next chapter.

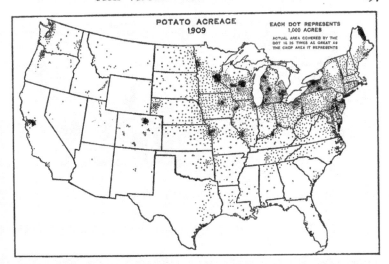

Potato centers, showing city locations in some cases and good agricultural locations in others. (O. E. Baker, *Year Book* of U. S. Dept. Agr., 1915.)

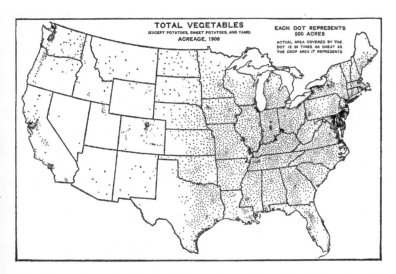

This industry is scattered by local city markets and special agricultural conditions. (Finch and Baker.)

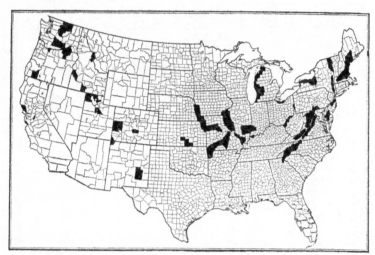

All important commercial apple growing in the United States is within the shaded areas. (Courtesy *Country Gentleman*.)

The location of our vegetable industry shows in part the location of the cities that furnish nearby markets, and in part locations where soil or climatic conditions favor the commercial growing of vegetables for distant markets or canning factories.

Even before the War garden campaign, school gardens had shown that city school children could get as much as ten cents per square foot per season from well worked little gardens where the produce was sold at city retail prices.

The family garden is a resource waiting for the American people when they start out systematically to attack the high cost of living. It furnishes food at the maximum of efficiency, because the food is fresh and of the best quality. It has paid no transport or delivery wagon cost, no retailer's and wholesaler's profit, no cost of expensive boxes. Digging in the ground is good exercise for indoor workers. It is also good for the soul of man. It gives one more field in which to achieve, one more thing to love.

It is a crime against nutrition, health, and national economy that men's dwellings in America are placed with so little regard to the possibility of a garden. In England there is a scientifically planned factory town, Letchworth or Garden City, where there is room for each of thirty thousand people to have a family garden and live where a short walk will reach wide spaces for running games.

centrated and non-perishable, which are grown and prepared in great quantities ($10,000,000 in 1914) on the semi-arid lands near the sea in southern California.

QUESTIONS

1. Name the two great food elements, their uses, and two sources from which each is obtained?

2. Is the potato a better crop than wheat for intensive agriculture and dense populations?

3. Do we grow potatoes on all the land suited to them? What would happen to the industry if we grew them on half the potato land?

4. Why does the potato price fluctuate less in Germany than in the United States?

5. How do the bacteria upon the roots of legumes enable us to use less meat?

6. What characteristic of the soil of the Atlantic coast plain adapts it to vegetable growing? Is it all so used? Why?

7. How does a climatic factor scatter the vegetable industry over the country?

CHAPTER IV

THE FRUIT AND CANNING INDUSTRIES

The standard fruits grown in the United States are not so nutritious as many of those grown in the Old World. The date, the fig, and the olive, so important in countries on the Mediterranean, are far more nutritious than the apple, the orange, and the peach, the leading fruits of the United States. Despite their low nutrition, the production of fruits is an extensive industry and one of especial interest to the student of geography because of the very great influence of the geographic environment upon it.

1. THE GRAPE

Origin of American varieties.—When the European colonists landed upon the shores of the United States and stocked their gardens with the plants and trees of Europe, the grape vines promptly died from a mysterious blight that destroyed the leaves. This was due to fungi which thrive in the heat and humidity of the eastern American climate, but which the vines had never been subjected to in cool west Europe or dry south Europe. Yet the colonists found in the American forests wild grapevines climbing to the tops of tall trees and growing to enormous size, their stems often reaching a thickness of half a foot or more. From this stock the people of the eastern part of the United States have in three centuries evolved a number of varieties of edible and of wine grapes, their names, Concord, Niagara, Early Ohio, etc., showing their American origin.

Location of the American grape industry.—There are now two widely separated centers of commercial grape growing in the United States: the eastern, near the Lakes, growing American varieties; and the western, in California, growing European varieties. The eastern grape belt lies close to the shores of Lake Erie, Lake Ontario, and the five slender north and south lakes of central New York, called the Finger Lakes. The vineyards of the Finger Lake district are upon the southern and western slopes of the hills along the eastern shores of the lakes, the prevalent west winds blowing across the waters in spring, giving the cool temperature necessary to retard the growth of the vines in the spring until the danger from frost is past. Along the southeastern shore of Lake Erie, especially on certain islands in the lake, and even on the Canadian shore, the vineyard is much the most important field upon the farm and is often the entire dependence of the grower. This eastern region produces table grapes which are far cheaper and sweeter, and therefore more generally liked, than are the edible grapes of central Europe.

California, with her Mediterranean climate, has become a second Mediterranean country in other respects than as a producer of citrous and dried fruits. The climate has attracted colonies of Italian and Swiss vine growers who grow the European grapes which thrive in this part of America. Two hundred and fifty thousand acres of land, mostly in the Great Valley, are devoted to grapes. This land is comparatively level, in marked contrast with the vineyards of Italy and Switzerland. Its deep soil gives a greater yield per acre than that of any other region in the world.

2. The Citrous Fruits

The citrous fruits, including the orange, lemon, lime, grapefruit or pomelo, and several others of small commercial importance, are the advance guard of the tropic fruit supply. These fruits can be transported to the markets of the north temperate zone because of the tough, thick, oily, and bitter skin which serves as an effective protection against insects, bruises, and decay. A host of other delicious tropic fruits remain practically unknown to commerce because they lack such natural protection, but quick transportation and modern methods of refrigeration are rapidly extending their use. The recent successful import into Germany from Kamerun, in Equatorial Africa, of fresh pineapples packed in peat dust is very suggestive.

The orange, a native of southern Asia, grows throughout the tropics and on the sub-tropic edges of both temperate zones, and is everywhere much prized as an article of food. Like many other fruits it attains its finest quality near the colder limit of its production, so that the orange of the United States is superior to that of the West Indies. It is to be had at almost all seasons of the year, since the orange tree carries ripe fruit and green fruit at the same time that it is in blossom. Its wide distribution makes possible an almost unlimited production, but inasmuch as the fruit is quite bulky and its commercial handling expensive it, like the banana, can enter into commerce in large quantities only where transporta-

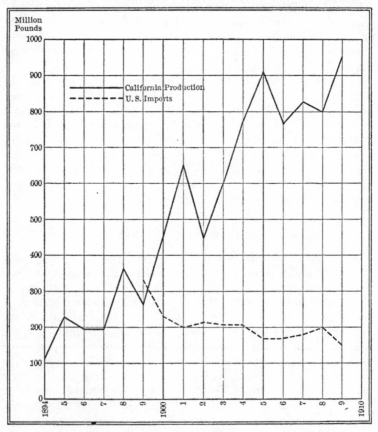

FIG. 57.—United States production and imports of citrous fruits.

tion facilities are of the best. Consequently, the world's commercial supply is from a few localities readily accessible to the world's great markets. It is possible that more oranges waste beneath the tropic orange trees than are eaten by the people of the temperate zones.

About 1835 our sailing vessels first began to bring us oranges from Italy and Sicily, and later from the West Indies, but the home supply has now about stopped the import (Fig. 57). Between 1880 and 1890, when through railroads were built to the south, it was discovered that Florida could grow oranges and ship them to northern states. The product of this southern region is excellent, but the orange growers have had much trouble with the occasional cold waves coming from the center of the continent and bringing freezing temperatures to the Gulf shore and to nearly all of Florida. If not in rapid growth at the time, the orange tree can resist some frost, but the moisture of the Gulf climate may make the tree grow rapidly at any time during the winter. Thus on January 1, 1894, a single cold morning altered the prospects of the state by killing practically all the orange trees in the northern part of the peninsula and bankrupting many of the growers. Groves were renewed and despite occasional injury to crop and sometimes to trees, there has been no other such destruction as that of 1894. Many growers now protect their crops by burning oil or charcoal in the orchards when frost threatens, and the industry is again extensive.

Florida's misfortune in 1894 proved to be California's advantage. The northern limit of the orange in Florida is about 30° north latitude, while in California, owing to the oceanic climate of the Pacific Coast, the tree grows as far north as 37° near San Francisco. However, the region in which the industry has had its largest development is south and west of the coast range in the Los Angeles-Pasadena district of southern California. Here the cold wave of the Mississippi Valley type is almost unknown and the danger of a destructive freeze is much smaller than in Florida, although frosts that destroy the crop are not uncommon in many localities. The astonishing freeze in the California citrous fruit belt in January, 1913, had not been duplicated in 40 years. The loss of fruit, estimated at from $20,000,000 to $40,000,000, tends to even up the competition between California and Florida.

California oranges are grown with the most perfect care on irrigated land of high value, the orchards often being valued at $1,000 and more per acre. This very high value is due not to scarcity of land, but to scarcity of water, which amounts to scarcity of land, since unirrigated lands cannot grow oranges. Great pains are taken to get and save water for the irrigation of the California fruit orchards. Tunnels are sometimes dug back in the hillsides to strike the underground flow; wells are dug and pumps lift the water sometimes several hundred feet to the orchards where it is often carried in pipes and put around the base of each tree so that the smallest possible amount may make an acre productive (Fig. 58). The great distance from the eastern market has made transportation costs high, so that only the best fruit can be shipped.

FIG. 58.—Irrigation of Arizona citrous fruit tree by the basin method, economical of water. (U. S. Reclamation Service.)

To attend to these matters the fruit growers have formed associations which are good examples of cooperative enterprise. They ship thousands of carloads (45,000 in 1914) largely to Chicago, New York, and Boston, for distribution throughout the East.

The lemon.—In the southern part of the California citrous district the lemon is now being extensively grown for the American market, but our import of about $3,000,000 worth per year, almost entirely from Sicily, shows that the home supply is well under the demand.

The grapefruit, appreciated for its bitter tang, is grown chiefly in Florida. It furnishes one of the most striking examples of the sudden development of a new industry through the creation of a demand for a hitherto unappreciated product. The output has increased several fold in a decade.

The future supply of citrous fruits.—California is using for oranges only one-tenth of her suitable orange land. The total area in bearing in 1914 was 37,000 acres. The total area planted was but 64,000 acres, just 100 square miles, one-fifteenth of 1 per cent of the area of California. Florida, with but 12 per cent of her area in cultivation, with only fourteen persons to the square mile, an abundant rainfall, and about half of her area in reclaimable swamp of great fertility, has a much higher ratio of possible expansion than has California. We could thus easily expand our orange and grapefruit crops by many, many fold.

Manifestly the limit of orange production in the United States is to be set, not by resources, but by prices. Unchecked production in Florida and California can easily produce the same low price that prevails in the tropics where oranges lie unused on the ground.

3. THE DATE, THE FIG, AND THE OLIVE

The date, the fig, and the olive have been found to grow well in southwestern United States (Fig. 59), where the climatic conditions resemble those of western Asia, southern Europe, and North Africa. Their culture has scarcely passed the experimental stage in the United States, but the results are very promising. It is expected that the 20,000 acres of olives in California will be increased 50 per cent during 1915. The success of date-culture in Arizona (Fig. 60) indicates that the American imports of these Old World dry-land fruits may in time entirely cease, for we have abundant land to supply all our needs. The Imperial Valley near the mouth of the Colorado River has from that river an abundant supply of water, a climate almost identical with that of the best date oases of the northern Sahara, and an area as great as the combined area of most of the oases of that desert. California figs are also being sent to the eastern markets.

The long failure and final success of fig growing in California depended on the study of an insect. For many years the fig trees had grown well but bore no fruit because of the absence of a certain insect that lives in Mediterranean lands, and by crawling into the hollow cavity of the fig fertilizes the many blossoms therein contained. The establishment of fig growing in California waited for the successful acclimatization of the insect. This was finally accomplished after much difficulty and many expensive attempts.

Fig. 59.—Olive orchard in Salt River Valley, Arizona. Alluvial soil, irrigated from a government reservoir. (Photo U. S. Dept. Agr.)

4. THE APPLE

The apple is the most extensively grown fruit in the United States. The tree is the longest lived and, excepting the cherry, the largest of all our common fruit trees. It is hardy and is adapted to a wider range of conditions than any other important fruit tree. A large tree will often produce ten to twenty barrels of fruit in a single season. From New England to North Carolina it is not uncommon to find trees healthy and bearing at the age of 100 years. The tree will grow well in practically all parts of the United States except the extreme South and the region just west of Lake Superior. There is reason to believe that selection, breeding and new methods of cultivation will give satisfactory apple trees for this latter location. Commercial production is carried on in districts where the climate is especially favorable and where industrial pioneers have proved the success of orcharding.

FIG. 60.—Eight-year-old seedling date palm with phenomenal yield of 400 pounds fruit.   Phoenix, Ariz.   The trunk gets longer each year until it becomes a tall tree.   (Photo W. T. Swingle, U. S. Dept. Agr.)

New York is the leading state in commercial apple growing; four counties on the shore of Lake Ontario in western New York have for a number of years been the most important apple-shipping district in the United States.   The Erie Canal and the railroads that followed it gave this region an early advantage in transportation to New York and other eastern markets.   This same waterway aided western competition, and made unprofitable the former staple products of New York farms, grain and live stock.   In addition to this disadvantage for growing staples, and the advantage for apple transport, this region has also a climatic advantage in the production of apples. The large bodies of water with their melting ice in spring tend to delay the blossoming time until the danger of injury from frost has passed. Although apples are the chief money crop of this district, there is no county in which the orchards cover more than a tenth of the land surface, a rather surprising fact, tending to show how rarely a locality depends upon a single crop.

The lower peninsula of Michigan is important in the production of apples for reasons very similar to those prevailing in western New York.

Virginia has two apple districts with probably quite as large a proportion of the land planted in apples as is to be found anywhere east of the Rocky Mountains. The first is in the Great Valley of Virginia and West Virginia not far from the cities of Winchester and Martinsburg. Here upon a low ridge, called Apple Pie Ridge, an enthusiast some 50 years ago planted a large field in apples which eventually brought him many thousands of dollars. Seeing his success his neighbors also planted apple trees, until now the ridge for 25 miles is almost an unbroken succession of apple orchards, and they are being extended to the ridges to the west of the Great Valley. The second apple district of Virginia lies along the eastern slope of the Blue Ridge Mountains in the central part of the state. From this district large quantities of finely flavored varieties are annually exported to England. Neither of these Virginia apple districts has any known advantage either in production or transportation over much other territory in the United States where the business has not happened to get started. The same thing may be said of nearly all American fruit localities.

The open Mississippi Valley and the Ozark plateau.—On the southern edge of the corn belt in Illinois, northern Missouri, Iowa, and Kansas extensive apple orchards have been planted, some of them covering more than a square mile, but the sweeping cold waves that come unimpeded down the open Mississippi Valley have frequently frozen the fruit buds in April and May, and for this reason some of these apple districts are not prospering. On the other hand the nearby Ozark plateau and the ridges of southern Missouri and north Arkansas, an old worn-down mountain system, are ill suited to grain farming, but very well suited to the produc-

tion of fruit. The elevation and the protection of mountain location against sweeping cold winds cause it to escape many of the
freezes that are so destructive in the open plains to the north and
east. The ridges have the advantage of "frost drainage," so important in giving the mountains an advantage in fruit growing.
Cold air is heavier than warm air and on still frosty nights it settles
to the lowland where fruit buds freeze while the hills remain frost-
free. This advantage is so pronounced that at times a difference of

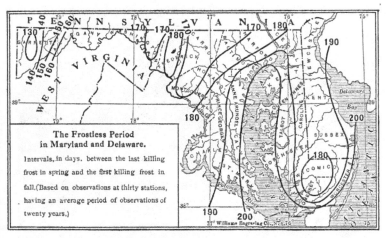

FIG. 61.—Note the influence of water and of moderately elevated ridges to
lengthen the growing season, and of high plateaus to shorten it. There are
ridges in Frederick and Allegany Counties, and high plateaus in Garret County.
(After O. L. Fassig, U. S. Weather Bureau.)

10 feet in elevation saves a crop. In the year 1907 the crop in the
open valley from the Appalachians to the Great Plains and from
the Ozarks to Canada was almost entirely destroyed by cold waves;
but a single Arkansas county in the southern Ozarks, immune from
these particular May cold waves, produced over $2,000,000 worth
of apples.

The Rocky Mountains and the Northwest.—In the newly settled
states of the Rocky Mountains and north Pacific coast there are
many irrigated apple-growing districts. Some of these, as the
Hood River Valley in Oregon, the Yakima and Wenatchee Valleys
in Washington (Fig. 62), and Delta, Colorado, have already become

well known in the eastern part of the United States through the beautiful fruit they send out. Parts of Idaho, Montana, and a few sections of California are equally well fitted for the growth of this fruit. Because of the bright sunshine of the semi-arid district, the apples grown there are the most beautiful produced in America.

Under good storage conditions some varieties of apples will keep

FIG. 62.—Furrow irrigation of four-year-old apple trees at Wenatchee, Washington. (U. S. Dept. Agr.)

well for a full year, so that cold-storage warehouses, refrigerator cars, and refrigerator ships have made possible not only the easy distribution of American apples all over this country, but also their export to Europe, and have also made possible their sale and use every day in the year.

5. THE PEACH

The peach tree, unlike the apple, yields well only in restricted localities under special climatic conditions. The peach buds are less capable of resisting spring frosts and low winter temperatures than those of the apple. The fruit requires a warm summer and much sunshine for proper ripening (Fig. 63). This condition does not exist in Germany, Holland, Belgium, the north of France or Great Britain, and the tree can only be grown in these countries under the artificial conditions of hothouses or on the south side of walls where the tree is trimmed so that it spreads out like a fan against the flat surface, thus catching the direct rays from the sun and the heat reflected from the wall.

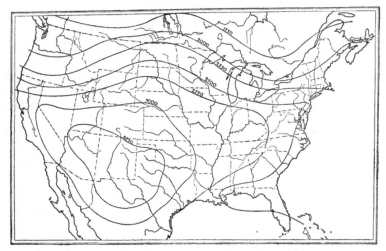

FIG. 63.—Map showing mean annual number of hours of sunshine in the United States. (After Van Bebber.) (From Salisbury, Barrows, and Tower.) Sunshine has great influence on plant growth, and aids greatly in giving color to fruit.

In the United States the peach industry has sprung up in eight localities, where the danger from spring frost is slight.

The peach belts of the Great Lakes.—Two of these localities are near the Great Lakes, whose cold surface makes the cool spring temperature that serves to delay the blooming of the peaches until after the frosts. The first of these is in the part of western New York where apples are important. Its production is rapidly increasing. The second peach belt, determined by the Great Lakes, is on the eastern shore of Lake Michigan where the prevalent west winds, blowing inland from the lake, give the necessary temperature control over a belt, less than 10 miles in width. In the same latitude upon the opposite shore of the lake the peach is of small importance.

The Chesapeake Bay and the Allegheny regions.—A third peach belt is in the peninsula east of the Chesapeake Bay in the states of Delaware and Maryland. Here, upon sandy soil thought to be ill suited for growing grain, grass, or live stock, and somewhat protected from frosts by the adjacent waters, arose shortly after the Civil War the first great centralized peach business in the United States. It has been discovered within recent years, however, that the climate of the ridges in the Allegheny region, to the west of the Great Valley, is better for peach growing than that of the coast plain. The coolness due to elevation causes a later start in spring growth and the slopes have also the advantage of frost drainage. Due to these advantages the fourth peach belt is developing rapidly upon the mountain slopes of the Blue Ridge and the Alleghenies in the Potomac drainage basin in southern Pennsylvania, western Maryland, and the eastern part of West Virginia.

New England.—The ability of the peach to do better upon mountain tops than upon lowlands has led to the discovery that it can be grown upon many of the higher hills of southern New England. Consequently prosperous orchards are now yielding good crops on the hilltops overlooking the Connecticut Valley in the state of Connecticut, an area which has never before known a commercial peach production. This is the fifth peach belt in the United States.

The Ozark region.—In the central part of the country the Ozark ridges furnish some frost protection in the vast plain where cold waves are perilous to the peach. This gives rise to a sixth peach district in Arkansas and southwestern Missouri, with a very large output.

The southern peach districts.—The seventh peach district is in the South. Since fast freight service has been established upon the railroads, it has been found possible to grow fine crops of peaches on southern cotton land (in central Georgia and Texas) and market them in northern cities some weeks before the crops of Maryland, New York or Michigan are ready. The industry has developed to important proportions in central Georgia and in Texas. The chief advantage of the South in peach growing is the absence of rival producers when its crop is ready to market, rather than greater certainty of production.

California peach growing.—California has the eighth and last peach belt in America. Bordering upon the Pacific Ocean with the mild winter produced by the prevalent even-tempered westerly winds from that great body of water, this state has a normal oceanic climate free from the cold waves and strong winds that spread over all territory east of the Rocky Mountains. Peaches can, therefore, be cultivated with fair assurance of getting a crop, although frost destruction is sometimes known there. California peach orchards are of great extent, and, owing to the perfection of the methods of picking, packing, and shipping, California peaches, in seasons of short crop in the East, are sent to all the larger eastern cities and at times even as far as London. But when there is a full crop in the eastern districts it is impossible for California growers to pay the transport cost, and millions of pounds of the fruit are then dried or canned.

6. COMBATING PESTS

The fruit trees are mostly exotics and the trees as well as fruits are often tender and very suceptible to insect and fungus attacks. As a result of our world commerce and the introduction of new varieties of plants, each locality also gets nearly all of the world's weeds and other agricultural pests. Thus came many insects, fungi (rusts, blights, mildews) and other plant enemies which combine to destroy nearly all the fruit that forms on the trees of the unprotected orchard. Fortunately they can usually be held in check by skillful care, much of which consists in spraying poisonous liquids on the trees (Fig. 64). This makes the pioduction of good fruit one of the most scientific of all pursuits, and is transferring it from the small orchard of the general farmer to the large orchard of the specialist in the better located fruit districts.

The history of peach growing in the Michigan district gives an excellent example of the dependence of industry upon science. A mysterious, incurable, and fatal disease called "the yellows" spread from tree to tree. Unchecked it worked destruction in the west Michigan peach belt and reduced the number of trees in one county from 600,000 in 1870 to 30,000 in 1884. This reduced the value of land to $10 or $20 per acre when it had been worth from $50 to $100, and brought communities to the verge of bankruptcy. At this point it was discovered at the State Agricultural Experiment Station that if every tree having the yellows was removed when the

disease was first discovered, only 1 or 2 per cent of the trees
per year would be killed, and the peach industry could thrive.   After
the adoption of this precaution the county that had but 30,000
trees in 1884 had over a million in 1906, and throughout the peach
belt prosperity again prevailed.

Fig. 64.—Spraying an apple orchard in Virginia with poisonous mist to kill
insects.   (U. S. Dept. Agr.)

7. Dried Fruits

Dried fruits in the domestic epoch.—Before the coming of steam
transportation, when each locality lived to a great extent upon the
local resources and the farmer's family lived almost entirely upon

the products of its own farm, the drying of fruits in humid America and Europe was almost as common as their production. But in damp or cloudy weather it often spoiled in the process; the humidity made it dark and unattractive in appearance. The only other

FIG. 65.—A rainless summer helps to locate the dried fruit industry by permitting it to be dried upon trays in the orchard, California. (U. S. Dept. Agr.)

methods of preservation were the then expensive ones of preserving them in sugar, brandy, or spice, or of pickling them in vinegar, which latter process made of them merely a condiment. Steam transportation and world commerce have worked a quick revolution by developing a large traffic in dried fruits from those parts of the world having unusually favorable conditions for their production.

Dried fruits in the modern epoch.—It has become easier to dry fruit in the sunny and rainless summer of countries having the Mediterranean type of climate (Fig. 65) and ship it great distances than to combat the difficulties of drying it in less favored localities with artificial heat in evaporators. The only exception to this is the drying of apples, an industry still centered in New York State, where large quantities of apples otherwise unsalable are utilized in this way.

In almost any grocery store in the United States today, boxes of dried prunes, apricots, peaches, dates, raisins, figs, and currants may be seen, and the names and addresses stamped on the boxes will show that they have come into these American communities from many distant parts of the world. They are nearly always from districts with a long dry summer, in which fruit exposed on trays beside the trees is dried by the constant sunshine with great ease and no labor except piling the trays and covering them on those rare occasions when rain threatens.

Distribution of the dried-fruit industry.—The dried-fruit industries grew up first in southern Europe and have very recently come to southern California, where they have developed with surprising rapidity and now supply nearly all of the home demand. In the case of dried prunes, raisins, and apricots, there is now an export of several million dollars per year in place of a quite recent heavy import of prunes from France, and of raisins from Spain. The Santa Clara valley alone produced 28,000 tons of dried prunes in 1914 and the total California crop was over 50,000 tons. The apricot is a fruit much like the peach, except that it is more susceptible to frost and also more perishable in transportation. These two fruits are grown so abundantly in California that when dried they sell for 4 cents per pound at the point of production.

8. CANNING OF FRUITS AND VEGETABLES

The importance of canned foods.—The canning process, perfected about the middle of the nineteenth century, is one of the great boons to humanity. Canning consists in hermetically sealing the food product after heat has destroyed all bacteria. Under these conditions the food keeps almost indefinitely. By 1883 the methods of doing this work had been so improved that machinery did nearly all the work, including the soldering of the cans and even the pasting and trimming of the labels (Fig. 66).

Before the coming of railroads and steamboats and the process of canning, a crop of tomatoes could be consumed only within a few miles of the place in which it grew and within a few days from picking time. After transportation by rail and boat was organized and improved, the tomatoes might be carried several hundred miles, but they still had to be consumed within a few days. After the

FIG. 66.—Cans of food filled by machinery and automatically carried past inspectors, finishers, and solderers who complete the closing of the cans. (Joseph Campbell Co., Camden, N. J.

canning process was perfected and developed into an industry, the perishable products of field or orchard could be preserved for consumption at any time within 2 or 3 years and in any corner of the world to which they could be cheaply carried. This elimination of the time limit on perishable commodities has revolutionized agriculture in many localities by suddenly giving perishable products access to the world market. The distribution of perishable crops now depends upon geographic and economic conditions which make certain localities best able to produce certain products rather than upon the more artificial conditions that until recently compelled their production close to the market of the nearby city.

The importance of the canning process in consumption is even more marked. Most parts of the world can now have many kinds of cheap foods previously unused or even unknown. The workers in a paper mill in the woods of Maine may now eat the tomatoes and peaches of Maryland, the cherries and apricots of California. The same is true of the gold digger upon the Klondike, of the engineer on the Panama Canal, of the rubber gatherer in the jungles of the Upper Amazon, and the whaler who spends a season in Bering Sea. When Nansen and his men drifted in the Arctic ice for years in an attempt to reach the north pole, they returned in perfect health because they were nourished with all kinds of canned and preserved meats, vegetables, fruits, fruit juices and extracts.

Canning, more than any other invention since the introduction of steam, has made possible the building up of towns and communities beyond the bounds of varied production. In New York City the money spent for canned goods exceeds that spent for bread and milk combined.

The extent of the industry.—Practically all classes of food—fruits, vegetables, soups, fish, meat, and even bread and pudding are now preserved by canning and they are often cooked ready to eat. The canning factories of the United States prepare yearly from 20 to 30 pounds of fruits and vegetables for each man, woman, and child in the country. Among the vegetables the tomato is most important, corn ranks second, and peas and beans third, while among the fruits the peach leads, followed by pears, apricots and apples. The output amounts to over 100 million dollars per year, and is produced in nearly all parts of the United States. Canning tends to be scattered in small towns wherever a surplus of some product is available, such as may occur in a truck farm or orchard district.

The Atlantic Plain.—Although widely scattered, the canning industry in the United States has three distinct belts showing greater development than other regions. The first of these regions to develop the industry was the Atlantic Plain. Maryland is the center and most important part of this canning district which extends from North Carolina to New York. This section has become important for the same reasons that made it important in the shipment of truck crops to the city markets, namely, the sandy soil which is exceptionally suited to vegetables, and not well adapted to the growth of other agricultural staples, especially wheat and grain. Baltimore is the leading center because of its remarkable facilities for assembling farm products. They are brought in steamboats from points as far away as Fredericksburg, Richmond, and Norfolk, in Virginia, and a great number of places on both sides of the Bay in Maryland, while the Chesapeake and Delaware Canal opens a way for the Baltimore fruit boats to go up the navigable creeks of New Jersey to such towns as Salem and Bridgeton.

The Baltimore canneries have another advantage in the fact that oyster canning gives employment to both labor and equipment in winter season—a cost factor of great importance.

The New York, New England, and Lake region.—New York, which is both a great agricultural state and a fruit grower, is the center of the northeastern canning belt, the second region of great importance. This state leads all the others in the canning of apples, pears, and corn. It is rather remarkable that this state and the New England States exceed the corn belt in the canning of corn. But the New England summer is almost too cool and short to ripen the grains well. For that reason Maine with a very small corn acreage cans a great deal of corn, since corn for canning does not need to ripen but is harvested a full month earlier than it could be if sold as ripened grain. The somewhat cool summer that makes parts of New York, Michigan, and Wisconsin second-class corn producers, makes them first-class producers of peas which are here extensively grown and canned.

Pacific coast.—California leads all other states in canning. It has become important from the combined influence of the climate, which is excellent for the growth of fruits and vegetables, and the great distance from eastern markets, which makes it possible to ship in the fresh condition only an uncertain fraction, and that the most perfect, of the total crop. This state supplies nearly all the canned apricots that appear in our markets, many of the canned peaches and other fruits, except apples and berries, and is very important in the output of canned tomatoes, peas, and asparagus. The canning industry also has large possibilities in the other Pacific coast states.

The possibility of increased production and of overproduction.— The possibilities of increase in the production of fruits, vegetables, and canned goods in the United States are very great. Of the sandy Atlantic Plain, so admirable for the growth of small fruits and truck crops, but a small portion is now used, and the production is only kept down by the unprofitable low prices which result from the rather frequent overstocking of the market. If, for example, the farmers of the United States could be assured 10 or 12 cents a peck for tomatoes at their farms for the next 10 years, it is probable that tomato production would be increased tenfold, for they are now commonly grown for less than that price and occasionally the crops are so great that the factories cannot handle them and they rot upon the ground by the hundreds of tons. Practically the same thing is true of all the other vegetables, including potatoes. This is a great deterrent to industry.

Even with the aid of the outlet afforded by canning, the small fruit and vegetable industries yield so enormously that overproduction, with its glutted markets and frequent losses, is a factor which, like frost, is ever in the mind of the producer and almost annually visits each locality of varied production.

QUESTIONS

1. What trouble did the early colonists of the United States have with the grape industry? Why? How was it overcome?

2 Can Massachusetts compete with New York as a grape grower?

3. Compare Florida and California as orange-growing states.

4. State and explain the influence of the Great Lakes on the location of the apple and peach industries?

5. Should the people of Illinois plant large apple orchards? Would it be any better to plant them in West Virginia?

6. How have climatic factors caused a decline in the eastern dried-fruit industry?

7. What is the canning process and what has been its influence on the time limit and the space limit for the use of perishable foods? Its effect on the adjusting of farming to resources?

8. Why is peach growing an important industry in western Michigan, but not profitable just across the Peninsula on Lake Huron?

9. Suppose all the good orange land in the United States were immediately put into orange groves, how would this affect the industry?

10. Explain "frost drainage." How does this become a factor in locating suitable orchard land?

11. Why is it necessary to kill bacteria in the process of canning?

CHAPTER V

SUGAR AND TOBACCO

1. SOURCES OF SUGAR

Sugar is one of the few foods that are all nutrition. Its general use among the people of the temperate zone is a recent development. It has rapidly passed from a luxury to a necessity, and its use is increasing rapidly. In 1589 a pound of sugar in England cost as much as a quarter of veal. Today its cheapness places it in reach of every family.

Nearly all plants, even onions, have sugar in their sap at some time in their growth, so there are many sources of sugar. Some of the more important of the sugar-storing plants are beets, carrots, and parsnips, which hoard it for use in the second year of their growth to make their heavy tops, blossoms, and seeds. In the tropical zone several palms are used to some extent for sugar manufacture. But sugar cane is the greatest sugar plant of the world. It is a plant much resembling an earless stalk of corn filled with sweet juice, and it grows throughout the moister parts of the tropics. In its natural condition it is so superior to other sugar yielders that (excepting honey) it was practically the only source of commercial sugar supply until the nineteenth century, when beet sugar came into prominence (Fig. 67). Throughout the tropic world a section of the stalk of the sugar cane from which the sweet sap can be sucked is a prized but common morsel and an important article of food.

2. CANE SUGAR

Climatic requirements and distribution.—Sugar cane is as distinctly limited to warm climates as the beet is to cool ones. It will grow on the sub-tropic edges of the temperate zones in such districts as Louisiana, Natal, New Zealand, and Cape Colony, but it is cultivated in the frost zone only where there is a long growing season, and where tariffs or bounties give freedom from competition with the Tropics. The best cane yields require such conditions as exist in Cuba, Java, Brazil, and India, where there is a temperature of 75 or 80° F. the year round and a rainfall of 60 inches or an equivalent amount of water by irrigation. The necessity of much sunshine gives irrigation a great advantage.

FIG. 67.—World production of cane and beet sugar, 1853–54 to 1910–17. Note the varying leadership and the recent triumph of cane.

The superiority of the tropics for cane growing is in climate rather than soil. In the frost-free climates there are records of fifty yearly cuttings from one planting, and the Cuban plantations regularly cut eight or ten crops from one planting. Those of Louisiana, because of our freezing winter, yield but one good harvest followed by a much smaller one, and one-third of a crop is required to furnish the cuttings for planting the next crop. Cold rains in December recently caused a loss of 8 million dollars in Louisiana in a single year. Owing to these climatic limitations cane-sugar production in the United States attains importance only in the southern third of Louisiana, in a coast strip in eastern Texas, and in a few locations in Florida. The sugar territory of southern Louisiana is part of the swampy flood plain of the Mississippi River. The only tillable land is within a mile or two of the streams, where the flood-deposits have built up a strip of land a few feet higher at the river bank than it is a short distance away where it merges into the flat, untillable swamps.

Methods of cultivation.—Cane does not require such careful handwork as the beet. It is cultivated with plows, not hoes; by men, not by women and children; and even the steam plow may do much of the work, as has been proved in the British island of Trinidad, and in Hawaii. The method of planting consists in putting cuttings in the ground, or, as is the practice in Louisiana and Cuba, in laying in the bottom of a furrow a row of cane stalks which send up sprouts from every joint. After 8 months or more of growth and cultivation the leaves are stripped off, and the stalks are cut by hand and carried away to the factory.

Products obtained from cane.—In the sugar factory the cane is crushed to extract the juice. The juice is boiled until most of the sugar crystallizes, and these crystals are refined and packed for the market.

After the sugar crystals have been removed there remains an uncrystallizable residue called molasses, which may with ease be distilled into rum, long an important export of the sugar-growing West Indies. The importation of West India molasses and the manufacture of rum was an important industry in colonial New England. England's interference with this trade was one of the causes of the Revolutionary War. The market for molasses is limited, and now much of it is used for the distillation of industrial alcohol and the preparation of a cattle food, which, under the name of molassquite, has of late become of increasing importance. Molassquite is made by causing the spongy pulp that comes from the heart of the cane to absorb the sugar of the molasses.

When it is considered that but one-fourteenth of the possible sugar area of Cuba is in use, we see the possibility of an important trade with the live-stock producing countries of the temperate zone; for, owing to the rising price of cattle foods, wheat bran and corn are now nearly as expensive to produce as cane-sugar, which is as nutritious and as acceptable to the ruminants as to man. There is no natural reason why we may not in the near future have a very important commerce in sugar and its by-products from the tropic countries, which will help to make cheaper meat, milk, and wool in the temperate-zone countries.

The extraction of cane molasses for local use is a simple process rather widely distributed in the Gulf region of the southern states, and a little cane is grown for this purpose as far north as Arkansas and eastern North Carolina.

Hawaii.—The Hawaiian Islands, with a total area nearly as great as Massachusetts, are second only to Cuba as a source of sugar import for the American market. The sugar yield per acre is the largest in the world, due first to the virgin fertility of the phenomenal soil, decayed lava from the great Hawaiian volcanoes. Fine yields are further guaranteed and produced by irrigation on the lee or dry side of the islands. In the absence of suitable rivers at the right elevation for stream diversion the water is gathered near the sea level from streams and wells and pumped up, sometimes hundreds of feet, through iron pipes and spread over the fertile lava slopes, making some of the most spectacular plantations in the world. Hawaiian crops have averaged over 9,000 pounds of sugar to the acre, twice the harvest of West Indies or Java, and these islands in turn yield better than cane fields upon the rich delta of the Mississippi where the climate is too cool for the best growth of cane.

Hawaii has had the especial advantage of receiving a higher price than any other sugar exporter except Porto Rico. This high price was due, before the islands were annexed in 1898, to the reciprocity treaty of 1876, admitting Hawaiian sugar to the United States without the payment of duty. The 11,000 tons produced in 1875 grew to 250,000 in 1899, and 506,000 in 1911. Since annexation all of the export goes to the United States free of duty.

This special privilege to the sugar growers of Hawaii has led to high profits and the suppression of other industries in the islands. These profits began when the islands had a few thrifty white people and many easy-going natives, giving an admirable opportunity for the formation of great estates which loudly called for workers. These came from China until the Chinese exclusion treaty shut them out in 1898. Then came Japanese until the Japanese government checked their emigration to the islands. Then came laborers from the Philippines, Portugal, and Russia.

As an accompaniment and cause of this population condition the sugar is grown on a few vast estates. One company reported for 1910 having harvested 6,448 acres yielding 56,856 tons of sugar, an average yield of 8.76 tons of sugar per acre. Only 6.89 tons of cane were needed to make a ton of sugar (U. S. Con. Rep., May 4, 1911). This cane is exceptionally rich, the yield phenomenally large, as were the plantation profits of $2,261,000.

3. BEET SUGAR

Science and beet culture.—The beet-sugar industry affords one of the best examples of the service that science renders to man. The stoppage of tropic trade during the Napoleonic wars started a search among French plants for a European sugar supply. This resulted in definite attempts to increase the sugar content of the beet which was then about 3 per cent. In 1836 it took 18 pounds of beets to make a pound of sugar; in 1882 about 10 pounds sufficed; in 1904 less than 7 pounds yielded a pound of sugar. This great improvement has been brought about, chiefly in Germany, by the practice of systematic selection. Within the life span of a man it has trebled the sugar content of beets and, along with improvements in the process of sugar extraction, made possible one of the great agricultural industries of the temperate zone. The improvement has not yet ended. In 8 years the amount of sugar produced per ton of beets in the United States increased 14 per cent (Fig. 68).

Requirements for the beet-sugar industry.—The conditions for beet-sugar production are exacting—a moderate amount of spring and summer rain, a summer of moderate heat, and a cool, dry autumn. Corn-growing climates, for example, are in the main too warm in mid-summer so that beets and corn do not grow best in the same localities, the beet belt being on the cooler margin of the corn belt. The irrigated regions of the West, where the autumn is dry and the nights are too cool for corn, furnish the best conditions for beet growing in the United States.

The growth of the sugar beet requires much care and labor. The soil must be fertile, mellow, rich in lime, and neither too clayey nor too sandy. It must be finely prepared, and plowed so deeply that a sub-soil plow must often follow the ordinary plow. Caring for the crop is most laborious because of the large amount of hand labor required. The young plant is so small that only human fingers can

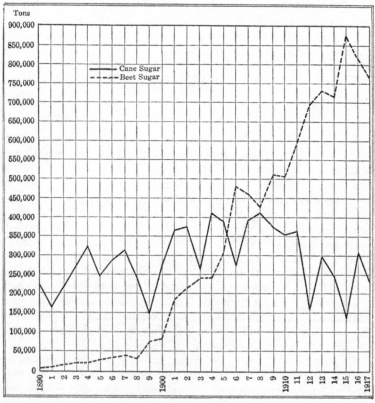

FIG. 68.—United States sugar production, 1890–1917.

rescue it from the up-springing weeds, so that men, women, and children go into the fields in nearly all beet regions and spend days upon their knees weeding the young beets (Fig. 69). A little later, when the plants have become established, they must be thinned out with the hoe. Thus far the inventors of machinery

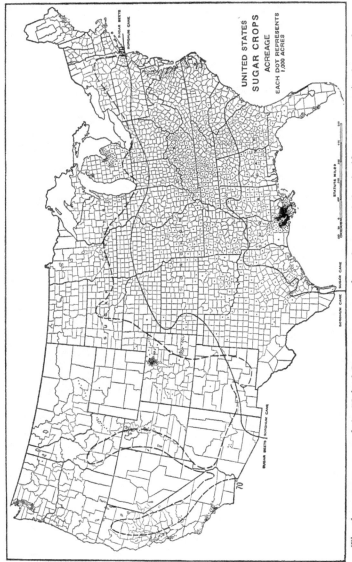

The three sugar zones of the United States—cane, sorghum, beet—and the significant summer isotherm of 70. (Finch and Baker.)

Leading Countries in Acreage.

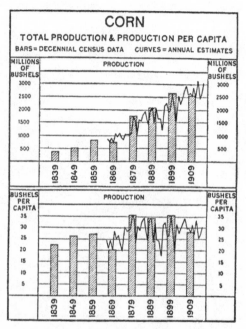

The declining per capita production of corn is one of the base facts that explains the rising cost of living and the rising price of land. As the land is limited in quantity increase in production henceforth must come by increase of effort.

have been unable to replace either of these kinds of hand labor.

It is quite common in the beet-growing districts of the United States for the hand labor to be done on contract by newly arrived immigrants. A peasant from Roumania, Hungary, or Poland, accustomed to the growth of beets, will contract at so much per acre to take care of the beet fields. With the assistance of his wife and children, he then takes entire charge of the crop for the American farmer.

After the plant is established there must be many cultivations, and in the late autumn the beets are plowed out of the ground and the tops pulled off. The roots are then piled in heaps which are

Fig. 69.—Women and children weeding a sugar-beet field, western United States. (U. S. Dept. Agr.)

covered with straw and sometimes with earth, to await their delivery to factories throughout the winter months. Here the beets are ground to pieces, the sugar soaked out of them in hot water, and finally crystallized and sent to the refinery to be put into final form. The beet-sugar factory, to be economical, must be large, costing a million dollars or more.

Distribution of the beet industry.—As a natural result of the intensive labor and the peculiar climate required, the sugar-beet industry was late in becoming established in the United States. With its heavy labor requirements it did not interest the American farmer, while corn land was still to be had for the taking. Here as in

Europe it could only compete with cane by the aid of a tariff. We
had a production of but 3,000 tons in 1890, but, stimulated by a
high tariff-made price, it passed the cane crop of the United States
in 1906 (see Fig. 68), and the crop of 1912 was 690,000 tons. Yet
the import of sugar is the greatest item in our import trade (see table
of food imports in appendix). The possible beet area of the United
States is several times as large as the possible cane area, and seems
to follow rather closely the July isotherm of 70° which traverses
the United States for nearly 5,000 miles (Fig. 70). The principal

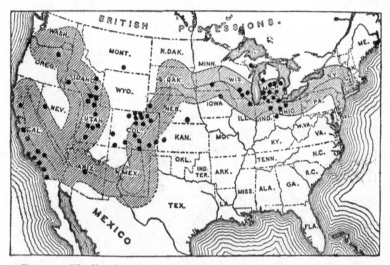

FIG. 70.—The line through the shaded area is the July isotherm of 70° F. The
shaded area shows the zone in which the sugar beet grows best and the dots
indicate the location of the beet-sugar refineries in the United States.

beet producing localities in the United States are in the four irrigation states of California, Colorado, Idaho, and Utah, and in Michigan,
and to a lesser extent in Wisconsin on the glacial areas too far north
for corn and not well suited to grass. Michigan and Wisconsin
have areas of light sandy soil excellent for beets, but not well
adapted to other staples.

In northern and central Europe, where the populations are dense
and the climate suits the beet and does not suit corn, there are
stronger reasons for growing the sugar beet than we have in the
United States. Especially does its heavy yield per acre make it a

suitable element of an intensive agriculture. It thus becomes a great crop from northern France through Belgium, Germany, Austria, Poland and Central Russia.

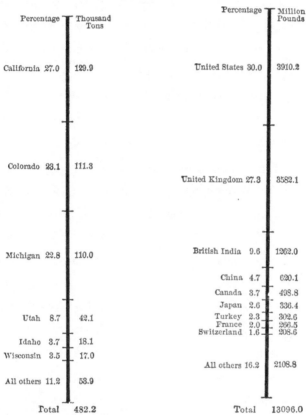

Percentage	Thousand Tons
California 27.0	129.9
Colorado 23.1	111.3
Michigan 22.8	110.0
Utah 8.7	42.1
Idaho 3.7	18.1
Wisconsin 3.5	17.0
All others 11.2	53.9
Total	482.2

Percentage	Million Pounds
United States 30.0	3910.2
United Kingdom 27.3	3582.1
British India 9.6	1262.0
China 4.7	620.1
Canada 3.7	498.8
Japan 2.6	336.4
Turkey 2.3	302.6
France 2.0	266.5
Switzerland 1.6	208.6
All others 16.2	2108.8
Total	13096.0

FIG. 71.—United States beet-sugar production, three-year average, 1909–10 to 1911–12.

FIG. 72.—World's sugar import, three-year average, 1908–10. This shows the inadequacy of the United States crop.

4. SUGAR FROM SORGHUM

Another sugar plant, sorghum, a member of the corn family and resembling both corn and cane, has long been grown in southern, central and southwestern United States for the manufacture of syrup for local use. The juice is extracted and treated in the same way that sugar-cane juice is extracted for syrup making. A century ago this plant exceeded beets in the sugar content of its juice, but progress in improving it has been slow. Experiments carried on for many years at Fort Scott, Kansas, have at last resulted in the making of satisfactory sugar from it. Now that the laws of plant breeding are better known, the sugar content of sorghum may be capable of as great an increase as has taken place in the beet. It is quite possible that a century hence it may rival or even displace beets and sugar cane in the United States, because it grows like corn in the corn belt and beyond (see chap. on cereals) and can be cultivated with work animals and machines.

5. MAPLE SUGAR

Maple sugar is produced by the evaporation of the sweet sap of several varieties of maple which will grow over large areas of eastern and northern United States, where it was a very important factor in the days before world commerce in sugar. Maple sugar costs more than either beet- or cane-sugar and would have no place in the world market at all but for its peculiar flavor and fine quality, which make it something of a luxury and enable it to command a higher price. The sap flows only in quantities sufficient for satisfactory sugar making where the early spring days are bright and sunny and the nights are cold. This climatic factor limits sugar orchards to the region from Indiana east and north. It is particularly important in the White Mountain region of Vermont and New Hampshire and the adjacent parts of Canada.

The sugar maple tree that yields from the time it is 20 or 25 years old till it is 75 or 100, on rocky land without cultivation, certainly has all other sugar producers distanced for permanence, but the yield is at present low. Much of the output of the "sugar-orchards" is marketed in the form of the more easily made maple syrup, a highly prized table delicacy.

6. TOBACCO

Few commercial plants grow over so wide a range of the earth's surface as does tobacco. It is injured by frost, but it grows in a comparatively short season, so that profitable crops ripen as far north as Wisconsin, southern Canada and England, while it is at home throughout the tropics. Probably no other commercial product possesses more grades and commercial varieties. One field of Sumatra tobacco may be classified into as many as seventy-two different market kinds. The quality of the soil affects it in a remarkable degree, as does temperature, humidity, and especially the fermentation and other chemical changes that take place in the process of curing the leaf. The resulting strength or weakness of flavor, the kind of flavor, the thickness, brittleness, elasticity, texture, color, size, perfection and relative weight of the leaf, its specks, its dustiness, gumminess and ripeness are some of the factors that decide whether the tobacco will bring 2¢ or $2 per pound.

Tobacco's commercial service.—The commercial service of tobacco has been great, likewise its injuries to man and to his resources. The Jamestown Colony in Virginia was about to fail in its early days because the settlers could find no money crop, nothing to sell to the mother country in return for the imports they must buy from her. England, being then essentially an agricultural land, had an abundance of wheat, oats, barley, rye, and all agricultural staples as well as manufactures. The colonists tried to grow silk, but failed. The grape also failed (see chap. on fruits) and despair ruled in Jamestown. Then a trial shipment of tobacco which the Indians had shown the colonists how to grow, brought a good price in England. It promptly became the great staple of trade, remained so throughout the whole Colonial period and to a very considerable extent down to the present time. As late as 1810 it was one of the few crops that could be sold by the people of Kentucky and Tennessee, whose export market was New Orleans, reached by flat boats which were floated down the Ohio and Mississippi Rivers.

The use, spread, and consumption of tobacco.—The increase and spread of the use of tobacco have been phenomenal, and of late years new industrial uses for it have been discovered (Figs. 73 and 74). The dust made of tobacco stems is a fertilizer rich in potash and the nicotine also kills the destructive aphis on the roots of fruit trees. This nicotine, which is the cause of the injury that tobacco inflicts on its users, has of late given rise to the manufacture of poisonous extracts for use as sprays in exterminating insects on the leaves of trees and shrubs.

Tobacco growing belongs to intensive agriculture. The tiny black seeds, three or four hundred thousand to the ounce, are sown in seed beds, and the little plants were, until the recent introduction of a new machine, transplanted by hand to their place in the field, where constant attention and hand labor are necessary to protect them from the cut worm which cuts off the young plant, the leaf worm which eats holes in the leaves, and the stalk worm which destroys the central stalk of the plant. The blooms must be picked

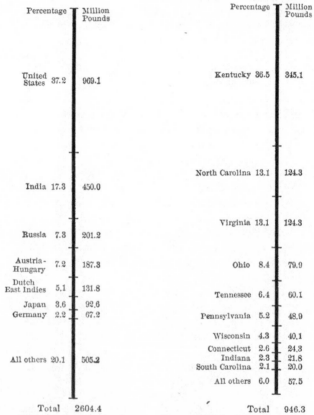

Percentage	Million Pounds		Percentage	Million Pounds
United States 37.2	969.1		Kentucky 36.5	345.1
			North Carolina 13.1	124.3
India 17.3	450.0			
			Virginia 13.1	124.3
Russia 7.3	201.2			
Austria-Hungary 7.2	187.3		Ohio 8.4	79.9
Dutch East Indies 5.1	131.8		Tennessee 6.4	60.1
Japan 3.6	92.6			
Germany 2.2	67.2		Pennsylvania 5.2	48.9
			Wisconsin 4.3	40.1
			Connecticut 2.6	24.3
All others 20.1	505.2		Indiana 2.3	21.8
			South Carolina 2.1	20.0
			All others 6.0	57.5
Total	2604.4		Total	946.3

FIG. 73.—World's tobacco production, three-year average, 1908–10.

FIG. 74.—United States tobacco production, three-year average, 1909–11.

off, so that the energy may go to leaf rather than seed. For the same reason, the suckers or side shoots must be pulled off, while the process of picking, curing, sorting, grading, and packing is laborious and requires much skill.

Tobacco as a crop.—The farm value per acre of the tobacco crop in 1913 was $100, eight times that of wheat. As much of the labor of tobacco growing requires watchfulness and care rather than strength, it can be done by women and children as well as by men, and as a result it is rarely grown on an extensive scale but usually in small fields, cared for by the members of the farmer's family. The tobacco farmer of Virginia and Kentucky usually raises enough corn to feed the horses that work his lands, the pigs that make his meat, and the cow and chickens that help feed the family. He sometimes also raises some other supply crops, but all his money he usually expects to get through the sale of tobacco.

FIG. 75.—Plantation of cigar-wrapper tobacco growing under artificial shade in fine sandy loam, Norfolk, Florida. (U. S. Dept. Agr.)

The leading tobacco belts of the United States.—For a long time the Virginia-Carolina tobacco belt running from southern Maryland through the middle part of Virginia and North Carolina was the leading tobacco belt of the United States (Fig. 75), but Kentucky has now become the first state, producing in 1911 over three-fourths as much as all of the states east of the Appalachians. Special grades of tobacco are grown in small quantities in restricted districts in Wisconsin, Connecticut, Florida, and Louisiana, but the limestone lands of Kentucky are the chief seats of tobacco production in the United States, and Louisville, their natural commercial center, is the greatest tobacco market in the world. Much

Kentucky tobacco is exported to European countries, for the United States is by far the greatest exporter as well as the greatest tobacco grower in the world. Louisville has many factories for the manufacture of tobacco into the various forms for final use from cigarettes to insecticides. In the eastern field, Richmond is the greatest center, while Petersburg, and the Carolina towns of Winston-Salem and Durham have enormous tobacco factories.

Tobacco injury to American soils.—The ready export market for tobacco has resulted in great injury to the soil resources of most American tobacco-growing districts. Because of the good profits, tobacco has been grown year after year without rotation of crops until its great demands for potash have exhausted the soil for a time and the fields have often been abandoned because land was so cheap that more could be had by cutting down and burning the forest. Then the heavy downpours of the summer thunder showers reduced the bare and abandoned tobacco field to useless gullies before the old-field pine could again make a forest there. This wasteful policy brought great poverty to southern Maryland and middle Virginia, and from these sections the people emigrated in such large numbers shortly after the Civil War when western farm lands were opened up, that there was a general loss of population throughout the old Colonial tobacco district. This region today has less land in cultivation than it had a century ago, and many localities have less population.

QUESTIONS

1. How may science give us new sources of sugar?

2. How does the supply of seed enter in as a factor in the competition of cane and sorghum?

3. Name and describe two minor sources of sugar supply.

4. Discuss molasses and molassquite as factors in the cost of living.

5. Why does tobacco suit a tenant farmer better than sugar cane does?

6. Discuss tobacco from the standpoint of a money crop, both at the present time and in colonial days. What by-products are there?

7. What effect does the heavy cost of a beet-sugar refinery have upon the beet farmer's market?

8. What by-product of sugar cane is used in feeding cattle? Mention by-products of industries treated earlier in the book, that are used in feeding cattle and pigs.

9. Ten pounds of mill (black strap) molasses from cane with the addition of 2 pounds of cotton-seed meal, make almost the exact equivalent as stock food for 10 pounds of corn. At the present price of corn and cotton seed in your town what would be the price of molasses to make the two rations of equal cost.

CHAPTER VI

FISHERIES

If judged by the products it gives us the sea is very barren as compared with the land. Although it covers three-fourths of the world's surface, it furnishes but a small proportion of our food supply. Fish are the cattle of the sea. They derive their support from the vegetable life of the waters. Even the clear water of the sea has countless millions of minute plant organisms, which are eaten by many small animal organisms. These in turn are eaten by each other and by the fish, but the support of the whole pyramid of marine animal life, like the life of land animals, is based upon vegetation.

The word fishery is applied to the catching of practically any animal that is taken in the water, as oysters, lobsters, whales, and even seals, which are often taken on shore. Sea fishery is considered the cause that first led man to sail upon the ocean, and from this beginning, all maritime peoples have had their rise—Phoenicians Greeks, Norsemen, Dutchmen, Englishmen, and New Englanders. The schooner, the fastest of all sailing vessels, was invented and is yet used by the fisherman of Gloucester, Mass., and in recognition of the importance of the sea industry to the state, a dried codfish has, since colonial days, hung over the desk occupied by the speaker of the Massachusetts Senate.

The fishing industry, through its connection with sea power and the romance and charm of the ocean, tends to be overestimated as to its real importance. All the fish that are caught by American fishermen ($54,000,000 worth, 1908) are less valuable than the tobacco crop, and not one-tenth as valuable as the poultry and eggs annually produced in the United States. The fish of all the world are only two-thirds as valuable as the poultry and eggs of the United States.

The location of fisheries.—Most of the world's fishing industry depends upon two habits of fish which enable us to catch near the land those that may have passed most of their lives hundreds of miles away at sea. The first is the spawning habit of many species

137

which lay their eggs only in rivers or in the shallow waters near the
shore. The second is the congregation of fish to feed upon the
bottoms, in shallow waters, commonly called "banks." The
occurrence of such banks near the shores of northeastern Asia,
northeastern North America and northwestern Europe is responsible
for the three greatest fishing regions.

The fisheries of northeastern North America are based on a rich
combination of rivers, bays and shallow off-shore banks (Fig. 76).
Especially important are the Grand Banks of Newfoundland and
smaller banks off Labrador, New England and New Jersey. The

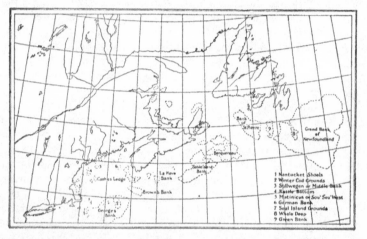

FIG. 76.—Map showing principal fishing grounds off the coasts of New
England, Nova Scotia, and Newfoundland. (After MacFarland.) (From
Salisbury, Barrows and Tower.)

Newfoundland banks were known to the fishermen of the French
province of Normandy and Brittany within a dozen years after
Columbus had returned to Spain from his first voyage. Scores of
vessels sailed back and forth from France to these Newfoundland
banks each year for a century before the French made settlements
on Canadian shores.

Proximity to these banks has made the New England fishing
industry equal in value to that of all the rest of the United States
together (Fig. 77). Massachusetts and Maine are the leading
states in fisheries. Gloucester, Mass:, was long the greatest fish

port in America, nearly the whole population being engaged in the catching, curing, buying and selling of fish. Boston with its better marketing facilities has recently surpassed Gloucester as a fishing port.

The cod fisheries.—The most important fish on these and other northern banks is the cod, a fish which feeds along the bottom and is commonly caught on a "trawl" which consists of baited hooks attached to short lines that are fastened at intervals of 4 feet to a longer line sometimes 3,000 feet in length. These trawls are attended to by fishermen in rowboats called dories that put out from the schooners. The men in the dory take up one end of the trawl, which is anchored and marked by a float, pass the boat along under it, and let it down in the water again after the fish have been taken off and the bait replenished. Fishing on the Grand Banks is an exceedingly dangerous calling, as the banks are one of the foggiest places in the world and the schooners often collide with each other and with icebergs. The men in the dories often lose their bearings and drift away to death, while a single fearful storm sometimes drowns scores or even hundreds of fishermen. To complete the chapter of dangers the fishing banks are in the path of the great transatlantic vessels which sometimes run down the small fishing craft in the fogs.

Shore and river fisheries.—A number of marine animals such as the oyster, clam, lobster, and sponge live in shallow waters where they can easily be caught. Many rivers and bays have a fishing value out of proportion to their area because of the sea fish that annually enter the stream for spawning and become the rich harvest of the fishermen.

The salmon, of which there are several species, is easily the king of

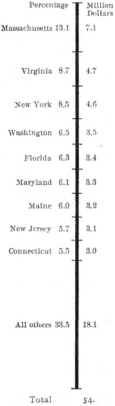

	Percentage	Million Dollars
Massachusetts	13.1	7.1
Virginia	8.7	4.7
New York	8.5	4.6
Washington	6.5	3.5
Florida	6.3	3.4
Maryland	6.1	3.3
Maine	6.0	3.2
New Jersey	5.7	3.1
Connecticut	5.5	3.0
All others	33.5	18.1
Total		54.

FIG. 77.—United States fishery products by states, 1908.

all river running fish.   It is said to ascend only streams having their
sources in lakes in which the females deposit their eggs, and experiment has shown that the salmon returns to the stream where it
was born.   Salmon are found to some extent in New England and
east Canada, but the rivers of the north Pacific, between San
Francisco and Japan, are the chief source of the world's supply.
In Alaska they have for an unknown period been almost the only
winter food supply of the natives, who at the time of the annual
run put away the year's supply of smoked salmon in little houses on
high poles, out of the reach of wolves and dogs.

For many years salmon canning has been an important industry,
first established in California, Oregon and Washington, then in
British Columbia and finally in Alaska, where in almost every river,
especially the great Yukon, salmon are exceedingly abundant.
Large salmon canneries have been built at the mouths of various
streams along these coasts so rocky and cold as to be undesirable for
human habitation throughout most of the year.   As the season
for the salmon running approaches, sailing vessels loaded with
empty cans and carrying many workmen, usually Chinese, leave
San Francisco, Portland or Seattle for the cannery.   In a few weeks
hundreds of thousands of pounds of salmon are canned, loaded into
the sailing vessels, and brought back to the home port for distribution throughout the United States, the United Kingdom, Australasia, and many other countries.   Salmon is the chief fish export of
the United States (1911, 40 million pounds, $4,000,000).

The shad, probably the most highly prized of American commercial food fish, ascends each spring the rivers from Florida to the
St. Lawrence.   The herring also ascends these same rivers in such
numbers that at times their scaly backs cause the surface of the
water to shine almost like a mirror.   The abundance of this fish
causes it to be an important article of diet in the eastern part of the
United States.   On the Maine coast small herring are packed in sar-
dine style.

Shell fish.—The oyster, of which the United States has from five-
sixths to nine-tenths of the world's product, is the most valuable fish
product in America, furnishing about one-third of the total catch.
This delicious shell fish lives on the sandy and gravelly bottoms of
shallow bays and estuaries.   It is found to some extent on the
Pacific coast of the United States, but the numerous bays between
Cape Cod and Galveston, with their large expanses of shallow

water of suitable temperature seem to be the best places in the world for oysters. The Chesapeake Bay, an old river valley into which the sea has flowed, is the most important oystering district of all, while Long Island Sound is second. The oyster, after being hatched from the egg, swims around for a time and then attaches itself to some firm substance, such as gravel, an old shell, or sunken wood. For 2 or 3 years he eats whatever the tide brings him, and is then scooped up with long-handled tongs in the hands of an oysterman or by a steam-drawn dredge. During the 7 or 8 months of the oyster season they are shipped in barrels and sacks to many parts of the United States and even to Europe. At Baltimore there is a large canning industry for shipment to small interior towns and foreign countries. The natural supply having been found inadequate, oyster culture has been established. Beds of young oysters are sometimes planted, that is, put down to grow large; another method is to lay old oyster shells and the bushy tops of trees upon the bottoms of the bays so that there may be something to which the floating spawn may attach itself and grow. The possibilities of the extension of the oyster industry in Long Island Sound, and in Delaware, Chesapeake and other bays are very great.

The importance of fish to the Atlantic Plain of the United States.— In the central part of the Atlantic Plain of the United States, these unusual fish resources combine with many other resources, to make the peninsula between the Chesapeake Bay and the Atlantic Ocean one of the most favored places in the United States, or, indeed, in all the world, for the easy support of the human race under physical conditions that place no serious handicap on man. The climate is wholesome; the varied soil, the abundant, well-distributed rainfall and satisfactory temperature permit the commercial production of an unusual variety of grains, fruits, and vegetables, while fish products reach their maximum of abundance. It is the greatest oyster, shad, and herring locality in America, and many minor fish are caught. Herring are so abundant that the laboring man may in the spring time buy a thousand for from $3 to $6, and with a sack of salt and a barrel they can be preserved for the entire year. As herring and corn bread make a sustaining meal (materials costing two cents) for a working man, living is exceedingly cheap. The shores of these waters are in many places marshy, making excellent feeding grounds for wild ducks as they pass in fall and spring between the wilds of

Canada and the swamps of the tropics. Consequently, along the Chesapeake, in addition to its resource of land and water, hunting is still an important source of support of the population, who thus make use of the emigrating product of another locality.

This peninsula differs but little from the tidewater region on the west of the bay and its advantages are in the main typical of the entire Atlantic coastal plain that extends from the fall line (see page 86) on the Atlantic rivers, to the ocean, and includes Long Island and Florida. The Gulf Plain differs from it but little except that it is warmer.

Open sea fisheries.—The mackerel and menhaden are two fish that are unusual in that they are caught in nets near the surface of the open sea, chiefly between Florida and Newfoundland. The net is a large one many hundred feet long commonly dragged by a small steamer at each end. The menhaden is unusual in that it is not eaten. Instead, ship loads of the fish are taken to factories along our Atlantic coast. From these factories, some of which now steam from port to port, the menhaden emerge as barrels of fish oil and sacks of fertilizer (dried pulverized fish).

Seal and whale fisheries.—American ports serve as the outfitting place of ships that prosecute these distant industries. In the first half of the nineteenth century, when whale oil supplied the family lamp, whaling was of very great importance. In those days New Bedford and Nantucket in Massachusetts, and New London in Connecticut, were the great outfitting centers of an industry that was prosecuted in all oceans of the world so persistently that the whale was nearly exterminated by 1860. At that time the fortunate dis- covery of petroleum lessened the demand for whale oil. Some whale fishing is still carried on, but the whalers of Nantucket have changed their base to San Francisco, so that they may be nearer the home of the whale, now chiefly caught in the Arctic Ocean near Bering Straits.

The seal gets its living (fish) in the sea, rears its young upon the rocky shores and is the prey of man on both sea and land. It is such a valuable quarry that extinction seems to be its fate where it is not protected by strictly enforced legislation. The greatest center of fur seal fishing is the Pribiloff Islands, an American possession in the Bering Sea. Here each year many thousands of seals gather from distant seas, and remain for a few weeks during which time the seal pups are born and grow large enough to swim with their mothers. Each year a certain proportion of the young males, 2- to 4-year olds are killed, according to strict regulations, by hunters who pay the government a license for the privilege. Most of the valuable skins are shipped to the London market. Unfortunately for the seals no country has in past years had any jurisdiction beyond 3 miles from its coasts. The seal at sea was therefore like the whale, beyond the protection of government. While the United States could and did protect the seals during their stay on the rocks of the Pribiloff Islands, the mother seals daily swam to the open sea for fish, and during many months the whole herd was scattered widely over the Pacific Ocean. When more than 3

Fig. 78.— A new conquest of science. Bits of sponge wired fast to cement frames have grown nicely in Florida waters.

miles from shore they fell a prey to the rifles of the pelagic sealers from Canada, Japan or the United States, who sailed the seas in search of them and waited at the 3-mile limit. As a result the mothers of many little seals were shot while gathering food, leaving the young to starve on the rocks. Thus the number of seals in the Pribiloff herds rapidly declined and extinction seemed only a matter of years, just as unchecked and uncontrolled sealing had practically exterminated, many decades ago, the countless thousands of seals that lived on several uninhabited rocks in the Antarctic. However a recent treaty (1911) between the United States, Japan, and Canada has probably averted repetition of such an economic insanity in the Bering Sea.

Extension of the fish supply.—Science is able to increase the fish supply. With the aid of refrigeration, fish are now caught in the teeming waters of Florida or the West Indies, frozen at once, and marketed weeks later in New York and Europe. Similarly fish are now marketed in the winter season in those markets from the waters off Vancouver Island and other distant places. We may, therefore, anticipate a development of the fishing industry in southern waters, which are more prolific than those of the North.

Another aid comes from fish culture, an art long ago perfected by the Chinese. The threatened extermination of many valuable species of fish has led to systematic fish culture by the United States government. Thus far it has been devoted chiefly to fish hatching and caring for the fry for a short time. Billions of fish eggs are hatched and the fry released in streams and lakes to replenish the supply. There are several salmon hatcheries in Oregon and Washington, shad hatcheries on the eastern rivers, lobster hatcheries upon the New England coast, and the Great Lakes fisheries receive more aid in this respect than any other locality. The young shad or salmon thus released by the United States Fish Commission goes away to pasture in the sea and returns fattened for our food supply.

QUESTIONS

1. How do the topography of sea bottoms and the habits of fish combine to make an industry for Newfoundland?

2. How do the habits of oysters and of salmon make it profitable for private individuals to increase the supply of these fish?

3. Why is a square mile of river more valuable as fishing ground than a square mile of sea?

4. Why has the fishing industry received so much more aid from governments than some more important industries?

5. How has a treaty probably saved the Bering Sea seals from the fate of the Antarctic seals?

CHAPTER VII

THE FUNDAMENTALS OF MANUFACTURE. *A.* ABUNDANCE OF LAND

FACTORS CONTROLLING MANUFACTURES

The basis of manufactures.—The manufacturing industries result from a combination of conditions largely geographic in their
origin and covered by the terms raw material, power, labor, markets
and capital. Of these factors capital is thoroughly mobile and
goes wherever some advantage in one or more of the other three
dictates. Raw materials light in proportion to their value go to
places where power or labor abound, as iron from Pennsylvania to
the Connecticut factories, where firearms, typewriters, and other
costly metal ware are made. Heavy raw materials sometimes tend
to locate an industry near where they are produced, as Birmingham
in the midst of the Alabama coal and iron ore area. Fuel and its
resultant power are also great factors in locating manufactures as at
Pittsburgh, which has an abundance of nearby coal for fuel, but
which has to bring the necessary large supplies of heavy iron ore
from the Lake Superior country several hundred miles away.
Nearly all great manufacturing districts are near to sources of fuel
or waterpower, for to them come capital, labor and raw materials.
It by no means follows that all coal fields are seats of manufacture.
Most of them are not, chiefly because of the lack of the human
element, labor, and especially the skilled labor necessary to manufacturing. The relative abundance of labor and natural resources
exercises a strong control over manufacturing. Nearness to market
is another important item in determining the location of manufactures that are difficult to transport, especially of food products as
in the great city bakeries, and of very bulky and very heavy products, as in mining machine factories at Denver. But nearness to
market is a factor of decreasing importance as transportation facilities increase and improve.

RELATION OF LAND AND POPULATION TO MANUFACTURE

Cheap land opposes manufacturing.—We all get our living directly or indirectly from the land. Land is therefore man's great opportunity. Where there is little of it per person, there is less opportunity to work; therefore, other things being equal, less return for labor, lower wages, and a necessarily lower standard of life. This is usually the most important fact in explaining the industrial history and industrial condition of a nation.

Manufacturing is chiefly carried on by people who work for others; but in America, from the date of earliest settlement to the present, there has been, because of our scanty population and cheap and abundant land, much greater opportunity to work for one's self and less necessity to work for others than there has been in Europe.

When the first English settlers established themselves as tobacco growers at Jamestown in Virginia, each had the same opportunity to take up free land and each man preferred to work for himself rather than work for his neighbor. If newcomers were brought from England they too could work for themselves, and thus every energetic man wanted many laborers and could get few or none. Out of this labor scarcity slavery arose, whereby the Englishman could control his labor. Similar situations tend to produce somewhat similar problems wherever they arise.

Throughout the eighteenth century and down to the year 1815, while manufactures were developing and manufacturing towns were arising in England, the young man of America could choose between working for someone else in a manufacturing plant or remaining his own master and acquiring wealth and property by taking a pair of oxen, a wagon and a few implements and going into the forests of western Massachusetts, New York, Pennsylvania, Virginia, or across the Alleghenies. Here by felling trees, building a log house and clearing a field, he could make a valuable farm. The fertile forest land was to be had for the taking, and the young men of America chose to build frontier settlements rather than to go to factories and cities.

The free land of the nineteenth century.—With the limited means of transportation then in use, most of our available land was occupied by 1810. Profitable farming depends upon good transportation, and good transportation in the United States at that time depended on natural waterways. Since farm products could only be shipped from near the banks of navigable waters, desirable land was comparatively limited in amount and therefore the people were turning to manufacturing. Then came the steamboat, and the railroad followed soon after. The American people who had been clustered along the seaboard and navigable rivers suddenly found themselves able to take possession of the whole continent, and the vast flat prairies of the Mississippi Valley at once became available for settlement. For decades the land was given away by the government to the homesteaders and three generations of Americans triumphantly and truthfully said that "Uncle Sam has a farm for every one of us." From 1816 to 1890 people went from the East to the new West by tens of thousands each year. The record of this movement of settlers exceeds anything that had previously occurred in the history of the world. The population of Iowa increased from 192,000 to 674,000 in the decade 1850 to 1860. That of Nebraska rose from 122,000 in 1870 to 452,000 by 1880 and to 1,062,000 by 1890. In the next 10 years it remained practically stationary because the waves of emigration had rolled on to a newer empty frontier, and Oklahoma, for example, newly opened to settlement, increased from 258,000 to 790,000 people.

So excellent were the opportunities to go West and get fine land for nothing, that in many parts of the East people abandoned their farms and the population of Maine and New Hampshire actually declined between 1860 and 1870—typical of what has happened in many agricultural districts throughout the East in the same period and since. Eastern farm lands, often as productive as ever, declined in selling value because of the competition of the western land, and the man who wished to farm could begin easily either east or west. So rapid was this settling of western farm land that by 1890 it may fairly be said that there was for a time overproduction of agricultural products. Corn was so cheap in the new country that it was cheaper at times to burn it for fuel than to sell it and buy coal.

Since 1895 the irrigation settlements in the region beyond the 100th meridian have kept before the American people the opportunity to go West and since 1900 the Canadian government has advertised widely the fact that it is giving away good farms. History has quickly repeated itself. The Mississippi Valley that was filling so rapidly in 1850 has for a time begun to empty itself into other frontiers (Fig. 79).

So rapid has been the emigration to Canada that the young man of the corn belt has been able to choose between taking up a free farm in Canada or working for high wages in Iowa.   Thus farm laborers in the northern Mississippi Valley near to free land get nearly twice as much wages as those in the valley of the Potomac, where there is no free land.   Owing to this chance to get land it is plain that the

Fig. 79.—Map showing, by black cross, the counties in four corn-belt states that lost population between 1900 and 1910. This is in part a tribute to the efficiency of agricultural machinery and part to the cheap land of the farther West.

factory that succeeded in getting workmen had to pay high wages to make them stay, and for that reason American wages became and have remained high.   Because of these high farm wages, manufacturers have made small progress in the upper Mississippi Valley, and only by increase in wages could the laborers be kept in the East.

New resources have the same effect as new land.—The effect upon wages and industry of abundant natural resources and especially of newly discovered or newly utilized resources, has been sharply illustrated many times in the settlement of this continent. When gold was first discovered in California, there was an enormous rush of miners from every state of the Union and every country of the world to dig up this gold from the sands of the California rivers where a man could sometimes find $10 or $15 in gold per day. This was often too strong a temptation for the sailors on the incoming ships, and large numbers of them deserted. At one time there were 100 idle ships lying in San Francisco Bay because the crews had been tempted away by the higher returns to be secured by working for themselves in the gold diggings.

At Cape Nome, Alaska, on the shore of the Arctic Sea, report of gold discovery a few years ago brought a rush of thousands of men who when they got there strove for the chance to work for $3 a day in the few claims that made up the one gold-yielding creek. Others gladly worked for their board. Suddenly it was discovered that the sands of the seashore were full of gold where each man could wash out $10 worth per day, and that sum promptly became the rate of wages in all the settlement.

The opposite influence has been lately shown in southern California, whither thousands of people have gone from the East to benefit their health, or for pleasure, in the gentle climate of the south Pacific coast with its warm and even-tempered winters and dry summers. The sudden influx of persons attracted by the search for health rather than by resources has caused many occupations to become overcrowded. Salaries, therefore, have become surprisingly low in comparison with the general level in the western country.

The ease of living in a sparsely peopled country and its influence on manufacture.—Where population is scarce and the climate favors vegetation, many things grow naturally and are to be had for the taking—so-called free goods. These conditions prevail to a greater or less extent throughout many parts of the United States, but especially south of Pennsylvania and the Ohio and Missouri Rivers and west to the limit of the eastern forest area. This whole region was originally forest covered, and more than half of it is still covered by some kind of forest growth. Logs and timber are still abundant for house building, and the winter, milder than that of the north, permits a cheap house to suffice. The same climatic conditions make less demand for fuel, and this the abundant woods still furnish in most rural communities.

It is in the matter of foods that the free goods are most abundant and most helpful in cheap living.   From the Rio Grande to the Delaware Bay the first bright days of spring bring a run of fish upward from the sea in thousands of creeks and rivers (see chapter on

FIG. 80.—Mazzard cherry tree on campus of Swarthmore College. This variety, often very productive, grows wild in much of the East and South, and the fruit is so abundant that anyone may pick all he desires—free goods.

Fisheries), and in these regions a man can procure fish as surely by sitting on the stream bank and catching them as he can by sending to a city market and paying money for them.   The herrings which can at this season be caught in nets by the millions are sold so cheaply that $5 will buy enough to fill a barrel and supply a family with salt fish for the rest of the year. Before the frosts are over various wild spring greens duplicate the spinach and lettuce of the city market. The family cow, giving from 4 to 12 quarts of milk per day and pasturing at from $1 to $2 per month, is a cheaper source of supply than milk served in cities and costing from six to fifteen cents per quart. In May and June, wild strawberries are to be had

FIG. 81.—French roadside. No free goods. Wheat comes clear to the gutter. The trees along the road are grafted English (Persian) walnuts. A good tree rents for as much as an acre of land. In the distance at the left grafted chestnut trees line the fence rows.

for the picking, as are also the black heart and red heart cherries (Fig. 80). These cherries grow naturally and bear plentifully along the fences and open woods from Pennsylvania southward. After the strawberries and cherries come raspberries, and the raspberry season merges into the blackberry season. The blackberry season merges into that of the huckleberry. These berries grow in such abundance in swamps and on mountain sides that they usually have no sale value whatever until they are picked and carried to market. After huckleberries come peaches, which, like the cherries, grow wild along the fence rows in some localities. In autumn comes the persimmon, sweetened by freezing, to hang upon the trees all winter waiting to be eaten, and the black walnut, rivaling in nutrition the high-priced English walnut (Persian walnut), is so common that it often lies ungathered on the ground. With the first frost the chestnut burrs are opened and this sweet nut is not only an important food supply, but also becomes a money crop of no mean importance. The people roam at will through the woods gathering chestnuts for shipment to the cities of the northern and central part of the country.

As for the meat supply, in late August and September the young squirrels are full grown, and a good hunter can at times get five or ten in a morning. Colored men in the south sometimes report a catch of sixty opossums in a single autumn, thus getting a meat supply which is quite as abundant as could have been bought with the wages earned by arduously working on a trolley track on a noisy street. With the falling leaves the oak trees shower down their acorns, the natural food of the hog. Often allowed to run at large in the forests, by December these hogs are fat enough to slaughter for the year's supply of ham and bacon.

In addition to these free offerings of nature there is a garden by almost every house in the country districts and small towns of this part of the United States, so that the working man in this region has two alternatives. He may work regularly, get wages and buy food or he may work occasionally at the spasmodic labor of the farm and get an equal amount of food by going hunting, fishing, or berrying—facts of profound influence in checking the development of manufacture.

The exacting demands of manufacturing.—Manufactured goods are produced in a factory that should start Monday morning at the sound of the whistle and work on a schedule until Saturday afternoon. This is an exacting demand upon labor. Throughout the sparsely peopled districts, with the abundant free goods above mentioned, labor is apt to be not only scarce, but unreliable, for most of the laboring population think they are just as well off if they occasionally stop work and go fishing or berrying or hunting, and when the desire comes, off they go.

These conditions help to explain the absence of large manufacturing industries in these territories, which, in the manufacturing resources of raw materials, power, and natural ease of transport, are superior to those of busy New England.

In the colder North nature demands more of man. On the treeless prairies of the Mississippi Valley, there is no free house material, no free fuel, the fertile level prairie is all cultivated, and man must depend more upon his own efforts than is necessary in the South. This is one of the reasons why manufacture has developed more in northern than in southern states.

FIG. 82.—Corsican mountain side as steep as a house roof. No free goods as in America. Every tree is a grafted chestnut and the crop makes the land worth $200 per acre.

The European labor supply.—The chief difference between the life of the people in America and in Europe is explained by the factors already mentioned in this chapter—resources. Hence conservation is one of the most vital and most patriotic movements in America. In Europe the result of density of population is clearly marked. In the United States the average population is less than 50 per square mile, in Germany it is 290; in Holland, 454; and in Belgium, 645, or more than one person to each acre. It is a region of little land per man. He who eats the product of the land must either produce it with much labor or buy it. Food prices are high because there is little land on which to produce, and wages are low because people are plenty. Under these conditions people must work, and work regularly, and the great difficulty is to get a chance to labor. Thus the factories can get an abundance of laborers cheaply, and northwestern Europe with its dense population is a veritable hive of manufacturing industries. These points of difference between Europe and America serve to explain nearly all the great emigration movements of all times, and one who would understand manufacturing industries must have clearly in mind these vital and underlying facts.

QUESTIONS

1. Would it stimulate or retard manufactures in England if 100,000 square miles of adjacent sea bottom suddenly became farm land? Why?

2. How does the speed of settlement of the United States show the service of coal?

3. Can a manufacturer produce cotton cloth more cheaply in a rich country than in a poor one?

4. Why are wages lower in populous Sicily than in sparsely peopled Canada?

5. Is the large amount of free food to be found in North Carolina an aid to manufacture?

CHAPTER VIII

FUNDAMENTALS OF MANUFACTURE. *B.* BASIC METALS

Manufacturing depends on iron and steel.—The abundance of these metals is regarded as a sign of national wealth. Iron and steel are especially important in the manufacturing industries. Without their extensive use no nation can develop great manufactures.

Iron, the most useful, is also one of the most universal of metals. Man has found it in many parts of the world and used it since before the dawn of history, but we have of late turned to the earth's stores of iron with renewed eagerness and within a few decades increased our use of it many fold.

Our ever-increasing list of manufactures is almost universally produced by machines of iron and steel, while the same material is entering in increasing quantities as a raw material for the equipment of factories, farms, and homes, and all kinds of industrial equipment (Fig. 87). Iron was an industrial luxury a century ago. Now it is an industrial commonplace, since recent improvements in production have reduced the cost and permitted a great increase in production.

Coal is the twin of iron in the production of the new world commerce, because this commerce is carried in vehicles made chiefly of iron, driven by power derived from coal. Coal also furnishes heat for the reduction of iron, and power for driving the machinery employed in its manufacture.

The formation of iron ores.—Iron ores are plentiful, but the metal is never found even in a reasonably pure state except in recently fallen meteorites. It is dissolved from almost every hillside by the leaching rain waters, and where a stream of water with iron in solution enters a stream of water with lime in solution, iron ore is deposited. For this reason we have a string of iron deposits in the United States from northern Vermont to central Alabama (Fig. 83). They are scattered along the edges of the limestones which are so common throughout this whole region, especially in the Great

Valley from Lebanon, Pennsylvania, to Chattanooga, Tennessee,
which has many deposits of limestone throughout its extent. Where
the conditions suitable for the deposit of iron ore continue undisturbed for great periods of time, we have large deposits, veritable
mountains of ore, such as exist in the rough country south and west
of Lake Superior, in the iron mountains of Mexico, the mountains
near Santiago, Cuba, near the Cantabrians of northern Spain, in
northern Sweden, and in many other parts of the world.

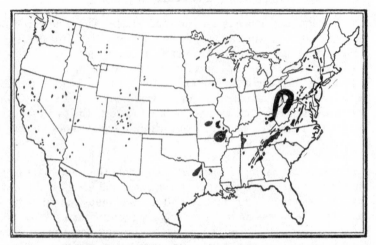

Fig. 83.—Map showing general distribution of iron ore in the United States.
(From Salisbury, Barrows, and Tower.)

Iron is melted out of the ore by being put into a huge stack or
furnace sometimes 100 feet high and filled from bottom to top with
roaring fire that rushes upward through layers of coke, ore and
limestone. The draft is provided by a blast of air driven by pumping
engines (Fig. 84). Hence the name blast furnace. The limestone
makes it melt at a lower temperature and unites with the dross to
form slag or cinder which is much like lava. The iron being heavier
collects in the bottom and is drawn off at intervals of a few hours.

Iron making in America.—The United States is the leader in iron
making in the twentieth century, as was England during the nineteenth century. This leadership has come as the result of a number
of rapid transformations of the industry in this country. In George
Washington's time the little forges or small blast furnaces with a

Fig. 84.—A Blast Furnace. Ore bins and freight cars at left; skip hoists (inclined planes) going up to furnaces in center; white hot molten metal running into ladle cars at both sides of furnace. (Bethlehem Steel Co.)

draft forced by a water wheel were scattered from New England to Georgia and from the seacoast to the Appalachian valleys in what now seem to be remote and isolated locations. Iron was made wherever the local blacksmiths needed it, and a small ore bank, a water fall, and the American forest, almost universal in the East, furnished the necessary raw materials, which the farmers hauled at odd times.

Fortunately for the American iron industry, the first coal field to be developed was the anthracite, which, by its purity and hardness, served well for smelting purposes without being made into coke. Here was a factor that gave one region a heavy advantage over all others and after 1840 we had a rapid concentration of the iron industry in the Schuylkill Valley and other regions adjacent to the anthracite coal mines of the Scranton-Wilkesbarre district in eastern Pennsylvania. The old forges survived longest in locations remote from the places of superior manufacture as in the isolated mountains of western North Carolina and other parts of the southern Appalachians, where some of them were running for purely local supply as late as the year 1900.

Pittsburgh and the Upper Ohio Valley.—The supremacy of the eastern iron districts was short lived because of the building of railroads through the soft coal regions of western Pennsylvania and the introduction there of coke making. Coke is the best iron smelting fuel, and the coals of the Connellsville Basin are particularly adapted to making it. The iron industry promptly rose in that region, and Pittsburgh, at the head of the Ohio Valley, rapidly became the center, first of the American and then of the world's iron industry. The importation of the richer iron ore from the Lake Superior district began in 1884. In America as in England, the old English adage holds true in most cases that "the ore goes to the fuel," so that Pittsburgh held the leadership, although the source of ore supply suddenly shifted from the valleys of Appalachia to the pine woods along the shores of Lake Superior.

A new process of coke making now enables the iron maker to get good coke from many other fields than the Connellsville basin. This fact has destroyed the regional monopoly that existed when all coke was made in the old beehive oven (see section on coal) and that from Connellsville coal was without a rival. Iron making is again spreading territorially in response to this widened fuel supply.

There is, at present, a tendency to shift the iron and steel industry using Lake Superior ores from Pittsburgh to Lake Shore points, such as Buffalo, Cleveland, Chicago and Gary. The whole of the triangular region between Buffalo, Chicago, and Pittsburgh, is dotted with towns having some of the iron industries, such as bridge plants, nail mills, wire fence works, steel car plants, and other varieties of iron work. The tendency of the industry to shift to the Lake Shore points is due to the economy that results from having the blast furnace located beside the ore dock where the lake steamer unloads; this is possible at any point on the shores of the lakes from Buffalo to Chicago. Manufacture under such conditions requires one less handling of the ore than is necessary at an inland point like Pittsburgh, or Youngstown (Ohio). This was an important factor in causing the United States Steel Corporation to locate at Gary, Ind., on the lake shore near Chicago, the largest and most complete steel plant in the world.

In northern Alabama, Birmingham, named from the iron city of England, possesses iron-making facilities that permit lower costs of production than at any other place in America, for here are found in the same district (see Fig. 94, Map of Birmingham District), within very short hauls of one another, the necessary ore, coal, and limestone, while fairly good transportation facilities place the district within easy reach of the rapidly developing southern markets for iron and steel products. For these reasons the Birmingham district ranks close to the Pittsburgh district in the value and importance of its output, and is a leading factor in the industrial development of the South.

Several minor producing districts exist in the United States. At the head of Lake Superior iron plants are arising to supply the northwestern market. They use the local ores and coal brought chiefly from Pennsylvania, because the vessels that have carried ore eastward to the Pennsylvania furnaces would otherwise usually have to return to the ore docks empty. Some iron is made of local ores and western Pennsylvania coke on the shores of Lake Champlain, in northern New Jersey, and in eastern Pennsylvania, as at Pottstown, Bethlehem, Lebanon, and Steelton. The eastern Pennsylvania plants are mixing local ores with some from Lake Superior and from foreign countries. The recent importation of ores into Atlantic ports indicates a revival of eastern iron making. Despite our great riches in iron ore there is an advantage in iron quality resulting from mixing ores. There are many qualities desired in iron, and various mixtures of ore make it possible to produce them

easily. Our chief ore import is from the district of **Santiago, Cuba,**
whence several ships a week sail for Baltimore and Philadelphia,
while lesser quantities are brought from Newfoundland, from
Sweden, from Spain, from the island of
Elba in the Mediterranean, and scatter-
ing cargoes from the coasts of the Black
Sea, South Africa, and South America.
Americans have recently purchased and
begun to develop valuable ore lands in
Chile.

In Colorado, which has local coal and
ore, there is another new iron center,
which, being a thousand miles from any
other iron-producing district, is of great
importance in the Rocky Mountain
region, but the output is as yet only
about 1 per cent of the total product of
the country.

The Pacific Coast, with its scarcity of
fuel, high wages, and convenient access
to water-borne cargoes of structural iron
from eastern plants, has developed only
a very small iron-smelting industry. Its
shipyards and foundries import most of
their material from the eastern States
and from Europe, a process that is
made easier since the opening of the
Panama Canal in 1914.

The Lake Superior iron ore fields produce far more than any other because of
the great size of the deposits and the ease
with which they can be mined. Many
of the ore beds are so near the surface
that they can be taken from open pits,
and so pure that they can be scooped up
with steam shovel and loaded on freight cars according to the method
followed in digging railroad cuts. It is never lifted by human muscle
or touched by human hand until it is finished iron or steel. "Up
by steam and down by gravity" is the motto. The ore car runs
out onto a high dock, drops the ore through its bottom into ore

Percentage | Million Long Tons

United States 36.5 | 46.3

Germany 20.3 | 25.8

United Kingdom 12.0 | 15.2

France 8.4 | 10.7

Spain 7.5 | 9.5

Russia 4.4 | 5.6

All others 10.9 | 13.8

Total | 126.9

FIG. 85.—World iron-ore production, three-year average 1908–10.

pockets, thence it drops into the steamer alongside to be lifted out by clam-shell buckets working like human hands but lifting tons at a grab.

Steel making.—Steel is merely a kind of iron which is hardened by an admixture of definite amounts of alloys, mostly carbon. There are three processes of making it. An old and excellent process called cementation begins by putting cast iron into a puddling furnace, which is a sort of basin with flames beating over it. The puddler stirs the molten iron in the basin with a rake while the flames burn the carbon out of the iron. When the coarse carbon of the casting is nearly all burned out, the iron, then called wrought iron, is very tough, malleable, and ductile. In the cementation process the wrought iron, cut into 1-pound chunks, is packed in air-tight boxes with charcoal (carbon) and the whole box kept red hot for a few days, during which the carbon in right amounts and quality is slowly absorbed by the iron. This ancient method has not been improved upon when the very best of steel is to be made, such as is needed for cutlery, firearms, and instruments of precision.

But the railway and the steamship require a cheaper metal; the great development of world commerce could not begin until after the invention, in 1860, by an Englishman, Sir Henry Bessemer, of the so-called Bessemer process. By this process 20 tons of steel are made in a few minutes by putting molten iron into a large retort through which a current of air is blown violently. The oxygen of the air unites with the carbon in the iron and burns it out. The product is then virtually wrought iron, which is changed to steel by the addition of the proper amount of carbon in the form of high-carbon iron called "spiegel-eisen." This quick method makes the cost of Bessemer steel but a small fraction of that of making cementation steel; and so for the 50 years since its invention, Bessemer steel has been of great service in making rails for railway tracks, and beams for bridges, buildings, and elevated railways.

Bessemer steel, however, sometimes breaks without warning and the great weight of the present-day locomotive requires a better rail than can be made by the Bessemer process. This new demand is met by a newer, slightly more expensive metal called open-hearth steel. This is made by putting molten iron in a basin over which flames from a gas-fed fire beat for 8 or 10 hours or until the carbon content is reduced to just the right amount, which can be determined by testing. This stronger and more uniform open-hearth steel is used for boiler plates, ship plates, and the best steel rails now used, and is rapidly displacing Bessemer steel. This open-hearth process, enabling the removal of the phosphorus impurity which occurs in many of the Birmingham ores, has greatly aided that district in taking a prominent place in the American steel industry.

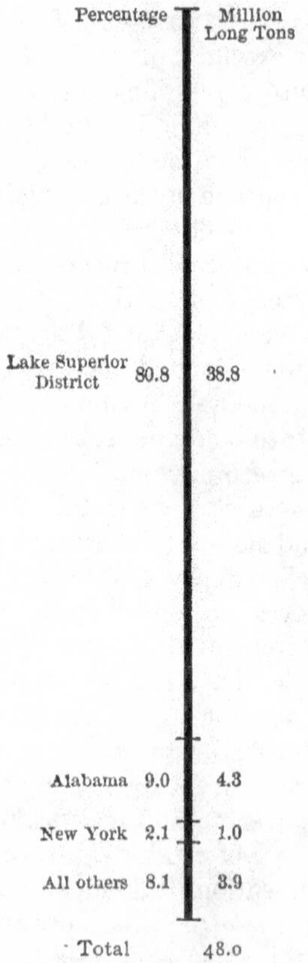

Various special steels, made by alloying iron with other substances than carbon, are produced in small quantity for special purposes, as nickel steel for armor plate, vanadium steel for automobiles, chrome and tungsten steel for the cutting parts of machine tools. Through this superior cutting quality a few hundred tons of tool steel have multiplied several fold the efficiency of thousands of machines and machinists.

Iron as a world industry.—Extensive iron making is an industry of countries advanced in manufacturing. It requires excellent transportation facilities, many laborers, much capital to build and operate the enormous plants, and the large market which only a vast population can give. It very distinctly is *not* a frontier industry, and this is just as true in the new states of the United States as it is in Australasia or South America. As a result, six countries dominate the iron making of the world, and three of these are of distinctly minor importance (Fig. 85). The United States, Great Britain, and Germany make four-fifths of the world's supply (Fig. 85); Belgium, France, and Russia are the next group, and after they have been named, there is little left of the world's iron industry as at present developed. South America, Africa, Asia, Australia, the East Indies, all the islands of the sea, and all the countries of the Mediterranean do not together make as much iron as a single Pittsburgh

	Percentage	Million Long Tons
Lake Superior District	80.8	38.8
Alabama	9.0	4.3
New York	2.1	1.0
All others	8.1	3.9
Total		48.0

FIG. 86.—U. S. iron-ore production, three-year average, 1908–10.

company, though nearly all of these countries have large quantities of ore.

World commerce in iron.—While the large production of iron is localized in a few districts of eastern America and western Europe, its commerce is world wide. All peoples who trade use it in many forms, so that from England, Germany, France, and the United States the manufactured products go to every country. The European countries, with their older industries and their cheaper labor, produce the more highly manufactured forms such as cutlery,

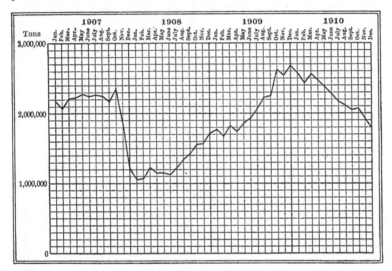

FIG. 87.—Production of pig iron in United States by months, 1907-10. (Iron Trade Review.)   The iron industry is called the Industrial Barometer. What is the percentage of variation?

tools, instruments, and the finest machinery. From the United States, which excels in raw materials and labor-saving machinery, the heavier products are shipped, such as railroad rails, bridges, girders, plates, and pipe. Pittsburgh rails and bridges are to be found upon the railways of Mexico, and Manchuria, on the upper Nile at Khartum, upon the African lakes in Uganda, in Australia, in Japan, and in Ecuador. The steel mills of Europe and America will continue for many decades to equip the new countries of the world.

The future of the iron industry.—Despite the many shiftings of the iron industry it has as yet used but a small fraction of the total ore-supply. The amount of ore throughout the world is very great, some of it being of good quality, but much the greater quantity is of relatively low grade such as we have not as yet learned to use because we have not as yet been compelled to do so. The iron industry, being comparatively young, has thus far drawn only upon the best ores.

Ocean steamers now render such cheap service that the ores near the coast of distant lands such as Central America, Brazil, South Africa and Sweden are in terms of freight rate much nearer to the furnaces of Pittsburgh or Baltimore than are the ores of Colorado. Thus the Sparrows Point smelters of Baltimore bring much of their ore from Cuba, although the Lake Superior mines are only two-thirds as far away. This condition makes a world supply of iron ore and indicates that the increasing American import of Swedish and Spanish ores is not an exception but part of a world movement. The United States Steel Corporation has purchased the famous iron mountain of Durango, Mexico, said to contain 300 million tons of iron. Six thousand miles by steamer and 1,000 miles by rail is not an over-expensive haul, and it is one that will make nearly all the earth accessible to one or the other of the great manufacturing regions of the future—the Orient or the North Atlantic.

The electric smelting of iron ore has long been experimented with and seems to have reached a profitable stage in Scandinavia where abundant waterpower is available for cheaply generating the powerful current. A ton of iron per year for each horse-power of electric energy is made at Jorpland, Norway, and this power costs but $6 at the waterpower plant. It is calculated that ores of only 40 per cent. purity can be utilized by the electric method. This possible emancipation of iron making from a fuel supply is a matter of great significance.

Copper and aluminum.—These metals are rapidly increasing in importance because of the many new uses to which invention subjects them. Bronze, an alloy composed of copper and tin, is a most durable metal prized alike by prehistoric and by modern man. A mixture of copper with zinc makes brass, but it is electricity and electrical manufactures which have made us so suddenly dependent upon these rarer metals. Fortunately we have increased our ability to get them.

Machines, power, explosives, chemical processes, and the large corporation have, within 50 years, transformed the winning of the less abundant metals to an extent comparable to the changes in the making of textiles. In some kinds of mining, operations are on a gigantic scale and the miner is no more of an industrial unit than the weaver. A recent mining enterprise in Nevada expended $20,000,000 in the purchase and equipment of two mines including 141 miles of railroad, a smelter, three towns, and a concentration plant to get copper, gold, and silver from a low-grade porphyry ore.

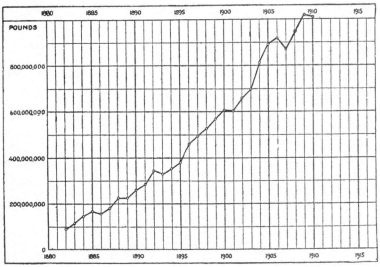

Fig. 88.—The production of copper in the United States from 1882 to 1910 (in pounds).

The production of copper approximately doubled between 1888 and 1898, and again in the succeeding decade—the total world production now being nearly 1 million tons a year (Fig 88). This increase in copper production is in response partly to the universal demand for copper in electrical work and partly to our ability to use low-grade ore due to the very rapid improvement in mechanical devices, and processes for the extraction of the metal. This source of increased supply is shown by the newly won ability to use large deposits of porphyry ores that are known to exist in Nevada, Arizona, Utah, and Queensland, but which were of no value at all a few years ago.

Constant discoveries of copper ore and new methods of smelting assure sufficient supplies for the immediate future.

The occurrence of copper.—Copper occurs in nature both as a metal and as an ore. It usually occurs in combination with many other substances. A single copper mine in Utah, for example, contains silver, gold, and iron. Other mines, especially in Colorado, have the copper in combination with silver and lead. Sulphur is one of the commonest substances with which copper occurs, and it is usually driven off by roasting the ore, which causes the sulphur to unite with oxygen of the air in the fire and pass off as sulphurous gases very injurious to the comfort of the people living in the vicinity, and destructive to the vegetation for miles around, as at Butte, Montana. The sulphur of these furnaces can be made into sulphuric acid at a cost, in Tennessee, of $2.25 per ton, but this manufacture was only begun under compulsion as a measure to protect vegetation and there is no market for it at Butte, despite its great importance in chemical manufacture.

The upper portion of Michigan was for many years the leading copper producer of the United States and of the world. In the old rocks of this glaciated district, there exists a large copper deposit, unusual in that some of it is pure. Here the copper occurs in nuggets, often of great size, and in small grains, scattered through the rock, which have to be crushed to release the metal. Easy transportation to this region by the Great Lakes caused early and profitable development of mining. Some of the mines are now a mile deep and their productivity is declining.

Due to the one great deposit in the hill at Butte, Montana has surpassed Michigan in output, to be in turn surpassed in 1910 by Arizona, on account of recently discovered deposits which now yield one-third of the American output. This metal is much more valuable per capita to the sparse population of Arizona than is wheat in North Dakota or iron in Pennsylvania.

Nevada and Utah are apparently just beginning as important copper producers. Recently found Nevada deposits of the newly conquered porphyry ore can be mined by steam shovels as are some Lake Superior iron ores.

Arizona copper fields are continued in the adjacent Mexican State of Sonora, where mining progress has been rapid, making Mexico the second copper-producing country.

The import of copper ores.—In addition to being the greatest producer of copper, the United States also smelts a great deal of copper ore produced in foreign lands. This is due partly to our great wealth in the necessary coal and also to the fact that from many sections ships returning, practically empty, can carry the ore cheaply. For these reasons, New York, Baltimore, Norfolk, and other coast cities smelt hundreds of thousands of tons of copper ore brought from Labrador, Newfoundland, Spain, Germany, Italy, Peru, Cuba, and Canada. Although the metal is destined for export, our copper imports are greater than the combined production of any two foreign countries.

Aluminum.—Aluminum is the newest of the important metals. It is especially attractive because of its lightness, toughness, and noncorrosiveness, being strong in qualities in which iron is weak. As one of the six commonest elements of the earth's crust, it exists in enormous quantities in the ordinary clay. Hence, great hopes for the future are entertained, but the extraction of the element in its metallic form is very difficult. In 1880 the price was $10 per pound and the world's production only 2 or 3 tons per year. In 1907, as a result of new processes of manufacture, its price fell to 42 cents per pound, and in 1909 to 22 cents, and the production now exceeds 20,000 tons a year. The manufacture is still costly. An aluminum plant at East St. Louis requires 1 ton of bauxite (aluminum ore), 1 ton of coal and 1 ton of very pure limestone to make half a ton of alumina (an oxide of aluminum). This requires further treatment in the electric furnace, a process requiring a large amount of electricity, by present practice about 1 horse-power for a day to produce a pound of aluminum. The world's aluminum is, therefore, made most easily where power is cheap, namely, the regions of great waterpower. Five companies working in Europe are located in the mountainous districts of Savoy, France (western Alps), of Germany, and of Italy. One of the American companies has plants at Niagara Falls, using 40,000 horse-power, others in Massena, New York (on the St. Lawrence), using 20,000 horse-power; and Shawinigan Falls, Canada, using 15,000 horse-power. With the reduced price, come new demands. For example, aluminum is an excellent transmitter of electricity; more efficient than copper. Now that copper and aluminum are not unlike in price, the possibility of competition at once appears. One aluminum electric transmission line 180 miles in length has already been erected in California. Automobile construction and aerial navigation open a new field for the lightest kind of strong construction, and give us greatly enhanced dependence upon the new metal. Probably the metal is most popularly used at the present time in the construction of camera bodies. New alloys are constantly discovered and each new alloy gives new uses.

QUESTIONS

1. How have inventions helped to concentrate and to scatter the iron industry? Give several examples.

2. Is Pittsburgh a better place than Cleveland for a new iron plant?

3. Why was Gary, Indiana, chosen as the site for the largest steel plant in the world?

4. What has been the influence of new alloys of iron?

5. How does it happen that the United States with the largest iron production of any country is also an ore importer?

6. Why is it that we are greater smelters of foreign copper ores than is Great Britain?

7. Why might Butte, Montana, be a good place to start an industry requiring sulphuric acid?

CHAPTER IX

THE FUNDAMENTALS OF MANUFACTURE. *C.* POWER

1. Coal

Importance of power to manufacturing.—In the development of manufactures iron is important, but the possession of some source of mechanical power is a much more potent factor in deciding a nation's rôle in manufacturing and in civilization, for the iron can be imported much more easily than the coal which has thus far been our chief dependence for power. We depend upon mechanical power in a way not unlike the dependence of young children upon their parents.

Our absolute dependence on coal.—If some wizard should, upon the first moment of an incoming year, banish all coal from the world, instant darkness would settle over the streets in most of the world's great cities and their inhabitants would rise the next morning to find their houses cold, and nearly all their factory wheels motionless. The starvation that immediately faced them would kill millions of people before another January first had come. Witness the plight of Belgium in the war, winter of 1914–15 (see appendix, table of food imports). England would be the worst sufferer, because coal-driven steamships and railroads bring to that country much of the food and raw materials upon which her people depend for sustenance and industry. There would be no escape from the panic-stricken island because the coal-driven steamships of the world would lie helpless, sailing vessels and oil burners would be grossly inadequate, and the building of more vessels would require iron and wood, neither of which could be had without the use of coal. The people of Germany, Holland, and Belgium, New England, and New York City (this city alone used over 15 million tons of coal in 1909) would be in nearly as bad a plight as those of England.

World commerce is now coal-driven commerce, and world manufacture is carried on chiefly in the steam-driven factory. Coal is thus back of both factors which have enabled man in the nineteenth and twentieth centuries to separate so widely his home space from his sustenance space. All the modern nations have at their disposal me-

169

chanical power, chiefly coal driven, which far outranks the combined muscular force of all their men and all their beasts, and the increase in its use is very rapid (see table, Appendix).

Late and rapid development of American coal mining.—During the first two-thirds of the nineteenth century, while England was busy manufacturing with coal, the people of the United States were chiefly employed in settling and farming the free lands of the Mississippi Valley which the United States Government was giving away to settlers. Our manufacturing industries started, before the improvement of the steam engine, in New England, where many streams tumbling down from the highlands made abundant waterfalls and good water power, as evidenced in the names of old New England mill towns, such as Fall River, Chicopee Falls, Rumford Falls, Bellows Falls, and many others. For domestic fuel the American people for two centuries burned wood, while England, old and relatively populous, had been short of forests in Queen Elizabeth's time and was using coal. In 1660 the British consumption was two-fifths of a ton per capita, a quantity not equaled in the United States until after 1850.

Coal mining in America was of slow growth. As late as 1820, Pennsylvania anthracite had a production of but a ton a day. But these deposits served as a magnet to attract the pioneers at both canal and railroad building, a highway of each type being built up the Schuylkill River from Philadelphia to the southern edge of the coal fields. Owing to the improvement in transportation facilities our coal consumption increased rapidly after 1850. The per capita consumption in 1850 was 0.287 ton, in 1870, 0.960 ton, in 1900, 3.530 tons, in 1910, 5.100 tons, or over 25 pounds per day for every man, woman and child in the United States (see Fig. 90).

The influence of coal on the settlement of America.—It was coal and steam that enabled the American people to finish the conquest of the American continent. In the two centuries between the founding of Jamestown and the marketing of coal in Pennsylvania, the colonists had slowly struggled westward through the forests and mountains and settled the river districts of western Pennsylvania, Kentucky, and Ohio, but the conditions of transportation in the West were such that no populous commonwealth could arise (Fig. 89). Exports of grain and meat and a little lumber went to New Orleans down the Ohio and Mississippi Rivers in flat boats, which were knocked to pieces because they could not be pushed up stream against the swift current. Imports were brought in wagons over the Allegheny mountains to Pittsburgh and thence down stream to the points where they were consumed. Economic and social progress was difficult under such conditions. In 1812 the steamboat changed all this by ascending the Mississippi River and making a two-sided commerce.

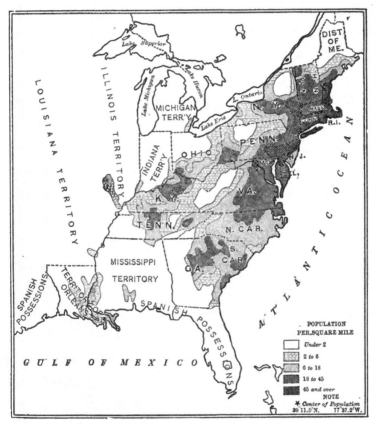

FIG. 89.—Distribution of population in the United States, 1810, before the age of railway transportation.

It enabled American people emigrating by the power of steam to attack the heart of the continent in a hundred places on the great navigable system of the Mississippi between Pittsburgh, Kansas City, Minneapolis, and up-stream points on many smaller rivers. Two

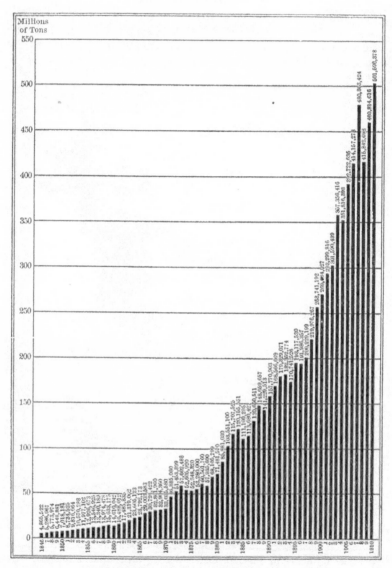

FIG. 90.—Production of coal in United States 1846-1910, a rate of increase that can not and should not be maintained.

decades later the steam-driven locomotive broke the shackles that had for ages held civilized man by the river bank and seashore, so that in half a century the American people spread five times as far as they had in the two preceding centuries.

Pennsylvania anthracite.—The first coal to be extensively developed was in the anthracite fields of eastern Pennsylvania (Fig. 91), which have the best coal in America. In this region we have now an annual production of nearly 1 ton of this valuable coal per capita for all the population of the country. Thus the supply is being rapidly reduced. The scattering remnants of a deposit once of

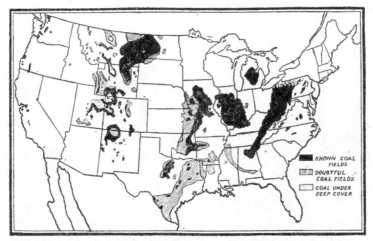

FIG. 91.—Map showing general distribution of coal fields in the United States. (U. S. Geol. Surv.)   (From Salisbury, Barrows, and Tower.)

greater area are divided into three fields covering an area of but 475 square miles with the cities of Scranton, Wilkesbarre, Pottsville, and Shamokin as the chief mining centers (Fig. 92).

The Appalachian bituminous coal field.—The Appalachian coal field (Fig. 91), reaching almost without a break from northern Pennsylvania into northern Alabama, contains the finest bituminous coal lands in the world (see Fig. 91, Coal Map of the United States). The coal area in western Pennsylvania alone is larger than Massachusetts, Rhode Island, and Delaware combined. Ohio River nagivation opened this rich fuel deposit to the world and caused many new

towns to spring up in the wilderness to shelter the miners. Pittsburgh, standing where the navigable Ohio was formed by two navigable branches, was the most convenient point of access to this coal
field and the natural place for its earliest development. Each
year acres and acres of barges of Pennsylvania coal float down

FIG. 92.—A large building is required to prepare anthracite coal for market and
the earth is encumbered with refuse. Eastern Pennsylvania.

the Ohio and Mississippi, carrying millions of tons to Cincinnati,
New Orleans and other cities along the great waterway.

The central part of this Appalachian coal field in West Virginia,
eastern Kentucky, Tennessee and part of Virginia was not developed
so early because it was more difficult of access. At the present time
there are in eastern Kentucky 10,000 square miles of this Allegheny
plateau underlaid with coal. But this plateau has been carved by

its many streams into a succession of steep mountains and sharp gorges, which are so difficult to travel that there is no railroad, and therefore no commercial coal mining. The people thus isolated are living the life of the pioneers and backwoodsmen of the Revolutionary period.

No more striking illustrations of the dependence of progress and welfare upon transportation facilities can well be found than the contrast between the poverty and ignorance of these isolated

FIG. 93.—Coal tipple, beehive coke ovens (right center) and miners' village in bituminous field, West Virginia. (Philadelphia Museum.)

mountain people and the prosperity and progress of their kinsmen and neighbors upon the lowlands beyond the mountains.

West Virginia, not so inaccessible as Kentucky, but far less accessible than the Pittsburgh district, now has, as a result of recent railroad building, a rapidly increasing coal output. The West Virginia coal fields are difficult for railroads to cross and the valleys are so narrow that the houses of the mining towns are perched row after row upon the steep slopes that rise directly from the streams (Fig. 93).

The southernmost of these eastern coal fields is in Alabama near

Birmingham (Fig. 94). It is very accessible to adjacent markets and hence has greater development than any field south of West Virginia. The recent building of locks and dams in the Warrior River, which permits the carriage of this coal in boats to Mobile for the supply of steamships and for export to Gulf and Caribbean ports, greatly increases the opportunity of this district for profitable development.

Pennsylvania bituminous coal was worth but $2.50 per ton at New York Harbor in 1909, and Virginia Pocahontas (used by the United States Navy because it is one of the best steam coals in the world) was $2.15 per ton at Hampton Roads. Atlantic coast cities thus

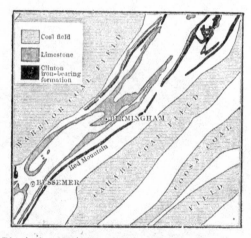

FIG. 94.—Birmingham District, Alabama, showing a relation of iron ore, coal and limestone which permits the cheapest iron manufacture in the world, about ⅓ of a cent. per pound. (Map after Brigham.)

have a very cheap fuel supply in the Virginia coal brought to tidewater by the Virginian railway and taken to New England by boat from Hampton Roads for sixty cents per ton in competition with coal taken from Philadelphia and New York by all rail shipments.

The interior coal fields of America.—The eastern interior field (see Figs. 91, 95, 96), southern Illinois, southern Indiana and western Kentucky, is second in importance only to that at the headwaters of the Ohio. The coal (bituminous) is not of as good quality as that of the Appalachian fields, but its nearness to Chicago, St. Louis, and the many manufacturing centers of the North Central States makes it the chief dependence of those regions and the output is greater than that of Pennsylvania anthracite.

It is an interesting fact that the quality of American coal declines

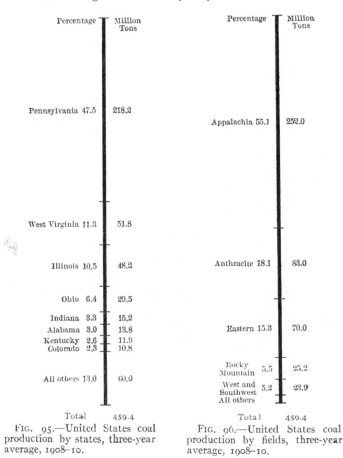

Percentage		Million Tons
Pennsylvania 47.5		218.2
West Virginia 11.3		51.8
Illinois 10,5		48.2
Ohio 6.4		29.5
Indiana 3.3		15.2
Alabama 3.0		13.8
Kentucky 2,6		11.9
Colorado 2,3		10.8
All others 13.0		60.0

Total   459.4

FIG. 95.—United States coal production by states, three-year average, 1908–10.

Percentage		Million Tons
Appalachia 55.1		252.0
Anthracite 18.1		83.0
Eastern 15.3		70.0
Rocky Mountain 5,5		25.2
West and Southwest 5,2		23.9
All others		

Total   459.4

FIG. 96.—United States coal production by fields, three-year average, 1908–10.

as we go west until the Rocky Mountains are reached.   The large western interior and southwestern fields, extending from central Iowa to central Texas, are inferior to those of Illinois and Indiana and are not so extensively mined.   Beyond these the yet inferior coal that underlies vast areas of the plains of Dakota, Montana and Wyoming is mined only for local use. The Rocky Mountains, embracing with their adjacent plateaus almost one-fourth of the United States, are a region of such sparse population and vast extent that their resources are not fully explored. Each year the scientists of the Geological Survey find thousands of square miles of additional coal, and it is already known to exist in every state from New Mexico to

Fig. 97.—Man standing in front of coal seam outcrop in banks of Yellowstone River, Montana. Blocks of fallen coal in foreground. In some parts of the West, farmers go to such banks and load their wagons. (Campbell, U. S. Geol. Surv.) Man is ½ inch from left margin of picture, feet, arm, and hat most visible.

the Canadian boundary (Fig. 97). The total quantity is doubtless very great and some of it is anthracite of good quality. Much of this western coal land still belongs to the United States Government, and should be held as a reserve for the future needs of the nation. It is hoped that it will make comfort for all the people rather than colossal fortunes for a few and misery for many. It can be leased to mining companies by the Government quite as easily and more satisfactorily than the present practice of leasing coal lands by individuals to mining companies.

The Pacific coast and Alaska.—The Pacific coast is the only part of the United States which suffers from lack of coal. For this reason the development of manufactures was greatly hampered in California, until the discovery of petroleum in large quantities in 1901 ended this fuel scarcity for a time.

Our incomplete knowledge of Alaska is being rapidly extended, and one of the surprises of this erstwhile little-esteemed region is its valuable deposits of coal and copper. This source of supply, inaccessible at the present time, is likely to prove a boon to future generations if not developed at once by the government railway already provided for.

American commerce in coal.—Despite our enormous coal resources and world-surpassing production, the coal export of the United States is relatively insignificant, because the coal carrying vessels can get no return cargoes. Nearly all of it goes to Canada, but small amounts are sent to Mexico, Cuba and the West Indies. Regular lines of vessels have long carried coal from Norfolk to Tampico for the supply of the Mexican railroads and mines.

The small export should not for an instant cause one to lose sight of the enormous part that coal plays in American railroad traffic. The entire wheat crop of the United States does not weigh half as much as the coal produced in Illinois or West Virginia. The entire cotton crop of the United States only weighs a quarter as much as the coal product of Alabama and only an eighth as much as the coal imports of New England.

Most of the present transportation of coal is entirely unnecessary. Central power plants at the mine mouth could generate power quite as cheaply as in more expensive town locations. Experience has shown that power can be transmitted at least 200 miles in the form of electricity, at a very low cost. Most of the people and most of the cities of the United States are now within that distance of coal mines. We need transmission wires and gas mains to replace freight trains, thus saving much unnecessary and expensive handling, as well as the fuel used by the engines now hauling the needless coal trains.

America, the richest nation.—The coal resources of the United States are much greater than those of Europe. Coal underlies nearly one-sixth of the area of this entire country, over 400,000 square miles, Russia has only 20,000 square miles and the United

Kingdom but 11,900. Germany, with less than 2,000 square miles, is, next to England, the greatest European producer, because Germany has within the last 40 years had an enormous development of manufacturing that requires coal. China is our nearest rival in coal riches.

Methods of mining coal.—The methods of mining coal vary greatly. In western Pennsylvania and West Virginia the coal lies in a high plateau through which the streams have cut valleys so that the

Fig. 98.—The little mine car brings the coal to the wasteful beehive ovens and the box car carries away the coke. Western Pennsylvania.

coal outcrops on the hillsides, making the entrance to the mines exceedingly easy (Fig. 97, Coal Seam on Hillside). Pennsylvania anthracite lies in the folded and bent strata of mountains, the pressure of mountain-making having turned the coal to anthracite or hard coal. It may outcrop in some places, as at Hazleton, so that it can be quarried from the surface. Nearby it is buried 3,000 ft. in the ground, requiring deep shafts which go below the level of the sea and involve much moving of rock, pumping of water and lifting of coal.   Anthracite coal also requires much sorting, cleaning, and preparing to get it clear of the shale.

The mines west of the Appalachians are mainly shaft mines of no great depth; those of Europe are almost universally deep, some of the shafts descending nearly a mile into the earth.

Coal utilization.—The ordinary methods of using coal as fuel in grates and furnaces are very wasteful, as much, of the heat value of the coal goes off up the smokestack, unused, in the form of gas and smoke.   In gas making much waste often occurs in similar ways, ard

FIG. 99.—Power plant where mechanical devices **carry** coal from car to furnace, feed the furnace, and load the ashes on the cars.

many valuable by-products are often allowed to run to waste for lack of suitable means for their recovery, but recent improvements in furnaces, smoke consumers **and** especially in gas engines, the most economical form of power generation, and a new process of making the gas called producer gas, promise to be revolutionary in increasing the usefulness and life of our coal deposits.   The producer gas plant can get the combustible carbon in the form of gas from any of our coals, even from Texas lignite, or from peat itself, from wood, from tan bark refuse, and even from dried sewage, although these latter have not yet been used on a commercial scale. This process of using low-grade fuels offers great power possibilities to many lands poor in coal but rich in peat, such as Ireland, where one-fifth of the surface is covered with peat bogs. Peat also covers large areas in Scotland, Sweden, Denmark, Russia, Canada, and New England.

The recently perfected process of briquetting enables the use, as fuel, of coal dust and fine fragments which would otherwise have to be discarded as mine refuse. Briquettes are compressed lumps of coal made by mixing small particles of coal with some adhesive material and pressing it in moulds so that it holds its shape until burned. In Germany 17 to 18 million tons of briquettes are made annually, while the industry is only getting started in the United States after many years of trial. It should enable us to save millions of tons of coal now wasted.

Coke, gas, and gas by-products.—Iron making requires the use of coke. Coke is made by heating coal in closed retorts where the gas and liquid matter are driven off as vapor and the coke is left in big lumps that are harder than the coal itself and therefore hold up the burden of the ore so that the fire in the blast furnace does not smother. By the old coke methods, the coal was roasted in simple "beehives" or conical kilns of brick (Fig. 98), and the gas and liquids were usually allowed to escape as undesirable refuse. The modern "by-product plants" are elaborate and expensive but they quickly pay for themselves by converting this refuse matter into a great variety of useful and valuable products. In coke-making sometimes as much as 10,000 cubic feet of gas per ton of coal may be entirely wasted by the old-fashioned beehive oven, or saved by an improved by-product coke oven. The purification of the gas from the by-product coke oven and also from the producer gas plant gives several pounds of crystallized ammonia and several gallons of tar per ton of coal. The ammonia is a valuable fertilizer; the tar is used for roofs and roads besides furnishing a host of chemicals and dyes.

The Germans, scientific, thrifty, and poor in coal, lead the world in the manufacture of by-product coke, coal-tar by-products and gas engines. Meanwhile we in America are wasting fuel in the old-fashioned beehive coke plant, in wasteful steam engines and in wasteful mining. These facts in combination with the rapid increase of manufacture and commerce are causing some alarm for fear of the exhaustion of our coal resources at a much earlier time than we previously thought possible. The price of coal is rising and must continue to rise. This turns our attention again toward substitutes, of which the chief are water-power and petroleum, now both.in active competition with coal. Of these, the oil may have an advantage of cheapness while it lasts, but all the minerals are at best an accumulation soon robbed and are but ephemeral in comparison to water-power which, depending upon the sun, the sea, and the high lands, remains an enduring source of power while climate and land endure.

An example of this competition between the coal mine and the waterfall comes from the Rocky Mountains.

On the extension of the Chicago, Milwaukee and St. Paul railroad to Puget Sound, the many waterfalls combined with the long and heavy haul necessary to provide coal for locomotives, have led to the great undertaking of installing electric power on the entire system over the mountains. This work is in progress (1914) and if successful, may revolutionize railroad engineering wherever water-power is available. The initial cost of such equipment is enormous, but there can be no doubt of its final advantage over coal.

2. WATER-POWER

Water-power resources.—The water-power resources of a country are chiefly its lakes and its streams. These are affected by many circumstances. For the best results in developing water-power a stream must have water enough and fall enough to turn the heavy waterwheels, and most important of all, the flow of water must be constant (Figs. 100, 103, 104). The seasonal distribution of the rainfall may give 3 months' flood and 6 months' drought in which torrents become, at times, dry stream beds, a condition found in monsoon countries and regions where the Mediterranean type of climate prevails. Here water-power plants may be idle a large part of the year unless there is some kind of water storage to supply the necessary uniform flow.

The water runs away more quickly from hilly than from level land. Even where the rainfall is well distributed throughout the year, there is, in small short streams, a great variation in volume because of the quick running off of the water after rain. A large river system tends to even up these inequalities.

A most important factor affecting water-power value of a given rainfall is some form of natural water storage. The spongy leaf mass of the forest floor holds water and makes more even stream

flow and better water-power on the forest stream than is furnished
by one draining tilled lands. Swamps and marshes are better yet,
and lakes are the best of all for natural water storage. Man improves streams by building dams to hold the water, but the
natural reservoirs of lakes are many fold better; they hold waters
that would otherwise be wasted in freshets, and let it out in time of
drought. As most of the world's lakes are due to the work of
glaciers, the fact that an elevated region has been glaciated is,

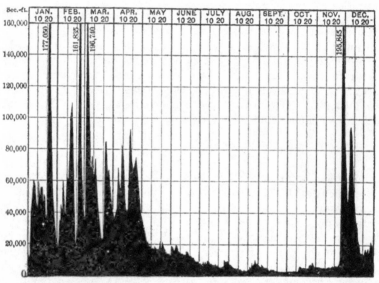

Fig. 100.—Discharge of water in 1900 from the Susquehanna at Harrisburg, a river
with a practically lakeless basin with much steep land. (U. S. Geol. Surv.)

granted rainfall, the most important thing in deciding the worth of
its water-power resources (Figs. 103, 104). Thus the Niagara
River with its wonderful natural reservoirs varies but 35 per
cent in volume, while the lakeless Potomac varies according to the
amount of rainfall from 1,000 to 250,000 cubic feet per second.

Snow fields and glaciers are second to lakes as natural reservoirs
and they have the particular advantage of releasing the water in time
of summer drought, and holding it tight in a period of excessive winter
precipitation. These factors, combining with a heavy rainfall and
the high Coast Range, Cascades and Sierra Mountains, give the

Pacific coast states nearly half the water-power resources of the United States.

The use of water-power.—The use of water-power has had its ups and downs, depending on industrial conditions and inventions. It was a factor of great importance in the American Colonies, furnishing as it did a means to grind flour and saw lumber. The old-fashioned overshot water-wheels (Fig. 101) so common in 1800 were largely dis-

Fig. 101.—Abandoned grist mill in Tennessee.   Old-fashioned overshot water-wheel, cornfield in background.

placed in the latter half of the nineteenth century by improved steam engines and cheap coal[1]. But water-power is again coming into use since the invention of the new turbine and **Pelton** water-wheels, and the ability to transmit power in form of electricity many miles to a convenient place of consumption. The easy construction, effectiveness, and permanence of well-built cement dams (Figs. 102,

[1] Small country mills were abandoned by the thousand as a result of this change.

105) are factors whose influence in water-power installation is just beginning to be felt.   This influence alone is enough to give us a new epoch.   Since 1890 the use of water-power has increased both in absolute amount and in proportion to coal-derived power.   An excellent example of this new competition of water-power with coal is to be found in Pennsylvania, the greatest coal-producing state in the world.   The Susquehanna River, whose tributaries drain two great and active coal fields, is harnessed by an enormous dam at

Fig. 102.—Concrete dam built in sections across Susquehanna River, Mc-Calls Ferry, Pa.   Power-house and forebay at the right.   Tail race sheltered behind island to left.   200,000 horse-power within reach of Baltimore, Philadelphia and Washington.   (Penna. Water & Power Co.)

McCall's Ferry, near the Maryland boundary (Fig. 102).   The power can easily be sold as far away as Philadelphia and Baltimore, in which latter city it runs the street cars.   This dam is merely one of many that might be built on this river.   Even the navigable Mississippi has been dammed at Keokuk, Iowa, where 200,000 horse-power will be developed while boats pass through locks beside the dam.

If we take a long point of view, the water-power of the glaciated region of northeastern United States (Fig. 103) is likely to have a much greater value than all the coal of Pennsylvania. Coal will go and the water-power will stay. The best example of this is to be seen at Niagara Falls, where the glaciers diverted a single stream across a cliff of rock, forming the Falls which will develop about 7 million

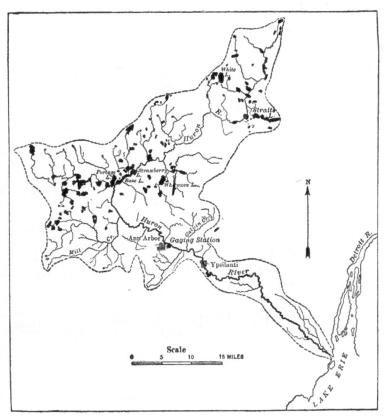

FIG. 103.—Basin of Huron River showing the natural reservoirs afforded by glacial lakes. (Newell.)

horse-power day and night if they are fully utilized. Hundreds of smaller falls combined have a greater power than even Niagara and many of them are already in use, as in the wood pulp and paper industry which is scattered from Niagara Falls to eastern Maine. It was this glacial water-power which started New England manufacturing. The state of Maine itself is said to have waterfalls that will yield a possible total of 6 million horse-power, that is, about 40 horse-power for every family in the state. In addition to this we are just learning how to utilize the energy of tides from which it is estimated that a half million horse-power may be developed on the coast of Maine.

New York state is about to begin making a series of state-owned reservoirs on the headwaters of some streams from which stored

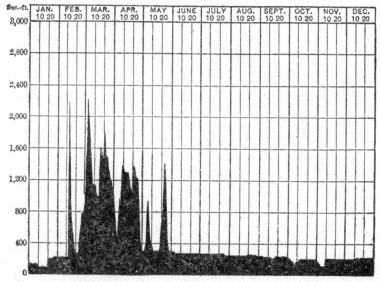

Fig. 104.—Discharge of water in 1900 from the Cobosseecontee, a river drain-ing many lakes in the Maine woods. (U. S. Geol. Surv.) The attempt to make a river discharge a uniform stream is one of man's supreme combats with the uncertainty of deadly nature. Compare the per cent. of variation of this stream with that of the Susquehanna (Fig. 100).

water will be released to be used many times as it passes through a succession of water-wheels on its way down to navigable water levels.

A few of the waterfalls of the Sierra Nevada mountains in California are already harnessed, power being carried sometimes as much as 200 miles to serve California cities, the water that produces it going on down to raise crops by irrigation on the lowlands. Water-power is particularly valuable in these states because of the absence of coal, and it is being utilized rapidly.

The competition of water-power with coal has in some places, such as California, been suddenly interrupted by the gushing wells of petroleum. There has been a sudden and great increase in the production of this mineral fuel, along with increased knowledge as to means of utilizing it efficiently. New engines of the Diesel type

Fig. 105.—Modern hydro-electric power plant, Cazadero, Oregon. Cement dam, steel tube penstocks. Type of construction for high fall. (From Power Development by F. Koester.)

developed in Germany promise to permit petroleum to replace even producer gas. Such a change may give somewhat cheaper power to a generation or two of men; but it is likely to deprive future generations of the irreplaceable petroleum of which our supply is much more limited than that of coal. Since nothing now in sight can replace it in many of its uses, particularly for lubrication, this new means of using petroleum is of questionable benefit to the race. The sudden new onslaught on petroleum as a source of power comes at the end of half a century **during** which this wonderful fluid has been of service in other capacities, chiefly as a source of light.

3. PETROLEUM

The use of petroleum.—Petroleum has helped greatly in spreading civilization over the world. All the world loves light, which is so

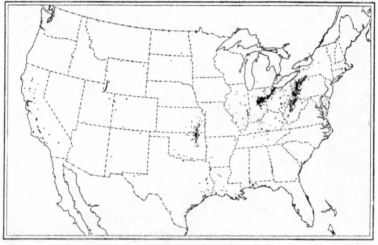

FIG. 106.—Map showing general distribution of petroleum and natural gas fields of United States. (Day, U. S. Geol. Surv.) (From Salisbury, Barrows, and Tower.)

necessary for the reading habit and the spread of civilization, and kerosene made from petroleum is, in every continent, the most common illuminant for the family lamp. The lighter parts of the oil serve for illumination. The heavier parts oil the wheels of the world's machinery, and the process of refining breaks it up into a surprising number of by-products.

Petroleum collects deep down in the earth, especially in porous sandstones, with water and natural gas, the gas, being lightest, on the top, the oil next, and the water at the bottom. When the boring machine breaks the impervious cap that seals the oil sands, the oil

Triplane.

Petroleum serves to show us how very new indeed is the world in which we live and try to do our thinking. It also shows us how our thinking is changed by mechanical, industrial, or economic things. In 1859, petroleum was gathered in blankets as it floated on the surface of oily springs, was squeezed out, and sold in bottles as a kind of cure-all ointment. Fifty-five years later it had given rise to one of our greatest industries, one of our best-known industries, and it had made the Great War different from all other wars. Three new things, each in itself revolutionary in the art of war, depended upon petroleum. These were the airplane, the submarine, and the motor truck. The Allies planned to deluge Germany with explosives in the year 1919, with the aid of multitudes of airplanes from American factories. The winning of the war before this happened was due in a large part to the Allied superiority in motor truck transportation.

We can see how oil has changed our thinking when we note how the submarine changed all ideas of international law, brought America into the war, and brought mankind to the serious consideration of that dream of many ages, a League of Nations.

We can see how petroleum has changed the daily life of nations when we think of the service that millions of automobiles and motor trucks now render to the people of America and of Europe, and how much more they will render in a few more years when they have been made cheaper and better, and placed within the reach of almost every normal family that is willing to work and save.

The gas engine has become a part of ordinary farm machinery until it is found today on millions of farms, and it is not at all unusual for a farm to have two or three of them.

All of these uses raise this vital question. Will the supply of petroleum for gasoline last? The answer is short. It cannot. (See graph of petroleum production.)

Two reserves, however, stand between us and alcohol. One is oil shale. It exists in great quantities in the Rocky Mountain region, and from it petroleum

Submarines.

can be obtained at a somewhat greater cost than we now get it from wells.   The other reserve is benzole, of which every ton of soft coal can be made to produce several gallons, along with ammonia and gas, by a new process of heating it before it is finally burned as soft coke.

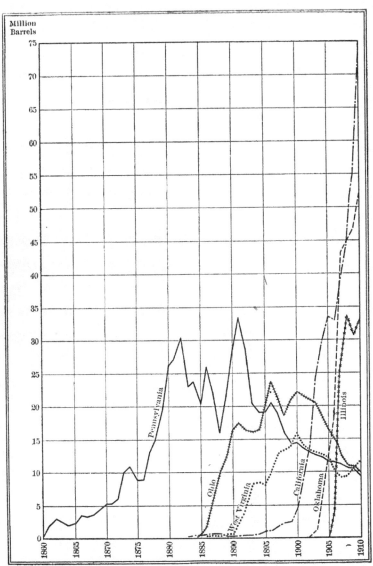

FIG. 107.—Petroleum production of leading states, 1860-1910 (barrels of 42 gallons). (U. S. Geol. Surv.) Petroleum is a meteoric industry. Note the changes in leadership.

gushes from the earth, due to the great pressure of the gas imprisoned
with it. This sends the oil forth as soda water blows itself from a
bottle.

The American oil fields.—American prominence in oil production
has been due in part to the fact that it was first discovered and developed here, but more especially to the discovery of field after field, a
process which may give us abundant oil for several decades or possibly generations. The oldest American oil field, runs from southeastern New York, southwest through western Pennsylvania, southeastern Ohio, and the adjacent parts of West Virginia (Fig. 106), a

FIG. 108.—Oil well, derricks and pipes discharging crude petroleum into a pool
containing many thousand barrels, Muskogee, Okla. (Standard Oil Co.) This
wasteful method is often necessary where every land owner works wildly to dig
wells on his land, and the wells gush (20,000 to 60,000 barrels per day), so much that
even pipes cannot carry it away.

territory 160 miles long and from 25 to 40 miles in width. Within
40 years after the discovery of the first well, this field had 20,000
deep wells and 4,000 miles of pipe line to collect the oil in storage
tanks and carry it to refineries. Large towns bearing such suggestive
names as Oil City, Olean, Petrolia had from small beginnings grown
large, rich, and prosperous. But oil prosperity is like a mushroom,
so short is the life of the fields (Fig. 108). The ephemeral nature
of the oil industry is well shown in the case of Texas, which produced
4 million barrels in 1910, 28 million in 1905, and 9 million in 1909.
Different states succeed each other rapidly in the position of first
place, and, following the decline of output, comes the emigration of

population, and the dilapidation and decay of temporary structures which mark the worn-out oil fields with desolation (Fig. 107).

The second discovery of importance in the United States was the Ohio-Indiana field, which crosses the northern part of the boundary between these two states with its center in Lima, Ohio. Then the first decade of the twentieth century witnessed a number of discoveries; in 1901 the Beaumont field in southeastern Texas; then came California, which in a short time surpassed in production all older states, to be in turn suddenly rivaled by the new fields in Kansas (see Fig. 107), Oklahoma, and Illinois, while in northern Mexico a still more spectacular field was almost immediately discovered (see chap. on Mexico). The first California oil field, located in the southwestern part of the state, practically underlies the city of Los Angeles where back yards bristled with wells and derricks. Some wells were even sunk in the Pacific to strike the oilbearing rocks beneath the waters (Fig. 109). The chief fields of California are in the southern part of the Great Valley. California oil is of especial value to the State because it is a heavy oil good for fuel purposes in a region surprisingly devoid of other forms of fuel.

Transportation of petroleum.—The fact that petroleum products are used in almost all countries and exported from so few necessitates large transportation. The problem of handling this inflammable fuel has been difficult. At first, barrels were used, then came iron tank railway cars, and lastly pipe lines where the traffic is great. Iron pipes 3 to 6 inches in diameter are laid over long distances to connect oil fields with great markets and ports of shipment. Thus Oklahoma oil is now piped to the Gulf Coast or to St. Louis, Chicago, Philadelphia, and New York. The recent large production of the California fields has resulted in several pipe lines from the wells to the Pacific coast. The natural accompaniment of the pipe line is the tank steamer, holding hundreds of thousands of gallons and loaded by merely letting the liquid flow in from the pipes. Such vessels connect with the pipe line at Port Arthur, Texas, and carry crude petroleum to the refiners of England, France, and Spain, as well as New York and Philadelphia.

Petroleum as a source of power.—The first great use of petroleum was for illuminating oil and then for lubrication, but with the opening of the twentieth century it has rapidly increased in use as a source of power. First came the engine run by gasolene, one of the petroleum products, now so important in the automobile. Then came the

FIG. 109.—A California oil field, Summerland. Calif. (Southern Pacific Railway). This multitude of wells on town lots where a few wells would have secured all the oil is one of the reasons favoring the leasing of oil lands by the government in the interest of conservation.

use of crude petroleum as ordinary boiler fuel. This has had its chief use in ships where oil tanks take up less space than coal bunkers and the crew can be reduced because the flowing of the liquid replaces the labor of coal passers.

Oil is also a good locomotive fuel, and as the great oil fields of Oklahoma and California are at the ends of a region where coal is scarce, the cheap oil of the new fields was quickly utilized by the railroads. It now drives the locomotives on 17,000 miles of railway between the Gulf of Mexico, Oklahoma, Utah and California.

The third and newest use of petroleum as a source of power is in the German invention of the Diesel engine, an internal combustion gas engine which has the great advantage (in cost) of being able to use the crude petroleum as it comes from the earth. It is so efficient that a gallon of oil costing from 2 to 5 cents will develop 15 horse-power hours. This invention promises to make oil a great power fuel while the present cheap oil lasts. In Germany this engine is also being used to develop power from tar oil derived from the tar produced by the by-product coke ovens and the producer gas plants.

Natural gas.—Natural gas, the most volatile of the petroleum products, is the best and most convenient of all fuels, the cheapest and most convenient of all sources of power. It separates itself from the oil as cream separates from milk, but it accompanies the oil in practically all fields. The greater part of this gas, which is richer in heat than that manufactured from coal at so much expense in most cities, has been wasted, owing to the heedlessness of man in failing to provide proper means for preventing its escape; and to the inherent difficulties of handling the problems presented by a new and untried industry. To properly control the industry so as to prevent this needless waste is a problem that must be handled by legislation. The conservation of petroleum and natural gas is a peculiarly difficult problem where every one owning as much as a back yard is free to dig a deep hole in the earth and let them run out. Thus the desire to get some oil causes every land owner to dig a well. Thus twenty wells (at $15.000 each) may be dug where one would get all the oil. In 1910, the gas thus going to waste from oil wells in the United States was probably worth at city prices over half a million dollars a day. In the American oil fields this gas has been of very great industrial importance in the iron and glass industries as boiler fuel and as city gas. It has been piped to many towns and cities outside the regions of its production. Most unfortunately the life of the gas well

is short and the supply is exhausted in a few decades, but it furnishes
an astonishingly cheap fuel while it lasts. It is often sold as low as
10 cents per thousand cubic feet. This resource has been the fourth
element in making western Pennsylvania more liberally supplied with
fuel than any other place in the world. In that region a thick forest
covered the hills which were underlaid with the magnificent coal deposits of the Appalachian field, while further down was crude petroleum, and the natural gas that drove it spurting from the orifices in
the rocks. The gas from this field is now about exhausted, the forest
is practically gone, the oil output has greatly declined, the coal is being rapidly used up, and scenes of desolation face the traveler. No
wonder the American people are beginning to consider the question
of the conservation of natural resources.

Refining of petroleum.—Crude petroleum is very complex chemically and the process of refining consists of distillation. Every
year many new commercial products are being separated from it.
Among them are many kinds of oil from light naphtha to heavy
paraffine oils, wax, paraffine, tar, and finally coke. Each product is
capable of separation into others by redistillation, some of the products being vaseline and other ointments and drugs, so that altogether the modern petroleum refinery sells, in addition to kerosene,
several hundred by-products, including tar which may be made into
thousands of aniline dyes. Thus we see why the refinery must be
a large plant.

Our foreign trade in petroleum.—The American trade in petroleum
products is as wide as the world. Our oil makes better illuminating
oil than that of Russia, and is sent, in the crude form, to some of the
more important countries, while in the form of kerosene or refined
petroleum for lamps it is distributed more universally than any other
product of American export. It goes alike to Greenland and New
Zealand, Norway and to the tribesmen in Italian East Africa. The
ordinary 5-gallon cans of American refined oil are distributed throughout the interior of China in places where the face of the white man
has never been seen. In 1910 the export of illuminating oil was about
a billion gallons and that of lubricating oil and crude oil each about
a sixth as much.

Considering the United States as a whole, it is a country with excellent equipment for manufacturing. Our resources of coal, iron,
water-power, petroleum, food, and wood (see next chapter) are unexcelled. Yet the very abundance of our land and land resources

serve as a drawback to the development of manufacture because of the opportunity they give for alternative employment.

QUESTIONS

1. How has the invention of producer gas been a relatively greater possible benefit to Dakota than to Pennsylvania?

2. Explain why an American coal miner gets out more coal per year than a miner in Europe?

3. How does it happen that water-power has varied so in importance in the United States?

4. Which is more valuable, the water-power of New England or the coal of Pennsylvania? Give reason.

5. Why is it more difficult with our present land laws to prevent waste in winning oil than coal?

6. Give some reasons why water-power is likely to increase as a source of power even where coal is available.

7. How is it possible to utilize water-power even at a considerable distance from its source.

8. Give some reasons why crude oil is shipped to European refineries rather than first refined and then shipped to Europe. On the other hand why is the refined product shipped to such countries as New Zealand, Greenland, East Africa?

CHAPTER X

THE FOREST INDUSTRIES AND PAPER

Civilization could scarcely exist without wood. Wood has been useful in all stages of man's progress and the more civilization advances the greater becomes the service it renders. Each day some inventor finds a substitute for wood in one of its uses, but at the same

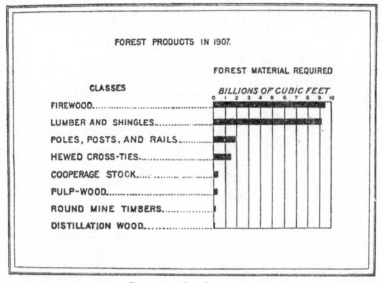

FIG. 110.—Lumber uses.

time other inventors find corresponding new uses for wood, so that our dependence upon it is increasing day by day (Fig. 110). It has even become essential to the spread of knowledge, for practically all our books and magazines are printed on paper made of wood pulp.

The American forests and their destruction.—America is the richest of all continents in useful wood. Through much of our history

our people have had to fight the forests. Against them the first
effort of the new colonist was directed. He worked laboriously to
clear away the trees before he could plant a crop (Fig. 111). He then
had to struggle for years with the stumps before he could have a
smooth field in which to grow his food. Decade after decade, through
the seventeenth and eighteenth centuries and the first half of the
nineteenth, the settlement of the country east of the Mississippi went
steadily forward, accompanied by the wholesale destruction of the

FIG. 111.—Cornfield made by the Indians' method of deadening the trees and
letting them stand. Rail fence in foreground. Slopes of Blue Ridge, Mitchell
Co., N. C. This process still goes on. (U. S. Forest Service.)

forests by felling and firing to make room for the plow. Throughout
this period of most active forest clearing the necessary lumber was
usually made in little saw mills on local streams where the water-
wheel drove a big upright saw up and down and ripped off the
boards one at a time for the man who brought his logs to the mill.
Recently, great improvements have been made in the manufacture of
lumber. The circular saw has replaced the upright saw, and in some
cases the rapid double-cutting band saw has replaced the circular

Fig. 112.—A modern sawmill. The band saw runs over the large wheel at the top and rips off a board with great speed. The squaring of the log wastes much wood. (U. S. Forest Service.)

saw, especially for working up the large logs in the western mills (Fig. 112).

The rise in the price of lumber.—About the year 1900 America began to reach the end of an epoch in the lumber supply. For 50 years the price of lumber had been steadily rising in Europe, while we in America had been cutting down the forests, burning up the timber to clear the land, using lumber prodigally and letting the forest fire run almost unheeded, to the destruction of the young trees that should have made the lumber of the future. Older states like Ohio and Indiana had long been supplying part of the lumber for the treeless northern Mississippi Valley with its thousands of towns and hundreds of thousands of farms. Suddenly there came an end to this lumber supply in these older states and they began to import heavily from distant places. At the same time northern and eastern lumber regions began to show signs of exhaustion, and lumber operators from New England, New York, Pennsylvania, and Wisconsin began to buy timber lands in the South and West, driving up the price by their competition.

Conditions for the lumber industry.—In the past the price of lumber has usually been much less than a cent a pound, so that lumber making for the market has always been dependent upon very favorable conditions of transportation, being most profitable when it could depend, in part at least, upon water transportation. The big log is more difficult to transport than the smaller boards, so the saw mills are situated as near as possible to the place where the trees grow. The mill is often portable, moving about the woods sawing the logs of a few acres in each place, thus minimizing the log hauling. A large saw mill is usually found only where the logs can be floated down a river or brought in by rail, so that it can draw its supply for many years from a large territory.

Forests will grow in latitudes ranging from the heart of the tropics to the edge of the Arctic far beyond the grain line. Granted moisture, evenly distributed throughout the year, no soil is too poor, too sandy, too rocky, or too steep, if the tree can once catch hold with its roots. A tree will stand in the very face of a precipice.

Within the forest the trees vary greatly in their suitability for lumber, most of which is made from a few species that are especially adapted by form and quality for such use. The shade trees commonly seen along the city streets of America and Europe are the broad-leaved deciduous trees. They are usually poor timber trees because their trunks are apt to be crooked and a great proportion of their wood is in the branches. The cone bearers are better timber trees because they have tall, straight trunks with small branches. They can also thrive in lower temperatures and poorer soils. As a result our familiar broad-leaved trees do not furnish over a quarter of the lumber used in the United States or in Europe.

The forest regions and lumber districts of the United States.—The natural forest region of the United States comprises practically all the country between the Atlantic coast and an irregular line extending from the mouth of the Rio Grande, to the Canadian border near the western boundary of Minnesota (Fig. 113); a large area in the higher regions of the Rocky Mountains; and the Pacific forests on the Sierra Nevada and Coast ranges. It is too dry for tree growth on the lower lands of California, of the Rocky Mountain region, the Great Basin, and also on the Great Plains. The prairie fires set by Indians to remove old grass from the pastures are supposed to have kept down the forest in large areas of the Mississippi Valley where trees now thrive, when man gives them a chance. There are seven important lumber districts in the United States (Figs. 118, 119), although the forestry map based on varieties of trees gives five forest regions.

Northeastern district.—The first of these is the northeastern district, comprising the upper New England and Adirondack forests, occupying a highland with a climate rather too cold for satisfactory agriculture of nineteenth century type. Much of this cold country is impossible of tillage because it was made rocky and swampy and sandy by the work of the overriding ice in the glacial epoch. But its rocky, swampy and sandy soils can, if properly cared for, give us crops of wood indefinitely. This lumber district, being easy of logging and near to cities, was the first in the United States to be largely developed. The cold winter and heavy snow of this northeastern highland are essential factors in the lumber industry because the swamps and rocks, impassable by wagons in summer, are frozen firmly and covered by the deep snows of winter so that teams are able to sled the logs out to the stream bank where the melting of the snow in spring furnishes the freshets which carry the logs downward to the mills (Fig. 114). Thus Bangor, Maine, on the Penobscot, became a saw-mill center.

The most important timber tree of this forest region is the white pine, a good timber tree yielding one of the very best of woods. It is prized for its lightness, strength, durability, freedom from warping, cracking, or shrinking, and the ease with which it can be worked.

FIG. 113.—Natural forest regions of North America. (U. S. Forest Service.)

The spruce is second, and the hemlock third in importance. The broad-leafed trees, including the maples, beeches, birches, chestnuts and oak form but a small part of the forest growth in this and the next lumber district.

The Great Lakes district.—The second lumber district is that around the Great Lakes. Climatically, geologically, and industrially it is a westward but separated extension of the New York and New England field. The lumber industry of this district shows the westward development that has accompanied the advance of the American people across the continent (Fig. 115). Lumbering in this dis-

FIG. 114.—Snow is almost as good as railroads for the Northern Lumber Industry. Thief River Falls, Minn. (U. S. Forest Service.)

trict began in the lower peninsula of Michigan, then went to the upper peninsula. Then Wisconsin succeeded Michigan as the leading state, but, as her forests diminished she was in turn succeeded by Minnesota. Minnesota has now been surpassed by the rapidly rising lumber districts in the south and on the Pacific coast. The exhaustion of the white pine especially has been the impetus to make the lumbermen emigrate to new fields (Fig. 116).

The logging enterprises of the Upper Lakes have been a link in a

peculiar industrial chain.   The one-crop farming that has characterized the grain-producing farms of the Mississippi Valley has made a
great demand for labor at harvest time, so that a farm having upon it
one man in winter suddenly needed two or three more at harvest time.
The total result was a demand for tens of thousands of men for a few
weeks in a locality which needed them no more until the next season.

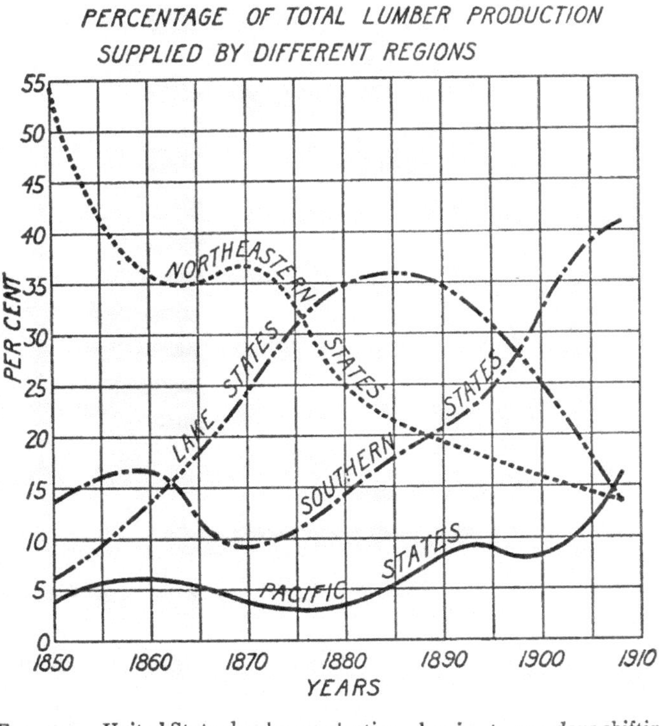

PERCENTAGE OF TOTAL LUMBER PRODUCTION
SUPPLIED BY DIFFERENT REGIONS

FIG. 115.—United States lumber production, showing tremendous shiftings
of the industry.

For many years thousands of men passed the winter in the logging
camps in the Upper Lake forests, felling trees and hauling logs to
the stream bank.   With the spring thaw, many of the choppers rode
upon the log rafts down the Mississippi to St. Louis or New Orleans.
In late May they began the summer's work as harvest hands in
wheat fields of Texas, and followed the advancing harvest season

northward through Oklahoma and into the wheat belts of Kansas. They also harvested hay and oats in that state and in Nebraska through July and early August, and then took up the harvesting of spring wheat in South Dakota, southern Minnesota, the Red River Valley of the North, and Manitoba. They followed the threshers through the frost of the autumn, and with the coming of winter rode eastward on the grain-carrying railroads to take up their axes once more in the lumber camps.

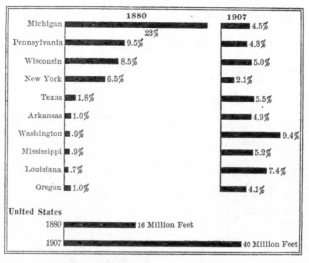

Fig. 116.—The shifting lumber supply as shown by percentage of output by states in 1880 and 1907. (U. S. Forest Service.)

Appalachian highlands.—The third lumber district is that of the Appalachian Highlands, reaching from southern New York to the northern parts of Georgia and Alabama. This region of plateau and mountains, becoming higher as it goes south and reaching its maximum elevation in North Carolina, extends the temperature of New England far into the south, and with it the trees of New England. In this Appalachian district the steepness of the mountains and the small amount of snow make impossible the extended use of sleds as in the New England, Adirondack and Great Lake forests, and the logs are moved to the mills on wagons or, in some cases, on chutes of logs or steel down which the logs slide from precipitous hills sometimes to a temporary railway in the valley below (Fig. 117). The timber has been almost entirely exhausted from the more accessible parts of this region. Carloads of lumber are now regularly shipped into Pennsylvania districts from which 25 years ago it was sent out by the trainload.

FIG. 117.—Log slide to the river.   Priest River National Forest, Idaho.
(U. S. Forest Service.)

Hardwood forests.—The fourth lumber district is the middle region of hard woods extending from New York to Alabama and from Alabama to the Ozarks, in Missouri and Arkansas, and to the lower Great Lakes.   The evergreens, spruce, pines, and hemlocks hold the top of the Appalachians, and pine trees grow naturally upon the sandy Atlantic plain, but between these two on the lower slopes of the Appalachians and the hilly country leading up to them on both the eastern and western slopes is a large area where the forest is made up of the broad-leaved trees, oak, hickory, chestnut, tulip, black walnut, and to a lesser degree ash and basswood, classed as hard woods by the forest service[1] (see central forest in Fig. 113). This is the region from which the American supply of these hardwood timbers has chiefly come. Chattanooga, and Evansville, Indiana, are great lumber markets, while Memphis is the greatest hardwood market in the world.

Southern pine forests.—The fifth lumber district is that of the southern pines, extending in an almost continuous forest along the Atlantic coast plain from Long Branch, New Jersey, to Austin, Texas (see Fig. 113). The most important tree in this district is the yellow or hard pine. The strength and hardness of this pine make it much prized for flooring and many other uses. In 1910 it furnished 35 per cent. of all the lumber cut in the United States. Other pine trees also grow in this belt, particularly the short-leaved or old field pine, one of the fastest growing trees in America, which, between 1860 and 1900, covered many abandoned corn and tobacco fields in Maryland, eastern Virginia, and North Carolina with a growth large enough for the saw mill.

Much of this southern country is sandy and level, some of it gently rolling, but none of it is rugged. A very large proportion of it is yet in forests. The warm moist climate makes this one of the best sections for the trees to replace themselves if they are properly cared for. Lumbering is much easier in this area than in New England or the Appalachian district. Much of it is done on temporary railroads which are put through the woods about 2,000 feet apart so that a donkey engine winding a cable 1,000 feet long can draw logs from any part of the woods to the side of the railroad track.

[1] Commercial woods as classified by the forest service.

Soft Woods	Hard Woods	
Pines	Oak	Cottonwood
Firs	Maple	Ash
Hemlock	Poplar	Hickory
Spruce	Gum	Walnut
Cypress	Chestnut	Sycamore
Redwood	Beech	Cherry
Cedar	Birch	
Larch	Basswood	
Tamarack	Elm	

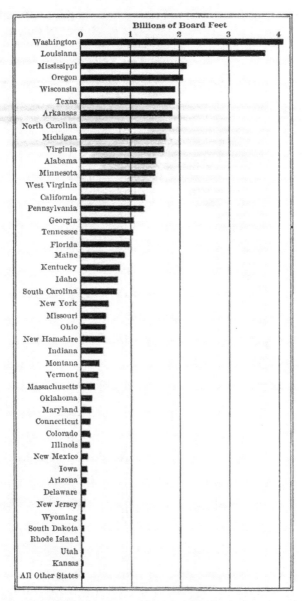

FIG. 118.—Lumber production by states, 1910. (U. S. Forest Service.) A chart with many surprises, as when one notes the relative positions of southern states.

The combined coastwise and export trade in this southern lumber makes large shipments from the ports of Mobile, Alabama; Pensacola, Florida; Brunswick and Savannah, Georgia; Charleston, S. C.; New Berne, N. C.; and Norfolk, Va.; while the new town of Gulf-

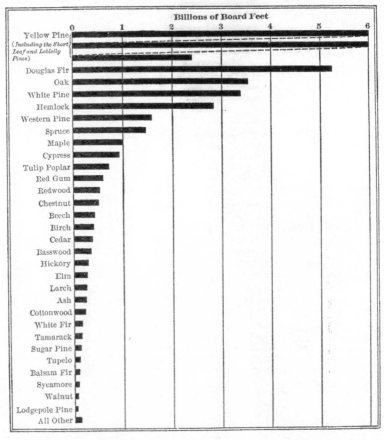

FIG. 119.—Lumber production by varieties, 1910.   (U. S. Forest Service.)

port, Miss., is actually for the time being the greatest lumber-shipping point in the world.   Vast quantities of southern pine are also sent by rail into the Ohio and Mississippi Valleys.

Another important timber tree in the southern field is the cypress, used for shingles and interior work. It is one of the few trees that will grow in a swamp, where its roots must be under water. The shifting source of cypress well illustrates the growing shortage of lumber, and the reasons for its rise in price. Norfolk used to be the great cypress market, but the comparative exhaustion of the Dismal Swamp supply caused Florida to succeed Norfolk, whereas scarcity in Florida has been followed by the rise of New Orleans as the chief market for the product of this swamp forest tree from the swamps of the Mississippi bottoms. Of increasing importance, too, are the gum trees, including tupelo, which, formerly considered worthless for lumber, were left standing while the cypress was being taken out.

The Western Mississippi Valley and Rocky Mountain District. —The central part of the Mississippi Valley north of the Ozark Mountains and west of Indiana was almost treeless when occupied by the homesteaders in the second and third quarters of the nineteenth century. Exception should be made of the moist lowlands along the streams where the scattered growth of broad-leaf trees was of great value to the early settlers, furnishing them with wood for buildings and for fuel. At the north the humidity in the glacial swamps and the lakes had preserved forests west of the source of the Mississippi (see Great Lakes district above) and at the south, the Gulf rains had extended the southern forests over east Texas and the hardwood forests over the Ozarks. Thence to the Rocky Mountains, Canada, and the Rio Grande was a timberless area with one oasis of forest on the small highland, where the Black Hills of South Dakota and Wyoming, with a greater rainfall, supported a rather inferior tree growth (see Fig. 113).

Owing to the slight rainfall at low elevations, the Rocky Mountain forests grow only in high elevations (**Fig. 122**), particularly in the south, but the lessened heat and evaporation make the area of the forest increase in Idaho and Montana. These Rocky Mountain forests, because of their dependence upon elevation, occur in scattered patches (see Fig. 113, Forest Map of United States) which increase in and toward the north. The percentage of forest area is comparatively small in New Mexico, but it has many more square miles of forest than has New Hampshire. There are even several hundred square miles of fine forest upon the plateaus of northeastern and central Arizona, and there are large extensions of this same plateau forest in the mountains of northern Mexico through which new railroads under American management have been partly built between the Rio

Grande and the Gulf of California. Owing to the prevailing coolness resulting from elevation, the Rocky Mountain forests are mainly coniferous; they include chiefly the western yellow and lodge-pole pine, spruce, Douglas fir, and western red cedar. Seventy-five per cent. of this area remains uncut.

The Pacific slope.—The seventh forest district of the United States and the finest in the world is that near the Pacific coast.

RELIEF MAP
of
CALIFORNIA

PACIFIC OCEAN

FIG. 120.—Relief map of California. The treeless central plain is conspicuous in a state that is largely mountainous—an explanation of the importance of her timber resources. (From Salisbury, Barrows, and Tower.)

This forest belt begins about latitude 35° in California, where it occupies the Sierra Nevada and Coast ranges, but low rainfall causes the great valley of that state lying between these mountains to be treeless (Fig. 120), as are the lowlands farther south and east. In northern California, parts of Oregon, and central Washington the forests cover not only both mountain ranges, but the rather high and rough valleys between. The second range of mountains from

FIG. 121.—Western pine, 20,000 feet per acre. The collection of centuries.
(Blackwell Lumber Co., Coeur D'Alene, Idaho.)

the sea sharply limits the rainfall so that, except upon the higher ranges, there is no forest in the Great Basin between the east front of the Sierras and the Wasatch Mountains of Utah, nor between the Cascade Mountains of west central Washington and Oregon and the mountains of Idaho.

FIG. 122.—V-shaped board flume floating sawed lumber out of impassable Rocky Mts., Canyon, Wyoming. At the right center a creek adds to the water supply. At the right of the flume is a running board for workmen. (U. S. Forest Service.)

The even climate, a good rainfall, freedom from windstorms, and a dry summer, checking fungus action, permit the trees of the Pacific forests to grow for ages and attain great size, as is shown by the well-known big trees of California. But commercially more important than these forest giants are large areas of forest in all three of the Pacific states where there is a thick stand of redwood, Oregon pine or

Douglas fir trees from 4 to 8 or even 10 ft. in diameter with straight trunks 100 ft. and even more in length. It is difficult work to get these huge logs to the saw mill. Because of this difficulty much fine timber is wasted. As it is utterly impossible to haul them on an ordinary wagon, they are sometimes dragged by donkey engines or long teams of oxen over a road bed paved with small logs. Oftener they are taken on temporary railways, and sometimes they are allowed to slide by gravity down log chutes. The largest must often

FIG. 123.—One of our crimes against posterity is this Georgia sawmill slab fire that burned for 25 years without stopping. (U. S. Forest Service.)

be split by blasting before they can be moved at all. The lumber is manufactured in the largest and most perfect lumber mills in the United States, some of them using every particle of the log that is brought to their wonderful machinery. A typical mill produces shingles, lumber, and match-sticks from the finest portions of the logs, while the sawdust and bark feed the engine fires. Sailing vessels have for years loaded at Seattle and Tacoma, Wash., Vancouver, B. C., Eureka and Humbolt, Cal., to carry this most excellent timber to markets of South America, Australia, Japan, South

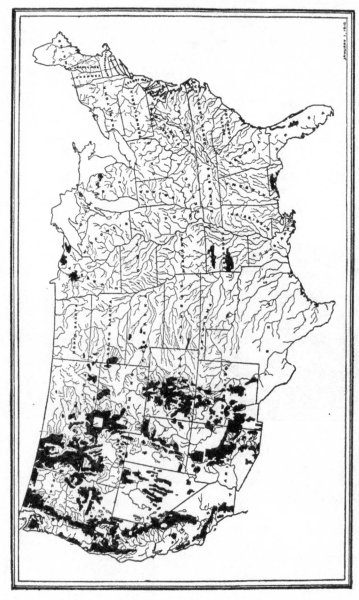

FIG. 124.—Map showing distribution of the National Forests (1910). This total area is greater than that of England, Ireland, Scotland, and Wales.

Africa, and even to England, France, and Germany, a voyage much longer than half the distance around the world.

The increased price of lumber in the United States permits the Pacific coast lumber to be carried across the continent to Chicago and even to New York, and it has become an important article of freight eastward upon the transcontinental railways.

Alaskan forests.—The forests of Alaska are a continuation of those of British Columbia.   In the southern part of Alaska, especially on the rather narrow Pacific slope, there is a heavy rainfall and a considerable area of evergreen forests.   In the interior of Alaska there is also forest growth along most of the streams, and the wood thus supplied has been of great aid in the operation of steamboats and in hunting for gold along those streams.   But little of this timber of interior Alaska is large enough for the saw mill; its rate of growth is slow and it has had serious fire injury.   However, it offers possibilities for paper making, for which purpose small trees are as suitable as large ones.

The forest policy of the United States.—The European experience of deforesting, timber scarcity and the resulting soil loss, tree planting, and forestry has at last been heeded to some extent by the United States, especially since the rising price of lumber, beginning about 1900, has called the attention of all classes to the impending scarcity of timber.   Careful estimates by forestry experts indicate that at the present rate of use our timber supply will last possibly 50 years (Fig. 121), and that the rate of use is likely to increase rather than to decrease.   Therefore our national government has begun a policy of setting apart as national forests those parts of the government land which are unfit for agriculture but which have trees upon them.   The map of the national forests (see Fig. 124) shows that they comprise large areas in the West, being nearly five times as large as New England, and comprising about one-fifth of the standing timber of the United States.   The national forests of California alone cover 43,000 square miles, an area more than two-thirds as great as New England.   Many of our states also own timber lands, but these are chiefly burnt-over stump-lands which have reverted to the state because no one will pay the taxes. Our forest policy is as yet in its infancy and its chief function thus far has been the merely preventive one of fire protection, which after all is the most important thing in all forestry (Fig. 125).

If their care is kept up, we may expect a steadily increasing output

of lumber from national forests chiefly by the sale of full-grown trees
to saw-mill owners under conditions of cutting that will not destroy
the growing trees.   Our timber needs will compel us, as our population advances, to take better and better care of our forests, and to
use less timber per person, as is now the case in Europe.   We have
thus far been chiefly in the hunter stage so far as lumber production
is concerned.   Just as the hunter goes out and shoots a wild rabbit,
so the woodsman cuts a wild tree which nature similarly has provided.
The systematic care of the forest increases its productivity several

FIG. 125.—"After man the desert." These rocks were covered with trees,
roots and black soil before the forest fire.   Mt. Tabor, Rutland Co., Vt.   (U. S.
Forest Service.)

fold.   Great increase is also possible through the introduction of
foreign trees.   The bamboo, the great mainstay of the Japanese,
thrives in parts of the Gulf region.   The camphor tree grows well in
Florida, and in California the eucalyptus, an Australian genus, has
been found so profitable that good agricultural land has been planted
with it.   This tree is phenomenal in that it grows to great size with
great speed and at the same time makes a very durable wood.
Owing to its peculiar oil the wood is comparatively free from the
ravages of boring insects and it is especially desirable for marine

piling in docks and wharves, because the oil protects it from the effects of insect and water.

Naval stores and tanbark.—Important among the many minor industries of the forest is the preparation of naval stores, the name applied to turpentine and resin, products of the sap of certain pine trees. Resin is the remaining product after turpentine has been distilled from pine sap. The chief center of production is in the long-leaf pine forests of the southeastern United States; Charleston, Savannah, Pensacola, Mobile, and Fernandina, Fla., being important points of shipment. The manufacture of naval stores, as carried on in the southern United States, is very injurious to the forests. The sap gatherer makes great wounds in the base of the tree from which in a few years it bleeds to death. During the process it is exposed to easy destruction by fire, and is easily overturned by wind storms. A newer method of "boxing" the tree does not gash it so deeply, and so, greatly prolongs its life and yield. Inasmuch as the slabs which are burned or wasted around many southern saw mills (Fig. 123) also contain large quantities of sap, as do the small branches and tops which are left in the woods, it is likely that the near future will see more economic methods of gathering naval stores. Some processes already discovered take all this refuse wood, soak the sap from it for distillation and leave the pulp thus purified for making paper.

Another industry which has caused great destruction of American forests is the gathering of bark for tanning. The chief bark trees are the hemlock and certain species of oak growing from Pennsylvania southward on both slopes of the Appalachians. Millions of good trees have been cut down for their tanbark alone, the trunks being allowed to rot. This shameful waste of logs still goes on to some extent in the eastern country and also in California, where in the Coast Range there is considerable collection of tanbark from one of the western oaks that grows among the redwoods. The tanbark district of Wisconsin and Michigan (chiefly hemlock) is second to the Appalachian in output. More detailed information about this industry will be found in chapter on Leather.

Wood manufactures.—The manufacture of the heavy log into rough lumber naturally clings to the forest, although special conditions cause some export of logs, especially of such high quality woods as mahogany and walnut. The further manufacture of lumber, usually carried on in planing mills where the rough boards are finished, tends to concentrate near the market in or near centers where building operations are largely carried on, since the rough lumber is more easily moved and stored than the easily injured dressed plank or the sash, doors, blinds, and special shapes that the planing mill turns out.

The same factors tend to locate furniture manufacture in great centers of consumption, especially in timber-importing countries. Thus London is both market for product and center for raw material because the imported wood is unloaded there from the ships. Owing to an early start when near-by timber supplies were abundant, and to very low freight rates since, we have had a great furniture industry developed near the former area of wood supply in Grand Rapids and other towns of the Lower Peninsula of Michigan, in Evansville, Indiana, and more recently the same industry is rapidly increasing in North Carolina. The recently perfected "knock-down" system of furniture making, which has been extended to boats and even houses, has enabled many such cities to maintain their wood-working industry even after the near-by timber supply has been exhausted. The expense of importing the raw lumber is balanced by the saving in freight made by the "knock-down" system. Furniture is expensive to ship, not so much because of its weight, but because of its bulk. "Knock-down" furniture can be taken to pieces, permitting economy of space in shipping. In this same way the parts of boxes and barrels (called shooks) are shipped ready to put up.

The sudden increase in the manufacture of veneer and its use for cheap industrial purposes is suggestive of the advancing economy of wood that scarcity and high prices are forcing upon us. Veneer is wood sliced into thin sheets like pasteboard or even like paper.

"Formerly veneer making was confined to a few hardwoods selected for beauty of grain and used as an exterior finish for high-grade furniture and cabinet work. With the improvement of veneer machinery and methods of drying there has developed a large demand for veneers cut from cheap woods and used for packing boxes, berry cups, fruit baskets, veneer barrels, drawer bottoms, filling in three-ply lumber, glass backing, and novelties, such as butter dishes, wooden plates, and fancy confectionery packages.

"On account of the constantly increasing price of hardwood lumber used for making furniture, fixtures, and cabinets, built-up lumber, which is usually made of three-ply veneer, is being extensively substituted. In manufacturing this built-up material, it is possible to use woods which heretofore have been but rarely used, owing to their tendency to twist and warp when sawed into lumber" (*Bureau of Forestry Report*). For many purposes this built-up lumber is better than the "natural" lumber.

Paper.—In 1870 when cotton, linen and woolen rags were the chief dependence of the paper manufacturers, it would have seemed preposterous to place a discussion of the paper industry in a chapter dealing with forests and forest industries, but this is an industry which has been completely transformed by changes in raw material since that time.

Paper is made of matted fibers, mostly vegetable. Nearly all plants have fibers in them and as indefinite numbers of vegetable materials will make paper, the actual choice of materials is decided by the relative quality and cheapness. For two or three centuries cotton, linen, and woolen rags were the chief dependence for paper making. In 1857 an Englishman invented a process of making paper from a tough grass called esparto, which grows well on arid, sandy, and rocky land and is found wild over large areas in the Barbary States of north Africa and in Spain. In less than 30 years after its introduction, it assumed an importance in English paper making greater than that of rags. By 1901 esparto was far outranked by the predominating wood pulp, which is now making an ever increasing part of the world's paper.

Paper is made by grinding up the rags, grass, or wood until the fibers are almost microscopic in size. They float in water which is kept at a uniform soupy thickness by stirring. For centuries paper making was a handicraft carried on by the paper maker and his family, who dipped sieves into vats of floating fiber and carefully lifted out upon the wire gauze enough fiber to produce a sheet of paper when properly dried. Now machines turn out more than 500 feet per minute and send it away from the factory in sheets often miles in length wound upon spools into rolls 3 or 4 feet in diameter. If the paper is to be used for writing purposes, the spaces between the fibers are closed by a process called sizing, which fills up the pores with material chiefly composed of china-clay, resin, alum, and talc, a process that greatly adds to the weight of the paper. While the expensive hand method of paper making prevailed, its price was high, and demand for it small. Machines have greatly cheapened paper, thus greatly increasing its possible uses, and the resulting rapid increase of consumption has in turn called for new kinds of raw materials.

Paper from wood.—The manufacture of paper from wood pulp was begun in the United States in 1867, and tree trunks now make the greater part of the world's paper. The cheapness of this material greatly depressed the trade in, and reduced the price of esparto grass, which had been a staple export of many of the Arab tribes of north Africa. The resultant hard times produced discontent, which, as is commonly the case, was blamed upon the Government, and the French rulers of Algiers had serious trouble with the tribesmen who found themselves poverty stricken through the loss that followed the decline in the esparto trade.

Before the pulp era, our paper mills, like our woolen mills, had been clustered along small streams in the vicinity of centers of population. The great increase in the use of wood pulp for paper in the United States since 1890 has caused the transfer of the center of the paper industry away from the market to the forest districts of the New York and New England highlands. The spruce wood originally so common in this region furnishes three-fifths of the wood pulp in this country, and two-thirds of the paper mills of the country use water-power because, when available, it is the cheapest source for the great amount of energy required to grind the wood into pulp. So important is this relationship of water-power to paper making that over 60 per cent of the water-power utilization in the United States is in the paper mills. The combination of water-power and spruce logs makes the states of northern New England and New York the greatest paper-manufacturing district in the United States. Clear water is very important in paper making. Massachusetts has excellent water and water-power, a skilled labor supply, cheap transportation of pulp from the northern forests, and is also near centers of population which furnish a ready market for the output as well as a supply of rags for the better grades of paper. Massachusetts leads in the making of rag and fine writing papers, for the manufacture of which Holyoke, on one of the falls of the Connecticut, with its twenty-four paper mills, is the most specialized center in the United States.

The cheapest wood pulp paper is simply ground wood which makes the flimsy and perishable newspaper. The better and more expensive kinds have the fibers loosened and the quality improved by the action of chemicals producing "sulphite" or "soda" pulp. The better grades or book papers are made largely of poplar (tulip) wood, which has a longer fiber and supplies scattering mills from New York to Carolina. Two-thirds of the newspaper, practically all made of spruce, comes from the Adirondack and New England highlands, while three-fourths of the remainder is made on the southern edge of the upper lake forests in Wisconsin.

Paper industry leads to forestry.—A paper mill with its water-wheels and heavy machines is expensive, and the impossibility of moving it makes it necessary that a paper company shall be sure of its wood supply. To do this they must often own the land, and, since they cannot flit from tract to tract after the manner of lumber manufacturers, some paper companies have become the foremost foresters in the United States, owning large areas of spruce land which they care for, and cut systematically. As their enterprises are often located in the deep forest, the companies must sometimes even build and own the towns in which the people live who make their paper. A good example of this is afforded by the town of Millinocket, Maine, where the largest paper mill in the world, turning out 250 tons of paper per day, was located far in the forest beside a great water-fall. A special railroad was extended to it, and the town built around the mill. The plant cost $25,000,000—an excellent evidence of the impossibility of moving and of the consequent necessity for conservation of wood supply, both by avoiding wasteful cutting and by replanting the cut-over lands, but above all by the stopping of fires.

The paper industry is undergoing rapid change in the source of its raw material, since it has been demonstrated that practically all of our native woods can be used. Already twenty species including pine, chestnut, and cottonwood are in use. Slabs and mill waste are also being utilized and soon there will be no excuse for the frightful wood waste of the past (see Fig. 123).

Paper from straw.—In the eastern part of the wheat belt in Ohio, Indiana, and Illinois, there is a considerable paper industry using straw, chiefly wheat straw, which makes cheap wrapping paper and strawboard, the so-called pasteboard of common use. This is an industry which might easily move west and northwest with the moving wheat fields. It has already declined in New York.

Our commerce in paper.—No other people in the world use so much paper as do the people of the United States with their large consumption of newspapers, magazines, books, wrapping paper and advertising. We import rags from Europe by the hundreds of millions of pounds, and from Canada a quarter of a million tons of wood pulp annually, about equaling in value ($5,000,000) the European rags. One of the surprises of commerce is the import by the United States of a quarter of a million tons of wood pulp from Europe, chiefly Norway and Sweden. It is common practice in both America and Europe for one mill to make the pulp which is shipped great distances to become the raw material for the paper mill. Despite our large manufactures, our import of high-grade paper from Europe, especially from Germany, is about as valuable as our export of newspaper and book paper, which we send to the United Kingdom and to almost all countries of Europe, Central and South America.

QUESTIONS

1. Are planing mills and saw mills commonly found in the same localities? Why?

2. Would the Upper New England forests be more valuable or less, if they had the winter of Tennessee or Maryland?

3. Explain from the map why Chattanooga, Evansville, and Memphis each ranks high as a lumber market.

4. Explain how environment makes different methods of logging.

5. The big tree (species sequoia) grows well in some eastern locations. May we expect it to get as large as in California?

6. What is the effect of the discovery of chemical tanning materials on the future price of lumber?

7. Why do different manufacturers using wood regard forestry differently?

8. Should a factory for the manufacture of fine furniture be in a big city or a big forest?

9. How did an invention in paper-making cause rebellion in another country?

10. Explain how "built up lumber" is made of three-ply veneer. Can you find out how the three layers of veneer are arranged so as to avoid warping that would occur if the same wood were used in the ordinary way? Mention several articles of furniture in which you have seen "built up" lumber.

CHAPTER XI

FIBERS, TEXTILES, AND CLOTHING

The United States, with its preponderance in cotton raising, is the greatest factor in the production of raw material for the world's clothing. The United Kingdom has a similar leadership in the textile manufactures, one-seventh of her workers being employed with textiles and clothing, while in the United States but one-sixteenth are so employed. The clothing of mankind is the product of wide-reaching world industries, which, with the production of the raw materials, touch in varying degrees all countries. A multitude of fibers contribute, but cotton is much the most important. In 1911 we used over thirteen times as much raw cotton as of scoured wool, its closest rival.

1. THE SUPPLY OF RAW COTTON

The universal use of cotton.—It is probable that few readers of this book ever saw a person into whose clothing cotton did not enter in some part, for it is alike the raiment of princes and of savages.

Cotton was in extensive and general use in India as much as twenty-seven centuries ago. Unlike most other important plants, its distribution throughout parts of the world suited to it took place at a very early time, probably by natural means, for Columbus and other discoverers found it in general use in the West Indies, Brazil, Mexico, and the Pacific Islands.

Until the end of the eighteenth century it was one of the most expensive of fibers, because hand labor was the only method of separating the fiber from the seed. The difficulty and slowness of this work made cotton more expensive than wool and linen, and caused it to be relatively more expensive than silk now is. The poor of 1790 had to choose between wool, linen, and leather, and this last material, in the form of workmen's clothing, played a much more important part than now in man's raiment.

Revolution through the cotton gin.—Before the invention of the cotton gin in 1793 a day's work was required to pick out the seeds from 1 to 2 pounds of cotton fiber. The cotton gin did this work rapidly, and so reduced the price of cotton that it descended from a luxury to a necessity and a great industry sprang up.[1] The gin and tillage machinery promptly transferred it from the class of garden and hand-labor crops, to the class of machine-grown field crops. The cheapened production and increased demand shifted the cotton-growing area from a region of cheap labor to one of cheap land, from the populous Indies to the broad fields of the almost empty South. The year before the invention of the cotton gin the American crop was so insignificant that the United States had in a treaty willingly promised to export no cotton to Great Britain, but within less than forty years we were sending Britain over two-thirds of her imports. It was the leading article of American export for many decades, during which it was frequently declared that "cotton is King." While it is not now so relatively conspicuous or so politically dominant, its export is more valuable than ever, having reached 585 million dollars in 1911, while meat and dairy products were 150 million and flour 50 million.

During the century following the invention of the gin, cotton has become the well-nigh universal clothing. It has almost entirely replaced linen, is with increasing success competing with wool in the soft and warm flannelettes and canton flannel, and it is also very generally mixed with wool in the production of cloth, to which it adds cheapness and in some cases durability. Other cotton fabrics, such as sateen, greatly resemble silk, while mercerized cotton is often sold as silk, so that cotton is being used as a substitute for this more expensive fiber also.

Natural cotton regions.—Cotton is a woolly fiber attached to the seeds of a shrubby plant and contained in a pod or boll, which at ripening time opens so that the white fiber protrudes in a mass about the size of a small apple (Fig. 126). Naturally tropical and sub-tropical, the plant will grow almost everywhere throughout the world between 40° north and 30° south. The northward growth of cotton is limited by the requirement of about seven months of frost-free weather (see Fig. 56 of frost-free periods). It also needs a good summer rainfall without too great an excess of rain, a uniformly warm summer without too excessive heat, and bright sunshine. A frost-free season from April 1 to Nov. 1 is thus a necessity unless the plants

---

[1] The influence of cotton on slavery and of slavery on the history of the United States is an interesting bit of the economic explanation of history.

are started under glass. Owing to combinations of geographical and industrial conditions, it is exported as yet from few and comparatively small areas and thus in its distribution throughout the entire world, it gives rise to a great commerce.

The possible cotton area in the United States.—It is estimated that 700,000 square miles of the southern part of the United States have the climate suitable for cotton. Owing to the ease of injury by too

FIG. 126.—The branching habit of the cotton plant and its uneven ripening has long baffled the inventors of picking machines. (U. S. Dept. Agr.)

much rain and cloudy weather the coast districts of South Atlantic States are not so well fitted as the districts further inland where the greatest centers of cotton production are found (Fig. 127). The small proportion of cotton states actually in cotton at one time shows great possibility of increased production. In 1879, 20,000 square miles were in cotton. This was practically doubled in 1898, but by 1911 it had not reached one-fifteenth of the total 700,000 square miles of possible cotton land. It is thus evident that the cotton output can be increased several fold while other crops can also be largely grown in the same belt.

Method of growing.—The cotton seeds, about the size of a small pea, are planted thickly in rows in March and April. As soon as the plants are established, they are thinned with hoes, after which frequent cultivations with the plow or cultivator are needed to keep down the weeds and to break up the top soil to stop evaporation.

The picking of the fiber, which has thus far baffled all machinery, must be done by hand. Because the cotton does not all ripen at

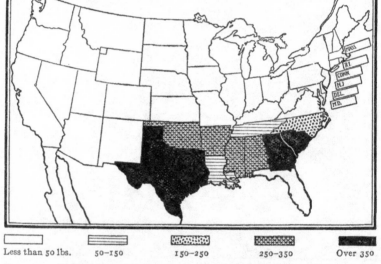

| Less than 50 lbs. | 50–150 | 150–250 | 250–350 | Over 350 |

FIG. 127.—United States cotton production in pounds per capita by states, three-year average, 1909–11. (U. S. Dept. Agr.) Pop., 1910.

once, the field must be "picked over" several times before the crop is all harvested. The large amount of work involved makes picking the limiting factor in cotton growing. Owing to the light nature of the work, much of it is done by negro women and children.

The cotton-growing industry has been seriously threatened by an insect, the cotton boll-weevil (Fig. 128). It came to us apparently from Mexico and destroys the crop by tunneling through the unopened boll and blasting it. The damage has amounted to scores of millions of dollars, but a compensating feature is that it is forcing the

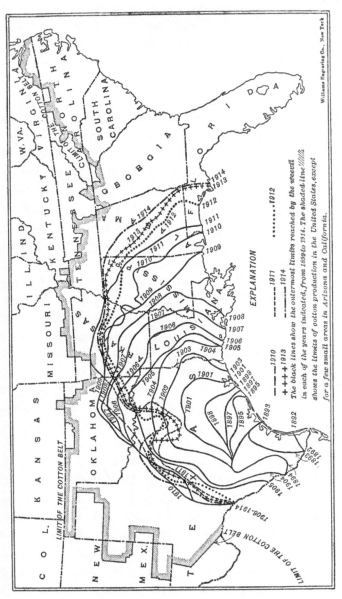

FIG. 128.—Spread of the Mexican cotton boll weevil.

EXPLANATION

------ 1910   ········· 1912

------ 1911   ------ 1914

+++++ 1913

The black lines show the outermost limits reached by the weevil in each of the years indicated, from 1899 to 1914. The shaded line //// shows the limits of cotton production in the United States, except for a few small areas in Arizona and California.

Williams Engraving Co., New York

South to develop a more diversified agriculture. The ease with which the grower's cotton crop, keeping indefinitely, easily handled, and king of money crops, could be mortgaged, and the great difficulty of mortgaging any other crop were factors in the establishment of the great crop-mortgage system in the South after the Civil War.

This mortgage system still continues to some extent and has been an important factor in the continuance of a one-crop agriculture in which very few supply crops are grown, so that even the hay eaten by the mule that plows the cotton is often imported in bales from north of the Ohio or west of the Mississippi. The man who advances the

FIG. 129.—Cotton acreage map.

money to the cotton grower does not encourage the growth of other crops, nor the development of a more rational agriculture, because no other crop is so easily mortgaged, so easily kept or so readily salable as cotton. Thus the South, which has excellent natural facilities for the development of live-stock industries and the growth of forage crops, continues to import mules, hay, corn, butter, cheese, and pork, which it might produce as cheaply as any other part of the world, if not more cheaply (see chapter on live stock).

Important cotton districts.—Cotton is grown from Norfolk, Va., to Austin, Texas, and up the Mississippi to Memphis (see Fig. 129), but three localities with unusual soils stand out conspicuously. One is the rich, black prairie of Texas, another the so-called Mississippi "bottoms," a term chiefly applied to the alluvial land to the east of the Mississippi River between Memphis and Vicksburg, which is occasionally fertilized by the mud deposited when the river overflows its banks and floods the whole region. The third district in which the natural fertility of the soil suffices to give a crop nearly double the national average of about 200 pounds per acre is the so-called "Black Belt" of Alabama. This is a wide valley, running from east to west a little above the central part of that state and having a fertile limestone soil of exceptional productivity for cotton, which, like many other crops, does its best in soils rich in lime. The center of cotton production has steadily moved to the west during . the last sixty years, until recently it shifted to the eastward, due largely to the influence of the weevil. But despite this pest, Texas yet produces more cotton than any other state.

Kinds of cotton.—The fibers of the ordinary upland cotton, the chief product of the United States, are a little less than 1 inch in length, but a variety known as Sea Isle cotton, considered the best in the world, has fibers as much as 2½ inches in length. This produces a superior thread and commands a high price for use in the manufacture of fine fabrics. Sea Isle fiber is chiefly grown along the low sandy islands (barrier beaches) off the coast of South Carolina and Georgia, and seems to require heavy rain, much moisture, and the slightly saline soil and air of shore districts. It also does fairly well for some distance inland in southern Georgia and northern Florida.

Because of the dry climate, Egyptian cotton is superior to our own for knit goods, and for this reason is imported into the United States in quantities (178,000 bales, 1910) greater than our total cotton consumption of 1830. Within the last few years it has been found that the conditions of the Yuma district of the lower Colorado basin in California and Arizona, because of the great similarity of climate, produce cotton that is quite the equal of that of Egypt. It is not likely, however, that the labor conditions of the Southwest with its high wages will favor cotton growing in competition with the Egyptian Fellahs.

Probable improvements in America.—With the continued rapid spread of more scientific agriculture, with crop rotation and animal husbandry in the cotton belt of the United States, the production can be increased several fold during the present century. The invention of a successful cotton-picking machine, which now seems assured, would work a great revolution by removing the greatest labor element in its production and putting it on a par with wheat, oats, and corn, in all of which crops machinery has made possible the working of

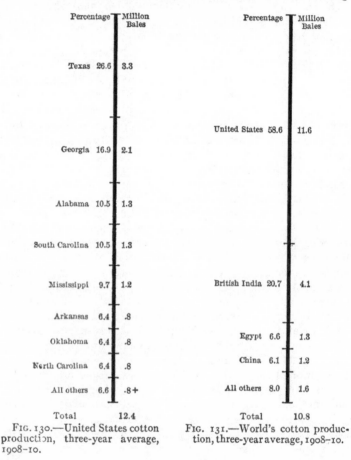

Percentage	Million Bales		Percentage	Million Bales
Texas 26.6	3.3			
			United States 58.6	11.6
Georgia 16.9	2.1			
Alabama 10.5	1.3			
South Carolina 10.5	1.3			
Mississippi 9.7	1.2		British India 20.7	4.1
Arkansas 6.4	.8			
Oklahoma 6.4	.8		Egypt 6.6	1.3
North Carolina 6.4	.8		China 6.1	1.2
All others 6.6	.8+		All others 8.0	1.6
Total	12.4		Total	10.8

FIG. 130.—United States cotton production, three-year average, 1908–10.

FIG. 131.—World's cotton production, three-year average, 1908–10.

many acres by a single individual. The cotton gin brought great emancipation to cotton growing, but cotton picking still depends upon human fingers. This alone restricts the possible production to a fraction of what it might be with a successful machine picker.

The stimulus to the breeding of early maturing varieties of cotton, produced by the boll-weevil outbreak, is likely to permit the northward extension of cotton growing in this and other lands.

By-products from cotton.—The cotton seed, one of the most nutritious of substances, was for a long time thrown away, or even burned. Later it was returned to the fields as fertilizer. Then came the discoveries that the oil in which it was so rich could be extracted and put to many and rapidly increasing uses. The manufacture of cotton-seed oil is now an important by-product industry throughout the South. The seed, more than 130 million bushels, and worth nearly a dollar a bushel, is hulled, ground, and run through heavy presses to extract the oil of which a ton of seed makes 40 gallons. The great richness of this cotton-seed meal in proteid, of which it is now the cheapest available source, has led to its appreciation as food for dairy cows, for which it is shipped to every important center of butter and cheese production in the United States, Canada, and Europe. Its satisfactory use as a breadstuff for human food has already begun in a small way. The oil is largely used for food in various manufactured forms as cottolene and other lard substitutes, and also as a direct substitute for, and adulterant of, olive oil, which it greatly resembles in food value. Unfortunately this oil, unlike olive oil, becomes rancid when exposed to the air for a few weeks.

2. MANUFACTURE AND TRADE IN COTTON CLOTH

Spinning and weaving in the hand-labor era.—Fibers of any sort, when twisted around each other, tend to cling together and form a thread, string, or rope. Cotton, being a flat hollow tube, has unusual spinning qualities. Primitive peoples in every continent have some method of spinning, also devices for weaving. For ages thread laboriously spun by hand was woven into cloth in hand looms, the industry being carried on in the homes of the workers even when the product was intended for sale. Some people were spinners, others did the weaving, and cloth making for sale was a common household by-industry throughout the western world in the middle of the eighteenth century. Late in the eighteenth century three machines revolutionized the clothing industry of the world and also the history of the United States and of England. One invention demands and usually produces another. The spinning machine

(1764), by providing more yarn than could be woven by the older
methods, demanded weaving machines (1787) (Fig. 132), and the
weaving machines in turn demanded more cotton. In answer to
this demand came the cotton gin (1793), which, as we have seen,
greatly increased the production of the raw material, six years after
the power loom had made cotton scarce. Cotton quickly became
cheap. This combination of spinning machines, weaving machines,

FIG. 132.—A modern loom. Spools of yarn to the right. Card-board patterns overhead at left. Roll of finished cloth near floor at left. (Crompton
Knowles Loom Works, Worcester, Mass.)

cheap cotton, and the coal and the iron resources of England, enabled
that country to forge rapidly ahead in cotton manufacture while all
the continent of Europe was disturbed with the turmoil of Napoleon's wars. In 1785, the export of cotton goods from England was
worth a million pounds sterling (about 5 million dollars); in 1815 it
was 22 million pounds, and during this period it increased from 5 per
cent of British exports to 38 per cent.

That short period of thirty years produced greater change in

British industry than many previous centuries had made. It has been well called the Industrial Revolution, and, like inventions, machines, and styles, it has spread and is spreading to all manufacturing countries. Before this revolution, man used little artificial power and the manufacturer often lived in the village or in the country where he gardened, kept some live stock, and worked on near-by farms. He was near to the food supply and had opportunity to use his extra time to good advantage. After the Industrial Revolution, the worker found himself living in a city tenement to be near his steam-driven machine in the big factory. He was away from the earth, the one great resource. He had no chance to produce food in his odd moments and was dependent upon the factory wage and imported food.

It is entirely erroneous to think of the machines of modern manufacturing as having completed their evolution. Mechanical improvement is going forward as rapidly now as ever, and to this improvement the textile industry is no exception. The completed modern cotton mill is large and often costs more than a million dollars. While one plant often completes the process, it is still a characteristic of the cotton-manufacturing industry that the yarn is made in one place and the cloth in another, as was done in the days of the wheel and hand loom. Thus, England is sending yarn to the Far East to be there woven into cloth; Japan and India are sending yarn to China; the mills of Massachusetts are sending yarn to Philadelphia, and the mills of Philadelphia are sending yarn to Rhode Island, while a wagon carrying yarn from mill to mill is a common sight in every cotton-manufacturing city. All this means a great waste of effort and consequently higher prices for cotton goods than necessary.

Present distribution of cotton manufacture.—During the nineteenth century, cotton factories have spread to many countries, and cotton cloth has traveled to the ends of the earth. The spinning wheel has disappeared before steam-borne commerce in ever-widening circles, until now it lingers only in exceedingly remote locations, where it continues, not because it is impossible to transport cotton cloth, but chiefly because it is impossible to send out any product with which to pay for it. In the United States, the old method still persists in the heart of the Appalachian plateaus of eastern Kentucky and North Carolina.

Relation of cotton manufacture to density of population.—The world's cotton mills produce many varieties of cloth, from the coarsest to the finest, and the distribution of the different kinds is an admirable illustration of the effect of dense population upon manufacturing industries. A pound of raw cotton may, with much fabrication, become several dollars' worth of the best machine-made lace, or it may become a yard or less of coarse, heavy cotton duck. Several times as much labor and capital are required to produce the finer of these two products, even if machine made, while if the lace is made by hand it takes vastly more labor than that required for machine lace. Brussels has been the center of the world's hand-made lace industry for the natural reason that it has been the metropolis of the most densely peopled nation. Much of the lace is made by the Belgian peasants in the intervals of their farm work—a means by which they retain the great advantage of the domestic system—steady employment.

The United States has an instructive distribution of the industry into regions of coarse and fine production. The average annual consumption of raw cotton per spindle in the South in 1880 was 155 pounds, in 1905, 119 pounds, while in Massachusetts it was 72 pounds, and in England 38 pounds. The cloth of the southern cotton mills was therefore much coarser than the British or the New England product. Speaking broadly, the South is, in its cotton cloth, exporting primarily its raw material. New England and Old England are exporting primarily their labor. The product of the Middle Atlantic States, as might be expected, is midway in fineness between that of New England and the South.

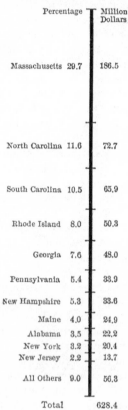

	Percentage	Million Dollars
Massachusetts	29.7	186.5
North Carolina	11.6	72.7
South Carolina	10.5	65.9
Rhode Island	8.0	50.3
Georgia	7.6	48.0
Pennsylvania	5.4	33.9
New Hampshire	5.3	33.6
Maine	4.0	24.9
Alabama	3.5	22.2
New York	3.2	20.4
New Jersey	2.2	13.7
All Others	9.0	56.3
Total		628.4

FIG. 133.—Value of United States cotton manufacturers, 1909.

In the United States the manufacture of cotton is concentrated in the region east of the Appalachians, in a long belt from Maine to Alabama, with its greatest centers in New England and at the eastern base of the Appalachians in the Carolinas and Georgia, with a lesser center in Philadelphia (Fig. 133). New England, with 17 million spindles, is the leader in cotton manufacturing and is likely to be for an indefinite time to come, although the southern states with 11.5 million spindles are already consuming more cotton in a single year than does New England. In 1910 Massachusetts alone had 34 per cent of the spindles of the United States, and the Carolinas had 24 per cent. But New England is making finer and more valuable fabrics.

The leading cotton-manufacturing city in the United States is Fall River, Massachusetts, where the little Fall River tumbles down to the sea and develops enough power to start the first mill. Being at the head of a bay, it has a good harbor and can take advantage of ocean transportation for the importation of cargoes of cotton, and of coal, which now drives practically all the machinery of the city, the water-power having long ago become insufficient for the many mills.

Southern cotton manufacture.—The cotton manufacturing belt of the southern states is located near the fall line which marks the boundary between the Piedmont district and the Atlantic Plain, and also in the Piedmont district, where it has been able to take advantage of many waterfalls. In Alabama it is close to the coal fields. Its nearness to the raw product which is often grown in the immediate vicinity is an advantage shared by no other important cotton manufacturing district in the world. But owing to the fact that freight rates are usually less on raw than on finished products, this is a questionable advantage for the southern cotton mill when manufacturing for other localities.

It was the cheaper labor that was the chief factor in locating cotton manufacture in the South. The Appalachian Mountain district had a white population, dense in relation to the resources, and therefore with inadequate opportunity for employment, so that wages were much lower than in the North and West. So when the cotton mills gave an opportunity for profitable employment these mountain people migrated in large numbers to the mills just as the people of Quebec and Europe migrated to the mills of New England.

The South with its product of coarser cotton sheetings and cloths, a product requiring a large amount of raw material with a small amount of labor, has entered more largely into supplying our exports than has any other district, because coarse uncolored cloth constitutes the chief bulk of our exports. Our best cottons stay at home and our export is consumed in largest quantities in countries where, like China and Africa, the coarse cloth is desired by a poor population. China alone has in some past years taken the greater part of our entire export of cotton goods, and we furnish the scanty raiment (loin cloth, 3 × 10 feet) for some of the tribes of Africa.

Cotton manufacture in other sections of the United States.— Many English textile workers have settled in Philadelphia, where their imported skill has made possible the introduction of textile industries that had not previously flourished in America, such as lace, hosiery, tapestries, chenilles and other cotton goods that require skill in coloring.

The dependence of the textile industry upon labor more than any or all other factors has caused the amount of cotton manufactured west of the Alleghenies to be very small, and it is not increasing.

3. THE WOOL-MANUFACTURING INDUSTRY

Wool and its qualities.—Wool was originally the under coat of the sheep. Many animals have an outer coat of coarse hair with a shorter warmer coat under it. The seal skin of commerce is such an under coat. On the sheep this under coat has the character we call wool, and by long breeding and selection sheep have come to have a coat which is chiefly wool, although this animal also has some hair and in some hot countries it has hair only, like a deer or cow. Wool differs from hair and other fibers in being crinkly or curled, so that it makes an elastic cloth, and also in being covered with minute scales, whereas hair is smooth. These scales overlap each other as do shingles on a roof, and when the natural grease is scoured from the wool, the scales catch each other and hold the wool together as a tangled mass. This quality is utilized in making a matted thread-less fabric called felt, produced by beating, shaking and rolling the fibers together. This felting process is also used in making hats, both soft and hard.

Woolen clothing is the best for cold climates because it prevents the escape of heat of the body, permits the moisture of perspiration to pass through and yet does not become wet so easily from rain as do fabrics made of other fibers. .

The process of manufacture.—The fleece as it comes from the sheep has grease and other impurities which amount to half or three-fourths its total weight. It is washed to get rid of the loose dirt, scoured to remove the grease, combed and carded to get rid of other foreign substances and to lay the fibers out straight ready for spinning the yarn for final weaving into cloth. In its relation to household industry and the industrial revolution, wool manufacture is like cotton and the other textile industries, except that it is older and much more widespread than cotton manufacture.

Woolens, worsteds and shoddy.—The term "woolen goods" as used in the trade, includes only those woolen fabrics which do not show upon their surface the intertwining threads of ordinary woven goods. Woolens are woven but the fact is hidden by a process called "fulling" in which the cloth is beaten to give a felting effect and finally the fibers are pulled up by being gently combed with teasles so that the surface has a uniform, smooth, almost furry appearance. The chief woolen fabrics are broadcloth, cashmere, tweed, blankets, flannels and shawls. "Worsted goods," made of woolen yarns, show upon their surfaces their woven origin and are gaining in popularity over woolens. "Shoddy" is thick, warm cloth made of re-manufactured wool fibers obtained by tearing up tailors' clippings and woolen rags, mixing them with new wool, and weaving all into a warm cheap cloth.

Wool manufacture in the United States.—In the United States we see the effects of the colonial importance of the woolen industry, for its manufacture is the most widely scattered of all the textile industries. Small mills, comparable to the rural grist mill and driven by small water-wheels on insignificant streams, were established in the last half of the eighteenth and the first half of the nineteenth century over almost all the settled country, and small factories are to be found today in every state of the Union, although in many of them the output is insignificant. The large scale manufacture of modern type, with big factories, is concentrated east of the Alleghenies, north of Maryland, in an almost continuous belt reaching from Wilmington, Del., and southeastern Pennsylvania, through northern New Jersey, southeastern New York, and lower New England into southern Maine. These factories, like the modern American wool industry, have largely arisen since 1865. In this concentration of the wool industry, we see another example of the dependence of textile manufacture upon dense population, the valuable wool of Montana, New Mexico, Ohio and distant foreign countries being carried thousands of miles to the place where abundant labor exists to manufacture it. Philadelphia is the greatest single woolen manufacturing center in the United States, but almost every city of importance in this eastern belt has woolen mills.

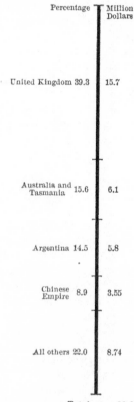

Percentage ⌐ Million Dollars

United Kingdom 39.3 | 15.7

Australia and Tasmania 15.6 | 6.1

Argentina 14.5 | 5.8

Chinese Empire 8.9 | 3.55

All others 22.0 | 8.74

Total 39.9

FIG. 134.—United States import of raw wool, three-year average, 1909–11.

Four hundred and fifty million pounds of wool were required by American mills in 1909, and we imported a little more than a third of it as has long been our custom (Fig. 134). Seventy million pounds of wool are also re-used in making shoddy. The declining importance of wool is indicated by the fact that the woolen mills of the United States recently used in one year 110 million pounds of cotton.

Carpets and hats.—Wool is important in carpet manufacture, but only inferior carpets are made of pure wool. The better ones, such as Wilton, Axminster, and even Brussels have a strong web of linen or hemp into which the wool is woven. Philadelphia has long been noted as the great carpet manufacturing center of the United States and although the carpet industry there is steadily growing, the increase of carpet mills in some north-eastern cities has caused Philadelphia's share of carpet manufacture to decline from nearly a half to about two-fifths.

Hats are classed with wool manufactures, but they are made chiefly by felting rather than weaving. The usual material is the hair of fur-bearing animals, especially rabbits obtained in Belgium and France. The fur of the beaver is used for the finer "top" hats. The coats of domesticated hares and rabbits of North France and Belgium are the mainstay of the American hat industry. This branch of the American woolen industry amounts to nearly $40,000,000 a year, of which one-half is paid for the furs. Hat manufacturing is chiefly centered in the district between Connecticut and Philadelphia, with the New Jersey cities in the vicinity of New York giving the leadership to their state. **The limitation of raw materials.**—Wool, like leather, is scarce and becoming more so with small prospect of adequate increase of supply to meet increasing population. Wool is largely a by-product of the meat industry, and the conditions of the wool manufacturing cannot affect the raw material supply so directly as cotton manufacturing can affect its raw material, since cotton is a product grown for its own sake. A 25-per cent increase in the price of wool, say from 20 to 25 cents per pound, amounts to 20 or 30 cents increase in income per sheep per year—a factor of small importance. A similar increase in cotton, from 10 to 12½ cents per pound, changes the entire basis of the business and causes great increase of output, for the cotton grown to meet the new demand would be on the market in a year or even less, while the wool resulting from a desire to increase the output would have to await the maturity of animals yet unborn. The cotton and wool industries have, therefore, fared very differently in the past 25 years. While cotton production and manufacture have been going up by leaps and bounds, the production of raw wool throughout the world has increased but little, and has at times remained stationary or even declined. As a result, cotton has been substituted for wool in many of its uses. If the process of **substituting** other fibers for wool does not continue, we are likely to have much higher prices for wool, because of the large amount of **land** needed to produce it.

The industrial awakening of China and Japan, and their adoption of western ideas and methods, will increase rather than diminish the world scarcity of wool. European styles demand wool, and Japan, with practically no wool supply, is beginning to import and manufacture some foreign wool. China is now exporting her small crop of wool because the native styles of clothing can be supplied by cotton and silk, chiefly cotton. The adoption of western styles of clothing by modernized China may be expected to produce a demand for wool in that country, as it has already done to some extent in India, which now makes nearly $2,000,000 worth of wool cloth and imports $10,000,000 worth besides. These oriental changes of style are likely to be permanent in contrast to the seasonal changes that beset the world trade in clothing, especially woolen clothing.

Substitutes for sheep's wool.—The other animal hair fibers used for fabric seem destined to continue in a very secondary place—as the alpaca wool with its resulting fabric, the Cashmere goat's hair with its fabric. Mohair, the fleece of the Angora goat, native of the province of Angora in central Asia Minor, shows well the process of invention and substitution. Its main use is for plush, as for car seats, but of late it has been used to make imitation fur of such reality that detection is difficult.

Percentage / Million Dollars

Japan 59.6   44.1

Italy 19.8   14.3

China 16.4   12.2

France 3.4   2.5
All Others 1.3   0.9
Total   74.0

FIG. 135.—United States imports of raw silk, three-year average, 1909–11.

4. SILK

The United States leads in silk manufacture though we do not produce a bale of the raw material. We import raw silk from the other side of the world, a fine example of the labor factor in locating industry. A freight rate of 3 cents per pound is about 1 per cent on raw silk and the same freight is from 150 to 200 per cent on wheat valuation. The freight is, therefore, an almost negligible factor in sending silk half-way around the world from the place with the most desirable conditions for the production of raw silk to the place with the most desirable conditions for its manufacture. Thus it easily comes from countries with very cheap labor (see chapter on Japan).

Over half of the total value of silk production is expended for the raw silk which is furnished to the United States as follows: Japan nearly two-thirds, China one-fifth, Italy one-seventh, France one-thirtieth (Fig. 135).

Relation of silk manufacture to other industries.—Silk manufacture is comparatively light work, and the percentage of women operatives in the silk mills is higher than in any other branch of textiles. This predominance of women gives the silk mill a tendency to be what is sometimes called a "parasitic industry;" that is, it is located because of the presence of other industries which employ large numbers of men, so that the wives and daughters of the workmen make a labor supply which encourages the starting of silk mills. Paterson, N. J., an important place for the manufacture of various classes of iron goods, which employ only men, has for this reason long been the most important silk-manufacturing town in the United States, having produced over a quarter of the total silk product in 1890 and about a fifth in 1905. This relation of the silk to heavy industries is well shown in Pennsylvania, where the silk mills are located chiefly in and near the coal-mining towns, especially Scranton and Wilkesbarre, and the cement-manufacturing towns of Allentown and Easton in the Lehigh Valley, and in the agricultural-implement-manufacturing town of York, and more recently in the coal and iron region of western Pennsylvania.

Artificial silk.—The silk worm makes silk by drawing the fine threads from a jelly-like mass in its head. This material is made from the cells in the worm's vegetable food, as changed by the chemistry of its body. Man has copied the worm's process. By the chemistry of the laboratory, sawdust or cotton waste may be converted into a jelly much like that from which the caterpillar makes its silk. By air pressure this cellulose is driven through very small apertures in glass and wound by machinery. Each aperture makes filaments so small that, as with silk, it takes ten to twenty of them reeled together to make a thread. This process, which began in France, has spread to Germany and Switzerland, England and America. The output is increasing with a suggestive speed, and the price of silk is declining. In 1909, the output of artificial silk was 3 million pounds, and in 1911, it was 13 million or nearly a fourth as great as that of real silk. It should be noted that this fiber, now in its infancy, is made chiefly from cotton, an abundant raw material.

5. The Plant Stalk Fibers

Practically all the larger plants have stalk fibers some of which are of good quality for textile use if they could be secured in cheap abundance, and several dozen kinds of such fibers are actually in extensive use in various parts of the world. This group of fibers is of unknown antiquity and because of gin-cheapened cotton it has probably been of less relative importance to man in the last century than in any century for thousands of years. It has been displaced for the time being, but there is no guarantee of the continuance of cotton's leadership in plant fibers. Some stalk fiber cheapened by machinery may compete with it, but just at present the use of plant stalk fibers is at a low ebb, despite their superiorities over cotton.

Flax and its preparation.—Flax is now, as in the past, the most important plant stalk fiber entering into our clothing. This plant, a member of the nettle family, has to our certain knowledge been yielding linen since the pre-historic Lake dwellers inhabited the Swiss lakes, and the mummies, bound up in linen cloth, were placed in the Egyptian tombs four or five thousand years ago. In 1790, when cotton was less used in manufacture than China grass or ramie now is, flax was the most important of all vegetable fibers. It was grown on almost every European and American farm, and in many an old American home the implements for the preparation of flax are still to be found. The introduction of cheap cotton caused the disappearance of flax from gardens at about the time of the passing of the spinning wheel and the hand loom.

The fiber as obtained is from 8 to 50 inches in length, strong and durable, but the labor of getting it out of the stalk has, since the coming of cotton, made its production impracticable wherever wages were high and the import of commercial products easy. Thus linen is limited to special uses for which it is peculiarly fit, as collar and cuff manufacturing. This is one of the most important American industries using linen, and this branch of manufacture shows a most astonishing concentration in the city of Troy, New York, where nine-tenths of the entire product of the United States is made. This concentration is best explained by the fact that, if a new collar and cuff factory is to be established, the best place in which to find labor already trained for the work is in the city of Troy. (It is stated that the wife of a Troy blacksmith first made shirts with detachable collars about seventy-five years ago, and that a Methodist minister encouraged this home industry. See R. H. Whitbeck, *Journal of Geography*, Oct., 1909.)

The range of the flax plant and the flaxseed industry.—Although flax produces a valuable seed (linseed), the plants grown for fiber are pulled before they blossom so that flax fiber districts have no valuable by-product of seed as is the case with cotton growing. Flax thus gives rise to two industries: one, fiber; the other, grain. The plant has an exceedingly wide range, having produced good fiber all over the eastern United States and in Europe from Scotland, Sweden, and Russia to Italy.

The cultivation of the flax plant, like silk culture, shows fine responses to labor conditions—density of population (Fig. 136). Varieties producing poor fiber but fine seed are grown in several of the important wheat regions, as the Argentine Republic (one-third of the world's crop), Central Russia (one-fifth of the world's crop), the spring wheat belt in the valley of the Red River of the North (one-fourth of the world's crop), and northern India (one-eighth

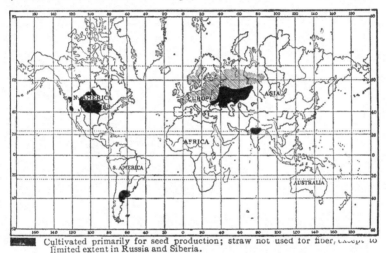

▬ Cultivated primarily for seed production; straw not used for fiber, except to limited extent in Russia and Siberia.

▨ Cultivated primarily for fiber; straw used for fiber and seed for oil, except in Ireland where seed is usually not saved.

FIG. 136.—Distribution of flax in cultivation.   (Original by Lyster Dewey.)

of the world's crop). In all these districts, with a total crop of 100 million bushels, flax is, from the agricultural standpoint, not a fiber but a cereal planted like wheat, harvested with the most improved reaping machinery, threshed by steam, and handled in every respect like wheat with no thought of saving the fiber that is in the straw. Indeed, the straw is often burned. The laborious hand processes of harvesting in sparsely peopled countries like Dakota and Argentina are entirely impossible, but fit well into the scanty opportunities of north Russia where the Archangel district produces most of the flax fiber.

The seed, upon being crushed, yields linseed oil, much used as a raw material for the paint and varnish factories of Philadelphia and other eastern American cities. The "oil-cake" that remains is highly valued as food for livestock, and is shipped in thousands of tons from Dakota by way of New York, Montreal, Boston and Philadelphia to feed the herds of dairy cows in Holland, Denmark, and England.

A possible revolution in linen.—By a recently perfected process it is claimed that much of the old and expensive labor of preparing flax fiber can be entirely avoided by a speedy mechanical operation which may be likened to the threshing of wheat, or the ginning of cotton, and which extracts the fiber from flax straw in a few hours.

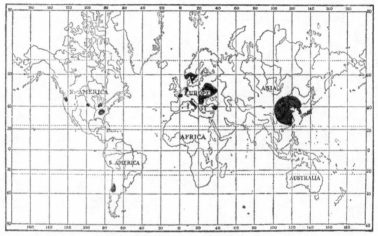

FIG. 137.—Distribution of hemp in cultivation. (Original by Lyster Dewey.)

Unfortunately the long fibers are broken into lengths of less than an inch. This limits its uses, but a Massachusetts factory has been built for its preparation and manufacture; this fact suggests great re-adjustments due to the competition of cheap flax produced upon the world's frontier grain fields and sold at a much lower price than the cotton which is still expensively picked by human fingers and sold at 10 to 15 cents a pound. The success of the cotton-picking machine and the flax decorticator, if both should come into use, will enable mankind to reap the benefit of a greatly cheapened clothing supply.

Hemp.—Hemp, the fiber of common cordage, is closely allied to

flax, of which it is really but a coarser variety and therefore fitted
for coarser uses.   It is chiefly produced in the flax districts of Russia,
and is used in almost every rope factory in the United States and
Europe (Fig. 137).

FIG. 138.—Cutting hemp by hand in Kentucky.   A machine has recently been
invented to do this work.   (U. S. Dept. Agr.)

The American hemp district, in the bluegrass section of Kentucky,
has for a long time had a declining output due to the competition of
cheaper labor in other hemp-growing countries, but especially,
through the competition of cheap jute.   Recently, after a long series
of failures, a hemp-breaking machine has been invented which is
responsible for the large-scale growth of hemp in northern Indiana.

Ramie or China grass.—The best of plant fibers is that known as rhea in India, ramie in Malay countries, and China grass in many other parts of the world. It is twice as strong as the best Russian hemp. It excels all other fibers in its resistance to the influence of water, and is used to make sails for racing yachts, where expense is no consideration. In appearance it rivals silk. It may be used for a host of purposes from the ship's cable and sail cloth to velvet or lace. It is much worn as summer clothing in China, and factories produce fabric from it in England and other European countries. In comparison to cotton the climatic range of the plant is wonderful. It thrives in the torrid zone and as far north as Normandy, where it is grown to a limited extent. It will thrive in many parts of the United States, is grown commercially in Mexico, but chiefly in China. The reason this wonderful fiber has not been extensively used is the great difficulty thus far experienced in separating it from the stalk of the plant in which it grows, and from the gummy substances which adhere to it. Cheap ramie, grown almost anywhere and decorticated by a machine, may, in combination with cheap flax, give unthought of competition to cotton even if picked by machinery.

6. Clothing

Similar development of the textile and clothing industries.—At the end of a century and a quarter of machine manufacture and world commerce, the making of clothing is now passing through an evolution similar to that which has occurred in the textile industries. The cloth was at first made in the homes of the workers from materials which were given out on contract. Later the whole work was done in the large factory with the aid of machinery. Some clothing is now made by the old domestic system, some on contract in the homes of the workers, and some in factories and shops.

The first decade of this century was, as a consequence, a period of rapid increase in the manufacture of men's and women's ready-made clothing in factories rather than in sweat shops. In the sweat shop five persons usually work on a coat, each doing a particular part. In some of the great factories, as many as a hundred persons work on each coat, and the total amount of time required to produce a given output has been reduced to one-third or even to one-tenth of that required before the introduction of the greater division of labor, new cutting machines, and the electric-driven sewing machines.

Clothing manufacture belongs to large cities (Fig. 139) because of the double advantage of nearness to labor and to market. It is an advantage to be near the center where the product is sold, and the successful selling of ready-made clothing requires a market where vast numbers of persons are supplied, so that, by the law of averages, all of each of the many sizes of clothing may be called for. As the market widens, it permits the finer and finer subdivision of the sizes, and the greater possibility of an exact fit for each person. The large city also possesses the labor which is so large a factor in this industry with raw materials so easy to transport. The manufacture of clothing is concentrated to an astonishing but declining degree in the city of New York, the greatest distributing center of the United States, where it is the leading industry, with an output valued at nearly half a billion dollars per year and equal to that of all the other cities of the country. Chicago is second, Philadelphia third, Baltimore fourth, Cincinnati fifth, Rochester sixth, and Boston and St. Louis next in order. This great predominance of New York is due in large part to the unusual labor condition that exists because it is the chief place for the landing of the new immigrant. Tens of thousands of these people know nothing of the language and little of the country, and they are accustomed to low wages and inexpensive standards of life. The clothing factory, where each person does a small operation, offers these helpless ones an opportunity to acquire in a few days the skill to make a better wage than they had in Europe, so they herd together in the cities. In one block on Broadway, New York, covered with twelve-story structures, 40,000 people are engaged in manufacture, largely clothing. The industry in all the American centers is usually carried on by foreign-born persons newly arrived in this country.

Percentage

New York 50.6

Chicago 10.8
Philadelphia 5.1
Baltimore 3.8
Cincinnati 2.8
Boston 2.8
Rochester 2.5
Cleveland 1.7

All others 19.9

FIG. 139.— United States clothing manufacture by cities, 1905.

The standardizing of clothing is steadily advancing and with it new additions to the list of manufactured articles. Thus the small tailor is suffering from the competition of the great factory through the competition of made-to-measure mail-order business. By this innovation, a country merchant in Texas shows a book of samples to a customer, measures him, and the suit is made in a New York, Rochester or Chicago factory.

QUESTIONS

1. How does the commercial excellence of cotton help to make poorer the man who grows it?

2. Will a heavy increase in demand for clothing fibers be met equally by increase in wool or cotton?

3. What would be the influence upon clothing supply of a successful cotton picker? a successful Ramie decorticator?

4. Is Alabama with plenty of cotton and coal a good place to start a mill for the manufacture of the finest cotton goods made in America?

5. The silk worm and the mulberry tree both do well in Indiana. Is it a good place for the production of raw silk?

6. Does the modernizing of China have the same effect upon the world supply of wool and silk?

7. Explain how the supply of fibers is in an unstable condition.

8. How did the European war which was then in progress destroy the value of the 1914 cotton crop? How did it affect the value of corn? In this instance, show the particular advantage enjoyed by the Southern farmer who rotated his crops? What are some of the other advantages of crop rotation in cotton lands?

9. How has the boll weevil outbreak stimulated the breeding of early maturing varieties of cotton?

10. Why has the cotton manufacturing industry not advanced west of the Alleghenies?

11. What changes of style in the orient may stimulate sheep raising in America?

12. Explain how freight charges are an almost negligible factor in the cost raw silk.

CHAPTER XII

LEATHER AND RUBBER

1. Raw Materials and Manufacture of Leather

Hides and skins.—Leather is made by cleaning and treating skins so that they will keep, and the skins are furnished by a great variety of animals. Naturally the domestic animals—the ox, sheep, goat, horse, and pig—lead, but many other animals contribute their small quota.

Leather is as old as trade and the industry contributes to the commerce of every nation and every people, sometimes in the form of hides and of raw materials for tanning, sometimes as finished leather, which is the raw material of shoe factories and other leather works, and finally in the form of shoes and other leather manufactures.

The term hides is applied to the skins of cattle and horses; skins, to those from sheep, goats, and smaller animals. The United States leads all other countries in the manufacture of leather; and the import of hides and skins, amounting to nearly $100,000,000 a year, is one of the greatest items of our foreign trade. Practically every country in the world contributes some of these raw materials, and of goat skins alone we import over a hundred million a year. We get hides and skins from poor countries like Venezuela and India that do not even have tanning industries. We also get them from the richest and greatest manufacturing nations in the world—England, Germany, and France, where the fuller utilization of resource, due to a dense population, has produced a scarcity of tanning materials in which the United States is the richest country in the world.

Tanning processes and materials.—Tanning usually consists in treating the skin with a strong astringent, tannin, a very common vegetable substance which unites with certain elements in the hide and changes it from a material prone to decay, to one of great durability. Tannin, like sugar, is widely distributed among plants,

253

and has long been found in workable quantities in all continents. Tannin is secured from many parts of the plant; as myrobolans, the dried fruit of a leguminous tree from India; valonia, the cup of an acorn in Turkey and Asia Minor; the sumac leaf from Sicily and Appalachia, and also from wood itself, as is done in the chestnut extract mills in the forests of both Europe and America.

Until a half century ago, the peoples of Europe and America depended for tannin chiefly upon the bark of oak in southern, and hemlock in northern, locations. The growing scarcity of forests and the increased supply of hides which world commerce produced, has created a lively trade in other tannin-producing materials, so that now no less than fifty of them are in use. With the increase in distant commerce there is a growing tendency to ship these materials in concentrated forms or extracts, thus lessening transportation costs.

The chief part of tanning consists in scraping the skins to get rid of all flesh and fat and then soaking them in liquids strong with tannin or other tanning material.

The United States makes over $300,000,000 worth of leather per year (Fig. 140). While still importing small quantities ($5,000,000 in 1911) of special European makes, the United States is doubling its leather export ($40,000,000 in 1911) every 10 years. The industry, which gives employment to 50,000 people, is one that has undergone greater changes in material than in method. The forest with its bulky bark determined the location of the American tanning industry until the end of the nineteenth century. The valuable hides and leather were easily portable. Tanneries were often small affairs like the little country grist mill, and were scattered in rural hamlets and mountain valleys throughout Appalachia and New England.

We have two bark-tanning belts, one reaching the whole length of the Appalachian Mountains from New York to Georgia and including Virginia on the east and Tennessee on the west, the other in the hemlock region running from Massachusetts to Wisconsin, both of which are important leather states.

Chemical tanning and its effects.—Fortunately for the forest resources of the United States and the world, a new tanning industry has arisen practically independent of vegetable materials because it depends upon chemical compounds of chromium. This chrome process was first developed in Philadelphia, where it has grown with great rapidity and has helped to make that city the greatest leather-manufacturing center in the world. Philadelphia's specialties are patent and enamel leathers and vici kid. The chrome leather industry, depending on factory products, labor, and markets,

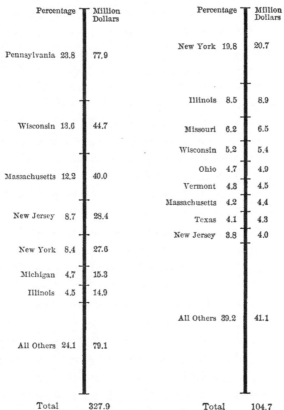

Percentage	Million Dollars
Pennsylvania 23.8	77.9
Wisconsin 13.6	44.7
Massachusetts 12.2	40.0
New Jersey 8.7	28.4
New York 8.4	27.6
Michigan 4.7	15.3
Illinois 4.5	14.9
All Others 24.1	79.1
Total	327.9

Fig. 140.—Leather tanned, cured and finished in United States, 1909.

Percentage	Million Dollars
New York 19.8	20.7
Illinois 8.5	8.9
Missouri 6.2	6.5
Wisconsin 5.2	5.4
Ohio 4.7	4.9
Vermont 4.8	4.5
Massachusetts 4.2	4.4
Texas 4.1	4.3
New Jersey 3.8	4.0
All Others 39.2	41.1
Total	104.7

Fig. 141.—Leather goods other than shoes manufactured in the United States, 1909.

tends to locate in manufacturing centers rather than forest districts and since it depends almost entirely upon imported goat skins for its raw material, there is some advantage in being near the ports of entry. Some kinds of leather must still be made with bark.

2. LEATHER MANUFACTURES

Leather manufactures include belting for driving machinery, harness, and finishings for carriages and automobiles. It is also used for a host of small trinkets and many industrial purposes (Fig. 141), but the making of boots and shoes is much the most important use.

During the first half of the nineteenth century shoes were made by hand all over the country. During the last quarter of the nineteenth century factories began to roll out shoes through the aid of very complex machinery, and a minute division of labor, in which many persons worked on each shoe. The passing of the roadside shop was followed by a surprising concentration of manufacture. The state of Massachusetts produces three times as many shoes as any other state. The two cities of Brockton and Lynn together produce about as many shoes as any two states outside of Massachusetts, while Haverhill, Marlboro, and Boston are other important shoe centers. Manchester, New Hampshire, and Auburn, Maine, are really a part of the same shoe district, which sends shoes to every state in the Union and to many foreign countries. As with the ready-made clothing, so with ready-made shoes, a wide market and large sale make possible the production of a great variety of shapes and sizes so that greater and greater proportions of the people can be fitted with the factory product. This factor in combination with the smaller cost of machine-made goods in comparison to hand output, helps to explain the great and quick concentration of the industry.

The foreign trade in shoes seems destined to be small. The superior fit and comfort of American shoes is appreciated and a few years ago a large trade seemed to be in prospect, but the export of American shoe machinery to Europe has been followed by the ability of Europeans to compete in the one respect in which they were lacking—style. This, in combination with preferential tariffs, has cut down the American shoe export to New Zealand, alone, six-sevenths in 6 years. In connection with shoe export, the tropic habit of going barefoot should not be overlooked. Shoes are almost unthought of by races that buy cottons by the million yards. Many nations that buy nearly all their cotton and woolen goods make nearly all of their shoes.

Tendency of shoe industry to spread.—High freight rates and the heavy expense of shipping a bulky though valuable commodity like shoes help to explain the rise of new centers nearer the western markets, New York, Rochester, Cincinnati and Columbus, Ohio, and St. Louis.

Glove manufacturing in the United States.—While many fine gloves come from France, Germany, and England, there is a production, chiefly for home use, of something like $20,000,000 worth in this country. The glove industry is remarkably concentrated, the two towns of Gloversville and Johnstown, in Fulton County, New York, neither of which has 20,000 people, making nearly half of the gloves in the United States. These towns, founded by Scotch glove-makers, had the advantage of an early start.

The future supply of leather.—There is no sign of any lessening in the demand for leather. As standards of living rise, the people of Holland, Belgium, and Germany tend to lay aside wooden shoes, as do the Chinese and Japanese their leatherless foot-gear of straw, cotton and wood. But leather is rising in price because it depends on the supply of animals, and animals are now becoming relatively scarce and must continue so. The world does not possess the leather to make western shoes for the Chinese. In the United States, which draws upon the world, the number of hides and skins used increased 16 per cent between 1899 and 1909, and their cost increased 59 per cent. Leather substitutes should be welcomed.

3. FURS

Furs comprise a branch of the leather trade that tends to go down rather than up as the population of the world increases. This is because nearly all the furs are taken from wild animals many of which are carnivorous. As a further limiting factor most of them live in forests and the forests are being cut. Thus the woods of our two northern forest belts are the chief home supply of furs, but the chief part of the world's product comes from the great subarctic forest that practically girdles the world from southern Alaska to Labrador and from Finland to Kamchatka. Throughout this vast and frosty region the wandering trapper annually makes deep journeys into the wild forest and emerges at the end of weeks or months with a bale of fox, muskrat, mink, martin, sable and other skins. These are nearly all sent to the two fur markets of Liepzig and London. So great is the monopoly of these centers that the war of 1914 caused the entire stoppage of the trade. The price of furs went to almost nothing and the manufacture of steel traps at Oneida, New York, suddenly stopped. Fur farming which has at last begun in a small way in Canada (see chapter on Canada) is in response to a keen and normally increasing demand.

4. RUBBER

The origin and utilization of rubber.—While primitive man long ago learned to use the tannin from many plants, the rubber that many other plants contain had to wait for the modern man with his laboratory.

The coagulation of the sap of trees into a sticky or gummy substance is a familiar occurrence, and the sap of many tropic trees produces the chemically complex substance we call rubber. For 80 years it was used only as an eraser. Then the inventions of MacIntosh (1823) and Goodyear (1842), mixing rubber with sulphur, made it suitable for waterproof clothing, shoes, and boots. A large percentage of sulphur makes the hard rubber used for combs and a great variety of electrical and industrial articles.

The recent increase in rubber consumption.—Goodyear's invention started the rubber boot and shoe industry, which now amounts to about one-tenth the value of the leather boots and shoes. The import of crude rubber and gums has gone up rapidly from 5,000 tons in 1870 to 72,000 tons in 1911. The chief supply comes from Brazil but nearly all tropic countries produce some rubber. About the year 1890 rubber consumption entered upon a period of great increase due to the adoption of the pneumatic tire. The sudden and large development of the bicycle and automobile industries followed. There has also been a steady increase in the amount of rubber used for electrical insulation and other new industrial work, and the enlarged demand for raw rubber has raised its price to phenomenal figures and caused it to be supplied by many countries where its production had previously been almost unknown (Figs. 142, 143, 144).

As a result the cultivation of rubber as a crop has started, and the chemists have also succeeded in making synthetic rubber in the laboratory. This has not yet been reduced to an industrial basis, but few things seem more certain than that, between the output of orchards and factories, as well as the old forests, our rubber-using industries are upon the eve of a new era in raw materials. (For rubber planting see chapter on Expansion of Industry.)

Rubber manufactures.—The prospective cheaper and larger supply of raw materials will be fortunate for the United States.

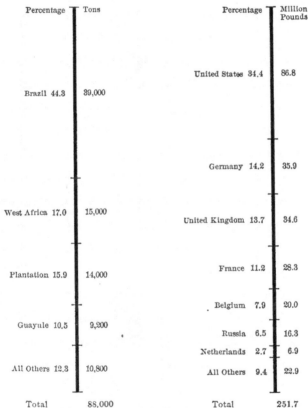

Percentage	Tons
Brazil 44.3	39,000
West Africa 17.0	15,000
Plantation 15.9	14,000
Guayule 10.5	9,200
All Others 12.3	10,800
Total	88,000

Percentage	Million Pounds
United States 34.4	86.8
Germany 14.2	35.9
United Kingdom 13.7	34.6
France 11.2	28.3
Belgium 7.9	20.0
Russia 6.5	16.3
Netherlands 2.7	6.9
All Others 9.4	22.9
Total	251.7

FIG. 142.—World's production of rubber, 1911. (India Rubber World.)

FIG. 143.—World's india rubber import, three-year average, 1908–10.

Already our rapidly growing rubber industries take nearly a pound of rubber per capita for all the 90-odd million people in this country. The enormous increase in the automobile industry promises to demand much more.

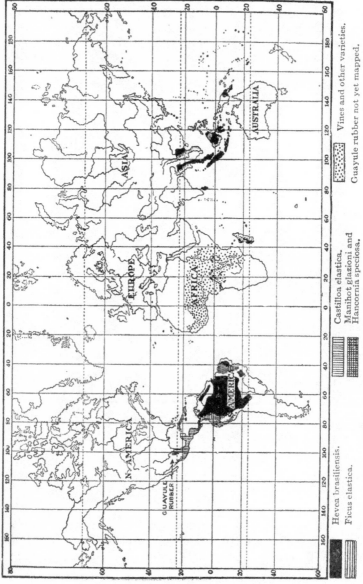

FIG. 144.—Distribution of leading varieties of rubber plant. (From A. Vincent, Industries du Caoutchouc et de l'amiante.) Few products are produced by so many plants over so much of the earth's surface.

The rubber boot and shoe, the best known of our rubber products, are produced almost entirely in the factories of southern New England. Massachusetts, Connecticut, and Rhode Island make nearly nine-tenths of the entire American output, but the industrial uses exceed those of foot wear in the quantity of rubber used in the United States. Rubber tires are everywhere manifest. Rubber hose is a universal necessity, filling a thousand uses; the airbrake system of every train requires it. Rubber packing in engines, pumps, and valves, and rubber electrical supplies, show how universal is the distribution of manufactured products of rubber which thus go wherever steam goes and water is lifted. For these purposes the products of American rubber factories are sent to every country in the world. The countries next in importance are Great Britain and Germany, but our rubber consumption exceeds that of any two foreign countries.

QUESTIONS

1. Where should a tannery be located?
2. From what kind of countries do we import hides and skins?
3. Explain how an invention revolutionized the rubber industry.
4. Compare the prospects for cheap rubber and cheap hides.

CHAPTER XIII

THE MACHINERY, SHIP-BUILDING AND METAL INDUSTRIES

1. FACTORS OF LOCATION

Ship-building must be done where the ships can be launched, but the location of other classes of machine building is influenced by two factors which often tend to conflict, but which sometimes coincide—labor and the market. It is easy to see how a carload of iron, steel, or wood is much less bulky than the same materials made up into machinery. It is therefore a transportation advantage to have the factories located near to the market rather than near to the raw material. In some classes of machinery, such as cheap and bulky agricultural machinery, the transportation cost is heavy in proportion to the value, and the dominating influence of the market is strong. So, Chicago, in the midst of the great wheat and corn fields, has the main plant of the International Harvester Company. In other classes of machinery, such as clocks and watches, the freight element in the cost to the ultimate consumer is relatively small and the labor element is large, with the result that the labor element has strong influence in the location of the industry. Waterbury, Conn., and Waltham, Mass., have thus maintained their watch factories in the East, where, for decades, their workmen have been trained.

The manufacture of machinery for factories is nearly always a sort of second stage in industry, the first stage being the growth of the industry which uses the machinery, thus developing the market for it.

2. THE MANUFACTURE OF AGRICULTURAL MACHINERY

The origin and service of agricultural machinery.—Large areas of cheap land in combination with the consequent high wages have dominated industrial conditions in the United States and made it impossible for the farmers, under the old system of hand labor and simple devices, to cultivate as much ground as they could easily secure. Necessity has in this form been the mother of invention of agricultural machinery, which has been perfected to a greater degree in this country than in Europe. The thoroughness of our invention and the scope of our agricultural machine works is shown by the virtual absence of imports of machinery of this class, while we have exports far greater than any other country.

In 1850 we produced 1 ton of cereals per person. In 1900 with a smaller proportion of the population engaged in agriculture, we produced 1½ tons of cereals per person. This increase in the

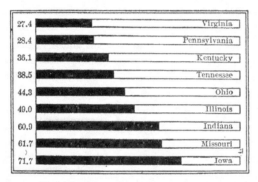

FIG. 145.—Percentage of counties losing population in nine great agricultural states 1900–10. Iowa probably leads all states in its exclusive dependence upon one of the most modern and thoroughly mechanical types of American agriculture. Its effects upon population are startling.

efficiency of the producer of breadstuffs is due largely to the machinery he has used. It has replaced hand-labor in production as the locomotive has replaced the wagon in transportation, and the two classes of machinery together have given the world cheaper food and raw materials than it ever had before.

The census of 1910 showed astonishing changes due to agricultural machinery. Within 10 years the rural population of Ohio, Indiana, Illinois, and Iowa had declined 6 per cent. (Fig. 145). This was due to the use of machinery which increased 50 per cent. in value per farm. It was accompanied by an increase of 5 acres in the size of the average farm, an increase in the number of horses and a decrease in the number of people per farm. Where it can be used agricultural machinery removes man from the land (Fig. 146), as shown by a population of seventy-one persons per 1,000 acres on the best level Ohio land and seventy-four per 1,000 acres on the poorer hilly lands of southwestern Ohio.

Manufactured near the market.—Agricultural machinery is very bulky, and the consequent high freight rates give a great advantage to the factory located nearest to the place where the machinery will be used. Therefore, this industry has always kept close to the edge of the great farming region, especially the grain belt. For a time the leading center of manufacture was in the city of Auburn, New York, then Columbus and Springfield, Ohio, on the edge of the vast level plain of the corn belt, which has been the compelling force to make men use farm machinery. With the further westward move-

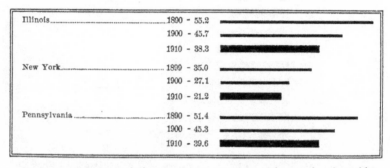

Illinois	1890 - 55.2
	1900 - 45.7
	1910 - 38.3
New York	1890 - 35.0
	1900 - 27.1
	1910 - 21.2
Pennsylvania	1890 - 51.4
	1900 - 45.3
	1910 - 39.6

FIG. 146.—Rural population: per cent. of totals. The supply of machine-made agricultural products has combined with the factory lure to cause a steady decline in the proportion of our population that lives on farms.

ment of the market, the industry centered in Chicago, the greatest agricultural market and the greatest railway center in the world. Chicago's leadership is due to her location in the heart of the corn belt, the hay belt, and the oats belt, and also near the wheat regions. These influences have made Chicago's manufacture of agricultural implements five times as great as that of any other city in the country.

The westward trend of the industry is shown by the fact that Springfield, Ohio, once the second city in importance in implement manufacture, has recently been surpassed by Moline, Illinois—a town on the banks of the Mississippi River distinctly to the west of the important manufacturing part of the United States. Peoria, Illinois, and Richmond, Indiana, are other important centers.

Interchangeable parts.—The manufacturing of agricultural implements has received a great impetus from the practice of making machines with interchangeable parts, so that one machine in the factory turns out one piece which will fit any one of thousands of a given kind of completed machine in the field. This enables the farmer in any land to feel independent of the location of the factory and to take advantage of the fact that the American machines have been adjusted to the various kinds of lands that exist in the United States or elsewhere. Thus we send machines of the so-called "stump jump" types to the newly cleared Australian "Bush."

The combination of patents, adaptation, and low prices gives us one of the few branches of manufacture in which America has outstripped foreign countries which have cheaper labor and approximate equality of raw materials. American agricultural machinery is much used in Argentina, Russia, Canada and Australia, countries with conditions much like our own.

3. Carriages, Wagons and Automobiles

Relationship to the agricultural implement industry.—The carriage and wagon output exceeds the agricultural implement output, and the two industries have a kind of economic kinship. Wood and iron are the raw materials in both; both are relatively bulky when completed, and, therefore, need to be made near the market, which is located primarily in the same region. Every farmer must have one or more wagons. The fitness of the North Central States for leadership in both industries is therefore explained.

The raw material.—The deciduous trees or hard woods (see chapter on Lumber) furnish nearly all our carriage woods. Second growth hickory, which was picked out by Peary to make the sledges for his dash over the Arctic ice fields toward the north pole, is one of the monopolies of the United States. This wood, unrivaled for strength combined with elasticity, grows from New York to Georgia and Missouri, and is almost universally used for making the spokes and hubs of light carriage wheels.

The carriage industry, like the manufacture of agricultural implements, has moved westward with the centers of agriculture and population. It has actually declined in New England; remains nearly stationary in New York and Pennsylvania; and has greatly increased in the West where six states—Ohio, Indiana, Illinois,

Michigan, Wisconsin, and Missouri—manufacture more than one-half of the total product of the country. Cincinnati is the leading wagon and carriage manufacturing city in the United States; St. Louis, near the Ozark lumber and the prosperous southwest is second; while South Bend, Indiana, a part of the Chicago manufacturing district, is third.

The manufacture of carriages and wagons has gone through the process of concentration similar to that which has occurred in the shoe and textile industries. Two generations ago the country blacksmith and wheelwright had their shops side by side. One did the woodwork and the other the ironwork, and they manufactured wagons for their neighbors, while the shoemaker next door made the shoes. As shoe machinery has replaced the shoemaker, so automatic woodworking machinery has displaced the country wagon-makers whose hand-made product can no longer compete with the cheaper product of the factories in the North Central States, which send their output to every state and co 1 ty in the Union, and, in limited amounts, to foreign countries.

The automobile industry.—The autom ile affords the newest of the important industries in the United States. The first modern automobiles were made in France in 1891. By 1900 they had proved their efficiency and the new industry was established in America, where it has increased since that time with astonishing rapidity. The American output for 1914 was estimated at 700,000 machines each worth $2,000 and the total product exceeds in value all the other vehicles and agricultural implements combined. The automobile differs from carriages in being much more predominantly of iron and in being much more complex. Its parts are numerous, they must be of exact material and proportions, and are therefore difficult to make. Consequently it is inexpedient for each plant to make all its parts. For example, such an item as the ball bearings require for their manufacture a large and expensive plant. One in Philadelphia, extending for two city blocks, is capable of making enough ball bearings for dozens of automobile works. Similar expensive plants and careful processes are necessary in making many other automobile parts, so that the industry is, to a considerable extent, an assembling industry—that is, many of the parts, sometimes fifty or one hundred or more are bought and combined with others made at the factory to form the completed machine.

It was very natural for the carriage makers of the agricultural

Middle West to take up the manufacture of this new kind of carriage. It is apparent that they are dependent not so much upon the lumber of Tennessee as they are upon the machine shops of New England, New York, and the North Central States.   Therefore, this species of vehicle-making clings to the northern edge of the region that has long manufactured our carriages and wagons.   Detroit and Cleveland, together producing over a third of the entire output of the United States, are the leading centers.   The three cities next in importance—New York, Buffalo, and Indianapolis—are also located on main lines of railroad between New York and Boston and Chicago.   There is some automobile manufacturing in Connecticut, Massachusetts, and eastern Pennsylvania, and some in and around Chicago.   The great dependence of the automobile factory upon other factories gives a strong tendency for these industries to cluster around one great center.   This seems to be occurring at Detroit, which is now far ahead of all other cities, and the rapid increase in the allied industries in and about the city tends to make it the most favorable place in the country for a new automobile factory to locate.   Some automobile works are even moving there.

Foreign trade in automobiles.—The automobile was first made in France, but the Americanization of the industry has been complete. This is shown by the fact that, as a result of our rapidly increasing industry, our imports, at first largely from France, have decreased and our exports increased until in 1911 they were greater than that of all other countries in the world combined.   This appears to be due largely to the factors that have operated in the export of agricultural implements—the extensive use of automatic machinery, cheap construction through interchangeable parts, and the adaptation through rapid invention of our automobiles to hill climbing and bad roads, both of which are important factors for American automobiles.

4. MACHINERY FOR MANUFACTURING

The manufacture of machinery for manufacturing tends to occur near to the place where it is used.   Aside from the advantages of freights and transportation, there is a great convenience resulting from the increased ease of running back and forth to see that specifications are carried out and repairs promptly delivered.

Textiles, our oldest modern industry, give ample illustration of these factors in the location of their machine supply industry. The bulk of the English textile machinery is made in Manchester, Bolton, Oldham, Accrington, and Rochdale, all of them in the Lancashire cotton district. As this district has led the world in making cloth, so it has led the world in the export of textile machinery, in which Britain far exceeds all other countries together.

Worcester, Massachusetts, near the center of the New England textile field, is the leading American city for the manufacture of textile machinery. Other cities of southern New England, especially in Massachusetts and Rhode Island, share in this manufacture, and as the textile industry is growing in Philadelphia, so also is the manufacture of textile machinery springing up there.

Importance of machine tools.—The machine tool is the keystone of machinery manufacture. It is a recent invention for the easy shaping of the wood and iron parts of the machinery upon which manufacturing depends. The fashioning of wood and metal can be reduced to a few simple mechanical operations—planing, boring, turning, milling, and slotting, which have for ages been done by hand or by very simple mechanical aids. For each of these operations large, heavy, expensive, but exceedingly efficient machines have been devised. These mechanical units have been combined into a class of machines called turret lathes which perform a number of different operations by having tools arranged on a rotating wheel, each of which automatically comes in turn to do its part of a finished whole. Thus a rod will be made into a series of perfect bolts, nuts, or screws of exact dimensions. These mechanical means produce the many parts which, upon being put together, make the complex, efficient machines of the modern factory.

Many of these machine tools have been improved to the point where they become automatic. This condition is attained when a machine will take pieces of material and turn out a uniform product. Thus a roll of wire is fed into one end of a machine and finished wire nails or screws come out at the other.

The manufacture of machine tools.—The machine shop is the market for machine tools, and the machine shop is located where machinery is to be repaired or made. It is plain that repair shops, even more than plants for new construction, must cling to the places where machinery is used. The machine-tool industry is therefore located by the machine users, and interesting responses of location result. It is an industry without any great center. In seeking its market it tends instead to scatter itself over the whole region of manufacture, with its greatest western centers at the centrally located cities of Cincinnati, and Cleveland, Ohio. Hamilton and Dayton are also important points.

In the East, Philadelphia is a center for this line of manufacturing, because of the need of her textile mills, her engine factories, her locomotive works, and the shipyards of Camden, Chester, and Wilmington upon the Delaware. Chicago, the heart of a rapidly increasing manufacturing district, is also rising in importance in the manufacture of machine tools, while New England is largely supplied from the cities of Worcester, Mass., Providence, Hartford, and New Haven.

Engines and motors.—Engines or electric motors are used in almost all kinds of factories, and also in nearly all mines and on many farms. Their market is not quite so restricted as that for machine tools, but their manufacture is located by the same factors and is distributed in the United States from Lake Michigan to the Atlantic and southward to southern Pennsylvania. The leading centers of manufacture are Milwaukee, Wisconsin, Pittsburgh, Philadelphia, New York City and environs, and Schenectady, New York, all of which have excellent transportation facilities.

5. MACHINERY FOR TRANSPORTATION

Railway cars.—Transportation, which plays so vital a part in this country, employs an enormous number of people. The mere building and repairing of the 2 million freight cars employs as many laborers as does the woolen industry in Great Britain, and the number of workers, 300,000, far outranks the 175,000 in the American woolen industry. The annual value of this work exceeds $400,000,000, an amount greater than the value of the product of the American blast furnaces. Although every railroad has repair shops scattered along its lines at junction points and at ends of divisions, this work is, so far as possible, concentrated in the best locations, Chicago, St. Louis, Pittsburgh and Philadelphia being important centers.

Locomotives.—In the manufacture of locomotives, Philadelphia leads every other city in the world. One plant there makes about one-third of the output of the country, and, with the assistance of plants at Pittsburgh and Scranton, gives to Pennsylvania one-half the entire output of the United States. Philadelphia's leadership is due to no one cause. It is an industry which, so far as the general situation is concerned, is almost equally at home anywhere between Chicago and New York. The Philadelphia plant has a unique labor organization, the city has excellent supplies of coal, is reasonably near the sources of iron, and being in a city of homes, has an abundant supply of workmen. The great locomotive works of Philadelphia have outgrown their city location and are gradually moving to a more roomy suburb on the bank of the Delaware. New York state produces one-fourth of the locomotives of the country, the most important center of manufacture in that state being the city of Schenectady, which also produces so much electrical machinery.

Few important industries approach locomotive manufacture in the extreme degree of fluctuation in prosperity. In periods of promising traffic and easy borrowing, the railroads order locomotives, and at other times they do not. The booming prosperity of 1906 resulted in the manufacture that year of 6,592 locomotives in the United States. After the panic of 1907 the output of 1908 fell to 2,342.

6. SHIP BUILDING

How ships are built.—The ship is the largest object that man can move, the most complex of all his devices, and the one with the most thoroughly correlated parts. The usual method of building a ship is to lay down its keel or back bone upon a series of inclined blocks (Fig. 147) called a "way," from which the ship is finally allowed to slide into the water when the hull is completed. As it lies in the water the masts and machinery are added and the finishing work is done. The method of ship construction shows the necessity of locating ship yards upon deep, quiet rivers with an abundance of available land along the shore. It is better that the ship-building river have fresh rather than salt water, because it is less injurious to the hull of the ship. All of the important ship-building localities are near to iron- steel- and machine-manufacturing districts.

Influence of different ship-building materials.—The American ship-building industry has had its ups and downs, due partly to the influence of the change in building materials. From 1800 to 1850 the world's ships were wooden sailing vessels, for which New England, with her pine forest, not far from the oak supplies of the Middle Atlantic States, had the best and cheapest material in the

The Hog Island shipyard, the largest in the world, stands for two terms new in shipbuilding. These are *standardization* and the *fabricated ship*. The necessity of building ships to beat the submarine required the fastest possible ship building. To do this, we adopted the policy of standardization, which gave the shipbuilding industry access to the machine shops of the whole nation rather than making them dependent upon works immediately beside the river bank. Ship design had for some time been at the point where the vessel's entire frame, floors and plates, could be cut in lengths sufficiently short to be shipped on freight cars to any point where it was desirable to assemble them into a complete ship. This permitted any steel mill to make plates, angles, shapes of standard dimensions, with holes punched $\frac{1}{8}$ or $\frac{1}{16}$ of an inch scant allowing for reaming after the plates were in place, all reaming, riveting and caulking being done by engine power through the aid of pneumatic tools. Thus standardization of design led to distant manufacture of parts, like knock-down houses, and the putting of these parts together wherever it was most suitable. By assembling parts made to fit, the first Liberty motor designed for airplanes was made in twelve factories scattered between Connecticut and California. The same thing was done with ships.

Thus we have the so-called "fabricated" ship. This is a tremendous contrast to practices that have prevailed in most shipyards whereby each plate, angle, and shape was a law unto itself in dimension, form, fitting, and the number of fastenings required to secure it in place, so that the ship was built as a house is built, by pieces made to fit on the spot, whereas the fabricated ship of the war emergency shipyard is put together like a knock-down house or the parts of a steel skyscraper.

This gave the shipyard access to the steel plants and machine shops of the entire nation. Forty-nine steel works were making the larger parts for the ships in one of the fabricating yards even before the yard was done. It is doubtless true that if all the various plants busy on some minute part, such as valves, pumps, compasses, electric apparatus, etc., were counted, the total number of plants would reach into the hundreds. This enables a bridge plant in Pittsburgh, a boiler plant in Ohio, a structural steel mill in West Virginia, and a plate mill in Illinois, to specialize and adjust machinery to make hundreds or thousands of duplicate pieces for hundreds or thousands of duplicate ships. So an automobile plant here, a windmill plant there, an engine shop yonder, can make some of the parts of the marine engine and the rather numerous small machines that are needed in a ship, such as small engines to hoist cargo, pumps for water, pumps for oil, fans for ventilators, pulleys, cables, compasses.

The world's shipyards will not keep all of these war hurry measures, for the world's traffic desires a greater variety of ships, but they will keep many of the economies of standardization and fabrication learned during the war. The changes in the amount of shipping possessed by different nations has been remarkable. (See table.)

world. All along her coast, especially in Maine, many ship yards were turning out vessels that were better and cheaper than those built in Europe. About the middle of the nineteenth century it was discovered that iron ships were better for most purposes than wooden ships, and their use rapidly increased. Iron was later replaced by steel. In the supply of the raw material for this new type of ship, England, with her leadership in the iron industry, was far ahead of the United States.

Fig. 147.—Steamer in dry dock at Fifty-fifth Street, Brooklyn, after collision off Massachusetts coast. Steel construction preventing shivering of ship and water-tight compartments prevented filling and sinking. Ships are sometimes built in dry docks like this one.

Within the United States similar changes occurred. In 5 years, 1857–61, in the wood ship era, the output of the New England yards was nearly twice that of the Middle Atlantic and Gulf Coast, but the latter, adjacent to iron and steel supplies, had triple the New England output in the 5 years of 1907–11.

Britain builds ten times as many ships as we do. Her leadership during the latter part of the nineteenth and early part of the twentieth century is due partly to cheaper raw material, partly to cheaper labor, partly to abundant capital, the limitations of home opportunities, and the desire to invest in ships, and partly to the economy which comes from the great size of the industry. In America and on the continent of Europe vessels are commonly built one or two at a time, but in the large ship yards in the British ship-building centers upon the River Clyde in west Scotland, the Tyne in northeast England, and the Irish harbor of Belfast, a half-dozen or a dozen steamers all alike are built at one time. As each part is duplicated several times, the cost for each ship is less than when built singly.

While the building of a wooden ship is largely a matter of carpenters and workmen, the building of the iron ship requires a large

Fig. 148.—A ship-building plant. (Courtesy of the Newport News Shipbuilding and Dry Dock Co.)

amount of expensive machinery and equipment. The modern ship yard is so costly and of such great extent that the building of one large yard at Newport News near the mouth of the Chesapeake Bay in Virginia practically gives that state leadership in the amount of capital invested in this industry (Fig. 148). Two New England ports, Bath, Maine, and Quincy, Mass., have the equipment to build the largest vessels, but the many yards at Brooklyn and other points upon the waters of New York harbor, make that the greatest single shipbuilding center in America. The Delaware sometimes called the American Clyde, with yards at Philadelphia, Camden, Chester, and Wilmington, is the most important ship-building river in America.

Other American yards.—Shipping upon the American Great Lakes renders great commercial service and its construction comprises half the American ship-building industry. As the vessels cannot leave lake waters, they are built upon the lake shores. The most important centers are at Cleveland, Chicago, Detroit, and Buffalo. Although the Pacific states produce practically no iron, the need of equipment for repair work and the building of battleships has caused the establishment of first-class, modern shipyards at San Francisco, Los Angeles, and Seattle, but the output of new shipping is limited almost entirely to war vessels.

7. SMALL METAL MANUFACTURES

Relation to good labor supply.—An inspection of a hardware store reveals a collection of hundreds and even thousands of articles, such as saws, axes, cutlery, fire arms and ammunition, plumbers', tinners' and carpenters' tools, and that very long list of articles known as builders' hardware, nearly all of which are made of metal. A jewelry store reveals a collection of still more valuable metal products in which, as in the hardware, the metal plays a relatively small part, and the labor a large part in the cost of production. This high labor and small material value means that these articles are likely to be produced where population is abundant, as in New England, not where it is scarce, as in Virginia, Kentucky or Iowa.

The distribution of the industry.—The manufacture of most of these small articles, in the making of which machine tools and automatic machinery are very important, particularly in America, originated in England and in Germany. It soon started up in this country, in southern New England the home of the so-called "Yankee Notions," and has gradually moved westward through New York and Pennsylvania into the North Central States. New England is holding a leading place by making more and more refined articles as regions farther west take up branches of the small metal manufacture. Springfield, Mass., continues to be a great center for the manufacture of fire arms and ammunition, and a large part of the jewelry made in the United States is produced within 30 miles of Providence. Rhode Island, being the most densely populated state, becomes a natural home for such an industry, in which labor is seen to dominate when we consider that both the valuable raw material and the finished product can be transported so easily.

Silverware has its center of manufacture in some of the towns of Connecticut, which state also leads in the manufacture of clocks and watches, especially the very cheap models.

Standardization and interchangeable parts.—The New England clock business has been made possible by the American system of manufacture, in which standardization and interchangeable parts have replaced the old hand methods by which every clock was different. Switzerland has long been famed as the best watch-making country in the world, Geneva and vicinity being the center. These watches are made by hand, each wheel carefully fitted to the next wheel, so that if one breaks, the new one has to be shaped by hand to fit its mates. By the American method of interchangeable parts, fifty watches can be taken to pieces, each piece put into its own bin, and the watches may then be satisfactorily reconstructed by chance selection of the necessary parts. Thus, Connecticut can make alarm clocks and watches at fabulously low prices, because of new methods of manufacture, perfected largely through American inventions.

Apparently such industries can only be kept up by the continued improvement of the patterns and methods, for if an article, like a microscope for instance, falls into the class where it is a plain matter of labor and skill, it is made where skilled labor is cheapest. Thus America has never thought of establishing a wood-carving business. It belongs in Europe just as the still more difficult ivory carving belongs in India with its yet cheaper labor, and as silk production belongs in China and Japan with the cheapest of all labor. Indication of this adjustment of industry to population is shown by the complaints of German makers of cheap clocks, that Japan is selling them in China at prices no European manufacturer can meet (United States Con. Rep., July 18, 1911).

Questions

1. Compare Kansas City as a place for the starting of an agricultural implement factory and a jewelry factory.

2. What is the influence of farm machinery on the number of farm population?

3. How has the environment made the United States lead Germany in the production of agricultural machinery?

4. Why does Germany lead the United States in the manufacture of microscopes?

5. Do the wagon and automobile manufactures have the same degree of concentration?

6. Explain some shifts of the ship-building industry due to inventions.

CHAPTER XIV

CHEMICAL MANUFACTURES

Chemical action.—Squeeze a few drops of lemon juice on some common cooking soda and something will happen. We call it chemical action. The lemon juice contains acid, and the acids are a large and important class of chemicals. Soda is one of the alkalies, another large class. These two kinds of chemicals start chemical action easily and are therefore very important in manufacture. The commonest of the acids is made of sulphur of which we use 18 pounds per person in the United States. The commonest of the alkalies is soda, of which we also make a vast quantity, using chiefly salt and coke. The soda plants are thereby located over the salt deposits of New York and Michigan.

The laboratory and the factory.—The chemist produces the painter's colors, the dyes of the weaver, the tannins of the tanner, the fertilizer for the farmer, the drugs and medicines for the physician, and raw materials for almost every factory. Things that are experiments in the chemical laboratory are coming more and more to be done in factories on a large scale. They are the basis of a rapidly growing industry so important in manufacturing that it is to be likened only to the use of power.

1. The Fertilizer Industry

The heaviest of all the chemical industries is that devoted to the production of chemical plant foods known as fertilizers. Of the several substances necessary to the growth of plants, three—namely, phosphorus, potassium, and nitrogen—often exist in the soil in insufficient amounts or in unavailable forms, and must be supplied if prolific crops are desired (Fig. 150). These three substances in many different forms and commodities are the main raw materials of the fertilizer manufacturer, and he ransacks the world to get them.

Phosphates.—The bulkiest, cheapest, and possibly the most important of these plant foods are phosphates, which furnish phosphorus to the plants. Much of the relatively minute amount of

277

phosphorus of the world has been concentrated as phosphates in the bones of animals. Consequently, it is from animal sources, directly or in fossil form, that nearly all available phosphorus is obtained. Phosphorus is now chiefly obtained by man from the fossil remains of animal life, known as phosphate rock, from which, by the aid of sulphuric acid, fertilizer is made.

No other country approaches the United States in phosphate rock resources. The mining of it started near Charleston, S. C., where the rock can be dug from pits. The greatest development now is near Tampa, Florida, but new discoveries have been made in central Tennessee, and recently deposits of great extent have been found in the arid plains near the boundary of Wyoming and Idaho, not far from the Yellowstone National Park. In addition to supplying the American market, we export over a million tons a year, chiefly to England, France, and Germany. The port of Tampa alone sends about half of the export.

Of late years the so-called basic process of purifying iron and steel has given us a new source of phosphorus. The limestone linings of the furnace draw the phosphorus from the molten iron and steel, and are later ground up and sold under the name of Thomas slag or basic slag, quite largely used as fertilizer in England and Germany. It is used less in the United States because of our fossil phosphates.

Potash.—The second great raw material in the fertilizer industry is potash, of which we are heavy importers (586,000 tons, 1911) from Germany, which country has, under present conditions, almost a world monopoly. Potash differs from phosphorus in that there are vast quantities of low-grade material as a possible future dependence. Mountains of rock (feldspar) in various parts of the world contain about 8 or 9 per cent of potash; but it is unavailable under the existing state of chemical knowledge. So the whole world depends upon the mines of Stassfurt, near the Elbe River, in Germany, where, overlying a large deposit of common salt, is to be found the only important collection thus far known of available potash salts, of which there are several varieties.

Very promising, however, is the potash from Kelp or seaweed, of which several hundred square miles exist off the Pacific coast of the United States. Conservative estimates place the output of 100 square miles of this kelp at 1 million tons of chloride of potash, worth $35,000,000 per year, or nearly twice our present imports from Germany. This output permits the permanence of the beds because they feed upon the exhaustless chemicals of sea water. This accounts for the high yield, $50 per acre, year after year upon thousands of acres, which puts agriculture to shame (*Year-book*, United States Department of Agriculture, 1911, p. 108). The manufacture of this potash has begun in California, Scotland, and Norway.

Nitrogen.—The third, and most expensive, of the fertilizing materials is nitrogen, of which, despite the apparent scarcity, there are many and unlimited possibilities of output, because this rather inert element comprises three-fourths of the air, and we can draw upon it as we do upon water. Until recently we have had to draw upon the indirect sources of nitrogen. All animal matter is more or less nitrogenous, and fertilizer factories receive as raw materials the inedible animal products from the butcher shop, the slaughter house, and the fish cannery.

The greatest nitrogen-supplying raw material at present is nitrate of soda, which, like guano (and probably potash also) accumulates in commercial quantities only in deserts, where the rainfall is insufficient to dissolve and carry it away. Some is produced in Death Valley, California, and the other deserts of California and Nevada, where it is found in small quantities as a white crust along with borax on or near the surface of the earth, and only needs to be hauled away and refined. But the supply of the nitrate in commercial quantities is practically a monopoly of Chile, where the Nitrate Trust controls a supply that is variously estimated to be sufficient for a few decades or possibly a century. Fortunately this monopoly is not destined to pass into a world famine, but into an era of plenty through new inventions. Ammonia, one of the by-products of coke making, yields approximately as much nitrogen pound for pound as does nitrate of soda. It is one of the by-products of coal distillation, and the total output of about 1,200,000 tons in 1911 (Fig. 149) was about half that of the nitrate product, and had doubled in 8 years. The more economical use of our coal would enable the United States to make a half million or a million tons of this product. While the coal may be exhausted some day, the air and waterfalls will not. The air is our final source. Manufactured nitrogen is now being exported from Norway, which can already make 330,000 tons of these nitrates per year. This is a product of the free air caught in the electric furnace by the electric spark from a hydroelectric current, and produced by German capital in the defiles of the Norwegian mountains. Nitrate of calcium, called cyanamid, is now being made at Niagara Falls, but its production did not develop there until after it had reached a considerable amount in Norway and France, where water-power is cheaper than in America.

These atmospheric supplies of nitrogen depend upon power. A very small population is required for the operation, and any distant source will do. For this purpose a 410,000 horse-power plant is being erected beside an Iceland waterfall and another in a fiord on the coast of Labrador.

The fertilizer industry and its location.—It is plain why the fertilizer plant, drawing each of its staple raw materials from a

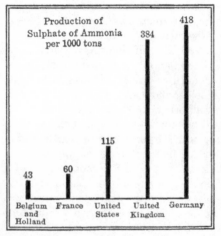

Fig. 149.—World production of sulphate of ammonia, 1911. This chart is one measure of the conservation of coal.

different continent, finds the best location upon navigable arms of the sea, so that a ship-load of potash from Germany, bones from Buenos Ayres, nitrate from Chile, or fossil phosphate from Tampa, can be unloaded direct from ship to factory. We thus find fertilizer plants established in or near almost every Atlantic port from Maine to Florida. Here fertilizer plants are also near their greatest market. Since fertilizers are so largely used by the truck-crop growers throughout the Atlantic plain and on nearly all farms east of the Alleghenies, fertilizer manufacture is as yet essentially an eastern industry. Georgia is the leading state in the manufacture, chiefly

FIG. 150.—Experiment showing the value of fertilizer at State College, Pa. For 29 years these three plots have been planted in the following rotation: corn, oats, wheat, and hay. The plot at the left has received ground limestone; that at the right, nothing; that at the center, a "complete" fertilizer of dried blood, ground bone, and muriate of potash. The yield of hay for left plot is 1840 lbs. per acre; center plot, 4640 lbs. per acre; right plot, 1320 lbs. per acre.

because it is an important cotton state, and the exhaustive one-crop plantation system of growing cotton makes the use of chemical fertilizers imperative.

The future of fertilizer and fertility.—We are just entering the era of artificial fertilization in the United States, because we have an increasing population, soils of decreasing fertility, and the new science of agriculture which is being disseminated with great rapidity (Fig. 275). The comfort of our future depends upon commercial fertilizers more than upon coal or iron. Granted the ability to grow plants abundantly, science can probably adjust and meet man's wants, but without plants, nothing. Without any one of the three constituents, potash, phosphorus, or nitrogen, a field rich in every other requisite of plant growth lies barren. Even the careful Chinese have to abandon otherwise good land where they can get no fertilizer. It is therefore fortunate that we have, even without the aid of the nitrogen-gathering bacteria upon plant roots, unlocked indefinite stores of nitrogen and potash. With phosphorus it is otherwise. Speaking in terms of generations its supply is scanty and no ultimate reservoirs are yet in sight. Phosphorus is therefore probably the point of man's weakest hold upon the earth, and its waste in sewage, the loss of animal manures, and soil leaching, is a form of resource destruction with which the future must deal unless perchance we can open some avenue of phosphorus recapture from the great reservoirs of the sea.

2. Soap-making and its Materials

Soap is produced by the action of soda or potash upon fats. This chemical reaction causes soap manufacture to be classed among the chemical industries. In the United States the product amounts to over $100,000,000 per year or something over a dollar per person, and in Europe it is nearly as important. Oils and fats used in soap making, like many other raw materials, seem to be of especial importance in countries of comparatively undeveloped industry. Tallow, olive oil, cottonseed oil, oil of sesame from India, groundnut or peanut oil, and cocoanut oil, are all the basis of large commerce. Many other fatty substances of animal and vegetable origin are also used, even including the grease that is removed from sheep wool in preparing it for the loom.

3. Coal-tar Dyes

One of the chemical manufactures most typical in its scientific nature, its importance, and its relation to other industries, is that of dye stuffs. These are now manufactured almost entirely from coal tar, one of the by-products of the by-product coke oven. In 1906, on the fiftieth anniversary of the discovery of the coal-tar dyes (aniline) over 62,000 of them were in existence. From this same tar other chemicals are prepared, including carbolic acid and many drugs. The artificial (but perfect) indigo made from coal tar has so nearly replaced natural indigo that the exports of that staple from India decreased from 21 million pounds in 1896 to 2 million pounds in 1910, and the average price dropped from eighty-five to fifty-five cents per pound with corresponding hard times for the indigo districts. The chemical industry arising from coal-tar products has an output of $100,000,000 per year, but the share of it outside of Germany is relatively insignificant. There are a few plants in New Jersey and in New England, but about 95 per cent. of the industry is German. The European war of 1914 has given a great stimulus to the chemical industry in other countries, notably America, by temporarily cutting off the large imports from Germany.

4. Explosives

Explosives, long used for destruction only, have at last entered industry, and are performing rapidly increasing services. Without dynamite and gunpowder the prosecution of the mining and quarrying industries, and the building of our railways, tunnels, subways, and canals would be impossible. Our per capita consumption of explosives amounts to over 5 pounds per year. The danger and consequent cost of transport is the dominating factor which scatters the centers of manufacture as freight costs scatter cement plants. Among the raw materials for this industry nitrate of soda is important along with nitric and other acids, sulphur, and charcoal.

5. Products of the Electric Furnace

Another new and important group of chemical products is that produced by electricity or electro-chemistry. The great heat of the electric furnace is used in the manufacture of a number of crystalline substances, such as calcium carbide which is used for the generation of acetylene for lighting. It is manufactured at Sault Ste. Marie, Michigan, and at Niagara Falls, where the great power plants, run by the waterfalls, produce also all the carborundum made in America. These same crystals are produced in Norway and Sweden, where the moist Atlantic winds blowing against the high mountains give an abundance of rainfall and cause numerous swift streams that yield excellent water-power for the production of the cheap electric current, which seems to be the locating factor in this industry. Similar water-power advantages have developed the industry to large proportions in Switzerland which shares with Scandinavia the leadership in exports of this nature.

QUESTIONS

1. What is the relation of aridity to the supply of chemical raw materials?
2. Name two foreign trusts from which invention is likely to emancipate us.
3. Which is the better location for a fertilizer factory, Baltimore or Harrisburg?
4. What is the basis for the advice of conservationists that the export of phosphate should be prohibited?
5. How may a new source of inedible oil influence the price of edible oil?

CHAPTER XV

THE MINERAL INDUSTRIES

The mineral industry has long shown an increasing importance of the baser materials. Coal and iron together make more than half of the total value of all minerals. The mineral industry of the entire world employs 6 million persons, yet its output is not over one-half as valuable as the product of the farms of the United States alone (Fig. 151).

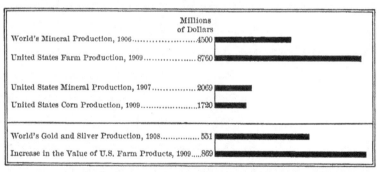

                                        Millions
                                      of Dollars
World's Mineral Production, 1906......................4500
United States Farm Production, 1909....................8760
United States Mineral Production, 1907...............2069
United States Corn Production, 1909.....................1720
World's Gold and Silver Production, 1908...............551
Increase in the Value of U.S. Farm Products, 1909.....869

FIG. 151.—Comparison of mineral and agricultural production. (Commercial Museum, Philadelphia.)

1. BUILDING MATERIALS

The scarcity of wood and the resulting increase in price that came with the twentieth century are forcing the people of America, like those of older countries, to find building materials in the earth's crust. After our nineteenth century saturnalia of tree slaughter and cheap wood, we are being driven more and more to adopt the building material used in Ancient Rome and used now in most parts of Europe, Asia and north Africa. It is merely a sign of the declining ratio of land to man that necessarily accompanied the increase of population.

The abundance of stone and clay permit quarrying and brick

making to be widely distributed in response to local demand. The low value and great weight of these materials make them expensive to transport. In its wide distribution in response to scattered demand, the making of common brick resembles dairy farming. Of the total output of nearly $60,000,000 in 1910, nineteen states had each over $1,000,000 worth, and but five over $2,000,000, and only two over $5,000,000 each. The regions of high output are the regions of large population—New York, Pennsylvania, and Illinois. Thus, New York, the state with the greatest city population has also the greatest amount of brick manufacture. This industry is located chiefly in the Hudson Valley between New York and Cohoes where both railroad and river navigation furnish easy access to the enormous market of the cities about the mouth of the Hudson River.

The brick yard, with its smoking kilns and clay-mixing machines that shoot out the bricks by the mile and cut them off into lengths, is usually an industry with a very limited local market, although at Milwaukee and a few Ohio points special bricks are made for distant markets.

Although brick must be manufactured while stone is merely taken from the earth, the building stone is often more expensive to use because of the large amount of labor involved in quarrying and shaping, or in fitting rough stones together in the wall. There are several places in the United States where stones of peculiar merit or unusual accessibility give rise to large quarrying industries with a distant market. For this reason, Maine has important quarrying industries along the sea coast where the scraping glaciers have exposed bare hills of slate, limestone, and granite. These quarries have access to the best possible transportation facilities, namely, that afforded by the sea-going vessels that can practically come to the side of the quarry in many sheltered bays upon the indented coast. Massachusetts, with conditions like those of Maine, is the third granite producer and Vermont is first. Quarrying is more important to this state than any other. Its granite for buildings and monuments is shipped to great distances as are those of New Hampshire; and its leadership in marble is most pronounced, the output being four times that of Georgia, its nearest rival.

The marble industry of south Vermont near Rutland is one of the greatest in the world (Fig. 152). A splendid marble deposit is almost as accessible to the quarrymen as are the granites of Maine or New

Hampshire. As in other extensive quarries, the rock is cut and lifted by mechanical methods and the product is sent surprising distances when one considers how many other good unused marble

FIG. 152.—Marble quarry, Proctor, Vermont. (Vermont Marble Co.)

deposits there are in the United States. It is a clear case of the influence of an early start, an established reputation and good organization in continuing the success of an industry.

The beautiful marble is far less important than the rougher, more rugged stone. Its output is no greater in value than that of trap rock, the hardest of all, which is quarried in immense quantities and crushed for road surfaces. Common limestones, used for road making, railroad ballast, concrete, and building stone are five times as valuable as the marble output. The limestone most used for building in the United States is the Indiana limestone (Bedford

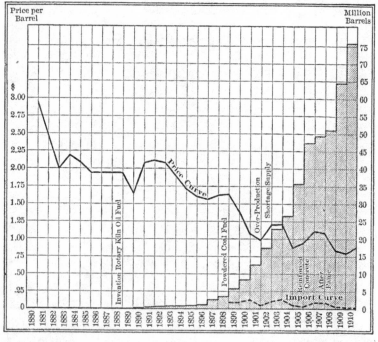

FIG. 153.—Price, production and import of cement in United States. (After R. Malcolm Keir.)

oölitic), from Bedford and Bloomington. This stone is widely used in eastern states because of its durable character and the ease with which, when first quarried, it can be sawed and worked into blocks and other desired building forms. Upon exposure to the air it hardens, as do some Ohio sandstones. Although they send their products to great distances, these important quarry centers produce but a small amount of the total building stone, which is commonly dug from the quarry most nearly available to the place of consumption.

FIG. 154.—Rotary cement kiln. (Atlas Cement Co., Northampton, Pa.)

Cement.—Cement is a mixture of lime and clay burned to drive off the water. Upon being wetted it absorbs water, hardens and

becomes as durable as rock.   Cement is now largely used in making
concrete, a mixture of cement, sand, and broken stone.   It was
the great building material of the Romans, whose experience has
proved it to be good for 2,000 years.   Chunks of it lie today in
wheat fields in Tunis and many other parts of the Roman world.
Three new factors, the reinforcing of concrete, the rotary kiln and
high-priced wood and iron, have combined since 1890 to produce
what is called the cement age in America.   When reinforced by

FIG. 155.—In the management of water cement renders irreplaceable service.
Trail Creek, Yakima Irrigation Project. (U. S. Reclamation Service.)

having a kind of skeleton of steel wires or steel rods within,
cement construction becomes a substitute for stone, for iron, for
steel, even for lumber, and can be used to build an entire house.
The resulting new uses brought increased consumption and the
demand for cheaper processes of manufacture.   This brought the
invention of the rotary kiln which has cheapened production (Fig.
154).   Cement has declined in price at the same time that its rivals,
steel, iron, and lumber, have increased in price.   The resulting
unprecedented increase in the industry has been one of the most
sudden of all industrial changes (Fig. 153).

At the present time we are losing by fire nearly half as many buildings as we erect and the life of past constructions has at best been
short. Good concrete buildings are permanent, and enrich the
nation by their durability as well as by the saving in other materials.
Cement has, in addition, exceptional ease of construction. Mixed by
steam power and poured into moulds, it is a natural product of machinery and unskilled labor. Its use for girders, boats, fence posts,
piles for driving into the ground, and shingles seems to indicate
that there is almost no limit to the service it can render (Fig. 155).

Fig. 156.—The location of the cement plants in the United States shows that the
industry tends to be a local one. (After U. S. Geol. Surv.)

Materials and distribution of cement making.—Fortunately the
raw materials, limestone and clay or limestone and shale, are to be
found in every state and the fuel for burning is also widely scattered,
so that there is the possibility of having many cement districts as
the demand spreads and increases (Fig. 156). The Lehigh Valley
in eastern Pennsylvania is at present the leading cement section of
the United States. Here the limestone and shale are close together,
at the surface, and only a few miles removed from the anthracite
coal fields and near an abundant supply of good labor (from the
adjacent Pennsylvania-German settlements). It is but 100 miles to
the great markets and ports of New York and Philadelphia.

But the Lehigh Valley is making relatively less and less of the American supply because of competition of newer plants as in the Shenandoah Valley of Virginia, in Georgia, eastern Tennessee, Pittsburgh, New York, Ohio, Michigan, Illinois, Kansas, and elsewhere. Like other building materials, cement tends to be a local industry, and is now being made in half the states of the Union. The price of a 380-pound barrel of cement in the Lehigh district (Sept., 1912) was $1.20. As a freight rate of $7 per ton will more than double the cost to the consumer, it is plain that a local plant has a great advantage over distant plants.

Cement from the iron furnace.—The making of cement from blast-furnace slag, with or without addition of other substances, is a recent innovation, important alike to iron and cement makers. Since the disposition of this practically useless by-product of the blast furnaces has been a serious problem at many plants, the making of it into cement is a double advantage and is being extensively carried on at Pittsburgh and Chicago and will doubtless soon spread farther.

2. POTTERY, PORCELAIN, AND GLASS

Utensils of earth materials are common even among savages. They were left by the Mound Builders and made by the Indians. The ancient Egyptians and Phœnicians were expert glass makers long before the beginning of the Christian era, and porcelain has been made in China for over a thousand years.

Glass is made by melting pure sand, which, by the aid of certain chemicals called flux, melts under high heat and remains transparent after hardening. Pottery, including its finer form, porcelain, is made by baking clay mixtures, which harden without melting. Pottery making in its simpler forms is a local industry which has survived the competition of the modern factory somewhat better than the textile industry has. The product is much more difficult to transport and clay suitable for some kind of pottery work is very common, although pure kaolin, the kind of clay used for the finest ware and which can be heated to 3,000 degrees without melting, is somewhat limited in its distribution. Large factories tend to concentrate the production of the better grades of product, but the cheapest grades tend to be made close to the market, as for example farm drain tile, made and used in the corn belt. Drain tile, short lengths of unglazed pipe, cheap, bulky, and difficult to transport because porous and weak, is mostly used as a sort of field sewerage system, to carry off surplus water from the flat lands, especially in the North Central States, and make them fit for tillage soon after the rain.

Pottery and porcelain.—The pottery and porcelain industries of the United States have increased very rapidly since the Civil War, but the best grades are yet imported from Germany, Austria, and France. The two cities of Trenton, N. J., and East Liverpool, Ohio, manufacture much the greater part of the good pottery produced in the United States. Trenton alone has more than forty potteries. The supply of raw materials for this city is diverse. The coal comes from the anthracite district of eastern Pennsylvania, and the local clay suffices for the coarser uses of the industry. Quartz and feldspar are brought from the Adirondacks and the southern highlands of New York. Some of the clay comes from distant southern states, the best from Florida. About half of the fine clay is imported from England, being brought back very cheaply by vessels which take out cargoes of American agricultural products and must otherwise come back well-nigh empty. The freight rate from Cornwall to New York is a dollar a ton, and from New York to Trenton by rail is another dollar. By wagon it costs a dollar to bring the local clay 4 miles from the pits. Trenton is one of the best places in the United States, if not the best, for a new pottery plant to secure adequate skilled labor and supplies—hence the concentration of the industry.

Ohio is the leading pottery state, with centers at East Liverpool, Zanesville, and Cincinnati. There are extensive deposits of good kaolin in North Carolina, Georgia and other southern states. Small amounts are dug in Delaware and Maryland, but there is no prospect of the industry moving to these southern supplies of raw material, which can be so cheaply and easily transported to centers of manufacture upon the edges of the coal fields.

Glass making.—The quartz sand and flint for glass making are commonly melted at about 2,500° F. with an alkaline flux, usually soda, to hasten the melting. The chief raw material, quartz sand, is most widely distributed. It occurs in practically all countries, and near all our manufacturing centers.

The United States leads the world in the manufacture of glassware. Like iron manufacture, the industry began in Colonial times with a wood-burning epoch, which caused it to be centered in New England

and the eastern states. There are now three important glass-manu-facturing districts in the United States; the eastern is in southern New Jersey and southeastern Pennsylvania. Millville, N. J., is one of the leading glass-manufacturing towns in the United States, and it is followed in importance in the eastern field by Bridgeton, Glassboro, and Philadelphia. These eastern glass centers have abundant sand, but they are at some distance from their coal supply which they use in the form of producer gas. The gas-fed flames play around the pools of melted sand as it waits its final shap-ing at the hands of the glass blower or glass machine. Owing to the great fuel advantage possessed by the natural gas region of western Pennsylvania, Ohio, and Indiana, great gains have occurred in these states, while the East has gained little in recent years. Muncie, Indiana, is the rival of Millville, N. J., and Gas City, Indiana, has had a great rise in glass making. The exhaustion of the natural-gas supply has centered attention upon bituminous coal as a fuel. As a result the Pittsburgh district with both coal and natural gas is now the greatest glass-manufacturing district of the United States, and Pennsylvania makes over a third of the product. The Ohio Valley dominates this industry as it does the iron industry and for the same reason—fuel.

Glass resembles pottery in the abundance of its uses and it presents even greater difficulties of transport. The necessary heat and suitable fuel are much more difficult to secure than for pottery, so it is not so widely distributed and is not, like pottery, an industry of very primitive peoples.

Commerce in glass.—The United States imports some European glass, especially the finest grades for lenses and for other fine work, but we also export to many countries the products of our inventive ability, in the form of our machine-made glassware. Our glass machines are being introduced into the German glass works—a proc-ess which will probably tend to cut off our exports, as was the case with shoes.

3. GOLD AND SILVER

On account of their remarkable malleability, durability, and beauty, these metals were highly prized for ornaments and coins even before the period of recorded history. The appeal gold makes to the imagination tends to cause an overestimate of its value. The world's output is of approximately the same value as the corn crop of the three states of Illinois, Iowa, and Missouri in 1911; yet, because of its use as the basis of all our commercial transactions,

FIG. 157.—Placer mining, Gibbonsville, Idaho. (Photograph by B. Willis, U. S. Geological Survey.) Placer mining tears down and washes away acres of land and chokes up river channels with its débris.

gold production becomes one of the most potent economic influences. Widely scattered in the earth's crust, gold is collected into veins of quartz in many kinds of rock. The destruction of exposed veins in the wearing down of mountains by streams has caused the transportation of gold along the courses of streams to great distances from the original veins. The miner's pan, not unlike a wash basin, suffices to extract the gold from the sand if there be water present in which to agitate the sand until the gold settles to the bottom so that the sand can be gradually separated from it. Large banks of sand and gravel, containing very small quantities of gold, are worked by the placer process (Fig. 157), which consists of washing

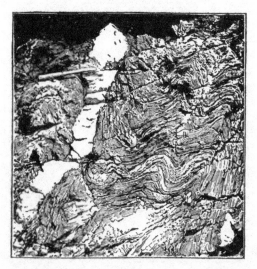

Fig. 158.—A quartz vein (the white band) in metamorphic rock. Muchals Caves, Kincardineshire, Scotland. (From Salisbury, Barrows, and Tower.) The uncertainties of mining are apparent.

down the gravel banks by the force of a stream of water from a nozzle. The water carries the sand through long sluice boxes, with crevices in the bottom, in which the gold is caught, because, being the heaviest of the materials, it gradually settles to the bottom. This method has been used extensively in many parts of the world, especially in California, where streams have been so choked by débris as to fill up valuable channels in their lower courses and to cover rich agricultural lowlands with worthless beds of sand and gravel.

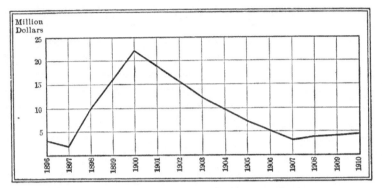

FIG. 159.—The fluctuating gold output of the Canadian Klondike.

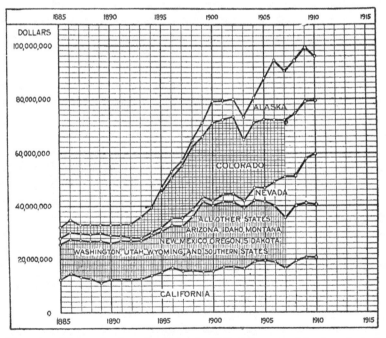

FIG. 160.—The production of gold in the United States and in the principal
states. (U. S. Conservation Commission Report.)

The most permanent kind of gold mining consists in the working of the ores that are found in the veins themselves (Fig. 158). The ore is usually ground fine by a stamp mill, and then washed by a process similar to that pursued in placer mining. This process does not, however, get out all the gold, and a newer method called the cyanide process dissolves the gold out of the pulverized ores by soaking them in tanks, and makes profitable the use of ores con-

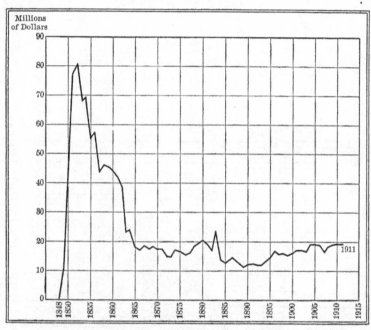

FIG. 161.—Gold production in California, 1848–1911. Compare this with previous gold production of the world. (Fig. 161.)

taining as little as $2.50 (less than one-eighth of an ounce of gold) per ton and possibly even less than that. This chemical process has greatly cheapened the extraction of gold from some ores and helps explain the increased yield which has practically doubled in each decade since 1886 (Fig. 162).

The uncertainty of gold and silver production.—While there is every evidence that gold production will largely increase, few industries have, on the whole, less permanence in any given locality (Fig. 159).

These quickly exhausted deposits of the Klondike were in sand and gravel along the streams where the individual worker could easily get the gold. The increase since 1907 marks the beginning of the period of large-scale production at the hands of a powerful corporation which built 62 miles of flume and pipe line to operate placers, and a water-power plant with 36 miles of electric transmission line. With this equipment, the Klondike will have a few more years of prosperity and then another decline which will be final unless the

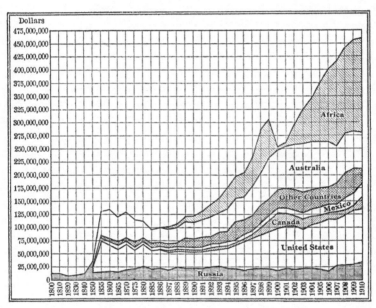

FIG. 162.—Gold production. The world and leading countries, 1800–1910.
(U. S. Conservation Commission.)

mother lode is found. The mother lode, if found, should last several decades before mining reaches its ultimate depth, which is now about 1 mile, and has been reached in the Victoria gold mines of Australia.

The population of Nevada fell from 60,000 in 1860 to 40,000 in 1890 because of the exhaustion of one mine—the Comstock mine near Virginia City. California, long the leading gold producer in the Union, shows the uncertainties of the industry by its frequent changes of base (Fig. 161). The gold discovered there in 1848 was in stream beds. These were soon exhausted, and the miners next discovered many old abandoned river beds and even buried river beds which could be reached by tunneling under lava deposits. Then came placer deposits. Finally the mother lode was discovered and at present two-thirds of California gold is coming from deep mines in the hard ore and the state which had been surpassed by Colorado with its vein mines was again the leader in 1910.

Colorado cities, depending entirely upon mining, have arisen in almost inaccessible places in the Rocky Mountains, such as Leadville, nearly 2 miles above the sea, and Cripple Creek, which produces about half of Colorado's present gold output.

Gold in Alaska.—Alaska, which in 1908 produced more gold than California, has three distinct fields. On the southeast are gold ores

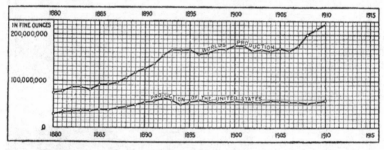

Fig. 163.—Silver production is unusual in that its output does not increase as rapidly as that of most other metals. This is due in part to financial legislation.

of low grade, at the Treadwell mines worked in stamp mills, operated by fuel oil at a total cost of $1.60 per ton of ore. In the Yukon Valley the centers at Klondike (in Canadian territory) and Fairbanks will doubtless be succeeded by other discoveries. Cape Nome (beyond the Arctic circle), on the west coast of Alaska, had a most unusual deposit. It was a sea beach so enriched by gold-bearing streams that a miner could pan $10 worth of gold per day from the sands.

Silver.—In the United States, second to Mexico in output, silver mining depends for its prosperity upon the output of gold, copper and lead, since silver is largely a by-product of such mines. The mines operated for silver alone are relatively few. The total output of silver in the United States, $30,000,000 in 1910 (Fig. 163), is but a third of the value of the $94,000,000 corn crop of Indiana (fourth in corn, 1911).

The future of gold and silver production.—Few industries have had so great a reduction in the cost of operation as has taken place in the production of gold and silver, especially of gold. Therefore, it has prospects of rapid increase in output. Much the greater part of the world has not been prospected adequately and deposits already known will provide for a largely increased output in the next few decades. This increase in production may take place too rapidly for the welfare of the world, owing to the disturbing influence that large production is supposed to have upon prices, probably the most interesting aspect of gold production. Anyone can take gold to the mint and have it coined. Thus most of the gold becomes money. Money is used to buy goods. If money is plenty it becomes relatively cheap, so that a piece of land or a piece of meat commands more money than formerly and we say prices have risen. As prices rise faster than wages, people who depend on wages or investments are made poorer.

QUESTIONS

1. Explain the location of brick yards and porcelain plants.
2. Explain the past and present relative position of the Lehigh Valley in the cement production of the United States.
3. Is cement of equal value to agriculture in the East and in the West?
4. What factors locate a glass plant?
5. How have improvements in gold mining made it difficult for people to get along on a fixed income?
6. How does placer mining interfere with the navigation of the lower courses of rivers?

CHAPTER XVI

THE TRADE AND ROUTES OF NORTH AMERICA

The internal trade of the United States is vast; the country is almost a world in itself, furnishing so large a proportion of its own needs that in comparison to Canada or England there is small reason to turn to the foreigner for his goods. This great, unmeasured domestic trade is favored by nature. The surface and contour of the North American continent offer easier paths for commercial routes than those of any other continent except Europe. Most of the habitable areas are comparatively near to, or are easily reached from, healthful coasts and suitable harbors.

The center of gravity in North American industry, population and commerce is, and will long continue to be, in the southeastern temperate region, the region comprising the Atlantic slope, the basin of the Great Lakes and the Mississippi Valley east of the meridian of 100° W. (Fig. 164). This section is especially favored for transportation within itself and for access to the sea. The slightly sunken coast line affords numerous good harbors, with value increased by a moderate tide. Inland waterways are afforded by the Great Lakes, the Mississippi, the St. Lawrence, and the rivers and bays of the Atlantic coast (Fig. 165). There are few mountain obstructions, and in the interior the Mississippi Valley is almost level, opens broadly to the Gulf and further has the phenomenal advantage of almost level passages to the Lake Basin, to the Atlantic slope and to the areas draining into the Hudson Bay and the Arctic Ocean. The problem of getting out to the Pacific, although of considerable difficulty, is easier than crossing the Alps or the chief mountains of Asia or South America. Excellent climate and natural resources in the temperate sections complete the conditions necessary for the development of trade routes unrivaled in the size of their commerce.

We have strangely failed to utilize all our advantages, especially our waterways, which are ahead of those of any other nation in extent, distribution, navigability, and ease of use. These little used resources consist of 25,000 miles of river now used to some

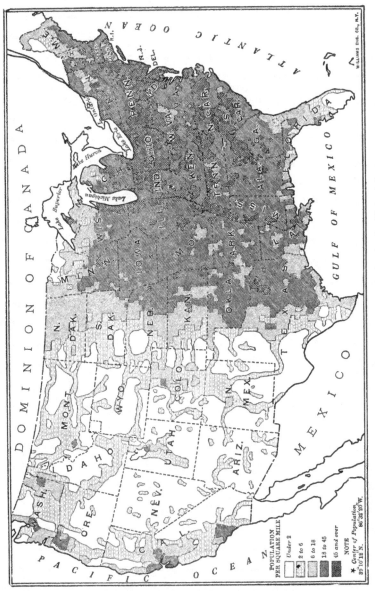

- FIG. 164.—Distribution of population in the United States, 1910.

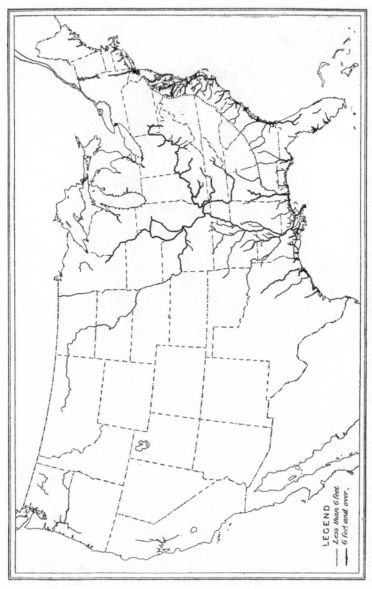

Fig. 165.—Navigable rivers of the United States.

LEGEND
Less than 6 feet.
6 feet and over.

extent; 25,000 miles that might be improved; 2,500 miles of largely abandoned canals and 2,500 miles of bays and sounds that need connecting by canals. The rivers and canals have languished and the railroads have thriven because we have been an individualistic rather than a social people. The individual or corporation could make a fortune from a railroad, while the river, free to all, merely interfered with the monopoly of the railroad interests and favored the shipper rather than the carrier. Before the coming of railroads, this country, like many others, was dependent upon rivers to an extent now little known. Thus the Ohio and Mississippi rivers were the first great avenues of trade, travel, and settlement in the country west of the Alleghenies, which they commercially dominated till 1850. But these streams were not adequately improved and the Great Lakes were; hence they have dominated the commerce of the last half of the nineteenth century as the Mississippi dominated the first quarter.

Influence of the Great Lakes in making routes.—The primary routes of the continent are those connecting the continental interior —the upper Mississippi Valley and the Great Lake Basin—with the Atlantic. On the south direct access from the distant Gulf of Mexico was all shut off until the steamer came (1812) and on the north it is still shut off by the Niagara Falls and the rapids of the St. Lawrence. The Ohio Valley frontiersman, in the day before the steamboat, took his flatboat load of produce to New Orleans, sold it, sold the boat because it could not be got upstream, and walked home with his silver dollars. His import goods he bought from another flat boat that came down from Pittsburgh, the end of a long wagon journey from the Atlantic. The Mohawk River, flowing out through the only complete break to be found in the Appalachians between Maine and Alabama, gave the key to the lake commerce. The completion of wagon roads across the state of New York about the beginning of the century was followed by the building of the Erie Canal in 1825, the first extensive canal in the United States. The tapping of the lakes by this canal was revolutionary for the commerce of the West. A barrel of flour, which before this had consumed its profit in paying wagon freight for a hundred miles, could now be taken from the lakes to the sea for a tiny fraction of the former prohibitive freight. A large territory in the heart of the continent was given commercial possibilities, because the new route made possible a commerce with Europe by way of New York. Lake shore points throve, having access to the sea through the canal. They also became the bases for the starting of railroad lines into the corn belt states a few years after the Erie Canal had virtually made a navigable river of the Lakes. The building of railroads to the West was most easily accomplished along the open route followed by the Erie Canal. This was a profitable place, too, for the building of a railroad, because here were already in existence the traffic-breeding centers of population that had grown up in the territory enriched by the canal that had made cities in the wilderness.

The Great Lakes thus have dominated the development of trade routes in the railway era. Along their shores are the greatest in-

Fig. 166.—Iron-ore dock, steamer, railroad terminal, ore unloaders and ore storage at a Lake Erie port.

terior populations and trade. The lake freight rates, which have been but a fraction of land rates, were a freight attraction that gave any lake port commercial command of the territory behind it. The lake shores have, therefore, always been magnets to the railway builders. Whenever possible these men have brought their lines to the lakes at some point or points so that they might forward to the eastward by boat and get a share of the water-borne lake traffic, going west. Consequently the Great Lakes have been the deciding factor in locating one terminus of most of the railroads of the central west (Fig. 167). The trade routes of this region may now be likened to a section of a thick cable woven of many strands which are untwisted and spread out fan-like at each end. The lakes, with their steamship lines and the competing and auxiliary railways that follow their shores, make the central or compact sections of the cable. The loose ends are represented by the many lines of railway that

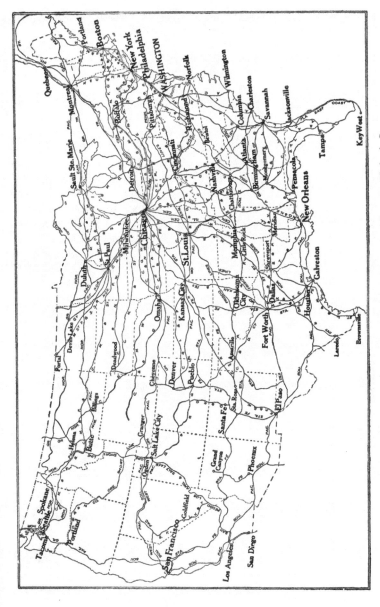

FIG. 167.—Map showing leading trunk railroad lines in the United States.

converge at the western lake ports, and by the other lines that diverge from the eastern lake ports to the Atlantic coast.

Once the railways have brought their grain, lumber, and ore to the lake ports, water transportation renders a great service. From Duluth, Port Arthur, and Fort William on Lake Superior, from Milwaukee and Chicago on Lake Michigan, and from Toledo on the Maumee near Lake Erie a vast fleet of steamers and barges busily and cheaply carry freight to and from Cleveland, Buffalo, and even Montreal on the east. But the railroads because of their greater speed are also busy with the east and west traffic. North of the lakes, between the lakes, and with many lines south of the lakes they keep up a constant competition with the lake vessels, and, in the winter months when the lakes are frozen, they must carry all the freight. The railroads also get at all seasons the vast amount of high-class freight for which there is need of haste. Thus, meat, one of the greatest if not the greatest single product in value in the whole Lake basin, goes eastward chiefly by rail from the great packing centers of Chicago, Kansas City, Omaha, and Sioux City. The eastbound grain from these same markets gravitates toward the lake steamer, since speed is not so important in its transit.

The traffic of the Lake region.—In numbers of tons per year the traffic through the American and Canadian canals around the rapids at Sault Ste. Marie at the eastern end of Lake Superior far outranks that passing through the Suez Canal (Fig. 168). The tonnage of freight passing Detroit is as great as the combined foreign trade of New York, London, and Liverpool, although it is of far less value per ton. The enormous shipments of iron ore are the largest single item. Shipments of lumber, coal, and grain also assume great proportions.

The Welland Canal at the other end of the Lake, with about one-twentieth as much freight, shows the limiting influence of shallow draught, 14 feet as compared to 21 in the channel at the Lime Kiln Crossing below Detroit.

Millions of tons of coal are carried from the southern shores of Lake Erie to the upper lakes at a freight rate of 30 cents per ton. The ore rate is commonly 65 cents from Duluth to Ashtabula, near Cleveland, and grain is carried nearly 900 miles from Chicago to Buffalo for 41 cents per ton. The lower rate westward is due to the competition of the many vessels for the relatively small return freight. In 1907, 80 per cent of the traffic through the

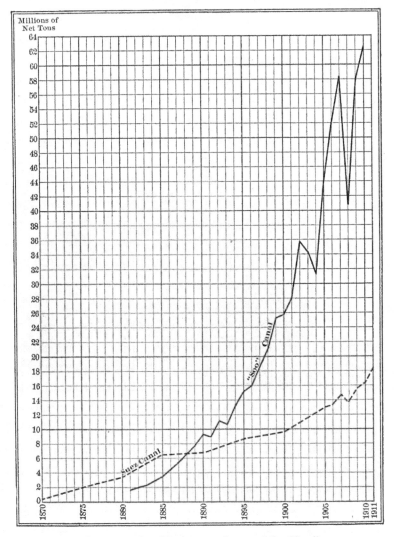

FIG. 168.—Canal Tonnage at Suez and the "Soo."

Sault Ste. Marie Canal was eastbound.   Important articles in this
total of 51.7 million tons were iron ore 35.3 million tons, wheat 84
million bushels, other grain 54 million bushels, flour 6.5 million
barrels, copper 107,000 tons, westbound 7.7 million tons bituminous
coal and 1 million anthracite.

The lake steamers are a highly specialized type.   They are just
as deep as the builders dare make them to pass through the 21-foot
channels that have been dredged in the shoals between lakes.
They are built with many hatches for fast loading, in which gravity is

FIG. 169.—Dumping carload of coal into steamer on Great Lakes.

the chief factor (Fig. 169).   In unloading the bulk cargoes, especially
of ore or coal, clam-shell grab buckets, some of them of 15
tons capacity, reach into the bottom of the ship and grasp minerals
as human hands would scoop up sugar (Fig. 170, Fig. 166).   Ten
thousand tons of ore have been loaded in 39 minutes, and 10,000
tons of coal unloaded at Duluth in 15 hours.   These factors of
economy explain why the Lakes draw the traffic, and why the Lake
cities have grown.

Chicago is at the tip of the lake that reaches farthest into the
corn belt.   All routes from the East to a large northwestern area
were compelled, in rounding Lake Michigan, to pass this point,

which naturally became the greatest railway center in the world (Fig. 171). Cleveland, Toledo, and Milwaukee had less commanding positions and grew less rapidly. Duluth, at the head of Lake Superior, is the gateway to a territory that, although much later in its development than that around Chicago and much less favored by climate, causes a large and increasing volume of freight, both outgoing and incoming.

Fig. 170.—Grab buckets of Hewlett automatic ore unloader lifting cargo from the hold of one of the Great Lake boats with its continuously open decks. (Wellman Seaver Morgan Co., Cleveland.)

West of the Lakes the railroads can and do spread out in all directions where there is traffic (see Fig. 167). At the east end of the lakes Buffalo holds a position as traffic distributor, corresponding to that of Chicago and Duluth as traffic assemblers. Trunk line railroads connect it with Boston, New York, Philadelphia and Baltimore, and the state of New York is spending over 100 million dollars in rebuilding the Erie Canal so that it can carry 1,000-ton barges and enable the port of New York to continue as the metropolis of lake traffic. The service of the Erie Canal is not to be measured in tons actually carried any more than we measure the value of a policeman by the number of arrests he makes. Every spring for many years the grain rates went down when the canal opened because the canal gave free competition on a cheap high-way. When the canal reduced the rate the railroads had to meet it. Thus the canal has reduced the rate on nearly all the hundreds of millions of tons of freight that have passed from the Lakes to the sea in the last 80 years—a service of incalculable value. This fact

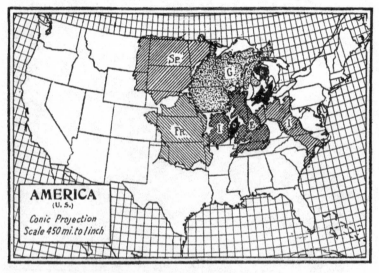

FIG. 171.—Dr. J. Paul Goode's graphic method of showing the commercial possi-bilities of Chicago and explaining why it is the greatest railroad center.

explains the bitter fights that the railroads have so often made to kill the canals (Fig. 172).

To the south of the Buffalo routes three other trunk routes of importance connect the Lake shore and the Ohio Valley with the Atlantic ports between Norfolk and New York.

This rather surprising number of routes to and from the Great Lakes is due to the remarkable topography of the basin of this group of lakes. They lie at the very top of the continental mid-region, *upon its very roof*, a reservoir and water transport system

on a level plateau. By the digging of a mere canal at Chicago the
waters are diverted to the Mississippi. The four southern lakes
are so nearly on a level with the general surface of the country, that
they can be approached by railway at almost any point suitable or
desirable for the landing of vessels. Hence, the multiplicity of
routes to them and from them.

The traffic on these east and west routes from the Atlantic Coast
States to the western plains is the heaviest railroad traffic in the

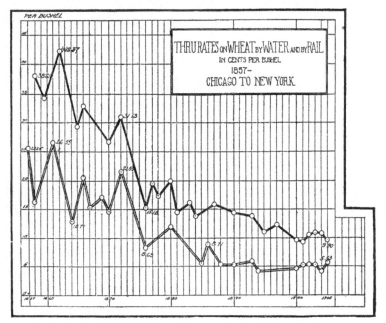

FIG. 172.—Water transportation is a controller of railway freight rates. (After
J. Paul Goode.)

world, and comprises in the main the eastward movement of
raw materials and food—grain, flour, lumber, ore, copper, meat,
and cattle foods in exchange for the westward moving manufactured articles and imports in almost infinite variety. The heaviest
single item going west is coal, chiefly the superior grades from
Pennsylvania.

Between the Chesapeake Bay and the Gulf there are no railroads of the first magnitude going inland from the Atlantic because there is no inducement to take export goods across the mountains to this corner of the continent. The region of the lower Ohio has sufficient natural outlets toward the Gulf or the Atlantic north of the Carolinas. Charleston, Savannah, and the lesser south Atlantic ports are fed by the local railways and the navigable rivers in the Atlantic plain. This limitation of hinterland gives them a prospect of permanently small size in comparison to that attained by ports having good connection with the center of the country.

The side doors of the continent.—This great sheaf of east and west routes bound together by the Great Lakes, and reaching into the center of the continent, has really included more territory than it can hold. As the result of transitory rather than permanent conditions of settlement, it has, in grasping for the vitals of the continent, overreached and placed itself in unstable equilibrium by taking trade that can, with the improvement of routes, go more easily by the side doors to the south and to the north—the Gulf of Mexico and possibly Hudson Bay.

The Mississippi River with its boats or the possibility of boats has rendered in its field a rate control service almost identical with that of the Erie Canal. The Mississippi Valley with its natural outlet toward the Gulf has created, first, New Orleans on the great river near its mouth, then at the sides of the valley, Galveston, Mobile, and Pensacola, which have become important with the building of the railways from the productive districts to the northward. These are all cities of the second class, but they are all at the end of promising lines of trade to the upper valley. Each also has a rich local territory in the cotton belt. Mobile has in addition, Alabama iron and coal, and Galveston can command Texas, Oklahoma, and Kansas grain. Although the routes to the Gulf ports at present are drawing but little freight from beyond the Ohio and Missouri Rivers, in the course of the coming decades these routes will be extended to the North, and perform a more important part in our foreign trade particularly with South American and Oriental ports. As the population and industries of the United States grow more like those of Europe, the commerce of the Central States will be relatively less with Europe and the East and more with the tropics. The opening of the Panama Canal is another strong factor helping to change the commercial front of the Mississippi Valley from the Atlantic to the Gulf. The lower Mississippi Valley, with vast undeveloped resources, also has great industrial changes before it, so that it is possible that by 1950 the Gulf routes will equal or excel in commercial importance those that connect the Great Lakes and the Ohio with the north Atlantic. These predictions are by no means dependent upon pure speculation. These changes are already in evidence and are progressing rapidly. Nature is with them.

This does not mean that we shall see any great decline for the eastern roads. Under present normal conditions they are and must be congested, crowded, overburdened with a prosperity that arises from the great growth of commerce which has come to stay. New trade will go to the Gulf. For example, the wheat trade of Kansas City is already greater than that of Chicago, and Kansas City is distinctly in Gulf rather than Atlantic territory. The distance from Kansas City to Chicago is 458 miles and the wheat rate 12 cents per hundred; from Chicago to New York, 908 miles, wheat rate 13 cents; from Kansas City to New Orleans, 880 miles, and to Galveston 851 miles, and the rate to both is $18\frac{1}{2}$ cents per hundred pounds as against 25 cents to New York.

The trans-continental lines.—Between the Pacific coast and the more populous East lie the Great Basin, the Rocky Mountain plateau, and the Great Plains, now crossed from east to west by seven railways, with others building (see Fig. 167). They are commonly known as the "Trans-continental Lines," but with one exception they lose their identity at the middle of the Mississippi Valley, which may really be considered their eastern end. They here serve as feeders to the Lakes and eastern routes described above, which forward the freight from any and all of them to the Atlantic coast points. In the competition for the trans-continental trade, the northern and southern routes are more favorably located than the central; and the most southerly route, the Southern Pacific, has, in some respects, the best location of all, and in other respects the worst. This route, having its termini at San Francisco and San Diego in the west, and at Galveston and New Orleans in the east, has the shortest land carriage, but it has the disadvantage of crossing the most arid part of the United States. Travelers commonly call it desert. From Galveston and New Orleans the route is in reality continued to New York by regular lines of steamers operated by the same company. This combination of railways and steamship routes secured much California trade with the East before the opening of the Panama canal. The three northern routes, Canadian Pacific, Great Northern, and Northern Pacific, with their termini on Lake Superior, utilize the cheap water transportation of the lakes, operate steamers to Buffalo, and have regular traffic arrangements with the railways from that point eastward. The Canadian Pacific also has steamers from Atlantic tidewater to Europe. The northern routes are also shorter than the lines that cross the central or widest parts of the United States as may be seen by reference to a globe.

The development of transportation facilities in the region has been most rapid. In 1849 caravans of gold seekers' wagons crossed it en route to California. The first regular transportation service across the Great Plains was the "Pony Express," relays of galloping horsemen carrying small packets of letters and valuables. This was succeeded by wagon trains that set out from St. Louis, Kansas City, and Omaha for New Mexico, Utah, and California. In 1869 the first railroad (from Omaha to San Francisco) was built through the aid of the United States Government at a time when the buffalo still held possession of the Plains. The present number and striking appearance of the trans-continental railways, when shown upon a map (see Fig. 167), tend to give an exaggerated impression of the part that they play as through carriers of freight. The strictly trans-continental traffic, aside from passengers and mail, is not large. This is due to the prohibitively high cost. Thus the wheat rate is 35 cents per 100 pounds from Logan, Montana (111° W.), the traffic divide on the Northern Pacific, to the Pacific or to Duluth (1,055 miles). Either terminus of this road is thousands of miles from the price-setting market at London. The chief service of these routes is as carriers of the freight produced along the lines, or of coast traffic consigned to interior points.

There is, however, a large traffic of an essentially trans-continental character. Thousands of carloads of oranges, peaches, apples, and grapes with some dried fruit are annually carried from points west of the coast range to points east of Chicago and even to the Atlantic coast cities. Manufactures of great value are taken from the manufacturing east to the essentially non-manufacturing Pacific coast. There is also considerable overland shipment of Oriental teas, mattings, and silk, but the heaviest traffic across the Rockies is in lumber, chiefly from the state of Washington. This traffic is increasing rapidly, for Washington lumber is becoming common not only in the Mississippi Valley, but also east of the Alleghenies. The efforts of the railroad managers to get return freight for their lumber trains have caused the shipment of a large amount of exports to the Orient via Pacific ports. In this way cotton has been exported from Texas to Japan via Seattle.

The people of the mid-region of the trans-continental railroads are great traffic producers. They are almost exclusively engaged in agriculture, mining, or lumbering. They are far from their markets and their sources of supplies so that a single farmer's family is reckoned by some railroads as contributing $500 a year income to the company.

The routes of the Pacific Coast region.—The trade routes of the Pacific States are simple. The centers of population are near the coast. Aside from the southern coast settlements, and the northern lumber towns, California consists essentially of a long valley extending to the north and south, opening at San Francisco Bay and drained by the Sacramento and San Joaquin Rivers. A railway net spreads over these valleys and the lines follow the rivers to the sea at San Francisco. In the south the coast range is low and it has not been difficult to build railroads which pass out of the San Joaquin Valley and reach the sea at San Pedro, the port of the populous and prosperous Los Angeles district, and also at San Diego, but neither has developed large ocean trade. In the northwest the chief productive regions (aside from lumbering) are the Columbia and Willamette Valleys, which also furnish routes for railways to the port of Portland. The Columbia is also navigable to the eastern boundary of the state of Washington; but the great excellence of Puget Sound for the development of great harbors and ports, combined with the richness of its immediately adjacent territory, and the shorter route to a rich interior, marks it as the site of the coming commercial metropolis of the Pacific coast of all America. In 1911 the vessels engaged in foreign trade, and entering Puget Sound ports, had a tonnage of over 2 million, while those entering San Francisco amounted to less than 1 million tons.

The nearness of the Pacific coast population to the Pacific causes the Panama Canal to be easily effective in stimulating their trade, which with its raw products, is so dependent upon the markets of populous regions.

Alaska.—In Alaska the arctic interior of the continent has been invaded by modernized trade routes, and the dog sledge and the human pack carrier have been succeeded on the main line of trade by the railway and the steamboat. The Klondike gold fields, lying upon the upper Yukon on both sides of the Alaska-Canadian boundary, were at first reached by the trail over the mountains near the coast, of South Alaska where a short but fearful journey separated sea and river navigation. Within 2 years after the important gold discovery on the Klondike (1897), the railway, beginning at the harbor of Skagway, had crossed the mountain pass and connected the steamer on the Fiord coast of south Alaska with the brave stern-wheeler that risks the shifting sands of the Yukon. But this river is open only in the summer months and must be *entered* from St. Michaels, across a part of the Bering Sea. The lower river route to the Klondike is hundreds of miles longer than the more direct one over the mountain ranges that separate the upper Yukon from the Pacific. Other railroads are now building to reach the middle Yukon from the center of the south coast of Alaska. One of them is to be owned by the United States Government.

The possibilities of travel in the interior of Alaska are being greatly improved by the domesticated European reindeer, which has been introduced by the aid of the Government. This draught animal is perfectly adjusted to North Alaskan environment where it can also furnish meat and milk. It will be a great aid to prospectors and miners in the search for minerals in which Alaska seems to be so promising.

Seattle and, to a lesser extent, Tacoma and San Francisco are the chief trade bases for the vessels, mostly the steamers of two companies which carry almost the entire trade of Alaska. Alaska sends gold, fish (mostly salmon) and fur in exchange for the great list of foods, clothing, and supplies needed by white men in a cold land, not suited to agriculture.

Waterway improvements in the United States.—The United States needs more facilities for transport, as shown by the freight congestions that clog our railroads in times of prosperity. The experience of Europe has clearly shown the advantage of extensive expenditures on canals and river improvement, and there is a growing sentiment in the United States in favor of the improvement of our waterways. At present they are in an astonishing stage of neglect. The Mississippi River is one of the finest natural waterways possessed by any people. It is 1,156 miles from New Orleans to St. Louis and thence 697 miles to Minneapolis and 406 to Kansas City. There is no steamboat line running the whole length of the stream, and except for coal barges and rafts it is very largely neglected at a time when we need new facilities and it is known that railway transportation is several times as costly as water transport. St. Louis, served by twenty-four railroads, and receiving 3 million loaded cars per year, and Kansas City, served by thirty-nine railroads, are connected by 406 miles of navigable river which for years was entirely unused.

The waterways can only become effective when effort is made to have through routing of freight and this the railroad companies have usually refused to do as a part of their diligent policy of thwarting the development of water transportation. Another element of success with waterways is the necessity of uniform and far-reaching system in the construction of locks and the maintenance of depths. The pork barrel system of waterway legislation so prevalent in the United States has put locks of varying sizes on the same stream, made a stretch of good navigation here and there that connected with nothing and leaves to us such monuments as the canal at Mussel Shoals on the Tennessee River. In 1908, 12,000 tons of freight passed through it at a cost to the government of $4 per ton for repairs and maintenance and $7.50 per ton for interest (at only 3 per cent.) on the cost of installation. Granted systematic construction and compulsory through routing of freight by the railroads, the waterways of the United States have a busy future. The possibilities of the Mississippi River are enormous. At the head of its navigable Eastern branch, the Ohio, is Pittsburgh, the capital of coal, iron, and glass with the astonishing traffic of 150 million tons a year. These figures become more significant when it is remembered that the United States has never yet produced 4 million tons of cotton or 30 million tons of wheat in one year. The total world export of wheat is less than 20 million tons (1911) and the entire world's crop of wheat is about 100 million tons a year. The Chicago Drainage Canal gives connection with the Great Lakes, and the Mississippi itself flows through the heart of the corn, oat, meat, and hay belts and reaches at Minneapolis the edge of the spring-wheat country and the greatest flour-milling center in the world. The continued neglect of such a waterway is an almost inexplicable waste of resource. We need less triple tracking of coal, wood, iron, and life-wasting railroads and more construction of resource-saving waterways for which the geographic conditions of the country are so favorable.

QUESTIONS

1. What was the matter with George Washington's plan for a canal from tide water on the Potomac to the Ohio River?

2. Compare the commercial future of Charleston and Galveston.

3. Which is needed more, the double tracking of some of the existing transcontinental railroads or the building of another one?

4. Compare the prospects for through traffic for railroads to be built from an Ohio River city to Mobile and to Norfolk—granted equality of freight rate.

5. Compare the traffic future of San Francisco and Seattle.

6. Why would the railroad traffic manager rather have a colonist settle in the Rocky Mountains than on the Pacific Coast?

7. What is the most important first step to get our waterways used?

PART II

FOREIGN COUNTRIES

CHAPTER XVII

CANADA

Canada an extension of the United States.—To understand Canada one should remember that it is geographically the northward extension of the United States. The glaciated and forested New England landscape with its meager agriculture, good water power, and fishing coasts, extends into Canada. The similarly forested and glaciated upper lake states are matched by more land of the same sort to the north of the Lakes. The old lake bed that lies to the west of the Minnesota forests and makes the Red River Valley famous for wheat, has the greater part of its area in adjacent Manitoba. The Great Plains of Dakota and Montana extend northward into Canada for hundreds of miles, and owing to the better water supply there, they are undoubtedly a better place for grain growing (Fig. 174). The only important part of the United States along the boundary that is not duplicated in Canada is the open Columbia river basin. The Canadian mountains here widen out so that with their forested slopes they cover most of the territory from the eastern front of the Rocky Mountains to the Pacific. Most important of all is the similarity in race and in institutions, including government. Except for the French population of Quebec, these too are in the main a continuation of those of the United States.

Climatic limitations.—The fact that Canada is farther north than the United States places agriculture, especially in the East, under a greater handicap. This causes the fishing industry on the Banks, which are closer to Canada than to the United States, to assume an ever greater relative importance in the maritime provinces than in New England. Northward from South Newfoundland the sea is full of southward floating ice, the air is cold and damp, and agriculture is limited to gardens and even gardens are a rarity in Newfound-

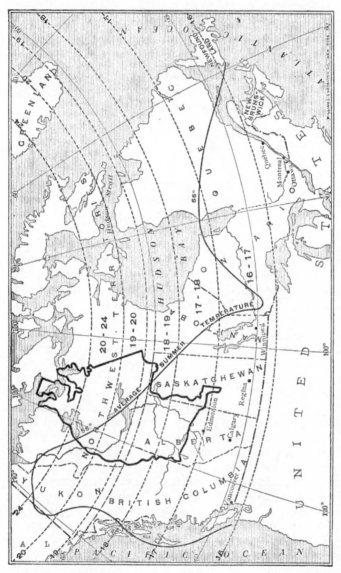

Fig. 173.—Map of Canada showing by dotted lines the number of hours' daily sunshine in June. A moderate summer temperature prevails in high latitudes because of the long days and short nights. The space enclosed in black line shows the areas of the Siberian province of Tobolsk in its proper latitude, which produced in 1907 nearly 72,000,000 bushels of wheat. This shows what may be expected of Canada in the future.

iand. Thus Newfoundland and Labrador offer one of the best modern examples of a people living from one resource—so great is their dependence upon fish. There is a little iron mining, a little lumbering, and some paper making, but eight-ninths of the exports are fish products and nine-tenths of the workers are busy with fish. The people who are not at sea catching cod, or herring, are busy curing them. Some of the cod are sold fresh, but most of them are cleaned and salted as soon as they are brought to the schooner by the dories, and when the schooner reaches its port they are dried in the sun upon sheds which stretch conspicuously along the coasts. The herring is salted or cured by smoking over a slow fire.

The fishing industry.—The fishing industry of Nova Scotia equals that of Massachusetts, the leading fishing state of the United States, and the total Canadian catch ($25,000,000, 1907) is slightly greater than that of New England. Nova Scotia with her many good harbors partakes somewhat of the character of Newfoundland but, though she catches nearly one-third of the fish of Canada, the warmer climate of this province enables the people to engage, to a considerable extent, in agriculture, and they ship sheep, cattle, and horses across the straits to the people of Newfoundland.

Fishing fleets from Europe still visit the Grand Banks, and although Newfoundland belongs to Great Britain, the French fishermen may, by treaty right, fish along the shore of the greater part of Newfoundland. They may also land and dry their fish, although no permanent French settlements may be made. France also owns two small islands, Miquelon and St. Pierre, situated just south of Newfoundland, with a population of a few thousand, dependent entirely upon the fishing industry. This single product serves to give these islanders an exceedingly heavy trade, many times as heavy per capita as that of the United States.

A seal sought for its oil and leathery skin is common in Labrador and Arctic America, and a fleet of steam sealers sails from St. Johns, N. F., on an annual fishing voyage. Single vessels have been known to bring back 30,000 skins.

Agriculture of East Canada.—The agriculture of East Canada like that of New England has been handicapped by the glacial topography and soil and almost wrecked by the competition of cheap products from the rich and level West. Where it has survived, it has been by intensification through dairying and the development of specialties. Thus Prince Edward Island is famous for its potatoes.

In this province also a suggestive new industry is arising. The enormous prices paid for the furs of the black fox have caused 10 million dollars to be invested in fox farming, several thousand dollars being paid for a single fine breeding fox. This is an industry to which the nearby fisheries contribute an important food supply. Again, in that part of Canada lying between Lake Huron, the city of Quebec and the American boundary, comprising the populous parts of the provinces of Ontario and Quebec, the people have reached a high degree of success in dairying. The provinces of Ontario and Quebec have more than 4,000 factories where butter and especially cheese are manufactured. Great care is taken to maintain the high quality of the product, and it is consequently much esteemed in Great Britain, whither four-fifths of the cheese go, making up half of the British import of that article. Canadian competition, aided by the inferior quality and bad repute of American cheese, has greatly lessened the export of the American product.

Canadian apple growing.—Canada is also an apple exporter of nearly as great importance as the United States. The apple does well from Lake Huron to the mouth of the St. Lawrence and two localities have utilized their especial advantages for developing the apple as a money crop for the foreign trade. The most famous of these is the Annapolis Valley in Nova Scotia (crop 1911 estimated 1,500,000 barrels). This valley 8 × 80 miles in the western part of the Peninsula is protected by the Bay of Fundy and a sheltering mountain range, and is well suited to the apple. There is an official record of one tree that yielded 35 barrels of fruit. These advantages, together with convenient access to the seacoast, relative unfitness for other forms of agriculture, and an early start at apple-growing have given this region a development of the industry which has made its product famous in Britain. The export apple is the chief money crop and financial dependence of its people. The second Canadian apple district is near Niagara Falls on the peninsula between Lakes Erie and Ontario, where it has the protecting influence of the water similar to that which benefits New York's lake shore apple belt, of which it is really an extension separated only by the Niagara River. It is surprising to think that this part of Canada is a better place for the growth of peaches and grapes than many parts of the United States.

Manufacture.—Canadian manufacturing has not been able to fully overcome the temptation of the people to emigrate to the western provinces and to the United States. The small population has left the industries without an adequate labor supply and limited them largely to lumber and wood products and some wool manufacture. The unused opportunities for iron manufacture furnished by Nova Scotia coal and Newfoundland iron, both near tidewater, are almost unrivalled. Canada seems destined to develop large manufacturing because of her wealth in wood and water-power.

Canadian forests.—Four of the forest belts of the United States touch and extend across the Canadian boundary (see Fig. 113). The Pacific and Rocky Mountain forests combine in Canada, extend northward through British Columbia and on to the Yukon, a vast region crossed as yet by but two railroads, the Canadian Pacific near the United States boundary, and the Grand Trunk Pacific farther north, so that most of it is unsettled and much of it is even unexplored by any but the unscientific trapper and prospector. It contains, along with some land good for agriculture, many forests that await the building of railroads to get the product upon the world's market. The treeless belt of the Mississippi Valley goes northward through Canada, until in latitude 60, the moisture conditions for forest growth are found and there is a connection between the Rocky Mountain forests and the forest region north of the Great Lakes in a subarctic forest belt 200 to 300 miles in width.

The whole of the country from near Winnipeg to the Atlantic was originally a forest of which but a fraction has been cleared for settlement and that is all in the region between Lakes Erie, Ontario, and Lower Huron, and in the St. Lawrence Valley. North of this small inhabited belt is one of the great forest reserves of the future reaching from near Lake Winnipeg to the mouth of the St. Lawrence and from Hudson Bay to Georgian Bay, the Ottawa River and the banks of the St. Lawrence itself. Much of it is upland; it is well sprinkled with lakes and marshes, and is practically unsettled except by a few Indians, fur trappers, and summer fishermen. A railroad is being built across it from the south end of Lake Winnipeg to Quebec, and branch lines have been built northward from the Canadian Pacific to reach silver and nickel mines in the newly discovered Algoma district north of Lake Superior, otherwise this great forest is yet without industry save lumbering on its southern edge. For this the Ottawa River gives a good outlet and the city of Ottawa is an important lumber producer and lumber market.

A continuation of the New England forests occupies most of the

Canadian territory between the St. Lawrence and the Atlantic. . Forests cover much of Newfoundland, and wood products are the only plant products exported from that cold, foggy, and sparsely peopled island.

There is extensive, but as yet almost unused, water-power on the many streams flowing from the lakes and swamps upon the large lake-strewn plateau between the St. Lawrence River system, the Atlantic Ocean and Hudson Bay. The province of Quebec alone has, according to the estimate of the Canadian government, 17 million horse-power—Ontario 3 million and the entire Dominion 25 million. It is nearly equal to the entire amount of artificial power developed in the United States. Less than 2 per cent. of the water-power of Ontario and Quebec is now utilized.

These extensive forests with their water-power make possible an enormous industry in wood manufacture, of which paper is a type and already one of the important exports of the region. New mills are being erected in the entirely unagricultural lands north of the Gulf of St. Lawrence and in Newfoundland. Electric smelting of aluminum, nitrates, etc., is another industry that has begun and for which the water-power furnishes the current.

The Western Canada wheat country.—The plains west of the Lake Superior forests are the new and now best-known Canada. Here is a vast level plain of almost unbelievable extent, and much of it still awaiting the settler to whom it is being given away in homestead tracts of 160 acres each. Day after day one may ride on new railroads across open, empty, treeless plains where the new settlers are again beginning with continuous wheat growing which will last for one, two, or three decades before they too must take to other crops and to cattle keeping. In the meantime these wheat crops on the virgin prairie soil of the harvest frontier are larger than those of the Red River Valley. It is possible that the Canadian region suitable for the extension of wheat growing reaches 60° north, and extends from Lake Winnipeg to the Rockies (Fig. 173). If experience proves this to be true, the wheat-growing possibilities are enormous, and the continuous cropping method will have land to support it for several decades.

For several years prior to 1914 the building of new railroads across this Canadian plain went forward with great speed. Many thousand settlers came each year from Europe and from the United States. The Canadian Government actually opened bureaus of information in cities of the United States and advertised in American farm papers that she had farms to give away.

Winnipeg with a location at the end of a lake, as has Chicago, is destined to be the Chicago of the great wheat country. It is already a hustling, thriving, booming metropolis with Regina, Calgary and Edmonton far beyond it to the westward rising in importance.

Canada's rise as a wheat grower is indicated by the yield of Saskatchewan—4 million bushels in 1900, 34 million in 1908 and 121 million in 1913. There is as yet little reason to modify Dr.

FIG. 174.—Grain elevators at a railroad station on the agricultural frontier 101° W. The first stage in the journey of grain from the farmer's wagon to the distant user.

Saunders' reasonable prophecy of 1904—that wheat grown on one-fourth of the land suitable to it in the Canadian northwest, with the acre yield of Manitoba for the previous decade, would bring a crop of more than 800 million bushels, which, as he shows, would feed 30 million people in Canada and supply three times the import need of the United Kingdom. The remaining three-fourths of the land would provide room for a vast animal industry with soil enriching crop rotations.

British Columbia, the northward continuation of the climate and lands of Washington State, has enough fruit and agricultural land to support, if in Europe, a nation of second-class power.

Mineral resources.—Canada is not so blessed in mineral resources as is the United States. Of the Appalachian coal fields there is no extension in Canada. There is only a small coal field in Nova Scotia so that most of the St. Lawrence basin is naturally tributary to the coal of Pennsylvania whence there is a large import.

Similarly the United States got the lion's share of the Lake Superior iron ores although recent discoveries show that Canada has large amounts in comparison to any possible home demand. The destruction of all surface features of most of the land in the eastern forests by glaciation makes prospecting very difficult, but there have nevertheless been recent discoveries of silver and nickel.

Parts of the western plain are underlaid by a deposit of coal that is probably larger than that of any European country and is already of great service in driving the locomotives on the long railroads that connect the new wheat lands with the steamers on the Great Lakes. In drilling a recent artesian well in Manitoba 100 feet of coal were found within 1,000 feet of the surface.

British Columbia also has some coal in the immediate coast district whence it was exported to California in considerable quantity before the California oil discoveries. There is some gold mining in the British Columbia mountains and a vast area of unprospected mountain country.

Transportation in Canada.—The settlement of this ready plain of West Canada has caused a general industrial boom, and a tremendous development in railroad building. These new enterprises were financed quite largely by foreign countries, but the money went to Canada in the form of goods and in a recent year showed itself in imports worth $351,000,000 while the exports were valued at $227,000,000—figures which showed Canada to be in the borrowing and equipping stage of industrial development.

With the large development of grain-growing West Canada has raised great hopes of utilizing the Hudson Bay Route for grain export. Fort Churchill, on the western shore of Hudson Bay, near the mouth of Nelson River, is 100 or 200 miles nearer to Liverpool than New York is and 1,400 miles nearer than New Orleans. The Hudson Bay Route's advantage of distance is modified by the winter ice, which closes the passage to the Atlantic for the greater part of the year, and may possibly prevent any extensive use of the route. At present nearly all of Canada's commerce with Europe passes through the port of Montreal when the St. Lawrence is open, and through

Halifax, St. Johns, N. B., Portland, Me., Boston and New York in the winter months when the St. Lawrence is frozen.

The far country.—North of these south Canadian lands of the white man is the greater part of her area that has for generations been the trading ground of the Hudson Bay Company which had posts and carriers to gather furs from the Indians. For a long time this historic company, with such an interesting history, was both trader and governor but it has now given the governing over to the Dominion, although it still has a virtual monopoly of trade in hundreds of thousands of square miles of cold forest and still colder barren grounds beyond. There is a sparse population of Indians and French and Indian half breeds who gather a considerable share of the world's furs.

This land of fascinating unmapped rivers abounding in fish and game remains in its primitive condition, with its primitive industry. (For other possibilities see chapter on Extension of Industry.)

Canada the complement of the United States.—There are many commercial reasons why Canada and the United States should forever be friends. We want her goods, she wants ours. There is every prospect that we will shortly be a wheat importer. Canada has the wheat. We already want the wood pulp and lumber from her vast eastern forests and the chemicals and metals made by her water-power plants. She wants our oranges and cotton, our coal, steel and machinery to supply her needs and develop her resources. We are her best customer; she is one of our best customers.

QUESTIONS

1. Why do the fisheries of Newfoundland and Labrador seem more important than those farther South?

2. For what industry do two resources fit the plateau north of the St. Lawrence?

3. What two sections of Canada are climatically fitted for apple growing?

4. Why may we expect west Canada to have a larger wheat yield per acre than North Dakota?

5. Why has a country of such great resources imported more than it exported?

6. Why will west Canada have a greater advantage as a wheat producer than as a meat producer?

CHAPTER XVIII

MEXICO

Northern Mexico is the southward extension of the natural features that characterize the southwestern United States—arid plateaus broken or walled by high mountains. The mountains of western Texas and of Arizona extend southward increasing in height until they meet south of Mexico City, which thus has its location on a walled-in plateau. While this city is in the tropics, its elevation of a mile and a half on the high plateau robs it of the tropic climate. It is on this plateau 700 miles long and 200 to 300 miles wide increasing in height as it goes south that nearly nine-tenths of the Mexican people live. As in Arizona, so in adjacent Mexico, mining is the chief dependence of the people and the chief basis of foreign trade. On the higher mountains are pine forests, on the plateaus scanty pasturage and vast cattle ranches, and here and there irrigated oases of alfalfa, vegetables, corn, and cotton. A little wheat is also grown, but cattle are the chief agricultural export of this plateau.

Lower California, a peninsula 700 miles long, the extension of the dry land area of south California is almost a desert. It is on the leeward side of the continent in the zone of trade winds and there are no mountains high enough to make precipitation of value to agriculture.

Population and living.—The population of all Mexico, one-sixth as numerous as that of the United States, is composed of 38 per cent native Indians, 43 per cent of mixed race and 19 per cent of pure or nearly pure white race of Spanish stock. As the Spaniard prefers official and military life to industry, all Mexican industries except the simplest are operated by foreigners. Americans, English, Germans and French plan the railroads, mines, and oil wells, and supervise the native peon in building and operating them. Foreigners also run practically all of the trains. The bulk of the native Indian or half-breed people have a very low standard of living. The simplest shelter suffices, and, rather than work much, they content themselves with a diet consisting chiefly of beans, one of the most easily grown of vegetables, and corn, the cereal which they can most easily and cheaply grow. In Mexico and other Spanish-American countries the commonest form of corn bread is the "tortilla" or hot corn cake which can be baked over an open fire. Despite this use of corn, Mexico will not be a corn exporter. That part of the country north of San Luis Potosi is steadily importing more and more corn as its mineral resources and railroads give employment to workers. Except for a mine or two of low quality product, near the Texas boundary, there is no coal in Mexico, and the scant rainfall of the plateau limits tree growth. As a result fuel is very scarce; wood and charcoal are often hauled many miles on mule back. The destruction of the forests in many locations has been very thorough.

Tropic Mexico and the forest.—On the outer slopes of the central plateau there are many delightful warm temperate valleys producing export coffee, but most of southern Mexico and the eastern shore plain is fully tropic with enough rainfall to produce the much overpraised tropic forest (Fig. 175). The woods here as in other tropic forests are in great variety and many are of surprising beauty and hardness, but most of the trees are crooked and useless for lumber. They are often worthlessly soft and weak, and the good ones are almost always mingled with many other species which makes their removal a very difficult matter. This mixture of species is a striking and important contrast to the practically solid stand that exists in the pine or spruce forests of Maine, the fir of Washington, the cypress of Louisiana, or the oak of West Virginia. Those who gather tropic logs usually find but one tree of a kind in a place, surrounded by hundreds of useless specimens of other varieties. To make matters worse, the heavy rainfall and the heat produce such a wealth of bushes, small trees, and vines that a man can only force his way through by first cutting a path. Thus the machete, a long-handled knife, is the most universal tool possessed by the inhabitants of many tropical countries. With it they cut paths through the forest in which each tree is often bound by creepers to a dozen others, so that the felling of one tree is a most difficult process. As the jungle is often swampy, the lumberman is tortured by insects, and it is evident that a wagon can rarely enter to carry logs because the wheels would sink into the soft earth even if roadways could be cut. The nearest approach to the northern blessing of snow with its sled transportation is the annual floods of the rainy season, which permit the floating out of those logs which grow on overflowed land and are light enough to float. Those that are heavier than water, and most of the tropical cabinet woods with their great strength and beauty are

FIG. 175.—Tropical forest in southern Mexico. Good logs are scarce and industry quails before the task of extricating them. (Salisbury, Barrows, and Tower.)   Photo by W. L. Tower.

heavier than water, must rot where they grow, or be dragged out at great expense. Consequently, the chief timbers exported from the tropics are the mahogany and cedar (buoyant enough to float), of which the United States imported $3,000,000 worth in 1911, while all other cabinet woods imported were not one-tenth as valuable.

One vast belt of solid green girdles the earth wherever the land emerges from the equatorial sea, yet this equatorial forest has thus far been of less use to man than if it were a desert with an occasional oasis. To this the forests of the Mexican lowland are no exception. The population is scanty—a few sickly coast settlements and scattered Indians in the forests.

Rubber.—Some wild rubber is found in the Mexican forests and some rubber plantations have been started, but the chief rubber output of Mexico comes from the plateau. It is furnished by the unique guayule, an herbaceous plant of the sunflower family, from a few inches to 3 or 4 feet in height, growing over the prairies of northeastern Mexico and even the southwestern part of the United States, oftentimes in regions so dry that there are no forests and all ordinary agriculture must depend upon irrigation. Guayule has sprung into sudden importance since the automobile put up the price of rubber. In 1904 it was in the experimental stage and in 1911 our imports of it, entirely from Mexico, were one-fourth as great as our imports of the so-called "india rubber." The extraction of the gum requires large quantities of water which necessitates taking the plant to large factories for the purpose

Two things about this source of raw material for the rubber industry are very suggestive for the future era of rubber cultivation. First, it is a small herbaceous plant offering the possibilities of a crop with steady returns once in 8 or 10 years. Second, it grows in a region where white men can live and work. The largest factory, employing 700 men and turning out 6,000,000 pounds in 1911 is at Torreon on the Mexican plateau in the latitude of the mouth of the Rio Grande. In the states of Durango and Coahuila, land which was considered absolutely worthless for pasturing cattle has in the last few years produced fabulous sums from the sale of the guayule shrub.

A part of Yucatan near the port of Progreso differs from the rest of the eastern lowland in rainfall and usefulness. It is a semi-arid limestone plain with a busy commercial life depending on one crop— the henequin or sisal, yielding a cordage fiber much used for binder twine (Fig. 176). The plant is an agave, close kin of the century plant, that does well in dry, spongy soils, particularly if they are calcareous. It requires no cultivation other than the occasional chopping down of rival plants, and yields an annual harvest for from 6 to 25 years. The rise of the henequin or sisal grass industry is due solely to the invention of a machine which effectively extracts the fibers from the long, fleshy, spiny leaves. In years of shortage of the local corn crop, the sisal growers import corn from the United States in considerable quantities as food for both man and beast.

FIG. 176.—Cutting agave leaves to extract sisal fiber. Yucatan.
(U. S. Dept. Agr.)

Several other stalk-fiber yielding plants are produced to a small extent in various parts of Mexico.

The busiest part of all Mexico is the oil field on the coast plain near Tampico.[1] There is great rivalry here between the English and

[1] On the fourth of July, 1908, the greatest oil well of the world, up to that time, was struck at San Geronimo, on the Gulf of Mexico, 67 miles north of Tampico. When struck, the oil gushed so rapidly that before the fire in the boiler of the engine running the drilling machinery could be extinguished, the flowing oil reached it and burst into a mass of flame which for two months burned 60,000 to 75,000 barrels of oil per day with a flame from 800 to 1,400 feet in height, and 40 to 75 feet in width, making light enough to be seen by ships 100 miles at sea, and to permit a newspaper to be read 17 miles away. After the

American oil companies. Several tank-ship loads of oil per day often leave this port for the North Atlantic ports of the United States and Europe.

The trade and routes of Mexico.—The trade routes of Mexico are, in part, a continuation of those of the southwestern part of the United States. Three railway lines from the United States enter the plateau by the easy ascent from the north. These are the Sonora Line of the Southern Pacific to Guaymas on the Gulf of California, the National of Mexico, an extension of the Santa Fe from El Paso through the Central Plateau to Mexico City with numerous side lines, and the eastern division of the same connecting at Loredo with the Internatonal and Great Northern. Three other lines, from Tampico, Vera Cruz, and Puerto Mexico climb the steep escarpment from the Gulf coast. The northern routes carry an active overland trade with New Orleans, St. Louis, Kansas City, and Chicago; but a larger and more valuable trade goes to the Atlantic ports of the United States and Europe by steamers from Tampico and Vera Cruz. The imports comprise the great variety of supplies and machinery used in a country that has little manufacturing of the factory type.

The Pacific coast of Mexico is inadequately supplied with trade routes. The western Cordillera is high and abrupt, making railroad building difficult. A number of lines have been projected, and the first one completed (1902) connects Guanajuato on the plateau, with Manzanillo, at the seacoast. The Pacific coast (less humid than the East Coast) is a promising region for tropic and sub-tropic agriculture, and the mountains of western Mexico are rich in minerals. The opening of the Panama Canal will give this region a short route to the Atlantic and will stimulate the building of railways in western Mexico. At present there are only mule trails from a number of ports to the mines 100 to 200 miles inland.

Mexico has, in the Tehuantepec Railway, a most efficient transcontinental line. This road connecting Puerto Mexico, on the Gulf, with Salina Cruz on the Pacific, was built by an English company for the transfer of freight from ocean to ocean. The line of American steamers that had for 8 years (1899–1907) been

loss of $3,000,000 the fire was put out, but the oil flowed so rapidly that it could not be carried away or put in tanks, and the English owners saved their oil only by confining it in a reservoir one-fourth of a mile long made by heaping up earth embankments to keep the oil from flowing away like water. Even this well was later surpassed by the Potrero del Lano No. 4 well near Tuxpan, Mexico, which yielded 160,000 barrels a day for some time.

rounding South America, at once turned to this route and the traffic capacity of the single-track railway was reached within a few months after the formal opening. The local traffic of this road is now increasing, owing to the new coffee and rubber plantations along the line.

Mexico's foreign trade will continue to depend as now chiefly on export metals, silver, copper and gold. She is the leader in the world's silver production, has long been so and will likely continue to lead, unless she returns to her old political chaos. The mineral resources in her western mountains appear to be enormous, and many foreign owned mines have been opened. In the past she has been pre-eminently a silver producer, partly because of the great number of silver deposits, and partly because these deposits can be mined in remote localities of a dry and rugged country where ores are concentrated by the simple device of the arrastra—a stone floor on which ore is crushed by a stone wheel, rolled around upon the ore by beasts of burden. From the crushed ore the silver collects in the cracks of the stone floor and in this concentrated form is carried scores or even hundreds of miles on pack mules. The building of American railways into Mexico has made possible the opening up of mines using the most improved machinery and processes, and has caused rapid increase in the output of gold and copper.

The future of Mexico.—Since Mexico became independent from Spain she has been in almost constant civil war except during the rule of one man Porfirio Diaz who was a successful despot and kept the peace during the period of 1876–1911. His practice of giving concessions to friends and foreigners amounted to graft and confiscation that dispossessed the natives of their land. Whether or not the great riches of Mexico can be developed is now (1915) an unsettled question. Without peace and security commerce and industry on any important scale are almost impossible.

Questions

1. What climatic contrast causes the native of Mexico City to suffer in Vera Cruz?

2. For what two reasons is the Mexican plateau poorly supplied with forests?

3. How is the aridity of Yucatan more profitable commercially than the more humid coast to the westward?

4. What facts about Mexican industries have given the people of the United States and England so great an interest in the Mexican civil wars?

5. With peace and abundant capital will Mexico become a grain exporter? a cattle exporter?

6. What industry is, and will be, most important in Mexico's foreign trade?

CHAPTER XIX

THE CARIBBEAN LANDS AND THE GUIANAS

1. Geography, Climate, and Population

The Caribbean Sea with the Greater Antilles on the north, the Lesser Antilles on the east, northern South America on the south, and Central America on the west, washes the shores of many little worlds. These include nine independent countries, two American protectorates, and many colonies owned by England, France, Holland, and Denmark. The numerous islands, the differing ownerships and races, and the divided condition of the extensive mainland have combined to give a great variety of industrial conditions to the lands touched by the Caribbean.

These lands have in common the tropic climate which permits a great range of products. It enables the family to grow its cane sugar in the garden; it shuts out wheat and the white potato, but permits in their place the sweet potato, the yam, the banana, and the cassava, a plant with a long starchy root widely used in the tropics as food and also for the manufacture of our tapioca. Corn, beans and many other plants thrive, and there is a great profusion of wild and domesticated tree fruits. The great yielding power of these plants has permitted in Panama and elsewhere the development of a satisfactory agriculture without the use of plow or beast of burden. Poultry, dogs and pigs are the only domestic animals in many localities (Figs. 177, 183).

These Caribbean lands also have in common the trade wind climate. This means a warm northeast wind with heavy rains on the northeast side of mountains and light rains on the southwest side (Fig. 178). It means heavier rain in the summer time, and tangled jungle on coastal plains such as those upon the western and southern shore of the Caribbean and some of the larger islands. The absence of such unwholesome plains upon some of the smaller islands is a great advantage to them.

Nearly all of the Caribbean lands are high in parts, having on the plateaus the great advantage of a cooler and more wholesome climate

337

than the neighboring lowlands. It is upon the plateaus of Central America, Colombia and Venezuela that nearly all of the people of those countries live. This makes access to the sea and its commerce difficult. In Colombia the Magdalena River, with its steamboats,

FIG. 177.—Panama farmer's family, home, and all the tools of agriculture—a machete (in man's right hand) to cut the bushes and weeds and a sharp stick to make holes for seeds. These people are from another world, the tropic world. They have not developed from savagery through the pastoral or animal-tending state. That is the Aryan method. These tropic people seem never to have used animals to any important extent but developed at once a hand agriculture depending largely on starchy roots, sweet potato, yam, manioc, taro, caladium and others which have been tilled so long that they have lost the power of producing seed. The banana, corn, and sugar cane are important additions to this untilled soil-preserving agriculture. (Photo H. H. Bennett, U. S. Bureau of Soils.)

serves as a trunk route to which several short railroads and many long pack-mule trails are feeders. Over such routes only valuable goods can pay the freight, and all goods must be in such packages that two of them will balance across the back of a mule. So the chief exports are limited to coffee, cattle hides, gold, and other easily portable goods representing large value for small bulk. Thus some tobacco reaches Germany from interior Colombia sewed up in two layers of raw cowhide, to protect it from the drenching rains en route on the forest trails. These commercial conditions are as true of much of Central America as of Colombia, for while the distances from the sea are not so great, transportation is very difficult because of the rough topography, high altitude and the dense vegetation.

In Venezuela the plateau with the center of population happens to be near the coast instead of an inland river as in Colombia. Short railroads connect with the ports.

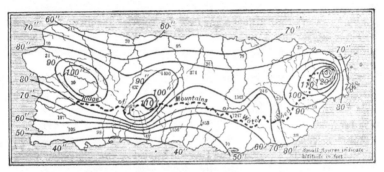

Fig. 178.—Porto Rico, mean annual rainfall, 1899–1909. A typical trade-wind island. Explain its rainfall distribution. (U. S. Weather Bureau.)

The Great Orinoco Valley, open, treeless, and covered with grass, has millions of acres of unused lands in the interior of Venezuela and Colombia. It seems to be a great reserve cattle range for the future.

It has been said that the poor transportation, low industrial conditions, and frequent civil wars of Colombia and Venezuela are due to the fact that it is ruled by the Spanish race, but adjacent Guiana ruled by the English, Dutch, and French, is even more empty. It affords an interesting comparison, and strongly suggests how man is dominated by nature—in this case, climate.

The white man in the tropics.—The population of the Caribbean lands in combination with their history shows that they are better suited to the colored than to the white races. As a result of the African slave trade of former years, the West Indies, excepting Porto Rico and Cuba, are largely populated with negroes in spite of repeated efforts at colonization by various races from Europe. In Hayti the population is almost exclusively black.

Thepopulation of Jamaica shows an interesting analysis at the end of three centuries of repeated colonization by various races from Europe, Africa and Asia—from the temperate and from the tropic lands. That island has a large amount of plateau with its cooler climate, it has had the advantages of 250 years of British rule, and British control of industry. A recent census shows a population of nearly 200 per square mile and 2.3 per cent white, 76 per cent black, 19 per cent "colored" (mulatto), 1.8 per cent East Indian. Within 20 years the increase of the colored races has been over 200,000 and the white population is now about 15,000. The experience of Jamaica shows that unless some new discoveries are made the tropics are not fit for the Caucasian to inhabit. The tropic world scarce affords a more favorable place than Jamaica, and many are far less favorable.

In Central America the bulk of the population, like that in Mexico, is still Indian, and there, as in the whole of the Caribbean countries and Mexico, the large industries are owned and operated by people of the temperate zone—United States and Europe. The Germans own extensive coffee plantations in the Central American highlands, especially Guatemala, and the English have for two centuries owned many sugar plantations in the West Indian Islands. For over a century these islands exported chiefly sugar (Fig. 179), molasses, and rum distilled from molasses. In the last quarter of the nineteenth century the competition of European beet sugar put down the price and made it difficult for the less efficient parts of the West Indies to compete. Hard times followed, but in some localities the newly arisen banana trade has replaced the lost sugar prosperity.

2. THE BANANA

The banana, a rival of the potato, the sweet potato, rice, and cassava, is one of the great starch foods of the world. It has been cultivated so long that it has ceased to produce seed. Wherever the climate is always warm and the rainfall suffices to support a dense tropic forest, the banana, in some of its many forms, is at home. There are seventy varieties in the Philippines, and equatorial Africa is rich in bananas. The banana belt goes round the world and reaches slightly into the north temperate zone. This plant stands almost without a peer among nature's gifts to man. Wheat, rice, and the potato we get by arduous labor and tillage, but one may stick the root of a banana tree in the favorable tropical earth, give to nearby rival plants a few blows with the machete to keep the young banana plant from being overgrown, and, in a few months, gather its great gift of fruit. For years thereafter the shoots which the original plant sends up continue to furnish abundant food throughout most of the year. The amount of food per acre is greater than from any grain, but far less than is often reported. Three hundred bunches per acre is considered a good crop in Jamaica, and the drain upon the soil is less than that made by a small crop of wheat.

The banana in commerce.—Owing to the perishable nature of the fruit and consequent necessity of quick transportation, it has not been long known to many people in the temperate zone. It is a gift of the tropics delivered to the temperate zone by the coal-driven steamship which is destined to bring us many other valuable gifts of a like perishable nature. The consumption of this fruit in the United States doubled every 5 years between 1870 and 1900. Since that date its use has steadily increased, because it is in many places the cheapest food that can be bought in America today. It competes with the cereals, to a limited extent with our home-grown fruits, and with the potato, of which it is almost a duplicate in nutritive content. (See table of food values, Appendix.)

Because of the difficulty of transportation, only certain favored locations in the tropics are near enough to the markets to export the banana. The supply in Europe is inferior to that in the United States because that part of the tropics lying nearest Europe is the desert of Sahara, where the banana cannot grow. The European supply has for a long time come from the Madeira, the Cape Verde and the Canary Islands off the west coast of Africa; but within recent years fast steamers have begun to carry the product of the West Indies and Central America to England.

Importance of the banana in Caribbean countries.—The nearness of the United States to the steaming hot plains that border the Caribbean Sea and the Gulf of Mexico has given us a favorable place from which to draw our supply of bananas. Owing to the unwholesome climate along the Central American coasts, nearly all the people live on the more healthful interior plateaus and the best banana lands have long lain idle. The comparatively new banana commerce, however, has caused recent rapid increase of settlements (mostly

West Indian negroes, with white supervisors) and of commerce along the low eastern coasts. American enterprise and capital have built railroads and established plantations near many of the ports and have sent ships to carry the product. When shiploads of bananas reach our ports, they are hurried on express trains to the interior. As a result of this highly organized international trade, a hungry man on the streets of many American cities can be better fed on 3 cents worth of bananas (usually two or three bananas) than he can on 3 cents worth of bread.

This comparatively new trade has been little short of revolutionary in the effects it has had in making new industry in the vicinity of Boca del Toro, Panama; Limon, Costa Rico; Puerto Barrios, Guatemala; Port Antonio, Jamaica; Santa Marta, Colombia, and other Caribbean ports. Four and one-half million bunches exported from Boca del Toro in 1910 made up practically all of the exports from the large territories of Panama. There is plenty of room on the Caribbean for more plantations as demand arises.

Drying the bananas, which has been begun in Jamaica, gives the possibility of producing the fruit in indefinite quantities because the ease of transporting the dried product will permit localities remote from port to send them to market. The banana is the chief export of Jamaica, but it is even more important in many places as a local food supply. Thus, the million inhabitants of Porto Rico who were supporting themselves almost entirely by agriculture, on a hilly territory less than half as large as New Jersey, were upon the verge of famine for nearly a year after a West Indian hurricane in 1899 beat all their bananas to the ground. But within a year another banana crop had sprung up from the roots of the old plants. Yet the Porto Ricans then as now did not export the banana largely. It was a supply crop for home consumption while they produced coffee, sugar, and tobacco for the foreign market.

3. CUBA

Cuba has two great staples of export, tobacco and sugar. It is second only to India as a cane producer, yields at times one-fourth of the world crop, and leads all others in the amount exported. About half of all the cultivated land in Cuba is in cane fields, which shows the great dependence of the people upon this crop (Fig. 179, 180).

Cuban sugar plantations are usually of large extent, mostly owned

by Europeans or Americans. The use of portable plantation railroads with locomotives to haul the cane to large factories is quite
common. The plantations are being enlarged, and improved machinery is being put in to reduce costs since labor cost is rising and

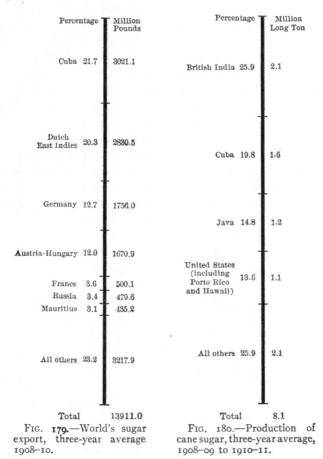

Percentage	Million Pounds
Cuba 21.7	3021.1
Dutch East Indies 20.3	2830.5
Germany 12.7	1756.0
Austria-Hungary 12.0	1670.9
France 3.6	500.1
Russia 3.4	479.6
Mauritius 3.1	435.2
All others 23.2	3217.9
Total	13911.0

FIG. 179.—World's sugar export, three-year average 1908–10.

Percentage	Million Long Ton
British India 25.9	2.1
Cuba 19.8	1.6
Java 14.8	1.2
United States (including Porto Rico and Hawaii) 13.6	1.1
All others 25.9	2.1
Total	8.1

FIG. 180.—Production of cane sugar, three-year average, 1908–09 to 1910–11.

the price of sugar declining. The present price of 2¼ cents per pound
at the plantation leaves some profit.

Cuba has been able to produce such great quantities of sugar because she has had a fairly stable government, a population superior

to that of most tropic countries because largely Caucasian, and an abundance of good, rich, well-drained sugar land. As only one-fourteenth of the sugar land is now in use, cane can be grown on this shiftless one-crop basis of the frontier farmer. When land is exhausted the industry is able to move, generally to the eastward from Havana where the industry had its first center. The increasing labor scarcity is at present setting the limit of Cuban sugar growing.

Cuban tobacco is famed throughout the world for its fine flavor, which gives Havana cigars their peculiar excellence. The amount produced is about half as great as that of Virginia. The Havana tobacco is the peculiar product of the south slope of the Sierra de Los Organos, a mountain range running from east to west throughout the whole length of the Province of Pinar Del Rio in the west end of Cuba. This tobacco is the one means by which the people of this district, called the Vuelta Abajo, are now able to buy products of the entire world. Innumerable attempts to grow the same quality of tobacco in other parts of Cuba and in other countries have resulted in failure, the nearest approach to success having been the shade-grown Florida product. Most of the Cuban tobacco is used for cigars, and Havana is a great cigar-manufacturing center.

4. AGRICULTURAL SPECIALTIES

In Porto Rico sugar is grown in the coast lands, and the advantage of the free admission of the crop to the protected American market made great increase in the output between 1899 and 1914. There was a corresponding decline in coffee from the highlands. It had been shut out of Spain by tariffs after the annexation of the island to the United States. There is some early vegetable growing in Porto Rico for the American market, and some tobacco is produced.

The little worlds on the Caribbean have many examples of special crops and unusual conditions. Thus Barbados presents the remarkable spectacle of 1,200 people to each of its 166 square miles, living largely by agriculture, chiefly sugar, corn, and potatoes. Trinidad has an important export of cocoanuts, and asphalt from its asphalt lake; Montserrat and Dominica, with calcareous hills, grow limes for export; Jamaica pastures are shaded by the allspice tree from which boys break off the fruiting twigs. In the Blue Mountains of Jamaica a very much prized variety of coffee is produced.

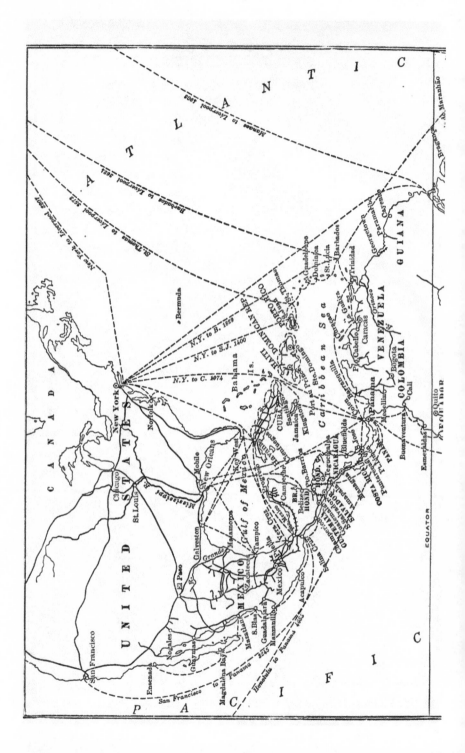

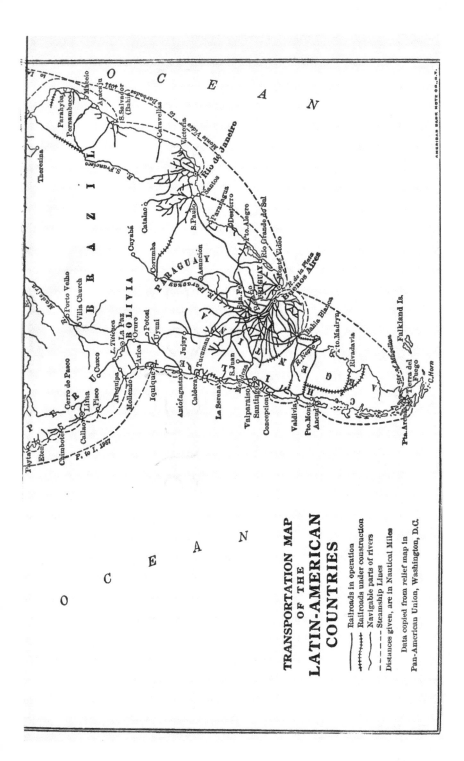

TRANSPORTATION MAP
OF THE
LATIN-AMERICAN
COUNTRIES

Railroads in operation
Railroads under construction
Navigable parts of rivers
Steamship Lines
Distances given, are in Nautical Miles

Data copied from relief map in
Pan-American Union, Washington, D.C.

5. TRADES AND ROUTES

The Caribbean countries, being alike in climate and resources, have almost no trade among themselves. Nearly all commerce is with the United States and Europe (Fig. 181). Nearly all of the many steamer lines make a circuit of several ports. The lines from Europe usually enter at Barbados or St. Thomas (both important coaling stations), while those from New York enter between Cuba and Hayti and call at La Guayra (Venezuela), Puerto Colombia, near the mouth of the Magdalena, Colon and Kingston (Jamaica). Direct

FIG. 182.—Native house and unplowed corn patch in Panama on land that has been cleared, put in crop and abandoned for a time and then recleared, for four centuries and probably many more. The land has never been plowed and man's action has not aided erosion—a fact which on its conservation side puts American agriculture to shame. (Photo H. H. Bennett, U. S. Bureau of Soils.)

lines of steamers go from New York to Havana, Cuba, and San Juan, Porto Rico, also from New Orleans to the Central American ports, Limon and Puerto Cortez for bananas. The opening of the Panama Canal is causing a great increase in the amount of shipping that sails these waters, but most of it will go directly through.

The canal zone, a strip of land on each side of the canal, has the advantage of being under a firm government from the outside, and also it will have a great opportunity to forward produce to all parts of the United States and Europe. Further, it will have many laborers who have been on the canal work. From these advantages it may be expected to develop a considerable export of agricultural produce, although the provisioning of passing ships will be a very considerable trade. It is now inhabited chiefly by negroes, some Chinese, some Indians, some Spanish descendants, and governed by people from the United States (Fig. 182).

FIG. 183.—The codfish from Newfoundland, dry as a bone, hard as wood, and keeping indefinitely is admirably fitted for the tropic market. (Photo by Miss Helen Fogg.)

6. THE GUIANAS

The Guianas do not touch upon the Caribbean, but since physiographically and climatically they are an eastward extension of Venezuela, they may be conveniently discussed here. They consist of three small countries belonging to Great Britain, the Netherlands, and France respectively, with a total area of 170,397 square miles, somewhat larger than the state of California. They have a hot, moist, densely forested lowland backed by an escarpment rising to a plateau covered with tropical vegetation and savannas, and inhabited by a sparse Indian and negro population.

The British Colony of Guiana is one of the most interesting of cane-sugar producers, showing intensive cultivation and the untouched wilderness side by side. Considerable areas of coast swamp have been reclaimed from the sea along the north shore in the same way the Dutch (the original settlers of Guiana) have done in Holland. This is the more unusual because most of the country remains a great forest absolutely uninhabited, save for a few savages. The explanation of this unused land is to be found in the climate which is so ill suited to white colonists that they number but 5 per cent of the total population and merely occupy the government positions and manage the stores and plantations. In the attempt to people this fertile desert and work the productive soil, the government has permitted the recent importation of thousands of East Indian coolies accustomed to growing rice and sugar cane. This has led to the rapid increase of rice-growing along with the continuance of sugar-cane growing which has been for many years the main export product of this colony. The reclaimed swamp land is very fertile, has a large rainfall, and, in addition, the flat and level dyke lands are easily irrigated for both sugar and rice. Further than that, the drainage ditches serve as canals for the boats that carry the cane from field to factory. Dutch and French Guiana differ from British in that they have no East Indian immigrants, and less industry.

QUESTIONS

1. Why is this region one of such varied industrial conditions?
2. Why do coffee, hides and gold fit into the foreign trade conditions of Colombia?
3. How does Guiana show that the poor condition of Colombia is not due to the Spanish race?
4. What does Jamaica show about the future of the white race in the tropics?
5. How has the steamship influenced the banana trade more than it has the sugar trade?
6. What two races are chiefly engaged in the Central American banana industry?
7. Why do other countries not compete with Cuban tobacco growers as they do with the sugar growers?
8. What is the most remarkable thing about Barbados?

CHAPTER XX

BRAZIL

Extent and population.—Brazil is larger than the United States, England and France, but has a population only equal to that of New York and Pennsylvania. Most of the country is so empty, so little known, that in 1914 an American-Brazilian exploring expedition discovered in the interior a new river a thousand miles long. The population, which is largely negro in the tropic sections, is fringed along the coast (see Fig. 3 cont.) and the foreign commerce depends chiefly on two great world staples, rubber and coffee, produced in widely separate sections of the country.

The Amazon rubber region.—The rubber which for several decades has supplied half of the world's market and set the standard of excellence is known as Para rubber, because it is shipped from the Brazilian city of that name at the mouth of the Amazon River (see Fig. 144). This city, practically upon the equator, is at the outlet of a valley, reaching from the Atlantic to the western wall of South America, containing the world's largest forest, and producing rubber over an area probably two-thirds as large as Europe. This rubber-yielding forest includes nearly half of Brazil and those large parts of Bolivia, Peru, Ecuador and Colombia which lie east of the Andes and receive the heavy rains brought from the Atlantic by the northeast and southeast trade winds. The center of the valley has the full equatorial or doldrum climate with its periods of daily thunderstorms and its persistent heat and humidity. Throughout the length and breadth of this enormous valley from Para to the Andes, and reaching beyond it into Venezuela and Guiana on the north, and Paraguay on the south, stretches an almost continuous forest through which the traveler must usually fight his way with knife and axe. Scattered here and there in this gloomy jungle are trees of the dozen or more varieties from which the natives gather the rubber to ship down the Amazon. Being shipped from Para, it is sometimes credited as being entirely the product of Brazil.

348

Transportation in the Amazon Valley.—The only transportation facilities through this continent-filling forest are furnished by the navigable streams. The Amazon and its many branches afford altogether several thousand miles of navigable waterways—and the amount might be largely increased by the removal of trees which overhang, fall into, and choke up the smaller streams. The native and half-breed rubber gatherers have to work in a fearfully unwholesome climate in a jungle full of insects, serpents, and wild beasts. The greatest difficulty in gathering this rubber is to cut paths from one tree to another in the tangled jungle. A few miles back from the navigable streams the jungle shuts out man by a tangle through which he could not afford to cut even with rubber at the unreasonably high prices of 1910, when for a short time it was $3 per pound. The prosperity of the whole valley is menaced by the competition of plantation rubber from the East Indies where the labor supply is so much more abundant.

Other products.—In this Amazon Valley, which might rival or double China in population if it were utilized, man has used only a few of the forest by-products, sarsaparilla, nuts and rubber, and the sickly population probably numbers less than one to the square mile. In addition to rubber gathering, some Brazil nuts and cocoa are exported. The recent increase in the use and price of rubber has (for a time, at least) brought prosperity to the Amazon Valley, its three ports, Para at the mouth, Manaos 860 miles upstream, and Iquitos, 1,100 miles beyond in eastern Peru, having a busy trade. For the number of people involved, the trade of the Amazon is heavy, and, upon its import side, varied. The people of the tropic settlements produce little but their exports; and import from the Portuguese farmers in the mother country surprising quantities of fruits, vegetables, and other products of agriculture. Steamers from England, calling en route at Portugal, regularly go as far up as Manaos, 15-foot boats going to Iquitos, while some of the branches are served by smaller steamers.

Cacao.—The climate of the Amazon Valley also makes it a prime place for the growing of cacao. Like the Para rubber tree it thrives in the doldrum heat and humidity, and the fertility of river alluvium. The valuable seeds or beans, to the number of thirty to sixty, are produced in a greenish or reddish pod, 3 or 4 inches in diameter and 6 to 10 inches long. This heavy, melon-like fruit is attached in clusters to the trunk and larger branches of the tree (Fig. 184),

FIG. 184.—The heavy fruits of the cacao tree cannot mature in a windy location.
(Photo Walter Baker & Co.)

and a strong wind beats the immature pods about until they fall useless to the earth. By this peculiarity the area over which cacao can be a profitable crop is limited to regions clear of heavy winds —the equatorial regions, and the latitudes below the trade winds and below the zone of tropic hurricanes which begin just south of the Greater Antilles. It is grown in sheltered valleys in Trinidad and Hayti. The Amazon Valley is the greatest cocoa-producing region in the world.

From the Amazon to Rio Janeiro, a distance as great as from the tip of Florida to Nova Scotia, there is no important trade route into the interior. There is a succession of coast ports, the largest being Bahia (population, 230,000) and Pernambuco (population, 130,000), each the outlet of a nearby region of rather dense population, largely negro, and exporting sugar, tobacco (second only to the United States), cotton and hides.

Coffee.—Brazil's leading export, coffee, of which she furnishes over half of the world's supply (Fig. 185), is shipped from the two ports of Santos and Rio Janeiro— a city about the size of St. Louis. The coffee district occupies a broad plateau and has a railway system which has developed into the only railway network in tropic America, reaching by devious routes points as far inland as Cleveland and Columbus, Ohio, are from Philadelphia and Baltimore.

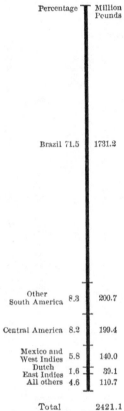

Percentage		Million Pounds
Brazil 71.5		1731.2
Other South America	8.3	200.7
Central America	8.2	199.4
Mexico and West Indies	5.8	140.0
Dutch East Indies	1.6	39.1
All others	4.6	110.7
Total		2421.1

FIG. 185.—World's coffee production, three-year average, 1908–10.

Coffee plant and the coffee region.—The coffee tree cannot endure any frost and is therefore limited, with a few insignificant exceptions, to the region within the tropics, although the greatest coffee region, that of Brazil, is close to the edge of the temperate zone. The plant requires a hot climate, yet in many coffee regions the full blast of the sun is too hot for it, particularly for the young plants, and high

FIG. 186.—Brazilian coffee plantation. (Reproduced by permission of the Philadelphia Commercial Museum.)

shade trees are scattered for protection over many plantations. The climate must be moist as well as hot, with a rainfall of from 75 to 120 inches, and the soil must be rich and also well drained, which practically limits coffee growing to hills and highlands where the streams have rapid fall to give the necessary drainage (Fig. 186).

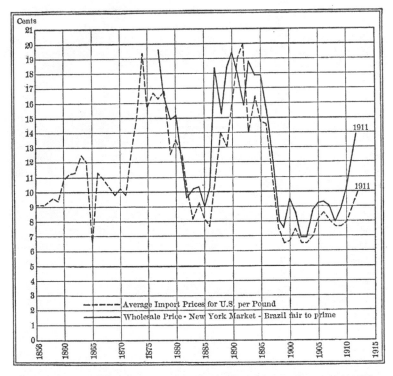

FIG. 187.—Cycles in price of coffee—a product capable of easy overproduction (Idea from Chisholm). High price, over 12 cents, means prosperity. The resultant heavy planting and enlarged crop makes oversupply, low price and decline of orchards until demand catches up and makes high prices to start another cycle.

Immediately back of the narrow unwholesome trade-wind plain on which Rio Janeiro and Santos are located rises a mountain wall, so steep that cable railways are used. Back of this coast range sloping gently toward the distant Parana River in the interior is a large plateau between 600 and 2,500 feet above the sea. Here are thousands of square miles of a rich red soil capable of producing several times as much coffee as the world needs (Fig. 187). The southeast trade winds bring from the south Atlantic an abundant rainfall, completing the natural conditions for coffee production.

The Brazilian coffee estates are often of enormous size, so that in some cases private railways run through them to carry the workmen and the coffee from one place to another. As the land is cheap, careless cultivation prevails, and the heavy rains do enormous damage to the resources of the country by the washing away of the fertile soil. Italian immigrants as laborers on these plantations have begun to replace the negroes, who are drifting to the coast settlements north of Rio Janeiro into the full tropics.

While the cultivation of the soil is heedless, as it is in many parts of the United States, the process of preparing the coffee for market is most scientific. Much elaborate machinery is used—a practice which the large size of the plantations permits. The city of Sao Paulo on the plateau back of Santos is the metropolis of the coffee district, and a very much Europeanized city, largely peopled by Italians, and supplied with electric power from nearby waterfalls.

Central and South Brazil.—The Brazilian coast runs on over 800 miles into the temperate zone, a beautiful forested country relatively unsettled except for a few German colonies. Much of the central and eastern interior of Brazil is shielded from the trade winds by the coast ranges and is too dry for anything but cattle ranches. It was but little used even for that until the recent building of a railroad. The interior province of Matto Grasso was only reached by a steamboat journey up the Parana River longer than that from New Orleans to Minneapolis.

Minerals.—There is a little gold and diamond mining inland from Rio Janeiro. Some manganese ore (used in iron making) is exported, but the most promising mining enterprise is iron ore. Docks are now being constructed at the port of Victoria to export millions of tons a year. Unfortunately Brazil has no coal.

Trade.—As the United States is the largest user of coffee and rubber, our imports from Brazil are very large. Her imports are more divided, the greater part of them coming from Europe. The United Kingdom alone sends about a million tons of coal, and many vessels make a triangular voyage from Europe to Brazil and thence to the United States.

QUESTIONS

1. Why is the most productive of Brazil's land so little used?

2. Why will rubber cultivation, for which she has so much suitable land, probably injure her?

3. Why is Para, situated in the edge of one of the greatest forests, a lumber importer? (See Mexico.)

4. Would it help the coffee district of Brazil if the coastal plain at Santos and Rio Janeiro were wider?

5. How does it happen that there is a large arid area in Central Brazil?

6. Has the cattle industry or the coffee industry the greater possibility of satisfactory extension in Brazil?

CHAPTER XXI

THE RIVER PLATA COUNTRIES

Climatic Conditions.—The countries on the River Plata, Argentina, Uruguay and Paraguay, comprise a region rich in sheep, cattle, wheat, corn, and alfalfa, and find their closest duplicate in that part of the United States between the Mississippi and Missouri Rivers and the Rocky Mountains. Argentina alone is half as large as the United States. As in any agricultural region, one must know the facts of rainfall (see Fig. 2), and to understand this it is necessary to note the main facts of the winds. Southern South America has, south of latitude 35°, the prevailing westerlies which drench the west coast and give scanty rain to Patagonia, the region east of the mountains. As we approach the tropics the southeast trade winds blow off the south Atlantic, giving to Uruguay, Paraguay and a part of Argentina some of the same abundant rainfall that blesses southern Brazil. Between these two rain-bearing ocean winds is a large arid strip (see Fig. 2) which comprises much of Argentina and crosses over the Andes to make the deserts of North Chile and Peru.

Parts of this region, Mendoza for example, being under the same world wind system that gives the California (Mediterranean) climate, produce the same products—scanty pastures on that great proportion of the land that cannot be irrigated and on the rest, alfalfa, dried fruits, European grapes, and wine. Unfortunately the arid area is large, but, as in the trans-Missouri region, it merges on its eastern edge into a wheat belt and then into a corn and alfalfa belt. Like our own prairie and plains country it was unforested, covered with good grass, and very accessible to the settler. It was as though the American settlers had landed from ship at Kansas City.

The live stock industries.—Forty or fifty years ago, when there was a great demand for haircloth, herds of horses valued at $2.50 each were driven into pens twice a year by their owners to have their manes and tails clipped to furnish horsehair for the crinoline looms in England and France. Then came the merino sheep, whose wool and tallow, skin and bone also went to Europe, while his meat was

356

thrown away because there was no possible market for it. Later came the refrigerator ship resulting in the export of mutton. The pastures of the Parana Valley are so fine that the sheep fatten entirely on the rich pampas grass.

Cattle and sheep.—In addition to being a natural pasture, this plain seems to be adapted to growing alfalfa. This makes it one of the finest places in the world for sheep and cattle, for alfalfa is the best of foods for these animals, and it makes possible an increase of their

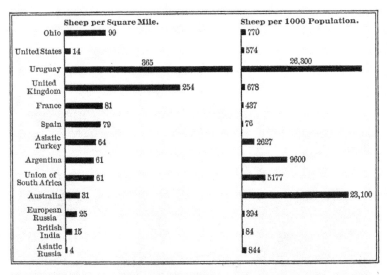

FIG. 188.—Ratio of sheep to land and to population, in leading countries.

number from three- to six-fold when it replaces natural pastures. The mild open winter, a characteristic of the southern hemisphere, permits the animals to run at pasture without sheltering barns.

For every person in the country there are five horses and cattle and ten sheep (Fig. 188) (see chapter on Animal Industries; compare United States), and the meat allowance of the guacho, or half-breed Indian cowboy, is 5 pounds per day, as much as many American families have for a week.

The temperate climate of Argentina makes it a white man's land that is now receiving heavy immigration from Spain and Italy. Its capital, Buenos Ayres, the largest city in the southern hemisphere, is a fine Europeanized city, nearly the size of Philadelphia. Owing to the progressiveness of the Argentina ranchers, the live stock industry is as modern as the capital. European breeds thrive and many thousands of dollars are paid for prize-winning specimens of English sheep and cattle to be used as breeding-stock. Now that the refrigerator ship can carry meat to Europe and the United States, there is great attention to beef breeds of cattle and mutton breeds of sheep with their coarse wool. This change from wool to mutton varieties

Fig. 189.—An Argentina wheat field. (Photo by W. Webber, courtesy International Harvester Co.)

is very disconcerting to the manufacturers of fine wool cloth who had previously secured fine merino wool there.

Influence of refrigeration.—Before the invention of refrigeration the sheep industry of the Parana or River Plata countries produced wool, skins, and hogsheads of tallow. The cattle industry had advanced beyond the shipment of hides, tallow, and bones by the manufacture and export of tasajo and beef extract. Tasajo is a peculiarly well-preserved kind of dried beef cured in the sunshine of the great pampas pasture plains. It has the quality of keeping indefinitely in such hot, humid climates as Cuba and Brazil, so that transportation becomes easy. For many years tasajo has had a wide distribution over tropic America.

Fresh meat goes in shiploads to Europe, and because of the increasing scarcity in the United States, regular shipments of Argentina meat to New York began in 1913. Since then the United States has continued to draw heavily upon the Plata countries for meats, and bids fair to increase her imports.

Fig. 190.—Load of Argentine wheat on way to market. (Photo by W. Webber, courtesy International Harvester Co.)

Wheat.—About 1870 wheat growing began and increased so rapidly that Argentina is now a great exporter. The resources are magnificent. This fertile treeless plain is one of the most level and most easily tilled tracts of land in the world (Fig. 189). In one place a railroad runs 278 miles in a perfectly straight line, and the traveler can ride for 2 days on a train and see nothing to break the flat line of the horizon. Here the Italian immigrant, mostly a tenant-farmer, grows wheat with American machinery in the usual one-crop land-robbing way of the frontier, which produces large yields for a short time. Already the wheat exports of nearly 100 million bushels a year about equal the combined wheat and flour exports of the United States. The proportion of the crop exported is significant. In 1910 the United States exported 9 per cent of the crop, Canada 28 per cent, and Agentina 52 per cent. There is great room for the expansion of the crop (Fig. 190).

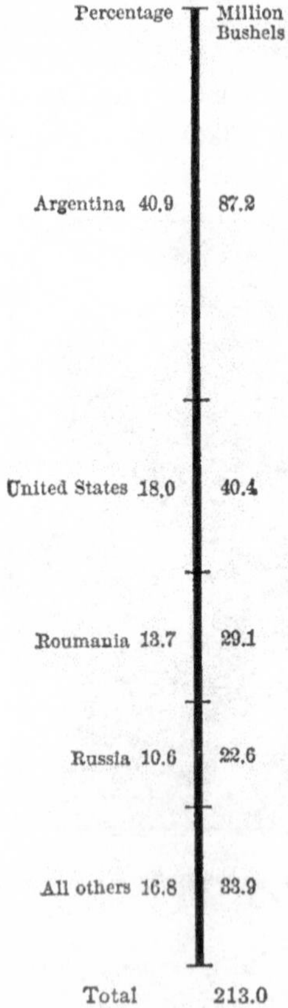

Corn.—The people of Argentina, about as numerous as those of Illinois, have of late begun to grow corn. The country exports at the present time a larger proportion of its corn crop than any other country of the world (Fig. 191), because the people do not yet use it largely as food, and for the fattening of live stock alfalfa generally suffices. During the four-year period 1907 to 1910 Argentina exported 77 million bushels per year, or almost exactly one-half her crop, while the American export of 52 million per year was a little over one-fiftieth of the total crop. The possibilities for the relative increase of corn production are probably better in the Parana Valley than in any other corn zone, because of the sparse population and the large area, of which only a tenth is yet in cultivation. The present production is about equal to that of the Mediterranean countries or of Ohio. As compared with the United States there is, however, a disadvantage in the less regular rainfall, which will be a permanent hindrance to great production because of the uncertainties of the harvest. Thus the fine crop of 1905, 195 million bushels, and nearly 30 bushels to the acre, led to enlarged plantings the next year, but the crop fell to 72 million and the yield to 13 bushels per acre. This caused a reduction in the area planted.

Percentage	Million Bushels
Argentina 40.9	87.2
United States 18.0	40.4
Roumania 13.7	29.1
Russia 10.6	22.6
All others 16.8	33.9
Total	213.0

Fig. 191.—World's corn exports, three-year average, 1908–10.

Patagonia is a frontier country of low rainfall, too low for grain growing, but suitable for sheep ranches. The climate is such that the sheep do not have to be housed. The country is being settled by British people from the nearby Falkland Islands. Many of the sheep ranches of Argentina, like most of the railroads, belong to British capitalists, while the slaughtering plants of the eastern cities belong to the same persons as do those of Chicago and Kansas City.

Forests.—In the northeastern part of Argentina, corresponding to the forested region near the mouth of the Mississippi, but reaching nearer the equator, is the Gran Chaco—an extensive, unsettled tropical forest containing much quebracho wood (the name means axe breaker). The tree is medium-sized, with a very hard wood containing 20 per cent or more of tannin, which renders the wood almost indestructible in the ground, thus making it very valuable for railroad ties. Its richness in tannin has caused a rapid increase in the shipment of the extract to the tanneries of England, Germany, and the United States, over 80 million pounds now being used annually in the latter country. There is a great supply of quebracho in Argentina. One tract in the Chaco gives employment to 30,000 workmen and also produces cattle, a fact that indicates the destruction of the forests. Since the wood is heavier than water and is very difficult to get and transport, the extracting plants are, like saw mills, located as near as possible to the place where the trees are cut. When used alone the quebracho extract makes inferior leather, but in combination with other materials, its results are better.

The entire absence of coal, the possession of great land resources, and the small population, indicate that Argentina will remain an agricultural country.

Uruguay, across the Parana River, from the best part of the Argentine Republic, is from end to end an undulating grassy plain closely resembling Nebraska in population and area. There are a few grain growers near Montevideo, the capital, but twenty-five times as much land is devoted to sheep and cattle pastures. The number of sheep doubled between 1880 and 1900 and their products make up the great bulk of the exports of the country.

Paraguay.—This tropic country, beyond the Argentina part of the Gran Chaco, of which it also owns a part, has four times the area of Cuba, but only one-third as many people. They are mostly of mixed Indian, Spanish, and negro races, and have suffered greatly from wars. Owing to the tropic climate, it has not shared the European immigration that has come to Argentina. Much of the country is in forests or in large cattle ranches, cattle being as numerous in proportion to people as they are in Argentina. Owing to the moist tropical climate, sheep are almost non-existent, but there is an important commerce in oranges and early vegetables that go by steamer to the cities down the Parana, which is the sole commercial outlet of the country. Oranges are used for fattening hogs in locations where shipping facilities are not good.

A rising export of Paraguay is maté, the dried leaf of a bush of the holly family. It is used as tea in the four countries adjacent to the Parana and is now being exported to Europe. Tobacco is also exported to Europe.

Trade and routes.—It is easy to see why the fertile plain of Argentina to the west of the lower Parana and Plata, low, healthful, of easy access to the sea, rich in sheep and cattle, wheat and maize, possesses the best railway net in South America. The foci of these lines are the ports of Buenos Ayres and Rosario. Rosario has such well-equipped harbor facilities that grain sacks slide by gravity down chutes from the warehouse on the bank to the steamer in the river. Buenos Ayres has an artificial harbor with splendid docks and warehouses that compare well with anything in America. It is as busy as New York. Westward from longitude 64° west, where the rainfall is insufficient for agriculture, the network of railways gives way to four single lines going directly across the plains to the irrigated districts at the foot of the Andes. Two of these roads lead to the northwestern province of Tucuman, the sugar producer, 900 miles from the Atlantic ports. A third railway is the Trans-Andean line, finished in April, 1910. It shortens by many days the winter journey between Buenos Ayres and Santiago, which had previously required a steamer journey through the Straits of Magellan because the mountains could not be crossed.

A new port, Bahia Blanca, has recently been opened to the southwest of Buenos Ayres. It is a kind of Galveston to the Argentina—a southwestern exporting point.

From the Plata ports of Rosario, Buenos Ayres, and Montevideo, there are many and frequent steamers sailing to the United States and Europe (Fig. 192), the great markets for their agricultural products and the sources of their supply of manufactures. From England alone are imported a million tons of coal per year, from the United States shiploads of agricultural machinery. This trade promises to continue, for these countries are new, with little capital, sparse population and much land. If they should contemplate manufacture it will have to be with fuel from the northern hemisphere for there is not $\frac{1}{500}$th as much coal mined in all South

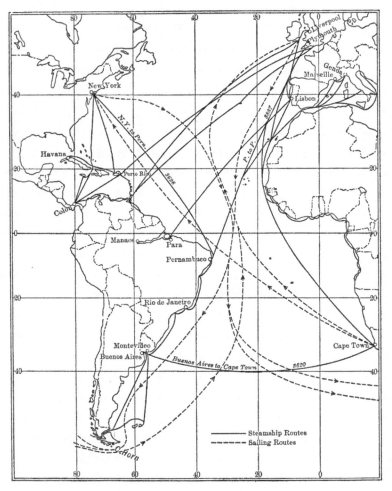

FIG. 192.—The vessel tracks of the Middle and South Atlantic.

America as in the United States. The Plata countries are peculiarly devoid of known deposits of workable minerals.

QUESTIONS

1. What is the cause of the great difference in the rainfall of eastern and western Argentina?

2. How does it happen that Argentina exports a larger proportion of its wheat than does the United States? Of corn?

3. For what climatic reason do the European immigrants prefer Argentina to Brazil?

4. Is it easier to export wheat from Argentina than from Saskatchewan or Montana?

5. What change have they made in the kind of sheep grown on the Argentina ranches?

6. How have the Argentina forests lessened the gathering of tan bark in the American forests? [What other use is made of the principal Argentina tree; why?]

7. If we liken Argentina to Nebraska, what state does Paraguay become?

8. Why did a German firm manufacture beef extract in Uruguay many years ago?

CHAPTER XXII

THE ANDEAN COUNTRIES

Topography and climate.—The Andes Mountain system runs without a break through Ecuador, Peru, Bolivia, and Chile—extending as far south from the Equator as Sitka, Alaska, and north Scotland are to the north of it. As a barrier to man's activity, it is second only to the Himalayas. Through most of its length there are several ranges enclosing a plateau between them. In Chile the elevation of the plateau descends until we have a great valley resembling that of California. Though not so extensive as the California Valley it has the same climate and its products are the same. Toward the equator, as in southern California, the rainfall declines, and the tremendous wall of the Andes shuts off the trade-wind moisture so absolutely that the Pacific coast of South America from the tropic to near the equator is desert, in places the most rainless desert known.

When we consider that this plateau region is cut off from the sea by swamps as in Ecuador, or desert in Peru and north Chile, and that the plateau is separated from this forbidding coast plain by precipitous trails that no wheel ever climbed for over $3\frac{1}{2}$ centuries after the white man came, we begin to understand why the countries are backward. Further, the people of the plateau are nearly all Indians who were fearfully abused by their Spanish conquerors and made to work the gold and silver mines to enrich Spain. Since they gained their independence from Spain there have been many wars and revolutions, so it is a land which geography and history have combined to keep undeveloped. But the climate is much better than that of most countries in tropic latitudes.

Desert industries.—The rainlessness of north Chile and Peru has caused the collection of large deposits of guano and nitrate of soda, which would otherwise have been dissolved by rain and carried away. Guano, an accumulation of the dried excrement and dead bodies of birds, is highly prized as a fertilizer and was exported in great quantities. These guano deposits of sea birds on the bare rocks called the Chincha Islands, off the coast of Peru, yielded $600,000,000 between 1830 and 1880, but are now about exhausted, only an annual product of 40 to 50,000 tons a year is now available. The method of mining the nitrate of soda is simple. After the removal of a little sand and earth from the surface, it can be shoveled up like clay and gravel and taken away in carts or temporary railways to the nitrate works, where it is dissolved in water, boiled down and crystallized. A byproduct of the nitrate industry is iodine, a valuable chemical, and Chile having a practical world monopoly of both nitrates and

Fig. 193.—Putting nitrate into bags for shipment.

iodine at the present time, limits production and fixes prices almost at will.

While there is some copper produced in nearby districts, the nitrate fields produce Chile's chief export. By export duties on nitrate they produce most of her revenue, and by their food demands, most of her domestic trade. The nitrate towns have been enabled to secure a water supply by laying pipe lines to the Andes, sometimes more than 100 miles away. But the desert destroys all possibility of any local food crops. Everything for the use of man and beast in the nitrate fields must be imported, so that Iquique, the nitrate metropolis, a city of about 50,000 inhabitants, and many smaller towns and nitrate works, are depending upon the farms of central Chile, several hundred miles to the south of them, for every potato, cabbage, bale of hay, or loaf of bread, necessary to support the daily life of these thousands who are extracting from the desert the nitrate accumulations of the past (Fig. 193). The same dependence upon foreign support applies to the nitrate, manganese, and borax works in the same vicinity but across the boundary in southwestern Bolivia. The desert miners sell minerals in Europe and the United States; these countries send manufactures to central Chile to pay for the food and forage sent thence by coasting steamers to the dwellers in the desert. "The meat supply for nitrate camps of northern Chile is derived by driving herds of live animals from Salta and Jujuy in northern Argentina. The animals are driven summer and winter over passes 15,000 feet high, where they sometimes have to spend 3 days without food in the desert."[1]

The United States imports 300,000 to 400,000 tons annually of the nitrate, about a fifth of the whole. Most of it goes to west Europe.

The Peruvian shore plain, though desert, has a number of streams that are fed by Andean snows and flow for half the year, giving rise to agriculture by irrigation. There is a considerable export of cane sugar and a small export of a peculiar brown cotton of a curly character that fits it admirably to mix with wool. Chinese immigrants have a rice industry that is one-third as great as that of the United States.

The Ecuadorean shore plain is a great contrast, for it is in the doldrum belt of heavy rains and is as damp, forest clad and unhealthy as any trade wind coast. Guayaquil, the chief port, has long been troublesome as a pest center. In the 20,000 square miles of forest there is a little gold digging, some gathering of palm nuts for export to the button factories, but the chief export has arisen from the excellence of the locality for the production of cacao. For a time Ecuador was the chief exporter, but Brazil and the Portuguese slave islands of St. Thomas and Principe in the Gulf of Guinea have lately surpassed her. Ecuador has plenty of room, but the labor supply is scarce.

"Some idea of the magnitude of the cacao crop may be gained from the fact that the main streets of this city (Guayaquil) are almost wholly occupied by cacao beans, placed there to undergo the neces-

[1] From Isaiah Bowman; *Bulletin American Geographical Society*, Vol. XLVI, March, 1914.

sary curing process, and the wharves are covered to a height of several
feet with the beans in bags ready for export. The enormous yield
is the result of the increased acreage and greater number of trees
planted in the last few years."[1]

The Andean plateau on which most of the people of Ecuador,
Peru, and Bolivia live is another world. It is mostly from 2 to 3
miles above sea level and while it is by latitude in the tropics, it is
by temperature so cold that in places the natives of Bolivia wear
wool masks to protect themselves from the biting winds. As the

Fig. 194.—The Llama. A beast of burden in Andean countries.

rainfall of much of this region is slight, there are no trees, but
potatoes are grown for local use, and there is a scanty pasturage.
Such a climate is the natural home of fleece-bearing animals and
wool export fits admirably into the conditions of pack train transport.
There are several million sheep and considerable numbers of three
native wool bearers, the llama, the vicuna, and the alpaca. Two of
these, the llama and alpaca, furnish for export some very fine, long,
soft wool, but the animals themselves have never appealed to the
people of other countries as suitable for propagation. The llama, a
small animal resembling both the sheep and the camel, is used only
for carrying packs, which cannot exceed a hundred pounds in weight
(Fig. 194). He is sure-footed and can pick his scanty living like a

[1] *The Journal of Geography*, December, 1914, p. 126.

camel. It is possible that the llama might be a source of profit in some other mountainous regions.

Metals are the great resource of the Plateau, especially in Bolivia and Peru. The silver mines of Potosi are justly famed for their almost fabulous riches. Yet this region, like the rest of South America, is practically undeveloped, and the recent construction of railroads from the Chilean ports of Antofagasta and Arica, and Mollendo in Peru, permitting the introduction of mining machinery, promises great developments. The tailings left in past centuries make good mining for well-equipped modern enterprises. Bolivia is one of the foremost tin producers of the world, and copper and gold are also found in many places. There is a little coal near the Peru-Bolivian boundary, but the quality and quantity both have much to be desired and the coast ports are still coal importers.

Before the discovery of America this plateau and also the shore plain of Peru were the home of dense population with advanced industry that has left many interesting remains.

Life on the Ecuadorean plateau.—The difficulties of Andean travel and the service that the railroad is rendering, and will increasingly render, is shown by the conditions and the recent changes that have occurred in Ecuador. The equatorial climate of the plains causes the center of Ecuadorean population to be in the enclosed plateau, about 40 by 300 miles, lying between the ranges of the Andes, containing the world-famous volcanoes Cotopaxi and Chimborazo. Here nearly a million people lived until near the end of the first decade of this century, entirely cut off from all communication with the commercial world, except by a pack trail descending from the 10,000-foot plateau by perilous ledges, and crossing swamps that often become impassable in the rainy season. A 350-mile railroad has at last been constructed by American capital from Guayaquil to Quito, the capital. It opens no new trade routes, but will revolutionize the methods and commerce of an old one. It makes possible, for the first time, the participation of these people in the world's commerce. This road practically annexes to the commercial world a new province containing a million people who have been living in the homespun epoch. Their commerce is likely to be of limited extent because they live in the temperate zone climate of the high plateau where the country is so rough that there is small likelihood of their having any surplus of wheat, corn, or beans to send any farther than to their neighbors of the tropic plain, if perchance they can compete even there with temperate zone breadstuffs. Their exports are, therefore, likely to continue largely of hides and wool, a little rubber from the eastern forests, and minerals, of which the country claims considerable store. The imports comprise the whole list of manufactures and supplies needed in a modern city and in a surrounding farming district.

The region east of the Andes.—Ecuador and Peru have trackless eastern territories in the Amazon Valley from which they have been cut off so absolutely that the Peruvian governors sometimes go out to their port at Iquitos on the upper Amazon by way of Callao, Panama, New York, Lisbon or Liverpool and Para. Great amounts of water power might be developed on the Amazonian headwaters that make the 10,000-foot descent from the Plateau. In Bolivia some of the eastern plain is pasture land, and a railroad has recently been built around the falls of the Madeira River so that 3,000 miles of navigable streams on its headwaters may be connected with Para.

The opening of the Panama Canal will stimulate enterprises in the Andean countries which have usually carried on their commerce by steamer around South America.

QUESTIONS

1. How does it happen that the west coast is so dry at latitude 15° south and so wet at latitude 1° south?

2. How has aridity made north Chile rich?

3. What are the points of resemblance between Chile and an American state?

4. Explain the three-cornered trade of agricultural Chile.

5. Why is the Andean plateau a natural place for the production of wool?

6. Did the Spanish exhaust the mines in the 16th, 17th and 18th centuries?

7. What resources has the Andean plateau region for electric smelting?

8. Why are hides well suited to the foreign trade of the Andean countries?

CHAPTER XXIII

THE UNITED KINGDOM

(With Introductory Comparison of United States and Europe)

I. EUROPE AND UNITED STATES COMPARED

Agricultural products.—Europe is roughly the same size as the United States, which it far exceeds in the proportion of the area that has sufficient rainfall for agriculture (Fig. 195). Partly from this cause, but chiefly because the population is four times as great as that of the United States, the agricultural output of Europe is much greater than that of the United States. The United States, Canada, and Mexico have 83 million cattle; Europe has 129 million. In other branches of agriculture the figures are as follows:

	U. S., Canada, and Mexico	Europe
hogs	67,000,000	73,000,000
sheep	58,000,000	176,000,000
horses	27,000,000	43,000,000
wheat	941,000,000 bu.	1,926,000,000
corn	2,740,000,000 bu.	585,000,000
oats	1,780,000,000 bu.	2,598,000,000

The United States has more of all of these products per person than Europe, and it is probably true that the United States has greater possibility of supporting people than Europe, because we have the large area of our South with the long growing season, high temperature, and summer rain, permitting, if needed, the growth of from two to four crops per year. This, south Europe, with its summer drought (Mediterranean type of climate), cannot do except in those small and favored locations where a little tract of land can be irrigated. The United States also has another advantage in the ability to grow corn. Most of north Europe is too cool for it, and in its stead barley, beets, and turnips are grown in vast amounts for stock food.

371

Agricultural methods.—The effect of the density of European population shows itself in the laborious preparation of rough land for garden agriculture by terracing, in the great cultivation of the

FIG. 195.—Rainfall, June, July, and August. (After Mark S. W. Jefferson.)

▨▨▨▨ Heavy—more than 10 inches of rain and melted snow in the three months.
▦▦▦▦ Light—from 6 to 10 inches in the three months.
▭▭▭ Scant—less than 6 inches in the three months.

This map shows Europe's splendid rainfall. No other continent is so uniformly blest.

potato in north Europe (see chapter on Potato and Vegetables), and in the very limited use of pasture because the ground yields more in cultivated crops. For this reason the cattle are commonly

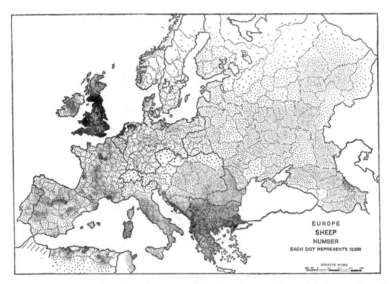

The value of sheep in humid Britain, semi-arid North Africa, and the rough and semi-arid Balkans, is apparent. (Finch and Baker.)

Comparisons of sheep industry in some European countries. (Finch and Baker.)

The wool supply during the war was one of the things which showed how greatly Europe and even the United States depend upon foregin regions for supplies of great importance. The man at war needs much more wool than the man at home. His uniforms, his coat, his blankets, make it require seventy-four pounds of wool to equip one American soldier. Then there is hard usage and much waste. To meet these needs, the British government and the American government took entire possession of the wool trade of their respective countries. As armies always plan against the worst possibilities, the war ended with great stocks of wool in the possession of the army and very little in the possession of civilians, who had only received it as doled out by the Quarter-master General of the United States Army.

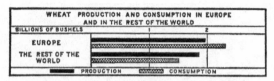

Wheat Production and Consumption in Europe.

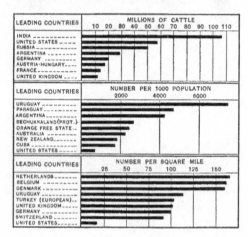

Cattle Statistics.

The great number of cattle per square mile in Europe was like the bread supply of the Allied countries in being dependent upon over-sea trade. Each year
ships from North America, South America, Russia, and India had brought millions
of tons of forage grains, corn, bran, cottonseed and linseed meal, and other food
to west Europe.

The necessities of supplying armies made ships so scarce that there was not
enough space to carry food for both men and beasts, so the herds of England,
France, and Italy were reduced in number to meet the reduced food supply.
Holland, Denmark, and Norway each had plenty of ships to bring food for all
the cattle they had, and Germany gave a splendid market for butter, cheese,
and meat. After the United States entered the war, our government's control
of trade through the War Trade Board stopped this indirect supplying of Germany. The resulting fodder shortage greatly reduced the numbers of cattle in
the countries of the northern neutrals.

kept in barns except where the ground is too rough to cultivate.
As a result of these conditions the sheep flocks of Europe are declining in number, and the land is being
used for breadstuffs, beets, and hay, while
the easily transported wool comes from
distant pastures on the frontiers of agriculture.

Forestry is another result of the density of population. Wild forests as we
have in America would no more suffice for
timber than would wild animals suffice
for meat, so they are carefully and systematically managed, giving a much greater
yield than the wild forests. This the
United States is just learning to do.

Labor supply and manufactures.—In
the greater dependence on manufactures
we see another result of the density of
population. The young man in Holland
or Belgium cannot find an opening in
agriculture unless he replaces some one or
engages in a more intense kind of farming.[1] His alternative is to get a factory
job or emigrate. Hence the great European strife for markets for factory output,
the great emigration, and the great and
terrible land-hunger and land-grabbing
that in part lay back of the fearful European war of 1914. We see this greater
dependence on manufacturing taking the
same forms of intensity that we find in
agriculture—the making of a refined and
much labored product, fine goods, and
instruments, not reapers—lace, not unbleached cotton.

Percentage | Million Bushels

United Kingdom 33.9 | 219

Germany 13.6 | 84.9

Belgium 11.4 | 71.2

Netherlands 10.7 | 66.7

Italy 6.6 | 41.1

Brazil 2.7 | 17.0

All others 21.1 | 130.2

Total 622.2

Fig. 196.—Wheat and wheat flour imports, three-year average, 1908-10.

Trade.—Any commercial comparisons of Europe and the United
States are apt to be misleading unless we should think of the trade

[1] One must not get the impression that there are no unused agricultural
resources in Europe, for there are surprising undeveloped agricultural resources
in parts of that continent, especially England, France, Spain, Portugal, Turkey
and Russia.

of the United States as it would be if it were cut into twenty independent pieces with one big piece between the Mississippi River and the Rocky Mountains to take the place of Russia. A shipment of butter from Wisconsin to New York is local trade, from Denmark to London is foreign trade; of oranges from Spain or Italy to Berlin is foreign trade, from Florida to Chicago is local. Most of the vast foreign trade of Europe, so-called, has in the United States as in China a counterpart of unrecorded local trade, because the United States and China are continental in size and resources.

In matters of race and government the differences between United States and Europe are trivial. The one great difference between United States and Europe may be summed up in one word, opportunity, and that means resources—resources with which the people can work. The conservation movement in the United States is therefore one of the most vital things that has happened.

2. The United Kingdom

The United Kingdom has been for a century and a quarter the greatest manufacturing country in the world, but she was a great agricultural country for many centuries before that, is one now, and will be more so in the future. The British climate is oceanic, much like that of our north Pacific coast, and it is one of the best in the world. The prevailing westerly winds coming from the ocean give a mildness to the winter and a coolness to the summer unknown in the United States east of the Rocky Mountains where the climate is continental rather than oceanic. This cool evenness of climate with little extreme weather and light snow fall permits sheep to live all winter in the open, even in Scotland. This climate is undoubtedly a strong contributing factor to the Briton's love of outdoor sports for which his climate is much better than that of New York or Chicago.

Live stock.—Along with comfort and wholesomeness is an abundant and evenly distributed rain. If rain interferes with British agriculture, it is usually by too much rather than too little rainfall, and that produces a fine growth of grass which has made England rich in flocks and the foremost country in the world in the production of breeds of domestic animals. The names of the breeds of sheep show their British origin—as Lincoln, Dorset, Southdown, Hampshiredown, Oxforddown, Leicestershire, and Highland. The judges of the highest English court have for centuries sat upon a wool sack—symbol of the commercial importance of that commodity, which for many centuries was the chief export of England in the time when Holland and Flanders were the great wool manufacturing center of Europe.

Many breeds of cattle and horses also bear British names, including the Shetland pony (Fig. 197), a dwarf produced by a meager

FIG. 197.—The Shetland pony with its long coat is an interesting response to an environment, the cold raw Shetland Islands. (Photo C. S. Plumb, Columbus, O.)

diet[1] of heather and grass on the cold, raw hills of the Shetland Islands.

Grain growing.—With a wheat yield per acre more than twice as heavy as that in the United States, Britain shows that she is an excellent country for the small grains. The hills and the rain of northern and western England, Scotland, and Wales, and the rains

[1] In many parts of the world a scanty food supply has produced local breeds of ponies, just as the abundant food of England and France has given us the big heavy draft horses to be seen on any city street.

of Ireland cause wheat growing to be of small importance in those parts of the United Kingdom. Eastern and southern England are the chief British wheat districts. With their suitable climate, level plains, and fertile soil these districts are about equal in wheat output to any corresponding area of the United States.

Oats and barley are largely grown for animal food, and Irish bacon is even imported to the United States because the meat of the barley-fed hog is so much leaner than that of the corn-fed hog of the American corn belt.

Forests and pasture.—England's access to seaports has enabled her to import wood for a long time, so that she has less forest (see Appendix) than any other civilized country. Instead of forest, her hills and even her mountains, such as the Scotch highlands, are sheep pastures, and the heavy rain promotes a thick covering of grass, fern, and heather, so that the soil is held intact. Similar pasturage of French mountains where the rainfall is less, has resulted in such rapid erosion that tree planting had to be done on an extensive scale to hold earth on the slopes. The English people prize mutton, especially British mutton, and Great Britain, with three-fourths as many sheep as people, has more sheep in proportion to population than the United States.

The condition of agriculture.—The United Kingdom was practically self-supporting in food until the origin of the factory system, and the consequent development of cities early in the nineteenth century (Fig. 196). Then followed a long political fight for free import of foods (cheap food), which resulted in British free trade about 1850. Then followed, from the Mississippi Valley, that same deluge of cheap grain and meat that so depressed farming and farm values in the states along our Atlantic seaboard (Fig. 198). As there is much unused land in New Jersey and Virginia, so is there, from the same cause, much unused land in England, although the recent rise in the price of foodstuffs is causing the British to become more interested in agriculture as are the people of the eastern United States. This revival of agriculture is very marked in Ireland where Sir Horace Plunkett has rendered a great service by the establishment of co-operative societies that have guaranteed the quality of eggs and butter produced by the members, and thus greatly increased the demand for the products. This help was sorely needed, for this island, devoid of coal, has not had the manufacturing development that has taken place in England and Scotland. Ireland, called the Emerald Isle

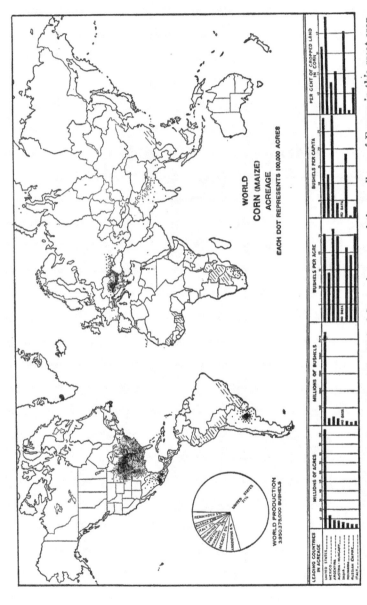

The world map shows the leadership of the United States in corn and the smallness of Europe in this great crop. This makes clear the basis of the great export from America to Europe of corn and its derivatives, pork, lard, and beef European climate is fine for small grains, but forbids any large corn area.   (Finch and Baker.)

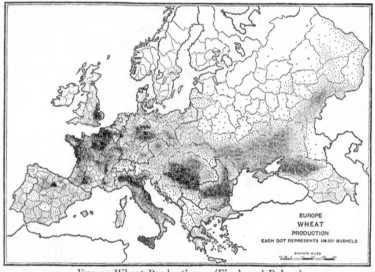

Europe Wheat Production.   (Finch and Baker.)
Compare wheat areas of United States and Europe to see how good Europe is.

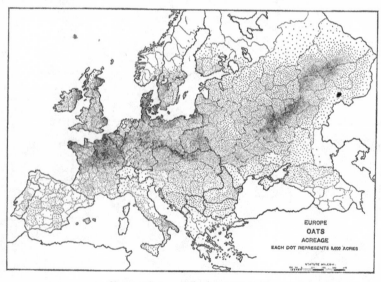

Europe Oats.   (Finch and Baker.)
Europe is also rich in her oat area.

because of the greenness of her well-moistened pastures, is chiefly engaged in the export of meat and dairy products to English cities. Much of England also is in pastures producing mutton and milk for 'her city millions, so that the 50 million bushels of wheat she produces is but a fraction of the bread requirements. She could grow much more grain than she does. In Germany 26 per cent. of the area is in grain. In the United Kingdom it is but 11 per cent.

In addition to the import of bread and meat, Britain has a heavy import of cheese and of butter from Denmark, Russia, and France, and of fruits and vegetables from the Mediterranean countries. Since bread and jam is an important article of British diet there is also a large manufacture of jams and preserved fruits. Examples of serious overproduction of small fruits in Great Britain give surprising verification of the menace of overproduction in agriculture (see chapter on Potatoes and Vegetables).

Being thus dependent on imports, a blockade of her coasts would starve her into submission in a few months. Hence her feverish insistence on a navy larger than that of any possible enemy.

Coal and iron.—England's twentieth century condition results from the fact that in the nineteenth century she led all nations in the abundance of capital and the ease of getting out her coal and iron. These factors resulted in the development of manufactures. England, already a coal user when the steam engine

Percentage | Million Dollars

United Kingdom 58.4 | 57.0

Germany 15.7 | 15.3

Cuba 5.6 | 5.5
Netherlands 4.2 | 4.1
Belgium 3.1 | 3.0
Canada 2.8 | 2.75
Mexico 1.1 | 1.05
All others 9.1 | 9.0

Total 97.7

FIG. 198.—Distribution of United States exports of hogs and pork, three-year average, 1909-11.

was invented, quickly took from Holland the leadership in power development, and then in manufactures, because she has large fields of good coal (Fig. 199) (bituminous) near to the sea and near to the iron, which is necessary for the harnessing of power derived from coal. England's supply of coal is estimated to be sufficient to last six centuries at present rate of consumption. Holland was coalless and had to depend on the wind for power. England had, in addition to power, and adequate labor supply, a stable government, and domestic peace. With these advantages the modern factory system quickly originated. It came after a number of mechanical inventions in the latter part of the eighteenth century made it possible to assemble many workers in one building where their machines could be run by a common engine. Previously, the English manufacturing had been done by hand machines in the cottages of people who lived in populous country districts and tilled some land. But coal and steam made easy the establishment of the factory system, and brought together these people into cities, usually to their physical injury, changed Britain from an agricultural to a manufacturing country and transferred the center of population and power from the agricultural southeastern plains to the rougher, more mountainous north-northwest and west with their coal and iron.

The examination of the map of the well-distributed British coal-fields shows (Fig. 200) how the well-known manufacturing cities have arisen by them.

The possession of good iron ores lying beside these coal deposits quickly made England the leading iron-making country in the world. The location of the iron and coal-fields on the east and west coasts of England and the southwest coasts of Scotland and of Wales, gave easy access to the sea for export, and later, when the ore supplies ran low in England, it was easy for the English iron industry to turn to a supply of

	Percentage	Million Tons
United States	37.5	459.4
Great Britain	24.1	294.8
Germany	19.6	240.7
Austria-Hungary	4.4	54.5
France	3.4	42.0
Russia	2.2	26.7
Belgium	2.1	25.8
Japan	1.3	16.4
All others	5.4	65.4
Total		1225.57

FIG. 199.—World's coal production, three-year average, 1908–10.

imported ore from the mountains near the north coasts of Spain and from northern Sweden.

Textiles.—Iron made the machinery, coal drove it, and caused England to lead the world in manufacturing by machinery, especially textiles. For more than a century the name of Manchester has been synonymous throughout the commercial world with cotton cloth. That city, the metropolis of Lancashire, has been the center of the greatest cotton manufacturing district in the world and it is still rapidly adding spindles to the equipment. The industry, established there as early as 1640, was partly due to the Atlantic winds which gave the moisture necessary to the best cotton manufacturing. Later these same Atlantic winds influenced the industry through the water-power of numerous small streams that descended from the central highlands and led to quick development after the invention of the new machines. Both of these advantages have now passed away. The moisture, like the temperature of the factory air, is now machine-controlled and the factories of Lancashire have long since

FIG. 200.—Coal map of England.

outgrown the water-power and turned to steam, for which the local coal fields are very convenient. The third factor in Lancashire's start was the convenient harbor of Liverpool, which has long had wide ship connection with regions producing and consuming cotton. The city of Manchester itself has now ceased to be so strictly a manufacturing city, and has become the sale and storage center for the product of many surrounding towns (Fig. 203). Liverpool, the natural port of entry for this region, is the greatest cotton port in the world because back of it lies the greatest cotton-manufacturing district. It is, indeed, surprising that in a century and a quarter, the British cotton industry should have spread so little beyond a radius of 40 miles from Manchester. This district clothes Britain and supplies 70 per cent of the world's export cotton cloth (Fig. 201). The intensity of the industry has given to Lancashire ten

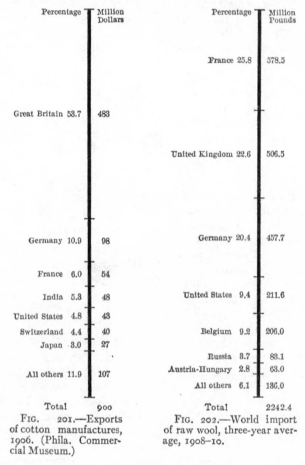

Percentage	Million Dollars
Great Britain 53.7	483
Germany 10.9	98
France 6.0	54
India 5.3	48
United States 4.8	43
Switzerland 4.4	40
Japan 3.0	27
All others 11.9	107
Total	900

Fig. 201.—Exports of cotton manufactures, 1906. (Phila. Commercial Museum.)

Percentage	Million Pounds
France 25.8	578.5
United Kingdom 22.6	506.5
Germany 20.4	457.7
United States 9.4	211.6
Belgium 9.2	206.0
Russia 3.7	83.1
Austria-Hungary 2.8	63.0
All others 6.1	186.0
Total	2242.4

Fig. 202.—World import of raw wool, three-year average, 1908–10.

times the population of Rhode Island, although its area is only 8 per cent greater. A son often succeeds to his father's place in the mill and the skill of the Lancashire operative may well be said to be hereditary, with factory work and school dividing the years of youth.

England sends fine cottons even into the best cotton manufacturing districts of the United States and of northwest Europe, the total British exports of cotton manufactures, $583,000,000 (1910), exceed by far in value the foodstuffs exported from the United States, $385,000,000 (1911).

England has been unable to secure such leadership in the world's supply of woolens as has been the case with cottons, nor is the industry so important. There is little difference in the amount of woolen goods produced in England, the United States, Austria-Hungary, Germany, and France (Fig. 202). The explanation of this greater equality in wool than in cotton manufacture is to be found

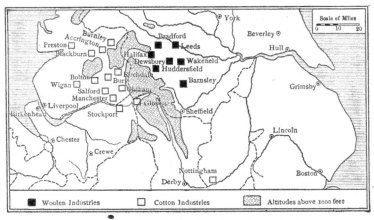

FIG. 203.—Location of cotton and woolen industry in England.

in the fact that wool manufacturing was a world-wide domestic industry before the factory system was developed. The Industrial Revolution found wool an established industry and merely transformed it. Wherever men made flour, they made woolen cloth, and the adaptation of primitive water-powers to the hand loom was a small change, much smaller than learning how to use a new fiber such as cotton. Cotton manufacturing was thus a new business, resulting from what was the practical discovery of cotton when Whitney's cotton gin made its production cheap. This came after the textile machines were established in England. That country, being in much the best position to manufacture textiles in factories, seized the new raw material and built up a world's trade in cotton, while wool, an industry as old as history, was still being made upon hand looms in millions of farm houses and in every textile village of Europe and America. With the tenacity which comes of an early start and the hereditary knowledge that lingers in families, wool manufacture has continued wherever, in the cooler parts of Europe and America, there is a population dense enough to develop any extensive manufacture. England, however, leads in exports of wool manufactures. The towns of Bradford, Leeds, Huddersfield in Yorkshire, just across a low mountain range from Lancashire, are known wherever fine woolen cloths are bought and sold.

Linen.—The manufacture of flax into linen is important in the United Kingdom. The north of Ireland (especially near Belfast), and the south of Scotland, which a century ago grew flax and manufactured it in hand looms, now are the centers of the world's finest factory operated linen manufactures, employing 100,000 people and giving excellent illustrations of the influences of an early start as the basis for an industry. The fiber is now produced in Russia, where labor is cheaper than in any other part of Europe suited to flax growing.

Silk.—The silk industry in England is peculiarly unimportant for a nation so great in textile manufacture. England's early lead in cotton was duplicated by the similar early success of France in silk manufacture, which enabled the mills of that country to compete with those of England even in their own market. Of late years there has been some manufacture of cheap silk goods in the cotton and wool districts of England, but the best silk goods used in England are imported, and the total number of silk employees is only about half as great as that in the United States.

Machinery and ships.—The possession of the coal, iron, and machine-using industries has given England the basis to build up a great machinery export, especially of textile machinery which goes to all countries as they begin on the textile industry, but ship building is the greatest iron manufacture in the United Kingdom. With the cheapest iron in the world, produced immediately beside the sea, her advantages for this industry were even greater than for the cotton industry. Her methods have also been the best. The large shipyards in the British ship-building centers upon the River Clyde in west Scotland, the Tyne in northeast England, and the Irish harbor of Belfast give a good example of concentration. The single city of Newcastle on Tyne built over a third more shipping (412,000 tons) in 1911 than the whole United States (291,000 tons) in the same year. The cities of Sunderland, Glasgow, and Greenock each rival the United States in output. The British total is greater than that of all the rest of the world, and British built ships are flying almost every flag upon the sea.

Shipping and trade.—It is plain that British imports must fill many more ships than do the leading exports. The imports of grain, meat (from Argentina and Australia), lumber, iron ore, cotton, and wool, are much more bulky than the cotton and woolen cloth, machinery, pottery, cutlery, and general manufactures that she sells. Even her exported ships can carry a cargo away with them if a cargo can be found. Fortunately there is coal to fill these empty ships as a kind of ballast cargo. Thus Britain becomes a greater coal exporter than all other nations combined. It goes by millions of tons to Brazil, Argentina, South Africa, the Mediterranean, and to the coalless countries nearer home such as Holland, Denmark, and Norway. This coal export is a fortunate factor for England. As the food vessel can earn money going out, it brings this food back more cheaply.

London the entrepot.—When she became the country with the greatest industry and the greatest commerce, Britain had, as a result, the best commercial connections. She was the first country to develop a good network of steamer lines upon the modernizing of commerce after the peace of 1815. Lines went to the Continent and to the United States, and from the days of the old British East India Company there had been frequent connection with the East Indies. London became the greatest trade center and the distributor of the products of Asia. Having developed routes for her own trade, the route via London often became the easiest way for goods or people from one distant country to reach another. We see the same thing in the way people living near a town must often make a detour and go through it to get from one suburb to another. Thus London became the greatest trade center or entrepot in the world.

But the importance of this intermediary or entrepot trade must not be overestimated, for it has always been subsidiary to the commerce that is essentially national in its origin or destination. This was true of London in 1865 when she was the undisputed world metropolis and it is true in greater degree in the present when her entrepot supremacy is passing away.

Other nations rise to commercial independence.—When Germany, Denmark, France, Belgium, or the United States wanted small shipments of Indian, or Oriental, or Italian goods, it was convenient and financially advantageous to get these goods in England, because Germany, Denmark, France, Belgium, and the United States had regular and frequent connections with England, and England had connections with the Orient. After a century of multiplication of commerce, London is still the leader, and richer than ever; but other cities are also distributing the products of the East since they have developed direct connections of their own. Half a dozen British ports have direct lines to the East. German lines go from Hamburg and Bremen, the French lines from Havre and Marseilles and the Austrian from Trieste. There are frequent and regular eastern sailings from Antwerp, Genoa and, once a month, from Copenhagen. New York also has regular connection with the Orient, Australia, Cape of Good Hope, the coasts of South America and the ports of the Mediterranean and the Baltic.

Other cities become entrepots.—Hamburg has, in large degree, succeeded London and Liverpool as the basis of foreign goods supply for Scandinavia and the Baltic; but almost before Hamburg is secure in her new trade possession, lines of steamers are beginning to carry the products of America and the Orient direct to Newcastle, Stockholm, to Copenhagen and to the Russian ports (see Fig. 234, 239).

London as a capital and export center.—As New York is the great center for the foreign trade and financial operations in the United States, so London buys and sells for the whole United Kingdom, and to some extent for many foreign countries. The London export house buys Manchester goods for shipment via Liverpool to customers in Bombay or Valparaiso. This might be called bargain center work, but there is another stage, the actual ownership.

Direct control of distant industries from the bargain center.—The capitalists actually carry on industries and manage them and sell the product through the headquarters in the capitalistic center. The Standard Oil Company from its office in New York buys lands in Mexico or Oklahoma through salesmen in New York. It buys pipes from Pittsburgh companies with offices in New York. The Jarri paving-wood industry of western Australia is all managed in two or three buildings in London. London has thousands of companies doing business abroad, and, if one walks through the business districts and reads the signs upon the office buildings, he can familiarize himself with geographical names in every continent, in almost every country or island with resources to develop and with inadequate capital. Britain has capital.

It should be emphasized that this capitalistic development has but begun. A mere corner of the world, say a half million square miles or 1 per cent. of the earth's land surface, has capital to spare; and all the vast remainder of the world must depend upon imported capital for the execution of any considerable enterprise; such, for example, as the building of a railroad. This is true of the entire continents of Asia, Africa, and South America, the East and West Indies, Australia, Central America, Mexico, west Canada, and most of the United States. We still use large amounts of foreign capital, although some of the American people have now begun to invest abroad, and there has long been much control of industry in our western states by eastern capitalists. Throughout the nineteenth century the countries of northwestern Europe were the sole exporters of capital, and Spain, Italy, Greece, the Balkan States, and Russia are still borrowers.

The income from all these investments, the earnings of the British ships that carry in every sea, come back to the English owners in goods. Thus England is able to import much more than she exports; likewise the other capitalistic investing countries—France, Germany, Holland, and Belgium (see table of values of Food Imports).

QUESTIONS

1. Explain what industrial changes are causing the sheep flocks of Europe to decline.

2. Compare the United States and Europe as to proportion of arid land.

3. Why does Europe grow more potatoes than we do?

4. State and explain the difference in the way forests are cared for in the United States and in Europe.

5. Is it fair to compare the foreign trade of England, France, and Germany with that of the United States?

6. How did a climatic factor make England an exporter of wool, and mineral factors make her later an importer of wool?

7. How does the English climate favor athletic sports more than the climate of New York?

8. Show the relation between an early start and the linen and silk industries of the United Kingdom.

9. Has Pittsburgh or Newcastle greater advantage for assembling raw materials for iron making?

10. Why does England's food supply make her anxious about her navy?

11. Why can the mountains of Scotland remain without forests while those of France cannot?

12. How does England's wealth enable her to import more than she exports?

13. Why is not the United States, the greatest coal producer, also the greatest coal exporter?

CHAPTER XXIV

FRANCE AND BELGIUM

Climate.—Beautiful France, as the inhabitants like to call it, has the oceanic climate of Britain, and finds its American counterpart in central and northern California. It reaches from the sugar beet zone in the north to the olive, prune, and trucking territory of the Mediterranean coast. The country is good from end to end (Fig. 208).

Agriculture.—The coal supplies are very meager and manufactures have as a result a minor place. France is still primarily an agri-

Fig. 204.—An example of French economy. An 11-pound cut flower basket for parcel post shipment made of split cane and requiring but a fraction of the material necessary for a box made of sawed boards. (U. S. Consular Bureau.)

cultural country and, stimulated by a high tariff on food, she almost feeds herself and has a foreign trade not over one-fifth as great as that of the United Kingdom. France is a well-tilled, well-kept looking country. The people are thrifty, saving, capitalistic, investing in enterprises in many lands. Her mountains are well and carefully forested to stop erosion (Fig. 204). Her sandy marshes along the Bay of Biscay have been converted into lucrative pine forests that are practically turpentine farms.

That France is primarily an agricultural country is shown by the fact that two of her great exports are from the farm—dairy products and wine. In the north the intensity of agriculture and density of population resemble those of Belgium. In other parts her agriculture is moderately intensive. With only one-sixth as much tillable land as the United States, the wheat crop is half that of the United States, and the acre yield is one-third greater. Yet in parts of rural France the methods are surprisingly unscientific and archaic, and there are large possibilities of increased production. French farms average 20 acres each, and those of the United States average 150 acres.

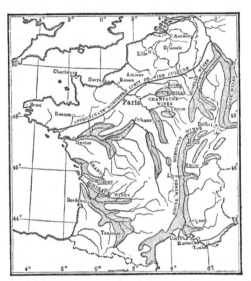

Fig. 205.—Chief wine-producing areas of France. Names of wine and brandy centers underscored. (After Brigham.)

Four times as many potatoes per person are raised as in the United States. As in England, barley and oats are grown and hay is important, because of the large animal industry. The Percheron horse, native in the department de Perche, the finest of the heavy draft horses, is bred in large numbers in the north of France.

Wine-growing is the most characteristic agricultural industry of France (Fig. 205), and the crop is worth more than half as much as the wheat crop. France, Spain, and Italy produce five-sixths of the world's wine, a peculiar dominance of an agricultural industry by the old countries. Wheat growing has shifted quickly to far frontiers. Not so with wine-making. This industry is hard to move. In the first place it is an intensive industry requiring a dense population, which frontiers rarely have. Like a garden crop it requires much labor to produce the grapes. The yield is great, in France about 200 gallons of wine per acre. In the second place, expensive appliances and much labor are required for the fermentation of the juice into good wine, and great skill is required to get the desired flavors in the product. Lastly, wines are sold by the name of the country or place producing them, as Burgundy, Madeira, Champagne, etc., and a long time is required to establish a reputation. If the growers of Burgundy wine should go to some other part of the world, they could not be sure that they would find the proper soil and climate to produce more Burgundy, for few crops are so affected by the soil, the moisture, and the temperature as is the grape. If the people from Burgundy made wine as good as Burgundy in California or Australia, it would take them two generations or more to establish the fact and get the price. But there is no guarantee that Burgundians could make Burgundy wine in a foreign land. Owing to the soil influence, particular varieties of grapes are often limited to narrow localities. Thus France remains the leader of wine-producing countries, and the good esteem of French wines, among them claret, burgundy, and champagne, makes wine, after textiles, the chief export of the country. The Phylloxera, a tiny insect of the aphis family, gets upon the roots of the grape vine and sucks the juices from then until the vine is killed. This pest nearly ruined the European wine industry about 1885. The only thing which prevented the practical extermination of grape and wine growing throughout the Old World, was the fact that in America, the home of the Phylloxera, there were varieties of grape immune to its attacks. These were imported to Europe, set out by millions in the vineyards which the Phylloxera had devastated, and tops of the European varieties were grafted upon their roots, making a composite plant with American root to resist the destroying insect, and a European top to produce the desired wine grape.

The French also import much Italian and Spanish wine which they mix with native wines and flavor, label, and export as French wines. They even import as much as 150 million pounds per year of the dried currants (grapes) from Greece, which are manufactured into wine for export.

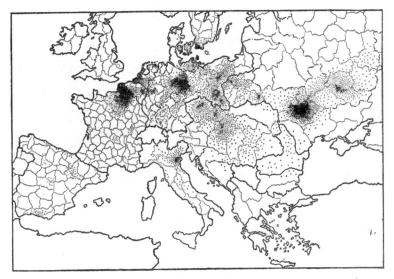

Europe. Sugar Map. (Finch and Baker.)

The European sugar map helps us to see that beet sugar is a part of the intensive agriculture. The great bread crop, wheat, covers a large percentage of the European fields as the wheat map shows, but the sugar map shows that a small area serves to give the continent of Europe all the sugar it uses in times of peace, with heavy export to England and even to America.

The location of the sugar fields was such that when Turkey came into the war nearly all the sugar land was shut off from the Allies, and the German invaders of France occupied a part of even the western-most important sugar region. It is hard for people in America to understand the privation to which this put the peoples of Europe. If you cut out five-sixths of your sugar, it seems to interfere with all your eating. In addition to this, the European people had reduced meat supply, reduced bread supply, and in Germany there was also a very great shortage of butter, lard, cocoa-nut oil, and all other edible fats.

Within the first few weeks of the war, the British government hired a great many ships and sent them to sugar countries and bought large amounts of sugar, so that England had enough to last her many months.

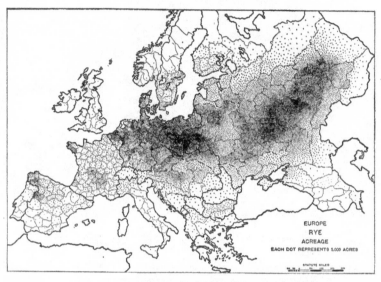

The rye map shows another of Europe's advantages.
(Finch and Baker.)

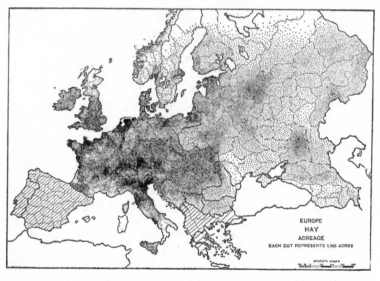

The hay map shows the extent of Europe's animal industry.
(Finch and Baker.)

The agriculture of Belgium.—The boundary between France and Belgium is as artificial as that between Indiana and Illinois. That is why the Germans came through Belgium to strike at France in 1914. French is spoken in both countries, and the two really comprise one industrial district. The chief difference is the greater density of Belgian population—over one person to the acre—and the greater intensity of the agriculture. This population is about twenty times as dense as that of the United States, and the country produces per square mile sixty times as many potatoes as does the United States. The garden farmer of north France and Belgium keeps hares and rabbits to which he feeds the weeds that are pulled from his crops. Hares have the advantage of being able to thrive in closer confinement than poultry, and they will feed on a very wide range of vegetable food. They are quite generally kept, both for their flesh and their skins and are exported to England by the hundreds of tons. The total British import of rabbits amounts to over $5,000,000 per year. The skins of these animals are an important material for the manufacture of hats, and as Belgium was the scene of the devastations of the early campaigns of the war of 1914, the American hat industry was disturbed.

All this intensity of agriculture means large product per *acre*, not per man (Fig. 206). It is estimated that the Belgian farmer produces on the average $508 worth of produce per year, and the American farmer $1004 worth. If the United States should suddenly produce as much per acre as Belgium, it would produce the most paralyzing panic ever seen. There would be no market for the produce, as there is now no market for the water of the road-side spring. The road-side spring would make its owners rich if beside a Sahara caravan route. Belgium therefore has a larger percentage of her population engaged in agriculture than we have in the United States.

Manufactures.—The best coal field in France and Belgium lies on both sides of the boundary of these two countries, as does the greatest manufacturing district. The industries of the Belgian are rather heavier than those of the French side, iron and cement being more important. Much fine glass is also made in this region, as are also the French porcelains known as Sevres and Limoges. Woolen and cottons are also manufactured, and Brussels is the market for a great deal of hand-made lace that is made by the peasant women in the intervals of farm and household labor.

Paris is a great manufacturing center, and the words "Paris

goods" stand for nicety and artistic qualities in clothing and personal goods that are known throughout the western world.

Lyons is the greatest silk manufacturing center in the world, and has been so for several centuries since the introduction of silkworms

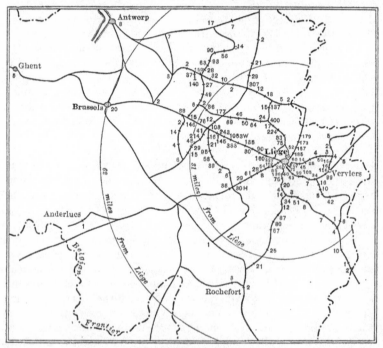

FIG. 206.—Distribution of city workers of Liege, to village homes. Figures represent number going from each station to Liege, June 1–5, 1906. Small agriculture is added to factory wages. By trades: miners 1832, factory men 2871, building trades 1440, unskilled 1493, dress-makers and milliners 360, apprentices 242, other trades 1167, railway workmen 520, total 9925, of whom 5830 went daily and 4095 weekly. (From "Land and Labor" by B. S. Rowntree.) Belgium is ahead of any other western nation in the scientific utilization of her resources. Her factory workers live upon the land to a degree unknown elsewhere. With his plot of ground there is room for production by the aid of women and children, old persons, and the spare time of the artisan himself. This garden product, the poultry, hares, and possibly the cows are great additions to a low wage and they conduce to the intensity of culture that gives large return per unit of land.

from Italy. It now manufactures more raw silk than France produces.

Marseilles has long been a center for the collection of the olive oil that is produced on all the shores of the Mediterranean. As oil is the chief raw material for soap, Marseilles has become a great soap-making center and a great market for many kinds of oils.

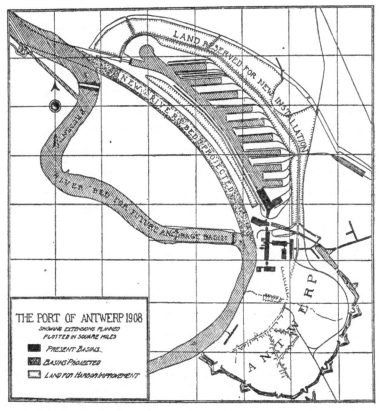

THE PORT OF ANTWERP 1908
SHOWING EXTENSIONS PLANNED
PLOTTED IN SQUARE MILES
■ PRESENT BASINS
▨ BASINS PROJECTED
□ LAND FOR HARBOR IMPROVEMENT

FIG. 207.—Antwerp has outgrown the fortifications put up as a defence against Napoleon III and before the war had port plans that are probably unrivalled for comprehensive system. America can show nothing like it. (After J. Paul Goode.)

The trade doubled between 1905 and 1910. In recent decades new industrial movements have given us other oils as rivals of, and substitutes for, the oil of olives. One of the most important of these new materials is cottonseed oil, produced chiefly in the cotton

districts of the United States, and in its purer grades, largely used
for food in south Europe as a substitute for olive oil, while the lower
grades serve as a soap material in the Marseilles markets and
factories.   The opening of the Suez Canal enabled this French port
easily to import new oils from the East, and the fat-seeded legum-

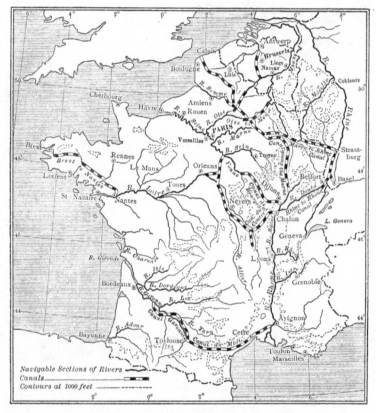

FIG. 208.—French and Belgian waterways.

inous groundnut or peanut is largely imported from Pondicherry,
India; from the French colony of Madagascar; from Mozambique,
East Africa; from German East Africa; from Senegal in West
Africa; and also from Brazil, Argentina, and Costa Rica.   The great
market for all these producing districts is Marseilles where peanut

oil, like cottonseed oil, is a rival of olive oil for both food and soap. The list of imported oil materials (see Appendix) shows the extent and phenomenal growth of the industry at Marseilles. It will be noted that the great increase is in the tropic products of peanuts and copra. The Belgian city of Antwerp is a greater port than Marseilles for it is the natural outlet of most of Belgium and also of a part of the Rhine Valley (Fig. 207). Its commerce has grown with great speed.

QUESTIONS

1. How have the resources of France left her behind England as a manufacturing country?

2. How does the foreign trade of France indicate her agricultural importance?

3. Why does the wine industry not follow the wheat industry to suitable new countries?

4. Why does Belgium have a larger percentage of farmers than the United States?

5. How may it be said that Paris goods show a quality of the French people?

6. How does the climate of southern France make Marseilles an importer of dried cocoanuts?

7. State two reasons why it would be undesirable for the lands of the United States to produce as much as those of Belgium.

8. What is the explanation of the fact that peanuts from British and German colonies go to Marseilles?

CHAPTER XXV

GERMANY

The war has taught millions that no nation is independent or can be. This, of course, has long been plain to anyone who closely examined the conditions under which modern communities lived, but the war has ground the fact into the minds of whole nations.

The Germany of 1914 was really a marvel in the success that had rewarded long, careful, and scientific labor to make a nation as nearly independent as possible on the rather slim basis of Germany's natural resources. To see that Germany is a poor country in comparison with the United States, compare the two countries in area, population per square mile, variety and area of staple crops, variety, production, and resources of important minerals.

The Germany of the future is difficult to predict with certainty, but there are good reasons to expect that most of her industries will resume, so that a careful examination of her condition in 1914 is as good a way as any to see what she will be as industry revives and readjusts after the war.

The meager resources of Germany.—Germany lies wholly within the zone having sufficient rainfall for agriculture. The northern half of the area is a coastal plain, much of it like parts of our Atlantic coastal plain, with sandy soil of low fertility, but the German plain has been made into fields of potatoes and rye, or well kept forest. In central and southern Germany are the Hartz and other mountains, low and well forested. There is very little mineral output aside from coal, iron, cement, and building stone. Germany is not naturally rich in soil and minerals like the United States. England has much more coal than Germany, although both countries have enough for the present. Both together are poor in comparison to the United States.

Scientific development of materials and men.—The conspicuous thing about the industrial life of Germany has not been her resources, but their scientific development. Never in the history of the world has a nation so systematically developed all of its resources, human

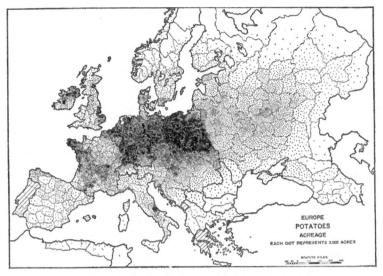

Germany's leadership in the world of potatoes is plain.
(Finch and Baker.)

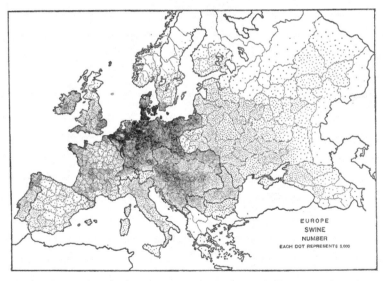

The swine region closely coincides with potatoes in Europe, corn in America.
(Finch and Baker.)

and material. Why was this? It seems plain that it happened because of the firm conviction in the minds of the German leaders that she needed to be a strong military nation. Located in an open plain in the center of Europe, she has been trampled by armies at frequent intervals from the time of the roaming Goths, Vandals, and Huns to the more recent period when Louis XIV of France, Gustavius Adolphus, the Swede, and the armies of Russia have in turn ravaged her territory. The final act in this series of pillagings because of her open location was the Napoleonic Wars, during which she was crushed to the dust, humiliated in the extreme, and from which she emerged with the conviction that she must be strong enough to defeat her neighbors. To be strong in the military sense, a nation must have strong, healthy, efficient men for her armies, abundant food, and varied industries to produce military supplies and support the civil population. To bring these ends to pass, Germany did five things: .

1. Educated her people to make them efficient in industry and the army.

2. Promoted social legislation to keep the people healthy and strong.

3 and 4. Promoted agriculture and manufacture by tariffs, bounties, and scientific investigation, to give herself varied industries.

5. Promoted the development of science because it stimulates industry and the development of war equipment.

She promoted education to the point where no other large nation had such a high percentage of its people educated so thoroughly.

As a part of her educational campaign, she promoted science, the branches of learning that make industry, rather than literature and languages, the branches of education that make culture or the mere, but really great, pleasure of being learned and knowing things. At a time when the colleges and universities of England and America taught almost nothing but ancient languages, mathematics, and a little history, the German universities were turning out doctors of philosophy in physics, chemistry, geology, and geography. No other country accorded such honors and rewards to the man who had made a real achievement in science, and it may safely be predicted that any nation will ultimately lead in proportion as it learns to honor and reward, and therefore urge onward, people who render it real service of a constructive character which improves the condition of the masses of its people.

Despite German attention to science, it has been repeatedly pointed out that they have not been so highly original as some nations where the individuals were left more free. Few really great inventions have come from Germany. An American, Morse, invented the telegraph. An American, Bell, invented the telephone. Americans, Langley and the Wrights, invented the flying machine. An American, Simon Lake, invented the submarine. Darwin, an Englishman, put the sciences of botany and zoology at the large service of man. But it was the Germans, with their thorough system of school and discipline who first taught a whole people how to utilize these things. This gave her industries a more scientific bent than those of any other country. She thus came naturally by her position of leadership in chemical manufacture such as the coal-tar dyes and other coal products.

The cessation of German trade caused by the war of 1914 brought great disturbance to the American supplies of dyestuffs, drugs, photographic supplies, potash, and other chemicals.

By skill, Germany's meager supply of brown coal is made usable by being compressed into briquettes. Much of it was made into coke by processes that left the gas and tar and gave the raw material for the dye industry. The Diesel engine that uses crude petroleum in place of gasoline is a German university product. So is the Zeiss glass that made nearly all the high-class lenses in the world before we were compelled to learn how to make it in this country during the war. One of the amazing results of the war was the way American scientists invented things and discovered things when they were given the chance, the equipment, and the time.

Germany's scientific agriculture.—On her area, which before the war was smaller than that of Texas (Fig. 209), Germany had twenty-

Millions of Acres
Area of Germany..133
Area of Corn and Wheat Fields in United States....148

FIG. 209.—An explanation of the fact that while Germany remained agricultural, there was large emigration of her people to the United States.

six more experiment stations than were to be found in the whole United States (not counting substations). The utilization of the beet and the potato are triumphs of great national importance. Her rough land is most scientifically forested. Her swamps are made into fish ponds where carp and trout are fed as we feed poultry in a yard. There are many fish growers' associations in the empire and the total area of fish ponds approaches 200,000 acres. In Saxony they cover one-half of 1 per cent. of the area. (Compare with the 3 per cent. under cultivation in Cuba or 5 or 6 per cent. in California.) The dog and the cow are made to work as draft animals (Fig. 210), and the growth of song birds, exported by the hundreds

FIG. 210.—In densely peopled Saxony the peasant women and the dog are draft animals. Factory labor is abundant.

of thousands by factory artisans of the Hartz Mountains shows an extreme development of the animal industries.

Grain.—In German agriculture, wheat and barley (see Chapter on Cereals) cover about equal areas, but owing to the poor sandy soil of her great northern plain she grows three times as much rye as wheat. Germany has had one-fourth, and Russia, into which the same plains extend, has had one-half of the world's rye crop. The peasants and factory workers of rye-growing countries eat the most of it in the form of black bread, which after all, is nearly as nourishing as wheat bread. But these people frequently substitute the superior and more highly esteemed wheat bread for rye bread, when they become able to buy wheat. The oat is also an important grain; with barley it partly fills the great gap caused by the absence of corn, for which the climate is too cold.

The potato is more important in Germany than any grain (Fig. 211). The failure of the potato crop would have brought on a

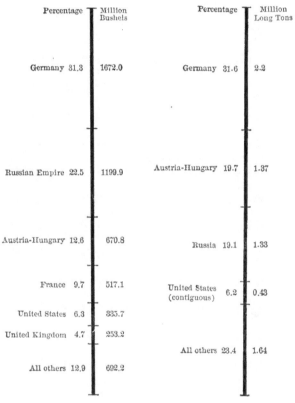

Fig. 211.—World's potato production, two-year average, 1910–11.

Fig. 212.—World production of beet sugar, three-year average, 1908–09 to 1911.

German collapse in any year of the war. The usual crop is 20 bushels per capita, Austria has 17, Belgium 11, the United States 4, and Italy 2.[1] Although the Germans eat three times as many

[1] The dry summer of the Mediterranean climate does not favor potato growing. This crop often requires irrigation in Italy.

potatoes per capita as we do, they eat only about one-fourth of the crop. The farm animals consume even a larger proportion. Potatoes are used for starch-making, for alcohol (a substitute for kerosene) and even before the war half a million tons were dried in more than 400 potato-drying factories. The product was used in chemical manufacture, in thickening soups, in bread and pastry making, as a substitute for corn meal, but chiefly for forage. These potato manufactures give stability to potato prices. There was a price fluctuation of 27 cents per bushel in Berlin in 5 years, while Chicago had a fluctuation of $1.34, with the result that the American farmer is afraid to grow potatoes. The stability of price afforded by these permanent outlets enabled the Germans to grow potatoes in great quantities. During the war the drying of potatoes and other vegetables increased enormously in Germany and was one of the things that enabled her to hold out as long as she did.

The sugar beet.—As the potato and the sugar beet leave the soil in splendid condition for a crop of winter grain, their cultivation tends to increase the grain yield. Because of this fact, it is probably true that Germany or any other country can grow more grain on a given area after adding potatoes and beets to the crop series than before. It is largely due to German selection that the beet has been improved to its high sugar content. Germany has a splendid beet climate (Fig. 212) and for several decades has exported sugar. Hence a part of the sugar shortage during the war.

The by-products of the beet field serve to enhance greatly the usefulness of this crop in the intensive agriculture of a populous country. The leaves and tops of the beets were worth in Germany, for cattle food, $4.50 to $5.75 per acre, which makes an interesting comparison with the $9.37 which was the farm value of the average acre of wheat in the United States at about the same time. The pulp from which the sugar has been extracted is taken back by the farmers and fed to cattle, and the average value of this in Germany was $10.40 per acre, whereas the average American hay crop was worth on the American farm $14.41 per acre, a figure that was less than the value of combined pulp and leaves of the German beet crop before the war had destroyed all old measures. It is therefore plain that beet growing plays an important part in the cattle-keeping agriculture of the small farms of north Europe.

German sugar production.—The map of beet production in Europe (see Fig. 213) shows that while its growth is scattered through

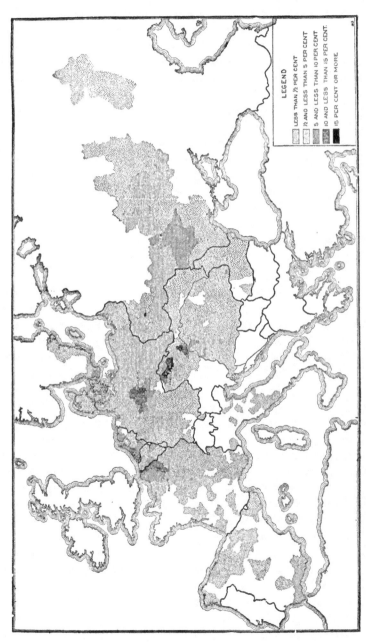

FIG. 213.—Proportion of the total arable land in Europe devoted to the sugar beet. (After U. S. Dept. Agr.)

LEGEND

LESS THAN ½ PER CENT
½ AND LESS THAN 5 PER CENT
5 AND LESS THAN 10 PER CENT
10 AND LESS THAN 15 PER CENT.
15 PER CENT OR MORE.

central Europe from northwestern Spain to Moscow, there are four centers of importance. The greatest is in central Germany, near Magdeburg where beets occupy from one-tenth to one-seventh of all the cultivated land. Here the beet fields spread in great expanses over the level, perfectly tilled plains and while the peasant children pull weeds, their mother may be seen plowing the beets, using at times the family cow for a draft animal. The most intense of all the sugar districts is in Bohemia, a part of Czecho Slovakia, where beets are grown as they are in Germany.

Poland, carved from these two great sharers of the Great Plain, is also a land of rye, oats, barley, potatoes, and beets.

Wine growing.—Germany has some fine vineyards and wine, but it is so near the northern limit of the grape belt that the desired heat and sunshine are obtained by planting the vineyards on the southward sloping hillsides (Fig. 214). In this way they are protected from the north winds and exposed, by the inclination, to the nearly perpendicular rays of the sun, and often get in addition the reflected sunshine from water surface as of the Rhine, the Moselle, and the Swiss lakes.

Manufacture and food supply.—Germany has stimulated manufactures more than any other nation, using tariffs, bounties, favorable rates on state railways, and a highly differentiated, technical education. No country excelled her in technical education. For the engineer, good training has been virtually free of tuition cost. The exporter goes to a commercial school, the weaver goes to a textile school, and in Pforzheim where there are 1,000 jewelry factories and 30,000 jewelry workers, there is a school for jewelers.

The progress of German manufactures since 1870 has been most rapid. Because of new jobs at home, emigration nearly ceased, so that despite the promotion of agriculture, Germany entered the class of nations dependent on imported food. At the outbreak of the war, the annual importation of agricultural products and foodstuffs into Germany amounted to $1,700,000,000 and the exports of goods of this class are worth about $400,000,000.

With a population of 64,000,000, the Germans had but 20,000,-000 cattle on the farms; whereas, the United States, with 100,000,000 population, had 61,000,000. We had 51,000,000 sheep, and the Germans 5,700,000; the American farmers owned 58,000,000 swine and there were less than 22,000,000 in Germany. As it is impossible to store food for many months, we see the basis of Admiral Mahan's statement that in any war between England and Germany the naval victor can starve the other out. This prediction, however, fails to note that by reducing the livestock figures by ⅓ there would be left enough barley, rye, and potatoes to enable the people to withstand a 5-year siege with unimpaired vigor, but on a nearly meatless diet. Germany's war hunger arose more from shortage

Fig. 214.—Stone walls hold the earth in Rhine slope vineyards worth $7000 per acre. Tower and castle of mediæval barons who lived by their exactions from Rhine traders. Freeing the Rhine was one of the great steps in modernizing Germany.

of man power than from the actual insufficiency of land to produce food. To make her land feed her people would have required an increase of labor. To get food cheaply she had been importing it from countries where it was grown easily.

The growing scarcity of animal food was being met by the Germans in a very effective and scientific way. Butter and cheese and meat are but digestible fat and protein (see table of food analysis, Appendix). Many vegetable oils furnish very similar fat and there are many cheaper proteins than those in cheese and meat. The oil of the olive has been an age-long peer of butter. Cotton-seed oil is now used as a substitute for olive oil, for butter, and for pork fat, and its use has spread so rapidly that in 15 years its price increased fourfold despite a doubled output. Even more promising rivals for dairy products are found in the oily cocoanut and the nutritious peanut, and the oil of the soy bean, all of which have sprung into commerce during the war scarcity.

FIG. 215.—German fence made of forest thinnings. Uprights are first thinning 1½-2½ inches in diameter, round. Cross pieces are second thinning split. Posts are larger round pieces. No saw dust or slab waste. The forest was planted with trees about as far apart as hills of corn in American fields.

Nearly half of the meat of the cocoanut is fat or oil, and the nut has the quality, unusual among oily vegetables, of keeping for many months without becoming rancid. The prewar rise in the price of animal products had caused increased attention to be given to the cocoanut as a source of food fat. A firm in Manheim, Germany, had put upon the market "Palmira," a hard snow-white vegetable cooking fat made from copra (dried cocoanut meats) and practically 100 per cent. pure fat. None of the rival animal fats (margarine, butter, lard, goose grease, etc.) contains less than 7 to 10 per cent. of water. The output of the factory increased in a

few years before the war from 700,000 to over 21 million pounds
per year.   The cutting off of the supply of vegetable fats, along with
the lard and bacon of America, was the most painful blow given
by the war to the German stomach.   The war showed that fat food
is more important than dieticians had thought.

In Austria, Holland, and England, and Scandinavia, the same
substitution of vegetable for animal fat is taking place.   The output
of European margarine factories using cocoanut oil as a base was

Fig. 216.—Potato harvest in Germany.   Even before the war the German
peasant woman worked in the fields almost as much as the man.   (Photo. by
Louis P. Robinson.)

put at 16 million pounds per week in 1913, an amount that then
exceeded the total European import of butter.   The war has reduced
the supply of butter while it multiplied the production of vegetable
fats.   The supply of cocoanuts promises to be unlimited because
of the great extent of unused land on nearly all tropic continents
and islands suited to the cocoanut palm, and the ease of producing
a product that falls from the tree and lies for weeks embedded in
its thick cushion of husk waiting to be picked up.   Peanuts and
soy beans are no less promising in their possibilities.

Iron and steel.—Germany is the second iron-manufacturing country of the world, having passed England in output about the end
of the nineteenth century, but the chief German iron district is
economically part of a district which extends through northern
France, Belgium, and the lower Rhine Valley, where local ores, coal,
and the dense population give the necessary conditions for modern
iron making. The navigable Rhine, with cheap transportation by
barge, makes possible the import of Swedish and Spanish ores
through Rotterdam, Amsterdam, and via canal from Antwerp, and
the export of finished product through these same ports, whose
steamship lines take the finished products at cheap rates to all the
world. The supplies of ore in nearby Lorraine are very great. The
town of Essen on the navigable Ruhr, a river reaching the Rhine
below Cologne, is the center of the world-famous German iron
industry owned by the Krupps.

Germany has not exceeded Great Britain as an iron maker because
of superior advantages. Germany's natural advantages are slightly
inferior, but government, science, and energy, and a large population,
have fostered the industry.

The growth of the German iron industry has been amazing. For
the world, there was a threefold increase in pig iron from 25 to 76
million tons between 1891 and 1913. In 1890 the output in million
tons was: United States, 9; United Kingdom, 7.8; Germany, 4.5;
in 1913, United States, 31; Germany, 19; while that of the United
Kingdom was less than in 1900. Here we see one of the reasons
why the world had reason to fear Germany. She had the stuff of
which munitions are made.

Other manufactures.—The German textile industry has advanced
rapidly, the linens of Westphalia being especially famed. For chemical manufacture Germany has had the great advantage of the world
monopoly of potash salts from the mines of Stassfurt near the Elbe
river. The potash shortage of the Allied world was such that prices
rose from $40.00 to $600.00 per ton. Many chemical works are
near the German potash beds. Germany leads the world in the
making of fine papers and fine leathers. In Germany, as in Holland,
Belgium, and France, we see in the leather industry an interesting
adjustment to the density of population. The scarcity of forests
long ago caused the establishment of willow plantations so trimmed
as to grow long slender twigs for weaving the baskets that replace
the boxes and barrels used in this country for the shipment of agri-

cultural and manufactured products. These same basket willows yield a bark suitable for tanning leather especially adapted for glove making. The dense population of Germany, France, and Belgium gives the labor supply to turn these good leathers into a large glove output. Germany also makes fine glass and has an important export of porcelain. In her great export of toys we see a combination of cheap labor, skill, and the domestic instinct so strong in the Germans. At the present time, she finds that Japan is copying her toys and porcelain and supplying many countries formerly·supplied by Germany.

Undoubtedly, the case of Germany, a nation that has slain millions and wrecked the world for a generation, is the strongest argument that can be advanced for the formation of a league of mankind that shall remove even from Germany the fear of war, or the possibility of war.

QUESTIONS

1. How have Germany's position and topography caused her to have a large army?

2. How has her manufacturing development aided in making a strong army?

3. Why is the price of potatoes more stable in Germany than in the United States? What is the effect of this on agriculture?

4. How is Germany meeting the high price of butter?

5. How has German esteem of scientific attainment enabled her to win some of England's foreign trade?

6. How does the Rhine serve the iron industry?

7. How does sandy soil cause the Germans to have black bread?

8. Name three ways in which German schools have made her army more effective.

CHAPTER XXVI

SWITZERLAND

Scenery as a Resource.—Switzerland is an example of prosperity in spite of poverty of resources. There are nearly four million people in a territory one-third the size of Pennsylvania, with no coal, 28 per cent of the surface covered with non-productive Alps, and 29 per cent so rough as to be fit only for forests, which by law are kept intact. Scenery, magnificent scenery, is the richest resource, and the ever-increasing tourist is the greatest crop. Right in the center of western Europe, and very accessible from America, Switzerland is the world's greatest playground with a summer tourist business that is a national asset.

Forestry.—This does not prevent the people from utilizing their other meager resources to the full. The land is very evenly divided among the small proprietors, of whom there is one to every nine of the population, an unusually high proportion. Some of the Swiss woodlands were carefully forested before Columbus set sail, and in the year 1910, 20 million trees were planted. The export of wood carvings is an example of full utilization of raw material.

Farming.—The chief field crops are rye, oats, and potatoes. Most of the bread and meat is imported, but Switzerland is able to supply herself with potatoes and sometimes even suffers from their overproduction. As further evidence of intensive agriculture, she has an astonishing proportion (18 per cent.) of her area in fruits. Of these, grapes, growing on the lake slopes, are so important that the wine output is one-fifth as great as that of France.

Dairying.—The Swiss have an interesting and unique dairy industry. Relatively large areas of land upon the high mountains, habitable only in summer, produce an abundance of rich grass as the melting snow recedes and lets the sun shine upon the saturated earth. The villagers of the valleys take their herds of cows to the higher pastures in summer and, because of the distance, stay with them through the whole season, spending the nights in little huts that have been built for the purpose. At intervals, members of their families bring up the necessary supplies and take away the accumulations of cheese and butter which the herders have produced. On the lower slopes of the Alps the water from snow field and glacier is often conducted out over the fields to fertilize and irrigate the grass for winter hay. As a result of this careful industry, Switzerland is an exporter of good cheese, Neufchatel being one of the best-known brands. She also sells annually nearly $2 worth per capita of condensed milk, some of it going to Canada, England, and India. Milk is also a large factor in the manufacture of milk-chocolate, in which Switzerland (like Holland) is important, sending abroad annually about three-fourths of the total product, valued at $10,000,000. On the per capita basis, Swiss cheese and milk exports exceed the entire exports of the United States in grain and grain products, animals and animal products. As some of the pastures are too rocky and steep for cows to climb, the Swiss have developed a very efficient breed of milch goats—animals that are, in proportion to their size, superior to cows as milk producers.

Manufactures.—For manufacturing Switzerland is blessed with water-power, and in hydraulic engineering she stands high. Swiss engineers designed the power plants at Niagara Falls. Her leading exports are fine cotton and silk fabrics, and machinery—all made of imported raw materials. The excellent hand-made watches of Geneva are the product of another industry well suited to a people who import their raw materials. The heavy expenditures of tourists and the foreign investments of her capitalists enable Switzerland to import 50 per cent. more than she exports, and the small variety of her resources causes her to have a foreign trade of over $100 per capita. At that rate ours would be about 10 billion dollars per year (see introduction to chapter on the United Kingdom).

Government and people.—Switzerland has one of the most democratic governments in the world, much more democratic than that of the United States. The people on the south slope of the Alps speak Italian. Those on the north, as at Basel, speak German, and those on the west, as at Geneva, speak French.

QUESTIONS

1. How do unproductive mountains become the best asset of Switzerland?
2. Why can she supply herself with potatoes but not with bread?
3. Are her industries on a more or less permanent basis than those of Germany?

CHAPTER XXVII

HOLLAND AND DENMARK

Utilization of resources.—Holland and Denmark are two thickly peopled bits of shore plain. Holland has an area of 12,600 square miles and 6 million population; Denmark, 15,600 square miles, 2,700,000 population. These little countries are examples of prosperity on lands reclaimed by arduous labor. Holland's well-known sea bottom reclamations are almost matched by the marshes and sand wastes that the Danes have converted into good pastures and fields. Holland also has considerable areas of infertile sand. Neither country has any coal or iron. The flatness makes water-power impossible, so manufactures must depend on imported coal. Materials and food for the worker must likewise be imported. We may therefore expect a full utilization of materials.

In this connection Holland has an agricultural industry that fits neatly into her situation. Bulbs of flowering plants, of which the culture of an acre costs over $1,000 per year, are raised by the carload and sent abroad to cheer the flower-lovers of every land. The export of millions of little forest trees and fruit trees to the United States and other countries is another example of much labor and income from little land. In a country where land is arable and too valuable to remain in forest, the extensive use of tile roofing is a good adjustment to resources.

Intensive agriculture through dairying.—While there is some manufacturing of diverse character and some fishing,[1] the countries are primarily agricultural, Denmark being a greater exporter of agricultural produce (per capita) than is the United States (Figs. 217, 218). This comes about through an intensively operated dairy industry. The moist climate promotes the growth of grass, the natural food of cattle, for which these regions have long been known.

Holland, with 454 people per square mile, has one-third as many horses and cattle and one-fourth as many sheep and swine as she

---

[1] The Dutch fishing fleet is manned by only 20,000 men, less than 2 per cent. of her male population.

has of people. In Denmark with 167 people per square mile, each of these two animal classes is nine-tenth times as numerous as the people. The state of Iowa, practically all arable, a strictly agricultural state in the midst of the corn belt, is far better fitted than

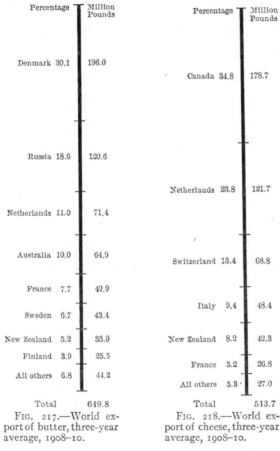

Percentage		Million Pounds		Percentage		Million Pounds
Denmark	30.1	196.0				
				Canada	34.8	178.7
Russia	18.6	120.6				
				Netherlands	23.8	121.7
Netherlands	11.0	71.4				
Australia	10.0	64.9		Switzerland	13.4	68.8
France	7.7	49.9				
				Italy	9.4	48.4
Sweden	6.7	43.4				
New Zealand	5.2	33.9		New Zealand	8.2	42.3
Finland	3.9	25.5		France	5.2	26.8
All others	6.8	44.2		All others	5.3	27.0
Total		649.8		Total		513.7

FIG. 217.—World export of butter, three-year average, 1908–10.

FIG. 218.—World export of cheese, three-year average, 1908–10.

Denmark to support livestock; but it has less of them per square mile than Denmark, having but forty persons to the square mile with a horse and cattle ratio of 300 per cent and a sheep and swine ratio of 330 per cent of this population.

Denmark, like Holland, had passed the limit in the number of

animals it can support on native food, and cattle foods such as wheat bran, cotton-seed meal, linseed oil cake, and other grain products are being imported in large and increasing quantities from the United States, Argentina, and Russia. In the attempt to feed her cattle, Denmark grows six times as much barley as wheat and Holland is increasing her area of oats and also greatly increasing her acre yields. Within 30 years her wheat yield has gone from 22 to 28.5 bushels per acre, and the potato yield from 136 to 203 bushels.

Meadows which the Hollander has won from the sea by pumping water off the rich Rhine mud, are too wet for tillage, but make pastures of great richness. Here drainage ditches separate from each other the little green fields, dotted with feed boxes from which the black and white cows eat bran and grains imported from America. The Dutch make 24 pounds of butter per capita per year. This is several pounds more than we make in the United States, but the Dutch being poorer, eat less of it per capita than we do. Their cheese output exceeds that of butter. The town of Edam, west of the Zuyder Zee, has given its name to a kind of cheese produced largely in that part of Holland, and, along with other Dutch brands, it goes to England, to the United States, and even to South Africa, and many other countries where the fame of Dutch cheeses has spread. Sweet butter also goes in large quantities to England.

In the production of this commodity Denmark is the teacher of the world. That little country, about half the size of Maine, is visited by the agricultural scientists of all the world who would learn in its best form the art of dairying. Forty years ago she was a meat exporter to Great Britain, but the necessity of greater output has turned this democratic kingdom into a vast dairy farm. The Danish peasant owns a farm of from five to twenty-five acres. More than half of the surface of the land tilled is in oats, hay, grass, and root crops to feed the cows. The increase of land used for forage has encroached upon the grain fields until there is not wheat land enough for bread. As a result, Denmark with a poorer soil rivals Holland in the race for world leadership in large number of animals per square mile. There are more than a thousand factories for making butter; the cows are inspected once a month to insure healthy stock; and the dread disease of tuberculosis, so common among housed cattle of the entire world, has been entirely stamped out of the kingdom. Over $50,000,000 worth of butter is sent each year to Great Britain alone. Danish butter preserved in tin cans has, through its excellence, become the standard article for consumption in the tropics and in all the remote corners of the globe where there is no local supply.

Danish bacon has an equally good reputation. All over Denmark it is cured by the same recipe, cut in the same way from pigs of the same breed slaughtered at the uniform size of 180–200 lbs.—the most economical size for a porker. This standardization of a product, agricultural or manufactured, is of great advantage in increasing trade.

QUESTIONS

1. Why does the United States export less butter than does Denmark?

2. Why is Holland less able to compete in manufactures than she was in 1650?

3. Why does Holland, with not enough land to feed herself, devote good grain fields to the growth of flowering bulbs?

CHAPTER XXVIII

NORWAY AND SWEDEN

Natural resources.—Norway and Sweden are, for Europe, large and sparsely peopled countries. Norway has an area of 124,000 square miles, 2⅓ million population, Sweden, 172,000 square miles and 5½ million population. The Scandinavian peninsula, which they occupy, is mountainous and extends far beyond the Arctic circle. The greater part of both countries lies farther north than Greenland and is only saved from frigid desolation by the amazing influence of the Gulf stream which enables the Arctic ports of Norway to be open all winter when on the eastern side of the Eurasian land mass the port of Vladivostok, in the latitude of Bordeaux, is frozen shut for months.

The arctic location, mountainous character, and recent glaciation explain the fact that 75 per cent of Norway is unproductive (except of water-power) and but 3.5 per cent is cultivated. Sweden, having a considerable area of plain, has 8.9 per cent cultivated. Forests, mostly pine, covering 21.5 per cent of Norway and 52 per cent of Sweden, are, after agriculture, the greatest source of employment and the greatest basis of export. Both countries are heavy exporters of lumber, pulp, paper, and other wood manufactures for which the snow-covered mountains furnish excellent water-power. The Swedes are able to sell power at the astonishingly low rate of $5.35 per horse-power year (U. S. Con. Rep., Jan. 23, 1911) in favored locations. This also accounts for the development of electric smelting and the manufacture of nitrate fertilizers in which these countries take a leading place (see chapter on Chemicals).

Fisheries.—The mountains and the sea meet along most of the coast of Norway which is, of all the nations, the most dependent upon fish. With its cool climate, its mountainous rocky land, and its coast full of bays, it duplicates in many respects Nova Scotia, Canada and Labrador, and like them has great fisheries of cod and herring. The cod are caught near the Lofoten Islands and the herring in the bays about Bergen in southern Norway. The catch of fish is about five times as great per capita as in Great Britain. Fish and fish products make up more than a third of Norway's export, and Norwegian codfish, codfish oil, and herring are known in many lands.

Iron.—Sweden is rich in iron ores, of which she mines more per capita than the United States. A railroad has recently been built from north Sweden across the arctic mountains to the Norwegian coast, so that the ore may be exported in the winter. Some of it comes to the United States; most of it goes to England and Germany. Sweden, with the large percentage (52.2) of her area in forests, has had the wood to keep on making charcoal iron, which is superior in quality to that of the coke-fed furnace, and is much sought by blacksmiths and machinists in many countries. For example, Sheffield (England) cutlery is made of Swedish iron, and the Swedish production of charcoal iron is now giving rise to the manufacture of high-grade machinery in Sweden.

Agriculture in the Scandinavian peninsula is a combat with rigorous nature. We see the influences of the cold in the relative value of the crops. In Sweden oats and potatoes come first, then rye, then barley, and lastly a little wheat. Most of the breadstuff is imported. The winter is long, and hay is so vastly important that the poor peasant must in some unfavorable locations actually spread the grass out under sheds to protect it from the rain until it dries, and then shelter it for winter use. To get it to the barn it is at times brought down from heights on trolleys, traveling on wire cables. Such laborious conditions of agriculture as this explain the emigration of Scandinavians to America, and we see why people who had been able to live in such a country quickly prosper in roomy America, with its more favorable climate and many opportunities.

The southern parts of Sweden, which are just across the sounds from Denmark, have also recently learned the art of making good butter; and this country, which in 1870 was a butter importer, is rapidly increasing its butter exports to Great Britain, over $6,000-000 worth being shipped there annually.

In the extreme north of Norway and Sweden there is more arctic moss than grass, and the reindeer becomes beast of burden, milk animal, meat animal, supply crop and money crop of the Laplander. This animal is the mainstay of arctic man from Norway to the Bering Sea.

Textiles and coal.—There is some textile manufacturing in Sweden, and manufacturing industries are developing scientifically and rapidly like those of Germany and Switzerland. There is a little coal mined in Sweden, but the supply is inadequate and several million tons are imported from England.

QUESTIONS

1. How do the natural conditions enable Sweden to make iron of unusual quality?

2. Why may we expect manufacturing in Sweden to develop more than agriculture?

3. Why did the geographic conditions of Norway produce a race of bold sea rovers?

CHAPTER XXIX

AUSTRIA-HUNGARY AND ROUMANIA

The empire of Austria-Hungary is made up of the kingdoms of Austria and Hungary and a number of minor states with so many races that eleven languages are officially recognized in the Imperial Parliament. (Austria has an area of 115,000 square miles and 26 million population; Hungary, 125,000 square miles and 15.7 million population.) Racial differences and strifes for dominance have made it a country of great political and social unrest, and greatly retarded its industrial and commercial development.

Austria, comprising the western end of the empire, is a continuation of Germany except in government. The navigable Danube flows from south Germany into south Austria. The navigable Elbe flows from north Austria into central Germany and carries Austrian commerce to Hamburg. As between Canada and the United States, so between Austria and Germany there is similarity of race, language, culture, religion, and form of government and absence of natural lines of separation. They use the same navigable rivers, the same railways, the same ports, grow the same sugar beets, have the same intensive agriculture, make the same substitute cocoanut butter, and have a similar manufacturing development in textiles, small metal wares and glass. Bohemian colored glass is famed. Austria has a much poorer commercial situation than Germany and is an insignificant iron maker because her ore and coal fields are separated, and the land transport necessary to assemble material of only moderate richness is too costly. Her iron-ore district is located in the populous and manufacturing state of Bohemia, in the Elbe Valley, adjacent to Germany, and the coal in districts to the southwest of Vienna.

The chief difference between these two Germanic states is that Austria, having the eastern Alps and other mountains has more forest (34 per cent to 24 per cent) than Germany and is an exporter of oak timber.

The Danube Valley.—Hungary, with its capital at Budapest, is primarily an agricultural country. The valleys of the Danube and its branch, the Theiss, spread out into a large expanse of level plain. This plain extends to the Black Sea, except for the interruption of the Carpathian Mountains, which separate Hungary from Roumania. In the lower Danube Valley and adjacent districts of the Black Sea basin is a corn zone second in importance only to that of the United States. The crop of this region is from 350 to 400 million bushels a year, about one-tenth of the world's supply, and about equal to the crop of Illinois, our leading corn state. Although occupied by several different nations, the lower Danube Valley is, like our corn belt, one economic region. Corn is extensively grown on the great fertile plains of Hungary and Roumania, also Servia, Bulgaria, and the nearby territory of Russia on the Black Sea. The greater part of Russia and the regions to the north of the lower Danube Valley and to the west of Hungary are too cold for corn growing. Farther to the eastward the climate becomes too dry, so that the Volga basin, near the Caspian Sea, does not produce any tilled crops.

The Black Sea basin is a land where droughts come with ever-increasing frequency as one goes eastward. The sure relation between labor and harvest in Illinois and the great uncertainty in Roumania are enough to explain why one region is filled with progressive and aggressive farmers and townsmen and the other with poor and rather backward peasants using oxen for work animals (Fig. 219). Despite these handicaps Roumania, by exporting two-fifths of her crop, manages to send to the foreign markets about one-third as much corn as does the United States.

Austria-Hungary produces about as much corn as Indiana, Roumania somewhat less than Oklahoma, and Russia somewhat less than South Carolina. The bulk of the population in this corn region is rather poor. They depend for breadstuff almost entirely upon corn, exporting to western Europe the wheat which they also grow. They also export some corn to western Europe. Of the cultivated land in Roumania one-third (or one-sixth of the total area) is in wheat and over one-third is in corn.

Roumania exported in 1907–10 from one-fourth to one-half as much wheat as did the United States. Steamers by the hundred load grain for west Europe at the ports of Galatz, Braila, and Sulina on the lower Danube.

Hungary grows nearly twice as much corn as Roumania (187 million bushels, 1910), but consumes nearly all of it within her own boundaries. The manufacturing populations of Austria also consume practically all of the wheat grown within the empire. The center of the Hungarian plain is rather arid, and so is largely given over to pastures, being well known for its horses and mules.

Roumania has an oil field with a small output. It is the only oil field in Europe except that in southeast Russia.

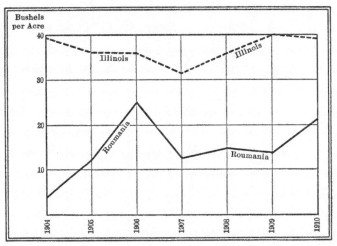

FIG. 219.—A comparison of the yield of corn per acre of Roumania and Illinois.

QUESTIONS

1. What are the natural conditions that cause Hungary to raise corn and Bohemia to raise beets?

2. How is Germany better equipped than Austria to make iron?

3. How does the climate make the corn growers of Roumania poorer than the corn growers of Illinois?

CHAPTER XXX

THE BALKAN STATES

History.—Bulgaria, Servia, Montenegro, and Albania, the four countries that divide the Balkan Mountains and part of the Danube plain to the north of it, have puzzled the world by their outbursts of hatred, valor, and rapine. Yet they are a natural product of environment and history.

In 1683 John Sobieski, the heroic Pole, helped the Austrians drive the Turks away from Vienna, which they were besieging in their westward conquering march. The Turks were driven back into the Balkans, an orderless, systemless chaos of mountains and little valleys, very difficult of access. Such places naturally lag behind in human progress, and the development of feuds between the people of different valleys is a common and world-wide occurrence. Long before the Turks got possession of the Balkans these mountains had been possessed and peopled by various branches of the Slavic race. On these peoples the Turks have exercised their genius for tyranny and misgovernment down to the present generation. This combination of conditions tended strongly to perpetuate the conditions of the Middle Ages.

Poverty of the Balkan peoples.—Meanwhile the people have remained poor, partly from misgovernment and tyranny, which have caused agriculture to be of the most primitive sort, and have limited manufacture to the household system. The latter condition still continues to a large extent. The possession of property in the land of the Turkish tax-gatherer is dangerous. It makes its owner risk loss of his property, and also torture if he does not surrender it quickly. The people are poor also from sheer overpopulation: 100 to 130 people to the square mile is too much for such resources and such industries to support in comfort.

The resources of the region are meager; much of it is semi-arid, and too rough for tillage, so that the mainstay of the people of the hills is flocks of sheep and goats, and of swine that eat acorns in the forests. In the valleys they grow wheat, barley, and corn, the latter being the mainstay. Thus Bulgaria and Servia are wheat exporters, and pork, sent largely to Austria, is the chief export of Servia. From the Servian forests oak staves for wine casks are exported to Austria and France. We see signs of the intensification of industry and limited resource in the export of plums, plum marmalade, and of silk from Servia, and in the production of attar of roses. The growers of Damascus roses in Bulgaria give to the western world its supply of this precious perfume. Its costliness results from the payment of from 3 to 5 cents per pound for the flowers, of which from 160 to 225 pounds are required to distill an ounce of the attar.

So mediæval, so undeveloped are parts of these countries that the people of Albania were in civil war in 1914 at the suggestion that they should pay taxes. Much of the Balkans has never had a census, and much of it is utterly without roads. As a measure of their poverty, it is estimated that there is one horse to eighty people in Montenegro. The common draft animal is the ox. This beast is slow, but is possessed of two prime requisites for a poor country. He does not need grain as does the horse. He can eat the straw while man eats the grain, and later man can eat the ox—the work beast of poverty.

The introduction of the long-range, high-power repeating rifle into this land of mediæval industry, mediæval concepts, poverty, ignorance, racial jealousies and old feuds, has produced untoward results in the fearful civil war that followed their successful war against Turkey. Their primitive industry enables them to carry on a war better than a richer commercial people might have done. At the end of harvest, 1912, the Balkan peasants and shepherds shouldered their rifles, took their bundles of homespun clothes, drove their flocks before them for food and let the wagon loads of grain follow. Thus were the armies equipped to drive the Turk from Europe in the first year that the Balkan peoples ever acted together. If ever people needed a benevolent despot, it is these 10 million who occupy about 100,000 inaccessible square miles in the Balkans. While benevolent despotism is the best kind of government, history records no means of keeping despots benevolent. For 500 years they have had malevolent despotism, and for the last half century they have been and still are the pawns of the European powers in the game of empire.

QUESTIONS

1. Why are the Montenegrins a pastoral people?
2. How has topography developed hatred in the Balkans?
3. Why is the slow ox preferred to the horse as a draft animal in some countries but not in the United States?

CHAPTER XXXI

THE RUSSIAN EMPIRE

Resources and people.—Writers like to call Russia, with its vast area of 8,647,000 square miles, and its population of 163 million people, sleepy, torpid, undeveloped. All these things are true, but if resources make men and nations, then the Russian Empire has a great future. With an area two and one-half times that of the United States, and twice as big as all Europe, this empire has greater proved resources, land and climate considered, than any other nation. She began in the kingdom of Muscovy near Moscow and gradually conquered her way northwest to the Baltic Sea, southwest to the Black Sea, eastward to the Pacific Ocean, southward to the backbone of Asia, and her rivals fear that she will get to the Indian Ocean through Persia.

She now extends from the land of reindeer to the land of corn and cotton, although there is not much corn or cotton. To make amends, she has the greatest wheat resources of any nation, possibly as great as any two nations, and it is in a climate that we know to be healthful and clear of any taint of enervation through too much heat, although some of it benumbs man by the severe cold of its continental winter.

Much of this land resource is unused. The nation is and has been a heavy borrower, as is shown by her imports of goods worth $410,000,000 and exports of $560,000,000 in which we see interest going to the owners of Russian enterprises, especially the French. Much of the human resource is also unused. Thus far the Russian has not acquired the proper attitude toward enterprise and as a result many of the factories and other capitalistic enterprises of Russia are not only owned, but are also managed by the foreigner—German, English, French, American. It is undoubtedly true that incompetence reigns in the government and in most organized Russian activities. Millions of the peasants are ignorant and the production of the country is therefore far less efficiently carried on than it might be (Fig. 220). But she has the resources, human and material, and a good climate.

428

The Russian Empire is still primarily an agricultural region. An iron production, mostly near the Black Sea, of a tenth that of the United States and a coal production of about a fifteenth that of the United States, prove the infancy of Russian manufacture. Her export of manufactures is negligible, and her import extensive and varied.

Russia is a region so devoid of any strong divisions by mountains that canals can cross Russia proper or Siberia in nearly all directions.

FIG. 220.—Russian thrashing floor of type common in eastern Mediterranean countries. The grooved stone rolls after the horse and shatters the grain from the straw. The man throws the straw out with a fork.

It is like the plains of Illinois and Canada. Even the Urals are low and easily crossed, but climatic differences divide the empire into natural zones of production.

Zones of production.—In the extreme north is the arctic tundra occupied by reindeer-tending Lapps, Samoyeds, and other tribes of Mongolian race (like the Eskimo). There, as in North America where the forest occupies the great central plain north of the Canadian wheat belt, the Eurasian forest finds, chiefly through the lessened evaporation of high latitudes, enough moisture to take possession of the plain. Thus the forests of Sweden are matched across the Gulf of Bothnia by the forests of Finland which continue almost without a break through more than a hundred degrees of longitude to the

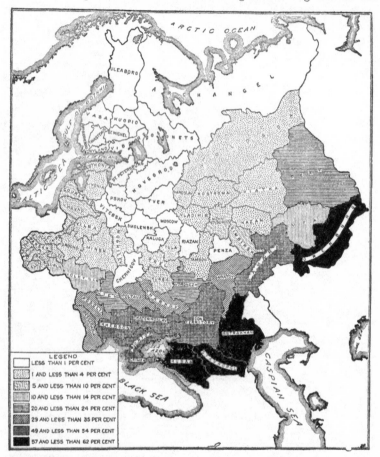

FIG. 221.—Map of Russia showing proportion of land in wheat. (From "Russia's Wheat Surplus," by I. M. Rubinow. U. S. Dept. of Agriculture, Bureau of Statistics, Bulletin 42.)

Pacific shores. The reason of Russia's large export of lumber from Baltic and White Sea ports to England, France, Germany, and Holland is thus very plain. It is also plain why her forests, like those of the United States, have been so ill cared for—they were so plentiful. The forests of European Russia alone, covering 40 per cent of her area, or 800,000 square miles, are greater in extent than the total area of the United Kingdom, France, Germany and Austria-Hungary combined. This forest zone is of large extent in Siberia between the tundra on the north and the grain-growing plains on the south. In the Amur Valley of eastern Siberia it is estimated that 20 per cent of the area of 400,000 square miles is forest covered. Compare this with the 55,000 square miles of German forest, or the 81,000 square miles of Austro-Hungarian forest, and we begin to grasp the magnitude of the Russian resources.

In this forest zone of northwest Russia is Finland, a conquered Scandinavian province with 3 million people. Aside from wood and wood manufactures, they are supporting themselves by agriculture, plainly marked by the sub-arctic climate (it is all north of Sitka and south Greenland). Oats and potatoes are the chief crops, followed by rye and barley, and there is not enough wheat grown to keep the people a week in the year.

As we go south from the land of the north Russians to the central region, we come to the eastward extension of the German plain with its German crops of sugar beets, rye, barley, oats, and potatoes, with grain exports to west Europe through Riga, Libau, and Königsberg on the Baltic. In southern Russia in the drainage basins of the Black and Caspian Seas are the black earth steppes or plains, famous for the production of wheat which is largely exported from Odessa and other Black Sea ports (Fig. 221). Altogether Russia produces more wheat than the United States—about a billion bushels. She usually ex-

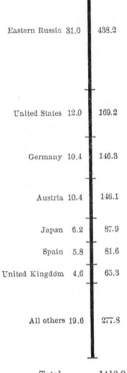

	Percentage	Million Bushels
Eastern Russia	31.0	438.2
United States	12.0	169.2
Germany	10.4	146.3
Austria	10.4	146.1
Japan	6.2	87.9
Spain	5.8	81.6
United Kingdom	4.6	65.3
All others	19.6	277.8
Total		1412.0

FIG. 222.—World's barley production, three-year average, 1909–11.

ports twice as much wheat as we do, because her own people eat the cheaper rye of which she raises half the world's supply. She nearly matches us in oat production, nearly triples our barley product (Fig. 222), but her total grain crop of about 4 billion bushels does not exceed that of the United States because of our huge corn production. The bulk of our grain crop, corn, is for animal food in a country of prosperous, meat-eating people, and the bulk of Russian grain crop is rye and wheat for human food in a country of poor people.

The arid belt so common in the middle of temperate zone continents begins with 300,000 square miles of cowboy pasture lands with nomad Cossacks in the Caspian basin, and goes on through Siberia to Turkestan and Mongolia, making the agricultural belt of Siberia much narrower from North to South than is that of western Russia. Nevertheless it is of vast extent, and there is little doubt that the great Siberian plain reaching nearly all the way from Lake Baikal to the Urals, and closely resembling in its black flatness much of the Canadian wheat country, is the most promising future wheat exporter of the Old World, and certainly a good rival of North America.

Now that the Trans-Siberian railway has made possible the export of grain the Russian peasant exploits these new lands in the same one-crop way that the Italian uses in Argentina and the American, in Dakota or Saskatchewan. After a time these Siberians also must rotate crops, keep cattle, and export butter and eggs to London, as do their brethren in the older and more developed lands of Russia and west Siberia.

The settlement of Siberia has but begun. It has only 8 million people, and the Trans-Siberian railway is newer than the Canadian Pacific. It is a great misfortune that the Siberian plains, drained to the frozen Arctic and shut off by mountains from the southern sea, have the worst situation of all wheat exporters with regard to the sea. The Siberian crop must make the long rail journey to the Baltic unaided by any such gift of nature as the American Great Lakes or the Danube River. For this reason the Siberian plain has been the last of the world's great plains to be settled. The recent railroads have enabled it to become a wheat exporter, but its crop combined with that of the adjacent provinces of central Asia amounted to but 62 million bushels in 1911, while that of North Dakota was 73 million (90 in 1910). But Siberia has the resources of great area, fertile soil, and the population of Russia promises plenty of immigrants.

The long cold winter and lack of corn keeps Russia from rivaling the United States in domestic animals. She has only one-fourth as many swine and about two-thirds as many cattle. The effort to get a crop to sell in central Russia and western Siberia is causing a large export of butter and eggs (marks of intensive agriculture) to the British markets.

The discovery and breeding of new crops that can extend agriculture farther into the regions of cold or aridity have enormous possibilities in an empire that stretches half-way around the world (the land part) with one cold edge and one dry edge. We already know how to utilize the low-grade coal which (as in Montana and Canada) underlies large areas of the Russian plain.

Minerals.—The flat nature of most of Russia tends to minimize the mineral wealth, but the Caucasus region is mountainous and has a considerable output of iron, copper, manganese, and petroleum. Evidences of petroleum exist from the Crimea in the Black Sea eastward along both slopes of the Caucasus Mountains and along the Persian frontier to the city of Merv, but nearly all the oil thus far produced in this large region has come from the small field around the town of Baku on the Apsheron Peninsula which projects into the Caspian Sea near the end of the Caucasus Mountain range. All the American fields together were at times distanced (before 1900) by this single great field of Russia. It has had a greater proportion of naturally flowing wells than any other field, and several wells have yielded as much as a million gallons of oil per day for several days in succession, a record that was unexcelled until the discoveries of the Beaumont, Texas, and the Mexican fields.

The Urals produce platinum, and the mountains of Siberia are the chief producers of Russian gold, the output of which is about one-fourth as valuable as that of the United States. The vast and largely unprospected area of the Russian Empire may be expected to yield many mineral discoveries.

The future of Russia.—There are reasons, based on Russia's natural resources, for the German plea at the outbreak of the year of 1914 that if she should be crushed, Russia would become the dominating world power. By mere flat size Russia ruined the mighty Napoleon.[1] But Russia will remain undeveloped until

[1] Holland, with ships and manufactures, was the great power in 1650 when England was agricultural and the Continent was landlocked. From 1815 to 1900 Britain, with coal, iron factories, and ships, was the great power. The war of 1914 is attributed to Germany's rivalry for this power, based on the growth of her industry, for which the materials are meager compared to those of Russia if they were utilized as well as those of Germany.

psychological and intellectual changes come to her people. Canada and the American West are also undeveloped, but they have the advantage of being peopled with the most progressive of west Europeans, while Russia has the handicap of a population of millions of semi-Asiatics who must be waked up, educated, and made over, as Japan is making over her millions.

QUESTIONS

1. Why does Russia exceed the United States in rye, but not in corn?

2. How do climatic conditions give Russia nomadic peoples in the northwest and in the southeast?

3. What natural reasons have kept Russia so far behind England in manufactures? Which has the greater natural resources for manufacturing?

4. Why does Russia grow flax for fiber and Dakota grow it for seed? (See chapter on Textiles and chapter on United Kingdom.)

5. Who owns Russian factories and what effect does it have on the relative value of her exports and imports.

6. Why does north Russia have the basis for the production of fine leather? (See chapter on Leather and Rubber.)

7. How does the surface of the country encourage transportation and how has it encouraged the growth of the empire? Compare with Balkans in this respect.

CHAPTER XXXII

THE NORTH MEDITERRANEAN LANDS

If South Carolina, Georgia, Alabama, and Mississippi happened to be four peninsulas jutting into the Gulf of Mexico, no one would think of giving each of them a complete description, because in

FIG. 223.—The donkey, servant of the peddler of American oil in Portugal (Standard Oil Co.) This wasteful pack transportation is used to a surprising extent in Spain and Portugal, and often where roads do not require it.

many respects they are all alike. The same is true of the Iberian, Italian, Greek, and Asia Minor peninsulas. They are bathed by the same Mediterranean, have the same climate, and therefore great similarity in products despite the great difference in their history.

The prime fact to remember about these lands is that they have a winter rain, a mild winter, and an almost rainless summer. This limits their extensive grain growing to wheat and barley (see chapter on Cereals). In addition to these winter grains agriculture depends first on irrigated patches where, in some little valley, water can be obtained. Where this can be had the hot summer permits the growth of rice and corn, but like wheat, the supply of these is nowhere sufficient for home use. Corn, being the cheapest of the grains, is extensively used as food—even cold corn bread, soggy at that, is relished by millions.

FIG. 224.—Herd of goats waiting to be milked at the door of the customer, Granada, Spain.

The next dependence of agriculture is on drought-resisting crops that can yield without irrigation or summer rain. The dry summer limits alike the agricultural land and the forest land, and leaves a large proportion of land for pasture, but this same drought, of course, leaves the pastures brown and dead except on the higher mountains where the rainfall is greater. The animals, like the crops, therefore tend to be of the drought-resisting sort. In place of the horse we find the mule and the ass, especially noted for their ability to survive coarse and scanty fare (Fig. 223). Spain exports the best breeding asses in the world. In place of the cow, the milch goat is a more common milk animal because it can get along without the green pasture. Bushes suffice for it (Fig. 224).

The olive is one of the neatest adjustments to the environment. It survives the drought because it is deep-rooted and evergreen, with a leaf hairy below and glazed above. It yields an oil that keeps for years and replaces butter and fat bacon in a land that is not well equipped to keep either cows or pigs. It is the great butter substi-

Fig. 225.—Land near Granada, Spain, ruined by erosion. The gullies are 200 feet deep. The shiny places on top are all that remains of the original surface.

tute of the Mediterranean climate. It grows everywhere and thrives in poor and stony ground. It lives for centuries, and in Spain it covers as much ground proportionally as does wheat in the United States. It is a tree crop, a crop type of which the Mediterranean lands make great use. "The almond is high in protein, the great factor in meat. The walnut is high in both protein and fat; the oil of the olive is more nutritious than butter and far more nutritious than any flesh of animals. The fig is a real food, containing some protein and much carbohydrate, and a greater amount of nutriment per pound than bread."[1]   The grape is a deep-rooting water searcher, so that wine production comes naturally into importance along the Mediterranean.

FIG. 226.—Part of the same slope as that in Fig. 225, steeper than a house roof, but, protected from erosion by oak trees. This forest is used as a range for hogs which fatten on acorns from the oak trees shown in picture.

All of these countries have been historic for over 2,000 years.   All have suffered great wasting of resources (Fig. 225), and all are over-populated in comparison to America and in relation to their resources.

[1] From *The Agriculture of the Garden of Eden*, by J. Russell Smith, in the Atlantic Monthly, August, 1914.

Being scantily forested, brick and stone are the universal building materials[1] (Fig. 227). All are without coal, and fuel is therefore scarce; suffering from cold is common in "sunny" Spain and "sunny" Italy. Being devoid of coal and meagerly supplied with water-power (because of summer drought), the development of manufactures has been greatly retarded and the heavy emigration from these countries to lands of greater resources and opportunity is most natural.

Fig. 227.—Underground houses. Thousands of people live in such homes in dry and treeless south-eastern Spain.

The heavy population and the climatic limitations on the animal industries make meat scarce. Italy has but 7 per cent as many cattle as people (compare the United States, see Animal Industries), and many of these are oxen. The ox is the commonest work animal of the north Mediterranean. The scarcity of protein food in the form of meat and milk causes the people of the Mediterranean to turn, therefore, to the cheaper forms of peas and beans. The gram or chick pea is said to be the leading article of diet in Spain, and is also greatly used by other Mediterranean people, including those of Mo-

[1] The Italian earthquakes are so destructive to life because the usual type of dwelling has arched masonry roofs and ceilings which fall upon the sleeping inhabitants.

rocco, Algeria, and Tunis, whence it is carried by caravans into the desert in exchange for dates. In the agriculture of the eastern United States we have no substitutes for the chick pea and, its partner, the fève or French bean. Both can survive some freezing and, like wheat, grow in the open rainy Mediterranean winter and ripen in the beginning of the rainless summer. These plants are priceless to such lands. Lentils, vetch, and lupine, other pod-bearing pulse plants somewhat like our peas and beans, are much grown throughout all Mediterranean countries, and from the Isle of Cyprus there is considerable export of the flat beans of the carob tree, a legume sometimes called locusts. It is widely used as a substitute for oats in horse feeding and is said to have been the food of John the Baptist in the wilderness.

The north Mediterranean countries are all mountainous, a condition which limits their agriculture; but they contain many little valleys protected from north winds by the mountains and warmed on the south by the sea thus much favored for the growth of early vegetables (Fig. 229). Where transportation to northern markets is good, as in Spain, Portugal and Italy, this gives rise to a trade with north Europe like that from Florida and California to northern cities.

Spain and Portugal.—Spain and Portugal depend on agriculture more than does Italy, yet Spain has not enough wheat or corn to feed her people. As Portugal is exposed to the Atlantic, it has more rain than Spain or Italy. Some corn is raised there without irrigation, but the yield is not high. The cattle and hogs of Spain are only one-ninth as numerous per capita as in the United States, but her sheep are slightly more numerous. Both of these countries have large possibility of increased agricultural production. Their backwardness arises chiefly from the fact that men of ability cannot attend to industry without losing social position. The Spanish and Portuguese have ruled subject empires so long that only military and official positions are considered honorable, and if not in office, one must at least be at leisure. Respectability demands that the gentleman must be at the café, which is his club, and his estate is in the hands of the ignorant. Thus scientific agriculture is still waiting to be introduced into much of these naturally rich countries. When one considers land, labor, and markets, the Iberian Peninsula offers some of the most wonderful openings in the world to the enterprising scientific agriculturist.

The people must work for low wages, because, through ignorance and bad methods, their output is small. A few years ago cork forests in central Portugal were being grubbed for the removal of undesired bushes by gangs of women from the more populous Oporto district. They worked for $3 per month and their board, slept on piles of evergreen brush around the central fire in a big circular hut, and ate nothing but corn-meal mush, fifteen parts to one part olive oil. They had all they wanted of it and it was better than they were used to, for they went back to their little farms in the spring in better condition than they came. This occurred on the very edge of large expanses of good but untilled land.

The railways of Spain and Portugal, the banks, the factories, the mines, and many of the landed estates usually belong to the foreigners—English, French, German. At the outbreak of the war of 1914 large hydro-electric works being constructed by English and American engineers near the Pyrenees were discontinued because the money supply, which came from France and Belgium, ceased.

The chief exports of Portugal are wine and cork. Cork is the outer bark of one of the oaks which lives for a century or two, and can be stripped of its bark, worth $75 per ton, every 9 or 10 years (Fig. 228). It is an excellent crop for the absentee landlord because it requires almost no care. It has probably helped to make the absentee landlord. He is further aided by the fact that these oaks and the evergreen oak (ilex) yield acorns which automatically produce half the pork of Portugal, since the hogs range the forests and gather them.

Spain also exports cork from her southwestern and northeastern provinces, and from the fertile shore plains by Cadiz, Malaga, Almeria and Valencia there is a great export of fruit, grapes, raisins, onions, wine, early potatoes and other vegetables by steamer to the North. Valencia oranges (irrigated) are famed. The agriculture on these favored plains is very intensive and is well carried on by small proprietors.

Aside from wine, the chief exports of Spain are minerals from the foreign-owned mines; iron on the Biscay shore at Bilbao, quicksilver at Almaden, and copper and sulphur at Rio Tinto. Spain is rich in minerals. Barcelona, the capital of Catalonia, is the chief port and a hustling manufacturing city with a growing export of textiles. The people of Catalonia are more enterprising than those of the south of Spain and are so democratic that they are a menace to the monarchy.

Italy has several advantages over Spain. Her past has left treasures that make her a cherished center of travel, and the beautiful

Riviera, the coast of the Gulf of Genoa between the protecting Alps and the blue Mediterranean, is, as a winter resort, the combined California and Florida of Europe. The southern Alps with their wonderfully beautiful lakes, Como, Garda, Lugano, and Maggiore, are also enriched by the tourist, but better than these as a source

FIG. 228.—Stripping cork in Portugal.

of human support are the water-power from the snow-fed Alpine branches of the Po and the irrigation of the fertile plain of Lombardy with its waters. Turin and Milan are manufacturing centers thriving on hydro-electric power and often using British capital. The Alpine streams furnish water for succulent pastures and hay crops, as many as 9 per year in some places. These are responsible for the famous Milan butter and for the few brands of Italian cheese that are well known in many countries of the world. One of these, the Parmesan cheese, is made of goat's milk. Cheaper cheeses are imported into Italy to feed her own people just as the Dutch and Danes import oleomargarine from Chicago for their own use and sell the butter that they make.

Even more important than these dairy exports are the silk exports which this same Alpine water produces through the indirect means of nourishing the mulberry tree upon the leaves of which the silkworm feeds.

Italy depends more upon grapes and wine growing than does any other nation. The limestone hills and dry summer permit grapes

to thrive better than most other crops (Fig. 231), and they are grown
in all parts of the country.   Vineyards cover not less than 15,000

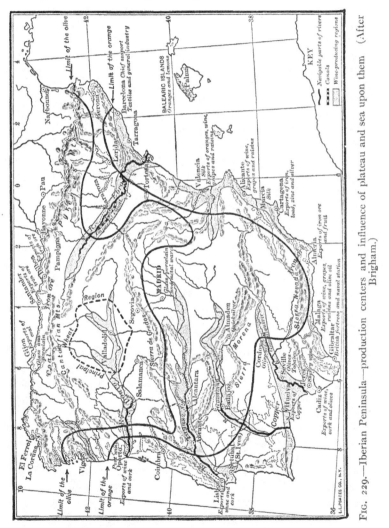

Fig. 229.—Iberian Peninsula—production centers and influence of plateau and sea upon them   (After Brigham.)

square miles of territory or about one-seventh the entire area of the
kingdom, one-sixth of all used ground, and one-half as much land

FIG. 230.—Italian wheat fields planted with trees which serve as vine supports. The trees are kept cut back except two long branches which are tied to those of adjacent trees. Land is prepared and crop cut by hand.

FIG. 231.—Terraced slopes of rich lava soil on Mt. Etna (elevation about 2,000 feet) used for vineyards, a vast monument to patient labor. One of the many small craters in the distance.

as all the grain crops combined.   These figures become more significant in comparison with the corn crop of the United States, which
covers about one-seventeenth the area of the country.

The citrous fruit industry is important in Italy.   There is an
orange or lemon tree for every two persons in the whole country.
Although the orange reaches its highest northern latitude for the

FIG. 232.—Slopes of Etna near agricultural limit (about 3,000 feet). At right,
clumps of chestnut shoots four or five years old, growing from a stump. The
twigs have been removed for fuel. When the shoots are seven years old they
will be cut for vine supports. Chestnut trees in foreground. The whole slope
is covered by blooming clover, ready to be cut for hay. It will be cut by hand
and taken down on pack animals.

world, 44°, on the protected coast of Italy not far from Genoa, it
is not important north of Rome, and the lemon, being more susceptible to cold, will not grow north of Rome at all.   Sicily greatly
predominates over the mainland in the products of both these fruits,
having almost a monopoly of the production of lemons, which have
for a century been distributed to the lemon-consuming regions of
Europe and America.   The Italian and Sicilian peasants give these

fruits the greatest care. South of Naples they can only be grown in those few spots that can be irrigated. The ground is usually cultivated with the hoe and the spade, while garden crops are often grown between the trees. Much of the soil is so steep that it is kept from washing into the Mediterranean only by the laborious building of terraces restrained by stone walls. It is chiefly this intensive kind of agricultural industry that has given to rugged and arid Sicily a population of 300 persons to the square mile (Figs. 230, 232).

It is interesting to note that it is south Italy, rather than north Italy with its water-power, that furnishes most of the emigrants. We see the Italian attempts to get along with little land in the manufacture of perfumery along the Riviera, oil of jasmine, oil of violets, oil of geranium, while in Sicily and Calabria they manufacture orange and lemon oil. There is still much household manufacture (Fig. 233).

Fig. 233.—Woman in an Apennine village spinning wool yarn by hand. She sets the top-like ball of yarn, which is wound upon a stick, to spinning and with her fingers regulates the fineness of the yarn. When she has spun three or four feet she winds it up makes a half hitch over the end of the stick and spins the ball again.

Greece.—(Area, 1910, 25,000 square miles, population, 1910, 2⅔ million.) Like Italy and Spain, Greece, rugged and mountainous, has its wheat, olives, wine, oranges, rice, goats, oxen, and backward agiculture. By far the greatest export is the currant so called, a dried grape grown extensively on certain peculiar soils. The production is over 150,000 tons per year and the chief use is for the manufacture of wine in west Europe.

Asia Minor and Turkey are in a sad economic condition, having suffered from the blight of the Turk, who has a genius for misgovernment (see Balkans). Tobacco is an important export from both European and Asiatic Turkey. Several million dollars worth of Valonia acorn cups for tannin are picked up annually in the forests and exported to west Europe. Smyrna is a great fig-exporting center and from the province of Angora in central Asia Minor, the home of the Angora goat, comes an export of the mohair produced by this animal. Asia Minor is more arid than the other north Mediterranean regions, and agriculture will be greatly benefited by the construction of large irrigation works for which the Young Turk Government has given concessions to European capitalists. Good cotton is being grown and the output will increase the importance of the Bagdad railway which is already built by European capital from Constantinople nearly to the Euphrates, and will help increase the already great importance of Constantinople as a metropolis of Levantine trade.

QUESTIONS

1. How have Spanish conquests in America injured Spanish agriculture?

2. Why do the north Mediterranean people use oxen? (See Balkans.)

3. How is the olive an adjustment to the environment and the needs of the Mediterranean peoples?

4. Why does Sicily have more emigration than Lombardy?

5. Compare Italy and the United States as to the chief sources of protein in food.

6. What industries do the Alps give Italy?

7. Who owns the important industries of the Iberian Peninsula?

CHAPTER XXXIII

THE TRADE AND ROUTES OF EUROPE

Comparisons with America.—The trade of the different European countries with each other is of great extent and closely resembles the trade of temperate North America. Each of these regions has, in the region of middle temperature, facing the Atlantic, a large territory with manufacturing people buying food and raw materials. In America it reaches from Chicago to the Atlantic, and from Canada to the Maryland boundary, and in Europe, from Berlin to Vienna, the Alps and the ocean. Farther in the interior lie the grain- and meat-producing plains, in the north are water-power and forests with their wood output, in the south the land of fruits and early vegetables. Europe lacks the corn and cotton belt, but has instead a great extent of wheat-, barley-, oats-, and rye-land in her mid region.

In the ease of this exchange of food and raw materials for manufactures, Europe has been favored more than North America, more than any other continent. The peninsular form and irregular coast lines, 20,000 miles in extent, make short and easy communications between the interior and the sea, the cheapest of all highways. Hence, it is natural that the greatest trade routes of Europe should be water routes, and that its railway mileage should be relatively low (Fig. 234).

Trade is further favored by the location of the inland seas that indent the European coast. In the north, as in the south, a succession of seas penetrates to the very center of the continent. The only comparison would be the American Great Lakes if they were navigable at all times by ocean vessels (Fig. 235). The Black Sea extends the advantage of the great ocean 50° eastward from western Spain. This may properly be called the most magnificent system of inland waterways in the world. Its waters give ocean transport to ten independent countries and many colonies. Through the navigable rivers of south Russia and the great Danube, it reaches far into the heart of Europe. The Baltic is almost equally favorable for northern Europe. Between these northern and southern seas,

448

Europe is but a great peninsula, fringed with a succession of smaller peninsulas, each having the particular commercial advantages of such

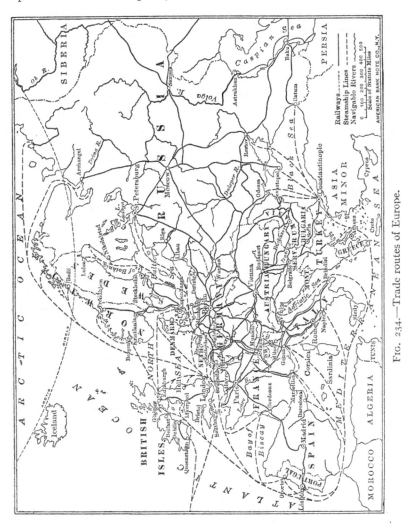

FIG. 234.—Trade routes of Europe.

a position. Further than this, Europe possesses no large isolated plateaus, and it is well supplied with navigable rivers.

Two sets of routes.—The commerce has developed two sets of commercial routes; first, the heavy-traffic routes, which are chiefly water routes; and, second, the fast-traffic routes, which are chiefly overland routes.

Two great heavy-traffic trunk routes are furnished by the southern and northern seas. The secondary heavy-traffic routes, the feeders

FIG. 235.—Navigable waterways in the North Central plain. Compare with Fig. 236. (After J. Paul Goode.)

to these main water routes, are the navigable bays and rivers and the railroads, which like the rivers, run in most cases toward the sea, and carry inland products down to the ports.

The great southern route.—From Gibraltar to Constantinople, the southern route is poor in the branches that navigable rivers furnish. There are two navigable rivers of third-rate importance, the Ebro and the Po, in addition to the second-class Rhone. The Po is practically choked with mud at its mouth—a condition which is usually found in rivers flowing into tideless seas such as the Mediterranean.

The Danube, draining the very center of Europe, and navigable throughout most of its length has had a canal cut through its swampy delta to avoid the dangers of its multitude of broad and shallow mouths, and permits the entrance of ocean-going steamers from west Europe. (See Austria Hungary and Roumania.)

FIG. 236.—An area of the German plain equal to that shown in preceding figure. (After J. Paul Goode.)

The Black Sea traffic is further enriched by the steamers on the Dniester, the Dnieper, and the Don rivers, and by the south Russian railways which help to assemble the Russian wheat and corn at the ports of Odessa, Kherson, Nicolaief, Taganrog, and Rostof, where the tramp steamers congregate in hundreds. Within the Mediterranean there is traffic between two distinct economic districts—a food-importing district and a food-exporting district. While Italy, France,

and Spain are great agricultural countries, they are also manufacturing countries and must import to some extent both food and raw
materials. The east Mediterranean region, comprising the Balkan
states, Turkey, Russia, and Hungary, which reaches navigation at
Fiume on the Adriatic and at the river ports on the lower Danube, is
essentially in the raw material producing stage. Grain and other
agricultural products are the chief exports, and to these, the east end
of the Black Sea with ports at Poti and Batum adds ores and vast
petroleum exports. This gives the basis for a lively exchange of
manufactures from the west for the wheat, corn, rye, oats, and oil of
the east Mediterranean.

The great northern route.—The northern waterway of Europe,
terminating at Petrograd and Lulea, is favored by receiving more
navigable rivers than its southern counterpart. Two of these are the
Rhine and the Elbe Rivers, which must be classed as of the first magnitude if measured by the commerce that they carry. The Elbe
carries down to Hamburg the products of central Germany and of
Bohemia. It is also connected with the Danube by canals. The
Rhine has with great labor and expense been made and kept navigable from the dykes of Holland to the waterfalls of Switzerland.
Other contributions of freight to the western and northern seas are
supplied by the Tagus, the Garonne, the Loire, the Seine, the Weser,
the Oder, the Vistula, the Niemen, and the Duna, as well as the canals
which thread the plain of north Europe from the west of France to
central Russia. The gentle topography and easy drainage of north
central Europe thus give many avenues to the sea, and make possible east-west waterways that duplicate to some extent the service
of our Great Lakes (Figs. 235, 236).

Especial emphasis should be laid upon the valleys of the Elbe,
the Rhine, and the Seine, the greatest industrial region on the continent, with efficient and extensive river transportation in addition
to the busy railroads.

The northern route is bifurcated, the lesser branch passing out in
the open sea around the coast of Norway and into the White Sea,
which, despite its Arctic location, has in its port of Archangel a
heavy shipper of lumber and grain, some of the latter from Siberia.
The ports of Norway add their contingent of lumber, also iron
ore, granite and fish.

The work of the heavy traffic routes.—The heavy traffic routes of
European commerce, skirting the continent, and fed by the secondary

routes[1] enumerated above, are served by a multitude of coasting vessels (Fig. 239), both steam and sail, large and small, giving access to every port of Europe and to every country except to Switzerland and Servia; Switzerland has Rhine boats and Servia has Danube boats. It is by ship that the heavy freight of Europe is carried; the traffic in which economy of cost is more important than economy of time.

Utilization of transport resources.—The manufacturing region of northwestern Europe has the most fully developed transport system in the world (Figs. 237, 238). It is a labyrinth of canals, and the rivers

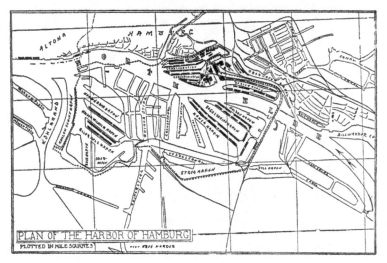

Fig. 237.—A big city on a narrow river must dig many docks. This harbor of Hamburg is typical of many European harbors. (After J. Paul Goode.)

have been improved at great expense. In an area of 800,000 square miles a billion dollars have been expended in waterways (Figs. 235, 236). This, however, is the trifling sum of $2 per acre and it has paid many times over in the increased ease and cheapness of commerce. The results of deliberate effort are shown by the upper Rhine navigation. In 1893 this river was navigable only 70 days between Mannheim and Strassburg, but owing to the deepening and care of the river by the governments of Baden and Alsace-Lorraine it was navigable for 356 days in 1910. In 1909 the Rhine carried 58 million tons of

[1] It is reported that "nearly" nine-tenths of the freight of the Magdeburg district of central Germany is carried by the Elbe. U. S. Con. Rep., No. 8, 1907.

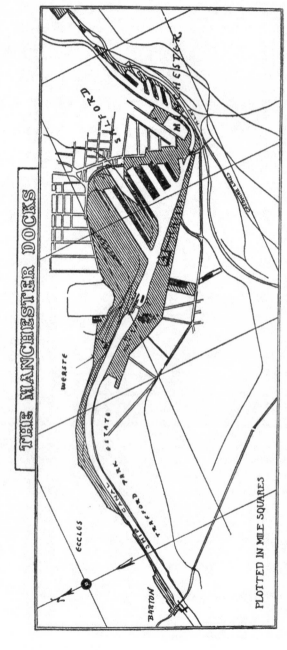

Fig. 238.—The port of Manchester has been made at the end of a 26 mile ship canal. The Trafford Park Estate is being developed for factories and commercial uses and the city is growing in that direction. Commerce is more systematically promoted in Europe than it is in the United States. (After J. Paul Goode.)

freight. The total for Germany of 118 million tons of inland water-borne freight was about six times the United States total of 19 million (exclusive of the Great Lakes traffic). Russia is reported to have 57,000 miles of waterways, Germany 11,000, France 7,800, Austria-Hungary 4,000, England 3,900, Holland, 3,200, Sweden 3,100, Belgium 1,400.

The efficiency of Europe's water routes and the important part that they perform in her commerce is shown by the comparatively small railway mileage. Europe has 20,000 miles less railway than the United States, although the area is slightly larger and the population is four times as great. The railways are not necessary where there is such a wealth of waterways so well utilized as those of Europe. Europe has no such problem as that presented by the transportation to the sea of the vast traffic that seeks an outlet from the American Great Lakes. If she had, her railway mileage would be much greater.

The Volga and the Caspian.—In the class with the great water routes of west Europe is the Russian inland system comprising the Caspian Sea and the Volga River. This is the nearest European counterpart to the American Great Lakes which they fully equal in length, but the commerce is by no means so vast even though the river and the sea stretch from the heart of Russia and Russian industry far into the confines of Asia, and offer an excellent avenue for the trade that arises in districts with heavy products and with reciprocal needs. In the northern part of the Volga's course its navigable western branches drain the manufacturing and commercial regions of Moscow and Novgorod. The northeastern branches come down from the lumber regions. The main course of the river traverses a grain-producing and, in its lower courses, a pastoral region. On the Caspian, the greatest petroleum district in the world lies at the point where the Caucasus Mountains project into the sea. Steamers pass from the coast of Persia to the heart of Russia and connect with canals that go on to the Baltic. There are great fisheries in the Caspian, and fish and petroleum are shipped upstream in exchange for lumber, grain and manufactures.

Express routes.—The mail, passenger, and fast freight service of Europe is well attended to by fast train service that radiates from London with many channel crossings and connects with every capital and important city in Europe. As in the United States there are New York-San Francisco expresses, so in Europe there are expresses from London to Madrid and Gibraltar, Rome and Palermo,

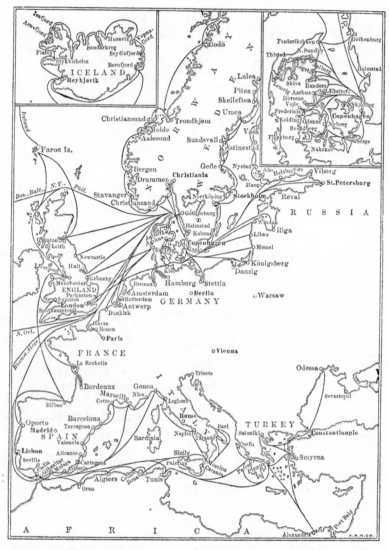

FIG. 239.—The steamer routes of, and ports served by, the leading Danish steamship company with headquarters in Copenhagen—a rising entrepot.

Belgrade, Salonika and Constantinople, Warsaw, Petrograd, Moscow and Siberia.

QUESTIONS

1. Europe has less railroad than the United States. Is this a measure of advantage or disadvantage?

2. Compare Canada and Russia with regard to the ease of exporting grain.

3. What transportation advantage would result if the Danube River had a 6-foot tide?   (See New York in Trade and Routes of the United States.)

4. Explain the basis for reciprocal trade on the Volga.

5. Same for Spain and England; for Germany and Roumania; Holland and Norway.

CHAPTER XXXIV

THE OLD WORLD DESERT AND THE DESERT'S EDGE

The trade winds sweep equatorward from latitude 30° to 35° north and south to about latitude 10° to 15°. They get warmer as they go, and if they come off of the land, they are drying, almost rainless, winds. Thus sand dunes are blowing into the sea at the west point of Africa and the dreaded Sahara envelops the whole width of that continent and

Fig. 240.—Bedouin home. Tent of camel's hair. Flowing robe of homespun wool. Basket of palm leaf fiber. The woman is turning the family mill. Fence of thorns at right to keep the animals out.

the desert is continued (eastward across Asia) by the deserts of Arabia, Mesopotamia, Persia, Afghanistan, Trans-Caspia, Turkestan and Mongolia. It goes on to the vicinity of Pekin where the mountains of Chili and Manchuria shut out the moisture-bearing monsoon winds from the Pacific. Throughout that almost inconceivably long stretch of 4,000 miles in Africa and 5,000 miles in Asia, there is an environment of great uniformity which by its severity holds man in an iron-bound control. Everywhere in this 9,000 miles man lives by means that are greatly similar. Here is the oldest social organization known, that of the Bedouin (Fig. 240) and here in the valley oases of Egypt and Mesopotamia arose the first recorded civilizations.

Here and there throughout the desert and its edges are oases where springs break forth, or ground water comes near the surface, or where streams flow in from regions of better rain as in Egypt and Mesopotamia. This water supply gives irrigation which, with the blazing

FIG. 241.—Desert edge vegetation, Tunis. Rainfall 5 to 10 inches per year. Bare ground with scattered bushes edible for sheep, goats, donkeys and camels.

sun, permits the world's most intense and productive agriculture. This supports oasis, village, and town population. No part of the desert is entirely rainless, and some of it has scanty vegetation (Fig. 241) which permits a little occasional pasturage. This increases in amount on the desert margins, and is finally interspersed with patches of land which will raise a little barley in good seasons. This northern desert's edge partakes of the character of the Mediterranean climate. The rain falling in the winter suits barley—where there is enough of the rain. The pasturage on the desert edge supports the same economic and social type, the nomad—Bedouin, Kurd, Kirghiz, Turkoman, Mongol, Afghan—according to his location.

The nomad, always facing starvation and other dangers, always on the move to find pasture, has been constantly schooled by his environment in the two great resources of the fighter—courage and transport. The environment has also given him hunger, a great motive to war or to plunder. "No episode in all the history of the land has been so common as the raid of the nomads (Fig. 242). From the treeless expanses they swooped down upon the dwellers of the oasis,

FIG. 242.—Wall around Sfax, Tunis, built as a defense against the desert nomads before they were reduced to order by the French.

and drove them forth. The roving nomad was always strong in attack, the dweller in the date garden was always easy prey. One cannot rightly guess the extent of the aeons during which human history in southwest Asia and north Africa consisted of one long and essentially unvaried series of captures and possessions of the oasis gardens, these captures being followed by yet other captures and expulsions at the hands of other hungry victors."[1]

The influence of this environment on the nomad's idea of morality is interesting evidence of the geographers' claim that environment makes man.

[1] "The Agriculture of the Garden of Eden," J. Russell Smith, Atlantic Monthly, August, 1914, p. 257.

"What is an Arab to do when his camels, his sheep, his wife, his children, and himself are all suffering the pangs of hunger? The only resource under such circumstances is plunder. The man who is starving has little thought of right or wrong. To have such thoughts would seem to him fatal. If considerations of humanity or any other moral idea prevent him from engaging in raids upon the tribes around him, the doom of his family is sealed, for his children die of hunger. Thus through the thousands of years since Semitic nomads first lived in Arabia, the hard conditions of climate have steadily weeded out all who withheld their hands from violence.

"The man who would succeed and who would keep his children in health must not only be ready to commit depredations and be utterly dishonest according to our standards, but he must also be strong in the endurance of heat, thirst, and the weariness of long rides; unfortunately, however, he has little need of steady industry or of strength to endure long physical labor. In a word laziness according to our definition of the word, is no great disadvantage provided a man is able to summon up his powers in a crisis when the camels have strayed far away, when they have been driven off by raiders, or when the man himself goes on a foray. Hence the Arab is lazy as well as utterly disregardful of the commonest principles of honesty. Just as he thinks of raids as a part of the ordinary routine of life, so he thinks of steady work as something scarcely to be demanded even of women and fit only for slaves."[1] The career of the Arabs in Spain under another environment is an interesting contrast. With good valleys and water to irrigate them they established and maintained rich cities, splendidly tilled farms, developed science, law and stability, having for a time the highest civilization in Europe.

The nomad lives chiefly on barley bread, milk, cheese, and meat and dates which he buys at the oasis. Being a rover he is in a fine position at intervals to trade wool, skins, animals, or homespun, for dates at the oasis, barley on the edge of the desert, or weapons at the ports. Nomads often stop for a time, raise a crop of barley, bury it for future use or load it on the camels in camel's hair sacks, and proceed.

Aside from the beasts of burden, the goat is the commonest of the nomad's animals. Algeria has 4 million, Asiatic Turkey 9 million, the whole world but 100 million. Cows are rare except in the oases, but fat-tailed sheep are common. The beasts of burden are varied. Throughout the arid region from Morocco to Pekin the mule and the donkey, the short distance burden bearers, climb the hills, thread the mountain passes, browse on the arid plains in companionship with the camel, which braves the worst desert, the ox that draws the creaking cart, and the horse that bears the proud chieftain.

The oasis life is easy, especially west of Persia, because of that wonderful engine of production—the date tree.

[1] From *The Arabian Desert and Human Character*, by Ellsworth Huntington, *Journal of Geog.*, Jan., 1912.

"Now, as for the last five or ten thousand seasons, the date-tree owner begins his year's work in the springtime by climbing his tall trees to fertilize their blossoms. The ascent is easy because of the natural steps furnished by the notchings left by the stubs of the leaves of past years. The blossoms of the fruitful female palm are fertilized by a dust of pollen shaken from a sprig of male flowers in the hand of the husbandman. This economical device permits a very small proportion of male trees to suffice and the garden can be filled to crowding with the productive female trees. Once the blooms are fertilized, little more is done for the tree but watering at rather frequent intervals, and this is often a light task, the mere diversion of a stream. Many of the palms are cultivated only one year in three, but with this small labor they are heavy yielders. The open feathery palm leaves permit much light to filter through, so that oranges, figs, and apricots grow beneath the palms, and garden vegetables can grow among these lesser fruit trees. The vegetables pay the cost, the rest is profit, hence the oasis garden sells for a very high price (Fig. 245).

Fig. 243.—Olive covered hill in Kabylia, northern Algeria.

"Thus the date garden leads all other kinds of agriculture in the amount of food produced, and this tree merits the title of King of Crops. Small wonder that the prehistoric Semite called it sacred. Pound for pound, the date is as nutritious as bread, and when the harvest is weighed, it is three- to twenty-fold that of wheat. After a score of years or less, the best wheat lands are exhausted by continuous production; but we know that certain oases have yielded dates regularly since they were visited and described by Roman writers, a score of centuries ago. They are today so prized that the Arab owner will refuse $5,000 in gold for an acre of good date garden. Its yield warrants the valuation. In May the oasis housetops beside the date garden are covered with drying apricots; in July and again in September the figs are drying; in late autumn comes the great event of the year, the date harvest.

"The surplus dates are sold to caravan traders, who bring barley for the coarse loaf, animals for meat, and manufactures from over the sea. Since the house of sun-dried bricks is small, and keeping it clean is no necessity, the secluded and unlettered woman has plenty of time to run the ancient spinning-wheel, and hand-loom."[1]

We have here the basis of the whole oriental rug business. The oases east of Mesopotamia differ only in the absence of the date tree, and the greater use of grains, so that throughout the whole arid region we have pastures producing camel's hair, goat's hair, wool, and nearby, the dense oasis populations, living the life that preceded Abraham, and with nothing much to do but weave. Further than this the valuable rugs and other fabrics can stand transportation

Fig. 244.—Oil press, oil mill, barley, and native on the outskirts of a Berber village.

any distance, anywhere by caravan, and they keep, with care, for centuries.

In north Africa is yet another type of interesting native life, that of the Berbers.

"The economic service that tree crops can render is well shown by the ancient Berbers who still live in the mountain territory of northern Algeria. They were never conquered by Roman, Goth, Vandal, Arab, or Turk. They made their first obeisance before the firearms of the French, 1857–61. Through all these millenniums they have lived in their populous villages perched high on the tops of steep hills (Fig. 243).[2] Around them in all directions is a zone of trees,

[1] "The Agriculture of the Garden of Eden," by J. Russell Smith, *Atlantic Monthly*, August, 1914, p. 258.

[2] It is such tribes as these, and the dwellers in yet more difficult fastnesses that make the campaigns in Morocco so difficult. Being nearer the Atlantic there is much good grain land in Morocco.

with pasture higher up, beginning at about three thousand feet, and the oft-conquered open valleys below.   Here for unknown ages the Berber has lived among and from his trees (Fig. 244).

"There are four staples of life in Kabylia—dried figs, olives, bread and meat. For miles and miles and miles there is one unending succession of villages set in this open forest of figs and olives (Fig. 243).   Here and there the better spots are picked out for grain fields and a few carobs are grown to spice up the donkey's diet of straw, and make a tidbit for the children (St. John's bread, we call it).   The sheep and goats which pasture beneath the trees furnish an occasional boiled or broiled joint and the much more important wool for the inclusive flowing robe of Arab style.   A diet of dried figs, coarse bread, olives, oil, and occasionally meat, may seem to us somewhat monotonous, but it has long supported a vigorous race.   A recent American agricultural explorer, Mr. Thomas Means, states that the population of this region is twenty-five times as dense where tree crops are the chief dependence as it is where the same people make their living on the same hills by depending upon the grains and grasses."

North Africa.—With European rule *western* industry is projecting itself into the midst of this native life at several points.   The French have conquered and colonized Algeria and Tunis.   They are conquering Morocco and the Italians are conquering Tripoli, a task made difficult by the mode of life prevailing there.   Half a million nomads or less in Tripoli have been harder for Italy to conquer than would have been 50 million oasis dwellers.   When the army goes to attack, there is no one there.   After it has camped two months it is suddenly attacked at dawn by a force of fighting fiends.

The immediate shore region of north Africa west of Tripoli is a plain with enough rainfall to grow wheat, olives, and wine, as do the lands on the other shore of the Mediterranean.   These crops the French colonists are growing largely with native labor, and along with cork, wool, and skins, they are the important exports.   The southern location also enables Algeria to export potatoes and other early vegetables, and oranges, to France and north Europe.

Tunis, which was for Rome an important source of supply for wheat and oil, is still exporting both and is having rapid extension of its olive orchards.

Several French railroads, largely military in their purpose of construction, have been built across the Atlas Mountains and into the Sahara in both Algeria and Tunis.   This is stimulating the date trade from the oases which had before depended upon the camel. There is a little trade across the desert, but it is insignificant for two good reasons: the great danger of robbers, and the greater ease of reaching the Soudan from the South.

Egypt, with an area of 400,000 square miles and a population of

10 million, is now as it has often been for the last 7,000 years, the world's greatest oasis. It has the Sahara climate, but is irrigated by the Nile, fed with rains in equatorial Africa (Fig. 246). The country is technically ruled by the Khedive, but virtually it is under British rule and is prospering. Under the continuous heat, sunshine, and irrigation, they regularly get two or three crops a year: wheat and barley in the winter, sugar, cotton, and rice in the summer, and rice, corn, millet, and vegetables in the autumn. There are excellent resources to grow sugar, but Egypt plays an unimportant rôle in this respect because her population of 930 per square mile of utilized

FIG. 245.—Road in the date growing oasis of Tozeur. Donkeys hauling loads of manure to and alfalfa from the gardens.

land demands rice, corn, and beans, whereof the acreage far exceeds the sugar acreage.

While the Nile Valley of Egypt is good for sugar, it is without question the best cotton field in the world. With alluvial soil of the Delta fertilized annually by the flood waters, with almost continuous sunshine and a climate in which there is a steady rise in temperature from spring to summer and a steady decline from summer to autumn, this valley produces 500 pounds of cotton per acre, which is double the yield of any other country. Unfortunately, its area is not great. The quality of Egyptian cotton, owing to its long, strong fiber, is better than that of any other except Sea Isle.

It commands a high price, and the production, which covered 1,350 square miles, or one-seventh of the cultivated area in 1885, increased to 2,670 square miles in 1908, an area greater than that of any other crop and covering one-fourth the fields of Egypt. Cotton is there a recent industry and can only be grown by frequent irrigation, which has been possible only since the introduction of modern engineering devices under European management (Fig. 247).

The greatest of these efforts at cotton extension is the building of the Assuan Dam, completed by the British in 1902 at an expense of $125,000,000. It holds back vast quantities of water from the season of flood until the time of need and permits irrigation at all seasons. Flooding of the Nile has annually spread a layer of mud over the Egyptian fields, permitting continuous cropping for many centuries without any other fertilization. Already there is complaint from the natives that the fields of lower Egypt are declining in fertility since the Assuan Dam shut off some of the floods and the mud.

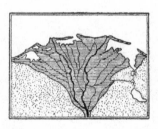

FIG. 246.—The Nile delta surrounded by the desert shown in dots. One of the first oases in the world with a close counterpart in the Imperial Valley of California.

We see the stubborn conservatism of the oriental agriculturist in the surprising fact that even in Egypt highways are little used, and that the donkey and camel are the chief means of carrying produce to the railroad and the steamboat introduced by the white man but *used* by the native.

Arabia, Palestine and Syria.—Most of Arabia is desert, so absolute that it cannot be crossed between Damascus and the Indian Ocean. In the extreme southern point is Yemen where mountains near the sea make a little area moist enough to be the home of Mocha coffee. Here the shade-loving coffee tree has the advantage of a mist, which arises on the lower plain almost every morning in the year and toward noon envelops the coffee-planted slopes in a haze which keeps off the full rays of the sun and also gives the proper moisture for the good development of the plant and the production of its seeds.

The fine quality of this Arabian coffee is due chiefly to the fact that it is carefully prepared, most of the crop being bought on the trees by Turkish and Egyptian merchants who personally superintend the harvest. The amount of coffee grown in Yemen is much smaller than that which is sold under the name of Mocha and it is much smaller than the demand. In Yemen coffee is purely a money crop, and is not used by the natives, who drink a decoction of the dried hulls. Only a small proportion of the Yemen land suitable for coffee is planted to that crop. Most of it is in dhurra, a grain resembling millet, which is the chief food of the people.

Fig. 247.—Lifting water by the rocker process in Egypt. One of the laborious processes by which the Eastern peoples get water to their crops.

Some oases on both sides of the Arabian Desert yield dates, particularly at Oman near Maskat, where they are an important export.

The Arabian horse, choice pet of the sheik or chieftain, sprang into literature from the Crusades. On the race course he is not so swift as the more carefully selected English breeds that are in part descended from Arabian stock.

Palestine and Syria are a fringe between the Mediterranean and the Arabian desert which holds sway beyond Jordan. They are much like Algeria or Greece, lands of wheat and barley, olives, wine, sheep, goats, and donkeys.

The region around the head waters of the Tigris and Euphrates is but an arid pasture like the highlands of Arizona or New Mexico. The methods and the difficulties of the live-stock industry in this region are shown by the following excerpts from a United States Consular Report from Harput, Asia Minor (June 17, 1911).

"A great portion of the cattle, sheep, and goats are owned by nomad tribes of Kurds that wander about this whole country with their flocks and herds. This last winter, however, was the most severe ever known in this country. The snow extended south even down into the sub-tropics, and over this winter-grazing land the snow was several feet deep and lasted throughout the entire winter. The people were helpless to provide against such conditions. There was no food procurable for the live stock and little for the inhabitants, 20 per cent. of whom and 70 to 80 per cent. of the live stock starved to death.

"Almost 300,000 head of sheep, 1 and 2 years old, were being driven from Suleimania, Kerkook and Mosul toward Aleppo and Alexandria (Syria) to be shipped to Alexandria (Egypt) for mutton; 90 per cent. perished en route."

Mesopotamia.—The flood plain of the Tigris and Euphrates, the site of Babylon and Nineveh, and the seat of many empires, has at times been a better oasis than Egypt. It has lain waste for several centuries since the Turkish conquests. The large and prosperous community, depending upon one irrigation canal for its very life, was a particularly easy victim for the Turk in the exercise of his genius for misrule. The farmer depending upon rainfall had at certain times certain crops that could be taken, but it is reasonably easy to keep enough to save life. The herdsman may get out of sight with his flocks, as the age-long strife of Bedouin and Turk attests, but the band of Turks at the head of the irrigation canal held over the heads of the irrigationists the power of life, death, and all exactions. Hence the desolation and unused possibilities of Mesopotamia with a fine navigable river flowing through its wasted midst from Bagdad to the Persian Gulf. In December 1913, an English built dam and a reconstructed irrigation canal were opened to service, through a concession granted by the Young Turk Government which was then in control at Constantinople. The valley is as good as it ever was and will make a home for millions. Some of the canals of the ancients only need repair. Persia owns a part of the lowland and produces largely of dates shipped by steamer from Bassorah on the lower Euphrates whence we get most of our supply.

Persia, with an area of 628,000 square miles and a population of 9,500,000, and Afghanistan with an area of 250,000 square miles and a population of 5,900,000, are high arid plateaus with scanty pasturage and occasional oases, connected by long and difficult pack trails.

Most of the Persian population is close to the Caspian sea where the rainfall is greater than in the rest of the country. Some of the oases produce silk and rugs, and skins are an important export. These countries remain independent, suffering from grievous oppression and misrule and devoid of roads or railroads because neither England nor Russia has dared annex them for fear of war with the other.

Central Asia.—The mountainous backbone of Asia, which skirts the northern boundaries of Persia and Afghanistan, becoming ever higher as it approaches the Himalayas, makes the aridity of central Asia more intense than that of Persia. Between the Caspian Sea to the upper Hoang-ho, a distance greater than from Boston to Salt Lake City, lie Russian Turkestan and Chinese Turkestan. At the bases of the mountains where the mountain streams flow out into the plains there are irrigation settlements, depending in size upon the size of the streams. Many of them are older than London, Paris or Athens, and they vary in size from mere hamlets to considerable cities like Kashgar, Samarkand, Tashkent, Bokhara (75,000 population) and Merv, names that are well known in the rug markets of the world. Some of these plains away from the mountains, especially in Chinese Turkestan, are so arid that crossing them is most difficult, but upon the mountains there is good summer pasture.

The Russians, who have recently conquered the native states of Turkestan, have built a railroad about 1,500 miles long to connect these oasis cities with the Caspian, and another to connect with Russia direct (see Fig. 257). Before this they had depended for ages on the slow and expensive caravans. The railroad has made two sudden industrial changes. Cotton and the dried apricot, which had been produced for local use from time immemorial, suddenly found a great market in Russia. Within two decades after the railway was built, cotton became one of the most important money crops from the irrigated fields of the oases which are fed by the melting snows of the high mountains of central Asia. The product, however (642,000 bales, 1910), is insufficient for the needs of the Russian Empire, and there is small possibility of its large increase because of the very limited areas for which it is possible to secure water. One-fifth of the irrigated land of Turkestan is in cotton, and the Russian government is trying to double this by arranging for an outside supply of wheat so that the wheat lands of Turkestan can be put to cotton. This poverty of cotton land shows up when compared with Louisiana where about one-twenty-fifth of the area is in cotton, and, with adequate drainage works, practically the whole state, 29 million acres, 45,000 square miles, is fit.

The whole of this region of the Old World Desert and the Desert's Edge is very promising as a field for future mineral development, excepting coal. Railroads, however, must come first. For instance, railroads in southwest Tunis bring to the port of Sfax large amounts of phosphate rock from low-grade deposits of vast extent. Persia especially seems to be rich in minerals.

QUESTIONS

1. Why is the desert's edge a natural place for the production of the hand-made rug?

2. What is the natural basis of conflict between the oasis dweller and the nomad?

3. Is the Bedouin a nomad because of his environment or because of qualities within himself.

4. Why does the United States with much cotton land import cotton from Egypt with little cotton land?

5. How have the English increased the area and reduced the fertility of Egyptian fields.

6. Predict the future of Mesopotamia.

7. What changes have recently taken place in the character of the exports of Russian Turkestan?

CHAPTER XXXV

CHINA, JAPAN, AND KOREA

The monsoon climate.—The vast land mass of Asia, more than five times the size of the United States, gets so hot in the summer that the heated air rises, causing rain-bearing winds to come in from the sea all the way from the Indus river in western India to northern

FIG. 248.—Intensive agriculture in China. Land completely occupied by crops, rendering effective service. Soy beans on the dividing lines, rice in the paddies treelised, pear orchards on the narrow, raised ridges. (From F. H. King, "Farmers of Forty Centuries.")

Japan. This three months' rain-bearing sea breeze is called the monsoon, and it is the most momentous single climatic fact affecting the human race, for it feeds the half of them. In discussing the Mediterranean lands it was shown that the dry summer was a great limitation to any land. The monsoon gives us the opposite, moisture where there is heat to make things grow. Because southeast Asia is soaked in summer by the monsoon rains, the crops and the people are there. In India and southeast of a line runn:ng from Calcutta to Harbin in Manchuria live half the people of the entire world. Vast Siberia and Asia west of the Indus are empty lands, with scarce 50 millions of people. Most of this part of Asia is too dry or too cold for great communities, the exceptions being the grain land strip across Central Siberia and occasional small and scattered areas elsewhere. With the exception of the Siberian wheat lands, it is a land in the main much like our arid west, where half the area of the United States has fewer people than some eastern states.

The abundant food supply of the land of summer rain has permitted dense populations to arise and persist for thousands of years. Thus, China proper, which does not differ greatly in size and resources from that part of the United States east of the Mississippi River, has five or six times as many people. For many generations their numbers have been so great that they could support themselves only by diligent labor, in agriculture and in household industries (Figs. 248, 249, 250). As a result the work habit is so thoroughly established among them that they are among the most industrious people of the world, the best of laborers. By their thrift and energy and ability to live on little, they are so able to crowd out the white races in economic competition that for mere self protection they are excluded by all white nations to whose lands they have attempted to emigrate in large numbers.

Isolation and completeness of resource.—For several thousand years China, Japan, and Korea have been a world apart. They have the great advantage over all other large groups of peoples in having the same written language. The Chinese characters are to the Mongolians as the Arabic figures are to the West, everywhere understood, but pronounced differently in different localities. These peoples have puzzled the West by trying to have nothing to do with us. But while they continued in their domestic system of household industry (compare United States Colonial epoch), each community was almost self-supporting. In a larger way this Mongolian region, even China alone, is almost a world in itself.

The summer rains of China stimulated agriculture, which used rich alluvial plains near the sea, while in the north were extensive deposits of fertile loess, the most indestructible of all upland soils

Reaching from the latitude of Havana to that of Newfoundland, her forests ranged from bamboo and oranges to pine and spruce; her grains from rice to wheat, corn, millet, barley and rye.   In the south was cotton; in the center, silk; in the north and west, the wool and hides from the flocks that roamed the 2 million square miles of arid and semi-arid ranges in the provinces.   The mines yielded coal, iron, copper, gold, and silver.   The careful husbandmen raised pigs and poultry in vast quantities and the fish supply of sea and river was supplemented by fish culture in which the Chinese have led the world. From north to south the Grand Canal passed between the latitudes of northern Florida and Philadelphia and connected a set of inland waterways probably better and more used than those of any con-

Fig. 249.—Canals in 718 square miles of Chekiang province, China.   Each line represents a canal.   (From F. H. King, "Farmers of Forty Centuries.")

temporary nation of 1800 or 1850.   While the domestic system of manufacturing continued in both East and West, the West had little for China but silver with which to pay for tea which the West de-sired, and which the western merchants took over the junk side in the Chinese harbors.   Naturally China wanted to be let alone by those who had nothing for her.   The discovery of petroleum and the invention of machinery, both of which China needs, have given to that country the desire for imports, the basis for a foreign trade. So complete has been China's isolation, so thoroughly has she been a world to herself, that she has had a set of prices all her own—low prices, so that the low-wage man bought low-priced commodities. A few years ago eggs cost 4 to 5 cash (2 cents, U. S. gold) per dozen at Yangtse ports.   Eggs were 5 to 6⅔ cents per dozen

at Shanghai in 1911. F. H. King (*Farmers of Forty Centuries,*
p. 180) found eggs in early April selling, near Shanghai, at 48
cents (American gold) per hundred; little chicks, $1.29 per hun-
dred. At the same place the wage of a man per 10-hour day was
24 cents, the price of four and one-sixth dozen eggs.

Peculiar industries.—In their long isolation these peoples have
developed a civilization, an art and an industry distinct from anything else in the world. Their great willingness to work, arising

FIG. 250.—Boatload of eggs on Chinese canal. Evidence of intensive agricultural industry. (From F. H. King, "Farmers of Forty Centuries.")

from the density of population and consequent scarcity of opportunity, has caused them to develop industries requiring great
labor. Of these the production of tea, silk, and rice are the most
conspicuous.

Tea, and factors affecting the distribution of its culture.—The
usual tea of commerce is the dried leaf of a tree native in the hills of
Assam, one of the eastern states of British India. It is quite hardy,
standing a frosty climate, thriving in central China and the cotton
belt of the United States, and many places where no tea is produced.

The large amount of skillful hand labor required in packing and preparing tea makes it necessary that it be grown in regions of dense population with its resultant low wage. This shows why the tea industry has not been developed in the United States, although it has long been known that the tea tree thrives well over an area 100 times greater than all the tea plantations in Asia. A little tea of good quality has for some years been produced near Charleston, chiefly by the labor of negro children, but naturally the industry does not expand in this region of relatively high wages. It costs 15 cents a pound to pick tea in South Carolina and the laborers there have been unable to learn a certain dexterous move that pulls a leaf without destroying the bud in the axis of its stem. To avoid this they pinch it off, leaving about one-third of the weight of the leaf. The plucking of the leaves, especially the young leaves, is one of the hardest things a plant has to stand, hence the tea only produces adequately where an abundant moisture supply and a warm summer promote growth.

Tea is widely grown in China and Japan in family gardens for home use, and is exported from both countries. The tea habit of the Chinese and Japanese seems to be an attempt to make pleasant the habit of drinking boiled water—a necessity recognized long ago by these peoples living on a land laden with germs resulting from the density of population and the habits of fertilization. After the picking, which is usually done by women and children, the leaves are wilted in pans over a fire. They are next rolled into balls by hand to squeeze out the sap, and dried upon screens, care being taken not to let the hot sun burn them. After this, they are further dried by "firing" in copper pans over a fire. The leaves are then hung up in sacks for a day, then picked over, sifted, assorted, and packed by aid of bare feet into tea chests for export. In some grades of tea, each leaf is rolled by human fingers. In Japan the export tea is now largely prepared by machinery.

Tea requires fertile soil, well drained but moist, a combination of conditions usually furnished best upon hillsides. This fact, in combination with the large amount of labor required, makes it a crop admirably suited for the Orient, where the vast demands for food cause the level land to be prized for rice and grain crops, and make tea growing in terraces upon the steep hillsides fit in admirably with the oriental economy. The tree naturally grows to 30 or 40 feet, but in the tea gardens it is kept down to 5 or 6 by trimming.

The best tea in the world is grown by Chinese people in the island of Formosa, which has belonged to Japan since the Chino-Japanese War of 1894. The eastern half of this tropic island is still possessed by head-hunting savages, and tea growing by the Chinese emigrants of the western half is a comparatively recent industry.

In the province of Szechuen, one of the western provinces of China on the headwaters of the Yang Tse Kiang, a poorer quality of tea is produced. The province has a very large population, estimated at over 16 million, a number about equal to the population of Brazil. They have supported themselves in that inland location for generations by household industries and agriculture, most of their few exports going down the rapids of the Yang Tse Kiang to Hankow and Shanghai, but they also send brick tea into Tibet. It is made by cutting off 12-inch twigs of the tea tree, roughly drying them in the sun, chopping them up, twigs, leaves and all, sticking all together with rice paste, and then compressing the mass into hard bricks for shipment over the fearful passes of central Asia upon the backs of coolies, mules, camels, and yaks. The greater ease of carrying this compressed form of tea accounts for its shipment by caravan into Russia at an early date.

The greater part of Chinese tea is grown in central China in the Yang Tse Valley, that of Japan in the southern part of the main island.

Silk.—Hundreds of species of insects spin cocoons in which to pass the chrysalis period of their lives. One of these insects, a moth when it is mature, but most commonly spoken of as the silkworm, makes a particularly fine cocoon, the fiber of which we call silk. The process of spinning is very similar to that by which the spider makes its web, except that the silkworm winds its thread around and around itself, as a result of which it can be easily unwound if the worm is killed—as it may be by roasting—before it cuts the thread by eating a hole in the end of the cocoon to emerge as an adult moth. The fibers are so fine that five are required for fine thread, and ordinary silk thread has ten to twenty fibers. The cocoons are soaked to loosen the fiber, the ends of several strands are placed together and the several cocoons easily unwound to make the thread of raw silk. This laborious process adds greatly to the cost of silk, which is ever the product of much labor.

The favorite and chief food of the commercial silkworm is the leaf of the white mulberry. The eggs of the adult moth are carefully collected, and upon hatching, the voracious young worms are kept indoors upon trays, which must be kept clean through the weeks during which the greedy worm devours his daily portion of fresh mulberry leaves, brought in at daylight, mostly by women and children. The worm can endure less cold than the mulberry tree, so the worms are kept in heated rooms in Europe and also in parts of China and Japan. Humidity and temperature must be closely watched or epidemics may carry the worms to a speedy death. When the worms have reached adult size, they crawl into bundles of straw to spin the cocoons which the women pick out by hand.

Throughout the whole life history of this insect and in the preparation of the fiber, the labor must not only be cheap, but careful, patient, watchful, and deft of hand. It thus becomes an industry that thrives where there is an abundance of the cheap labor of women and children, as in the densely peopled parts of the old world. It is easy to understand why the various attempts at silk growing in the United States and many other places have failed to start an industry, despite the many baskets of sample cocoons that have been produced, and despite the fact that the mulberry tree is widely distributed in all continents (Fig. 251).

The production of silk responds to this labor factor so surely that the industry is readjusting itself in accordance to it. The forcible opening up of China and the modernizing of Japan, and the resulting development of transport facilities have exposed the silk growers of the western world to Oriental competition. France and Italy have been

Percentage	Million Pounds
Japan 34.1	18.3
China 31.7	17.0
France 11.7	6.3
Italy 7.4	4.0
All Others 15.1	8.1
Total	53.7

FIG. 251.—Production of raw silk, three-year average, 1908–10.

growing silk for centuries; the governments are aiding the silk industry all they can, but their silk growers feel Oriental competition and the output has begun to decline. The greatest silk-producing region is China, where it is a household industry of the peasants centered between 30 and 35° north latitude. This corresponds roughly to the Yang Tse Valley, a region whose silk output makes its metropolis, Shanghai, the world's greatest silk market. Canton in south China is also a considerable silk center with many silk filatures employing 500 persons each.

Silk growing is very important in Japan, being particularly suited to the conditions that prevail in that country. The monsoon rains of summer give the moisture needed to make the mulberry trees yield abundant growth of leaves. The small proportion (less than a sixth) of the land that can be cultivated leaves plenty of room on the hillsides for the mulberry tree, and the overcrowded population furnishes the labor. It is natural, therefore, that this opportunity should, in a land of scanty raw materials, be eagerly seized upon, as is shown by a 50 per cent. increase in the export of raw silk within 5 years.

Rice growing is another industry that fits naturally into the conditions of the summer rain and dense population (see chapter on Cereals). In those parts of southeastern Asia, where the moisture is sufficient to its satisfactory growth, rice is the mainstay of the population. It is said to be the main food supply of one-third of the human race, but the extent of its use has been somewhat exaggerated through our contact with Oriental people at sea-coast points. Rice is the grain of the moist low plain, and contrary to the general opinion, it is a luxury to millions of Chinese and Japanese who live on the cheaper and less desirable millet, European small grains, and other cereals not known in America.

These European and other grains are raised where rice cultivation is impossible. Thus, in north central and northern China rice does not thrive, and wheat is extensively grown. In colder or more arid localities comes barley, and in the region of Pekin and southern Manchuria, corn, while many drier districts of central and north China have millet as their chief cereal. Southern Korea depends much upon rice, while in the rougher and colder north, barley, rye, oats, millet, and some wheat are grown. The same practices prevail in Japan. Wheat and barley are often grown on rice land in winter, and the two grain crops per year measure the intensity of production (Fig. 253).

Among the people of Europe and America, rice is used as an ordinary vegetable, as well as for pudding, and as a substitute for the potato in periods of shortage. Its great keeping quality and con-

venience in transport enable it to be used anywhere and it is consumed throughout the western world from Iceland and Greenland to

FIG. 252.—Forestry. Bamboo grove in central China where temperature falls
to 20° F. (Photo F. N. Meyer, explorer, U. S. Dept. Agr.)

Patagonia and New Zealand. This fact in combination with its
use in the Orient and the tropics probably makes it the most widely
used of human foods.

With peas and beans, rice furnishes almost the entire nourishment for hundreds of millions of Orientals. Peas and beans are widely grown by almost all eastern peoples who raise rice, and they are the substitute for meat, milk, and cheese of the West, while the starch of rice is the substitute for bread, potatoes, and many puddings as well. The unpolished rice eaten by the Oriental is much more nutritious than the shiny, white grain which we of the West insist upon eating. The process of polishing it takes off the most nourishing part, and is one of the numerous cases in which appearance makes the purchaser select the really inferior article.

FIG. 253.—Lifting water from well by hand power to irrigate Chinese gardens at Liao Yang, Manchuria. The fence in the background is made of sorghum stems, and is used as trellis for cucumber and bean vines. (Photo F. N. Meyer, explorer, U. S. Dept. Agr.)

The thousands of varieties of rice due to the age-long cultivation are divided into two classes, known respectively as upland rice and lowland rice. Lowland rice must be grown under water, while the upland rice is grown much like wheat or oats and chiefly where population is sparse and land abundant. Dense populations nearly always grow the wet variety of rice, because of the greater and more certain yield. Few crops are surer than the wet rice, and few more uncertain than upland rice. Wet rice must be grown by irrigation, and the devices used in fitting and keeping the land for this service are among the greatest monuments of human diligence in the world (Figs. 248–263). They are certainly the most creditable constructions produced by tropical peoples, the only rivals being the slave-built monuments of tyrants. Many an irrigated plain is divided by low banks into ponds of small area—rice fields, each of which has by great labor been leveled so that the water may be of uniform and proper depth for rice growing. As the traveler climbs the slopes of the hills, the rice patches continue, with smaller area and higher banks, turning at last into a giant flight of gentle water steps, one of the most beautiful landscapes that the world possesses. Many mountains in Java and Ceylon are thus terraced for rice far up their sides; and, in China and Japan, similar stupendous works have been constructed for the support of the dense populations which, like those of Java and of Ceylon, are mainly dependent upon agriculture in which rice is the largest staple. In Japan 56 per cent. of the arable land (11,000 square miles) is in these irrigated paddy fields.

The common treatment of the lowland rice is alternately to flood it and draw off the water during the early periods of its growth. It is kept under water during the largest part of its development, the water being entirely drawn off as it ripens.

The place of animals.—The labor of rice growing often involves the raising of plants in small sprouting beds and transplanting them in little bunches to the rice field itself. This work, like most of the other work in connection with terrace-grown rice, can be done only by hand. The small fields make it impossible to use such machinery as reapers, and at times even the ox. But beasts of burden are often unobtainable in a densely populated country like China. There is not land enough to raise food for many animals, so the spade in the hand of a man replaces the plough drawn by a beast, and the garden replaces the field of more sparsely peopled lands. This scarcity of animals is by no means universally true for there are millions of water buffaloes plowing rice fields in the Philippines and the mainland of southeastern Asia. Parts of China and Japan and India have reached the ultimate stage of agriculture, where man grows by his own labor the food for his support, and there is small possibility for increase of food production. Thus a crop failure makes famine for man rather than leanness or death for the beasts.

We have here some of the conditions that enable us to appreciate the great differences in man's relation to the land in the West and the East, in the sparse and the densely peopled country. The American

farmer grows corn and feeds it to cattle and then eats the cattle; but
one ox eats as much as five men and requires five times as much land
for his support, so the numerous Orientals often omit the animal-
feeding stage and grow rice and vegetables and eat them rather than
feed them to animals. Great increase in population could result
from the essentially vegetable diet and the omission of animal raising.
The ox that consumes as much as five men lives at least 2 years and
will not produce over 750 pounds of meat. It is reported that the
excessive amount of 5 pounds of meat per day is allowed the Argentine cowboy. Thus an ox represents in terms of land 150 days'
rations for the Argentinian vs. 3,650 days rations (10 years) for
the Oriental—one of the many striking results produced by difference in density of population.

Japan is peculiarly poverty stricken in animals. Although but
a sixth of the land is tilled, the apparent room for pasture does not
exist because of a "dense growth of bamboo grass wholly unfit for
food and impossible to eradicate." The effect of this absence of pasture and of this pressure of population in limiting the production
of domestic animals is most marked.

The soy bean.—In this agriculture that supports man by the almost meatless diet, the soy bean, now being introduced into American
agriculture with marked success, plays a surprising part (Fig. 254).
It has 18 per cent. of oil, used as butter and bacon substitute in China
and Japan, and the 10 pounds of this edible fat per bushel of beans
is a cheaper food than butter or bacon. In addition to the fat, the
bean is rich in protein, or nitrogen, substitute for lean meat. Thus
the bean becomes meat, its oil, butter, and the cake left after crush-
ing is a stock food and also for centuries has been much used as a
fertilizer for the Japanese fields.

In 1907 some of these eastern beans were sent to Europe. This
was due to the utilization of the oil in competition with cottonseed,
linseed, and soap-making oils which had suddenly gone up in price.

The suddenness with which this oriental farm product sprang
into importance is almost startling and shows what a resource we
have in the commerce with our Mongolian brother when we establish
a reciprocal relation. The trial shipments of beans to Europe in
1907 were followed by 100,000 tons in 1908, 245,000 in 1909, and
in 1910, 800,000 tons to England alone. Recent British experiments
have shown bean cake to be more economical stock food than linseed
cake or meal.

The industrial revolution in the Orient.—By hand agriculture and household industry Japan, China, and Korea had supported themselves for ages (Fig. 252).   Then came the contact with the westerners with their science, steam and machines.   This contact has turned to contagion and the industrial revolution which swept the West 100 years ago is now sweeping the East.   Japan being smaller than China, was easier to move.   She was also more crowded and more in need of industrial change.   Her insular location made easy the infiltration of foreign ideas and foreign goods which her meager re-

FIG. 254.—Chinese coolies carrying soy beans up to storage stacks for oil manufacture. Newschwang, Manchuria. (F. N. Meyer, explorer, U. S. Dept. Agr.)

sources caused her to import.   She adopted western learning and western machinery, and was seized with the ambition to be a world power.   This required armies, navies, arms, railroads, and the mechanical equipment of the inventive West.   In the attempt to equip herself with these things Japan realized her poverty, which was intense alike if she would buy or manufacture at home.   Her dense and diligent population could not wring a surplus from the scanty land (Fig. 256).   There was no surplus of rice, and it is now regularly imported, as are also flour, beans, tobacco, and most of the little meat that they eat, and even phosphate with which they fertilize the fields. To complete the list of her limitations we need but to point out the poverty of factory materials. There is no wool or leather, but little cotton, no rubber, no iron, and inferior supplies of coal. Yet the increasing population of Japan must support itself by manufacture, or emigrate, or starve. There were no suitable places for extensive emigration, so the demand for manufacturing and the trade in raw materials and finished products was imperative. Her fisheries were fully developed (Fig. 255).

As the Japanese realized that they must become like England and live by manufacturing, they appreciated the importance to themselves of Korea and Manchuria. They had long imported from these quarters beans, bean oil, and bean cake (for fertilizer), and the trade with these regions promised to be of prime and increasing importance as the country went over to the factory and commercial basis. Korea had unused rice and barley land, promising minerals, and good forests. In Manchuria, corresponding to our upper Mississippi Valley and part of the Canadian Northwest, is the finest stretch of unused farm land in the Mongolian world. Manchuria also has forests, coal, and other minerals. These regions would furnish Japan with food, take her manufactures and the thronging emigrants, and would put her in an independent position resembling that of China and the United States. It is in response to pressing need that Japan now possesses Korea, and also important concessions in Manchuria.

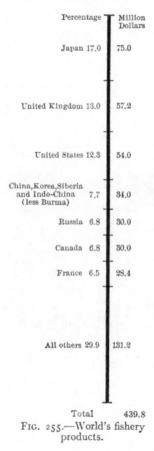

FIG. 255.—World's fishery products.

The change of Japan from the eastern to the western way of doing things is one of the most sudden changes in all history. The old industries have been laid aside or assisted by the modern ones.

For example, the Japanese are great users of paper, of which they make many remarkable native kinds,[1] but a new $4,000,000 pulp paper mill has recently been started at Tomakawai in the forested North Island of Japan, with a daily output of 70 tons. All of the electric machinery and 97 per cent. of the paper machinery came from the United States, most of the paper machinery being made at Watertown, N. Y., in the midst of the Adirondack paper district. The Japanese method is shown in that one foreigner only was employed, an American, to superintend the erection of the machinery.

Considering the admirable opportunity for coastwise vessels,

FIG. 256.—Irrigation in Japan by foot-wheel. (From F. H. King, "Farmers of Forty Centuries.")

Japan has a good railway net. She is supplied with cement plants, has shipyards to build a warship, guns and all, is using hydro-electric power and making a little iron from ore imported from central China near Hankow on the Yang Tse Kiang. The shortage of coal and iron is the one great weakness, the great point of difference between Japan and Britain, which she so greatly resembles in area, in latitude, in relation to the nearby continent, and in her economic problems.

The percentage of arable land in the Japanese Isles is much lower than in the British Isles, and this fact has made all the keener Japan's dependence upon manufacturing, in which the textile industry holds a prominent part. She is now importing raw cotton from Texas, China, and India, and is likely at an early date to de-

[1] Thick tough paper is made to serve as tarpaulins, for grain sacks, as walls of houses, and even as a substitute for leather (which Japan has not).

velop a much greater cotton industry than she now possesses. The American Consular reports fairly clamor with the accounts of the competition of Japanese cotton manufactures with the American, which they seem to be displacing in the markets of Manchuria and north China. The Japanese industry being comparatively new, competes directly with the low-grade American goods sent to the Chinese markets. If the Japanese labor is less efficient than the American, the wages as reported for certain Japanese mills for the month of March, 1912, 23 cents per day American money for men, and 15 cents per day for women, give a powerful basis for competition and explain the statement that the Japanese can use American cotton and produce the finished cloth at from 10 to 25 per cent. less than it costs in America. Japan was (1911) in competition with west Europe by sending socks, shirts, and imitation Turkish rugs to Salonica, Turkey. There is some land that can, by reclamation, be added to Japan's fields, but her chief economic extensions must lie along the line of manufacture and trade.

In many respects China resembles Japan, except that her resources are far greater, her population much larger, and apparently composed of better workers. The western way of doing things did not capture their minds so quickly—a natural result of the factors of size and isolation, but now she is following rapidly in Japan's footsteps.

China is as conspicuous for her riches in coal and iron as Japan is for her poverty in them. In addition to possessing, next to the United States, the most abundant supply of coal in the world, there is much evidence to show that iron ore exists in great quantities and good quality. A little iron has been manufactured in the primitive way for ages, and now that China is adopting modern methods the possibilities of the future iron industry are a matter of interesting speculation. Both iron ore and coal, the great raw materials, are there and also a labor supply exceeding in amount that of any three western countries. Already in a period of great prosperity and temporary shortage in the American iron market, the product of a modern blast furnace located at Hankow at the junction of the Han and Yang Tse Kiang Rivers has sent its product to the port of New York, where it could pay a heavy tariff in addition to a freight charge for transportation half way round the world and yet compete with the American product. The next century will probably witness a most astonishing competition between the Orient and the western world.

Chinese railroad building promises to transform Chinese industry so suddenly that it may almost be called a cataclysm. Three or four hundred million people, still mostly in the homespun stage of domestic industry,[1] will in a short time be subjected to the forces that have been gradually applied to the West during a period of one and one-half centuries, at the beginning of which time our populations were scanty. The West has in the main had an industrial evolution. China seems destined to have what we may in all propriety call an industrial revolution. One of its most painful features will be the sudden rise in prices as China connects with the world market.

The following excerpts from *Transportation in Interior China*, by Eliot Blackwelder, in *Journal of Geography*, Nov., 1911, describe the present conditions.

"If we look back to the seventeenth century we find our ancestors making use of methods of transportation, manufacture and agriculture which differ only in a minor way from those now used in China. . . . The horde of junks, large and small, which ply the waters of the canals upon the eastern plains, carry millions of tons, both of native and foreign goods, each year. . . . Along the river banks at nearly all of the large cities of eastern China there is a mass of junks and smaller boats so densely packed that the traveler is moved to wonder how each owner ever finds his own boat. The bare masts make a veritable forest around such great cities as Hankow and Canton. As is well known, these junks are used as permanent habitations by thousands of families who spend most or all of their lives in these movable homes. The internal traffic carried on by means of the junks is enormous in volume, but has never been reduced to figures. When the wind blows in the right direction, the skipper of the junk hoists the familiar sail strengthened with bamboo slats. But at other times—and these probably seem to the poor coolie all too numerous—the boat must be dragged or 'tracked' by the crew wearily tugging at the long hawser made of thin twisted strips of bamboo. . . .

"On land two vehicles are most in use for both freight and passenger traffic—the cart and the wheelbarrow. The carts are small cumbersome affairs, very heavy in proportion to the loads they carry. This heavy construction has probably been adopted because the roads are so bad that a lighter cart would be shaken to pieces. In western countries local or general governments build and maintain the principal roads, but in China this is not the practice. . . . Among the mountains, pack animals and men afford almost the only means of transportation. Carts are available locally in the broader valleys, but they cannot cross the rugged passes from one valley to another. . . . The idea of doing anything for the common good seems utterly foreign to Chinese thinking. Thus it happens that instead of improving roads so that large vehicles may be used and drawn at a fair speed, both the vehicles and the speed are adjusted to the inexorable demands of roads, which are usually as bad as they could possibly be.

"The great popularity of the wheelbarrow in China is probably due to the fact that a vehicle with one wheel can more easily take advantage of the best parts of the road than one with two; furthermore, it requires no draft animals.

[1] The completeness with which China supplies herself is shown by her imports, which are less than a dollar per person. The spindles in the new Chinese cotton factories are but 2 per cent. as many as those of Britain.

The freight-barrow used by the Chinese has a capacity of 600 to 800 pounds, and, like the cart, is a very stout, heavy machine. It is made of wood throughout. There is no more characteristic noise in China than the incessant squeak which arises from the ungreased axles of the wheelbarrows in town and country. The

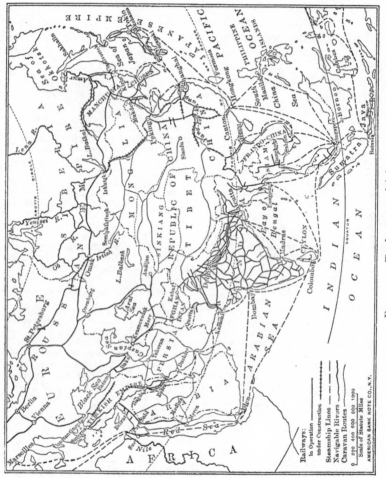

FIG. 257.—Trade routes of Asia

barrow is not always a one-man vehicle; often a donkey or a mule is hitched to the front of it, after the manner of a plow; and when the wind is favorable the thrifty coolie not infrequently rigs a sail to aid him in his weary struggle with a load which always seems much too big for him.

"There are coal mines in Shan-tung (one of the eastern provinces) whose entire output goes by wheelbarrow to cities and towns 50 to 100 miles away. In the case of coal, the rapid increase of the freight charges limits the sale to a small district. More valuable commodities are often carried much farther. . . . Low-grade commodities such as coal, building stone and grain cannot now be carried any great distance from their sources, on account of the excessive expense of coolie and cart traffic. . . . In 1900 a severe drought destroyed the crops in Shen-si province and soon reduced 3 million people to starvation. More than a third of these actually perished for want of food. And yet, at the same time, bountiful harvests were gathered in the eastern and southern provinces . . . The coal from Shen-si, carried on donkeys or coolies, is doubled in price every 15 or 20 miles, and so can have only a local market. For this reason one sees the peasants of the great Yellow River plain burning corn stalks for fuel in their cooking stoves and making no pretense of heating their houses during winter. Coal is beyond their reach now, but with railroads they might have an ample supply at $2 or $3 per ton. . . . The railroad will not drive out entirely the cart and the barrow, the donkey and the coolie porter. It will merely supersede them in long-distance hauling. In some districts China's dense population long ago used all the forests and often dug up the roots, with frightful results in floods and denudation."

At the end of 1911 there were in China proper 5,500 miles of railway in operation, and 2,800 miles of trunk line under construction (Fig. 257). Dr. Sun Yat Sen hoped to be instrumental in building 60,000 miles of railway in the next 10 years, giving China a complete network of main lines. Some observers predict that the next 25 years will see more railroad building in China than in all the rest of the world put together. This will give rate wars and the freight advantages of competitive points. This is the force that has done more than all else to pile up western populations in unwieldy cities, separate them from their food supplies, and increase the cost of living.

QUESTIONS

1. Contrast in facts and effects the rainfall of southeast Asia and south Europe.

2. Why did China maintain a policy of isolation?

3. Show two important points of resemblance between Japan and the United Kingdom; two points of difference.

4. Why have we not succeeded in introducing silk and tea production into the United States?

5. Why is a crop failure more serious in a country where there is no large animal industry than where there is one?

6. Explain the sudden entrance of the soy bean into European commerce.

7. Compare China and Japan in coal and iron resources.

8. What is the present and prospective status of the Japanese iron industry?

CHAPTER XXXVI

INDIA AND SOUTHEASTERN ASIA

Southeast Asia proves conclusively that (at least before the application of the white man's new sanitation) the rainy tropics were too much for man to conquer. In China the people are so numerous that they die by the hundred thousand in occasional famines. Yet they do not spread into the territory south of the edge of the tropics (in the latitude of Havana) although there is no more of a physical barrier than there is for the white man on the plains of Russia or Canada where the frost has stopped him. Similarly India extends from the tropic forests of her eastern borders to the arid western edge of the monsoon belt. In the west she has a population dense enough to perish by the million when the rains fail, but in her eastern territories, where the tropic forest holds the land, the population is sparse. The Ganges Valley near Calcutta is the end of the dense population and the native inhabitants there suffer much from malaria. Thence eastward to Hong Kong the country is mostly forest with settled patches, and the exports of the frontier, grain (rice) and lumber.

This unoccupied forest region comprises Burma, which the English have taken, Tonquin, Cambodia, and Cochin China, which the French have taken, and Siam upon which the two powers are gradually encroaching. In all this region, with many times the population capacity of Japan,[1] the settlements of trading people are all on or near the navigable rivers Mekong, Menam, Salween, and Irawadi, which constitute practically the only outlets and are served by both native craft and European steamers. Thus Rangoon, at the mouth of the Irawadi, Bangkok at the mouth of the Menam, and Saigon at the mouth of the Mekong become the great rice-exporting ports

[1] Siam 220,000 square miles, population 7 millions.
French possessions, 105,000 square miles, population 11 millions.
Burma, 237,000 square miles, population 12 millions.
Japan, 147,000 square miles, population 50 millions.

of the world. They also export much teak timber that has been floated down stream. The cultivation is largely limited to stretches of fertile, river-borne delta soil that lies favorably for cultivation by irrigation. It is very productive, and rice has become the money crop of the natives who grow large quantities of it in these unwholesome swamps. This surplus they carry in their native boats down through the winding waterways to Bangkok, Rangoon, and Saigon. Here, in the mills of English, German, French, and Chinese firms, the greater part of the world's export rice is cleaned for shipment. It is easy to let the facts of export cause unsound inferences as to total production. There is no necessary connection between the two. A small population, and a production small in comparison to other countries, permits countries like Argentine and Canada to appear large in wheat export, as French Indo-China and Siam do in rice export, although they produced respectively but 5 and 7 billion pounds in 1909 in comparison to 16 billion in Japan, 88 in India, and 50 to 60 in China.

British India (exclusive of Burma) is really a collection of countries. There are almost as many races and languages as in Europe, to which it bears considerable likeness in size and population. There is great variety of country—mountains, plateaus, vast plains, and the rainfall ranges from desert to swampy jungle. In such variety of natural conditions there is correspondingly much variety in production.

Excepting certain small populations in the Himalaya slopes and in the northwest, all the people are living under tropical conditions. Most of them are poor, living in densely peopled districts. They have a great variety of breadstuffs, wheat, rice, millet, sorghum, and native grains. Legumes are as important as in China and Italy, the great dependence being the lablab, a climbing bean used as food by man and beast. Swine and sheep are few, although the stamp of the desert is seen in the possession of a third of the world's hundred million goats. India leads the world in cattle (Fig. 258). She has 50 per cent. more than the United States and three times as many as Russia, the third cattle country in the world. They are used for work animals as well as meat animals and, excepting hides, there is no export of importance. In the humid parts of India the slow creeping water buffalo is the chief beast of burden. The statistics of draft animals for India, 17 million buffaloes, 78 million cattle

other than dairy cows, and 1.6 million horses show the great dependence on the bovine genus, which endures tropic heat and insects
better than the horse does, and in the end can be eaten. This fact
does not give an adequate meat supply to
India. Millions of her people are vege-
tarians, some from economic necessity, some
for religious reasons.

In northwestern India the dryer part is
the wheat region in the Indus Valley and
the plateau near Bombay. In bad years
India eats her crop and in good years she
has an export which equaled 26 per cent. of
that of the United States during the years
1907–10. Practically no wheat is grown in
the Ganges Delta or on the coasts of the
Peninsula. In the region of the Indus
Valley and the upper Ganges Valley there
is much irrigation, partly by capitalistic
enterprises with great canals built by the
British, partly by wells in a flat plain where
every farmer lifts the water for his little
patch as best he can.

Bombay, in a recent year the first port of
Asia in amount of shipping, is a railroad port.
Back of it is a fertile plateau where the
dense population produce for export large
quantities and many varieties of seeds, such
as castor oil seed, poppy, sesame, rape and
linseed, known as oil seeds because oils are
manufactured from them. Bombay is also
the port for Indian cotton export, which is
second in amount only to that of the United
States. The leading cotton area is located
on the plateaus between 1,000 and 2,000
feet above the level of the sea and lying east of the western Ghats Mountains. The crops depend upon the monsoon rains of summer, which in
this section are rather light, owing to the mountains which intercept the
rain-bearing winds. Droughts follow rains and no cotton could be
grown at all but for the very peculiar character of the so-called black
cotton soil, which in the rainy season is often flooded, becomes a tena-

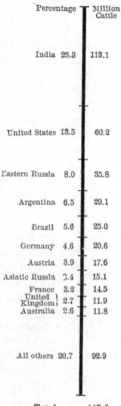

Percentage	Million Cattle
India 25.3	113.1
United States 13.5	60.2
Eastern Russia 8.0	35.8
Argentina 6.5	29.1
Brazil 5.6	25.0
Germany 4.6	20.6
Austria 3.9	17.6
Asiatic Russia 3.4	15.1
France 3.2	14.5
United Kingdom 2.7	11.9
Australia 2.6	11.8
All others 20.7	92.9
Total	447.6

FIG. 258.—World cattle
distribution, 1911.

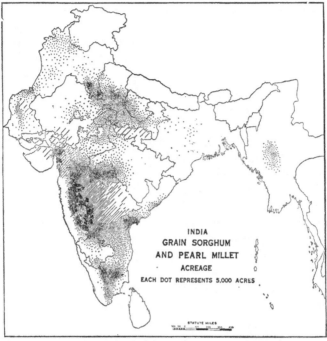

Compare this with a rainfall map of India. (Finch and Baker.)

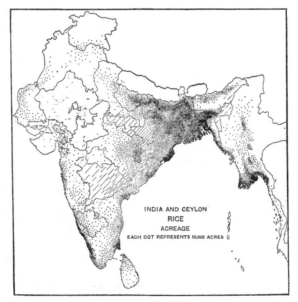

Compare this with a rainfall map of India. (Finch and Baker.)

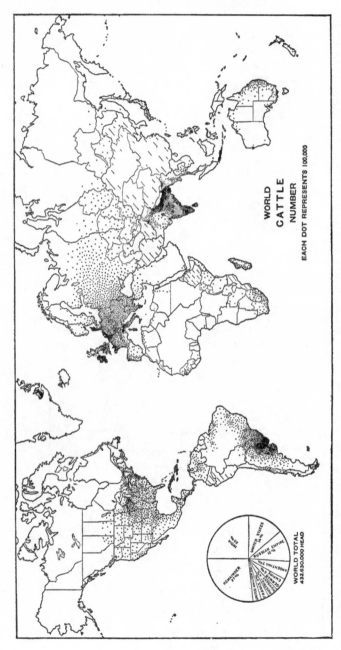

WORLD
CATTLE
NUMBER

EACH DOT REPRESENTS 100,000

WORLD TOTAL
432,630,000 HEAD

It usually comes as a surprise to us to learn that India has more cattle than the entire western hemisphere. The western hemisphere could be made to feed two or three or four times as many cattle as India, but India has more people by far than the western hemisphere, and their animal wealth is largely centered in cattle. (Finch and Baker.)

cious mud, and after the rains have ceased dries somewhat and is separated by countless cracks into hard lumps. This does not prevent the spongy soil from retaining sufficient water to mature the cotton, which is here sown broadcast like wheat, in a lava soil so enduring that some of it has been planted annually to cotton for centuries. The yield is only about half of that of the United States, and, because of the short staple, the quality is poorer. The influence of climate is shown by the improvement of Indian cotton when grown in America. Cotton can also survive standing in water in India, but in the United States it is fatal because of the smaller amount of evaporation by which the plants rid themselves of surplus moisture. In northern India, some cotton is grown in the irrigated districts along the Indus and Ganges.

In the drier part of India more extensive use is made of millet than of wheat. The millet area is nearly as large as that of the American wheat crop, but rice, grown chiefly in the humid east and northeast is the greatest crop of all India, having four times the area of her wheat crop. These grains are almost entirely for the home use of India's hordes, and the chief export of the Ganges Valley, the chief rice region, is jute, the cheapest fiber in the world. In northern and eastern Bengal near Calcutta, along the overflowing Ganges, there is the right combination of tropical climate, flooded land, and abundant labor to make a crop of this tropic plant. While adapted to all soils, most of the product is grown on the overflow land near rivers because the plants easily stand flooding. Like flax, hemp, and many other fibers that are not gummy, it is separated from the stalk by being soaked in water. After the bark is stripped off by hand, the plant tissue is washed away by beating the plant upon the surface of the water in which the laborer stands.

Jute has been long used in India where common gunny sack was first produced by hand looms. During the latter part of the nineteenth century, jute mills were established in the linen manufacturing centers of the United Kingdom, on the continent, in Calcutta itself, and also in Boston and Philadelphia. Calcutta is still the greatest center of manufacture, with total exports of raw and finished products amounting to $100,000,000—a greater addition to the wealth of India than the silk industry is to that of the United States.

India is also a tea grower, about four-fifths of the product coming from the northeastern part in east Bengal and Assam, regions tributary to the port of Calcutta (Figs. 259, 260). It is grown upon the hills sloping down from the great plateau of Tibet, and to some extent in many other places along the southern slopes of the

Himalaya Mountains, a district receiving tremendous summer rains as the monsoon sweeps northward.   In southern India on the Nilgiri hills is the most important tea district outside of Assam and Bengal. India is exceeded as a tea producer by Ceylon, an island (area

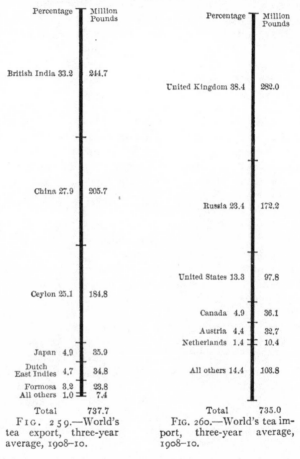

FIG. 259.—World's tea export, three-year average, 1908–10.

FIG. 260.—World's tea import, three-year average, 1908–10.

25,332 square miles, population 3,592,397) with a suggestive industrial history.   It has a better rainfall than any part of India, for it gets the northeast as well as the southwest monsoon, and has had the benefit of European energy, brains and capital, and abundant labor both native and imported from southern India (Figs. 261, 262).   In

1880 coffee was the chief export of the island, but a blight ruined the industry, and it was replaced by tea. A million pounds were exported in 1883 and 182 million in 1910. The prosecution of this industry on large plantations by European managers using every scientific device that was known so reduced the price that the export of conservative

FIG. 261.—Map of Southern India with the bridge and ferry to Ceylon. An example of the development of tropic resources under temperate zone leadership.

and thus far unchanged China fell away one-third, and a commission of Chinese visited Ceylon to learn how to grow tea.

The Ceylonese method of tea growing is typical of the most successful method of prosecuting tropical industries. More than half of the plantations are owned by corporations, and practically all are managed by English superintendents. By this means the average size of the plantation is raised to 300 acres, while in China it is probably a small fraction of an acre. The Ceylon tea plantation work is done by coolies, men, women and children, many of them being Tamils from southern India, and they usually return to their homes across the straits after a period of work gives them a little money. The intensity of the tea industry and its dependence upon a dense population is shown by the fact that less than 600 square miles of tea plantations employ about 400,000 coolies. This is one person to the acre, a strong contrast to the American corn belt farm of 160 acres, on which the proprietor often has but one hired man to help him and his machines grow and harvest 40 acres of corn, 40 acres of hay,

Fig. 262.—Viaduct between India and Ceylon, built entirely by native labor under white supervision. (Scherzer Bridge Co., Chicago) (See Fig. 261.)

40 acres of oats, and fatten 40 cattle and grow 60 hogs, besides raising enough horses for his own use with an occasional pair to sell.

The overproduction and low price that came with Ceylon's leadership as a tea exporter has stopped all new plantings, and the estate owners are turning to the two newer tree crops, cacao and rubber, which are in increasing demand at a high price. The production of both is rapidly increasing. Rubber is being planted out in some tea plantations so that the rubber trees will convert the declining tea plantation into a rubber orchard without cessation of income.

The hevea, or Para rubber tree, was first successfully cultivated in Ceylon. The most careful and scientific methods are there being applied to it, with the result that the cultivated Ceylon rubber already bears a better reputation and brings a higher price than that from Para itself. It has been found that a tree 10 years old can be depended upon to produce annually from 1 to 3 pounds; the tapping of the trees does not hurt the yield,which has actually increased with the age of the trees.

India has moderate coal resources, and has made more progress in manufacture (chiefly textiles) than any other tropic country. Most of the manufacturing is in the northern cities where access is easier. E. C. Semple (*Influence of Geographic Environment*) points out that the people of central and southern India are ignorant and superstitious because they are shut off from the rest of mankind by coasts difficult of approach from the sea, owing to poor harbors. Similarly, mountain walls shut off the rest of Asia. In contrast, Greece, open to the contact and ideas of all passers, developed the highest culture and learning. For a time India's scores and hundreds of millions of cotton wearers took about one-half of England's exports, but since that time the import has declined as a result of the introduction of cotton mills built by English capital, equipped with English machines and directed by English foremen teaching the cheap laborers. Her exports are now about half as large as her imports and comprise both cloth and thread sent to China and Japan. In the Presidency of Bombay alone there were, in 1911, 431 cotton factories. One hundred eighty-four of these factories employed 160,000 hands. In the same year the cotton employees of the United States numbered 387,000 and those of Britain 550,000. India even imports raw cotton from Texas and is competing at Aden with the American cotton cloths for the supply of Arabia and east Africa.

India imports largely of machinery, hardware, and fabrics from England and of petroleum with some iron and steel products from the United States. We get large quantities of jute. The gunny sacks made from it are the almost universal material used in the packing of agricultural products.

QUESTIONS

1. Compare the Indus and Ganges Valleys in the number of people (see population map, Chapter I, No. 18).

2. Compare Indo-China and India in the production and export of rice.

3. Is the population in these countries distributed in proportion to the ability of the land to produce food?

4. What is the most interesting fact in the agricultural history of Ceylon?

5. What is a geographer's explanation of the superstition of the people of Southern India?

6. Why do the people of one part of India eat wheat and those of another part eat rice?

7. What change has taken place in the Indian supply of cotton cloth?

8. Are the tea plantations of Ceylon being extended?

CHAPTER XXXVII

PHILIPPINES AND MALAYSIA

The Philippines, the Dutch East Indies and the Malay Peninsula are a vast collection of tropic or equatorial lands of heavy rain, forest, Malays, rice (Figs. 263–266), and carabao or water buffalo. Here and there the forest is cleared for a little area, and the resulting agricultural land feeds a dense population, but in the main it is forest, like Farther India. Fishing and a little agriculture support the Malays. The more energetic Chinese immigrants and a sprinkling of Europeans dominate commerce and large enterprises, while wild beasts and equally wild men possess the primeval forest. At least one of these peoples, those of Acheen in the interior of Sumatra, have been at war with Holland for decades and have maintained their independence.

The exports of this region are chiefly those of the agriculturist, the hunter, and the miner. The forest, which covers most of the area and possesses in the Philippines alone one hundred kinds of wood, is the tropic forest (see Mexico) and the forest exports are limited to a little wood, rattans (climbing vines) and gums, including rubber. One exception to this is an interesting forest substitute for one of our truck crops, the potato. In these far eastern tropics a form of starch is produced from the sago palm tree and extensively used as local food supply in Java, Borneo, Celebes, and adjacent islands. When a sago palm tree is about 15 years old it blossoms profusely and produces a large amount of fruit. Before blossoming all the material for the production of this fruit is stored in the trunk of the tree in the form of starch. To get this accumulation of years the Malays, just before the tree blossoms, chop it into pieces 2 or 3 feet long, soak out the starch, dry it, make it into flour for cakes, or the "pearled" rounded masses which are to be bought in grocery stores as sago.

The Philippines (area 127,853 square miles, population 8,276,802) are largely in forest, despite the average population three times as dense as that of Iowa. When under Spanish control (before 1898)

500

they were chiefly noted as exporters of sugar, tobacco, and hemp. The plain of Luzon, north of Manila, is the chief cultivated area, much of it being in rice, of which there is also considerable import from Indo-China. The tobacco is largely grown on the overflow lands in the Cagayan Valley in North Luzon and brought around to Manila by boat.

During the years of American occupation there has been a large increase in the exports of hemp and cocoanut. Manila hemp, the

FIG. 263.—Reflected light emphasizes some of the many water terraces that surround this Igarot village upon the slope of the tropic mountains. Sagada Bontoc, Philippine Islands. (U. S. Bureau Insular Affairs.)

best of common rope materials, is not hemp at all, but a coarse fiber sometimes 8 to 10 feet long, found in the pithy stalk of the abaca, a fruitless member of the banana family. This plant is cultivated only in the Philippines. It thrives best on the slopes of volcanic hills in a moist climate, and it will not do well in water-soaked or very dry soil. Its culture is easy. From time to time one can plant a few suckers of the abaca plant, and in 2 or 3 years he can cut them down, split them into strips a couple of inches wide, scrape away the pulp with a sharp knife and sell the long, white, shiny fiber to traveling Chinese merchants, who gather it up and take it to Manila. They pay sufficient cash to meet the small financial needs of the tropic family for a few days or weeks until pressing need makes it desirable to scrape a little more fiber. Attempts at introducing Manila hemp-growing into other parts of the world have thus far failed, and it is practically a monopoly of the Philippines, where there is a great abundance of admirable, unused abaca land. It makes the strongest of rope, which is especially prized in the rigging of ships, and when worn out for this use it is ground up to make the exceedingly strong paper known as Manila. It is also much used for the manufacture of twine used in binding up the bundles of wheat in self-binding reapers, for which purpose approximately $20,000,000 a year are expended in the United States for twine made of Manila hemp, and of its cheaper rival the sisal or henequin, which is the great money crop of Yucatan.

Fig. 264.—Cocoanut palm is one of the great automatic food machines. There is a saying in the tropics that when a man gets his cocoanut grove started he hangs up his hammock. (U. S. Dept. Agr.).

The increasing price of animal products and the new use of cocoanut oil as food (see Germany) has created a need which these archipelagoes are peculiarly fitted to meet. The cocoanut thrives especially well on the seashore of which the isles possess so much. There is unused land on nearly all tropic continents and islands suited to the cocoanut palm, and it would be difficult to improve on the ease of producing a product that falls from the tree and lies for weeks embedded in its thick cushion of husk waiting to be picked up (Figs. 264 and 267). In some places, ten nuts is the annual average per tree; 4,000 to 7,000 nuts make a ton of copra, now (1914) worth $120 per ton and yielding 100 gallons of oil. During the four years, 1906–09, the Philippine Islands produced 800,000 tons of copra. The rapidly increasing output is an important element in the economic life of the islands, and gives promise of becoming more important there and elsewhere (Fig. 265). As an industry it is no experiment. The tree grows universally in the tropic world, and the American

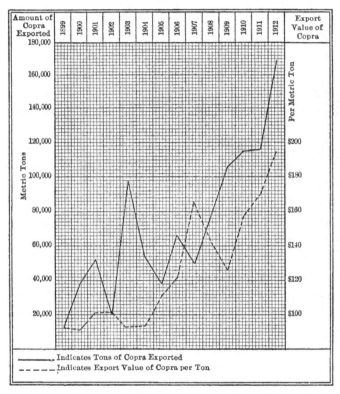

FIG. 265.—Graph showing rise in price and quantity of export copra in the Philippine Islands for the fiscal years 1899 to 1912.

planters of the Philippines are but copying the European planters of Ceylon where the area in cocoanuts is proportionally as great as the combined wheat and corn area of the United States.

The cocoanut promises to be one of the world's great crops. The crop of 1912 was estimated to be worth $350,000,000 and rapidly increasing. Eighty-four uses for the nut are already recognized.

As in adjacent regions, the chief food of the Filipinos is rice, of which there is usually an import from the mainland of Asia. The people find it more to their liking to grow tobacco, hemp and cocoanuts and buy rice, cotton cloth and of course the whole great variety of manufactures that are consumed in a large city like Manila.

FIG. 266.—Transplanting rice, Philippine Islands. Note the carabao or water buffalo.

The resources of the Philippines are very largely undeveloped because of the scarcity of laborers arising from the fact that we will not permit any more Chinese to come there.

Java, about the size of New York State, with a population one-third that of the United States, is best known for coffee, one of its minor crops. The Java coffee has a good quality because it is grown at an elevation of from 2,000 to 4,000 feet upon government plantations, where careful measures in harvesting the crop

are rigidly enforced. The total coffee crop of Asia and the East
Indies in 1910 (84 million pounds) was less than one-sixteenth that
of Brazil.

Sugar is a far more important crop in this interesting island, which
is the most thoroughly cultivated region within 15 degrees of the
equator. Forty per cent. of the land is cultivated, and its population of 30 million have food products for export. It furnishes about
one-fifth of the world's crop of cane sugar, being second only to
Cuba and India. In sparsely peopled countries like Cuba, sugar can
often be grown on newly cleared land, and as the cane will live for
many years with an annual cutting, new sugar lands are often
made to give six or eight or ten crops before replanting. In Java,
the larger area under cultivation makes it impossible to keep moving to new land, hence Java has the most scientific agriculture to be
found in any cane-growing region.

Since the first cutting of canes, following the plowing and planting, is always the best, a field is allowed to yield but one crop, as
is commonly the case in Louisiana because of frost. This is followed
the next year by beans, then by corn, then rice, then back to sugar.
Under this systematic cultivation and a complex system of government control which at times amounts to compulsory labor, the sugar
output increased threefold in the 20 years following 1884. The
sugar goes to the United States, China, Japan, India, Australia, and
other eastern countries, practically none of it going to the mother
country, Holland, or any other part of Europe, because of their
beet supply.

Sumatra (area 161,312 square miles, population 4,029,503) has
recently developed an important export of valuable wrapper tobacco. The Sumatra tobacco belt lies on the eastern plain extending 5 or 10 miles inland from the Straits of Malacca. The
industry is due entirely to the enterprise of Dutch financiers and
managers, a single company of Dutch capitalists having employed in
the island of Sumatra as many as 16,000 Chinese with 200 skilled
European overseers. They have cleared the virgin forests and
have taken such splendid crops of tobacco from the rich volcanic
soil that some of the companies have paid as much as 75 per cent
dividends per year.

Singapore is a little island just off the point of the Malay Peninsula. It is an English colony at the turning point of the route between the East and West, and it is also a junction point for numer-

ous local lines to and from such places as Siam, Cochin China, the Philippines, Borneo, Java, and the Celebes. It is the metropolis of the world of tin, spice, gums and rubber cultivation.

Tin is one of the scarcer metals, and the 2,500 years of working have about exhausted the deep mines of Cornwall, England. In the Malay Peninsula and adjacent islands, there are large areas bearing alluvial gravels in which 20,000 coolies work as the individual miner works placer gold. This mining is done very carelessly.

FIG. 267.—Opening cocoanuts for drying to make copra. (Bureau of Insular Affairs.)

The regions promise a great output in the future if the same lands shall be reworked with such a dredging device as that which now reworks the old alluvial gold fields of Australia. By this device, a centrifugal pump and six or eight men per shift can do as much work in 24 hours as do 500 Chinese under present hand methods. Alluvial deposits are usually trivial in comparison to the lodes from which they were washed. The first tin mine on the mother lode in the Malay Peninsula has been opened, and the era of deep mining such as is followed in Cornwall should be long.

Spices, despite their non-nutritious character, are so generally prized as an article of diet as to be of nearly world-wide interest. In the history of commerce they are of especial interest because the trade in spices long dominated the commerce between the East and the West. They were for centuries the only food products that could be transported far and they were of greater relative importance in the diet of ancient and medieval peoples because the small variety and poor flavor of their food made a greater necessity for something to improve its palatability. It was the spice trade that Columbus sought, and spice trees were among the early introductions to the New World.

While the New World took the Old World grains and cattle, and now dominates in the export of these products of sparse populations, our export of spices yet remains insignificant. Practically all the spices, with the exception of mustard, are limited in their production to the tropics, and are like tea in requiring tedious and painstaking labor in their production. As a result their export is limited to centers of dense population and good labor supply. These conditions are furnished by the settlements in the region tributary to Singapore, and much of the labor is Chinese. A large proportion of the 230,000 people on the 206 square miles of Singapore are Chinese coolies, the best laborers in all the tropical world. With them are many Europeans—a combination providing both workers and supervisors. Siam also has at least 200,000 Chinese in the vicinity of Bangkok. The Chinese coolies are also responsible for most of the pepper and other exports of Sumatra.

Pepper, the most important of all the spices, is the dried, unripe seed of a climbing vine and the white pepper is the same seed riper and with the skin peeled off. The common method of growing this plant is to sow the seeds in fields of rice, castor beans and other temporary crops. At the same time the seeds of rapidly growing trees are sown. In 2 years these trees are cut and stuck in the ground as poles, making a permanent support for the climbing pepper vine, which yields its crop in about 2 years. Nutmegs, mace, and ginger are other products of Singapore and adjacent regions.

Gums.—Singapore is the greatest center for the shipment of gums of a class known as copals, which are with difficulty soluble and therefore serve as the basis of varnish used for vehicles. Here also is gathered for shipment a large proportion of the world's rattan, the jointed stem of a creeping vine that runs for hundreds of feet through the tropic tree tops and helps to bind them together into the jungle mass. Properly split it makes the cane seats of chairs.

The gums are very closely allied in production to rubber, a product in which Singapore has peculiar interest. A great change in rubber supply is likely to come through the shifting of production from the isolated dying tree, to which the rubber hunter has laboriously cut his path, to the scientifically managed rubber plantations in which tens and even hundreds of thousands of rubber trees will yield an annual crop. Since the opening of this century when the automobile made rubber high-priced and caused a threatened rubber famine, there has been tremendous interest in rubber cultivation throughout the world. The possible rubber region is very large indeed, including the equatorial rain belt which encircles the world; while the Ceará (a state in East Brazil) rubber tree has demonstrated its ability to thrive on dry, stony tropic uplands, and the guayule bush of north Mexico, in the latitude of Texas and a climate of frost, grows and produces rubber in lands too arid for a forest or even the tilled or pastured field. Demonstrations of rubber cultivation have been made in many lands, and the labor factor will probably locate the great industry in Ceylon, India and Malaysia.

The Malay Peninsula which differs but little from equatorial lowlands everywhere, is quite as good for rubber growing as Ceylon. It has a rainfall of from 100 to 200 inches, and the almost daily shower of the monsoon season in combination with the steady heat and humidity of the equatorial latitude sometimes produces in 3 years a Hevea rubber tree 60 feet in height. These orchards can be grown with side crops of banana, corn, or even cacao.

The labor supply of Malaya is unique. The Straits Settlements (British) are a few settlements along the Straits of Malacca comprising a small fraction of the land area of the Malay Peninsula. Here the British Government has kept the ferocious natives in order, so that the Chinese, industrious, quick to seize opportunities, have gone there for the business opportunities in a climate they can stand better than Europeans. In 1911 the population (total 714,000) consisted of 7,200 Americans and Europeans, 8,000 Eurasians, 370,000 Chinese, 82,000 natives of India, 40,000 Malays, and 200,000 other Asiatics. In the native states under British control are 400,000 more Chinese. These Chinese laborers are doing the work on the rubber plantations. This makes Singapore, the metropolis of the Straits, the natural rubber metropolis in the cultivation era which is coming. Within a comparatively short distance of Singapore are the enormous labor supplies that can upon demand be furnished by the millions of China, of Java, and of India. The fare from China to Singapore was for years $2.50 per workman. These coolies are good workers and are at present content with 12 to 20 cents American gold per day, with the worker boarding himself. This kind of labor supply tropic America does not possess, and the feverish efforts of Brazil to enter upon the cultivation of rubber seem destined to poor success unless she imports Chinese laborers into her empty Amazon lands.

QUESTIONS

1. Are the forests of the Philippines with their fine woods more valuable than forests of common pine in Germany or Virginia.

2. Compare Para and Singapore as places to start a rubber export business.

3. How has the high price of cow feed in Illinois affected the cocoanut industry of the Philippines?

4. Why are there more Chinese in the small Straits Settlements than in all the rest of the Malay Peninsula?

5. Does the growing of Manila hemp cultivate the work habit as does dairying?

CHAPTER XXXVIII

TROPIC AFRICA

Right across the center of Africa runs the equator, with its accompanying zone of calms and rains and resulting jungle—a great equatorial forest like that of South America. As this Doldrum zone of heavy rains moves north and south a few degrees with the passage of the sun, it gives the annual floods of the Nile which have supported so many dynasties and so many millions of subjects in Egypt.

To the north and south of the Doldrums are the zones of the trade winds which here blow from over the land and are therefore desert-making winds resulting in the Sahara and Kalahari Deserts. Between these deserts and the forests are transition regions of plains or steppes with grass and occasional trees, and a climate far more wholesome than that of the humid jungle.

For a long time Europe was content to call Central Africa the Dark Continent and let it alone. Approach was difficult, for the coasts are swampy and unhealthy, and the rivers come down from the plateau with many falls making their ascent impossible. The climate is fatal to all our beasts of burden, so man was thrown back on his own muscle in an enervating climate (Fig. 268). Then, late in the nineteenth century, the fever of colonization suddenly struck Europe. Africa was partitioned off, and railroads and steamboats have pierced the Dark Continent with surprising speed. They have often been built by colonizing governments in advance of any adequate economic demand. Commerce is rising rapidly, but the natives, of whom there are many millions, do not have many needs or many industries. Thus far their exports have rarely even got down to agriculture, being composed almost exclusively of the forest products of ivory, rubber, palm nuts, and palm oil, some cacao and cocoanuts. Life has been too easy to compel the development of industries in the modern sense. The ease of banana production should be emphasized in its effect on tropical life. In the Congo Basin and other humid parts of central Africa, where the climate is so bad for the white man, the nutritious banana is said to be the main article of diet for many, probably scores of millions,

of the negro race. It merely replaces bread and the potato of the
north European peasant, and the rice of the southern Chinese.

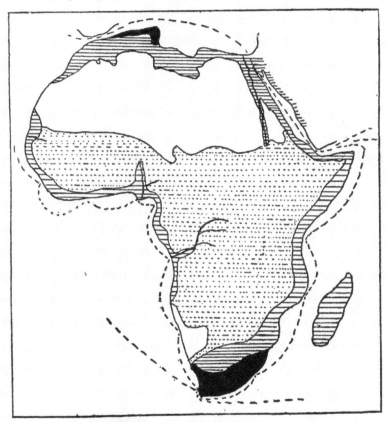

 Regions of large commerce.
Regions of important commerce.
Regions commercially undeveloped.
Desert or unproductive regions.

FIG. 268.—The trade zones of Africa. (After Robt. M. Brown.)

The Belgian Congo gives good examples of the whole commercial
movement. Of the $15,000,000 of exports, rubber comprises
$10,000,000, ivory $2,000,000, palm nuts and oil $1,000,000. They
import cottons, clothing, provisions, machinery, iron, steel and copper.

In Portuguese Angola, in 10° south latitude, the Benguela railway with terminus at the Lobito Bay, is being pushed rapidly eastward to tap the famous copper deposits of the Katanga district. From Loando and Mossamedes in the same colony, railroads are being pushed eastward in a country said to be rich in malachite, copper, iron, petroleum, and salt.

The Congo river route.—The Congo River is at present the longest and the greatest central African highway. Eleven steamers ply between the seaport of Banana at the mouth, and Matadi, less than 100 miles inland, where a 250-mile railway connects with the steamers of Leopoldville, on Stanley Pool above the numerous falls. The commercial changes of the new Africa can be easily inferred from the effects of the railroad from Matadi to Leopoldville. The journey used to require 20 days, with great loss of life. The freight rate was £2 (nearly ten dollars) per load of 65 to 75 pounds, about $250 per ton. The journey now takes 2 days and the freight rate is $3 per ton. From Leopoldville eastward the Congo is navigated for 1,200 miles to Stanley Falls on the equator. Here another railroad connects with several hundred miles of navigable waterway on the upper river, giving steam service 2,250 miles from the sea. Several branches are also navigable. Still further extensions are promised in railways now building to the central African lakes. Everywhere there is great similarity of imports; first cotton cloth, then hardware, trinkets, and varying amounts of machinery and equipment goods, depending on the new enterprises of the region in question.

The Guinea coast, so deadly to white men, has an increasing trade. Gambia is an exception to the rule in having an agricultural export, $4,000,000 worth of peanuts. The gold coast sends $8,000,000 worth of cacao, but there is a greater cacao production on the islands of Sao Thome (or St. Thomas) and Principe (or Prince's Island), lying under the equator in the Gulf of Guinea. While they have less than 45,000 people (of whom 96 per cent. are negroes) and have an area of but 360 square miles, they have the cacao climate and a fertile volcanic soil. In the year 1905, this tiny Portuguese Colony outstripped Ecuador and all other cacao-producing countries. This is not a measure of superiority of resources. It is a result of the fact that slavery still exists there and the task master can make the native work.

One of the most interesting of African products is the oil-yielding palm nut—exported from the west coast, between the upper part of the Gulf of Guinea and Fernando Po, from the east coast between Zanzibar and Pemba, near the Tropic of Capricorn, and also from the shores of the African lakes. The native climbs the 30-foot palm tree and cuts off its head of fruit, as big as a basket. The many small fruits are boiled, thrown into a kettle of water, and tramped by bare feet to crush out the oil, which is skimmed from the surface of the water. This is refined by further boiling, and used throughout much of Africa as a choice morsel of food, a substitute for the olive oil of Europe and the butter of America. It is also the chief money crop of west African countries and is one of the important articles of freight for the many steamers that skirt the African coast. The kernel of the seed is also quite largely exported for the manufacture of oil in European ports. At present it is used for soap, but we shall probably soon be eating it and calling it butter.

In the British colony of South Nigeria (about 80,000 square miles and 8 million people, of whom 1,650 are Europeans), palm products make up $20,000,000 of the $25,000,000 worth of exports. This colony also shows the advantage of a coast location, for it has six times the trade of North Nigeria, which is a larger and better country. Its trade, however, promises to increase because of the extensive commercial equipments now in progress. Akassa, the chief port, has several hundred miles of the navigable lower Niger adjacent to it, with twenty-two government steamers and many barges upon it; and, from the head of navigation, the government has completed a 400-mile narrow gauge railroad to Kano, a caravan trade center and commercial metropolis in the latitude of Lake Tchad in the Soudan, 900 miles (4 days) from the sea. This is one of the least known but apparently the most populous and promising parts of tropic Africa. The latest geographers report cities of 60,000 to 100,000 people, who are, for Africa, industrious; and the climate and the country are suited to live stock. It is a transition region between the desert to the north and the jungle to the south, and is said to be good for cotton growing. It is Africa's land of promise, with a cotton area in Nigeria alone five-sixths as large as that of the United States.

The French have recently established a rail and steamer route via the Senegal and upper Niger Rivers from Dakar on the west coast of Timbuktu. It seems to spoil romance to go to Timbuktu by steam.

East central Africa is a land of less population, but because of its greater aridity and elevation it has possibility of becoming in part a white man's land. We see the aridity shown in a soda lake at Megadi where the evaporation of the water has left a soda deposit covering 30 square miles and of almost incalculable amount. An output of 500 tons and later of 1,000 tons per day is expected. A special branch railroad, 95 miles long, has been built to connect it with the British line that goes from Mombasa to Lake Victoria.

The white man's land is limited by the plateaus of British East Africa where 5 million sheep are now reported, most of them of the native woolless variety. Experiments at breeding up from these hardy sheep are succeeding. The problem of producing the breeds of domestic animals before settlement can take place, shows the great handicap of Africa in comparison to the settlement of the United States. This securing of domestic animals is almost as important for the transplanting of civilization to Africa as it was for the first origins of civilization. It would seem that the moderns, if possessed of any spark of appreciation for resources, should duplicate the achievements of the ancients, redomesticate the elephant and give to central Africa the most powerful of all beasts of burden where it now has the least efficient—man.

Parts of Africa have some hope of a beast of burden through the probable fitness of a new hybrid, the Zulebra, a cross between the horse and zebra—an equine that resembles the horse quite as much as does the ass. The African tsetse fly kills all the domestic equines, but four species of zebra are native and immune—possible bases for an efficient new work animal for which several million square miles of middle Africa are sadly in need.

The Cape to Cairo railway, long a dream of Cecil Rhodes, the empire builder, will be completed before many years if some steamer links be included. It already extends from the Cape up to a point beyond the boundary of Belgian Congo. When completed it will have no through traffic, but will merely serve as a feeder to coast lines already built, as that from Mombasa or the one building in German East Africa.

Agriculture, settlement, and new industries come slowly in tropic Africa, but mineral deposits give quick traffic. A copper deposit in central Africa, known as the Star of Congo mine, affords an interesting example. Before the completion of the railroad to it, from Beira (1911), mining work was already begun, so that 1,000 tons of copper per month could be extracted as soon as the railroad permitted the erection of the machinery and a yield of 5,000 tons of copper per month was expected in a short time.

Central Africa, like the rest of the tropics, being nearly devoid of coal, has a compensating resource in the enormous water-power which its districts of heavy rainfall afford. Africa, a vast plateau, has rivers tumbling down to the sea in many cataracts, those of the Congo in west Africa rivaling Niagara in power, while engineers are already discussing the carriage of power from the falls of the Zambezi, 700 miles to the gold mines of Johannesburg in the Transvaal, and the diamond mines of Kimberley in Orange River Colony.

Because of the Tropic climate there is small prospect that this power will be used for anything but extractive work and the heaviest power-using industries, like the manufacture of nitrates. Thus Africa promises to stay in a condition of increasing trade because her development will be along the line of extractive industries requiring exchange with the manufacturing countries. Her development also will be strictly under foreign guidance as it now is. Thus nearly all the commerce and much of the industry of the east coast is carried on by a few thousand Hindoos. They have even transported thither an oriental spice industry, the production of cloves, of which Zanzibar is a great center.

"Formerly this spice was imported to the West in great quantities from the Moluccas, but now the trade has passed almost entirely to Zanzibar and Pemba which provide the requisite conditions for clove cultivation, viz., a dense population and a high temperature all the year around, rain at very frequent intervals and heavy dew. A month of dry weather with no dew would probably kill the stoutest tree."

Pemba: The Spice Island of Zanzibar. By Capt. J. E. E. Craster.

QUESTIONS

1. What part of tropic Africa promises to have the best cotton zone? What nation has made it accessible?

2. What surface and climatic features delayed the opening up of Central Africa?

3. Why is the eastern region north of the equator dryer than the corresponding region south of the equator?

4. With what temperate zone products does the African palm nut compete?

5. What industries make the heaviest freight traffic in tropic Africa?

6. How were the ancients ahead of the moderns in the domestic animal question?

CHAPTER XXXIX

SOUTH AFRICA

The part of Africa beyond the Tropic of Capricorn does not extend far enough south to get into the latitude of heavy rains produced by the prevailing westerlies. As a result it is a land of desert, made much worse by the mountains of Natal which shut off the southeast trade winds and limit the district of heavy trade wind rain to an eastern coast strip of relatively small area. The exports are therefore limited to minerals and the produce of arid agriculture, although the eastern coast is fitted by nature for the production of cane sugar, coffee, tea and other tropic and subtropic agriculture of which there is some development with the aid of East Indian coolies.

We see the aridity showing in an export of mohair exceeding that from Asia Minor, the home of the Angora goat, which, in Africa, pastures on the arid approaches to the Kalahari Desert. The better pastures on the great plains of the interior are given over to sheep and cattle ranches, but the total number of cattle in all Africa is less than that for Uruguay and Paraguay combined (about 12 million in 1910) and the most important part of the continent, British South Africa, has about as many (4 million) as Iowa. In Matabeleland, Rhodesia, north of the Transvaal border, a large grant of land has recently been made to a London company which is now building dipping tanks (for disinfecting live animals and removing vermin), digging wells, and stocking its ranch with cattle. Later it is planned to build a meat-extract plant. The location, as far from the Southern Sea as Chicago is from the Atlantic, and with no home market, is a natural one for the manufacture of so concentrated a product.

The aridity is too great for the growth of a home supply of wheat, an occurrence found in no other new land in a temperate zone.

In the seventeenth century when Holland was the great maritime, financial, and commercial power of Europe, as England was in the nineteenth, the Dutch settled South Africa as a provisioning station for their East India ships. Later, England took the Cape and the Dutch went inland and now the region has the two races mixed and under English rule. Except in the extreme South the black population far outnumbers the white, and the race problem is acute.

Cape Colony, Natal, the Transvaal, and Orange River Colony are a pastoral and mining region, resembling some parts of the western United States and having an area a little larger than Texas and New Mexico. This region is in the early stages of ranching and agriculture, is being rapidly settled, and has an expanding railway net. The railroads, which are so necessary, are building in many directions to develop a constantly enlarging frontier. The backbone of this railway system, the trunk line running north from Cape Town, is being pushed steadily northward and has five side lines connecting with the ocean at Port Elizabeth, East London, Durban, Lourenco Marques and Beira.

Southern South Africa, having the Mediterranean type of climate (see chapter on Fruits), is admirably fitted for fruit production, and has two advantages over any North Temperate zone region. One advantage is a very mild winter, because there is no land from which cold waves can rush in. The other advantage is the ripening season, which permits the shipping of fresh grapes, plums, and peaches to London and New York in March and April. Thus far the great distances and the time and cost involved have made prices so high that the export has remained small, but the natural resources seem excellent.

South Africa has developed one new agricultural industry—the domestication of the ostrich. It has almost a monopoly of the export of the plumes. This is an interesting example of a new domestic animal and a new industry. The plume-producing bird is a native of semi-arid Africa, being found over most of the Sudan and large areas in South Africa. The Hamar Arabs in West Kordofan, Sudan, keep a few birds in pens, but the feathers are inferior to those from wild birds which were until recently the sole supply in all lands. The British in South Africa are the real founders of the ostrich industry, having found that when enclosed by a strong fence and supplied with suitable food of grain and good grass the ostrich will thrive about as well in domestication as the sheep. In 40 years the Afrikanders have reduced ostrich keeping to a science, established systems of registry for pure bred birds and improved them to the point where $5,000 has been paid for a single bird for breeding purposes. The number of tame birds in the fields of Cape Colony farmers is estimated at 500,000, the best feathers sell at over $200 per pound, and the feather export at

FIG. 269.—Ostriches—the last important addition to our domestic animals. (Reproduced by permission of the Philadelphia Commercial Museum.)

$9,000,000 rivals that of wool even though the colony has 18 million sheep (Fig. 269).

In one irrigated district on the Grobbelaars river, 2 miles by 70, 80,000 ostriches are kept at pasture on alfalfa. They yield over $20 apiece per year and the land sells for $750 to $1,000 per acre. A change in styles might change all this.

The commerce of South Africa is predominantly dependent upon the gold and diamond industries. The gold output of Transvaal and Rhodesia far exceeds that of any other country. The producing district of the Transvaal, known as the Rand, is a long range of low hills, the leading gold district of the world, with Johannesburg as its chief center. It is in a semi-arid country like New Mexico or Arizona, where other industries are few and communities of hundreds of thousands of people must live by mining alone. The deposits are of great depth, and the companies can therefore plan to work for many years. It is the practice to bring men from great distances to work in these mines on time contracts. They come from interior Africa and from China, but the Chinese must be taken back to China by the mining companies when these contracts expire. In 1909, the total number of men employed on the Rand was about 220,000, and nearly 10,000 stamps were at work.

In the diamond output of the world Transvaal is even more predominant than in gold. Brazil was for a long time the leading diamond-producing country in the world. The Brazilian diamonds were found upon the interior plateaus of the state of Minas Geraes, near Diamantina, in a sparsely settled region where the diamonds had been left in the beds of streams by the same process which leaves gold in the stream, namely, the washing down from the mother lode. During the last quarter of the nineteenth century, South Africa vastly outdistanced Brazil, because of the discovery of several so-called diamond pipes in the vicinity of Kimberly, in the Transvaal. These deposits are believed to be the cores of old volcanoes with diamonds imbedded in the lava, now existing as a hard formation known as blue clay or diamond clay. The washing of the clay from these old volcanic necks produced diamonds so much more cheaply than the hunters of Brazil can find them that for many years South Africa has virtually supplied the world. Nearly all the product is furnished by two companies, which maintain one of the tightest trusts in the world.

There is prospect that the long diamond monopoly of British South Africa will shortly disappear. Further explorations in Africa have revealed new finds of true diamond-bearing earth in Rhodesia, while in German Southwest Africa, diamonds are secured in the sand on or near the seashore for 300 miles north of

Elizabeth Bay. Miners wash the sand for diamonds just as the gold miners wash the Cape Nome sand for gold. Unfortunately for the easy prosecution of the industry, this region is a desert, less so than that of similar latitudes in north Chile, but supplies must be brought hundreds of miles. Recent explorations seem to indicate the discovery of the volcanic neck from which these shore diamonds have been washed. Thus German Africa has had developments similar to the Transvaal, where there was for a time a large diamond industry on the shores of the Vaal River, where the searching for water-borne stones finally led to the discovery of the mother lode in the blue clay.

Foreign Trade.—British South Africa is served by several lines of splendid steamers working in unison and giving service from Liverpool, New York, London, Southampton, and the Continent. The liners engaged in the South African trade pay no heed whatever to all the rest of Africa, but steam directly from Europe and America to Cape Town and usually skirt the coast to Lorenco Marques, stopping at Port Elizabeth, East London, and Durban (Fig. 270).

The traffic of South Africa is a very peculiar one in the world's trade. Regions of sparse population and comparatively recent settlement are usually producers of large quantities of raw material and consumers of manufactures, which comprise a much smaller tonnage. Such has been the commercial history of practically every country in the New World; but, owing to the scanty rainfall, which precludes extensive agriculture in South Africa, and the great predominance of gold and diamond mining among the industries there, South Africa imports several million tons per year of coal, lumber, grain, flour, machinery, and general manufactures, and pays for them in such valuable commodities as gold, diamonds, ostrich feathers, wool, mohair, hides, and skins. The old saying that "good goods come in small packages" here holds true, so that a vessel carrying a cargo to South Africa faces the almost inevitable prospect of going away practically empty. The Cape is therefore a scattering point for vessels in ballast, seeking freight.

The future of the American trade with South Africa and Australasia is particularly bright, because these British colonies are in the same stage of industrial development as parts of the American West. We have had experience with their kind of physical problems, our agricultural machinery is adapted to their kind of land, as our mining machinery is adapted to their mines, and there is

every reason to expect a continued and increasing trade in American
machinery and supplies for the development of these new lands,

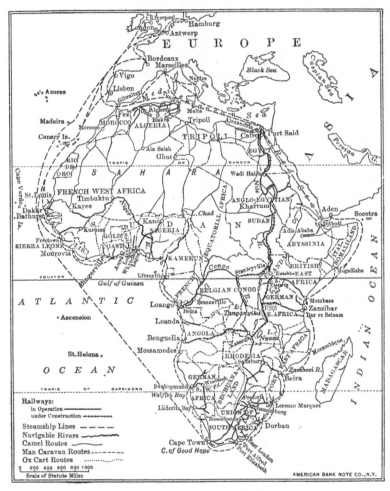

FIG. 270.—Trade routes of Africa.

while our mills and tanneries are increasingly dependent upon their
wool, hides, and skins.

QUESTIONS

1. Give a climatic explanation of the fact that South Africa imports more tons of freight than she exports, the influence of the mining industry on the same fact.

2. What advantages and disadvantages does South Africa have for the development of the fruit and vine industries?

3. How does the climate cause an export of mohair rather than pork or beef?

4. How have the South Africans established a new animal industry?

CHAPTER XL

AUSTRALASIA AND POLYNESIA

Australia has many points of resemblance to South Africa. It has the same latitude, the same trade wind desert, just missing the good rain-bearing west winds, and it even has a north and south mountain range along the east coast to shut off the winds which have in similar latitudes made such a fine country of Uruguay and part of Argentina. Fortunately this rain-checking mountain range is not so high as it is in Natal, thus permitting large areas to get enough rainfall to produce some pastures, although most of the continent is desert. (Figs. 271a and 271b.) Australia differs from South Africa in being entirely settled by whites and of British race.

The animal industries.—Australia has long been known as the greatest of sheep countries and the leader of wool exporters. It is about as large as the United States, but the mountain barrier parallel to the eastern coast shuts off from the interior most of the rain brought by the southeast trade winds, leaving only a narrow plain along the coast fit for corn and other agricultural crops requiring much moisture. Between the mountains and the grassless desert which occupies the central and western part of the continent are some of the finest sheep ranges in the world. The railroads that connect the ranches with the eastern ports reach almost to the desert and all the land that has any value has for some decades been occupied by the sheep flocks. (Fig. 272.) Australia is unfortunate in the arid nature of much of her territory and also in the irregular character of the scanty rainfall. Droughts sometimes last for long periods, cutting off both grass and water so that the sheep perish by millions, as in the period 1894 to 1898 when continued drought reduced the sheep flocks from 110 million to 84 million. The great dependence of the flocks upon rainfall and rainfall fluctuations is shown by the observations of a scientist who says that with 10 inches of rainfall per year, an Australian plain will support ten sheep per square mile; with 13 inches of rain, twenty sheep; and with 20 inches of rain, seventy sheep.

With less than 10 inches of rainfall, the land is of no value even for pasturage.

New South Wales possesses more than half the sheep of Australia, while Queensland, further north (partly in the tropics) has more

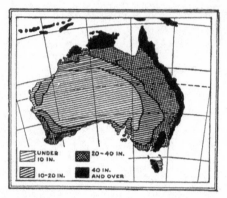

FIG. 271a.—Mean annual rainfall for Australia.   (Diercke.)

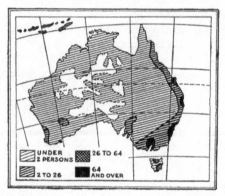

FIG. 271b.—Map showing density of population per square mile in Australia. (Lyde.)   (From Salisbury, Barrows, and Tower.)   Australia is almost an empty shell.

rain and heat and better forage, and therefore, a predominance of cattle over sheep, since they can stand heat and moisture better than sheep, and require better pasture.   South of New South Wales is Victoria, which lies far enough from the equator to be in the edges of the zone of prevailing westerly winds and gets more rain than New South Wales. It has better pastures and only one-quarter as many sheep. Because of the superiority of the Victorian pasture in a cool climate the farmers have enough grass to keep cows and make butter, of which much more is exported than is exported from the United States (see table of dairy products). The market for the butter, as for the frozen beef of Queensland and frozen mutton of

FIG. 272.—A flock of sheep in Australia. The fence is American.

New South Wales, is almost entirely in the mother country, Great Britain.

The large flocks of Australia (Fig. 272), like those of other southern hemisphere lands, help to give the South Temperate Zone 40 per cent of the world's sheep, although it has but 1½ per cent of the population. In Australia the sparse population of about 1½ per square mile has, for each 100 people, 280 horses and cattle and 2,100 sheep and hogs—chiefly sheep. These figures show why meat and other animal products make up such a large proportion of the exports of these sparsely peopled south temperate zone countries.

Since swine are meat animals of grain-growing lands, as the sheep is of grass-growing lands, pastoral Australia has 100 sheep to one hog, wnile Iowa, a great corn state, has seven hogs to one sheep. The production of sheep just suits these lands, but the fact that some of these lands are hot, and do not naturally suit the sheep, is another illustration of an industry in a place that is not best suited to it. The sheep with his warm coat is equipped for cold climates; the fleece degenerates in hot lands, the wool entirely disappearing in the tropics, leaving only the hair coat, of which all sheep possess a little. In Australia, the tendency to degeneration because of heat has been overcome by the constant importation of fresh breeding stock from England, Vermont and other localities where the sheep is at his best.

New Zealand, farther south than Australia, with the good rainfall of the prevailing westerlies and an open winter, is an excellent sheep country, and is largely given over to that industry.

Some of the mountain pastures upon the western coast of New Zealand, very wet from exposure to the sea winds, have such splendid grass that they will support five sheep per acre throughout the year. These mountains make the eastern side of that island drier, and thus cause the Canterbury plain on the east, the best stretch of arable land on the islands, to be largely used for wheat growing; but owing to the sparse population, less than a million people in a good grazing territory as large as New York, New Jersey and Pennsylvania, agriculture cannot be very much developed and the 23 million sheep and 2 million cattle are the chief wealth of the country. The good pasture and regular food supply of New Zealand causes the frozen mutton of that country to be considered the best that is imported into England. The sheep are often fattened by being turned into large fields of turnips from which they first eat the tops and then the entire root, and it is said that mutton can be produced at a cost of 3 cents a pound.

When the Australasian sheep ranches were first established in the middle of the nineteenth century, there was no thought of selling meat. Wool, skins, tallow and bones were the products. In the decade between 1880 and 1890, the perfection of cold storage and refrigeration suddenly caused a demand for mutton at Buenos Ayres, at Wellington, New Zealand, at Melbourne and Sidney, Australia, as well as at Chicago, Kansas City, and Omaha. The rising price of meat since 1900 has emphasized that demand and made the carcass more valuable by far than the fleece.

The merino sheep, with his excellent fleece, had no plump fat carcass, while the mutton-loving English had carefully bred and selected the Lincolnshire and the Southdown and other breeds for the ability to grow large and fat and make fine mutton, regardless of their coarse and meagre wool. The refrigerator ship suddenly made the big, fat sheep more valuable in the Argentine Republic, Montana, and Australia than was the fine fleeced little merino. As a result, the sheep breeders at once began cross breeding their flocks for mutton rather than wool, and in a little while the sheep were half Lincolnshire, then three-quarters, and often seven-eighths. As a result, the people of Europe can now eat antipodean mutton, but the wool market has been disturbed by the great increase of coarse wool and the decrease of fine wool. New Zealand and the Argentine Republic have changed the sheep more rapidly than Australia, which has clung longer to the wool sheep, because in the latter country the great droughts often make it impossible to fatten sheep for market.

Agricultural Industries.—The rather limited argiculture of Australasia is due in part to the climatic limitations, but even more to the scarcity of population. There is little doubt that New Zealand possesses agricultural resources superior to those of Italy, a country about the same size, with thirty times its population. But one family with 500 or 1,000 acres can do little more than herd its pasturing flocks, while one family with 3 or 5 acres must till it most intensively.

In Australia the moisture suffices for wheat growing only on the eastern, southern, and extreme southwestern sections, and her crop varies greatly with the fluctuating rainfall on this desert margin. New Zealand is a regular wheat exporter because it misses the belt of scanty rainfall which roughly follows the tropics of Cancer and Capricorn. It gets instead the regular rains of the west wind. Australia gets the rain of southern California, and New Zealand that of Washington state. Like England, in a similar latitude and climate, New Zealand has a splendid wheat yield per acre, about 30 bushels, in contrast to 10 or 12 bushels in southern Australia. There are a few scattered places where corn is grown to some extent, as in northern New Zealand, and in the eastern margin of Australia, but here it has to battle against droughts and scanty rainfall and is unimportant.

The New Zealand Government has taken great pains to inspect and guarantee the quality of exports of dairy products, with the result that its butter and cheese stand well in European markets.

Their export is more important than in Australia, which, being further north, and out of the latitude of steady rains, has her production of dairy products sadly interfered with by the droughts, and chiefly limited to Victoria, the most southerly, the coolest, and rainiest part of a warm dry continent.

Fruits.—Australia, like the other continents, has its region of summer drought and irrigation. In the state of Victoria, the irrigation colony of Mildura on the Murray River has under irrigation a quarter million acres of land under the same kind of arid climate that prevails in California, Spain, and Asia Minor, and the people are already producing dried prunes, dried peaches, dried apricots, dried currants, and raisins for the home market, and occasionally exporting to Great Britain, where they compete with the products of the Mediterranean countries and California.

Australia has large vine-growing areas near her arid interior, and it is admitted that the product of certain vineyards is practically as good as any wine in the world. In New South Wales, the farmers have been driven to grape growing because the droughts, although they ruin the wheat, will not prevent a crop of grapes. Owing to the sparse population of Australia, however, its wine production is insignificant. Export, which would stimulate production, still labors under the handicap that the reputation of Australian wines has yet to be made (see chapter on France and Belgium).

There also appears to be indefinite room for apple growing, particularly in the island of Tasmania, which is about as large as West Virginia. It much resembles this state in its mixture of mountain and valley, its good rainfall, and its suitability to the apple, and in its mountain orchards. Its orchard area is one-tenth as great as that of Britain. Tasmanian apples are sent to Australia and to a limited extent to England. South New Zealand with a similar climate sends more of them to the British market. The total export from the southern hemisphere, however, is small in comparison to that of the United States and Canada.

Sugar and cotton.—The sugar situation is very similar to that of the fruits, but the scarcity of labor is even more acute. In the warmer part of Australia there is a very large area of admirable cane land, especially in Queensland, but though the population is less than one per square mile, the strenuous desire of the Australian commonwealth to remain a white man's land has caused the enactment of laws stopping the admission of the colored laborers

(Hindoo, Chinese, or South Sea Islanders) who had been the planter's dependence. The white men who own the Queensland lands could superintend large numbers of East Indian, Polynesian, or Chinese laborers if they could get them. But this would result in Queensland becoming essentially an African or Chinese or Polynesian community, with but a small percentage of white people. This the other Australians do not wish, and, therefore, they will not permit the Queenslanders to import a single coolie. The North and South problem is there also a bitter one, as it was in America in 1861 when the South wanted slaves and the North did not. As white laborers will not go to the tropics, the Queensland sugar output is not increasing, and sugar is imported from Fiji Islands where imported Hindoos grow it at home under white guidance.

There also seems to be a large area of unused cotton land in Queensland.

Forests and lumber.—Australia has some of the largest trees in the world in her eucalyptus, a genus that grows with great speed and is of great value in many temperate lands. Except in the tropic north there is not much forest in Australia, and she is an importer of pine from United States and Sweden. Certain small sections in southwestern Australia produce two species of export wood. They are members of the Eucalyptus family, the karri and jarri, which, through their hardness and durability in the ground, are well suited for wooden pavements and are exported to European cities for that purpose. The northern island of New Zealand has some splendid forests of the gum-yielding kauri, a tree furnishing logs 8 to 10 feet in diameter and 100 feet long. New Zealand's lumber export, though small, is growing.

Minerals.—For half a century minerals have been very important in Australian trade. With a gold output of $65,000,000 per year (1910), she is third among the world's producers. The output of the newer west Australian fields, like that of the mines of Victoria, is declining, with the result that the total gold production for Australia fell off about $15,000,000 between 1906 and 1910. The Victoria deposits, first discovered in 1851, have been worked to the depth of a mile, which is about the limit for mining at present. It is expected, however, that the production of west Australia will continue at its present level, about half of the total, for a number of years, now that the surface deposits are collected and the working of the deep quartz has begun.

There is also some copper mining, but the most valuable of all minerals is coal, of which both Australia and New Zealand have enough for their own needs. Australia with mines near Sydney has considerable export of coal across the Pacific to Chile and California.

Manufacture and trade.—Although the coal and other resources of Australia and New Zealand are extensive, the population, small, practically stationary, and less than that of Illinois, does not furnish a labor supply adequate for any large amount of manufacturing. There are many small manufactures, but there is no

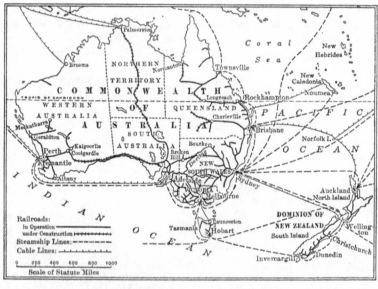

FIG. 273.—Trade route map of Australia.

iron making and the foreign trade is marked, like that of South Africa, by an extensive exchange of raw materials for a great variety of manufactures. Most of the railroads (Fig. 273), many of the ranches, and other industries, are owned by the people of the mother country, and we see the basis of a part of Britain's heavy imports in the Australian export in a recent year of $339,000,000 worth, while she (an interest-paying country) bought but $252,000,000 worth.

Polynesia.—The vast expanses of the Pacific between Australasia, Tahiti, Hawaii, Guam, and New Guinea (Fig. 274) are dotted with a multitude of islands, mostly very small, often uninhabited, often densely inhabited, and having two great resources—fish and cocoanuts. The cocoanut is most important to these South Sea Islanders, to some of whom it directly supplies an amazing variety of wants and furnishes the only means of purchasing the products of the outside world, which come to them in small vessels, veritable floating department stores that skirt the populous archipelagoes trading for

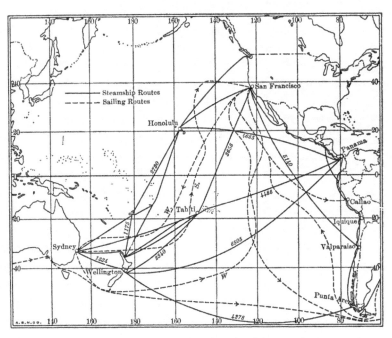

FIG. 274.—Routes of Southern and Eastern Pacific Ocean. W—winter. S—summer.

cocoanut meats and cocoanut oils, which finally find their way to the European soap factories—at Antwerp, Liverpool, Hamburg, and Marseilles. One of the leading manufactures of Sydney, the metropolis of Australia, is the new branch of a British soap company. The plant crushes 1,500,000 cocoanuts per week. The annual harvest of 23,000 acres of palm groves is brought to it by steamers which scour the Pacific from Christmas Island on the east to Solomon Islands on the west, including Fiji, Samoa, and Tonga. Some of these islands are never visited by any other ships. This one plant at Sydney makes soap, supplies Australia with cocoanut oil, exports much to Europe, and also has as by-products glycerine, and oil cake for cattle food. From New Caledonia comes the complaint that the natives can make a living so easily gathering cocoanuts ($100 per ton for copra) that they do not care to work for white men or dig in the chrome mines.

QUESTIONS

1. Why do Australia and New Zealand differ in the importance of the dairy industry?

2. Why do Iowa and New South Wales, two agricultural states with the same market, differ so much in the crops and animals produced?

3. Explain the status of the Queensland sugar industry and the political controversy that arises from it.

4. Compare Australia with Italy and France in grape-growing resources; in grape industry.

5. How has the refrigerator ship disturbed the wool manufacturers?

6. Australia has iron ore and coal. Why is there no large iron industry?

PART III

WORLD COMMERCE

CHAPTER XLI

EXPANSION OF INDUSTRY AND RESOURCES

1. THE BALANCE BETWEEN RESOURCES AND HUMAN NEED

There is frequent expression of the idea that opportunities for making a living are getting fewer, that the world holds fewer oppor-

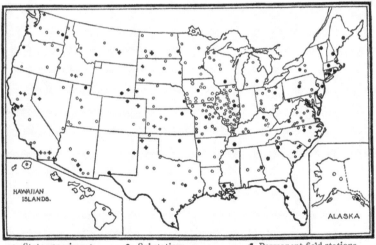

HAWAIIAN
ISLANDS.

ALASKA

● State experiment   o Substations.   ✿ Permanent field stations.
  stations.

FIG. 275.—Map showing the location of agricultural experiment stations and substations in United States. U. S. Dept. of Agriculture. (Bureau of Plant Industry.)

tunities per man than it previously possessed. This belief is not founded in geographic or scientific fact. A community needs for its support, land for the production of food and raw materials,

533

power with which to manufacture and transport goods, and a good climate to maintain vigor and health. While the actual material in the world is not increasing, our knowledge of ways to utilize it is increasing so rapidly that the unused opportunities for industry (resources) appear many fold greater than our needs, and they are increasing faster than population is increasing.

The degree of utilization of resources.—The question naturally arises, when are resources fully utilized, and when is a country fully occupied? It is difficult to say when a country is full because of the present practice of living by manufacturing and consuming the products of other localities. The question of the standard of living is a second factor making it difficult to determine when resources are fully utilized. If the population is content to live in small houses rather than large, to eat grains and vegetables rather than meat and other things requiring more land to produce, then the population can be large. Under the system of household industry many localities of Europe and Asia have become populated up to the food limit, the non-flesh food limit, and the record of famines in India shows that country to be far beyond the food limit in years of crop failure. Millions there have starved beside the railway, which could have brought them food if they had had goods or money with which to buy it.

Belgium, and other densely peopled western localities have passed the point where they can under present standards feed their people from their own land; but they have passed into the stage of buying raw materials, selling them again as manufactures, and importing food with the proceeds. The steady increase of commercial facilities, shows evidence of continuing growth in manufacture, population, and dependence upon the foreign markets and upon foreign raw materials. To a large number of people in manufacturing districts, their land is a home space, their sustenance space being, in part at least, in other lands.

The best example of a country approaching the full development of its resources is Japan, with meager mineral wealth, rugged topography, a small proportion of arable land, and a population of 2,200 per square mile of tilled land, nearly four persons per acre. Until the recent sudden shift to commerce, this population supported itself almost entirely by agriculture, with an average area of 2.6 acres per farm family. Upon this slim resource, the nation had maintained its physical and intellectual vigor and a high civilization; but to do so they have entered almost exclusively upon the ultimate stage of agriculture, namely, the non-flesh diet and the garden stage of hand labor, which would make Oriental wheat cost $4 or $5 per bushel if American wages were paid.

The mystery of the way in which China supports her millions is explained by a skilled American agricultural observer's account of a visit to the farms of the densely peopled province of Shantung. (*Farmers of Forty Centuries*, F. H. King.)

"Every scrap of vegetable matter and excrement is saved and returned to the fields, which yield a harvest of wheat or barley in June, and then, with the aid of midsummer monsoon rains, a second crop of millet, corn, sweet potatoes, peanuts or soy beans." The last two are nitrogenous meat substitutes and help explain the observer's statement that "One of the farmers in this province with whom we talked had a family of twelve people which he was maintaining on 2.5 acres of good farm land, keeping besides one milk cow (also used as a work animal), one donkey, and two pigs. The crops raised were wheat or barley, millet, soy beans, and sweet potatoes." This is at the astonishing rate of 3,072 persons per square mile and also on the same square mile 256 cows, 256 donkeys, and 512 pigs. It would be an impossible search to find an American square mile that could feed, under American methods, the animals alone.

2. Unused Agricultural Resources of the Temperate Zones

It is plain that there are two standards for the utilization of land— the *Oriental standard* of hand labor, largely non-flesh diet, and the *Western standard* based upon work animals, dairying, and other animal industries. Judged even by the western standards the temperate zones have large unused agricultural resources. In contrast to Italy, China, and Japan, we may class North America, the South Temperate Zone, and even parts of Asia as relatively unoccupied lands.

So little is farm land utilized and sought in the United States that in large areas east of the Alleghenies it is a common saying based upon fact, that when a man sells a farm he gives away either the value of the building or the value of the land, for the price obtained is often less than would be required to replace the buildings. Very little of the land cultivated in the United States has reached the intensive stage, and we have an advantage unique among lands of large resources—the great gift of corn for which we have a vast area. Over 1 million square miles of the United States can produce this king of forage crops, the most productive and easily grown of all the grains. Further, this grain lends itself to double cropping, the recourse of the crowded people (Fig. 276).

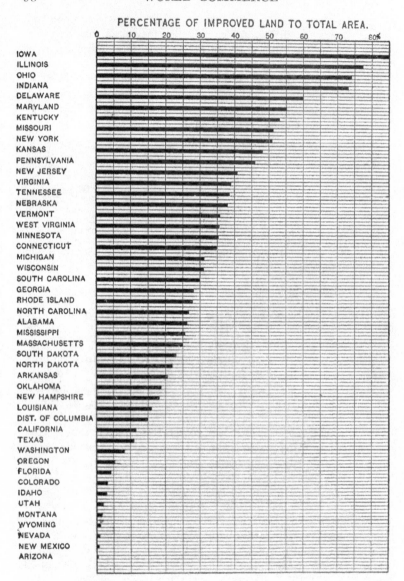

PERCENTAGE OF IMPROVED LAND TO TOTAL AREA.

FIG. 276.—This graph is more worthy of study than statistics of area. The low percentage of unimproved land in the regions of good rainfall show great possibilities as do the present low yields of much of the improved land. (Report of the U. S. Conservation Commission.)

In Japan and China, and wherever possible in Italy, the land is made to yield two crops per year, winter grain between October and June, and rice or other summer crop between June and September. Similar double cropping, now almost unknown in the United States, can be done, if need be, in most of the United States corn belt. For example, as far north as New Jersey a good crop of peas can be harvested in May and June, and young corn, sown between the rows,

FIG. 277.—Ditch digging by machinery on the Mississippi flood plain. Note the wheel, called caterpillar. It keeps the machine from sinking in the soft earth over which it travels as it digs. (The Bucyrus Co., Milwaukee, Wis.)

will ripen a full crop before frost. Even a third crop can be grown and agriculture yet maintain its western standard. Cowpeas, clover, and several other leguminous plants will thrive with the corn or cotton, enriching the soil with their roots, feeding animals with their tops and making possible a wealth of agricultural production now undreamed of in most of the United States and impossible in sunny Italy, with its rainless summer. Yet even there over 300 people per square mile succeed in extracting a living from the earth.

The American cotton belt, with its summer rain, now supporting only from twenty to fifty people per square mile and six times the size of Italy, has easily twice the abilities of Italy in the production of food, raiment, and timber and is many fold richer in minerals and water-power. We have in the United States 100,000 square miles of swamp lands, scattered among the old glacial lake beds in the northeast, in tidal marshes along the Atlantic coast, in cane brakes south of the Chesapeake and in the alluvial lands along the Mississippi and other rivers. These swamps and 60,000 square miles to be irrigated can be made twice as productive as uplands (Fig. 277).

It is possible to adopt much of the Old World intensification of agriculture and still keep the American large-scale machine processes (see Louisiana rice industry in chapter on Cereals) which permit large production per man and a high standard of life. The application of science to agriculture is just beginning in the United States and all other new countries, and is now being rapidly pushed forward by the governments of all the leading countries. The greatest work for the promotion of agriculture now is the teaching of science to the masses—not more discoveries, but the practice of what is now known, so that we may have an agriculture that is adjusted to resources and conditions. As an example of results of such endeavor, note the following great increases in average yield resulting from 25 years of teaching in Belgium (Fig. 275).

	1880–85, bu. per acre	1907–10, bu. per acre	Increases, bu. per acre
Wheat..........	24.54	38.55	14.01
Rye............	23.86	36.69	12.73
Oats...........	49.79	81.48	31.69
Winter barley ..	38.25	57.57	19.32

A comparison of these *increases* with the American yield is surprising.

What has been said of the unused resources of the United States might be said, with varying figures, of Canada, Alaska, Siberia, southwestern Asia, and the South Temperate Zone. For example, the South Temperate Zone with millions of square miles of land, has a total population less than that of Holland and Belgium. These large territories, while greatly limited by aridity, have a wholesome,

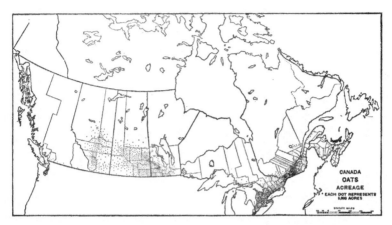

The universal growth of oats in eastern Canada finds its counterpart only in corn-less Europe. (Finch and Baker.)

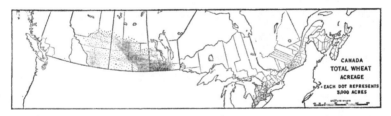

The location of the Canadian wheat area shows what a small proportion of that great has yet been utilized.

The area covered by the wheat crop and the oat crop in western Canada is no index either of the ultimate boundaries of this grain region or of the density of production. This land is new to agriculture. (It is not yet fully equipped with railroads. The world has not called for heavy wheat export from it.) If demand should increase, the crop here can be enormously increased by the addition of millions of workers following rational, scientific, and reasonably intensive agriculture, marked by rotation of crops, the keeping of cattle, preferably dairy cows, and the use of commercial fertilizers. This merely means the duplication of the agriculture of the best parts of eastern Canada and the United States, or whole belts of territory in Holland, France, Denmark, or Germany.

The same use of the wheat region in corresponding latitudes in Russia and Siberia offers interesting speculation.

The tractor, probably the major agricultural invention of the 20th century.

The beet, typical of the northern agriculture so little developed in America.

This New England field of forage beets is symbolical of the northern agriculture which has as two of its great staples the heavy yielding root crops—beets, carrots, turnips—as food for beasts and the heavy yielding potato crop as food for man. If at any time anyone fears the early approach of serious food shortage, let him consider the possibilities of this northern agriculture and take comfort.

So far as land resources are concerned, Europe may raise many more potatoes than it now grows and North America can easily multiply its potato area thirty-fold and then double the average yield per acre.

The potato is second only to wheat in the number of times per year that it is eaten in America, and in Europe it probably stands first. Analysis shows that it is very close to wheat in actual food value; but it contains so much water that we have to eat four times as much potato as wheat in order to obtain the same amount of nourishment.

The figures of possible increase may seem surprising but there is nothing unreasonable about them. The fact is we have developed in America a systematic warm land agriculture and have not yet reached the degree of food shortage that would compel us to develop a systematic cold land agriculture. The price of meat is the crop controlling factor in American agriculture. The chief object of American agriculture is feeding animals, for they eat the major part of the produce of the American farm. Up to the present, the price of meat has been so low comparatively that it would not pay us to grow potatoes and beets to feed farm animals, as is the case in Germany, Denmark and Sweden.

The potato and beets have revolutionized Europe; they raised Germany from a third-rate power to a world menace, and if need be they may revolutionize the economic status of a great section of central North America from central Ohio to the forests of the Ontario highlands, and from Newfoundland to Michigan, Manitoba, Alberta and Alaska.

The figure of thirty-fold increase in area is not so astounding when we realize that in the year 1919 we had 4,000,000 acres of potatoes and 113,000,000 acres of corn. We have but to put the potatoes a little above corn in acreage.

It should be noted that this astounding increase in the production of potatoes which we do not now want can aid in giving us an increase in the amount of grain and milk and meat produce. On this new price level the farmer in Maine, Ontario, Alberta or the Yukon Valley may have a hundred acre farm with crops as follows: 15 acres wheat, or rye, 15 acres barley or oats, 15 acres potatoes, 15 acres forage roots, 5 acres homestead, garden, etc., 20 acres rough land for pasture. From this farm wheat or rye and potatoes would go directly to market, everything else being consumed on the place by dairy cows, furnishing enormous quantities of milk, butter or cheese and some meat. The tractor may have a big place in this agriculture where there is such a long season of idleness for working animals.

There has now come on the scene a new factor, whose possible power to make wheat and many other crops is almost as little foreseen today as was the locomotive in 1840. It is the farm tractor. We have made great strides in the cheap production of wheat by getting tools that depend on the muscle of our strong beasts rather than on the muscle of our weak selves. The four footed harvester has reduced the cost of grain. The iron horse, hitched to the wagon and the boat, has made a new world. The iron horse (tractor) hitched to the plow is going to work another transformation, particularly in the world of wheat, probably also in the world of corn and potatoes. It has just begun. The wheat crop of the world is today dependent, with few exceptions, upon the muscle of beasts. The Italians are even still cutting much wheat by hand on their terraces and little odd-shaped patches on their steep and rocky mountain slopes. But most of the land for the world's crops is plowed by the horse, the mule, and the ox, who also draw the seeding drill and the reaper. Enough camels are helping to make the list picturesque. At the most, these farm animals may be needed for only six or eight weeks of work in producing the grain crop; but they must eat for twelve months. If there is a crop failure every third year they must eat for thirty-six months in order to make two crops; and if there is a failure every other year, they must eat forty-eight months in order to make two crops. Despite their months of necessary loafing they get tired when they work, and must rest. They get hot, they get sick, they go lame. The farm tractor does not get tired, it does not eat when it is not working. We can probably improve it to the point where it will not go lame. It can go night and day, and in the rush season a man who has had a long period of rest can work fifteen or sixteen hours a day for many days, and then someone else can take his tractor and, with our present knowledge of lighting, keep it going throughout the night. One man, instead of driving three or four horses, turns on the power of twenty or forty or sixty horses that will work twenty-four hours a day. The acreage of level plain that a family can plant with this new help is several times as large as that within the reach of man aided merely by beasts. It is already claimed that in level Dakota a man, with the help of his wife and one child, can plant 120 acres.

This enlarged acreage means reduction in the cost of wheat growing. It means that wheat can be grown in lands that we before thought worthless because of the uncertainties of rainfall. Take the case of some experiments of Cheyenne, Wyoming, which in three seasons produced respectively 9.3, 7.8, and 37.6 bushels because of the difference of four inches of rain in the growing season. The average was 18.2. Four of the low crops and one of the high would still average 14.3, a figure that looks well among national averages, made possible by one good season in five. Such farming would scarcely be profitable with the aid of beasts, but it is easily practicable with the aid of the tractor.

In lands of low rainfall it has been well proved that the wheat yield can be increased in quantity and certainty by the practice of summer fallowing, which means plowing the land one year and raising the crop the next. By this means no plant is allowed to grow during the fallow season and the water which would otherwise evaporate. through the growing plants (a surprising amount) remains in the subsoil, where it welcomes the next year's rainfall and combines with it to water one good crop out of the two year's supply. The trouble with this system is that it requires much cultivation. It is easy to see how the tractor helps at summer fallowing and so will push the wheat fields out into the lands of little rain and of frost. The tractor will enable wheat growing to become a dependable business in climates where frost or drought may almost spoil two crops out of three, if one bumper crop gets to the threshing machine; farms, towns, and food-supply may then be found in places where now the farmer gives up in despair.

There is no way as yet to reduce to figures what the tractor may do for us, but it probably will enable seven wheat-belts running through five continents to be widened out—toward the region of drought and frost through central Asia and central North America, and toward the region of drought through Argentina, Australia, and South Africa.

This possibility of development means that we are in the beginning of another century of spring wheat which has in the last sixty years made wheat more abundant in the commercial world than ever before.

Taken altogether, the undeveloped lands of the present wheat regions, the possible regions of the new wheat growing, the new varieties, the new fertilizers, the new knowledge, and the farm tractor, seem to promise that a wheat supply is within our reach for many, many decades if we can devote our powers to the conquests of nature rather than to the destruction of men.

invigorating climate, and resources that will permit a many-fold
increase in the population based on a many-fold increase in the production of grain, meat, dairy products, and fruits, Moreover, like
most of the world, their mineral resources are but slightly prospected.

3. SCIENCE CREATES RESOURCES

In the face of all these usable but unused resources comes the
great growth of science, which is yet young. Our new knowledge,
applicable alike to agriculture, manufacture, mining, and transport,

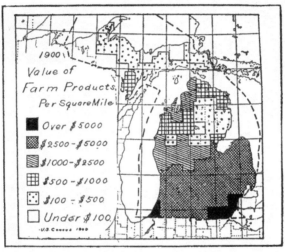

FIG. 278.—Farm products in Michigan. (After A. E. Parkins.) A good
illustration of the way glaciers have laid out the occupation of men—rough land
having prohibited plow agriculture. Most of it is, however, good for tree agriculture which has not yet been largely adopted.

gives us many new facilities for utilizing things heretofore unavailable. Science may be said to create resources of great aid to every
land from empty Australia to the teeming Orient, still depending
upon human muscle for bearing burdens and running the loom.

One of the great resource creators is chemistry. Suggestive of
progress from this source is the synthetic method of making indigo,
which is now almost entirely produced from retorts of coal tar rather
than the vats in which the people of India and Central America
fermented the stalks of the indigo plant. The indigo fields are now
free to produce food.

It therefore appears that in the twentieth century the human race looks out upon a new world—a world newer in the economic sense than the one Columbus showed to the sixteenth century—the world created by scientific industry and speedy transportation.

FIG. 279.—The mangum terrace —a great discovery in agriculture. It is a ridge going across the face of a slope so that water will follow it to the edge of the field instead of running down the field and carrying away the soil. While it retards erosion in plowed fields it does not prevent the use of farm machinery. (U. S. Dept. Agr.)

Old standards for the measurement of the value of lands to man are gone and the new scientific utilizations are changing that value by a series of improvements more rapid than we have ever before experienced, and the end is not in sight.

New resources for manufacture.—Aside from the production of food, the most important single resource for the maintenance of existing civilization is that which will give power to drive machinery. At the present time we are depending largely upon coal, which, being a mineral, is one of our surely perishable resources. Unlike the field which may yield thousands of crops, or the forests which may perpetually yield timber or the waterfall which will run on for ages, coal, once used, is gone forever. This most important mineral has recently had its economic value doubled by the discovery of the art of making producer gas, which utilizes inferior coal or peat itself, for the making of gas for the running of gas engines—much the most efficient means at present known of producing power from fuel.

Alcohol is, however, a more permanent fuel than producer gas. It can be produced from henequin pulp, corn stalks, potatoes, and a great variety of vegetable materials. We already know how to use it as a rival of gasoline and kerosene, and it is extensively used for these purposes in Germany, which has no petroleum and much potato land. Alcohol as a source of power permits us to go indefinitely, because it depends upon agriculture, the enduring industry.

The new turbine water wheel and the rapidly developing art of transmission of power by electricity are re-introducing a water-power era. The full utilization of power, which now flows uselessly to the sea, might enable many now sparsely peopled parts of the world to maintain large manufacturing populations.

If water-power should become inadequate there are many parts of the world in which the wind blows with great force and regularity. This has long been used as a source of industrial power in Holland, and modern windmills, if we choose to use them, are much more efficient than the picturesque Dutch pattern. The sun, the original source of all coal, all streams, and most of the wind, is, through its rays, showering upon the earth's surface unlimited energy, which we may shortly find to be the most easily obtained of all sources of power.

All other sources of power pale beside this great source—the direct rays of the sun which hurl into 9,000 square miles of Egyptian desert enough power to replace all the engines and water wheels in the world. Three different types of machines have utilized this power to a small extent. The success of such power development to the point of superiority to existing power sources offers interesting speculation as to where would be natural seats of empire when the best sources of power were within the zone of 200 or 400 mile power transmission from cloudless deserts.

Science increases mineral resources.—The application of science to the art of mining and purifying minerals and metals had produced changes quite as great as in other fields. As it is now possible to work deposits at least a mile in depth, and since, of the 50 million square miles of the earth's surface, we have prospected thoroughly less than 1 per cent, it is evident that we have scarcely touched the world's mineral resources.

New resources in agriculture.—Food is man's limiting factor. He absolutely requires a certain amount of it and the increase of the food supply is the thing that will permit man's numbers to add billion on billion in the peopling of the earth. Thus agriculture outranks all other industries in importance. By the creation of new resources in agriculture, science can give to man his greatest aids to increased support upon the earth.

Down to the end of the nineteenth century, man's progress in the increase of powers and the combat of difficulties was essentially the result of the unscientific effort of untrained workers and the enthusiasm of the individuals who tamed the wild animals of the forest, cultivated and improved by selection those plants that seemed most useful, and, by accident, made inventions and discoveries. We have now entered upon a new epoch, in which governments and institutions as well as individuals are promoting science and its applications.

We have recently discovered the laws of heredity and the art of breeding and therefore of improving the plants, and to some extent the animals, which furnish us most of our food, clothing, and raw materials. These plants become machines, man the mechanic, and the things he can create are of the greatest value. We understand the effects of environments in fitting plants to survive particular conditions. If the climate of Arizona is dry, we now know that each and every desert in the world has been developing plants to thrive in Arizona. For example, the date is an Old World adaptation of nature to the dry environment. Knowing this, we no longer depend upon chance introduction of plants by emigrants and plant-loving botanists. The search has become definite and organized. Thus a new alfalfa from Siberia, or a peach from Mongolia is hardy by the natural selection resulting from 10,000 to 10,000,000 raging winters. It is raw material for the plant breeder of the agricultural experiment station. By this work of the plant explorer and the plant breeder, we can get the new cold-resistant or quick-growing plant that pushes the farm line north, or the new drought-resistant plant that pushes the farm line into arid regions, or the better yielding plant for the fields now under cultivation. The sugar beet has had its sugar content increased several fold within a century—suggestive of changes for the better, that may come to any plant and are now actually in progress for many. Thus surprising results have been obtained in getting strains of corn to be (a) more vigorous and productive, (b) more oily, (c) more starchy, (d) more highly charged with protein than before. By the combination of the searching of the world's cold and arid deserts and the improvement of plants there found, new crops are already being produced and harvested in lands previously too arid or too cold for any use but scanty pasturages (see Kaffir corn in chapter on Cereals). Every mile the farm line is pushed westward in the Great Plains opens to cultivation 1,600 square miles of farms, which will, under existing American conditions, easily support 75,000 people, and in some countries of the world would support several times that number.

The domestication of new plants.—Vast additions to wealth, comfort, and industry are to come from the domestication of plants now unused or only produced by unaided nature. For two centuries cinchona was gathered from trees growing wild in the forest, and no one thought of questioning that the east slopes of the Andes had a permanent world monopoly of this precious product until, in 1852, the Dutch government introduced it into Java, and in 1860 the English introduced it into India and Ceylon. Java, with its populous valleys and humid mountain slopes, exported over 10,000 tons of cinchona bark in 1911. The price is one-thirtieth that which prevailed in 1870 when it was gathered wild upon the Andean slopes. The rubber industry seems to have in process the same changes that have transformed the cinchona industry.

New uses for plants long cultivated are equally suggestive. Thus the peanut is replacing corn on the edge of our Great Plains where the drought makes corn uncertain. At certain times corn is blasted by a shortage of water, while the peanut vine merely waits for rain and grows when it comes. Then the hogs root the crop up and fatten upon it. The peanut may be considered a partner of the cocoanut in the vegetable onslaught on the animal industries. While the cocoanut is a substitute for butter and other fats, the peanut (see its content in table of food values) is a substitute for butter, cheese, and meat. Taken together, these two nuts form an admirable example of the shift from animals to plants as sources of food supply (a step toward easy support of larger populations), and also a shift of support from cool to warmer lands.

Animal breeding.—Another great field where science affects agriculture is the breeding of animals. It follows the same laws as plant breeding, and has been understood longer. The work already done in this direction is easily appreciated by comparing the useful cow with the wild buffalo. By the application of known science to animal breeding, the efficiency of our domestic animals along many lines can be approximately doubled with little increase in the amount of man's effort in their behalf.

4. New Resources Through Tree Crops

Possibly the greatest of all agricultural benefits will come through the utilization of crop-yielding trees and the breeding of new ones— a piece of scientific work for which we are now ready.

The essential thing about the earth from the agricultural standpoint is its fertility. How to unlock it is man's problem. The key for this unlocking is vegetation, and vegetation must have as aids: first, heat; second, light; and third, moisture. The past insistence on a fourth factor, arability (ability to be plowed), has caused vast possibilities of fertility, heat, and moisture to be practically unused, and by the plowing of steep lands that should not be plowed, vast soil resources have been barbarously wasted and destroyed by erosion, to the permanent and profound injury of the earth as a home for man (Figs. 278, 279).

Man began agriculture at the wrong end of the plant kingdom. The grains upon which we feed are all weaklings. Harvest is often but a small handful in comparison to yields of tree crops— the engines of nature which have for ages been giving man the most astonishing object lessons of production, and inviting him to improve them rather than the feeble grains at their feet; but the grains are annuals—a profound advantage to the primitive man who started our agriculture.

Great productivity and profit of tree crops.—The chestnut orchards of Italy and Corsica yield *per acre* nuts in amount approximately equal to the per-acre yield of wheat fields in the United States. The wheat grows on the best and levelest and most easily tillable soil of America, while the chestnut orchards occupy at times the steep, rocky, untillable mountain sides. While the wheat lands must be plowed for each crop, the chestnut orchards produce their crop without tillage. The trees stand among the rocks and at their feet are pasturage and herds to match the laborious plowing and seed time of wheat culture. This tree crop is the

FIG. 280.—Tree crop agriculture. Grafted chestnut trees on granitic hillside in the Department of Ardeceh, 70 miles southwest of Lyons, France. Value $160 per acre, producing nuts, pasture for goats and cows, and bedding of leaves and Scotch broom.

bread supply and the money crop of many thousands of mountain dwellers in the higher regions of Mediterranean countries. The sale value of these chestnut orchards exceeds that of American wheat land (Fig. 280).

Despite this productivity of trees, we have until the present depended almost purely upon chance. Freak trees have arisen by accidental hybridizing here and there to become the parents of a variety.

Now, however, science has caught up. We need no longer depend upon chance, the well-tried method of the ancient nomad.

FIG. 281.—Fruiting branch of the wild persimmon in Georgia. The persimmon is very nutritious and grows wild over nearly a million square miles. It probably will become a great forage crop, as domestic animals like it and the tree is very hardy, growing on the poorest soil.

Plant breeding (scientific, not accidental) is a force that will transform agriculture as the steam engine has transformed transport and the factory. It will enable us to harness the trees, the great productive engines of the plant kingdom, and as a result tree crops, the crops of great yield, are to come out of the corners where they now occupy so inconspicuous a place. It is probable that the cultivated fruiting trees of all sorts do not cover over 2 per cent. as much ground as is given over to the less productive grains. As agriculture adjusts itself suitably to resource, the area of tree crops, with their great superiorities, will eventually far outstrip the grain crops. Already many crop-yielding trees are good enough to be made into crops without any plant breeding at all. Among these may be mentioned the pecan, shagbark, hazel, black walnut, Eng-

FIG. 282.—Evergreen oak in Portugal with an average annual record of 750 quarts of acorns. This acorn is nearly as good for stock food as some grains.

lish (Persian) walnut, persimmon, mulberry, sugar maple, pawpaw, and above all the oaks—so important in Spain and Portugal.

What New England and all hill countries need more than any other thing in the whole list of relations between man and nature is an application of science to give them an agriculture that is adjusted to their unplowable soils. The present agriculture of New England is an imported misfit from the lands suited to the plow.

Everywhere east of the Mississippi trees will grow where there is earth standing above the water level. With the properly improved varieties of tree crops there is no reason why Massachusetts might not, square mile for square mile, produce as much food as Kansas does now with her fat pigs or fat sheep or fat turkeys—possibly more. The proper succession of fruiting mulberries, persimmons, chestnuts, walnuts, pecans, hickories, shagbarks, filberts, and many other tree crops that might be introduced from this and other lands would give us an abundance of good food or one continuous succes-

FIG. 283.—A forest remnant with soil preservation. Soil destruction on the tree-stript slope opposite. Shansi province, China. (F. N. Meyer, explorer, U. S. Dept. Agr.)

sion of workless harvests to which the pigs, sheep, and turkeys could walk and eat if man himself did not want them (Figs. 280, 281, 282).

The benefits that tree crops can render the arid and semi-arid[1] land are equal to if not greater than those that may be conferred upon the hilly lands. The grasses, grains, and ordinary forage plants are ill

[1] See *The Real Dry Farmer*, by J. Russell Smith, Harpers' Monthly Magazine. May, 1914.

equipped to fight for life against the rigors and uncertainty of aridity. Corn, for example, must have water within a certain two weeks or it is blasted, but the trees can prepare for siege. In the first place, their roots can go down from 30 to 60 feet. These roots can store up energy, and when the time comes they can make fruit (Fig. 284).

One of the best examples of a new tree crop is the Hawaiian experience with the algaroba, a species of the mesquite which will grow

FIG. 284.—Olive trees planted by the Romans, in central Tunis more than 1200 years ago, still bearing good fruit without cultivation and with only 10 inches of rainfall per year. The tree is the most enduring productive device within the reach of man.

in considerable areas of the United States. Hawaii has, after many difficulties of a mechanical nature, learned to grind up the beans and pods of the algaroba bean, and thereby added an industry of great promise. The meal resulting from this grinding is worth $25 a ton as a stock food, and is the "mainstay" of the dairy industry of the Islands. The Hawaii Experiment Station states that an algaroba forest yields 4 tons of the beans to the acre per year, and 1 ton of wood. The labor of production consists of picking up the big beans, which grow upon a leguminous tree introduced about the middle of the last century from Peru or California.

The tree-crop possibilities of the fecund tropics are beyond description or even reference here, but it should be remembered that in comparison to it the temperate zone is a land of poverty of plant species, and that most tropic products are already tree crops—tea, coffee, cacao, rubber, cocoanut, palm nut, Brazil nut, allspice, nutmeg, cloves, cinnamon, cinchona, orange.

Man has thought of himself as depending upon a *field* in which to grow his food, but there seems abundant reason to believe that science can, through tree crops, now give him food from any land that grows a forest, and from much land which now grows almost nothing. Further than this, the tree crop will have a valuable by-product of wood, a material of which there is now a painfully increasing scarcity.

After man the desert.—The proper development of tree crops as indicated here will effect the greatest saving in the world conservation movement—the conservation of the soil, our greatest and irreplaceable resource. The Roosevelt country life commission uttered this warning: "A condition calling for serious comment is the lessening productiveness of the land. Our farming has been largely exploitational, consisting of mining the virgin fertility. On the better lands, this system of exploitation may last for two generations without results pernicious to society, but on the poorer lands the limit of satisfactory living conditions may be reached in less than one generation." The saying "After man the desert" is much too true, as the frightful desolation of most ancient empires attests. It has nearly all come through erosion, and tree crops with their earth-gripping roots will practically stop it all, for the tree is nature's method of holding earth on the rocky framework which erosion reveals so near the surface of our hills and mountains (Fig. 283).

The ultimate uses of land.—The final uses of land to get maximum return with conservation of the soil seem to be about as follows:

(*a*) Where heat, moisture, and fertility abound:

      1. Level or gently rolling lands will be tilled as at present, but planted to more productive varieties of plants; and

      2. Hilly, steep, and rocky lands will be put to tree crops.

(*b*) Lands that we now call arid or semi-arid can in many cases also be in tree crops.

(*c*) Cold lands where the cost of keeping warm is great will be left to produce our timber-yielding forests.

(*d*) Beyond the tree crop and forest zones will come cactus deserts and moss-covered tundra to be used as pasture ranges by animals suited to the conditions.

(e) The bare desert, the bare rock, and the snow field will then as now remain without harvest other than:

1. Possible minerals where the earth is visible.
2. Possible utilization of deserts for sun-power generators.
3. Snow-field water-power.

5. The Economic Possibilities of the Tropics

The temperate zones are dwarfed into insignificance when compared with the possible expansions of food supply and industry in the tropics. These regions are quite the equal of the winter lands, as a field for the creations of new resources by science. While the tropics have great possibilities in the new era of scientific industry, they have for ages lain practically unused. Considerable areas of the temperate zone, as in parts of Europe, China, and Japan, have approached the food limit, and most unfortunately a great part of the remainder of the temperate zones lies under the withering limitations of aridity or of low temperatures. In contrast to this, the torrid zone, which includes about half of the land surface of the globe, has far more than half of the area of abundant rainfall. Add to this its greater heat with absence of winter, and we behold possibilities of the growth of food plants and, therefore, possibilities of the support of population several times as great as that of the temperate zone.

Despite this richness, 90 per cent. of the tropic forest stands today virtually as undisturbed as in the day of our primitive ancestors. An excerpt from U. S. Con. Rep., Dec. 9, 1911, gives an interesting example of tropic emptiness.

"British North Borneo (area 31,000 square miles) is owned and governed by an incorporated company under a charter from the British government. The population of the colony is estimated at 180,000, made up mainly of aborigines, about 15,000 Chinese, and not over 400 Europeans.

"The natives clear small patches of the valleys and hillsides, where they plant rice and vegetables for food. For other foodstuffs they depend upon hunting and fishing. The manner of farming is decidedly primitive. The hoe is the main instrument, and there is no demand for agricultural implements or any kind of hardware except the hoe and a long knife used in war and in cutting the underbrush. In all Borneo there is not a cultivated tract of ground worthy of being called a farm. The greater part of the land is yet covered with large trees."

British North Borneo is about one-seventh of the whole island, which is as large as France and naturally several times as productive because the unending heat and moisture of the equatorial belt permit the continuous growth of crops.

With the exception of certain island colonies which have become populous under white man's influence, and a few minor exceptions chiefly in southeast Asia, the tropic forest in its full force has baffled man, and he has developed only the less productive corners, where nature goaded him with difficulties, stung him into action, made him work or starve, and then often starved him despite his pathetic efforts.[1] Man seems inclined to take his ease where he can and it seems to require intermittency in supplies to make him work. Thus he has, except under Caucasian influence, advanced in the tropics only on its arid edges and in southeastern Asia where the monsoon rains of summer make a season of growth alternating with the dry season of the winter monsoon. Under this stimulus and this limitation, India and South China alone in the tropics have become populous, and the occasional failure of the summer rains produces crop failures and famines—catastrophies inconceivable to us of the well-fed West. It is a curious commentary on man's relations with tropic nature that he should have become numerous where the famine comes to slay him, and that the equatorial belt with its abundant and regular rains should have remained idle until the Dutch showed us by their wonderful object lesson in Java that this is the world's natural belt of heavy population.

Since 1798, the Dutch government, leaving the forms of native government alone, has kept peace in Java and to a considerable extent directed and compelled the industry of the people to provide food for home use and export. As a result the population has increased more than fivefold in a little over a century. In Java and Madura (the population is mostly in Java) there are 50,000 square miles with 30 million people, over 600 to the square mile, and it is far from being fully populated. Only 40 per cent. of the land is under cultivation, and a recent European scientist has (for good

---

[1] Famine deaths, India (from William Digby, "Prosperous British India," pp. 130–1).

1800–25	5 famines	deaths	=	1,000,000
1826–50	2 famines	deaths	=	500,000
1851–75	6 famines	deaths	=	5,000,000
1876–1900	18 famines	deaths	=	26,000,000
	Total since 1800		=	32,500,000

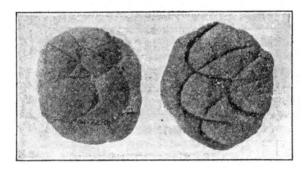

Sweetmeat—ground root of cassava sweetened with coarse, unbleached sugar called rapadon, purchased in market of Las Cahopas, Hayti, 1917. (U. S. Dept. Agr.)

There are hundreds of millions of people who do not eat bread, certainly not cereal bread, but that is no sign that they are savage, barbarian, or even heathen. They get carbohydrate and protein, but they do not get them in bread because the climate in which they live produces carbohydrate and protein most easily in other forms. The tropic regions are often said to have great possibilities for the support of human life. One evidence for this statement is the great abundance of starch-producing plants that are bread substitutes. Throughout the length and breadth of the damper part of the tropics several easily grown plants afford foods which are the essential equivalent of the bread so dearly beloved by the western world that two thousand years ago it got its place in the most widely used prayer in Christendom.

Cassava, one of the tropic bread substitutes, helps to fill the local need in many lands. It also produces for the peoples of the temperate zone the dried starch product called tapioca. Like the sweet potato, cassava is grown for its starch-producing roots. The native grates and dries it, making of it not only a nutritive equivalent of bread, but actually a piece of bread, although it is not the light bread to which the northern world is accustomed, but a thin, stiff cake, rather insipid to the wheat-eating palate. That, however, is a matter of habit.

In many Tropic lands, cassava cakes and boiled or baked cassava roots are standard articles of diet for the natives, partially taking the place of the corn bread of the American negro, the boiled potatoes and rye bread of the European peasant, and all the other breadstuffs of the temperate zone.

Very suggestive is a Hawaiian discovery, a war bread manufactured and sold for a time in all bakeries, there. It was made of thirty per cent. banana pulp and sixty per cent. white flour—the invention of a pastry cook in a Honolulu hotel. Perhaps the future bakers of Chicago and Christiana will for a part of their mixture roll out a cask of banana pulp, frozen in a fruit preserving factory on the banks of Albert Nyanza.

THE FOOD OF NATIONS

World Crop Comparisons for the Three-Year Period, 1911-13.

	Pop. per Sq. Mi.	Pop. per Sq. Mi. of Improved Land	Wheat Bu. per Cap.	Wheat Yield per Acre	Rye Bu. per Cap.	Rye Yield per Acre	Potato Bu. per Cap.	Potato Yield per Acre	Corn Bu. per Cap.	Corn Yield per Acre	Barley Bu. per Cap.	Barley Yield per Acre	Oats Bu. per Cap.	Oats Yield per Acre	Total Grain per Cap.	Cattle per 100 Pop.	Sheep, Goats per 100 Pop.	Swine per 100 Pop.	Horses Mules Asses per 100 Pop.
United States	26.6	222.	7.5	14.7	.4	17.8	3.7	102.	28.5	24.8	2.1	25.8	12.2	30.5	150.8	65.5	60.	67.6	30.2
Canada	1.9	124.8	32.7	21.4	.3	15.9	11.1	163.	2.5	59.	6.7	30.5	12.5	38.7	47.7	97.	32.	41.5	30.
British Australasia	1.5	195.	33.3	13.7	.04	14.8	4.9	121.	2.6	28.9	.9	25.8	6.2	25.	43.	30.4	2401.	29.6	65.7
Argentina	6.9	84.	21.5	10.3	....	....	4.8	139.	21.	31.	....	....	9.7	29.9	34.9	360.	1074.5	37.	123.7
Netherlands	504.	1020.	.8	35.3	2.6	27.7	21.3	301.	....	....	.5	50.1	2.8	50.8	11.5	25.	10.8	21.7	5.2
Belgium	652.	1200.	2.3	38.9	3.2	34.6	16.2	292.	....	....	.6	51.4	5.4	63.	20.9	89.		17.5	3.
Denmark	178.	495.	2.	37.1	9.2	28.8	18.	238.	....	....	8.2	37.7	1.5	42.3	21.4	31.6	10.9	71.3	4.8
Germany	310.4	637.	2.5	33.1	7.1	29.6	26.5	206.	....	....	2.5	42.2	9.3	54.7	14.	31.7	16.	35.9	7.2
Austria	247.	682.	2.2	20.6	3.9	22.2	15.6	145.	.4	18.1	2.5	29.	5.	31.7	28.9	28.8	12.7	22.3	8.7
Hungary	166.	368.	8.3	19.9	2.4	24.8	9.	180.	7.9	27.7	3.7	27.	6.6	33.2	18.1	28.1	135.6	31.8	10.4
Russia in Europe	70.	302.	5.3	10.	7.2	12.7	9.3	114.	1.9	19.6	1.6	16.6	2.1	21.9	6.7	26.	35.4	9.7	5.5
United Kingdom	375.	404.	1.3	32.2	.02	21.	5.8	259.	....	....	1.4	34.	4.	44.5	19.	35.3		8.5	8.3
France	189.5	....	8.3	30.2	1.4	18.8	12.8	128.	.5	21.	1.1	25.5	7.9	31.2	10.2	44.6		17.4	6.2
Italy	326.5	433.	4.6	12.5	1.4	16.5	1.6	97.	2.9	25.	.27	16.	1.	29.9	13.3	40.1		7.2	11.3
Spain	102.6	465.	6.1	13.2	1.2	12.6	4.5	145.	1.3	26.5	3.5	20.6	1.2	21.		12.8	94.	12.6	2.9
Japan	206.	2572.	.5	26.5	....	....	4.6	147.	.6	25.3	1.7	28.8	....	....	1.5	2.6	.2	.5	1.3
British India	223.	744.	1.5	12.2	....	....	....	....	....	....	....	....	....	....	i45.9	47.2	24.6	7.5	
Saskatchewan	1.9	....	33.8	21.1	.1	27.2	2.1	173.	....	....	5.7	31.9	.2	40.9	41.6		22.9	45.8	91.
Prince Edward Island	42.9	78.6	6.4	19.1	....	....	66.	171.	....	....	1.4	28.5	66.9	34.9	78.0	118.	107.	47.2	37.1

ᵃ Data for 1910, 1912, 1913
ᵇ Data for 1910, 1913, 1915
ᶜ Data for 1909, 1914, 1915
ᵈ Data for 1907, 1912, 1913

ᵉ Data for 1911, 1912
ᶠ Data for 1911, 1913
ᵍ Data for 1910, 1911, 1912

ʰ Data for 1908
ⁱ Buffaloes
ʲ Including Rice

This table merits careful study. Many comparisons can be made in the wealth of nations. Note especially the supplies of the various main classes of food. Compare the condition of countries from which emigrants go, Italy, Russia, Austria, with conditions in countries to which the emigrants go, United States, Argentina. To make the picture clearer, manufacturing resources should be considered also.

reasons, we believe) estimated that Java may easily support three times as many people as it now possesses. This would bring its density up to about 2,000 per square mile. By applying this figure to the whole Dutch East Indies, of which Java and Madura are a sample, comprising less than one-fourteenth, we would have a population three times as large as that of Europe, and ten times as great as that of North America. Population of this density over the suitable parts of the tropics would permit that zone alone to contain six or eight times as many people as the entire world now contains, and they would be far less liable to famine than they are in India today.

The inhabitants of the tropics.—If the tropic jungle becomes a field who will labor in it? If three centuries of colonization have shown us anything, they have shown that it will not be the white man. He can only come in as the ruler, the capitalist, the plantation manager, the engineer, the sanitarian, the expert, and the professional man.

The distribution of population in tropic America affords excellent illustration of the influence of climate on the white man, the location of his home, and his place in the development of the country. The white race has here retreated to the cool plateaus of the interior. It has always remained a small, very small, minority, and the native Indian makes up the bulk of the population, with the half-breeds the second element in numerical importance. But the handful of white people rules—a fact not without significance.

If these vacant tropic plains which we of the North claim, but may not inhabit, are to become peopled, it apparently must be by the various black, brown, or yellow races that have become adjusted to the tropic climate.[1] Left to their own devices, they have produced tribes of savages with sultans, wars, murders, piracies, slavery, pestilences, and disease that have effectively kept down population. They have never yet developed even a second-rate power or civilization and have fallen an easy prey to colony-annexing European powers. Given order and protection and guidance as in Java, they clear up the jungle, populate the earth, and have crops to sell. Thus, by the aid of the acclimatized peoples, and apparently thus only, will these untouched continents yield unlimited amounts of rice and rubber, sugar, cocoa, oil and nuts, cotton, hemp and other fibers, and a whole host of tropical products

[1] *Control of the Tropics*, by Benjamin Kidd. MacMillan.

which we can buy with our northern goods, especially with the products of factories located in comfortable climates.

Relation of tropic peoples to northern prosperity.—The development of the dense populations of Barbados, Porto Rico, Java, and Bengal shows that these lands are almost certain to remain essentially agricultural or, at best, in a low stage of manufacturing. The tropic lack of ambition means that they will probably stay indefinitely as colonies or in a low stage of political power. The white races of America and Europe would have nothing to fear from 3 or 5 to 10 billions of black, brown, or yellow people in the torrid zone. History seems to indicate that a small fraction of this population in a frosty climate would in time break out into a world-conquering foray; but in their monotonous tropic plenty they would be, as they now are, non-militant agriculturists carrying out, as now, the instructions of white men, and our trade with them, largely the exchange of manufactures for raw materials, would be a great source of temperate zone riches, and would easily enable northern lands to double their population. The sooner we recognize and act upon the fact that we have a brown man's world and a white man's world, the more comfortable we shall all be, provided the white race can without its own destruction keep on sending some people to the tropics.

QUESTIONS

1. Name several substitutes for coal.

2. Compare Italy and the United States cotton belt in the degree of utilization of natural resources; in amount of natural resources.

3. How may Arizona profit by plant introduction?

4. What happened to the cinchona industry of eastern Peru and Colombia? What does this suggest about rubber?

5. Compare the yield and value of French chestnut orchards and Dakota wheat fields.

6. Upon what factors does plant growth necessarily depend?

7. How may plant breeding extend the area of agriculture?

8. Explain the relation of tree crops to soil conservation.

9. How thoroughly are the equatorial regions now utilized by man?

CHAPTER XLII

THE LAW OF TRADE

Trade arises because individuals and peoples, having different goods, exchange their surplus to mutual advantage. This difference in the production of peoples arises from three main reasons—first, the difference in the peoples themselves; second, the differences in the stages of industrial development; and, third, the difference in the resources of their respective lands.

Section 1.—**Racial differences.**—The first reason for a difference in production arises from a difference in the peoples themselves. The Japanese and Chinese export to other countries their porcelains, lacquer ware, metal work, fancy paper goods, and other products, which have their distinctive character and value because they reflect a skill peculiar to these oriental peoples, whose culture is so different from our own. From India come many carvings and curios. The chief commerce of some American Indians is in basketry, blankets, birch-bark work, and other products of native arts and crafts. Among the peoples of western civilization, the French are conspicuous in commerce through the export of products which are valuable because of the French skill and taste which give them a superior artistic character, and make them precious to the lovers of the luxurious and beautiful everywhere. German commerce has reached an important position partly through the influence of the scientific attainment and thrift of the German people.

It may, at first thought, seem that the difference in the skill, genius, or culture of races is the greatest cause of trade; but this is not the case. Racial difference is the least important of the three main causes.

Racial differences and their commercial results tend to be evened up and to disappear. The relative advantage of German scientific leadership is passing because the Germans themselves are teaching other peoples their own sciences and arts. America, Japan, and England are copying German sciences and scientific instruction with all their might, while the Japanese art products are declining because of the influence of European and American machine manufacture under the factory system. The arts of the Indian and the tribesman everywhere tend to vanish before the machine-made product of world commerce. This is usually a great blow to tribal life.

SECTION 2.—**Difference in the stage of industrial development.**— The second cause, a difference in the stage of industrial development, is much more important in explaining the world's present commerce. The difference in stage or intensity of industrial development is largely a matter of the density of population. Two people to the square mile will inevitably support themselves by means which differ greatly from those that will be adopted by 200 people per square mile in the same kind of territory. The sparse population seizes upon the raw products of nature, or produces raw materials requiring the least labor. A dense population, having few raw materials per capita, must fabricate them to a high degree to make value. In the new forest lands, one person to two or three square miles, will make a satisfactory living by trapping fur-bearing animals and gathering gums, herbs, and roots. A population slightly more dense will cut down the forest and sell logs as lumber. A sparse population upon the open plain will employ itself in tending herds of sheep and cattle, and will export wool, hides, and animals. If the population increases and the climate is suitable, the level plain will be carelessly plowed up and sown to grain, which will be exported to the densely peopled region in exchange for manufactures.

This, in brief, is the explanation of the great commerce of the second half of the nineteenth century. The European peoples settling the comparatively empty lands of America have been producing wheat and sending it back to the better yielding wheat lands of Europe; they have been sending cattle, butter and cheese to the European countries, where the pastures are better and cattle more numerous per square mile; they have been exporting lumber to the countries where the forests are better kept, because the European population is dense and the American population has been, and still is, relatively scanty. This is the chief explanation of the commerce of the newly settled lands in Dakota, Nebraska, or Saskatchewan with the old country. We even send to and get from Europe articles of the same material but of different degrees of manufacture. Thus we export raw cotton and buy fine fabrics and lace; we export logs and planks and import wood carvings from

Switzerland, and the Black Forest region of Germany; we export sole leather and import the fancy tans of France and Germany; we sell steel rails and pig copper and buy cutlery and scientific instruments; we send coal tar to Germany and bring back the drugs and dyes that her chemists make from it.

Owing to the westward movement of the main line of migration and settlement we see, within the Old World itself, a duplicate of the trade that passes between America and Europe. The densely populated manufacturing parts of Europe, west of Vienna and Berlin, carry on a most active commerce with the territories of the Baltic and Black Seas, deriving from them products identical with those that come from across the Atlantic. These manufacturing regions have been sending to us and to eastern Europe, woolen goods, cottons, silks, leather goods, machinery of all kinds, metal manufactures, cutlery, gloves, lace, and the thousand products which reflect the great labor and the relatively small raw material of densely populated regions. The new outposts of Western civilization in Australia and temperate South America are to manufacturing Europe but two other Missouri Valleys, with grain fields and sheep and cattle ranges, inhabited by people who buy their manufactured goods and pay for them with grain and animal products. This trade will appear wherever these differences of population are found and land permits. Thus in Roman times, France and west Europe sent to Rome furs, cattle, timber, food and slaves in return for the more valuable goods of Rome. This basis of trade, like that depending on racial differences, from which it cannot completely be distinguished, has a strong tendency to disappear through the equalizing of population and industrial conditions throughout the world.

The United States and Germany, which for a time were England's great market for her manufactured goods, are now rapidly developing the same industries, and are becoming the great rivals of England. Within the United States itself the whole development is shown. New England duplicates old England in more than name. It is little more than a group of towns and cities whose people live by fabricating raw materials, most of them imported, and sending the product chiefly to the west and south in return for the food and raw materials of those newer and less populous sections of the country. Ohio, which, 50 years ago, was to New England both market and source of supply for food and raw materials, is now becoming her rival in manufacturing, and turns for her supplies to the yet newer West. The cotton industry of America, once centered in New England, is rapidly being built up in the south; and manufacturing of many kinds is being carried on in greater and greater quantities beyond the Alleghenies, so that the North Central States are coming to resemble New England as New England has come to resemble old England. Every state and every country desires manufacturing industries, and they are increasing in every state in the Union, and in almost every foreign country.

Immigration.—Lastly, but by no means the least important, comes the immigrant to even up the population physically and to complete industrial similarity, so far as it pertains to the labor supply. The cheapness of the Atlantic passage and the distribution of knowledge of American industrial conditions throughout Europe permit greater and greater movements of people to America, to take advantage of her industrial opportunities. Already more than a million have come in a single year, and there is no reason why, in a few generations, this country shall not become as fully peopled as is Europe.

This growing likeness in industries and population is accompanied step by step by the cessation of trade in those articles for which the necessity ceases as America comes to produce an article previously secured in Europe. A few decades ago most of our iron and steel was brought from England. Now we export it occasionally to England. The import of textiles, chemicals, and other manufactures is falling off in consequence of American production. The large import of sub-tropic fruits and dried fruits from Mediterranean countries had almost entirely ceased through the development of identical industries in California.

SECTION 3.—**Difference in resources.**—Trade arising from difference in resources is one of increasing importance and is one which man affects but little, a fact which will become of greater and greater influence the more fully we adapt our use of each section to its resources. The chief of these differences are those of topography, soil, moisture, nearness to sea, and temperature.

Differences in topography give rise to a trade which will endure. The products of the well-used mountain and of the well-used plain must forever be different. The rough, rocky and steep lands cannot be tilled; but they are the natural home of the forests, of wood and tree products, and of the mining and quarrying industries. The full utilization of mountain countries means therefore minerals, wood, nuts, fruit, water-power, paper, and the possibility of printing and publishing and the manufacture of varied light imported raw materials through water-power. But the mountain needs the agricultural products of the open plain, grain for bread, animals for meat, wool and cotton for clothing, and the many other products of agriculture, which can be paid for with mountain products. Such is the trade that does now and may for centuries pass between the prairies of west Canada and the glacial regions north of the St. Lawrence, between hilly New England and Appalachia and the level West.

Soil differences also make trade. Along the banks of the Mississippi, Ohio and other streams are glacial sand plains in the midst of the fertile black prairies of the corn belt. The sand plain, too poor to grow corn, just suits melons and sweet potatoes, which the farmers grow in large fields, and peddle in wagon loads across adjoining counties, or ship by train loads to adjacent states to be bought up by people who can grow corn, but who cannot, on their richer, heavier, more valuable lands, grow good melons or potatoes. This example is typical of the vast trade that is now developing between the sandy districts in the Atlantic plain and elsewhere, and the rest of the United States. Though the most conspicuous, this soil difference is but one example of many others.

The differences in moisture give us the humid and the arid lands between which there is a great and growing trade. Beyond the bounds of cultivation in all countries that verge toward the desert are the sheep and cattle ranges, where sparse population has two or three products to sell, and must buy most of its food from more favored farm lands, and must secure from the manufacturing towns all the other products that are to be purchased in the store. In the irrigated cases of the arid lands, dried fruit is produced most easily; and it is already being sent from these favored spots in Australia, in Argentina, in Chile, in Europe and in the United States to the more humid districts, which can with ease produce other products for exchange. This exchange of dried fruits and animal products for grain and manufactures is world wide and seems to be as enduring as the distribution of people and variation in rainfall.

The Shore Lands carry on an enduring trade in fish with the inland regions, of which the rocky and even untillable cold coast has at present a great wealth, enabling it to command in exchange the products of all other climates.

Temperature as a basis of trade is the most fundamental, the

most widespread, and, for the future, the most promising of great and
yet greater performance. No exchange of culture, no equality in
education or skill, no emigration of peoples evening up density of
population can change the temperature and make tropic fruit grow
in the land of arctic fur, or cotton grow in the land of spring wheat.
If America becomes a second Europe, Manitoba will have a lively
trade with Texas, because Texas can produce cotton and other sub-
tropic products, which the short summer forever bars from Manitoba.
Florida and other southern lands will send their oranges and vegetables to the northern lands of frost when the latter's agriculture
is frost bound; and the north will send in return its wheat, the red
apples from its hills and the myriad products from its mills. Examples in miniature often permit us to see the tendencies of the
time more clearly than larger and more complicated examples. Thus
the Canary Islands, snugly fixed on steamer routes in the frost-free
waters of the warm Atlantic, have within 30 years developed an
export of over 200,000 tons per year of bananas, tomatoes, and
potatoes, mostly to the English market (Fig. 285).

The future course of trade.—This north-south trade is the trade
of the future. It gives the things we cannot ourselves produce, and
is needed to round out the economic life of northern and southern
lands alike. Foods make the most important class of commodities
from tropic and sub-tropic lands. Northern peoples want their cane
sugar, cacao, coffee, rice, spices, bananas and other fruits; their
cocoanuts, Brazil nuts, palm nuts, tapioca, and many minor foods.
We of the temperate climates want, for our mills, their raw materials,
rubber, Manila hemp, jute, henequin and other fibers; their cabinet
and dye woods; their rattan, gums, palm oil and other forest products. In exchange for these the northern lands are sending machinery, clothing and all kinds of manufactures and some foods.
This is a natural trade.

At the present time the great bulk of our commerce depends upon
differences in the stage of industrial development—east and west
trade—but the future is indicated by changes now in progress. The
greatest rates of increase are taking place not along east-west lines,
but in the trade of temperate with tropic regions; and, if the present
rates of increase in this traffic continue throughout this century, it
will far surpass that on the east and west lines. The east and
west trade will probably not decline in absolute quantity, but will
gradually become relatively less important as the world's commerce

multiplies itself many fold, as it inevitably will if its present tendencies continue.

SECTION 4.—**Size of country and volume of foreign trade.**—Foreign trade, depending thus upon natural laws, modified by man's aid and interference, is of varying importance in different countries, with the general tendency to be least important in large countries and most

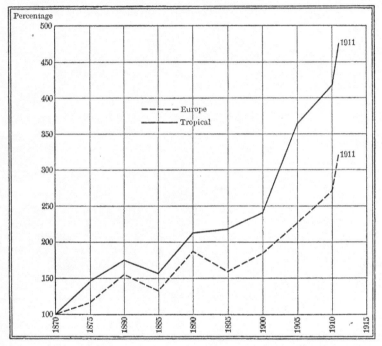

FIG. 285.—Comparison of increase of imports into the United States from Europe with increase of imports of tropic products. Tropical products according to United States Bureau Statistics classification are cocoa, coffee, fibers, rubber, indigo, ivory, licorice, olive oil, rice, silk, sugar, tea, tobacco, vegetable oils (using values in 1870 as base or 100 per cent.).

important in small countries. China peacefully and successfully ignored the foreign world for many centuries, because she is a world within herself. She scorned the world because it could give her nothing that she did not produce. Petroleum, cheap cotton cloth, modern machine manufactures and new machinery have tempted the Chinese to buy; but their foreign trade of less than $1 per person is insignificant today. The foreign trade, however, of a country like Uruguay, a little fertile cattle and sheep ranch, is over $60 per person, among the highest in the world, because Uruguayans produce essentially one class of articles, with which they must buy everything else which a civilized people consumes. Small countries like Switzerland, Belgium and Holland, with almost no variety in climate, and accompanying small variety of resources, have a relatively enormous foreign trade. So does England. If we had the figures of commerce that cross the southern and western boundaries of New England we would be astounded at the total. But most of New England trade is with other states of the Union, and disappears without statistical record in our vast domestic commerce, which is said to be more than twenty times as great as our foreign commerce. Our great area and variety of resources give us a smaller per capita foreign commerce than that which is shown by the countries of Europe, especially such small countries as Denmark or other western European countries.

To see commerce in its extreme development we should look at the Falkland Islands, a wind-swept sheep-range with an area of 6,500 square miles, and a population of 2,300 people, whose foreign trade is about $600 per person per year. This only slightly surpasses the little French colonies of Miquelon and St. Pierre—a few thousand fishermen and ship outfitters on two barren rocks in the cold Gulf of St. Lawrence, who import and export each year the enormous total of about $500 for every person in the colony. In contrast to this the per capita foreign trade of the United States is less than $40, and of Great Britain is about $100 per year.

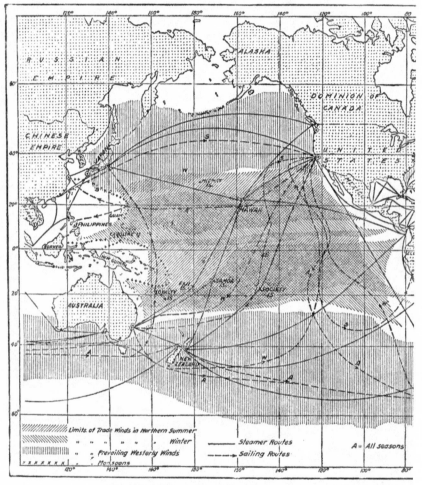

FIG. 286.—Principal world trading routes, steam and sail. (From

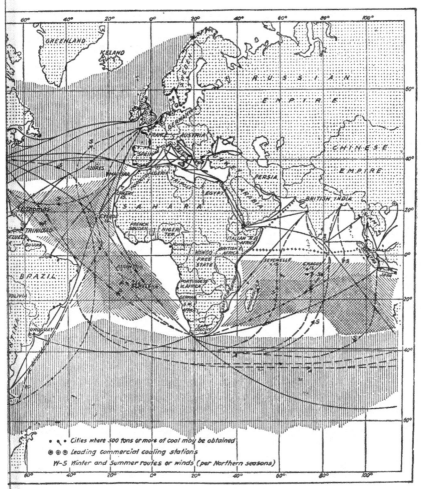

• .. • Cities where 500 tons or more of coal may be obtained
⊛ ⊛ ⊛ Leading commercial coaling stations
W-S Winter and Summer routes or winds (per Northern seasons)

Ocean Courier by J. Russell Smith, courtesy of G. P. Putnam's Sons.)

CHAPTER XLIII

THE WORLD HIGHWAY—THE OCEAN AND ITS CARRIERS

The sea, sea trade and sea power have always been of great interest to civilized man, and to understand world commerce we must first know the part played by the ocean. The nation that does not touch the ocean is like a house that is not upon the street, and some of the bitterest strifes of history have been enacted for the possession of bits of coast. Once a nation has reached the sea, it has possessed itself of a part of the world highway that reaches everywhere and belongs, according to international law, to each and all who own even a tiny strip of coast.

The freedom of the highway.—It is an adage that ocean transportation is cheaper than that on land, but it is difficult for the landsman to realize how much ocean carriage differs from land carriage in cheapness and in the freedom of competition. This freedom is chiefly due to the same cause which produces the greater cheapness of transportation, namely, the fact that the ocean carrier must furnish only the vehicle, while nature furnishes the roadway, and, in some cases, even the motive power—wind. Upon the railway the cost of the vehicle is an insignificant part of the total cost of service. The important thing is the way itself. On the ocean the way is free and also the place for the ship to unload is usually found with comparatively small expense to the ship, so that ocean transportation remains competitive and cheap both on the international high sea and within the shadow of the land. Terminals remain practically free or, at least, equally free to all ship owners because the desire of cities for trade is so keen that they bid for ships by getting harbors and docks ready for them.

The two types of ocean service.—This freedom of the highway and of terminals results in a great variety of traffic methods, but the whole of ocean commerce may be divided into two large classes.

1. The line traffic—with which everyone is more or less familiar—carries the passengers and mails and certain kinds of freight. It corresponds to the express, passenger and fast-freight business of the

railroad.   The line service is in the public eye and achieves a degree of attention which is much beyond its relative merits.   2.
Charter traffic—single vessels operating as units, as is any wagon
that is for hire on the street corner—handles the larger part of the
ocean's freight.   It is an individual matter entirely between the
shipper and the ship owner.   The individual ship, which is known

Fig. 287.—A tramp steamer in dry dock shows how nearly cubical she is—about
81 per cent.

as a charter ship, or more commonly as a "tramp," is on the list of
some ship-broker or brokers who secure a freight for her on commission, and she goes about her work unnoticed by the traveling
public or by the headlines of the newspapers.

The tramp vessel that is free to go when work offers, and to lie
in port when it does not offer, has a distinct advantage over the
line vessel, which must go on a certain date, full or empty, must
maintain a schedule and make sailings to ports of call, which in

themselves are often unprofitable, but which are necessary, since a line vessel must maintain a reputation, establish relations with shippers and form a clientele. The ambition of the liner is regularity and reliability; the ambition of the tramp is cheapness (Fig. 287).

The charter or tramp vessels.—The freedom of the sea makes competition easy, but it is especially easy among the tramp vessels. The owner of a single ship is in a position to compete in the world's freight market, and can take service on any sea, in any country and from hundreds of ports. The ocean is a world ocean; the ship market is a world market; the charter traffic is a world traffic; and the ocean rate a world rate. Wherever freight offers, there the ships may go and do go. If there is grain in volume in the Black Sea the ships go there, and the same is true of India, Australia, or South America.

This tramp steamer, which may be built and owned by anybody, and which may sail in all seas, and carry the products of any or all countries, is a remarkably free agent. It is to be had, however, only by those persons who can afford to load a whole ship; and that is about the only limitation upon the character of product that is carried by the tramp vessels. First in the class comes grain; then we have sugar, cotton, ores, coal, nitrate of soda, lumber, china clay, petroleum and many other bulky raw commodities. Only occasionally some manufacturer ships enough heavy goods, such as steel rails, locomotives and agricultural machinery, to fill a vessel, in which case he almost invariably charters a tramp. The regions producing the tramp freight and the regions consuming it embrace every important country in the world. There are hundreds of ports with freight for tramp vessels and there are thousands of ships scattered about the world to do this work.

The proper bringing together of the ships and the freight is a world puzzle, compared to which the game of chess is simplicity itself. The ships must move around the world in such a way that the freight is all carried and that the ships that do the work have as few empty voyages as possible, and keep constantly employed (Fig. 286).

The successful adjustment of this complicated situation is one of the results of the development of the ocean cable. Lloyd's agency in Great Britain, with its branches throughout the world, reports every observed movement of more than 10,000 vessels; maritime associations in commercial ports do the same work; so that the ship owner can easily know where his vessel is and where the vessels of his rivals are. It is necessary, however, in this work that watch be kept not only upon vessels but upon freight. Most of the products depend upon harvest and commercial conditions. If there is to be a good or bad grain harvest upon the Pacific coast or in the Argentine Republic, tramp ship owners must know it and place their ships accordingly. The differing times of ripening of the various crops in the different producing regions and other particular seasonal demands make each port or district have its busy season and its off season. Accordingly, the manager of the tramp vessel has a number of problems to consider as he guides his ship through the maze of world commerce.

He must consider more than one voyage when he makes an engagement to perform a certain voyage, for it is necessary that this ship be discharged in a place where freight is to be secured for another voyage. If such is not the case, he may have a long voyage in ballast, making cost without income. The result is that the probable second voyage affects the rates for the first. The manager seeks an engagement which will release his vessel near good prospective freights and he avoids engagements that take him into barren seas. Accordingly this master of applied commercial geography scans the world's horizon for prospective wheat crops or other freight supplies toward which he can work his ships with a chance of securing another freight.

Because of this free market, ocean freight rates fluctuate greatly. When cargoes are scarce rates sometimes decline to the point of heavy loss to ship owners, and, conversely, they may rise to great heights, for when the freight is plentiful and the ships are scarce the only limit to which the rates may rise is set by the limit that the shippers can afford to pay to get a particular cargo carried. Thus a tenfold increase in rates came within a few months after the outbreak of the European war of 1914.

The co-operation of tramp traffic and liner traffic in world commerce.—This tramp traffic bears a very fundamental relation to world commerce because it carries the heavy commodities—the raw materials and food—without which the manufacturing city and the manufacturing state as at present constituted could not exist. The era of world commerce in its present sense may properly be said to have begun about the middle of the nineteenth century, when

Great Britain began the heavy importation of food and the wide export of manufactures. At this time came the steamship, and lines were established between Europe and America, and between Europe and all other countries, and between New York and the West Indies and Colon, and from Panama to San Francisco and to Chile. These two types of ocean service work together like freight trains and express trains. The tramps handle the trade of vast quantity; the liners handle the trade of high value and the shipments of small size and great number. The lines, therefore, serve the greater number of shippers. They serve the multitude who cannot fill a ship with one consignment, and among manufacturers there must be thousands of small shipments of finished goods to one that requires a tramp to handle it. The manufacturing state may depend upon the thousand tramp ships that bring food and materials, but there is an equal dependence upon the 300 big liners that carry to market with greater speed the myriad small consignments of manufactured exports. Conversely the raw material producing country like Argentina depends largely upon tramps to take its exports and upon liners to bring its imports of valuable manufactured goods.

In most seas the line managers have been able to combine and control *line* rates to some extent. The tramp managers have been unable to do this.

It is also true that the line traffic is gaining on the tramp traffic and the development of some line enterprises has reached huge proportions. The law of growth among steamship lines works surely to the development of trunks and branches, a development which has already taken place, although the branches are fewer than upon railroads. The great ocean liners sail with precision and regularity. To secure the supply of freight for these great lines, their managers have been compelled to establish smaller lines to supply and distribute the necessary cargo. The largest trans-Atlantic lines are, without exception, thus equipped at one or both of their terminals. The North German Lloyd and the Hamburg-American connect at their European ends with lines running to South America, east Asia, and other distant parts of the world. They also connect with smaller lines plying to the nearby European ports and with steamers on the German rivers. These two German companies carry the same system even farther. Their trunk lines to east Asia are fed at Singapore and other eastern ports by lines of smaller German steamers which traverse the eastern archipelagoes and the Asiatic coasts and rivers, collecting cargo for the trunk-line stations of the large steamers bound for Bremen or Hamburg, at which ports it is distributed by the European distributors referred to above or sent on to America by the trans-Atlantic lines. The Wilson Line from New York to Hull connects in that city with an enormous fleet of small steamers which thread the coasts of the North Sea and reach all ports of importance in Scandinavia and along the Baltic. The French and Italian trans-Atlantic lines are fed by fleets of Mediterranean coasters and trans-oceanic liners at Havre, Marseilles, and Genoa. The ocean service of single companies at times circumnavigates the globe.

The best example of this wide-reaching world carrier was furnished by the Hamburg-American Steamship Company at the outbreak of the war of 1914. This one company dominated the metropolitan city of Hamburg and connected it with Montreal, Portland, Boston, New York, Philadelphia, Baltimore, Newport News, New Orleans, and Galveston in the eastern United States. It sent steamers to Mexico, Central America, Panama, Colombia, Venezuela, and several services to the Lesser and Greater Antilles. They went to the Amazon, to the ports of central and south Brazil, to Uruguay and Argentine Republic, to Chile and Peru and on up the Pacific coast of America to the ports of the United States. In Europe they circumnavigated the British Isles, skirted the coasts of France, Spain, Portugal, and Italy, to the head of the Adriatic; they went in the Baltic to Russia and Finland and Sweden, and out in the Atlantic to Iceland and North Cape, and on to Arctic Spitzbergen in the summer. In Africa it touched at Alexandria and down the whole west coast as far as the mouth of the Congo. In Asia it served Aden, the ports of Arabia, Persian Gulf, Ceylon, Calcutta, Straits Settlements, China, Korea, Siberia, Japan, and finally—and possibly most remarkable of all—it sent steamers thence across the Pacific to Portland, Oregon—a grand total of sixty-eight services crossing every ocean, touching all continents and every geographic and commercial zone. Extensions were in contemplation or contracted for.

CHAPTER XLIV

THE NORTH ATLANTIC ROUTE

The greatest of all ocean trade routes is that crossing the North Atlantic and connecting the two most commercial continents. To a person who has not given attention to the geography of the north Atlantic it might seem that this ocean possesses a multitude of trade routes. Yet there are certain geographical conditions producing a surprising similarity in the path followed by all of the ships going across this ocean from North America to northern Europe.

The greatest factor leading to the use of this common path is what the mariners call "the great circle line." This can be best understood by examining a globe, the only map that is accurate for large areas. By it one sees that in high latitudes the shortest line between any two points equi-distant from the equator is not on the parallel running due east and west, but along the arc of the circle passing through both of the points in question, and dividing the earth into two equal parts—a great circle. The farther apart the two points in question are, and the farther from the equator they are, the greater is the poleward curve of the shortest line between them. Consequently, there are almost no straight routes upon the charts to be followed by the mariner. He is forever following curves, because he is, of all men, the one who is most directly concerned with the fact that the world is round.

It is rather astonishing to discover that the positively shortest air line from Sandy Hook to Liverpool passes directly overland through New England and Canada, west of Nova Scotia. The more closely ships can approach this great circle line, the shorter is their voyage; consequently, as soon as it is possible, all vessels leaving New York abandon their eastward course and swing northward along the line of a great circle, the exact point for this turn varying with the seasons. At all times of the year the vessel must proceed eastward, sometimes hundreds of miles, before it is permitted to turn to the north. Only by this means can the navigators avoid the worst dangers of the Newfoundland coast and the fog banks. The great circle swing makes the vessels from New York, Halifax, and Montreal approach each other before mid-ocean is reached. For a part of the year, often less than half, the St. Lawrence steamers make an exception to this by going north of Newfoundland.

An examination of the globe, or a photograph of part of it shows that the east coast of the United States, of which we often think as

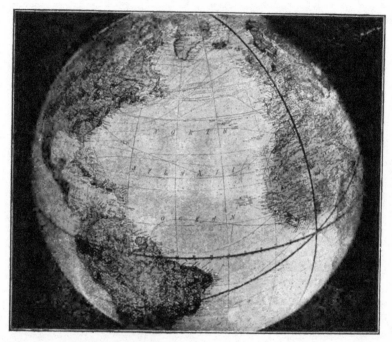

Fig. 288.—Globe showing narrowness of North Atlantic and cause of location of North Atlantic trunk. (Photo E. Stirling.)

extending from north to south, really lies so near east and west as to be practically a part of the great circle line from the Georgia coast and the Florida straits to Scotland; so that the ships from south Atlantic and Gulf ports follow the coast and take the same trunk route as those from the north Atlantic. Even Nicaragua is almost within the territory of this same north Atlantic route, for it is but 223 miles further from Greytown to Liverpool via New York than

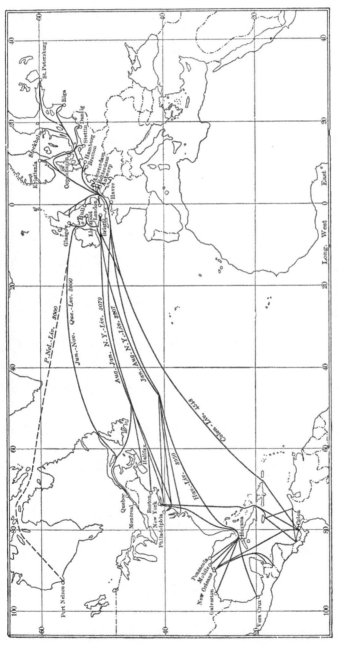

Fig. 289.—North Atlantic trunk route.

via the shortest possible route. It is thus plain that the north Atlantic route is a great trunk route with a string of branches for the different ports from St. Johns in Newfoundland to Havana, Tampico and Vera Cruz in the tropical Gulf (Figs. 288, 289).

It is, therefore, exactly in accord with these basal facts of location that there is now arising a trans-shipment trade at New York and New Orleans by which the products of the West Indies and Caribbean countries are being forwarded to Europe by the great trans-Atlantic liners, and return cargoes come by the same route.

It is a working out of the narrowing longitude of high latitudes that causes Quebec and Montreal, which we are inclined to think of as being far in the interior, to be nearer to Liverpool than are New York and Boston; while the distance is no greater to the trading posts located far in the center of the American continent upon the western shores of Hudson Bay—a fact interesting to speculate upon.

The north Atlantic route has the great advantage of being entirely devoid of islands with the exception of Sable Island—the so-called graveyard of the Atlantic—east of the Maine coast and a few small rocks on the Grand Banks. So universally are these skirmish posts of the continent dreaded that the route for the trans-Atlantic steamers aims to interpose 60 miles of clear water between the ship and these destroying landspecks. This is the more necessary because of the mingling together of the Arctic current and the warm Gulf Stream which produces well-nigh continuous fog on the Grand Banks. The handicap resulting from these difficulties is well illustrated in the St. Lawrence River, one of the feeders of the Atlantic route, where the narrow and rocky channel has been frequently the scene of great disasters and where at the present time ships must often tie up during the night. One result of these dangers is an insurance rate often several times as high as that for open-sea voyages.

The icebergs, almost continually afloat in the region of the Grand Banks, are a greater menace than a group of islands.

Another dangerous part of the route is Cape Hatteras, which really projects into the Atlantic and, with its long strings of sand bar reaching out to sea, must be rounded by hundreds of vessels from the south. In the temptation to save distance, many a good ship has ventured too near these bars and met her end.

Fuel supply.—In the present epoch of steam no route equals the north Atlantic in the abundance of the supply of fuel. Eastern America and north Europe are producing 95 per cent. of the world's coal and this supply is on both continents admirably distributed for the supply of steamers. The American supplies at New Orleans, Mobile, Norfolk, New York, and Nova Scotia, are known to the reader. The European end has a distribution of coal that is not less complete. Southern and western England with the ports of Bristol and Liverpool are supplied from the rich fields of Wales and Lancashire; Glasgow almost overlies the coal-fields of western Scotland. On the east lies Newcastle, synonym for coal; Antwerp and Rotterdam, the great ports of the Rhine, are in reach of Rhine-borne coal from Westphalia and Belgium; Hamburg and Bremen receive their coal very cheaply as return cargo in ships which carry sugar to England, and German coal can also come down the Elbe on barges from the east German coal-fields. Another fuel supply that should be mentioned is the oil of Texas, Kansas, and Oklahoma in the lower Mississippi Valley. This is now used to a limited extent and may at any time become of greater importance.

Traffic.—The north Atlantic route began as one over which emigrants left Europe to start new homes in America; and, strange to say, this traffic, which was the first over this route, is also the last and one of the greatest. In the first 10 years of the twentieth century, more immigrants by far landed from trans-Atlantic steamers than had succeeded in reaching America in the two and one-half centuries preceding the year 1850. In addition to this prodigious immigrant traffic it is also the greatest travel route of the world and the greatest freight route, and consequently the route possessing the largest, fastest, and most complete ships that ever floated.

The north Atlantic traffic has always been of a dual nature. The emigrating European has been finding a home, and the manufacturing European has been finding raw materials. This has given to the passenger and freight traffic a continual condition of unstable equilibrium. There are more passengers moving west than east; there is more freight moving east than west. Thus, there are, with the exception of certain short seasons of the year, unused passenger accommodations on the steamers setting out from America, and there is never even a temporary respite in the movement of empty freight vessels from Europe for American cargo. America has been sending raw materials in great bulk—cotton, wheat, corn, meat, lumber, copper, and cattle foods—and receiving manufactures of much smaller bulk. This was true in the first days of the Virginia colonists, tobacco ships, grain ships, and lumber ships; and, in the last decades,

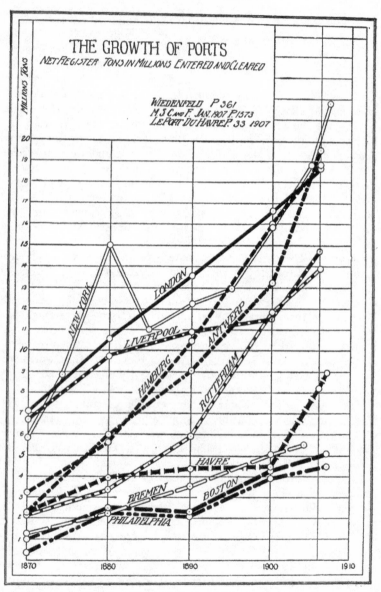

THE GROWTH OF PORTS

NET REGISTER TONS IN MILLIONS ENTERED AND CLEARED

WIEDENFELD P 361
M S C AND F. JAN. 1907 P 1573
LE PORT DU HAVRE P. 33 1907

MILLIONS TONS

NEW YORK

LONDON

LIVERPOOL

ANTWERP

HAMBURG

ROTTERDAM

HAVRE

BREMEN

BOSTON

PHILADELPHIA

FIG. 290.—The growth of world commerce. (After J. Paul Goode.)

American manufactures have added a new class of traffic, chiefly bulky products of wood and steel. Many vessels return with no cargo whatever except worthless ballast.

This traffic, in ballast, which makes a load valuable for its weight only has brought us hundreds of thousands of tons of sand and stone of less than no value; but the necessity of carrying something has caused the Atlantic ships to bring at times coal, iron ore, iron, chalk, china clay, and such bulky freight from Europe at minimum cost as ballast substitutes. (See British coal export in chapter on United Kingdom.)

The traffic future promises that our freight movement will not increase so rapidly as it has in the past. America, with her increasing population and her great mills, is using more and more of the raw material, has less and less for export to Europe. The fact that we are establishing manufacturing industries means also that we have a lessening demand for European goods, so both upon the side of production and on the side of consumption there is a prospect of lessened dependence of America upon Europe, and relatively lessened demand for commerce upon the north Atlantic trunk route. Although it is also scarcely conceivable that there can be any large extension of the emigrant traffic to America, there is every indication of the steady growth of travel between the two continents.

Ports.—The great increase in trade during the last quarter century has produced a multiplication of the lines of vessels, and consequently a great breaking down in the centralization that arose in the distribution and collection of the traffic to and from a few great ports which have been monopolizing it. There was a time when London and Liverpool almost monopolized the line traffic between Europe and America, but other cities rose to the position of claiming their share from America direct rather than through the intermediate ports. Liverpool saw Bristol rise to the south of her, Glasgow to the north of her, and Belfast across the Irish Sea. London has lost trade through the rise of Antwerp, Hamburg, and Havre, which ports in turn have established coasting lines and have snatched from London a part of the distributing trade of Scandinavia and Russia. But this was not the end. The establishing of coasting lines was scarcely complete at Hamburg and Antwerp, when the same process went further, and yet another set of rivals arose. There sprung up a direct trans-Atlantic connection that gave to Hull, Copenhagen, Stockholm, Petrograd, and

Bordeaux the ability to get some of their goods without dependence upon either the new intermediaries, Hamburg or Antwerp, or the old intermediaries at London or Liverpool (Figs. 290, 291).

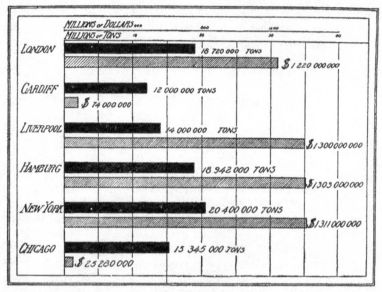

Fig. 291.—Variations in the foreign trades of ports. Comparison of net register tonnage and value of goods. Cardiff is a port for coal and ors. Liverpool for cotton and manufactures. (After J. Paul Goode.)

A similar development has occurred on the western end, where New York, while growing steadily in the annual amount of her traffic, is proportionally losing trade to her rival ports like Montreal, Boston and Baltimore, New Orleans, Galveston, and Pensacola.

CHAPTER XLV

THE NORTH PACIFIC ROUTE

The commercial newness of the Pacific.—As late as 1840 a man of international reputation stood up in the United States Senate and ridiculed the idea that the Pacific coast of what is now the United States could ever be of value. It is from the middle of the nineteenth century onward that the Pacific has risen swiftly to the important place it now holds in the attention of the civilized world. In 1848 came the gold discoveries in California and the making of a new commonwealth there promptly followed. In 1851 the gold cry went up from Australia and there was rush to that corner of the Pacific. In 1854 the ports of Japan were opened to the world; 15 years later our first trans-continental railway was completed to the Pacific coast; and throughout the last 50 years we have had continual interest in the north Pacific fisheries.

Since 1890 the intensity of interest in the Pacific has increased. In 1894 came the Japanese-Chinese War, which signified that there was an Asiatic power. In 1897 the Alaska gold discoveries placed emphasis on yet another point. We have become possessed of the Philippines and Hawaii, have watched the Russo-Japanese war, and all the leading powers of Europe have been striving to gain a foothold in China, the mysterious Celestial Empire that has proved so inviting to the exploiting and trading nations. And the United States has been digging away at the American isthmus to get a new gateway to the great Pacific.

Two steamer tracks.—All this recent interest centers around regions which are directly connected with the north Pacific trade route. This route is like the north Atlantic route in that the great circle factor is of much importance in locating it, and widely separated regions are brought by the factors of geography to use one and the same great route. The great circle factor is of much greater importance on the Pacific than on the Atlantic. Instead of America and Asia facing each other across a wide ocean, a globe shows that, because of the great width of the Pacific, the west shores of America

583

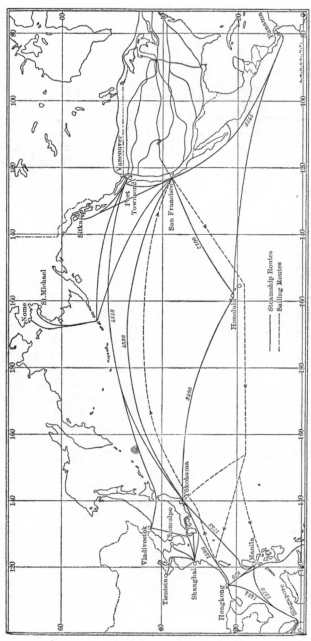

FIG. 292.—Routes of the North Pacific.

and the east shores of Asia are practically a continuous straight line. The steamer that attempts to pass directly from the ports of Puget Sound to Yokohama will wreck herself upon the rocky shores of the barren Aleutian Islands. Consequently the route is not a true great circle, but is flattened out to the southward from it, so that vessels may avoid the Aleutian Islands, in sight of which they pass. From San Francisco it is possible for the vessels to make a true great circle up near the Aleutian Islands. The effect of the great circle becomes yet more perplexing when the attempt is made to apply it to the route from Panama to Yokohama. The direct line between these two points goes northwestwardly through the Caribbean Sea, Yucatan, the Gulf of Mexico, Texas, Wyoming, Vancouver's Island, the Alaska peninsula and thence southward to Japan. A steamer compromising with these hard facts skirts the shores of the American continent until southern California is reached, and then across the north Pacific Ocean in the latitude of southern Canada. San Francisco is therefore much more nearly upon the actual short route from Panama to Yokohama than is Hawaii, which we are accustomed to think of as being exactly in the path. To stop at San Francisco would require a deviation of but 114 miles from the shortest possible steamer path and the deviation to Hawaii is over 300 miles. The one point that commercially commands the north Pacific route is the main island of Japan, for upon it is the great port of Yokohama, where practically every vessel crossing the north Pacific stops. Here every thread of this great commercial cable is focused to a single point. This spot is exactly on the route and is a great coaling station, being thousands of miles from any other port to the eastward which can have rendered service to the steamer. Manila is the last port of call for the steamers passing from America to Asia; Yokohama is directly on the route to it; and the Chinese ports of Hongkong and Shanghai are almost invariably sought by the same steamers on the out voyage (Fig. 292).

Coal supply.—The coal supply upon the route is fairly satisfactory, but the great length of the voyage requires that a steamer shall give up a comparatively large proportion of her space for coal purposes. There is practically none taken en route. Fortunately the Japanese coal, lying as it does part way between Asia and America, is admirably located close to the ports. Unfortunately there is no satisfactory supply thus far in California, and most

Fig. 203.—Great Northern Railway terminal on Puget Sound.

of the American coal comes from the region adjacent to Puget Sound. Some Japanese and more Australian coal is imported at San Francisco, and for many years before the opening of the Panama Canal cargoes of coal in sailing vessels regularly came around the Horn from Atlantic ports of America and occasionally from Wales.

Traffic.—The first part of the north Pacific route to attain modern importance was the link between Panama and San Francisco in the early days of the gold epoch in California. Many thousands of men engaged in producing nothing but the precious metal of coinage required a relatively great movement of commodities to supply their every want. Sailing vessels flocked around Cape Horn with supplies. Steamship lines were running from San Francisco to Panama and Nicaragua several years before the opening of the Panama Railway in 1856 and the completion of the Union Pacific in 1869 gave quicker communication with the eastern centers of population.

The north Pacific route has rendered its greatest service as a new road between the West and the East—a new rival to the old routes across Asia, around Good Hope and through Suez. Before the first trans-continental railway was opened in 1869 there was a steamer line from San Francisco to Japan and China. This original line has been followed by a half dozen more. These numerous steamers, which are among the largest in the world, carry outward a much greater amount of cargo than they bring on the return voyage from Asia (Fig. 293). A comparison of staples easily explains the reason. America exports coarse cotton cloth and gets silks in return; coarse lumber is exchanged for lacquerware, raw cotton for silk, canned goods and flour for drugs and essential oils, heavy machinery and petroleum for matting, Oriental art goods and fire crackers.

This lack of freightage balance upon this trade route has led to some peculiar movements. An European vessel coming out to China and Japan is in a sad plight for return cargo, so that many of the sailing vessels which go to China and Japan from the north Atlantic ports of Europe have discharged their cargoes (chiefly oil) in the Oriental port, crossed the north Pacific in ballast and returned to the north Atlantic via Cape Horn with a cargo of grain secured at Puget Sound, Portland, or San Francisco Bay. Within the past few years, British line steamers have continued their voyage from Great Britain to Japan by crossing the Pacific to Puget Sound, loading there with grain and other American produce, which is taken to Liverpool by way of China, Japan and the Suez Canal.

Hawaii and Alaska.—Hawaii has a place in the traffic of this route much greater than her area would indicate. The Hawaiian staple is sugar, which has reached quantities exceeding 500,000 tons a year. Most of this went around the Horn until the opening of the Tehuantepec Railway. Much of it goes to the port of Philadelphia, although some of it goes to the nearby ports of the Pacific mainland, which are also importing bananas, pineapples, and other tropical fruits from these islands. The frequent service from San Francisco gives that city an even greater importance as a base of Hawaiian supply than as a market for Hawaiian goods.

To the northward there is an additional stream of traffic. To supply the gold and fishing industries of Alaska, vessels pass both from San Francisco and Puget Sound, although the latter, because of its nearness, has a larger trade and a route which lies largely within the shelter of the archipelagoes that skirt the shores in this region.

Prospective traffic.—The prospects are for great increase of traffic along the north Pacific route. Every region adjacent to it is, in the modern sense, in its economic infancy. The chapter on China, Japan, and Korea showed the vast human and material resources of the Orient. Any industrial awakening there must mean enormous traffic over this route.

There is also indication that the mineral resources of Alaska are of large extent, requiring much import of machinery and other supplies from the South. The rapid increase of trans-continental railways can be taken as a prophecy for Pacific trade, for every trans-continental railway has some kind of trans-Pacific steamer connections at its western terminus, and the incompleted lines in both Canada and Mexico have contracts for new Pacific steamer lines to follow the common track to Asia.

CHAPTER XLVI

THE SUEZ AND PANAMA CANALS

Going round the world is usually a patchwork of several different journeys for the travelers, and until 1914 it was an unusual thing for ships to make a complete circumnavigation. Now, since the opening of the Panama Canal it is easy and common.

It was fortunate for commerce that the chance of nature so nearly cut the earth in two at its middle that we could finish it with canals. The Suez Canal (opened 1869) relieved the trade between the West and the East of a long and wearisome journey around Africa or an expensive portage at Suez. Before the canal was opened, thousands of camels transferred burdens between the Mediterranean and Red Sea steamers. The distance and scarcity of coal on the Good Hope Route restricted it at that time almost entirely to sailing vessels. About 1890 freight steamers began going to Australia that way while the mail steamers used Suez. The difficulties of the Red Sea have always kept the sailing vessel away from the Suez Canal, and it still rides around Africa before the unusually favorable winds that sweep the Atlantic and Indian oceans (Figs. 294, 295).

Judged by its relation to the earth's land mass and to the numbers of people served, the Suez Route goes through the heart of the world. It reaches lands containing most of the world's population. For Asia the total is nearly 800 million; for Europe it is 370 million; for Atlantic North America it is over 70 million, and Africa contributes enough to raise the total of the people served by this route to over 1,200,000,000—an astounding figure—more than three-fourths of the world's inhabitants. The only large masses of population that are not reached are the savages of Africa and the forty odd millions of South Americans.

While the American isthmus blocked access to the Pacific, that ocean was in a sense a sort of blind alley as evidenced by the tremendous journey made by vessels that went from London to Yokohama and Puget Sound and then turned to retrace their tracks. To-day the short cut home for that vessel is by way of the Panama canal, thus completing a round-the-world voyage which is to become typical. Europe's ships can go out to the Orient loaded and return

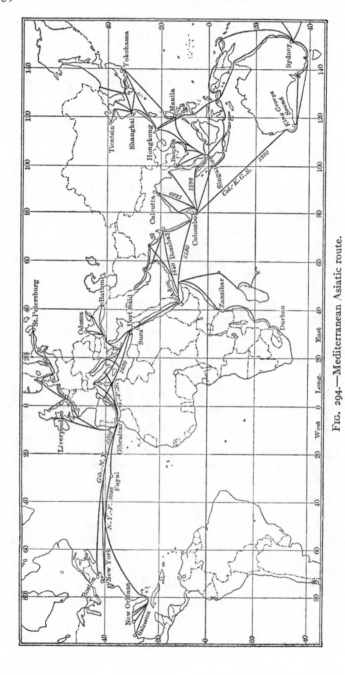

FIG. 294.—Mediterranean Asiatic route.

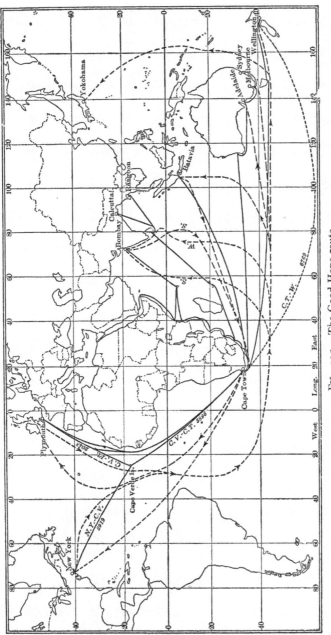

FIG. 295.—The Good Hope route.

(see **chapter** on North Pacific) with cargoes from the west coast of North America. Similarly the liner on the west coast of South America can circumnavigate that continent, coming or going by the Canal as circumstances warrant.

The canal affords a great relief (see table of distances, Appendix) to the trade of the United States Pacific Coast with Atlantic ports, which had long been compelled to pay high **costs for transs**hipment at Panama, or go around Cape Horn, the longest journey in the commercial world. The trade of New York and New Orleans with Australia also has much distance to save by the Canal. Even greater is the saving from the Atlantic ports to the Orient. The steady procession of nitrate ships and ore ships, mostly tramps, from western South America will use the Canal, but the tramp will make varying use of the new waterway. If freights are high it will be more profitable than when freights are low. Thus a ship may be making $25 or $250 per day, facts which would make her owner have differing regard for the canal tolls which might cost him $100 per day for the time saved.

These two canals have done much to enable the tramp and liner alike to get quickly from traffic zone to traffic zone and economically serve the world. The opening of each has been a world influence. Upon the opening of the Panama Canal there is no continent, almost no important country even, that does not find a rearrangement in the routes by which some of its goods go and come by sea. To their great relief, steamship lines by the score can rearrange their itineraries, and the tramp freighters by hundreds and thousands find themselves unloosed from harassing restrictions and free to work their way around the world with a freedom that will redound to the benefit of hundreds of millions of men. The start forward to this, the greatest readjustment of all time, is not unlike the general movement that follows the signal of a policeman in a crowded street when he releases two masses of waiting men or vehicles after a parade has passed.

QUESTIONS

1. Which of these canals is nearer to good coal shipping ports?
2. What oriental city is about equi-distant from New York by either canal?
3. How does the ocean freight rate make the tramp ship more or less dependent on the canal?
4. What facts about Pacific traffic make vessels circumnavigate the globe?

CHAPTER XLVII

WORLD TRADE DURING AND AFTER THE WAR

To understand world trade, and especially American trade, as it will probably work out in the decade after the war, we need to understand what has happened during the war and see the significance of this remarkable disturbance of trade.

The war had its unbelievably bloody battles, but it was also a war of goods—(a) equipment, (b) food, (c) transport.

(a) Equipment. We get some measure of the importance of equipment in this war when we recall that in November, 1914, after the deadlock on the western front and the digging-in of the armies. Lord Kitchener, head of the British armies, announced that the war would last three years. He missed it by a twelve-month, showing that even he did not realize how much time it would take to make the thousands of big guns, the millions of shells, the shiploads of explosives, the tens of thousands of motor trucks, and the other masses of material of which the mere enumeration gets us into figures beyond our understanding.

The United States, with its one hundred million people, its matchless and abundant resources, its machine shops and factory organization, spent four busy years making munitions for this war. Every European neutral was equally busy.

(b) Food. When Germany closed the Baltic Sea and, by getting Turkey into the war, closed the Bosphorus, she shut Western Europe off from her chief import supplies of bread and forage grains. This threw added burdens on the American market and it enlarged the wheat fields and corn fields of American farms. The people of Europe were so busy with fighting that they did not have time to plow and raise forage for all of their animals, so the demand fell upon America also for meat, and we increased our flocks and our exports of meat, as the appended chart shows.

(c) Transport. The war was as much a war of transport as it was of men and of munitions. The fleets of motor trucks that ground up the roads of France until they had to be rebuilt time and again came by the trainload from American factories and clogged

American ports. The sinking of ships by the submarine put us to feverishly building a navy and created the greatest burst of merchant ship-building ever seen. These trucks, these ships, this meat, this bread, these munitions, were all sold to Europe at unheard-of prices, and as a British official remarked to me in the fall of 1917, "You have here in America all the money in the world."

Europe had indeed imported and America had exported to the limit, indeed, beyond any limit that the world's financiers had before thought possible. Before the war we had regularly exported a few hundred million dollars a year (see chart) more than we imported. This surplus, commonly called a favorable balance of trade, was made up as follows:

1. Interest due the people of Europe who owned stocks and bonds in American enterprises.

2. Payment of freight to European ship-owners who carried our goods. Most of our commerce was carried in foreign ships.

3. Excess of travel expense, because the amount of American travelers expenses in Europe exceeded the amount of European travelers expenses in America.

4. Money taken back by Europeans who worked here for a time and returned. Also money sent by new immigrants back to their old homes in Europe.

Because of the war our balance of trade jumped up to an extent never before seen. Europe imported but did not export.

The chart of balance of trade shows how astonishingly Europe bought without sending us goods in return. Instead of sending us goods as is the habit of trade, they have given us promises to pay at some future time. First the British and French governments paid for these goods by giving their bonds (promises) to American individuals (bankers). When this had about reached its limit, the United States government borrowed the money from the American people and loaned it to the British government, which paid for our corn and iron with these credits.

It was the liberty bond that finally pushed up our foreign trade in 1917 and kept it there during 1918 and 1919. This unnatural trade without real payment cannot last. Promise must be followed by performance. The Europeans must pay the interest on their bonds and they must some day pay the bonds themselves. To do this they must resume their industries and their trade. They must make goods and get money.

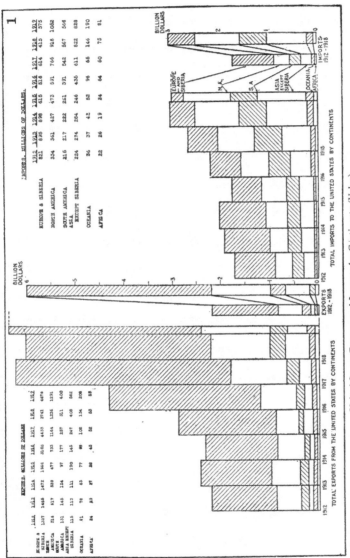

United States Exports and Imports by Continents (Value)

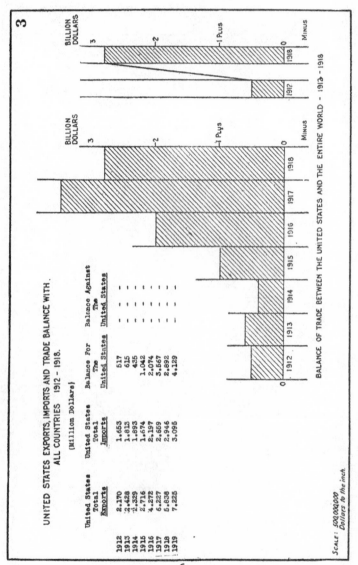

UNITED STATES EXPORTS, IMPORTS AND TRADE BALANCE WITH.
ALL COUNTRIES 1912 - 1918.

(Million Dollars)

	United States Total Exports	United States Total Imports	Balance For The United States	Balance Against The United States
1912	2.170	1.653	517	- - - - -
1913	2.428	1.813	615	- - - - -
1914	2.329	1.893	435	- - - - -
1915	2.716	1.674	1.042	- - - - -
1916	4.272	2.197	2.074	- - - - -
1917	6.227	2.659	3.567	- - - - -
1918	5.838	2.946	2.892	- - - - -
1919	7.225	3.095	4.129	- - - - -

BALANCE OF TRADE BETWEEN THE UNITED STATES AND THE ENTIRE WORLD - 1912 - 1918.

SCALE: $500,000,000 Dollars to the inch.

6

The period of readjustment.—The war is now over. The era of loans is drawing to an end. Business begins the post war period with a new basis of international trade, particularly American trade. The basis of American trade is changed profoundly in four respects:

1. The German indemnity.
2. Europe's increased ability to compete in foreign trade.
3. The changed balance of trade.
4. The change of price basis.

1. **The German indemnity.**—We cannot understand the prospective trade situation until we see what it means for Germany to pay to her late enemies for some of the billions of dollars worth of property that she so ruthlessly destroyed.

Through her indemnity payments, Germany may decide the export surplus of her late enemies. If they compel her to pay for the war destruction or the war costs or both, she can at the start borrow a little money in neutral countries as she has already done. This is merely to give her a little start. In this case the United States might send payment (goods) she owed a neutral, say Holland, for ship hire, to England or France, or Belgium because Germany had borrowed of Holland to pay England or France or Belgium. But in the main, Germany can pay her enemies in only one way—by producing goods, export goods. If she had all the gold in the world, other nations would have no money, and it would only be a drop in the bucket anyhow. What then? Goods. The facts of trade tend to make us forget that gold, like bank cheques and all other money, is but a medium for the exchange of goods. The only exception is when the gold happens to be the product of a mine in which case it is goods, like coal, for the country first producing it. Countries settle trade differences with gold, but they can only get the gold by digging it out of the ground or buying it with goods. As Germany is not a gold producer, she can only get it by buying it with goods— exports.

Her enemies wish to make her pay for the war. How may it be done? With regard to war settlement, Germany may pay four different ways:

(*a*) The payment of money which results from exporting to the world market.

(*b*) The payment in produce directly to her enemies.

(*a*) **Money payment.**—This merely means exports, selling goods abroad, the purchase with goods of bills of exchange on banks in

London, Paris, Brussels, or New York, and the handing of these
bills to the representatives of the collecting country. By this
process, Germany may send the goods to neutrals and transfer the
credit to England or France, as by sending cloth and machinery to
Argentina to pay for wheat and meat that went to England or
France. That is the way France paid Germany in 1872-73, chiefly
in bills on London, but it was paying none the less in exports, of
which France showed at the time a distinct surplus over imports.
To get the bills on London she sold goods in other countries. Germany, receiving all these credits, showed a financial inflation and
speculation which according to many authorities helped bring on
the panic of 1873, and made its effects in Germany much more severe
than in France.

Because of war settlements Germany may be compelled to show
an export surplus of a billion or two per year for a term of years.
If she does do this other countries will find it difficult to do the same
thing at the same time, for Germany will by this process become a
country of low prices, therefore, a country of low wages, a country
without luxury. It will be most difficult for countries with higher
prices and higher wages to compete with Germany in neutral markets on commodities where the competition is even; as in chemicals,
textiles, standardized machinery, machinery and other metal manufactures. The United States and the Allies will have high prices
due to the inflation of war loans. Germany will probably have to
repudiate all her internal debt, and therefore her currency will not
be inflated so much as that of other countries. This contrast will
make all countries having the inflated currency extra good markets
for German goods with which Germany will get credits to send to
London and Paris to pay the war debts of those countries. Germany
will in a sense be giving the goods away and the rest of the world
will be trying to sell them in competition with her. The result of
such competition is plain. It will make a lower price level throughout the world, because it will increase supplies and large supplies
always tend to reduce prices also. After 10 or 20 years of paying
for restoration, Germany will have the greatest export trade ever
seen except our recent war trade. She will have had to build up a
trade first to get the credits to pass to her enemies. Her enemies
will have the credits but Germany will have the trade.

Some people are much alarmed at this prospect. A part of this
fear arises from the widespread belief that exports are necessarily

a fine thing for a country and imports necessarily a bad thing. This 18th century idea called mercantilism was held so strongly by Napoleon Bonaparte that he freely permitted England to import grain from the Baltic in 1810-11, thinking that he was thereby injuring her. Really he let England strengthen herself to crush him.

If we look at it in its simple economic light, this payment looks good, very good. For a term of years, Germany becomes the servant of other nations to the extent of billions of dollars' worth of goods which she produces and sells for their account, turning the money over to them—wealth, national wealth. That certainly looks good. It would undoubtedly help in the payment of national debts. England and France would hand money over to their citizens in exchange for bonds. The people would take this money and buy things. German things perhaps. The Belgian Government could pay for the bread the Belgian Relief distributed through the terrible years of the war.

Here is the place where we must deal with the distinction between the Government and the citizens of the country. There are two kinds of danger in this situation—one industrial and the other financial. The industrial danger lies in the possibility of the citizens living on this restoration fund for a time and getting out of the habit of supporting themselves so that when the payments end they would be in the position of the rich young man who had lived on his father's money while it lasted and had not learned how to support himself when it was suddenly gone.

If the people of the fund-receiving country could keep up their work and their industries just the same this difficulty would not arise. This, however, is very difficult or impossible to guarantee. It depends on the individual choices of too many people. Some prefer to work and save; others prefer to work some and spend, and then from time to time industrial depression, the greatest ogre of modern industrialism, throws millions out of work whether they will or no. Here is a point where the financial danger of the restoration payment aggravates the industrial danger. It may tend to increase panics in the receiving countries as did the French payments to Germany, 1871-73.

There is little doubt that the receipts of hundreds of millions a year of foreign credits by England, France, Belgium and Italy will be a menace by making speculation, inflation and panic that will require a careful and vigorous control of governmental finances already over-inflated with war loans—paper money in fact. Undoubtedly one part of this financial control should be a continued, careful inspection and licensing of capital issues in all the countries receiving German money and probably in the United States also. Such a reform is already under discussion in the United States. It is much needed.

The ultimate industrial danger in the German restoration fund is that Germany will finish her payments with a huge industry and thoroughly established trade outlet for that industry, while her enemies have neither the industry nor the outlet. This danger, if it is a danger, can be partly avoided by having the payments on the fund taper off, after a time declining at a small percentage each month until it gradually disappears. Under no condition should the rate of payment be left to Germany. In 1871–73, France got Germany on the hip by handing her money faster than she could digest it, and if Germany were free to pay as she chose she might play hob with world finance.

The gradual ending of the payments would let international trade and industry make gradual adjustment to the great change, so that its ending would be unnoticed.

Gradual ending would also dovetail with a process of foreign investment. The restoration fund should be and probably will be largely invested in foreign lands. German cloth, cement, machinery, glass, paper and general consumption goods may now go to Spain for French and Belgian account, and let French and Belgian financiers resume the work on hydro-electric, irrigation, power and public service enterprises that stopped so suddenly in 1914 when French and Belgian supplies were cut off by war paralysis, and the American engineers who were doing the work were sent home. The building of a railroad in Brazil means that somebody furnishes equipment of the road and the goods used by the men and the families of the men as well as by the mules who do the work of building the road. Thus Germany will build a railroad in Brazil for English account by sending cars, rails, steam shovels, dynamite, cement, and locomotives to Brazil. She will also send clothing, shoes, pocket knives, playing cards and phonographs for the men and also gasoline, tobacco, flour, and bacon, mules and bales of hay which she may secure in the United States, Argentina and Brazil by sending potash to those countries. The financial records of the transaction will be wages paid and certain pieces of paper, bills of

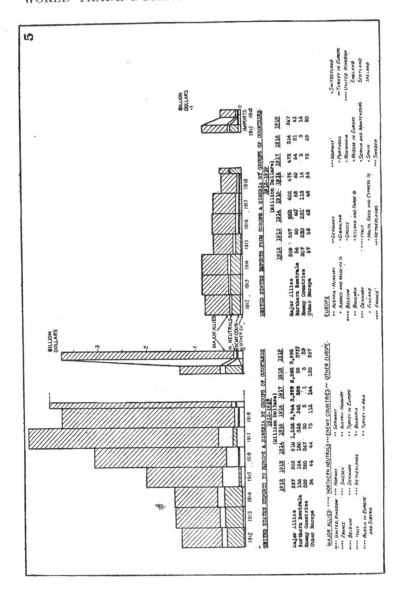

exchange, written in terms of gold. Thus the surplus exports which
produce Germany's restoration fund may be used to equip enterprises in Russia, Asia Minor, Brazil, and even the United States
for the account of English, French and Belgian investors who will
later fatten their imports with the return from these investments.
The income from these investments should gradually mount as the
annually payment of restoration money declines, so that its ending
would be unnoticed. The period of payment must end, however,
with Germany possessed of large producing capacity and large export, while England and France will in all probability have relatively
small export and large import—this surplus of imports meaning, of
course, that the nations were rich with foreign investments on which
they were receiving returns.

2. **Europe's increased ability to compete.**—Europe has lost
millions of workers, but their producing power has been much more
than replaced by improvements in the mechanical power and industrial organization that the goad of war necessity has forced upon
European industry. Europe's changed industrial basis may be
summarized under two points:

(a) She has greatly increased her use of agricultural machinery
which she had delayed adopting because labor was cheap and
abundant.

(b) She has learned to utilize the three American wonders of
standardization, specialization and mass production.

To understand these three words which have for the last twenty
years characterized American industry, and which refer to processes
that Europe has now learned, we can look at the building of a wagon
a generation ago. The wheelwright took his hand tools and shaved
the spokes, turned and chiseled the hubs, sawed and trimmed the
felloes. Perhaps his one helper fashioned the bed and the running
gear, but the wheelwright himself knew how, from start to finish,
to make a wagon, and he did it. Now two to three machines combine to make the spokes, other machines make the hubs and the
felloes. The bed is chopped out by standardized wood-working
machinery. Each piece is made by a specialist, and the wagon-
maker puts them together as a child does a house of blocks. This
is typical of the revolution which has given us the age of cheap
machinery. This standardization and specialization have given us
those miracles, the dollar watch, the Ford automobile, the phono-
graph, the telephone, and placed them all within the reach of the
average citizen.

Specialization and standardization are so much cheaper than the old-fashioned made to-order-way because they permit us to use the machine tool. This is the age of the machine tool, which has replaced in wood-working the various hand tools of the carpenter, and in metal-working the various hand tools of the machinist. Reduced to their lowest terms, the wood-working and iron-working processes are similar, and the elementary processes are few. The artisan bores holes, he shaves or planes, he saws, he turns in lathes, but the machinist or factory wood-worker of today does none of these things himself. If he wishes holes made, he puts a piece of wood or iron in a boring machine; if he wishes it smoothed, he puts it in a planing machine. No matter whether it be wood or iron, steel or brass, the process is the same with machines made to do the work in an infinite variety of sizes, shapes, and materials. The expert machinist, the old-style machinist, can take any kind of a machine and do any kind of work, but he is now as much out of date as the man who can make a watch or wagon from start to finish.

It is wasteful for one man or one machine to do many kinds of work. The reason of this is that the machines are elaborate; they must be adjusted and set for each kind of operation that they perform. Thus the setting of a machine to do a piece of work often takes more time than the actual doing of the work. Sometimes it takes a half-day to reset a machine. Sometimes it takes a week. It may take ten minutes to work up one piece after the machine is set. Thus the costs of shaping a particular piece of metal were, for one piece, 25 cents, for two pieces 15 cents each, for 5 pieces 10 cents each, for 100 pieces 5 cents each, for 500 pieces 3 cents each. Now we see why it is so much cheaper to make the valves for one of a hundred ship engines all alike, new style, than it is to make one or two for sister ships, old style.

Then, to cap the climax of this thing, these pieces made at such low cost are interchangeable, and will fit into any one of tens of thousands of machines of a certain type. It is by the utilization of these revolutionary processes, standardization and specialization that the Ford car, the dollar watch, and the American locomotive made by highly paid men, are sold in competition with the produce of men who work for lower wages but on the old unstandardized methods. We also see why the Ford car has not changed its design for years.

This enables a bridge plant in Pittsburgh, a boiler plant in Ohio, a structural steel mill in West Virginia, and a plate mill in Illinois to specialize and adjust their machinery to make hundreds of thousands of duplicate pieces for hundreds or thousands of duplicate ships. So an automobile plant here, a windmill plant there, an engine shop yonder, can make some of the parts of the marine engine and the rather numerous small machines that are needed in a ship, such as small engines to hoist cargo, pumps for water, pumps for oil, fans for ventilators, pulleys, cables, compasses.

Standardize, standardize, standardize; specialize, specialize, specialize. Thus we can win the war, *if we try*. Fortunately we can try harder than we are now trying.

The important point about this standardization and specialization and mass production is that the war has taught it to Europe.

The making of munitions forced England, France, Germany, Switzerland, Sweden, Denmark, and Holland to make over their machine-shop industries until they had specialization, standardization, and mass production carried to the finest degree of perfection ever attained on this planet. We boast in America of our war industries, but the facts are that the European munitions plants did more accurate work, and millions of workers were taught their simple parts in this copying of an industrial method first worked out in America.

What does this mean in the foreign trade? It means that Europe can now compete on terms of equality with America in one of the points where we had a kind of pre-war industrial advantage, in some cases one might almost say industrial monopoly.

As an example I may cite the case of a certain American safety razor which has long been advertised and sold at a price of several dollars. Exact duplicates of this razor made in Japan are being sold in South Africa and elsewhere for 38 cents. The American makers have withdrawn from the South African market. They can do nothing there.

In the matter of European use of the new factory system in this period of readjustment it should be remembered that technical education in Europe has been promoted more than in America, both before the war and since the war.

3 and 4. **Balance of trade and price basis.**—Our astonishing balance of trade due us must shortly stop piling up. Debts cannot mount much higher. Europe must cease to pay us in promises.

She must begin to pay us in goods. Already the long continuance
of buying on promises has so disturbed international finance that
this morning, November 26, a pound sterling was worth $4.06⅝ in
New York. This means that $4.86⅝ worth of American goods is
only worth $4.06⅝ in London. This gives to the British and other
Europeans whose exchange is low a great advantage when they sell

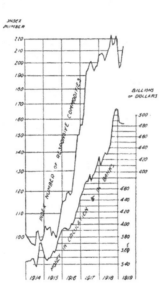

in foreign markets in competition with us. Our high price tends
to keep us out of foreign markets at all points where there can be
any competition.

In summary, we may state that America is now approaching the
period where she must give up her monopoly of war trade advantage.
For five years people have begged us for goods. We had not *sold*
them nor have the purchasers paid for them. We have *let people
have the goods* on credit. Now they must start to give us the back
pay in *goods*, the only thing in which payment can be made. We
have large import trade due us. When it comes to continued selling
abroad we find ourselves at a disadvantage in international exchange
and with rivals who have new powers of competition and a new
equality at the point where we had had something approaching a
monopoly advantage. There is a new era of trade ahead of us.

STATISTICAL APPENDIX

Persons desiring to go further into statistics are referred to the following sources:

I. Statistical Abstract of the United States, published by the Bureau of Foreign and Domestic Commerce, and to be had free from your congressmen.

II. Yearbook of the United States Department of Agriculture for agricultural statistics. (See congressmen.)

III. Mineral Resources of the United States, a large two-volume annual with very full accounts of Mineral Industries and Statistics of Mineral Production. (See congressmen.)

IV. The Statesman's Year Book, London, $3.00, contains an excellent brief account of all countries, with many well-chosen statistics.

TABLE I.—WHEAT TRADE AND PRODUCTION

Note the relative yields per acre in importing and in exporting countries

Importing countries	Million bu.		Yield in bu. per acre, 1913	Exporting countries	Million bu.		Yield in bu. per acre, 1913
	Crop, 1913	Import, 1912			Crop, 1913	Export, 1912	
Belgium..........	15.0	71.0	37.8	Argentina	198.4	103.3	11.6
Denmark..........	4.5	8.5	33.5[1]	Australia	94.9	40.4	12.9
France...........	321.6	26.7	19.9	British India....	358.4	68.8	12.1
Germany..........	171.8	85.0	35.1	Bulgaria........	45.0	14.5	16.2
Italy.............	214.4	58.6	18.1	Canada	231.8	104.3	21.0
Japan.............	27.1	3.0	22.0	Roumania	83.2	56.8	20.7
Netherlands.......	4.8	75.0	34.3	Russia[3]	962.6	100.5	12.9
Switzerland.......	3.5	20.0	13.4[2]	United States ..	763.4	109.5	15.2
United Kingdom...	58.4	229.0	32.6	Average			15.3
Average			27.4	Kansas.........	92.3		13.0
New York State.....	6.8		20.0				

[1] 1912. [2] 1911. [3] Includes ten provinces of Asiatic Russia.

607

TABLE 2.—CROP COMPARISONS, WITH ADDITION OF ACRE YIELDS

The relative dependence of different nations on different crops and the differing yields of these crops afford interesting subjects for explanation

	Population, millions	Population per sq. mile	Potatoes, bu. (1912)			Wheat, bu. (1913)			Barley, bu. (1913)		
			Acreage, 1,000	Crop, million	Yield per acre	Acreage, 1,000	Crop, million	Yield per acre	Acreage, 1,000	Crop, million	Yield per acre
United States.	92.0	30.9	3,711	420.6	113.4	50,184	763.4	15.2	7,499	178.2	23.8
Germany.....	65.0	310.4	8,257	1,844.9	223.5	4,878	171.8	35.1	4,087	188.7	41.3
Russia.......	138.0	69.2	11,167	1,356.8	121.5	74,512	962.6	12.9	31,197	574.0	18.4
France.......	39.6	189.5	3,863	552.0	145.8	16,169	321.6	19.9	1,890	48.4	25.6
United Kingdom.......	45.4	374.0	1,208	213.8	177.0	1,796	58.4	32.6	1,931	67.8	35.1
Belgium......	7.5	652.0	387	121.5	313.9	397[2]	15.0	37.8	84	4.1	48.8
Sweden......	5.6	32.2	378[1]	65.8	174.0	260[2]	7.8	30.0	446[1]	14.0	31.4
Austria......	28.6	247.0	3,092	460.8	149.0	2,998	60.1	19.9	2,699	75.9	29.4
Hungary.....	21.0	167.0	1,530	197.8	129.2	7,700	151.3	19.2	2,887	79.8	26.5
Italy.........	35.2	318.8	712	56.3	79.0	11,842	214.4	18.0	620	10.8	17.4
World crop...				5,898.5			4,124.9			1,616.2	

	Rye, bu. (1913)			Corn, bu. (1913)			Oats, bu. (1913)		
	Acreage, 1,000	Crop, million	Yield per acre	Acreage, 1,000	Crop, million	Yield per acre	Acreage 1,000	Crop, million	Yield per acre
United States.	2,557	41.4	16.2	105,820	2,447.0	23.1	38,399	1,121.8	29.2
Germany.....	15,849	481.2	30.4	....	....	......	10,967	669.2	61.1
Russia.......	74,990	1,002.5	13.4	4,233	72.8	17.2	47,512	1,135.7	24.6
France.......	2,958	52.7	17.8	1,177[2]	22.0	18.7	9,881	322.1	32.6
United Kingdom.......	58	1.7	29.1	....	....	......	3,961	181.1	43.7
Belgium......	650[2]	21.4	32.9	....	....	......	648[2]	41.0	63.2
Sweden.......	989[2]	23.0	23.2	....	....	......	1,952[1]	76.0	39.0
Austria.......	4,853	109.0	22.4	705	13.3	18.8	4,707	160.0	39.3
Hungary.....	2,668	52.0	19.5	6,129	182.0	29.7	2,884	99.8	33.7
Italy.........	307	5.6	18.2	3,888	108.4	27.9	1,251	43.5	34.8
World crop...		1,885.1			3,605.4			4,631.2	

[1] 1911 statistics.　[2] 1912 statistics.

TABLE 3.—POPULATION AND DOMESTIC ANIMALS IN THE UNITED STATES, 1870–1914

What does this table show about meat prices? How has the change in the number of people changed the relative numbers of different classes of cattle?

	Popu-lation, million	Cattle of all kinds 1,000	Per cent of popula-tion of United States	Milch cows 1,000	Per cent of popula-tion of United States	Other cattle 1,000	Per cent of popula-tion of United States	Hogs 1,000	Per cent of popula-tion of United States	Horses and mules 1,000	Per cent of popula-tion of United States	Sheep 1,000	Per cent of popula-tion of United States
1870	38.6	25,483	66	10,095	26	15,388	40	26,751	69	9,427	25	40,853	106
1880	50.2	33,258	66	12,027	24	21,231	42	34,034	68	12,930	25	40,765	80
1890	62.9	52,801	83	15,953	25	36,849	58	51,602	82	16,544	26	44,336	67
1901	77.0	62,333	80	16,834	22	45,500	59	56,982	75	19,648	25	59,756	77
1912	93.0	57,959	62	20,699	22	37,260	40	65,410	70	24,871	27	52,362	56
1914	98.1	56,592	57	20,737	21	35,855	36	58,933	60	25,411	26	49,719	50

TABLE 4.—DISTRIBUTION OF CLASSES OF CATTLE, 1914

What is the explanation of the different ratio of the different classes of cattle in the different regions?

	Milch cows, 1,000	Other cattle, 1,000
Populous East:		
New Jersey	146	68
New York	1,465	876
Pennsylvania	943	632
North Central Dairy Belt:		
Michigan	798	680
Wisconsin	1,549	1,158
Iowa	1,350	2,555
Cattle-fattening States:		
Kansas	698	1,565
Missouri	789	1,386
Texas	1,065	5,173
Range States:		
Arizona	37	739
Wyoming	41	546

TABLE 5.—INTERNATIONAL TRADE IN DAIRY PRODUCTS, 1912

How does it happen that a great agricultural country like the United States imports cheese while Canada and Switzerland export it?

	Exports			Imports		
	Butter, million lb.	Cheese, million lb.			Butter, million lb.	Cheese, million lb.
Argentina	8.0	....	Argentina		....	11.8
Australia	67.0	....	Belgium		15.0	31.0
New Zealand	33.0	49.0	Austria-Hungary		....	12.0
Canada	0.9	154.0	Brazil		4.0	6.0
Denmark	187.0	....	British S. Africa		4.9	5.0
Finland	27.0	....	France		14.0	47.0
Russia	159.0	8.9	Germany		122.0	47.0
France	37.0	1.8	Italy		....	10.0
Holland	86.0	131.0	Switzerland		11.9	7.9
Italy	8.8	67.0	United Kingdom		435.0	250.0
Sweden	48.0	....	United States		1.1	49.3
Switzerland	....	66.0				
United States	3.6	2.6				

TABLE 6.—POWER CONSUMPTION OF UNITED STATES, 1870-1905

Power used for manufacturing	Total horse-power, 1,000		Horse-power per wage earner		Horse-power used per $1,000 of output	
	1870	1905	1870	1905	1870	1905
Agricultural implements...........	26	106	1.0	2.2	0.5	1.0
Boots and shoes.................	3	62	0.1	0.4	0.1	2.0
Cotton goods....................	146	1,040	1.1	3.3	0.8	2.3
Flour and grist mill products......	576	780	9.9	19.9	1.3	1.1
Hosiery and knit goods...........	6,500	84	0.4	0.8	0.4	0.6
Iron and steel...................	170	2,725	2.2	11.2	0.6	3.0
Lumber and timber...............	641	1,500	4.3	3.7	3.1	2.6
Paper and pulp..................	54	1,125	3.0	17.0	1.1	5.9
Silk goods......................	2	79	0.3	1.0	0.2	0.6
Woolen goods...................	85	164	1.1	2.3	0.5	1.2
Worsted goods..................	8	130	1.6	1.9	0.4	0.8
All other factories...............	626	6,850	....	....	....	....

Increase { Power consumption, 300 per cent.
Power rates to population, 100 per cent.
Power rates to wage earner, 164 per cent.
Power rates to $1,000 of product, 137 per cent.

TABLE 7.—COAL OUTPUT PER MINER

Does this table prove or disprove the conservationists' claim that we should not waste our coal?

	Yearly output per miner in tons		Cost per ton at mine
	1899	1908	1909
England......................	311	279	$2.05
Germany.....................	264	246	2.45
France.......................	211	189	3.08
Belgium......................	173	160	3.11
United States:			
Anthracite..................	433	478	1.84
Bituminous.................	713	644	1.07

TABLE 8.—WATER-POWER RESOURCES

Very detailed figures of power development by streams and regions may be found in statistical abstract of the United States

Principal drainages	Drainage area, square miles	Flow per annum, billion cubic feet	Horse-power available	
			Primary or minimum of two low-est weeks	Minimum of six highest months
Northern Atlantic to Cape Henry, Va..	159,879	8,942	1,702,000	3,186,600
Southern Atlantic to Cape Sable, Fla...	123,920	5,560	1,253,000	1,957,800
Eastern Gulf of Mexico to Mississippi River...............................	142,220	6,867	559,000	963,000
Western Gulf of Mexico west of Ver-million River.......................	433,700	2,232	433,760	829,650
Mississippi River main stream.........	1,238,800	21,940	147,000	335,000
Mississippi River tributaries from east..	333,600	12,360	2,472,590	4,940,300
Mississippi River tributaries from west, including Vermillion River..........	905,200	9,580	3,948,970	7,085,000
St. Lawrence River to Canadian line....	299,720	8,583	6,682,480	8,090,060
Colorado River, above Yuma, Arizona...	225,000	521	2,918,500	5,546,000
Southern Pacific to Point Bonita, Cal...	70,700	2,193	3,215,400	7,808,300
Northern Pacific.....................	290,400	15,220	12,979,700	24,701,000
Great Basin..........................	223,000	....	518,000	801,000
Hudson Bay..........................	62,150	614	75,800	212,600
Total...........................	4,508,289	94,612	36,906,200	66,449,310

TABLE 9.—PETROLEUM PRODUCTION, MILLION BARRELS

Note the great changes in a short period

	1900	1909	1913	Per cent of world production, 1913
United States.......................	63.0	182.0	248.4	65.12
Russia.............................	75.0	65.0	60.9	15.97
Austria............................	5.7	14.9	....	....
Roumania..........................	1.6	9.3	13.5	3.53
British India.......................	1.0	6.6	7.5	1.98
Dutch East Indies...................	2.2	11.4	11.9	3.14
Japan..............................	0.8	1.8	1.0	0.51
Mexico............................	....	....	25.6	6.7
World production...................	....	285.0	381.5	....

TABLE 10.—FOREST AREAS

Explain the differences in relative forest areas in England, Russia, Denmark, France and New Hampshire

	Percentage of area in forests	Approximate area of forest lands, square miles	Total area, in square miles
United States...................	28.9	860,000	2,973,890
New Hampshire.................	67.6	5,628	8,315
Washington State...............	51.4	34,000	66,127
California.....................	20.0	31,250	155,652
United Kingdom................	0.041	5,000	121,391
England......................	0.052	2,680	50,890
Russia (European)..............	40.9	761.772	1,862,524
France.......................	18.0	36,000	207,054
German Empire................	24.0	54,000	208,780
Switzerland...................	21.0	3,355	15,976
Italy.........................	13.9	15,437	110,550
Spain........................	13.0	25,102	194,783
Austria.......................	34.6	41,100	115,930
Holland......................	10.0	1,264	12,648
Denmark.....................	4.8	750	15,582
Norway......................	21.0	26,900	128,129
Sweden......................	52.2	90,241	172,876
Japanese Empire including Formosa......	16.5	29,000	175,540

TABLE 11.—STATISTICS OF AMERICAN SILK TRADE, 1914

Is there any evidence here of density of population? Does the United Kingdom produce the silk she sends?

	Imports into the United States			Exports from United States
	Raw silk		Manufactured silk	Manufactured silk
	Amount in lb.	Value	Value	
Japan................	20,772,231	$71,755,416	4,246,724	....
China................	7,460,624	16,724,618	314,003	....
Italy.................	2,936,383	9,566,907	1,089,927	72,000
France...............	478,262	589,663	18,700,633	....
Switzerland...........	223,184	95,809	4,762,373	....
United Kingdom.......	1,716,670	431,907	4,346,649	349,150
Germany.............	66,592	18,150	5,010,727	76,130
Canada..............	767,526	1,686,983	38,548	1,228,196
Total............	34,421,472	$100,869,453	38,509,584	1,725,476

TABLE 12(A).—MILLIONS OF COTTON SPINDLES IN THE WORLD

Does this show anything about the relative fineness of cotton manufacture in the United States and Switzerland? Explain the relative amounts of export in the United States and Switzerland.

	1900	1912
Great Britain...	45.5	55.3
Continent, Europe......................................	32.0	43.0
Germany..	8.0	10.7
Total Europe......................................	77.5	98.3
United States:		
Cotton states..	4.3	11.5
Other states..	15.1	19.0
Total U. S...	19.4	30.5
British India	4.9	6.1
Japan..	1.2	2.1
China..	0.5	0.8
Canada...	0.5	0.8
Mexico...	0.4	0.6
Total world	105.6	141.0

TABLE 12(B).—COTTON MANUFACTURED, 1910

	Pounds of cotton per capita	Exports, million dollars
United States...............................	25.4	40
United Kingdom.............................	38.1	583
France......................................	9.4	63
Germany....................................	12.8	105 (1906)
Switzerland.................................	12.3	50
Spain.......................................	8.2	9
Japan.......................................	12.7	5
Italy..	11.3	5

TABLE 13(A).—MACHINERY EXPORTS OF LEADING COUNTRIES, from Commercial America (Phila. Commercial Museums)

This table shows how commerce has been able to increase so rapidly. Machines make goods

	1890, millions	1910, millions
Great Britain	$80	$142
Germany	15	119
United States	15	110
France	9	20
Belgium	8	12
Switzerland	4	14
Netherlands	3	6
All other	5	43
Total	$140	$468

TABLE 13(B).—CLASSES OF MACHINERY FROM LEADING COUNTRIES

Articles	1910, Great Britain, millions	1911, United States, millions	1910, Germany, millions
Prime movers of all kinds, steam and traction, including locomotives	$8.0[1]	$16.0	$29.5
Machine tools	3.4	....	....
Metal-working machinery	....	9.6	14.2
Wood-working machinery	....	1.8	3.0
Textile machinery	37.0	....	12.3
Sewing machines, and parts of typewriters	8.4	{ 9.0 9.8 }	10.2
Agricultural machinery	13.0[1]	24.6	5.2
Parts of agricultural machinery, and other agricultural implements	....	11.4	....
Printing presses and machinery	....	2.8	4.0
Mining machinery	6.2	7.0	....
Electrical machinery	8.0	8.0	....
Sugar machinery	....	....	2.3
Shoe machinery	....	1.6	1.5
All other	58.2	27.2	33.0
Total	$142.5	$129.2	$119.0

[1] Including traction engines.

TABLE 14.—WORLD'S MERCHANT MARINE (Figures from the Shipping **World** for 1915)

One of the explanations of the fact that the British are a wealthy people

Country	Tonnage in thousands
British.	19,988.0 (46 per cent of total)
German.	5,072.0
American.	2,380.0
French.	1,861.0
Norwegian.	1,914.0
Japanese.	1,680.0
Italian.	1,442.8
Dutch.	1,508.0
Russian.	970.0
Swedish.	1,016.3
Austrian.	1,016.6
Spanish.	876.0
Danish.	745.0
Greek.	830.0
Belgian.	347.0
Brazilian.	275.6
Argentinian.	163.7
Chilian.	86.4
Turkish.	116.0
Chinese.	87.0
Portuguese.	80.0
Total for all countries.	42,742.7

TABLE 15.—IMPORTS OF OIL MATERIALS AT MARSEILLES

Vegetable oils are increasing about as rapidly as mineral oils

Articles	1906, tons	1910, tons
Sesame seed.	61,416	90,979
Groundnuts:		
Shelled.	111,158	199,774
In shell.	78,677	148,242
Linseed.	19,634	10,128
Rape and ravison.	3,191	5,483
Poppy seed.	3,925	1,794
Castor seed.	13,554	13,487
Pulghere seed.	....	1,887
Cottonseed.	18,391	11,655
Niger and kapok seed.	2,375	1,788
Copra.	109,914	171,423
Palm kernels.	4,170	1,629
Mowrah, illipe, etc.	6,431	7,410
Total.	432,836	665,679

TABLE 16.—RECEIPTS OF GRAIN AT VARIOUS AMERICAN MARKETS

The development of the American West is shown in part by the relative position
of Chicago among grain cities

	Year[1]	Million bushels		
		Wheat	Oats	Corn
Winnipeg..................	1913	166.2	70.9	....
	1914	108.0	36.5	....
Minneapolis..............	1913	125.9	18.6	6.2
	1914	103.6	22.7	10.7
Duluth....................	1913	82.9	9.2	....
	1914	63.0	5.8	....
Kansas City..............	1913	48.3	7.7	16.9
	1914	31.0	11.2	27.4
Chicago..................	1913	44.1	144.2	131.7
	1914	50.7	106.0	84.8
St. Louis.................	1913	38.1	23.4	22.7
	1914	26.6	25.9	16.9
Omaha....................	1913	20.4	14.7	22.6
	1914	18.0	16.7	37.1
Tacoma...................	1912	14.5	1.1	0.2
	1913	11.2	0.8	0.2
Milwaukee................	1913	10.1	15.8	11.6
	1914	6.3	18.4	15.8
Seattle...................	1912	9.0	2.1	0.5
	1913	8.8	2.7	0.5
San Francisco............	1912	7.0	2.1	0.22
	1913	7.5	1.7	0.18
Toledo...................	1913	4.7	5.6	3.9
	1914	5.8	3.7	4.5
Peoria....................	1913	1.9	11.2	17.9
	1914	1.6	11.7	14.7
Indianapolis.......	1913	1.9	7.9	15.9
	1914	1.8	5.3	14.1
Detroit...................	1913	1.0	3.8	2.7
	1914	1.4	3.8	2.8

[1] Wheat year, July 1–July 1; corn year, Nov. 1–Nov. 1; oat year, Aug. 1–Aug. 1; but ı
San Francisco, Seattle, Tacoma and Winnipeg the period covered is calendar year.

TABLE 17.—DISTANCES SAVED BY THE PANAMA CANAL

If it costs an exporter $200 per day to hire a steamer by the month, and tolls cost him $2,000 for a passage, note how his attitude toward using the canal will vary with profits of $25, $100, or $150 per day.

	Nautical miles	Days at 10 knots	Days at 16 knots
Liverpool to Port Townsend.....	5,666	23.1	14.2
Liverpool to San Francisco.......	5,666	23.1	14.2
Liverpool to Honolulu..........	4,403	17.8	10.9
Liverpool to Valparaiso..........	1,540	5.9	3.5
Liverpool to Yokohama..........	−694	−2.4	−1.3
Liverpool to Shanghai..........	−2,776	−11.0	−6.8
Liverpool to Sydney.............	−150	−0.6	−0.4
Liverpool to Adelaide...........	−2,336	−10.8	−6.1
Liverpool to Wellington.........	1,564	6.0	3.5
New York to Port Townsend.....	7,873	32.3	20.0
New York to San Francisco......	7,873	32.3	20.0
New York to Honolulu..........	6,610	27.0	16.7
New York to Valparaiso.........	3,747	15.1	9.2
New York to Yokohama.........	3,768	15.2	9.3
New York to Shanghai..........	1,876	7.3	4.4
New York to Hong Kong........	−18	....	....
New York to Manila............	41	....	....
New York to Sydney...........	3,932	15.8	9.7
New York to Adelaide...........	1,746	6.7	4.0
New York to Wellington.........	2,493	9.9	6.0
New Orleans to San Francisco....	8,868	36.4	22.6
New Orleans to Yokohama.......	5,705	23.3	14.4
New Orleans to Valparaiso.......	4,742	19.2	11.8

TABLE 18.—COMPARISON OF IMPORTS AND EXPORTS OF TYPICAL PORTS

The statistical abstract of the United States gives interesting figures of imports and exports for various United States ports for many years

	Imports		Exports	
	Total value, millions	Per cent total U. S. or U. K.	Total value, millions	Per cent total U. S. or U. K.
New York..........	$688.0	57.6	$701.0	37.6
Boston..............	93.0	7.8	96.0	5.1
New Orleans........	42.0	3.5	159.0	8.5
Galveston..........	5.0	0.4	161.0	8.6
San Francisco.......	48.0	4.0	28.0	1.5
Puget Sound........	22.0	1.9	28.0	1.5
London.............	£209.0	32.4	£123.0	23.7
Liverpool...........	160.0	24.8	165.0	31.1
Glasgow............	15.0	2.3	30.0	5.0
Plymouth..........	1.5	0.2	0.17	0.03
Belfast.............	8.1	1.2	2.4	0.4
Dublin.............	2.7	0.4	0.1	0.01
Dundee............	5.7	0.8	0.9	0.1

TABLE 19.—AREAS, POPULATION, AND

(From the Yearbook of

	Area, 1,000 sq. mi.	Population, 1,000	Population per sq. mi.	Wheat		Corn		Oats		Barley	
				Crop, million bu.	Yield per acre	Crop, million bu.	Yield per acre	Crop, million bu.	Yield per acre	Crop, million bu.	Yield per acre
Maine.........	30.0	742	24.8	0.07	25.5	0.6	38.0	5.6	40.0	0.1	28.0
N. Hampshire...	9.0	430	47.7	......	....	0.8	37.0	0.42	35.0	0.02	28.0
Vermont.......	9.1	356	39.0	0.02	24.5	1.6	37.0	3.0	39.0	0.38	32.0
Massachusetts..	8.0	3366	418.7	......	....	1.9	40.5	0.315	35.0	......	....
Rhode Island...	1.0	542	508.5	......	....	0.4	36.5	0.05	26.0	......	....
Connecticut....	4.8	1114	231.3	......	....	2.3	38.5	0.30	28.0	......	....
New York......	47.6	9113	191.2	6.8	20.0	15.0	28.5	42.7	33.5	2.0	26.7
New Jersey.....	7.5	2537	337.7	1.4	17.6	10.8	39.5	2.0	29.0	......	....
Pennsylvania...	44.8	7665	771.0	21.9	17.0	57.0	39.0	35.7	31.0	0.18	26.0
Delaware	1.9	202	103.0	1.6	14.5	6.2	31.5	0.1	30.5	......	....
Maryland......	9.0	1295	130.3	8.1	13.3	22.1	33.0	1.2	28.0	0.145	29.0
Virginia.......	40.3	2061	51.2	10.6	13.6	51.5	26.0	4.1	21.5	0.28	26.0
W. Virginia	24.0	1221	50.8	3.0	13.0	22.7	31.0	2.7	24.0	......	....
N. Carolina	48.7	2206	45.3	7.0	11.7	55.3	17.5	4.4	19.5	......	....
S. Carolina.....	30.5	1515	49.7	0.97	12.3	38.5	17.5	8.4	23.5	......	....
Georgia........	58.7	2609	44.4	1.7	12.2	63.0	15.5	9.2	22.0	......	....
Florida	54.8	752	13.7	......	....	10.1	15.0	0.9	18.0	......	....
Ohio..........	40.7	4767	117.0	35.0	18.0	146.1	37.5	54.3	30.2	0.96	24.0
Indiana........	36.0	2700	74.9	39.0	18.5	176.4	36.0	36.3	21.4	0.20	25.0
Illinois.........	56.0	5638	100.6	41.0	18.7	282.1	27.0	104.1	23.8	1.4	26.0
Michigan.......	57.4	2810	48.9	12.8	15.3	56.1	33.5	45.0	30.0	2.1	24.8
Wisconsin......	55.0	2334	42.2	3.6	20.1	66.8	40.5	83.0	36.5	18.1	25.0
Minnesota......	80.8	2076	25.7	68.0	16.2	96.0	40.0	112.6	37.8	34.8	24.0
Iowa..........	55.6	2225	40.0	16.3	23.4	338.3	34.0	168.3	34.5	10.0	25.0
Missouri.......	68.7	3293	47.9	39.5	17.1	129.0	17.5	26.5	21.2	0.11	22.0
N. Dakota.....	70.0	577	8.2	78.8	10.5	10.8	28.8	57.8	25.7	25.5	20.0
S. Dakota......	76.8	584	7.6	33.9	9.0	67.3	25.5	42.1	26.5	16.7	17.5
Nebraska......	77.5	1192	15.5	62.3	15.0	114.1	15.0	59.6	26.5	1.7	16.0
Kansas........	81.8	1690	20.7	86.9	11.0	23.4	3.2	34.3	19.5	1.9	8.1
Kentucky......	40.1	2290	57.0	9.8	13.6	74.8	20.5	3.1	19.8	0.08	26.6
Tennessee......	41.7	2185	52.4	8.4	12.0	68.6	20.5	6.3	21.0	0.05	25.0
Alabama.......	51.3	2138	41.7	0.3	11.7	55.0	17.3	6.6	20.5	......	....
Mississippi.....	46.4	1797	38.8	0.01	14.0	63.0	20.0	2.8	20.0	......	....
Louisiana.......	45.4	1656	36.5	......	....	41.8	22.0	0.9	22.0	......	....
Texas..........	262.4	3896	14.8	13.6	17.5	163.2	24.0	32.5	32.5	0.16	24.0
Oklahoma......	69.4	1657	23.9	17.5	10.0	52.2	11.0	18.5	18.0	0.06	9.0
Arkansas.......	52.5	1575	30.0	1.3	13.0	47.0	19.0	6.3	26.5	......	....
Montana.......	146.0	376	2.6	20.6	23.6	0.8	31.5	21.7	43.5	1.8	31.0
Wyoming.......	98.0	146	1.5	2.2	25.0	0.4	29.0	8.3	38.0	0.39	30.5
Colorado.......	103.6	799	7.7	9.6	21.0	6.3	15.0	10.6	35.0	3.2	32.5
N. Mexico......	122.5	327	2.7	1.2	18.0	1.5	18.5	1.5	30.0	0.09	24.0
Arizona........	113.9	204	1.8	0.9	32.0	0.4	28.0	0.30	43.0	1.4	39.0
Utah..........	82.2	373	4.5	6.4	25.5	0.3	34.0	4.1	46.0	1.1	38.5
Nevada........	109.8	818	0.7	1.0	26.0	0.03	34.0	0.4	43.0	0.49	41.0
Idaho..........	83.4	326	3.8	14.0	27.6	0.4	32.0	15.1	46.5	9.5	42.0
Washington.....	66.8	1142	17.1	53.3	23.0	0.9	28.0	14.2	47.5	7.2	40.5
Oregon.........	95.7	673	7.0	15.0	20.4	0.5	28.5	15.2	42.3	4.2	39.0
California......	155.8	2377	15.3	4.2	14.0	1.8	33.0	6.6	31.6	33.1	26.0
United States...	2974.0	91972	30.9	763.3	15.2	2447.0	23.1	1121.7	29.2	178.1	23.8

PRODUCTION, UNITED STATES, 1913

the U. S. Dept. of Agr.)

Rye Crop, million bu.	Rye Yield per acre	Potatoes Crop, million bu.	Potatoes Yield per acre	Cotton Crop, million bu.	Cotton Yield per acre	Dairy cattle, 1,000	Other cattle, 1,000	Horses, 1,000	Mules, 1,000	Sheep, 1,000	Swine, 1,000	
....	....	28.0	220	....	....	159	100	111	....	177	97	Maine.
....	....	2.0	122	....	....	96	65	47	....	39	51	N. Hampshire.
0.01	18.0	3.0	127	....	....	265	165	88	....	111	106	Vermont.
0.05	18.5	2.8	105	....	....	162	82	65	....	31	106	Massachusetts.
....	....	0.6	130	....	....	23	11	10	....	7	14	Rhode Island.
0.13	19.3	2.2	92	....	....	120	72	47	....	20	57	Connecticut.
2.2	17.2	26.6	74	....	....	1465	876	615	4	875	753	New York.
1.2	18.0	8.9	95	....	....	146	68	91	4	31	158	New Jersey.
4.9	17.5	23.3	88	....	....	943	632	584	45	839	1130	Pennsylvania.
0.01	14.0	0.9	87	....	....	38	19	35	6	8	58	Delaware.
0.38	14.4	3.7	87	....	....	168	119	165	24	223	332	Maryland.
0.71	12.3	9.8	94	23	240	345	450	350	61	735	869	Virginia.
0.23	13.5	3.9	83	....	....	230	331	190	12	788	367	W. Virginia.
0.47	10.3	2.4	80	790	239	312	365	180	192	177	1362	N. Carolina.
0.03	10.5	0.8	80	1374	235	185	211	85	171	33	780	S. Carolina.
0.12	9.5	0.9	81	2315	208	402	660	128	319	166	1945	Georgia.
....	....	0.9	76	58	150	128	735	55	27	118	904	Florida.
1.6	16.5	10.2	64	....	....	886	838	901	24	3263	3467	Ohio.
1.5	15.2	3.9	53	....	....	640	707	854	86	1238	3961	Indiana.
0.80	16.5	5.7	46	....	....	1107	1216	1497	148	984	4358	Illinois.
5.3	14.3	33.6	96	....	....	798	680	653	4	2118	1313	Michigan.
7.4	17.5	32.1	109	....	....	1549	1158	678	3	789	2050	Wisconsin.
5.7	19.0	30.2	110	....	....	1163	1173	847	6	570	1430	Minnesota.
1.0	18.2	7.2	48	....	....	1350	2555	1584	57	1249	6976	Iowa.
0.24	15.0	3.2	38	67	286	789	1386	1095	326	1568	4250	Missouri.
1.8	14.4	5.1	85	....	....	305	468	748	8	278	428	N. Dakota.
0.6	13.2	4.6	78	....	....	419	912	730	14	617	1039	S. Dakota.
1.7	14.5	5.6	48	....	....	613	1883	1048	84	374	3228	Nebraska.
0.63	14.0	2.9	40	....	....	698	1565	1110	222	316	2350	Kansas.
0.27	12.4	2.4	49	....	....	389	527	443	229	1267	1507	Kentucky.
0.20	12.0	2.4	64	379	210	348	498	346	270	688	1390	Tennessee.
0.01	11.0	1.5	84	1494	190	388	514	149	278	124	1485	Alabama.
....	....	0.9	80	1307	204	421	490	241	286	202	1467	Mississippi.
....	....	1.7	70	442	170	263	448	191	132	180	1398	Louisiana.
0.03	15.0	2.3	52	3943	150	1065	5173	1216	753	2052	2618	Texas.
0.04	9.5	1.9	60	830	132	484	1097	766	269	75	1352	Oklahoma.
0.01	11.5	1.8	72	1071	205	376	475	273	235	124	1498	Arkansas.
0.21	21.0	5.0	140	....	....	104	753	372	4	4293	184	Montana.
0.07	19.0	1.6	140	....	....	41	546	171	2	4472	51	Wyoming.
0.34	17.0	9.2	115	....	....	186	949	340	17	1668	205	Colorado.
....	....	0.6	68	....	....	62	918	197	15	3036	56	N. Mexico.
....	....	0.07	75	....	....	37	949	112	6	1601	24	Arizona.
0.20	17.0	3.6	180	....	....	88	356	140	2	1970	85	Utah.
....	....	1.7	160	....	....	22	437	76	3	1517	33	Nevada.
0.06	22.0	5.7	170	....	....	112	354	234	4	2981	252	Idaho.
0.16	21.0	7.3	123	....	....	234	199	305	14	506	284	Washington
0.35	17.5	6.7	135	....	....	196	470	301	10	2670	300	Oregon.
0.12	15.0	8.0	119	....	....	515	1410	498	73	2551	797	California.
41.3	66.4	331.5	54.1	14,116	182	20737	35855	20962	4449	49719	58933	United States.

TABLE 20(A).—AGRICULTURAL PRODUCTION, 1913

	Wheat, million bushels	Corn, million bushels	Barley, million bushels	Oats, million bushels	Rye, million bushels	Potatoes, million bushels
United States................	763.4	2,447.0	178.2	1,122.0	41.4	420.6
New Brunswick..............	0.3	....	74.0	5.9	....	7.5
Ontario......................	19.8	16.2	14.6	105.1	1.5	22.7
Manitoba....................	53.3	....	14.3	56.7	....	6.1
Saskatchewan................	121.5	....	10.4	114.1	....	6.5
Alberta......................	34.4	....	6.3	71.5	....	5.7
Other........................	2.3	0.59	0.3	12.1	....	15.1
Total Canada............	231.7	16.8	48.3	404.6	2.3	84.9
Mexico......................	10.0	190.0	7.0	0.017	....	0.9
Total North America.....	1,005.0	2,653.7	233.5	1,526.4	43.7	507.9
Argentina...................	198.4	196.6	....	115.8	....	38.0
Chile........................	21.0	1.?	....	4.0	....	9.6
Uruguay.....................	5.5	4.0	....	0.8	....	....
Total South America.....	224.9	201.8	....	120.7	....	47.6
Austria......................	60.1	13.2	75.9	160.0	109.0	460.8
Hungary proper..............	151.3	182.0	79.8	99.8	52.2	197.8
Croatia Slavonia.............	16.9	24.0	2.9	6.1	2.5	21.6
Bosnia Herzegovina..........	3.8	7.5	3.9	5.9	0.6	3.4
Total Austria-Hungary...	232.2	226.9	162.6	272.0	164.5	683.8
Belgium......................	15.0	....	4.1	41.0	21.4	121.5
Bulgaria.....................	45.0	30.0	10.0	12.0	9.0	0 5
Denmark.....................	4.5	....	23.0	43.3	18.7	28.9
Finland......................	0.1	....	6.3	27.2	12.0	23.5
France.......................	321.6	22.0	48.3	322.0	52.6	552.0
Germany.....................	171.0	....	188.7	669.0	481.2	1,885.0
Greece.......................	7.0	....	....	....	....	0.5
Italy........................	214.4	108.3	10.8	43.4	5.5	56.3
Montenegro..................	0.2	....	....	....	....	....
Netherlands..................	4.8	....	3.3	20.0	15.3	121.9
Norway......................	0.3	....	3.2	11.7	0.9	29.8
Portugal.....................	5.5	15.0	....	....	....	....
Roumania....................	83.2	118.1	27.3	35.1	3.7	1.0
Russia (European)...........	962.6	72.8	574.1	1,135.7	1,002.5	1,356.8
Servia.......................	8.5	23.6	2.8	5.5	0.9	2.1
Spain........................	112.4	25.1	68.7	25.3	27.9	93.1
Sweden......................	7.8	....	14.0	76.0	23.0	65.7
Switzerland..................	3.5	....	....	....	....	46.7
Turkey (European)...........	18.0	....	....	....	....	....
United Kingdom.............	58.3	...,....	67.7	181.1	1.7	213.8
Total Europe............	2,276.0	642.0	1,215.3	2,920.9	1,841.2	5,256.3

TABLE 20(A).—AGRICULTURAL PRODUCTION, 1913
(*Continued*)

	Wheat, million bushels	Corn, million bushels	Barley, million bushels	Oats, million bushels	Rye, million bushels	Potatoes, million bushels
British India................	358.4	....	....	....	....	....
Cyprus.....................	2.1	....	2.1	0.5	....	....
Japanese Empire............	27.14	....	101.12	....	....	25.7
Persia......................	16.0	....	....	....	....	....
Philippine Islands...........	....	10.2	....	....	....	....
Turkey (Asia Minor)........	35.0	....	....	....	....	....
Total Asia..............	438.6	10.2	103.2	....	....	64.5
Algeria.....................	36.8	0.39	50.0	17.9	....	1.6
Egypt......................	30.9	57.5	....	....	....	....
Tunis......................	5.6	....	7.3	4.2	....	....
Union of South Africa.......	6.0	30.8	1.3	9.6	....	3.8
Total Africa.............	79.3	88.7	58.6	31.8	....	5.4
Australia...................	94.8	8.6	4.0	16.6	0.09	11.2
New Zealand...............	5.8	0.2	1.4	14.0	0.09	5.4
Total Australasia........	100.7	8.8	5.4	30.6	0.18	16.7
Grand total	4,124.9	3,605.4	1,616.1	4,631.2	1,885.1	5,898.5

TABLE 20(B).—DOMESTIC ANIMALS, 1913

	Year	Cattle, 1,000	Swine, 1,000	Sheep, 1,000	Goats, 1,000	Horses, 1,000	Mules, 1,000	Asses, 1,000
North America:								
U. S., on farms.........	1914	56,592	58,933	49,719	2,915	20,962	4,449	106
U. S., not on farms.....	1910	1,879	1,288	391	115	3,183	270	17
Hawaii...............	1910	149	31	77	5	28	9	3
Porto Rico...........	1910	316	106	6	49	58	5	1
Total U. S. (except Philippine Islands).	.....	58,937	60,358	50,193	3,084	24,233	4,733	127
Canada:								
Quebec...............	1913	1,455	662	603	......	370	......	......
Ontario..............	1913	2,601	1,652	706	......	903	......	......
Alberta..............	1913	779	351	178	......	485	......	......
Saskatchewan........	1913	663	387	115	......	580	......	......
Manitoba............	1913	410	185	43	......	304	......	......
Total Canada.......	1913	6,656	3,448	2,129	......	2,866	......	......
Newfoundland...........	1911	39	27	98	17	14	......	......
Mexico.................	1902	5,142	616	3,424	4,206	859	334	288
West Indies.............	....	2,971	404	59	105	627	46	14
Central America:								
Costa Rica...........	1910	333	70	1	1	60	3	......
Guatemala...........	1899	197	30	78	......	50	......	......
Honduras............	1912	420	118	5	6	88	15	4
Nicaragua............	1908	252	12	......	1	28	6	1
Panama..............	1907	65	28	......	3	17	2	......
Salvador.............	1908	284	423	21	......	74	......	......
South America:								
Argentina.............	1911	28,786	2,900	80,401	4,302	8,894	535	319
Bolivia..............	1910	734	114	1,449	468	97	45	173
British Guiana........	1912	72	17	18	11	2	......	......
Chile................	1912	1,760	166	4,169	273	421	37	33
Colombia.............	....	2,800	2,300	746	361	341	257	......
Dutch Guiana........	1910	7	3	......	3	......	......	1
Falkland Islands.......	1912	8	......	711	......	4	......	......
French Guiana........	1911	4	......	......	......	......	......	......
Paraguay.............	1912	3,000	24	214	214	183	8	......
Uruguay.............	1908	8,193	180	26,286	26,286	556	18	4
Venezuela............	1899	2,004	1,618	177	177	191	89	313

TABLE 20(B).—DOMESTIC ANIMALS, 1913 (Continued)

	Year	Cattle, 1,000	Swine, 1,000	Sheep, 1,000	Goats, 1,000	Horses, 1,000	Mules, 1,000	Asses, 1,000
Europe:								
Austria-Hungary......	......	17,788	14,540	13,477	3,074	4,374	43	59
Belgium	1912	1,831	1,349	....	....	263	......	......
Bulgaria............	1911	2,018	527	8,632	1,459	478	12	118
Denmark............	1909	2,254	1,468	727	40	535	......	......
Finland.............	1910	1,573	418	1,309	13	361	......	......
France.............	1912	14,706	6,904	16,468	1,409	3,222	196	359
Germany............	1912	20,182	21,924	5,803	3,410	4,523	2	11
Greece.............	1912	400	80	4,000	3,339	160	88	141
Iceland............	1911	26	......	574	1	44	......	......
Italy..............	1908	6,199	2,508	11,163	2,715	956	388	850
Luxemburg..........	1913	101	136	5	10	19	......	......
Malta..............	1912	4	4	15	18	9	......	......
Netherlands........	1910	2,027	1,260	889	224	327	......	......
Norway.............	1907	1,094	319	1,393	296	172	......	......
Portugal...........	1906	703	1,111	3,073	1,034	88	58	144
Roumania...........	1911	2,667	1,021	5,269	297	825	4	......
Russia (European).....	1910	36,302	13,521	48,176	1,179	24,652	4	......
Servia.............	1910	958	864	3,809	627	153	......	1
Spain..............	1912	2,562	2,571	15,830	3,116	526	929	829
Sweden.............	1911	2,690	951	946	66	588	......	......
Switzerland.........	1911	1,443	569	160	340	144	......	......
Turkey (European).....	1910	6,726	21	21,190	12,216	1,042	202	1,556
United Kingdom.......	1913	11,869	3,334	27,824	....	2,231	......	......
Asia:								
British India..........	1911	114,876	......	31,691	....	1,711	......	1,508
Cyprus..............	1912	61	40	256	271	69	......	......
Japan..............	1912	1,399	309	3	101	1,582	......	......
Formosa............	1910	176	1,308	....	137	......	......	......
Philippine Islands......	1913	388	1,822	103	515	182	......	......
Turkey (Asiatic).......	....	3,000	......	45,000	9,000	800	......	2,500
Africa:								
Algeria.............	1911	1,114	110	8,529	3,682	227	192	272
Egypt..............	1912	620	......	....	....	47	21	691
Tunis..............	1912	225	19	767	492	37	22	192
Union of South Africa..	1911	5,797	1,082	30,657	11,763	719	94	337
Australia...........	1912	11,577	845	83,245	99	2,408	......	......
New Zealand.........	1911	2,020	349	23,996	6	404	......	......

TABLE 21.—COMMERCIAL AND FINANCIAL STATISTICS OF PRINCIPAL COUNTRIES OF THE WORLD

These figures, the latest available, are taken from the 1913 statistical abstract of the United States and mostly for the year 1912

	Area, sq. mi.	Population, millions	Population per sq. mi.	Total imports, million dollars	Total exports, million dollars	Imports per cap., dollars	Exports per cap., dollars	Percentage of imports from U.S.	Percentage of exports to U.S.	Railroad mileage	Railroad mileage per 1,000 sq. mi.	Railroad mileage per 10,000 pop.
North America and West Indies:												
Canada	3,729,665	7.4	2.0	670.0	355.7	89.74	47.64	65.0	39.6	29,304	7.9	39.2
Central American States:												
Costa Rica	18,691	0.3	21.35	8.6	9.9	21.63	24.97	50.4	49.9	546	29.2	18.2
Guatemala	48,290	2.1	43.88	7.7	13.1	3.67	6.21	46.6	29.4	502	10.4	2.4
Honduras	46,250	0.5	12.24	4.3	3.0	7.63	5.44	67.0	88.4	150	3.2	3.0
Nicaragua	49,532	0.6	12.11	4.9	3.4	8.28	5.69	54.8	38.9	200	4.0	3.3
Panama	32,380	0.3	11.95	6.7	2.0	25.51	5.34	38.6	86.2	202	6.2	6.7
Salvador	8,170	1.7	208.94		9.9	3.97	5.82	33.3	29.7	122	14.9	0.7
Cuba	45,881	2.4	53.92	132.3	165.2	53.49	66.78	53.3	80.3	2,331	50.8	9.7
Haiti	11,072	2.5	225.79	11.4	17.2	4.47	6.91	65.4	4.9	140	12.6	0.6
Mexico	767,323	15.1	19.76	97.4	149.6	6.43	9.87	49.7	77.2	16,103	21.0	10.7
Santo Domingo	28,000	0.7	25.89	8.2	12.3	11.34	17.08	62.1	58.7	175	6.3	2.5
United States including Alaska, Hawaii and Porto Rico	3,627,557	98.4	27.14	1,813.0	2,428.5	18.41	24.66			258,033	85.2	26.2
Porto Rico	3,435	1.1	339.74							340	99.0	2.9
South America:												
Argentina	1,139,196	8.7	7.64	371.3	463.5	42.69	53.28	15.4	6.7	20,806	18.3	23.9
Bolivia	708,195	2.3	3.20	19.0	35.8	8.67	15.79	9.3	0.4	798	1.1	3.5
Brazil	3,291,416	24.3	7.39	308.6	303.6	12.70	14.94	15.6	39.2	13,848	4.2	5.7
Chile	292,420	3.4	11.85	122.0	139.8	35.24	40.38	13.8	17.5	3,606	12.3	10.4
Colombia	435,278	5.0	11.65	23.9	32.2	4.72	6.35	31.8	49.1	621	1.4	1.7
Dutch possessions, in America	50,282	0.1	2.98		4.4	33.77	29.89	26.0	37.6	117	2.3	7.8
Ecuador	118,627	1.5	12.64		13.7	7.10	9.15	23.8	28.9	350	2.9	2.3
Paraguay	97,722	0.8	8.19		4.0	6.36	5.11		24.5	232	2.4	2.9
Peru	683,321	5.8	8.49	25.1	45.9	24.33	7.92	14.3	23.1	1,719	2.5	3.7
Uruguay	72,172	1.2	16.99	51.1	50.4	41.65	41.11	39.1	5.3	1,639	22.7	13.4
Venezuela	393,976	2.7	7.00	19.6	28.7	7.14	10.44		34.2	634	1.6	2.3
Europe:												
Austria-Hungary	261,033	51.5	197.31	722.0	554.9	14.02	10.78	9.8	2.3		112.0	5.7
Austria (including Bosnia and Herzegovina)	135,606	30.4	224.58							15,631	115.2	5.2
Hungary	125,427	21.0	167.67							13,596	108.3	6.5
Belgium	11,373	7.5	666.40	956.8	762.6	116.26	100.62	8.3	3.7	5,402	474.1	7.1
Denmark	15,586	2.9	178.04	219.0	159.9	78.95	57.63	10.8	0.6	2,303	147.8	8.3
France	207,129	39.6	191.19	1,588.5	1,295.5	40.11	32.71	14.8	6.4	31,807	153.6	8.0
German Empire	208,794	66.0	316.56	2,544.5	2,131.7	38.36	*32.13	2.8	*8.8	39,157	187.5	5.9
Greece	24,064	2.6	106.79	33.4	27.1	20.20	10.20		*7.8	1,000	40.1	3.8
Crete	3,327	0.3	103.40	4.1	3.0	11.58	8.77		4.9			

These figures, the latest available, are taken from the 1913 statistical abstract of the United States and mostly for the year 1912

	Area, sq. mi.	Population, millions	Population per sq. mi.	Total imports, million dollars	Total exports, million dollars	Imports per cap., dollars	Exports per cap., dollars	Percentage of imports from U.S.	Percentage of exports to U.S.	Railroad mileage	Railroad mileage per 1,000 sq. mi.	Railroad mileage per 1,000 pop.
Europe:												
Italy	110,688	34.6	313.38	714.4	462.6	20.60	13.34	13.9	10.9	11,086	99.0	3.2
Montenegro	3,509	0.2	71.24	1.6	0.4	6.63	1.94			11	3.1	0.4
Netherlands	13,171	6.1	466.48	1,452.4	1,251.4	236.60	203.60	10.0	4.4	2,023	153.6	3.3
Norway	124,675	2.3	19.19	140.8	86.9	58.90	36.38	5.7	8.8	1,921	15.4	8.0
Portugal (including Madeira and Azores)	35,499	5.4	152.76	73.5	36.7	13.57	6.78	8.6	23.1	1,854	52.2	3.4
Roumania	50,715	7.2	142.92	109.9	133.5	15.17	18.42	2.3	0.03	2,338	46.1	3.2
Russia	8,361,708	167.9	20.08	782.1	782.1	4.66	4.66	7.5	0.2	46,586	5.6	2.8
Finland	144,249	3.1	21.77	90.6	65.1	28.88	20.76	2.9	1.2	2,338	16.2	7.4
Servia	18,650	2.9	158.55	22.2	22.5	7.53	7.63	0.9	0.2	912	48.9	3.1
Spain	194,794	19.9	102.39	189.6	186.8	9.52	9.37	4.8	3.6	9,381	48.2	4.7
Sweden	172,920	5.6	32.44	186.6	177.8	33.28	31.71	7.8	8.1	8,868	51.3	15.8
Switzerland	15,955	3.7	236.97	381.9	262.0	101.02	69.30	4.2	10.0	3,176	199.1	8.4
United Kingdom	121,316	45.6	376.31	3,623.7	2,371.0	79.38	51.94	18.1	6.2	23,441	193.2	5.1
Asia:												
China	4,277,170	336.0	78.57	360.2	274.8	1.07	0.82	7.5	9.5	6,123	1.4	0.2
French Indo-China	256,255	16.9	66.30	36.9	48.1	2.17	2.83	1.3	0.1	1,185	4.6	0.7
India (British)	1,773,088	315.1	177.73	522.3	782.4	1.66	2.48	3.2	7.8	33,484	18.9	1.1
Japan (including Pescadores but excluding Formosa and Sakhalin)	147,699	52.3	354.18	308.2	256.2	5.89	4.90	20.5	32.1	5,607	38.0	1.1
Formosa	13,839	3.4	250.23	31.1	31.2	9.01	9.02	27.2	7.8	296	21.4	0.9
Chosen (Korea)	84,103	14.8	176.30	33.4	10.4	2.25	0.70	7.6	0.5	836	9.9	0.6
Dutch East Indies	778,154	37.9	48.78	144.3	188.3	3.80	4.96	1.5	4.3	1,602	2.1	0.4
Persia	635,135	9.5	14.96	48.2	36.1	4.94	3.80	2.6	1.5	34	0.05	0.04
Siam	195,000	8.1	41.79	28.2	30.3	3.46	3.72	2.6	1.1	702	3.6	0.9
Philippine Islands	115,026	8.5	74.35	56.3	53.6	6.59	6.28	45.5	37.2	653	5.7	0.8
Africa:												
Algeria (French)	343,629	5.5	16.19	130.3	106.3	25.23	19.11	1.5	0.4	2,169	6.3	3.9
Egypt	383,899	11.2	29.40	128.0	170.9	11.35	15.14	1.6	11.9	3,674	9.6	3.3
Sudan	950,000	2.6	2.74	9.7	6.7	3.74	2.61	0.4	8.6			
Eritrea (Massana), Italian	52,162	0.2	5.35	3.1	1.4	11.33	5.04	0.1				2.7
Kongo (Belgian)	913,127	20.0	21.90	10.4	11.5	0.52	0.58	7.2		784	0.9	0.4
Liberia	36,834	1.5	40.72	1.0	0.9	0.70	0.64		17.2			
Libia (Italian)	406,000	1.0	2.46	5.3	0.7	5.36	0.78	0.5				0.5
Morocco	169,591	5.0	29.85	20.4	14.4	5.89	2.90	4.2	0.02			
Tunis (French)	64,633	1.9	29.85	30.1	29.8	15.64	15.47	0.5	1.0	1,027	15.9	5.3
Union of South Africa	473,184	5.9	12.62	183.0	316.6	30.64	53.01	13.8		8,393	17.7	14.1
Australasia:												
Australia	2,974,581	4.7	1.59	380.3	369.6	80.36	78.10	13.8	2.7	18,653	6.3	39.4
New Zealand	104,751	1.0	1.02	102.0	103.5	95.31	96.66	9.8	2.9	2,869	27.4	26.8

TABLE 22.—DISTRIBUTION OF THE UNITED STATES FOREIGN TRADE

(A) Exports of domestic merchandise, 1913

	Crude materials for use in manufacturing		Foodstuffs in crude condition and food animals		Foodstuffs partly or wholly manufactured		Foodstuffs for further use in manufacturing		Manufactures ready for consumption		Miscellaneous		Total value	
	Dollars, million	Per cent of class	Dollars, million	Per cent of class	Dollars, million	Per cent of class	Dollars, million	Per cent of class	Dollars, million	Per cent of class	Dollars, million	Per cent of class	Dollars, million	Per cent of total exports
Europe	594.6	81.26	138.8	76.31	224.8	70.01	263.6	64.49	239.4	30.85	2.5	29.42	1464.0	59.98
North America	97.7	13.36	33.3	18.34	61.7	19.21	95.4	23.36	301.9	38.89	5.7	67.38	595.9	25.04
South America	2.6	0.36	1.8	1.01	13.3	4.16	28.1	6.88	99.6	12.84	0.09	1.13	145.7	5.92
Asia	30.2	4.14	3.7	2.05	11.3	3.52	9.3	2.28	60.1	7.74	0.02	0.27	114.7	4.67
Oceania	3.5	0.49	0.9	0.54	6.3	1.98	9.9	2.43	58.0	7.48	0.05	0.61	78.9	3.21
Africa	2.8	0.39	3.1	1.75	3.6	1.12	2.2	0.56	17.0	2.20	0.10	1.19	29.0	1.18
Totals and per cent that total of class is to total exports	731.7	30.13	181.9	7.49	321.2	13.23	408.8	16.83	776.2	31.97	8.5	0.35	2428.5	100.00

(B) Merchandise imported

	Crude materials for use in manufacturing		Foodstuffs in crude condition and food animals		Foodstuffs partly or wholly manufactured		Foodstuffs for further use in manufacturing		Manufactures ready for consumption		Miscellaneous		Total value	
	Dollars, million	Per cent of class	Dollars, million	Per cent of class	Dollars, million	Per cent of class	Dollars, million	Per cent of class	Dollars, million	Per cent of class	Dollars, million	Per cent of class	Dollars, million	Per cent of total exports
Europe	242.7	38.21	26.2	12.40	76.5	39.42	217.2	62.18	317.7	77.84	12.3	86.50	892.8	49.25
North America	123.8	19.49	49.2	23.27	102.9	52.98	54.1	15.49	30.6	7.51	1.1	8.32	361.9	19.96
South America	71.9	11.32	113.3	53.52	0.8	0.43	29.4	8.43	2.0	0.51	0.1	0.89	217.7	12.01
Asia	147.8	23.28	21.0	9.96	9.0	4.64	43.5	12.46	54.5	13.36	0.4	3.28	276.4	15.25
Oceania	23.1	3.64	1.5	0.75	4.9	2.52	4.8	1.39	2.9	0.74	0.04	0.29	37.5	2.07
Africa	25.7	4.06	0.2	0.10	0.01	0.01	0.17	0.05	0.15	0.04	0.10	0.72	26.4	1.46
Totals and per cent that total of class is to total imports	635.2	35.04	211.7	11.68	194.2	10.72	349.4	19.27	408.1	22.51	14.2	0.78	1813.0	100.00

TABLE 23.—VALUES OF IMPORTS AND EXPORTS AND ESTIMATED VALUE OF PRO-DUCTION OF FOODSTUFFS IN COUNTRIES NAMED

(From Farmers' Bulletin 641, U. S. Dept. of Agr.)

The status of the United States in food supply will be a surprise to many.

[Figures represent approximately conditions in 1912 or 1913. Values for the different countries are made independently of each other—i.e., on different bases—and therefore are not strictly comparable with each other.]

Product	United Kingdom				France				Russia			
	Millions of dollars			Per cent production to requirements	Millions of dollars			Per cent production to requirements	Millions of dollars			Per cent production to requirements
	Imports	Exports	Production		Imports	Exports	Production		Imports	Exports	Production	
Edible grain	311	25	107	27	52	8	590	93	16	298	1477	124
Meats	326	19	350	53	31	23	540	98	13	7	876	99
Dairy products	151	5	243	62	13	16	193	101	1	38	412	110
Poultry and eggs	53	...	73	58	12	2	39	80	...	49	309	119
Vegetables	29	...	292	91	2	11	251	104	1	21	515	104
Fruits and nuts	87	...	24	22	13	14	58	102	21	3	77	81
Sugar	112	...	....	0	26	18	77	91	...	34	140	132
Coffee and tea	83	24	....	0	43	...	....	0	35	...	....	1
Fish	24	44	49	166	15	6	27	73	15	2	154	92
Other	63	83	24	540	25	11	2	13	...	...	25	100
Total	1239	200	1162	53	232	109	1777	93	102	452	3986	110

Product	Germany				Austria-Hungary				Belgium			
	Millions of dollars			Per cent production to requirements	Millions of dollars			Per cent production to requirements	Millions of dollars			Per cent production to requirements
	Imports	Exports	Production		Imports	Exports	Production		Imports	Exports	Production	
Edible grain	211	53	730	82	19	11	658	99	183	35	47	24
Meats	03	...	833	93	6	6	223	100	11	4	30	81
Dairy products	28	...	333	92	6	1	203	98	8	1	22	76
Poultry and eggs	53	...	107	67	15	32	122	115	5	3	8	80
Vegetables	13	5	714	99	6	6	424	100	15	17	77	103
Fruits and nuts	54	2	48	48	15	6	49	84	5	1	15	79
Sugar	...	62	143	177	...	52	90	230	...	12	19	272
Coffee and tea	54	...	....	0	68	...	....	0	15	5	....	0
Fish	...	...	....	0	4	1	4	53	5	1	7	63
Other	222	160	24	28	5	...	41	88	...	...	....	....
Total	698	282	2932	88	144	115	1814	98	247	79	225	57

Product	Argentina				Canada				United States			
	Millions of dollars			Per cent production to requirements	Millions of dollars			Per cent production to requirements	Millions of dollars			Per cent production to requirements
	Imports	Exports	Production		Imports	Exports	Production		Imports	Exports	Production	
Edible grain	3	101	163	249	6	141	240	229	19	160	766	123
Meats	4	66	234	136	6	15	120	108	40	148	1986	106
Dairy products	2	2	26	100	2	21	172	112	16	147	800	120
Poultry and eggs	...	...	....	100	3	...	50	94	4	4	650	100
Vegetables	1	...	17	95	4	2	70	97	20	14	554	99
Fruits and nuts	2	...	7	78	17	5	20	62	48	31	250	94
Sugar	2	...	22	92	18	...	1	5	217	4	69	24
Coffee and tea	2	...	....	0	9	...	....	0	130	...	....	0
Fish	1	...	....	....	3	20	35	194	20	14	148	96
Other	...	...	....	....	4	...	2	33	48	18	111	79
Total	17	169	469	148	72	204	710	123	562	340	5334	100

TABLE 24.—FOOD VALUES
(Figures from U. S. Dept. of Agr.)

	Refuse	Water, per cent	Protein, per cent	Fat, per cent	Carbohydrates, per cent	Fuel value per pound, calories
White bread.................	....	35.3	9.2	1.3	53.1	1,200
Wheat flour patent roller process, high grade and medium.................	....	12.0	11.4	1.0	75.1	1,685
Low grade.................	....	12.0	14.0	1.9	71.2	1,640
Rye flour.................	....	12.9	6.8	0.9	78.7	1,620
Corn meal.................	....	12.5	9.2	1.9	75.4	1,635
Rice.................	....	12.3	8.0	0.3	79.0	1,620
Beans, dried.................	....	12.6	22.5	1.8	59.6	1,520
Beans, baked.................	....	68.9	6.9	2.5	19.6	555
Potatoes.................	20.0	62.6	1.8	0.1	14.7	295
Sweet potatoes.............	20.0	55.2	1.4	0.6	21.9	440
Bananas.................	35.0	48.9	0.8	0.4	14.3	260
Apples.................	25.0	63.3	0.3	0.3	10.8	190
Almonds.................	45.0	2.7	11.5	30.2	9.5	1,515
Chestnuts, fresh...........	16.0	37.8	5.2	4.5	35.4	915
Cocoanuts.................	48.8	7.2	2.9	25.9	14.3	1,295
Peanuts.................	24.5	6.9	19.5	29.1	18.5	1,775
Chocolate.................	....	5.9	12.9	48.7	30.3	2,625
Date.................	10.0	13.8	1.9	2.5	70.6	1,275
Sirloin steak.................	12.8	54.0	16.5	16.1		975
Neck of beef.................	27.6	45.9	14.5	11.9	....	1,165
Cod, salt.................	24.9	40.2	16.0	0.4	....	325
Salmon (canned)...........	....	63.5	21.8	12.1	....	915
Eggs, hens' eggs.............	11.2	65.5	13.1	9.3	....	635
Whole milk.................	....	87.0	3.3	4.0	5.0	310
Cheese, full cream	....	34.2	25.9	33.7	2.4	1,885
Butter.................	....	11.0	1.0	85.0	....	3,410
Oleomargarine.................	....	9.5	1.2	83.0	....	3,525
Unrefined lard.................	....	4.8	2.2	94.0	....	4,010
Pure olive oil / Pure cocoanut oil / Pure peanut oil / Pure cottonseed oil	.....	....	....	100.0	....	4,040

INDEX